PERSPECTIVES AND PROGRESS IN
MENTAL RETARDATION

City Hall, Nathan Phillips Square, Toronto, Ontario.
(*Courtesy of Government of Ontario, Ontario House, London*)

PERSPECTIVES AND PROGRESS IN MENTAL RETARDATION

*Sixth Congress
of the International Association
for the Scientific Study of Mental Deficiency (IASSMD)*

Volume I

SOCIAL, PSYCHOLOGICAL, AND EDUCATIONAL ASPECTS

Edited by
**J. M. Berg, M.B., B.Ch., M.Sc.,
F.R.C.Psych., F.C.C.M.G.**

Technical Editor
Jean M. de Jong

University Park Press
Baltimore

UNIVERSITY PARK PRESS
International Publishers in Medicine and Human Services
300 North Charles Street
Baltimore, Maryland 21201

Typeset by Maryland Composition Company, Inc.

Manufactured in the United States of America by
The Maple Press Company

Library of Congress Cataloging in Publication Data

International Association for the Scientific Study
of Mental Deficiency. Congress (6th : 1982 : Toronto,
Canada)
Perspectives and progress in mental retardation.

Includes indexes.
Contents: v. 1. Social, psychological, and educational
aspects—v. 2. Biomedical aspects.
1. Mental deficiency—Congresses. I. Berg, J. M.
II. De Jong, Jean M. III. Title. [DNLM: 1. Mental
retardation—Congresses. W3 IN12T 6th 1982p / WM 300
I611 1982p]
RC569.9.I57   1982   362.3   83-14621
ISBN 0-8391-1952-6 (v. 1)
ISBN 0-8391-1953-4 (v. 2)

CONTENTS

SECTION I: ATTITUDES AND OUTLOOKS

SECTION II: INTERACTIONS AND RELATIONSHIPS

SECTION VI: DEINSTITUTIONALIZATION AND COMMUNITY LIVING

SECTION VII: PARENTAL PERCEPTIONS AND NEEDS

CONTENTS OF VOLUME II

SECTION I: EPIDEMIOLOGY AND SURVEYS

SECTION II: PRENATAL ENVIRONMENTAL HAZARDS

SECTION III: CHROMOSOMAL ABERRATIONS

PREFACE

The sixth Congress of the International Association for the Scientific Study of Mental Deficiency took place in Toronto from August 22nd to 26th, 1982. The remarkable interest in the subject is reflected by the fact that the Congress attracted 1,100 fully registered participants and their associates from many disciplines and from 60 countries. As Professor Hans Olof Åkesson and Dr. Robert McClure each indicated, in their opening presidential remarks and closing banquet address, respectively, it was a great opportunity to exchange ideas and information between workers from widely varying cultural milieus and socioeconomic circumstances; indeed, such a beneficial exchange was a hallmark of the Congress.

Some 500 presentations were made on many aspects that constitute the intricate mosaic of mental retardation, and 426 of these presentations were submitted for consideration for publication in the Proceedings. Financial and other practical exigencies precluded the publication of more than two volumes of Proceedings. This necessitated the inevitable exclusion of many worthy papers, which are listed by title and authors' contact addresses in the first of these volumes. The editor is indebted to the members of the editorial board (listed on page xviii) and the following additional panel of reviewers for graciously and generously assisting in the delicate selection process: Dr. J. Corbett, Dr. C. Cunningham, Dr. S. Einfeld, Dr. M. Feldman, Dr. J. Hogg, Dr. C. Kiernan, Dr. V. Markovic, Professor M. Partington, Dr. D. Reeves, Dr. C. A. Rubino, Dr. B. S. Scott, Dr. P. E. Sylvester, Professor M. W. Thompson, and Dr. A. Wellman. Their advice, individually and collectively, was invaluable, although such exclusion of papers as may be considered injudicious should be attributed to the editor, who personally read, and made the final decision on, every submission.

The papers accepted for publication fell conveniently, as in previous Congresses, into two main categories that provided the subtitles for each volume (Volume I—Social, Psychological and Educational Aspects; Volume II—Biomedical Aspects), under the overall heading of Perspectives and Progress in Mental Retardation. The division of each volume into subsections was undertaken for ease of reference and does not necessarily follow the order of oral presentation at the Congress itself. In making the selections for these proceedings, particular weight was given to papers that were considered to be of scientific interest, in keeping with the crucial component in the name of the Association under whose aegis the volumes are published.

It is a pleasure to express here special gratitude to two admirable ladies without whose enormous help and support the editor's task would have been well nigh impossible. Mrs. Jean de Jong, the technical editor, once again brought her wide-ranging talents and experience to bear, with characteristic grace and goodwill, in organizing and shepherding the editorial process through its multiple phases; only those who have been associated with her in similar contexts could know how large a debt is owed to her by the Association and the editor. Ms. Marika Korossy gave unstintingly of her time in facilitating the process, also with the characteristic good-natured competence from which the editor had benefitted greatly in more than a decade of work together. The pleasant and efficient collaboration of the production editor, Ms. Megan Barnard Shelton, and her associates at University Park Press also is gratefully acknowledged. It would be remiss not to thank as well my wife, Eva, for her patient tolerance during the countless hours devoted to the present undertaking.

J. M. Berg
Toronto, Canada

Officers of the
International Association
for the Scientific Study
of Mental Deficiency:
1979–1982

President: H. O. Åkesson, Psychiatric Department III, Lillhagen's Hospital, S-422 03 Hisings Backa 3, Sweden
President-Elect: G. A. Roeher, 21 Colwick Drive, Willowdale, Ontario M2K 2G4, Canada
Honorary Past Presidents: H. A. Stevens, 128 West Main, Evansville, Wisconsin 53752, United States
A. D. B. Clarke, Psychology Department, The University, Hull, HU6 7RX, England
M. J. Begab, University Park Press, 300 North Charles Street, Baltimore, Maryland 21201, United States
Vice-Presidents: I. Wald, Instytut Psychoneurologiczny, Al. Sobieskiego 1/9, 02-957 Warsaw, Poland
C. G. A. de Jong, Bartimeushage, Centre for Multiply Handicapped, P.B. 87, 3940 Doorn, The Netherlands
Honorary Officers: A. Shapiro, B. E. Cohen
Secretary: D. A. Primrose, The Royal Scottish National Hospital, Larbert, Stirlingshire FK5 4EJ, Scotland
Treasurer: A. Dupont, Institute of Psychiatric Demography, Aarhus Psychiatric Hospital, 8240 Risskov, Denmark

Officers of the
International Association
for the Scientific Study
of Mental Deficiency:
1982–1985

President: G. A. Roeher (*due to his untimely death, the President-Elect has become President*)
President-Elect: A. Dupont, Institute of Psychiatric Demography, Aarhus Psychiatric Hospital, 8240 Risskov, Denmark
Honorary President: H. A. Stevens, 128 West Main, Evansville, Wisconsin 53752, United States
Vice-Presidents: C. G. A. de Jong, Bartimeushage, Centre for Multiply Handicapped, P.B. 87, 3940 Doorn, The Netherlands
R. J. Andrews, Commonwealth Schools Commission, P. O. Box 34, Woden, Canberra ACT 2606, Australia
Honorary Vice-Presidents: A. D. B. Clarke, M. J. Begab
Secretary: M. Mulcahy, Medico-Social Research Board, 73 Lower Baggot Street, Dublin 2, Ireland
Treasurer: A. H. Bernsen, Demographic-Genetic Research Department, 8240 Risskov, Denmark
Honorary Officers: S. Krynski, A. Shapiro, B. Cohen, J. Veerman, I. Wald
Honorary Secretary: D. A. Primrose

Congress Organized by the
International Association
for the Scientific Study
of Mental Deficiency
in Association with the
Local Organizing Committee

Local Organizing Committee
Honorary Chairman: William B. Bremner
Chairman: Mrs. Louise Stuart, C.M.
Vice-Chairmen: Peter Cekuta, Helen Honickman, John McCrea, Margot
Scott, Dolly Tarshis
Members: Diane Anderson, Shirley Barron, Henry Botchford, Robin
Chetwyn, David Courtin, Shirley Crombie, Vince Gillis, John Haddad,
Shirley Ingram, Jack Pulkinen, Mike Solomonides, Steve Wace, Shirley
Walker

Scientific Program Committee
Chairman: G. A. Roeher
Members: H. O. Åkesson, M. J. Begab, J. M. Berg, A. Blanchet, C. G.
A. de Jong, G. C. J. Magerotte, A. H. Neufeldt, J. Pelletier, D. A.
Primrose

Proceedings Editor
J. M. Berg

Co-Hosts
The Canadian Association for the Mentally Retarded
The National Institute on Mental Retardation
The American Association on Mental Deficiency—Region VI and Ontario
Chapter

IASSMD Congress Publications

Proceedings of the First Congress (Montpellier, 1967):
Editor: Barry W. Richards
October 1968   982 pages
Distributor: editor, St. Lawrence's Hospital,
    Caterham, Surrey CR3 5YA, England

Proceedings of the Second Congress (Warsaw, 1970):
Editor: David A. A. Primrose
December 1971   774 pages
Distributor: Swets & Zeitlinger, B.V., Heereweg
    347B, Lisse, The Netherlands

Proceedings of the Third Congress (The Hague, 1973):
Editor: David A. A. Primrose
April 1975   2 volumes   875 pages
Distributor: editor, The Royal Scottish National
    Hospital, Larbert, Stirlingshire
    FK5 4EJ, Scotland

Proceedings of the Fourth Congress (Washington, D.C. 1976):
Research to Practice in Mental Retardation
Editor: Peter Mittler
July-September 1977   3 volumes   1718 pages
Publisher: University Park Press, 300 N. Charles
    Street, Baltimore, Maryland 21201,
    United States

Proceedings of the Fifth Congress (Jerusalem, 1979):
Frontiers of Knowledge in Mental Retardation
Editor: Peter Mittler
April 1981   2 volumes   870 pages
Publisher: University Park Press, 300 N. Charles
    Street, Baltimore, Maryland 21201,
    United States

Proceedings of the Sixth Congress (Toronto, 1982):
Perspectives and Progress in Mental Retardation
Editor: Joseph M. Berg
December 1983   2 volumes   960 pages
Publisher: University Park Press, 300 N. Charles
    Street, Baltimore, Maryland 21201,
    United States

PROCEEDINGS OF THE SIXTH CONGRESS
OF THE INTERNATIONAL ASSOCIATION
FOR THE SCIENTIFIC STUDY
OF MENTAL DEFICIENCY

Toronto, Canada August 22nd–26th, 1982
The Sheraton Centre

**Perspectives and Progress
in
Mental Retardation**

Published in two volumes:
Volume I: Social, Psychological, and Educational Aspects
Volume II: Biomedical Aspects

Edited by
J. M. Berg, M.B., B.Ch., M.Sc., F.R.C.Psych., F.C.C.M.G.
Professor of Psychiatry and of Medical Genetics,
University of Toronto
Director of Genetic Services and Biomedical Research
Surrey Place Centre, 2 Surrey Place
Toronto, Ontario M5S 2C2, Canada

Editorial Board:
M. J. Begab, Ph.D.
P. Berry, M.Ed., Ph.D.
R. I. Brown, Ph.D.
A. M. Clarke, Ph.D., F.B.Ps.S. and A. D. B. Clarke, C.B.E., Ph.D., F.B.Ps.S.
P. Mittler, C.B.E., M.A., Ph.D., M.Ed.
D. A. Primrose, M.D., B.L., C.A., F.R.C.Psych., F.R.C.P., M.R.C.G.P.
J. Stern, Ph.D., M.R.C.Path.

DEDICATION

Professor G. Allan Roeher died tragically in an airplane accident on 2nd June 1983. He was, at the time, President of the International Association for the Scientific Study of Mental Deficiency. As President-Elect of this Association and Chairman of its Congress Programme Committee, he gave unstintingly of his many talents and his time to ensure the success of the 6th Congress from which these Proceedings are derived. He was devoted, for many of his 58 years, to the welfare of mentally handicapped persons and their families to the great benefit of all concerned. His wise counsel will be sorely missed. As a small token of the well-deserved esteem in which he was widely held, the two volumes of PERSPECTIVES AND PROGRESS IN MENTAL RETARDATION are respectfully dedicated to his memory.

SECTION I
Attitudes and Outlooks

PERSPECTIVES AND PROGRESS IN MENTAL RETARDATION
Volume I—Social, Psychological, and Educational Aspects
Edited by J. M. Berg

SOCIOETHICAL ISSUES IN THE MANAGEMENT OF DEVELOPMENTAL DISABILITY

M. Adams

*Department of Child Health Research Unit, University of Bristol,
77 St. Michael's Hill, Bristol BS2 8BJ, England*

This paper gives a brief definition of the dominant ethical systems in western society and attempts to examine their influence on the practical management of developmental disability in the health field, with emphasis on issues related to prenatal diagnosis for at-risk mothers, intensive care for severely defective newborns, and general medical provision for developmentally disabled individuals at any phase of their lives. The conflict between formalist and utilitarian ethics is illustrated in regard to the welfare of the family and allocation of resources for different aspects of developmental disability.

Webster's Dictionary defines ethics as "the study of human behavior, characteristics and institutions as they relate to moral duty" or, put in operational terms, the assignment of rightness and goodness to human actions, policies, and the principles from which these derive. Western society is mainly influenced by two ethical systems, formalism (Ross, 1930) and utilitarianism (Mill, 1971). The cardinal principles of formalism are 1) acting justly, 2) keeping promises, 3) dealing honestly, and 4) refraining from purposeful injury, whereas the basic tenet of utilitarianism is to facilitate the best balance of pleasure over pain and the greatest good for the greatest number. To sharpen the focus of my topic I have added the prefix *"socio-"* to the adjective *"ethical"* because the practical application of ethical principles to a specific group of individuals, such as the developmentally disabled, is liable to generate social problems and dilemmas that bring into question the appropriateness, and even morality, of the ethical norm invoked. The observations that follow are an attempt to examine a number of social issues that are encountered in the management of developmental disability, with a view to seeing how well their resolution accords with, or transgresses, the ethical principles cited above.

The wide range of social issues involved in the care of the developmentally disabled stems from certain characteristics intrinsic to their condition—irreversible neurological damage and associated impairment of intellectual functioning and social competence, with resultant chronic dependency on others for their well-being, care, and survival. These features create an inherent vulnerability to exploitation that has to be countered by the observance of rigorous ethical standards in their treatment. This point is illustrated by the fact that the irreversible nature of the disability, with its connotations of diminished social competence and value, has led to the developmentally disabled individual's being deprived of many human and legal rights, with serious ethical and social consequences (Skarnulis, 1974).

RIGHT TO LIFE AND CONFLICTING ETHICAL VALUES

At the most fundamental level, this abrogation of rights extends to life itself (Himsworth, 1973; Dyck, 1974), initially through the now commonly accepted practice of prenatal diagnosis and its logical sequel of elective abortion (Powledge and Fletcher, 1979). This measure seriously compromises the right to life of the fetus by making its survival dependent upon an innate characteristic—the absence or presence of a defect with serious handicapping qualities. The same issue occurs again at birth when the question arises of whether a newborn infant with severe life-threatening neurological impairment should receive special treatment to promote survival (Duff and Campbell, 1973; *British Medical Journal*, 1981). The argument advanced for relaxing the principle of right to life for the defective fetus or newborn is that the predicted quality of life does not warrant the normal ethical practice of saving it (Fletcher, 1972; McCormick, 1974).

From the practical social angle, this issue of right to life introduces a number of conflicting factors, a primary one being the effect of the defective infant's survival on society—first on his immediate family, and second on the wider social system of which the family is a part. For example, the family may, for religious, cultural, or personal reasons, be anxious to preserve the child, irrespective of its deficits and limited future (Hosey, 1973), and will resist the recommendation to terminate the pregnancy (Bundy, 1978). This decision evokes several dilemmas: first, it is not feasible to try to impose abortion on a mother who does not want it; second, doing so would violate prevailing social morality that vigorously supports individual self-determination in regard to health, childbearing, and family arrangements (Brody, 1976;

Brieland, 1979); and third, women who terminate pregnancy under pressure are prone to subsequent psychological disturbance (Kuman and Robertson, 1978; Donnai et al., 1981). Against these cogent arguments is the ineluctable fact that a deliberate decision to produce a child with a confirmed serious handicap contravenes preventive health policies and increases morbidity.

A different facet to this controversial question raises the ethical point that to preserve life for a seriously compromised individual can be interpreted as not refraining from purposeful injury, because of the lifelong handicap that will be the sequel to survival. In ethical terms this can be construed as "wrongful life" (Engelhardt, 1973; Bayles, 1976). Furthermore, there is another social dimension to this concept that is not always recognized. This is that the disabled existence that constitutes a wrongful life for the afflicted individual may be equally injurious to the family responsible for his care, should this create demands and stresses that impede the healthy development of other members. Although the presence of a handicapped member is not necessarily damaging to the family (Gath, 1975), research has shown that the stresses involved can have that effect (Tew and Laurence, 1973; Gath, 1977). This possibility speaks to the utilitarian ethic because, if an entire family is penalized by the deficits of one member, the best balance of pleasure over pain has been negated and the greatest good for the greatest number bypassed.

SOCIAL AND ETHICAL CONNOTATIONS OF COST-EFFECTIVE HEALTH CARE

A second point that has an important bearing upon the ethical principle of right to life and the practical salvage tactics of critically ill defective newborns is that intensive perinatal care is costly in money, professional skills, and time and represents a high investment of resources (Lightowler, 1971; McCarthy et al., 1979). Moreover, if intensive care results in the survival of a baby with a severe chronic handicap, a further investment of resources will be required to provide the specialized services to maintain him, foster his development, and provide support for the family who undertake his care (Fry, 1981).

In the field of maternal and child health it has been suggested that funds at present allocated to intensive care nurseries might be better channeled into preventive community outreach programs. Such a measure would help to ensure adequate antenatal care for at-risk pregnant mothers that would increase their chances of producing full-term, normal-size babies instead of premature, low-birthweight ones at risk for cerebral damage (Davies, 1980; Hobel, 1980). Such a policy would exemplify the utilitarian ethic because, although a few at-risk newborns might not survive without intensive care, a much greater number of socioeconomically deprived babies of normal biological endowment would get a better start. This improvement in health and living standards would heighten the likelihood of their developing normally and is of particular relevance to our field in that children from poor socioeconomic backgrounds are susceptible to developmental retardation (Adams and Colvin, 1969; Rutter and Madge, 1976). If their depriving circumstances are not improved during their early formative years, these children run a very real risk of lapsing into permanent intellectual deficiency (Garber and Heber, 1977).

ETHICAL ASPECTS OF INEQUITABLE SERVICE PROVISION

The rights of the developmentally disabled have also been curtailed in regard to provision of services to compensate for their innate deficits. This inequity stems partly from a misconception of their needs, and partly from the conviction that, because their social potential was limited, it did not matter if it remained unfulfilled. A very common example is the policy of institutionalizing retarded children at a very early age in the belief that they would not benefit from normal family living (Shearer, 1980). Aside from its direct effect upon the developmentally disabled themselves, this approach has social repercussions that compound its obvious ethical shortcomings. At the simplest level, if a retarded child or adult does not receive training and care that will promote maximum development, at best he will be less productive than he might otherwise be, and at worst he will stagnate in a state of persistent dependency (King et al., 1971; Oswin, 1978). In residential settings, where this issue of right to treatment was first fought out (Amery, 1980), such reduced competence necessitates a much higher investment of resources in caretaking staff to carry out tasks that retarded persons could easily do for themselves if trained and supervised. With regard to the retarded individual living in the community, a shortage of services to supplement the family's efforts (Jaehnig, 1979; Wilkin, 1982) places a greater demand on their time and energies, with inevitable constraints on their own social life (Grossman, 1972; Wilson, 1972; Pomeroy et al., 1978). This constitutes an infringement of both the formalist ethic of acting justly toward the disabled person and the utilitarian ethic of promoting the greatest good for the greatest number, as embodied in the whole family.

This vigorous advocacy of good, which often means expensive, services for the developmentally disabled, may strike an illogical note when juxtaposed to my uncompromising stand against prolonging the survival of a chronically impaired child or adult. My rationale derives from the concept of human values and quality of life and their practical manifestations, which argues that it is not necessarily a denial of the unique value of a defective infant to withhold treatment that prolongs an inevitably crippled life. However, once the child has survived under its own steam and develops toward maturity, it is a gross devaluation of him as a human being to consign him to services that are unrewarding, unstimulating, and sometimes oppressive (MacAndrew and Edgerton, 1964; Morris, 1969). Providing effective care for handicapped individuals whose existence is already established would seem to represent a more genuine concern for the rights and well-being of this client group than the ideological espousal of the right to life irrespective of what that life will be like.

Besides these shortcomings in specialized care for the developmentally disabled, there are a number of ethical issues relating to general health and welfare services and the extent to which they are available to this patient group. Historically, the bias has been toward providing separate specialized services for the mentally retarded, often resulting in their being excluded from services available to the general population (Potter, 1977). The ethical flaw in this policy of specialized service provision is that excluding developmentally disabled persons from common services has tended to exclude them from common criteria about their needs, with serious inequities in treatment, the all-too-familiar example being the decision not to operate on duodenal atresia in a baby with Down's syndrome (Doyle, 1981). From the ethical perspective it is not acting justly or dealing honestly to restrict a service commonly available because the patient has qualities denoting social inferiority.

A different ethical dilemma associated with access to general health and welfare services concerns the problem of priority setting for treatment that is in short supply or costly to provide. This problem is not exclusive to our field (Freireich, 1980; Leaf, 1980; *Lancet*, 1981), but it bears upon it with greater weight because of the problematic social value attached to mentally retarded persons. In order to resolve this tricky issue both equitably and with good sense we must look at the social connotations of priority setting and make sure that the criteria that determine eligibility for our particular client group are based upon a relevant assessment of facts rather than a global preconception. In the hypothetical situation of whether complex, expensive treatment in short supply should be offered to a developmentally disabled patient, the following points should be borne in mind (Fox, 1981):

1. Will he be able to utilize it to optimal advantage?

2. Will it produce unduly distressing or painful side effects?
3. If it does, will the health benefits be sufficient compensation if the patient cannot appreciate them?
4. When considering treatment that prolongs life without curing the basic disease, how should the quality of life be balanced against increased duration if the retarded patient's limited comprehension of time and the future make the latter of less significance than enjoying a relatively trouble-free but shorter life?

SOCIETAL DIMENSION OF ETHICAL STANDARDS

Besides these issues directly affecting the developmentally disabled patient, it is also important to view his claims in the broader perspective of comparability with those of others, particularly in terms of productivity and social responsibility. However reluctant we are to confront these value-laden factors, they cannot be ignored, if only because availability of services for the disabled depends in the final analysis on society's having enough productive members to produce the gross national product from which to finance them. From this angle, we have to recognize that there is a vital difference between ascribing equal and absolute values to all members of society, irrespective of innate qualities, and our practical interpretation of the ethical norms of acting justly, keeping promises, dealing honestly, and refraining from purposeful injury, all of which are social concepts that must be related to other social influences, many of which seem remote from the actual clinical situation in question. Provision of intensive medical care depends on both the wealth of the social system and on how it decides to dispose of its resources—whether to expend £75m on the purchase of Trident II aircraft or invest that sum (or even a modicum of it) in health, education, and welfare services.

This point offers a good theme on which to conclude—the relationship of ethics to other dominant forces in society and the fact that their influence on social institutions, behavior, and attitudes will be largely determined by the social context in which they operate (Susser, 1980). Ethical theories and systems must therefore be constantly reevaluated in the light of social change to ensure that they remain relevant to vital social trends and, if necessary, are modified to meet new social mores and demands (Callahan, 1980). Only if this happens will ethical systems be able to serve their important social function of regulating social behavior and sustaining a requisite moral standard.

REFERENCES

Adams, M. E., and Colvin, R. W. 1969. The deprivation hypothesis: Its application to mentally retarded children and their needs. Child Welfare 48:136–141, 164.

Amery, I. B. 1980. The Rights of the Mentally Retarded and Developmentally Disabled to Treatment and Education. Charles C Thomas Publisher, Springfield, Illinois.

Bayles, M. D. 1976. Harm to the unconceived. Philosophy and Public Affairs 5:292–304.

Brieland, D. 1979. Bioethical issues in family planning. Soc. Work 25:478–484.

British Medical Journal. 1981. The right to live and the right to die. Br. Med. J. 283:269–270.

Brody, E. B. 1976. Reproductive freedom, coercion and justice. Soc. Sci. Med. 10:553–557.

Bundy, S. 1978. Attitudes of 40-year-old college graduates towards amniocentesis. Br. Med. J. 2:1475–1477.

Callahan, D. 1980. Shattuck Lecture—Contemporary biomedical ethics. N. Engl. J. Med. 302:1228–1233.

Davies, P. 1980. Perinatal mortality. Arch. Dis. Child. 55:833–837.

Donnai, P., Charles, N., and Harris, R. 1981. Attitudes of patients after "genetic" termination of pregnancy. Br. Med. J. 282:621–622.

Doyle, C. 1981. A baby's right to live—or die. The Observer, England, August 16th.

Duff, R., and Campbell, A. G. 1973. Moral and ethical dilemmas in the special care nursery. N. Engl. J. Med. 289:890–894.

Dyck, A. 1974. The value of life. Paper presented at the Third Annual Joseph S. Barr Intensive Care Unit Symposium—The Ethics of Newborn Intensive Care, Massachusetts General Hospital, February 26th.

Engelhardt, T. 1973. Euthanasia and children: The injury of continued existence. J. Pediatr. 83:170–171.

Fletcher, J. 1972. Indicators of humanhood: A tentative profile of man. Hastings Cent. Rep. 2:1–4.

Fox, R. C. 1981. The sting of death in American society. Soc. Serv. Rev. 55:42–59.

Freireich, E. J. 1980. Can we afford to treat acute leukemia? N. Engl. J. Med. 302:1084–1085.

Fry, A. 1981. Call for resources for those we keep alive. Community Care, September 17th, p. 5.

Garber, H., and Heber, F. R. 1977. The Milwaukee Project: Indications of the effectiveness of early intervention in preventing mental retardation. In: P. Mittler (ed.), Research to Practice in Mental Retardation, Vol. I, pp. 119–127. University Park Press, Baltimore.

Gath, A. 1975. Down's Syndrome and the Family: The Early Years. Academic Press, London.

Gath, A. 1977. Sibling reactions to mental handicap: A comparison of the brothers and sisters of mongol children. J. Child Psychol. Psychiatry 15:187.

Grossman, F. K. 1972. Brothers and Sisters of Retarded Children. University of Syracuse Press, Syracuse, New York.

Himsworth, H. 1973. The human right to life: Its nature and origins. In: B. Hilton, D. Callahan, M. Harris, P. Condliffe, and B. Berkeley (eds.), Ethical Issues in Human Genetics: Genetic Counselling and the Use of Genetic Knowledge. Plenum Publishing Corp., New York.

Hobel, C. J. 1980. Better perinatal health. Lancet 2:31–33.

Hosey, C. 1973. Yes, our son is still with us. Child. Today 2:14–17, 36.

Jaehnig, W. 1979. A Family Service for the Mentally Handicapped. Fabian Society, London.

King, R. D., Raynes, N. V., and Tizard, J. 1971. Patterns of Residential Care. Sociological Studies in Institutions for Handicapped Children, Chapter 7. Routledge and Kegan Paul, London.

Kuman, R., and Robertson, K. 1978. Previous induced abortion and antenatal depression in primiparae: Preliminary report on a survey of mental health in pregnancy. Psychol. Med. 8:711–715.

Lancet. 1981. Ethics and the nephrologist. Lancet 1:594–596.

Leaf, A. 1980. The M.G.H. Trustees say no to heart transplant. N. Engl. J. Med. 302:1087–1088.

Lightowler, C. D. R. 1971. Meningomyelocele: The price of treatment. Br. Med. J. 2:385–387.

MacAndrew, C., and Edgerton, R. 1964. The everyday life of institutionalised "idiots". Human Org. 23:312–318.

McCarthy, J. T., Koops, B. L., Honeyfield, P. R., and Butterfield, L. J. 1979. Who pays the bill for neonatal intensive care? J. Pediatr. 95:755–761.

McCormick, R. A. 1974. To save or let die: The dilemma of modern medicine. JAMA 229:172–176.

Mill, J. S. 1971. Utilitarianism. Longmans Green & Co., London.

Morris, P. 1969. Put Away: A Sociological Study of Institutions for the Mentally Retarded. Routledge and Kegan Paul, London.

Oswin, M. 1978. Children in Longstay Hospitals. Spastics International Medical Publishers, London.

Pomeroy, D., Fewtrell, J., Adams, M., Butler, N., and Gill, R. 1978. Improving the quality of life for families with a mentally handicapped child. Parents Voice 28:4–5.

Potter, R. B. 1977. Labelling the mentally retarded: The just allocation of therapy. In: S. J. Reiser, A. J. Dyck, and W. Curran (eds.), Ethics in Medicine: Historical Perspectives and Temporary Concerns. M.I.T. Press, Cambridge, Mass.

Powledge, T., and Fletcher, J. 1979. Guidelines for the ethical and social and legal issues in prenatal diagnosis. N. Engl. J. Med. 300:168–172.

Ross, W. D. 1930. The Right and the Good. Clarendon Press, Oxford.

Rutter, M., and Madge, N. 1976. Cycles of Disadvantage. Heinemann Medical Books, London.

Shearer, A. 1980. Handicapped Children in Residential Care: A Study of Policy Failure. Bedford Square Press of the National Council for Voluntary Organisations, London.

Skarnulis, E. 1974. Non-citizen: Plight of the mentally retarded. Soc. Work 19:56–62.

Susser, M. 1980. The works of George Rosen. Observations of a very small sample. Int. J. Health Serv. 10:323–328.

Tew, B., and Laurence, K. M. 1973. Mothers, brothers and sisters of patients with spina bifida. Dev. Med. Child Neurol. 15(suppl. 29):69–76.

Wilkin, D. 1982. A task-oriented approach to the assessment of the distribution of the burden of care, levels of support and felt needs in the family. In: B. Cooper (ed.), Assessing the Handicaps and Needs of Mentally Retarded Children. Academic Press, London.

Wilson, E. 1972. Exploited mothers. Soc. Work Today 2:6–7.

PERSPECTIVES AND PROGRESS IN MENTAL RETARDATION
Volume I—Social, Psychological, and Educational Aspects
Edited by J. M. Berg

MALTREATMENT AND MENTAL RETARDATION

R. F. Schilling and S. P. Schinke

*Child Development and Mental Retardation Center,
University of Washington, Seattle, Washington 98195*

The authors describe a still unfolding but important relationship between mental retardation and maltreatment that involves mentally retarded children, mentally retarded adults in the community, and their children. Retarded persons' dependency and cognitive limitations translate into increased risk of abuse, neglect, and exploitation. Mentally handicapped persons exist in poverty—of income, experience, and opportunity. These circumstances compound the likelihood of maltreatment of retarded individuals and children of retarded parents. Practitioners are beginning to apply strategies to prevent and ameliorate the effects of maltreatment. Modest pilot efforts point toward further applied research. Parents of mentally retarded citizens, retarded people themselves, and their children all stand to gain from a better understanding of these issues.

There is growing awareness that mentally retarded persons are at high risk of maltreatment (Friedrich and Boriskin, 1976; Schilling, 1981). Concurrently, it has been noted (Edwards and Wapnick, 1979; Schilling et al., 1982) that, in certain circumstances, retarded persons may harm those who are still more vulnerable—their own children, younger siblings, and fellow residents in group living facilities. Awareness of the relationship between mental retardation and maltreatment has not translated into a clear understanding of the nature and extent of these phenomena. This paper highlights three at-risk groups of mentally retarded people: children, adults in the community, and parents. For each of these groups, we discuss characteristics that increase the risk of maltreatment, and detail ways to prevent abuse, neglect, and exploitation.

Funding was by Clipped Wings, United Airlines Stewardess Alumnae Incorporated, Seattle Chapter, and by Grant No. 90CA902 from the National Center on Child Abuse and Neglect, Administration for Children, Youth, and Families, Office of Human Development Services, U.S. Department of Health and Human Services, awarded to the University of Washington Child Development and Mental Retardation Center, Seattle.

11

MENTALLY RETARDED CHILDREN

Risk of Abuse and Neglect

Ordinary standards about abuse and neglect are inadequate to meet the needs of mentally retarded children (Schinke et al., 1981). A developmentally disabled 13-year-old, for example, may be as dependent as a 6-year-old nonhandicapped child who would receive a higher priority by overworked protective service workers. Biological anomalies of some retarded children demand altered definitions of malnourishment. For example, the uncontrolled appetite in Prader-Willi syndrome (Holm and Pipes, 1976) means parents must strictly limit caloric intake. Mentally retarded persons with motor deficits require special clothing, furniture, prosthetics, and ambulatory devices. Tighter safety standards must be enforced when impaired balance and judgment mean higher risk of accidents. Such unique requirements of retarded children translate into a greater risk of physical neglect.

Mentally retarded children, more than their nonhandicapped counterparts, are at risk for emotional neglect. In dealing with parents of developmentally disabled children, practitioners are apt to hear, "I know he can understand me—when he wants to." In fact, some retarded children may learn simpler cues such as, "Wash-up, it's dinner time," far more easily than tasks with less immediate reinforcers. Mentally retarded dependents may be pressed into unreachable goals by parents who are unable or unwilling to accept their child's limitations. Sandgrund et al. (1974) argue that an "abuse-prone" parent is one whose poor self-image forces him or her into unrealistic expectations of children. A retarded child whose performance falls far short of demands reinforces such a parent's poor self-image, increasing the probabilities of abuse.

Physiological or behavioral characteristics of some mentally retarded children may adversely affect parent-child relationships. Retarded children who exhibit aggressive, noncompliant, or tantrum behavior may provoke parents into abusive responses (Robinson and Robinson,1976; Roberts, 1979). A Down's syndrome child's passivity and poor sucking reflex may clash with the mother's expectation of a reciprocal bonding process (Gordon and Jameson, 1979). Children with autistic features may be ignored at home as they engage in self-stimulatory behavior. Retarded children may risk punishment meted out by angry parents who are frustrated in their attempts to teach, manage, or communicate (Friedrich and Boriskin, 1976; Gaensbauer and Sands, 1979; Frodi, 1981).

Not surprisingly, mentally retarded children are overrepresented in child maltreatment statistics (Rose and Hardman, 1981; Schilling,

1981). Frodi (1981) cited numerous studies of child maltreatment with sample sizes ranging from 14 to 6,000 in which retarded children are disproportionately represented. Sandgrund et al. (1974) controlled for socioeconomic status and found that 25% of abused children were mentally retarded whereas only 3% of control children were retarded. Confounding problems of cause and effect cannot be ignored, but there is little doubt that retarded children risk maltreatment more than non-handicapped children (Nesbit and Karagianis, 1982).

For mentally retarded children, the risk of maltreatment increases because of stresses on their care providers. The physical, emotional, and financial burden of rearing a handicapped child results in family strain (Solomons, 1979) and increased risk of abuse. Parents of developmentally disabled children want and require extra support (Friedrich, 1979; Schilling and Schinke, 1983) but tend to be shunned by society, cut off from friends, and left unsupported by extended family (Berger and Foster, 1976). Parents whose children are less manageable, most difficult to teach, more demanding, and less rewarding are those who are without social supports that provide relief, encouragement, perspective, and empathy. Care providers in group homes and institutions, and to a lesser extent staff in sheltered workshops and developmental preschools, must also endure extraordinary stress, exacerbated by long hours, low pay, lack of training, and limited or nonexistent consultation, supervision, or backup support (Schinke, 1979). As a result of these factors, retarded persons, who are by definition vulnerable, are at even greater risk of maltreatment when adverse circumstances converge.

Intervention

Preventing abuse and neglect of mentally retarded children should be primary for clinicians and researchers. Despite acknowledgment of the problem, few efforts have been aimed at preventing and treating such abuse and neglect. Our pilot work indicates that parents of mentally retarded children can be taught to increase coping ability and enhance social supports. Group training encompasses facts about developmental disabilities, problem solving and decision making, coping skills, social supports, interpersonal communication, and advocacy. Participants learn through didactics, audiovisual and written materials, group discussions, modeling, practice, and homework. Groups are led by social workers experienced in group process techniques.

Participants are introduced to coping by discussing troubles of families of handicapped children. Leaders transform problems into vignettes, roleplay the situations, and verbalize coping statements. For example, when faced with a tantrum, a parent might say: "Oh, oh, I can feel my neck getting tight. Time to relax a bit. I'll go into the next room, sit in the big chair, and take a deep breath." Participants learn coping in subgroup simulations. They verbalize self-statements and think them silently. Families learn to push aside overwhelming feelings of rejection and fear by using positive self-statements ("Gee, I'm grateful for the good friends I have," or "Easy now, remember when we thought he would never walk?"). All the while, leaders and group members give coaching, feedback, praise, and instructions.

Family members require extra skill in establishing necessary but elusive social supports. Parents learn, via group discussion and testimony from experienced parents, to give up idealized images of parenthood. They come to understand social support and its significance for families of developmentally disabled children. They learn the importance of social supports and how extra efforts and skills are required to form an effective support system (Power and Dell Orto, 1980).

In groups, parents learn to identify present social supports and those they wish to cultivate. Using data provided by participants, instructors complete a composite support plan in group. Homework involves each parent or family making an individual plan, matching needs to possible supports. Next, parents implement a plan for developing and maintaining a social support network. Because few persons reach out to families of developmentally disabled children, parents learn to cultivate supportive relationships based on mutual need. One parent was successful in trading child-caring responsibilities with another parent of a handicapped child who also needed time away from the responsibilities of child care. Shared kinship reflects still other motivations, desires, and needs. In building a network parents learn to recognize and adapt to these differences in potentially supportive persons.

Increasing interpersonal communication skills helps families establish contacts and build social supports (Power and Dell Orto, 1980; Voysey, 1980). Employing elements of structured learning therapy (Sprafkin et al., 1980) and methods developed in other settings (Schinke et al., 1978; Schinke et al., 1980), participants systematically learn how to begin, carry on, and end conversations, follow up initial contacts via telephone, and accept and express appreciation. Later, participants learn to ask for help and, in turn, offer assistance.

Homework is a vehicle for applying new skills to everyday situations. Parents first bring social network plans to group meetings, and explain how new social supports would help meet family needs. They then tell of future opportunities for approaching potentially supportive persons. After practicing their coping and interpersonal skills in groups, parents test out new skills in their home, church, or neighborhood.

Later, they tell of successes and failures as they read from daily logs. Group leaders and members offer comments, praise, and encouragement for further action. After training, parents have first-hand experience solving problems, making decisions, coping, and effectively communicating. They know how to establish social supports and how to advocate for their child. Most important, trained parents understand how to increase the well-being of everyone in the family by managing the stresses of a developmentally disabled child.

Results

Pilot work with a group of eight parents showed positive changes following training. On written measures of anger, nervousness, and irritability, parents evidenced more self-control and calm. One measure asked parents to put themselves into an imaginary situation trying to manage an out-of-control mentally retarded child. When asked what they were thinking or saying to themselves, trained parents showed significant gains in positive self-talk, calming statements, and self-praise. On a pre- and posttraining videotape measure parents demonstrated their skill in engaging potentially supportive persons. Rated by judges who were blind to the purposes of the study, the performance test indicated that through training parents became more skilled in approaching and engaging would-be social supports.

Parents were faithful in attending meetings and carrying out assignments. They reported that as a result of the group training they had gained new social supports, and were better prepared to cope with stresses encountered in caring for their child. Three months after the last session six parents reported continuing contacts with one or more social supports gained during group training. Although these early data are promising, future projects must incorporate controlled research design and rigorous outcome measures (Berger and Foster, 1976; Friedrich, 1979).

MALTREATMENT OF MENTALLY RETARDED
PERSONS LIVING IN THE COMMUNITY

Risk and Normalization

Mentally retarded persons who may for years have endured inhumane treatment in institutions (Forssman and Åkesson, 1970; Braddock, 1977) may now be victimized in community settings. Haywood (1981) noted that, as retarded persons gain greater freedom, they become more vulnerable to personal, sexual, and financial exploitation: "A defining characteristic of mental retardation is the relative dependency of many retarded persons. That very dependency constitutes in itself a dimension of vulnerability, since whenever one is necessarily dependent upon others for essential aspects of one's life, that can only be defined as great vulnerability'' (p. 192). If mentally retarded persons are to lead richer, less protected lives, they inevitably must experience greater risks.

Consider moderately and severely retarded individuals who increasingly live in small group facilities: they may have difficulty grasping community standards of sexuality in regard to casual conversation, touching, public masturbation, and approaching children. In the workplace and in the residential setting, their vulnerability may result in economic exploitation, sexual abuse, and unhealthy living quarters. To date, strict regulation accompanying the deinstitutionalization movement seems to have prevented exploitation and maltreatment in community environments. In reality, the extent of maltreatment affecting retarded adults in the community is unknown. Current trends toward deinstitutionalization push more retarded persons into the community. Concurrent trends of service cutbacks may mean that these persons and the community will be ill-prepared for the transition. The potential for victimization exists for mentally retarded citizens who are becoming more independent.

Preventing Maltreatment

Normalization must find a balance between maximum social participation and minimum social vulnerability (Haywood, 1981). Unfortunately, little attention has been given to finding ways to deal with the vulnerability of mentally retarded persons. Preventing exploitation, neglect, and abuse of retarded citizens requires both changes in the environment and increased competence in those "newly arrived" citizens who are too often victimized (Brown, 1981). These twin objectives may be met within the same sphere or context. The authors are consultants to one such program that prevents adverse outcomes by both preparing the individual and adapting the environment. A food service training program (Moss, 1979) incorporates instruction for mentally retarded workers on how to handle their earnings and withstand pressure from those who wish to "borrow" money. In one training sequence retarded workers practice refusal skills while instructors or fellow workers roleplay an insistent borrower. Program staff who are responsible for placing trained clients in restaurant positions recognize that successful outcomes depend on a positive environment compatible with retarded persons' special needs. Accordingly, these staff members are careful to screen out potentially unethical employers who would circumvent health, safety, and wage standards. Although more worldly trainees have little difficulty working late hours in undesirable business districts, clients who have proved themselves especially vulnerable are placed in less risky circumstances. Restaurant managers who employ program graduates also learn how to provide minimum sheltering for retarded workers. For example, in some instances paychecks are mailed to the bank, rather than risk loss or theft.

Sexual conduct for all persons includes both rights and responsibilities—no less so for developmentally disabled individuals. Mentally retarded persons need to know that sexual behavior is appropriate only in certain contexts. They should be able to recognize and accept refusal from others and be able to demonstrate refusal skills when approached. Developmentally disabled persons must know to avoid such acts as public masturbation or inappropriate sexual contact (Landesman-Dwyer and Sulzbacher, 1981). Strict societal sanctions against deviant sexual behavior demand well-conceived programs aimed at retarded persons who are susceptible to exploitation and are more likely to overstep the bounds of acceptable sexual conduct. Perhaps because it is of such great concern to society, sexually proscribed behavior has not been left to chance for developmentally disabled people. One training sequence (Newton-Alrick, 1979) allows participants to anticipate potentially exploitative situations and plan prevention and escape responses. Mentally retarded persons should be able to demonstrate an understanding of the consequences of undesirable sexual behavior. Because didactic teaching is an ineffective way of training new skills in retarded individuals, instruction should emphasize demonstration, practice, and roleplay. As with other areas of exploitation affecting retarded persons, issues of sexuality afford preventive and ameliorative roles for parents, group home staff, police, informed citizens, and social workers.

CHILDREN OF MENTALLY RETARDED PARENTS

Environmental Risk

Despite methodological shortcomings, available data suggest that children of mentally retarded parents are at risk for abuse and neglect (Smith, 1975; Robinson, 1978). In a recent paper (Schilling et al., 1982), these authors critically reviewed studies linking child maltreatment to retarded parents. Although rigorous studies are lacking, considerable evidence indicates that mental retardation adversely affects parental ability. A subtle but important aspect of childrearing by retarded parents is their inability to provide cognitive stimulation (McCandless, 1952; Baroff, 1974). Concrete thinking may limit retarded persons' awareness of alternative child management techniques (Bruner, 1967; Baroff, 1974; Pearlin and Schooler, 1978). Similarly, communication deficits of retarded parents limit their ability to understand or talk to their children. Lacking reading skills, retarded parents are unable to turn to books and magazines on childrearing. Mentally retarded persons—both as children and as parents—have fewer opportunities to learn about childrearing through observation, discussion, or experience.

Our experience in a university-based mental retardation center and as consultants to a developmental preschool suggests that mentally retarded parents are disadvantaged in many ways. Indeed, retarded adults have low incomes, unskilled jobs, inadequate housing, and poor health (Hurley, 1969). These conditions, along with social isolation, increased stress, poor self-esteem, and expectancy of failure, result in a sense of impotence like that experienced by parents who abuse and neglect their children (Bailer, 1970; Justice and Justice, 1976). Therefore, even without considering the special characteristics of mental retardation, mentally handicapped parents are relegated to a socioeconomic status that fosters child maltreatment (Elmer, 1977; Pelton, 1978).

Although most children of retarded parents are not retarded, such parents are more likely than others to rear retarded children (Reed and Anderson, 1973). Such children require special care, and place added stress on parents who are least able to provide necessary economic, emotional, and cognitive resources (Crain and Millor, 1978; Solomons, 1979). Surely, for developmentally disabled children reared by retarded parents the possibility of optimal nurturance seems more remote than the likelihood of maltreatment.

Intervention

Recent pilot work by the authors was directed at mentally retarded parents referred following investigations of abuse or neglect. Parents met for eight twice-weekly group sessions led by a male-female team of social workers. Parental learning and behavior change was facilitated through a carefully structured presentation of target skills including repeated exposure to demonstration, practice, and feedback (Schinke and Landesman-Dwyer, 1981; Barth et al., 1983). Demonstration and modeling prepared parents for the next step of guided practice. In self-control training parents learned to identify and manage stressors. Parents came to recognize early cues of provocative situations, identify signs of anxiety or anger responses, pause and take deep breaths, employ alternative thoughts and actions, and reward their own effective coping. After a video demonstration showing a father in both controlled and uncontrolled responses to a child spilling her milk, the group leaders assumed parent and child roles. Initially guided by a script, then progressively without prompts, group members rehearsed the use of self-talk, impulse delay, and relaxation in the "spilled milk" situation. Before applying the skills to their own conflicts, parents practiced calming statements and self-reinforcement in additional preestablished role-play situations. Pretest-posttest scores showed important gains on written and video performance tests. At posttest, parents receiving a treatment package scored significantly better than an untreated contrast group. On the Anger Inventory (Novaco, 1975) anger levels of experimental group members declined more than those of controls ($F_{1,17} = 5.932$, $P < 0.04$). Self-reported ratings on the Becker Adjective Checklist (Becker, 1960) significantly favored treated parents ($F_{1,16} = 4.70$, $P < 0.05$). While being videotaped, parents responded to childish stress-producing behavior of a confederate. Blaming statements declined while "I" statements rose, yielding a significant positive change in the ratio between them ($F_{1,17} = 5.191$, $P < 0.037$). Although this modest effort demands replication, pilot results are encouraging.

Early casework descriptions report varying degrees of success in helping mentally retarded parents (Mitchell, 1947; Mickelson, 1949), but no published data report on the outcomes of current efforts (Madsen, 1979; Sherman and Flory, 1981). The Parents Are Learning Skills (PALS) project aims to prevent environmental retardation through in-home parent education directed at retarded parents (Nanis, 1978). Project Esprit (Sherman and Flory, 1981) is a criterion-based educational model for teaching skills to the mentally retarded parent. The comprehensive project covers parenting skills, independent living, and home safety, and includes an educator, a social worker, and five home visitors. Parent and child objectives are linked with activities and progress is measured over time. Like other projects (Madsen, 1979), these approaches are aimed at improving overall childrearing competence and preventing environmental mental retardation. Research and demonstration projects should continue, as investigators advance our limited knowledge on the efficacy of interventions with vulnerable families and practitioners press on with needed services.

ACKNOWLEDGMENTS

The authors warmly thank Anna Bolstad, Lois Holt, and Cheryl Kelso for assistance in preparing this manuscript.

REFERENCES

Bailer, I. 1970. Emotional disturbance and mental retardation: Etiologic and conceptual relationships. In: F. J. Menolascino (ed.), Psychiatric Approaches to Mental Retardation. Basic Books, New York.

Baroff, G. S. 1974. Mental Retardation: Nature, Cause, and Management. John Wiley & Sons, Inc., New York.

Barth, R. P., Blythe, B. J., Schinke, S. P., and Schilling, R. F. 1983. Self control training with maltreating parents. Child Welfare 62:313–324.

Becker, W. C. 1960. The relationship of factors in parental ratings of self and each other to the behavior of kindergarten children as rated by mothers, fathers, and teachers. J. Consult. Psychol. 24:507–527.

Berger, M., and Foster, M. 1976. Family-level interventions for retarded children: A multivariate approach to issues and strategies. Multivariate Exp. Clin. Res. 2:1–21.

Braddock, D. A. 1977. A national deinstitutionalization study. State Government 50:220–226. (Council of State Governments, Lexington, Kentucky.)

Brown, R. I. 1981. Development of integrated programs for mentally handicapped persons: The present and the future. In: P. Mittler (ed.), Frontiers of Knowledge in Mental Retardation, Vol. I. University Park Press, Baltimore.

Bruner, J. S. 1967. On cognitive growth I and II. In: J. S. Bruner, R. R. Oliver, P. M. Greenfield, J. Hornsby, H. J. Kenny, M. Maccoby, N. Modiano, F. Mosher, D. R. Olson, M. C. Potter, L. C. Reich, and A. Sonstroem (eds.), Studies in Cognitive Growth: A Collaboration at Center for Cognitive Studies. John Wiley & Sons, Inc., New York.

Crain, L. S., and Millor, G. K. 1978. Forgotten children: Maltreated children of mentally retarded parents. Pediatrics 61:130–132.

Edwards, J. P., and Wapnick, S. 1979. Being Me—A Social/Sexual Training Guide for Those Who Work with the Developmentally Disabled. EDNICK Communications, Portland, Oregon.

Elmer, E. 1977. Fragile Families, Troubled Children. University of Pittsburgh Press, Pittsburgh, Pennsylvania.

Forssman, H., and Åkesson, H. O. 1970. Mortality of the mentally deficient: A study of 12,903 institutionalized subjects. J. Ment. Defic. Res. 14:276–296.

Friedrich, W. N. 1979. Predictors of the coping behavior of mothers of handicapped children. J. Consult. Clin. Psychol. 47:1140–1141.

Friedrich, W. N., and Boriskin, J. A. 1976. The role of the child in abuse: A review of the literature. Am. J. Orthopsychiatry 46:580–590.

Frodi, A. M. 1981. Contribution of infant characteristics to child abuse. Am. J. Ment. Defic. 85:341–349.

Gaensbauer, T. J., and Sands, K. 1979. Distorted affective communications in abused/neglected infants and their potential impact on caretakers. J. Am. Acad. Child Psychiatry 18:236–250.

Gordon, A. H., and Jameson, J. C. 1979. Infant-mother attachment in patients with nonorganic failure to thrive syndrome. J. Am. Acad. Child Psychiatry 18:251–259.

Haywood, H. C. 1981. Reducing social vulnerability is the challenge of the eighties. Ment. Retard. 19:190–195.

Holm, V. A., and Pipes, P. L. 1976. Food and children with Prader-Willi syndrome. Am. J. Dis. Child. 130:1063–1067.

Hurley, R. 1969. Poverty and Mental Retardation: A Causal Relationship. Vintage Books, New York.

Justice, B., and Justice, R. 1976. The Abusing Family. Human Sciences Press, New York.

Landesman-Dwyer, S., and Sulzbacher, F. M. 1981. Residential placement and adaptation of severely and profoundly retarded individuals. In: R. H. Bruininks, C. E. Meyers, B. B. Sigford, and K. C. Lakin (eds.), Deinstitutionalization and Community Adjustment of Mentally Retarded People. Monograph No. 4. American Association on Mental Deficiency, Washington, D.C.

McCandless, B. 1952. Environment and intelligence. Am. J. Ment. Defic. 56:674–691.

Madsen, M. L. 1979. Parenting classes for the mentally retarded. Ment. Retard. 17:195–196.

Mickelson, P. 1949. Can mentally retarded parents be helped to give their children better care? Am. J. Ment. Defic. 53:516–534.

Mitchell, S. B. 1947. Results in family casework with feebleminded clients. Smith College Stud. Soc. Work 18:21–36.

Moss, J. W. 1979. Post Secondary Vocational Education for Mentally Retarded Adults. Council for Exceptional Children, Reston, Virginia.

Nanis, D. 1978. What Happens to Children of the Mentally Retarded? (brochure.) Community Association for the Retarded, Palo Alto, California.

Nesbit, W. C., and Karagianis, L. D. 1982. Child abuse: Exceptionality as a risk factor. Alberta J. Educ. Res. 28:69–76.

Newton-Alrick, G. 1979. Caring, an Approach to Sex Education. Author, Portland, Oregon.

Novaco, R. W. 1975. Anger Control: The Development and Evaluation of an Experimental Treatment. Heath, Lexington, Massachusetts.

Pearlin, L. I., and Schooler, C. 1978. The structure of coping. J. Health Soc. Behav. 19:2–21.

Pelton, L. H. 1978. Child abuse and neglect: The myth of classlessness. Am. J. Orthopsychiatry 48:608–617.

Power, P. W., and Dell Orto, A. E. 1980. Approaches to family intervention. In: P. W. Power, and A. E. Dell Orto (eds.), Role of the Family in the Rehabilitation of the Physically Disabled. University Park Press, Baltimore.

Reed, S. C., and Anderson, V. E. 1973. Effects of changing sexuality on the gene pool. In: F. F. de la Cruz and G. D. LaVeck (eds.), Human Sexuality and the Mentally Retarded. Brunner/Mazel, New York.

Roberts, M. 1979. Reciprocal nature of parent-infant interaction: Implications for child maltreatment. Child Welfare 58:383–392.

Robinson, L. H. 1978. Parental attitudes of retarded young mothers. Child Psychiatry Hum. Dev. 8:131–144.

Robinson, N. M., and Robinson, H. B. 1976. The Mentally Retarded Child. McGraw-Hill Book Company, New York.

Rose, E., and Hardman, M. L. 1981. The abused mentally retarded child. Educ. Train. Ment. Retard. 16:114–118.

Sandgrund, A., Gaines, R. W., and Green, A. H. 1974. Child abuse and mental retardation: A problem of cause and effect. Am. J. Ment. Defic. 79:327–330.

Schilling, R. F. 1981. Treatment of child abuse. In: S. P. Schinke (ed.), Behavioral Methods in Social Welfare. Aldine Publishing Company, Chicago.

Schilling, R. F., and Schinke, S. P. 1983. Social networks in developmental disabilities. In: J. K. Whittaker and J. Garbarino, and Associates, Social Support Networks: Informal Helping in the Human Services. Aldine Publishing Company, New York.

Schilling, R. F., Schinke, S. P., Blythe, B. J., and Barth, R. P. 1982. Child maltreatment and mentally retarded parents: Is there a relationship? Ment. Retard. 20:201–209.

Schinke, S. P. 1979. Staff training in group homes: A family approach. In: L. A. Hamerlynck (ed.), Behavioral Systems for the Developmentally Disabled: II. Brunner/Mazel, New York.

Schinke, S. P., Blythe, B. J., Schilling, R. F., and Barth, R. P. 1981. Neglect of mentally retarded persons. Educ. Train. Ment. Retard. 16:299–303.

Schinke, S. P., Gilchrist, L. D., and Blythe, B. J. 1980. Role of communication in prevention of teenage pregnancy. Health Soc. Work 5:54–59.

Schinke, S. P., and Landesman-Dwyer, S. 1981. Training staff in group homes serving mentally retarded persons. In: P. Mittler (ed.), Frontiers of Knowledge in Mental Retardation, Vol. I. University Park Press, Baltimore.

Schinke, S. P., Smith, T. E., Gilchrist, L. D., and Wong, S. E. 1978. Interviewing-skills training: An empirical evaluation. J. Soc. Serv. Res. 1:391–401.

Sherman, L. G., and Flory, R. H. 1981. Project Esprit: A Manual for Replication. Association for Retarded Citizens, Allegheny County, Pittsburgh, Pennsylvania.

Smith, S. M. 1975. The Battered Child Syndrome. Butterworth Publishers, Reading, Massachusetts.

Solomons, G. 1979. Child abuse and developmental disabilities. Dev. Med. Child Neurol. 21:101–108.

Sprafkin, R., Gershaw, N. J., and Goldstein, A. 1980. Structured-learning therapy: Overview and applications to adolescents and adults. In: D. P. Rathjen and J. P. Foreyt (eds.), Social Competence. Pergamon Press, Inc., New York.

Voysey, M. 1980. Impression management by parents with disabled children. In: P. W. Powers and A. E. Dell Orto (eds.), Role of Family in the Rehabilitation of the Physically Disabled. University Park Press, Baltimore.

PERSPECTIVES AND PROGRESS IN MENTAL RETARDATION
Volume I—Social, Psychological, and Educational Aspects
Edited by J. M. Berg
Copyright © 1984 by I.A.S.S.M.D.

PUBLIC POLICY FOR MENTALLY RETARDED PERSONS
Incompetence, Guardianship, and Advocacy

J.C. Moskop
Humanities Program, School of Medicine, East Carolina University, Greenville, North Carolina 27834

In this paper, it is argued that claims like "retarded persons are either (totally) competent or (totally) incompetent" and "formal advocates are the best representatives of retarded people" depend on an oversimplification of the situation and needs of retarded people. More complex and less rigidly defined alternatives that can be tailored to the particular circumstances of individuals are more likely to serve the best interests of retarded persons. Examples of such alternatives discussed are statutes that provide for limited guardianship and the recognition of different advocates for different kinds of decision making on behalf of retarded persons.

This paper examines two currently controversial issues regarding public policy for mentally retarded persons. These are the determination of incompetence and guardianship for retarded persons, and the determination of proper bearers of responsibility for persons adjudged incompetent. In both cases, I argue that flexible proposals that permit significant individual variation promise improvement over more general and rigid alternatives.

INCOMPETENCE AND GUARDIANSHIP

The Competence/Incompetence Dichotomy

Wikler (1979) examined the justification for denying full citizenship to mentally retarded persons by declaring them incompetent. He pointed

23

out that decisions about competency involve a trade-off between two fundamental values, freedom and protection from harm; that is, declaring a person incompetent denies him a wide range of freedoms, but protects him from harm caused by his inability to make fundamental decisions adequately. Wikler argued that, even if mental capacity or intelligence is a continuous endowment always admitting of "more" and "less," a nonarbitrary line can be drawn between competence and incompetence, because only a certain amount of intelligence is necessary to perform key life tasks. He then noted that the level of difficulty of these key life tasks is largely socially determined. Although these tasks could be made simpler, thus rendering many retarded persons fully competent, simpler conventions would be less useful for persons of average or above-average intelligence. The choice between changing social practices to make them safe for retarded people and denying retarded people freedom to act in a riskier environment is, Wikler concluded, ultimately a matter of distributive justice.

Wikler's claim that social practices could be made simpler to allow retarded persons to participate in them suggests one promising approach to reconciling the values of autonomy and protection. However, his argument assumes that competence, unlike intelligence, is an "all-or-nothing" property, "so that all standing above it are equally endowed and all falling below it are unendowed" (Wikler, 1979). I believe that abandoning the simple competent-incompetent dichotomy will offer other ways to reconcile autonomy and protection. In a footnote, Wikler acknowledged the value of a notion of "selective competence" with respect to specific tasks. Nevertheless, his general argument assumes "that many of the important liberties denied the mildly retarded require about the same level of intelligence." However, does it require about the same amount of intelligence to drive a car, manage an estate, rent and maintain an apartment, subscribe to a newspaper, complete a tax return, vote, marry, care for a child, and give an informed consent to surgery or to nontherapeutic research?

Consider, for example, the case of Mrs. Mary Fabre, decided in 1979 by the Louisiana Supreme Court (Wilkinson, 1979). Mrs. Fabre was a 31-year-old widow with a 2½-year-old child. After her husband died, her brother brought an action to interdict her, the Louisiana equivalent of a finding of incompetence. The case was described as follows:

> The testimony presented at trial provided an extraordinarily clear picture of the defendant's capabilities and limitations. Intelligence testing showed she was capable of doing work only at a first grade level or lower. The witnesses agreed that in domestic matters she was capable of performing a wide variety of tasks. For example, she kept an immaculate house,

maintained friendly social contact with neighbors and friends, cared and cooked for her son and herself, and maintained neat personal appearance and personal hygiene. In addition, she regularly went to the post office and the drug store to fill prescriptions, and brought her son to a pediatrician whenever he was ill. She mowed her lawn, changed the oil and gas in her lawnmower, had a boyfriend, and regularly watched television and understood the plot.

Mrs. Fabre's limitations were just as clearly set out. All the expert witnesses agreed that she was incapable of handling her financial affairs. She could not handle money or make major purchases, read, write, add, subtract, make change, or recognize numbers beyond ten. Moreover, she was incapable of telling time, reciting the alphabet, or describing the shape of a ball, and she did not know her age, address, phone number, or the number of months in a year. The experts disagreed on Mrs. Fabre's ability to abstract or reason constructively when left to her own devices. Two believed she had no ability in these areas. The third felt that she had some ability to abstract and discriminate in certain situations. (Wilkinson, 1979, p. 175, footnotes omitted)

Mrs. Fabre seems clearly competent in some important areas, and clearly incompetent in others. If this is generally the case, Wikler's assumption that exercising various important liberties requires about the same amount of intelligence does not hold, and the notion of general mental competence as an all-or-nothing property may be a procrustean bed that has been imposed on retarded people.

Wikler's use of competence and incompetence as all-or-nothing concepts has a long heritage. Incompetence and the related concept of guardianship were inherited from the English law of equity and became standard features of state law in the United States. Corresponding to incompetence in jurisdictions based on Roman law is interdiction, a term that more clearly suggests the broad deprivation of rights involved (Wilkinson, 1979). Under such laws, courts traditionally had only two alternatives: declaring a person incompetent and appointing a guardian to handle virtually all his or her affairs or *not* declaring the person incompetent, thus letting stand the presumption of total competence. However, this limited range of action has come to be viewed as a weakness; its application to the mentally ill (Sherman, 1980; Wear, 1980) and to children (Gaylin, 1982), as well as to the mentally retarded (Kindred, 1976; Dussault, 1978; Wilkinson, 1979; Sherman, 1980; McCullough, in press), has been challenged. These authors reject a strict competent-incompetent dichotomy and propose concepts of partial incompetence and limited guardianship in order to achieve a more satisfactory reconciliation of freedom and protection for each individual.

Concept of Limited Guardianship

Although the idea of limited guardianship is not new [it was proposed by the President's Panel on Mental Retardation in 1963 (Kindred,

1976)], most states that have enacted limited guardianship statutes have done so in the last 5 years. Several models have been used in such statutes. In five states, for example, limited guardianships are restricted to mentally retarded persons who are financially self-supporting (Wilkinson, 1979). Limited guardians may be appointed in these states to administer the person's property exclusive of wages or earnings. Other states, including Washington, Texas, Kentucky, and North Carolina, provide a much broader scope for the responsibilities of a limited guardian. These states typically require an inquiry into the nature and extent of an individual's disabilities over a broad range of activities, including living arrangements, employment, financial management, health care, education, and training. In North Carolina, this inquiry is carried out by a court-appointed multidisciplinary evaluation team including, at least, a physician, a psychologist, and a social worker (Turnbull, 1979). The evaluation team formulates a guardianship plan recommending that specific powers and responsibilities be assumed by the guardian and other rights and privileges be retained by the retarded person; this plan becomes the basis of the court's action.

According to traditional legal doctrine, if a person has been found incompetent, his or her consent is not effective, and the consent of his or her guardian is a necessary and sufficient substitute in most areas. Thus, the plenary guardian maintains substantial control over the life of his or her ward. Limited guardianship statutes like that of North Carolina make possible a less restrictive arrangement in which the guardian may add his concurrent consent to that of the retarded person in order to support his or her decision (Turnbull, 1979). In this case, the consent of the guardian would be necessary, but not sufficient, because the consent of the retarded person would also be required.

Limited guardianship laws are, of course, not without costs of their own. They must first be mastered and applied by the interested parties—judges, professionals, attorneys, parents, relatives, and friends of retarded persons. Because the procedures are more complex, they will require more work by attorneys and court-designated investigators and be somewhat more expensive than traditional methods. However, this approach promises significant benefits for retarded persons. In the case of Mrs. Fabre, for example, the State Supreme Court overturned the lower court's decision and ruled that she did not meet the conditions for interdiction (Wilkinson, 1979). This ruling recognized her ability to act freely, but, because the state of Louisiana made no provision for partial guardianship, it placed her and her son at greater risk of financial exploitation and loss because of her inability to manage her financial affairs. Through a better fit between actual capacities and formal legal standing, retarded persons are likely to gain both workable freedoms, with an accompanying increase in self-reliance and self-esteem, and needed protection in areas of greater disability. These important benefits warrant a look beyond the traditional competence-incompetence dichotomy toward more refined methods for determining legal standing and the protections of guardianship.

THE QUESTION OF ADVOCACY

As noted above, new limited guardianship laws seek to allow retarded persons to make decisions for themselves whenever they are able. However, substitute decision makers are still necessary where individuals are not able to decide for themselves; profoundly retarded persons, for example, may completely lack this ability. There remains, then, the question of who should make choices for retarded persons when they themselves are unable to do so. Roos (1979) has commented on the difficulty of deciding who these decision makers should be, and Rothman (in press) proposed a deceptively simple answer to the question. Rothman's strategy is straightforward: first, he considers in turn and rejects several traditional candidates for this position—professionals, parents, and attorneys. Then, he proposes and defends the notion of formal advocates as the most appropriate decision makers for retarded persons. I argue that this issue is more complex than Rothman allows and requires a more flexible, context-bound solution. First, however, I briefly review Rothman's argument.

Formal Advocates as Decision Makers

As evidence of the inadequacy of *professionals* as protectors of retarded people, Rothman cites a 1967 accreditation report on Willowbrook State School prepared by a "professional team of the American Association on Mental Deficiency." Although Willowbrook was at that time, according to Rothman, a desperately overcrowded, understaffed, woefully inadequate institution, the report appears to gloss over and minimize many serious problems. To illustrate this, Rothman cites passages from the report and suggests alternative formulations. For example, the report states: "The nursing staff is quite impressive. The institution has 59 nurses, but 113 vacancies remain." He offers this alternative: "Why are there twice as many places open as there are staff on hand? How can 59 nurses possibly care for 5,400 residents as handicapped as those at Willowbrook?" The point of this analysis, Rothman claims, is not that the professionals visiting Willowbrook were uncaring, but that they identified with the institution's administration, not with the clients. They were unwilling to "blow the whistle" on miserable conditions, but chose the more comfortable strategy of supporting fellow professionals and trying to work within the traditional system for gradual improvement. The historical record represented by this report, Rothman concludes, makes it unwise to trust the professionals who run and accredit institutions to represent retarded persons.

Rothman also finds deep-rooted conflicts of interest in the position of *parents* vis-à-vis their retarded children. Among the factors that often conflict with the interests of the retarded child he cites the needs of other children, the parent's own relationship, shame and guilt about the child's handicap or their decision to institutionalize, and feelings of powerlessness to effect institutional change. Given this complex agenda, Rothman claims that parents are not the "natural" representatives of the interests of their own retarded children.

Rothman turns next to public interest or civil rights attorneys, the *legal* advocates of the retarded. Although he acknowledges the importance of their role in the deinstitutionalization movement, he is concerned about their lack of detailed knowledge of retardation and their inclination to move on to new fields of interest. Rothman prefers the term *formal advocate* to describe his choice for the best representative of retarded persons, although he recognizes that it will usually be a lawyer. By means of this term, Rothman seeks to emphasize that the advocate "will press for rights and entitlements before a judicial or administrative body; he will be most comfortable with set rules and unambiguous regulations, preferring to define the authority and obligations of caretakers rather than to trust to their skills or benevolence." In defense of this choice, Rothman cites the considerable successes of class-action suits on behalf of retarded persons over the past 10 years. He also argues that better decisions will be made in the give-and-take of an open, public forum, and that set procedures and fixed rules for the care of retarded persons will be more likely to prevent abuse and neglect than the broad discretionary authority of professionals.

What Constitutes Advocacy?

Rothman proposes an answer to the question, "Who is best suited to speak for retarded persons?", but he does not discuss a prior question, "What does it mean to speak for retarded persons?" In fact, it is never clear just what kind of representation or substitute decision-making authority he has in mind. This makes it difficult to gauge the significance of his conclusion, because such authority can be ascribed in different ways and on different levels. Consider, for example, the differences between 1) formulating public policy for retarded people as a group, or for subgroups such as the mildly retarded, 2) making decisions for small groups, such as the residents of a single group home or of an institution for severely and profoundly retarded children, and

3) making choices for a particular retarded person as his/her appointed guardian.

Rothman largely sticks to the neutral terminology of "speaking for the retarded"; this allows him to shift back and forth between all three levels of decision making, i.e., for large groups, smaller groups, and individuals. He does specifically limit his concern to decision making for severely and profoundly retarded people, noting that mildly retarded persons can make choices for themselves. This suggests a concern with guardianship, because severely and profoundly retarded persons are most in need of guardians to make decisions for them. Moreover, his claim that "the agenda that parents face is too complex and lengthy to make them the natural representatives of the interests of their own retarded children" also suggests a concern with guardianship, since it appears to be an attack on the legal principle of parents as natural guardians. However, Rothman's major examples are broader public policy issues of reforming institutions, securing funding for increased social services, and developing statewide standards for the habilitation of retarded persons.

Because Rothman does not make himself clear on this important issue, let us consider several possible interpretations of his view. First, given his apparent references to various levels of substitute decision making and the unqualified way in which his conclusion is stated, Rothman might be construed to mean that formal advocates are best suited to make decisions for severely and profoundly retarded persons on all the aforementioned levels. This position is a weak one, however. Whatever the value of formal advocates for shaping public policy, it hardly seems necessary or even feasible to insist that only persons fitting this description may become guardians for retarded persons.

A second interpretation might hold that Rothman is concerned only with deciding who is best suited to represent the interests of severely and profoundly retarded persons in the formulation of public policy, and he is not interested in other kinds of decision making. The formal advocate is, after all, explicitly described as one who "will press for rights and entitlements before a judicial or administrative body." Moreover, this interpretation would not require large numbers of formal advocates to assume a guardianship role for individuals. This second interpretation also has several drawbacks, however. First, it cannot account for Rothman's discussion of parents, because in it he does seem to be concerned with guardianship and decision making for particular individuals. Second, this interpretation would to some extent trivialize his position, because many would grant that, when it comes to formulating public policy, individuals trained in law and formal legal advocacy ought to play the major role.

A third and bolder interpretation of Rothman's position is as follows: not only are formal advocates best suited to represent the interests of severely and profoundly retarded persons in public policy decision making, but all important decisions for persons in this group should be made at the policy level, leaving little or no discretion to professionals and parents or guardians. This interpretation, I think, comes closest to capturing Rothman's intention. It is certainly not trivial, but it is very controversial. Under this interpretation, all important life choices for severely and profoundly retarded persons would be made through the ascription of legal rights to that group and the specification of those rights by means of set procedures and fixed rules. This approach, Rothman seems to be saying, will best serve the interests of retarded persons because it will enable the identification of instances of abuse or neglect and make such instances violations of specific legal rights.

Importance of Personal Relationships

Recently, several authors have challenged the claim that an exclusive emphasis on the possession of rights will, in fact, best serve the interests of retarded people. Woozley (in press), Diamond (in press), and May (in press), among others, argue that too great an emphasis on rights may lead to neglect of important virtues of a more intimate nature, such as love, friendship, and charity. If retarded persons are viewed only as bearers of rights, Woozley claimed (in press), it may be forgotten that first and foremost they are unique individual persons. We should therefore foster relationships of love and friendship in which retarded persons are understood and appreciated as individuals. Diamond (in press) offered examples of attitudes toward retarded persons in other cultures in order to suggest that virtues of charity or kindness may inspire action on behalf of retarded persons as well as or better than an appeal to rights. Based on an analysis of the process of bonding between parents and their handicapped children, May (in press) argued that the bonded parent imparts a special value to his child. He claimed that this value, which is achieved in and through the creation of an intimate relationship, provides a much stronger foundation for the provision of care than does consideration of rights.

All these writers insist on the importance of personal, caring relationships for the well-being of retarded persons. Only in such relationships are retarded persons valued and cared for as individuals rather than as members of a particular class. However, this perspective is completely absent in Rothman's account, and, if the last interpretation of his position is accurate, there can be no place for it, because all important decisions for severely and profoundly retarded persons will be made at the policy level. If writers like Woozley, Diamond, and May are correct about the significance of more intimate relationships for retarded persons, then Rothman's position is too narrow—it should allow a greater role for parents, guardians, and others personally involved in caring for retarded persons.

Conclusions

What, then, should be the overall assessment of Rothman's position? His claim that public policy is essential in breaking through a tradition of neglect and providing a baseline for decent treatment is, I think, important and uncontestable. Furthermore, I see no reason to disagree with his emphasis on the value of formal advocates in developing public policy for retarded persons. However, I would add that policies are unlikely to achieve their beneficent goals fully unless advocates rely on the guidance of both professionals and parents. This omission is, I think, symptomatic of the most serious weakness of Rothman's argument; that is, it dismisses parents and professionals as representatives for retarded persons too quickly and too categorically. Rothman's apparent conclusion that all important decisions be made at a high level of generality (i.e., for a whole class of persons) does not take sufficient account of individual needs and preferences and of the importance of personal caring relationships. Recognition of these factors requires a more complex system in which important authority is delegated to parents, guardians, and professionals, each according to their role in caring for retarded persons, and to retarded persons themselves, insofar as they are able.

REFERENCES

Diamond, C. Rights, justice and the retarded. Paper presented at the symposium, Natural Abilities and Perceived Worth: Rights, Values and Retarded Persons, Greenville, North Carolina, October 2, 1981. In: L. Kopelman and J. Moskop (eds.), Ethics and Mental Retardation. D. Reidel, Dordrecht. (in press)

Dussault, W. 1978. Guardianship and limited guardianship in Washington State Application for mentally retarded citizens. Gonzaga Law Rev. 13:585–624.

Gaylin, W. 1982. The competence of children: No longer all or none. Hastings Cent. Rep. 12:33–38.

Kindred, M. 1976. Guardianship and limitations upon capacity. In: M. Kindred et al., (eds.), The Mentally Retarded Citizen and the Law, pp. 63–87. The Free Press, New York.

McCullough, L. B. The world lost and the world gained: Labelling the mentally retarded. Paper presented at the symposium, Natural Abilities and Perceived Worth: Rights, Values and Retarded Persons, Greenville, North Carolina, October 2, 1981. In: L. Kopelman and J. Moskop (eds.), Ethics and Mental Retardation. D. Reidel, Dordrecht. (in press)

May, W. F. Parenting, bonding and valuing the retarded. Paper presented at the symposium, Natural Abilities and Perceived Worth: Rights, Values and Retarded Persons, Greenville, North Carolina, October 3, 1981. In: L. Kopelman and J. Moskop (eds.), Ethics and Mental Retardation. D. Reidel, Dordrecht. (in press)

Roos, P. 1979. The law and mentally retarded people: An uncertain future. Stanford Law Rev. 31:613–624.

Rothman, D. Who speaks for the retarded? Paper presented at the symposium, Natural Abilities and Perceived Worth: Rights, Values and Retarded Persons, Greenville, North Carolina, October 1, 1981. In: L. Kopelman and J. Moskop (eds.), Ethics and Mental Retardation. D. Reidel, Dordrecht. (in press)

Sherman, R. B. 1980. Guardianship: Time for a reassessment. Fordham Law Rev. 49:350–378.

Turnbull, H. R. 1979. The Law and the Mentally Handicapped in North Carolina. Institute of Government, University of North Carolina at Chapel Hill.

Wear, S. 1980. Mental illness and moral status. J. Med. Philos. 5:292–312.

Wikler, D. 1979. Paternalism and the mildly retarded. Philosophy and Public Affairs 8:377–392.

Wilkinson, J. C. 1979. Interdiction reform: The need for a limited interdiction article in the Louisiana Civil Code. Tulane Law Rev. 54:164–193.

Woozley, A. The rights of the retarded. Paper presented at the symposium, Natural Abilities and Perceived Worth: Rights, Values and Retarded Persons, Greenville, North Carolina, October 2, 1981. In: L. Kopelman and J. Moskop (eds.), Ethics and Mental Retardation. D. Reidel, Dordrecht. (in press)

PERSPECTIVES AND PROGRESS IN MENTAL RETARDATION
Volume I—Social, Psychological, and Educational Aspects
Edited by J. M. Berg
Copyright © 1984 by I.A.S.S.M.D.

SELF-ESTEEM
Its Measurement and Some Correlates in Educable Mentally Retarded Greek Children

D. P. Stasinos

Psychological Laboratory, University of Ioannina, Ioannina, Greece

This paper examines, first, the nature of self-esteem in 90 middle- and upper-grade educable mentally retarded children attending special state schools in Greece and, second, the relationship between self-esteem and sex as well as between this trait and the amount of special schooling of these children. The results indicated that educable mentally retarded children were able to positively evaluate themselves, that sex was not related to self-esteem, and that the amount of special schooling was correlated significantly with the children's self-esteem.

In recent years, self-esteem became a subject of systematic research by psychologists. The interest developed from the clinical observations of Fromm (1939) and the experiments of Janis (1954) and Coopersmith (1967), which provided significant information about the important role of self-esteem in the personal and social adjustment of the individual as well as in the shaping of some forms of psychopathology.

Coopersmith (1967) stated that the term *self-esteem* refers to the individual's opinion and feelings about himself that he displays to others by his attitude and behavior. This feeling, according to Rosenberg (1965), stimulates one to adopt an attitude of approval or disapproval toward oneself. The term *self-concept* refers, according to Germain (1978), to the notion that an individual has about himself in connection with the environment in which he lives. Self-esteem, therefore, is a dimension of self-concept. According to Diller (1954), Stotland and Zander (1958), Gelfand (1962), Rosenbaum et al. (1962), Coopersmith (1967), Ziller et al. (1969), and Apostal (1970), self-esteem in the normal individual decisively affects his social behavior, and its degree depends directly on daily life experiences.

With regard to self-esteem in the educable mentally retarded (EMR) individual, Goldstein and Seigle (1961) theorized that such an individual tends toward self-devaluation because of a limited ability to assess his own capabilities and limitations realistically. Also, according to them, such a tendency to self-devaluation is due, at least in part, to failures he experiences. Results of experimental work employing a self-concept dimension with retarded persons suggest that: 1) the EMR individual has, according to Cromwell et al. (1963), a higher expectancy of failure than has the normal child [on this issue Diller (1954) found a change in a negative direction in several aspects of the EMR person's self-concept following an experience of failure]; 2) EMR children in integrated classes have higher self-esteem than such children in segregated classes (Monroe, 1975); 3) EMR individuals have lower self-esteem than normal individuals (Ringness, 1961; Meyerovitz, 1962; Collins and Burger, 1970); and 4) self-esteem in the EMR child can be increased by providing appropriate programs and school environment (Stasinos, 1981).

The nature of self-esteem in EMR children has received little systematic attention, largely because of a lack of standardized scales for the measurement of this trait, and because of a widespread, but prejudiced, disbelief in the potential of EMR individuals for success in life and for integration in society. These considerations led to the study reported here on self-esteem in EMR Greek children.

METHOD

Sample

The subjects consisted of 90 middle- and upper-grade EMR children (63 boys and 27 girls). They were drawn from 17 randomly chosen (Stasinos, 1981) special state schools in Greece, in the urban areas of Athens, Piraeas, Patras, and Jannina, during the school year 1979–80. The IQ range of the sample was 55 to 85 (mean = 71) and the children ranged in age from 10 to 16 years (mean = 12 years). Over 90% of the children's fathers were unskilled or skilled workers corresponding to the first two categories of socioeconomic status in Greece (National Statistical Service of Greece, 1975).

Instruments

The instruments used to measure self-esteem of the EMR children were the Self-Esteem Inventory (Form A) and the Behavior Rating Form, both developed by Coopersmith (1967) and translated into Greek by me. The rationale underlying the choice of these instruments stems directly from Coopersmith's definition of self-esteem, which states that "it is a subjective experience which the individual conveys to others verbally and with other expressive behavior." With regard to the quality of subjective experience, James (1890), Cooley (1902), and Mead (1934) postulated that the subjective self-estimate, regardless of its correspondence with the truth, determines the individual's level of self-esteem.

Self-Esteem Inventory (SEI)   The SEI contains 58 items, 50 forming the self-esteem measure and the remaining eight forming a "lie scale." The items are simple, self-reference statements such as "I always do the right thing." There are two response alternatives for each item: "Like me" and "Unlike me." For the purposes of this study I replaced them by "Yes" and "No," respectively. Four subscales were identified conceptually: General Self, Social-Self Peers, Home Parents, and School Academic. The same form was used for both male and female subjects.

For the purposes of this research, the SEI was administered orally and individually by the author to compensate for the reading deficiencies of the EMR children and to eliminate the possibility that they would misunderstand certain items. Responses were also recorded by me to compensate for the children's handicap in writing and to avoid any confusion of the subjects in relation to marking the two columns of the scale. There was no time limit for completing the SEI, as had been established by Coopersmith, because that would have greatly reduced the children's quality and quantity of responses.

Behavior Rating Form (BRF)   The BRF is a 13-item, 5-point scale referring to behaviors of the child as related to failure, self-confidence in a new situation, sociability with peers, and the need for encouragement and reassurance—that is, external manifestations of the individual's prevailing self-appraisal. The BRF consists of two parts. The first part is a 10-item scale that provides an appraisal of the behaviors mentioned above. The second part is a 3-item scale that provides an index of an individual's defensive behavior. The BRF was completed by the teacher of each EMR subject.

Statistical Analyses

The scores on the SEI and BRF scales and the amount of the EMR child's special schooling were analyzed statistically. (The amount of special schooling of each EMR child was calculated on the basis of the date of the child's first registration in a special state school in Greece and the date when the present research was started.) The means and

Table 1.   Means and standard deviations of scores on two self-esteem instruments for male and female EMR children[a]

	Self-esteem Inventory (SEI)		Behavior Rating Form (BRF)	
	Mean	SD	Mean	SD
Males (n = 63)	25.9	18.8	7.8	4.5
Females (n = 27)	27.7	20.8	9.15	4.6
Total (n = 90)	26.4	19.4	8.3	4.45

[a] The range of their scores, corresponding to the three levels of self-esteem (i.e., high, medium, low), was as follows:

Levels of self-esteem	SEI scores	BRF scores
High	35–55	15–25
Medium	14–34	4–14
Low	<14	<4

standard deviations of the scores of the subjects by sex and for the total sample were calculated for each scale. The means and standard deviations of the subjects' amount of special schooling were also calculated. The correlation between the variables (i.e., self-esteem, related school behavior, and the amount of special schooling) is expressed by Pearson's r coefficient. The t criterion was applied in order to test the significance of the difference of the means in the male and female EMR children. According to Paraskevopoulos (1973), the t test of significance should be used when testing the difference of the means between two independent samples (males and females) of a different number of subjects (i.e., unequal samples) when derived from a homogeneous population such as children.

RESULTS

The data obtained from the two self-esteem instruments and the calculation of the amount of special schooling provide information on: 1) the degree of the EMR subject's self-esteem; 2) the relationship between the measurement of self-esteem and the evaluation of the child's school behavior related to self-esteem; 3) the differences between the two sexes regarding their degree of self-esteem; and 4) the relationship between self-esteem and amount of special schooling.

Self-Esteem of the EMR Subjects

Table 1 presents the scores on the SEI and BRF scales of the male and female EMR subjects and of the total sample. The table indicates that, in contrast to the theoretical view of Goldstein and Seigle (1961)

Table 2.   Means and standard deviations of amount of special schooling

	Years of special schooling	
	Mean	SD
Males ($n = 63$)	4.5	0.54
Females ($n = 27$)	4.2	1.43
Total ($N = 90$)	4.4	0.86

mentioned above, these EMR Greek children had formed a positive opinion about themselves.

Relationship between Self-Esteem and Related School Behavior

The correlation (Pearson r) between these two variables was 0.33 ($P < 0.001$). Thus there was a positive correlation between the child's self-image and evaluated behavior in and out of school.

Comparison between the Sexes

Table 1 shows that the sex differences of the mean scores that the subjects achieved on the SEI and BRF scales were small. These differences were not statistically significant ($t_{88} = 0.39$ for the SEI scores and $t_{88} = 1.29$ for the BRF scores). Thus, sex appears not to have been a determining factor in the formation of the EMR child's self-esteem.

Relationship between Amount of Special Schooling, Self-Esteem, and Related School Behavior

Table 2 presents the findings on the amount of special schooling for each sex and for the total sample. The table shows that the amount of special schooling was almost equal in both sexes. The correlations (Pearson r) between the amount of the children's special schooling and their self-esteem scores, and between the amount of their special schooling and school behavior, were 0.34 ($P < 0.001$) and 0.43 ($P < 0.001$), respectively. These results indicate that the EMR child expresses in his school behavior how he feels about himself.

DISCUSSION

This study indicates that: 1) the EMR child is able to evaluate himself and adopt an attitude of self-approval or disapproval based particularly on personal experiences in daily life; 2) the degree of self-esteem is a subjective experience of the EMR child that is manifested to others verbally and behaviorally; 3) the degree of self-esteem of the EMR child is independent of the child's sex; and 4) there is a positive correlation between the amount of special schooling of the EMR child and the child's self-esteem and school behavior related to this trait.

That the EMR child who attends a special school in Greece is able to positively evaluate himself, and feel satisfaction as a result, is in contrast to Goldstein and Seigle's (1961) view regarding this issue. This finding could be interpreted as an indication that the EMR child's personal experiences in Greece are positive and play an important role in increasing the child's self-esteem. The parents and teachers of such children presumably show an affectionate understanding of the difficulties the children face in solving problems and especially in achieving normal integration in Greek society. Of interest in this regard is Nassiakos' (1977) observation, in Greece, that parents, and especially mothers, who belong to low socioeconomic classes are likely to be emotionally involved and to intervene to try to solve their children's problems. Such an attitude from the EMR child's parents and teachers could lead to the child's achievements, with concomitant increase of self-esteem. For this to be so, both parents and teachers of the EMR child must have basically realistic expectations. In this way, the child may also be able to form a realistic image of his mental potential (Grunewald, 1978).

The finding of a positive correlation between self-esteem of the EMR child and related school behavior contrasts with Coopersmith's (1967) observations on intellectually normal individuals. According to him, "the disparity between self-attitude and external manifestations of acceptance and success presumably reflects defensive distortions against the realities of inferiority." If this is so, the positive correlation between the EMR child's self-esteem and related school behavior is an indication that the child who attends a special school may not feel inferior presumably because the school does not require the child to compare his work with that of others with higher intelligence levels, as in a regular school.

The absence in the present study of a significant sex difference in the EMR children's self-esteem or their related school behavior is in keeping with the findings of Monroe (1975) in a sample of EMR children in the United States. In these countries at least, self-esteem does not seem to vary with the sex of EMR children, and teachers of these children apparently do not assign different scores on the basis of the sex of the children.

Finally, the positive correlation between the EMR child's amount of special schooling and the child's self-esteem and related school behavior can be interpreted as an indication that the special school plays an important role in increasing such self-esteem.

CONCLUSION

From the findings of the present study it can be concluded that: 1) helping EMR children establish realistic goals, praising their behavior, encouraging self-acceptance, and fostering participatory activities increases their self-esteem; and 2) an appropriate special school environment provides good opportunities to achieve these objectives.

ACKNOWLEDGMENTS

The author wishes to thank Professor J. M. Berg for his assistance in the reconstruction of this study, and also Professor M. Nassiakos for her critical reading of the original manuscript.

REFERENCES

Apostal, R. A. 1970. Objectives of elementary guidance. In: H. F. Cottingham (ed.), Elementary School Guidance. Reprint Series 1. American Personnel and Guidance Association, Washington, D.C.

Collins, H. A., and Burger, G. K. 1970. The self-concepts of adolescent educable mentally retarded students. Educ. Train. Ment. Retard. 5:23–30.

Cooley, C. H. 1902. Human Nature and the Social Order. Charles Scribner's Sons, New York.

Coopersmith, S. (ed.). 1967. The Antecedents of Self-esteem. W. H. Freeman and Company, San Francisco.

Cromwell, R. L., Baumeister, A. A., and Hawkins, W. F. 1963. Research in activity level. In: N. R. Ellis (ed.), Handbook of Mental Deficiency. McGraw-Hill Book Company, New York.

Diller, L. 1954. Conscious and unconscious self-attitudes after success and failure. J. Pers. 23:1–12.

Fromm, E. 1939. Selfishness and self-love. Psychiatry 2:507–523.

Gelfand, D. 1962. The influence of self-esteem on verbal conditioning and social matching behavior. J. Abnorm. Soc. Psychol. 65:259–265.

Germain, B. R. 1978. Self-concept and self-esteem reexamined. Psychology in the Schools 15:386–390.

Goldstein, H., and Seigle, D. 1961. Characteristics of educable mentally handicapped children. In: J. H. Rothstein (ed.), Mental Retardation, pp. 204–230. Holt, Rinehart & Winston, New York.

Grunewald, K. (ed.) 1978. The Mentally Handicapped. Hutchinson of London, London.

James, W. 1890. Principles of Psychology, Vols. I and II. Holt, Rinehart & Winston, Inc., New York.

Janis, I. L. 1954. Personality correlates of susceptibility to persuasion. J. Pers. 22:504–518.

Mead, G. H. 1934. Mind, Self and Society. University of Chicago Press, Chicago.

Meyerovitz, J. H. 1962. Self-derogations in young retardates and special class placement. Child Dev. 33:443–451.

Monroe, K. M. 1975. Self-esteem of educable mentally retarded students in segregated and integrated classes. Diss. Abstr. 36:788A.

Nassiakou, M. 1977. Mother's expectations, child's intelligence and the motive for success. Doctoral dissertation, the University of Thessalonica. (in Greek)

National Statistical Service of Greece. 1975. Statistics of Stated Income of Natural Persons and the Taxation of it during the Fiscal Year 1974. National Statistical Service of Greece, Athens. (in Greek)

Paraskevopoulos, I. (ed.). 1973. Applied Statistics in the Behavioral Sciences, Vol. II. Thessalonica. (in Greek)

Ringness, T. A. 1961. Self-concept of children of low, average and high intelligence. Am. J. Ment. Defic. 65:453–461.

Rosenbaum, M. E., Horne, W. C., and Chalmers, D. K. 1962. Levels of self-esteem and the learning of imitation and non-imitation. J. Pers. 30:147–156.

Rosenberg, M. 1965. Society and the Adolescent Self-image. Princeton University Press, Princeton, New Jersey.

Stasinos, D. 1981. The assessment of a training programme for the development of creativity and self-esteem in mentally handicapped Greek children. Doctoral dissertation, The University of Dundee, Scotland.

Stotland, E., and Zander, A. 1958. Effects of public and private failure on self-evaluation. J. Abnorm. Soc. Psychol. 56:223–229.

Ziller, R. C., Hagey, J., Smith, M. D. C., and Long, B. H. 1969. Self-esteem: A self-social construct. J. Consult. Clin. Psychol. 33:84–95.

SECTION II
Interactions and Relationships

PERSPECTIVES AND PROGRESS IN MENTAL RETARDATION
Volume I—Social, Psychological, and Educational Aspects
Edited by J. M. Berg
Copyright © 1984 by I.A.S.S.M.D.

DEFINING, DESCRIBING AND EXPLAINING THE SOCIAL STATUS OF MILDLY HANDICAPPED CHILDREN
A Discussion of Methodological Problems

G. M. Morrison[1] and D. L. MacMillan[2]

[1] *Graduate School of Education, University of California, Santa Barbara, California 93106*

[2] *School of Education, University of California, Riverside, California 92521*

Problems in research on the social status of mildly retarded children are discussed under three major topics: group comparison issues, measurement problems, and identification and definition of contextual variables. Group comparison problems include difficulties in finding homogeneous special education groups and a meaningful comparison group. Measurement problems are related to a lack of thorough descriptions of indices used and failure to relate the meaning of these indices to the final pattern of results. The importance of identifying and accounting for contextual variables is discussed.

Much of the work on the social status of mildly retarded children has been done in the context of questions about the efficacy of mainstreamed educational placements for these children. This work has used classroom placement as an independent variable on which to compare social and/or academic outcomes (Kirk, 1964; Corman and Gottlieb, 1979; Semmel et al., 1979). Although such a design seems appropriate to answer questions comparing mainstreamed versus segregated classroom environments, continual use of this strategy has deflected attention from important complexities within the environments (Kaufman et al., 1975) and from exploring the dynamics of the social relationships of the children involved.

This paper describes the complexities of understanding and analyzing the social relationships of mildly handicapped children and how these factors interact with research methodology for studying these relationships. The paper relies heavily on the experiences and research results that a group associated with the Mental Retardation Research Center at the University of California at Los Angeles have obtained in investigating the social status of mildly handicapped children.

The description of any social situation should include consideration of the person, significant others present, and the situational context in which these people find themselves. In the case of a mildly retarded child in a school situation we would need to consider the child and his or her characteristics, the characteristics and actions of the peers and teachers, and the school context in which interactions take place (MacMillan and Morrison, in press). The job of describing these variables would seem reasonable if not for the fact that no component in the model is static. Given the dynamic and changing nature of the variables, there are three major methodological problems to be faced in interpreting and conducting research in the area of social status of mildly handicapped children: problems in group comparisons, measurement, and identification and definition of contextual variables.

PROBLEMS IN GROUP COMPARISONS

When examining the social outcomes for mildly handicapped learners in different school settings, the typical design has been to compare children with similar characteristics in different environments on a dependent variable such as social status. The validity of this model is questionable on two major points. The first weakness is related to the assumption in classic research design that groups to be compared are homogeneous, between and within groups, according to specified characteristics. However, as Guskin and Spicker (1968) emphasized, mildly mentally retarded children who are educated in special day class placements as opposed to integrated class placements are likely to be a more severely "involved" (cognitively or behaviorally) group of children. In other words, the selection bias operates in determining classroom placement for mildly handicapped children.

MacMillan et al. (1980) described the process of selection for classroom placement (system identification) and crucial variables that influence this process. The critical point expressed by these authors that is relevant to this discussion is that educational placements are made to meet the needs of the mildly handicapped child, not to maintain neat, clean, researchable groups that fit strict definitional criteria. On the contrary, children progress through educational placements with varied sets of circumstances. Although all these children fail in some way to meet the expectations of the regular school environment, they may be affected differentially by teacher tolerances, relationships with peers, philosophies and procedures followed during referral and assessment, extent of cooperation by parents, and availability of resources and services to meet their needs. Therefore, not only is the final composition of special education classrooms heterogeneous, but the social process of failure, referral, identification, and placement has provided the children in these classes with unique experiences that set them apart from their cohorts in regular class placements.

A second problem related to the validity of group comparisons on social status is the social meaning of the comparisons made. Three common types of comparisons have been made in the social status literature related to the mainstreaming questions. In one design (exemplified by Thurstone, 1959), special day class educable mentally retarded (EMR) children were rated by their special class peers, and low-IQ regular class children were rated by their nonretarded peers. Since raters, ratees, and settings are different, the comparisons are confounded and of minimal social interest. Another approach (Goodman et al., 1972; Gottlieb and Budoff, 1973; Gottlieb and Davis, 1973) controls rater characteristics by having the same nonretarded children rate integrated and segregated EMR children. Again the social meaning of such comparisons is limited because of the differential exposure that raters have had to the two sets of retarded children.

A third design examines the same handicapped child in two settings (integrated and segregated) with two sets of peers (Lapp, 1957; Rucker et al., 1969; Morrison et al., 1979). Although this design has strength in that the comparison group is controlled (i.e., mildly retarded children are compared to themselves), the variable settings and the nature of the handicapped children's exposure to the different groups represents unexplained variability.

The point of the above discussion is that sensible comparisons for research design purposes may be difficult to achieve given the natural and imposed variability in educational groupings and settings. We do not need a great deal of sophistication to tell that mildly handicapped children are not socially successful in public school settings. We do need to recognize and document the effect that variations in peer groups and settings have on the social standing of these children so that we may eventually understand and improve their situations. In other words, instead of controlling these variables, the effect of their variability should be examined.

MEASUREMENT PROBLEMS

Another major problem in interpreting and conducting research on the social status of handicapped children is related to measurement. In general, researchers have been very loose in their descriptions of indices of social measurement, particularly in titles, abstracts, and summaries. Social relationships have been measured through the use of, for example, peer ratings of characteristics, classical sociometrics, attitude surveys, and direct observation of interaction.

Although each of these methods measures some aspect of the social lives of children, it must be remembered that each one measures from a *different* perspective and has unique strengths and weaknesses (Asher and Taylor, 1981; Gresham, 1981). One needs only to be reminded of the struggle in social psychology to determine the relationship between attitudes and behavior (Wicker, 1969) to realize the importance of distinguishing between the various perspectives. An example of the need to specify the use of indices of social relationships is in the examination of the development (in nonhandicapped children) of attitudes and acceptance toward mildly handicapped children. Gottlieb and Switsky (1982) found that the attitudes of nonhandicapped children toward retarded children improved between the early and later elementary years. In contrast, Morrison and Peck (in preparation) documented the decrease in the level of social acceptance that mildly handicapped children receive from early to later elementary years. The different patterns seen between these two studies may be due to the method of social measurement. Whereas Gottlieb and Switsky (1982) measured attitudes toward mentally retarded children in general, Morrison and Peck (in preparation) were measuring specific feelings of acceptance or rejection that children have for each other. Although it may become more appropriate to verbalize accepting attitudes toward handicapped children with increased age, specific accepting and rejecting responses or friendship choices may become more discriminating in terms of similarities in characteristics and interests. This example highlights the importance of carefully describing and *distinguishing* the type of social measurement used.

Looking more specifically at the use of sociometric measurement to measure all outcomes of mildly handicapped children, measurement issues also are significant in interpreting substantive results. For example, the two major methods of sociometric measurement used with young children are the peer nomination method and the roster and rating method (Asher and Hymel, 1981; Asher and Renshaw, 1981). Morrison (1981a) found that these methods of measurement revealed different patterns of relationship between mildly handicapped and non-handicapped children depending on the classroom placement arrangements for the handicapped children. That is, the results of the nomination method revealed low levels of social acceptance *and* rejection for special day class children, who generally spent very few hours a week with the nonhandicapped children. However, higher levels of acceptance *and* rejection were obtained for mildly handicapped children who attended resource rooms and spent most of their day with the nonhandicapped children. The roster and rating method revealed a different pattern of results, indicating similar levels of acceptance for special day class and resource children but highlighting a greater amount of rejection toward the resource room children. Given these different patterns of acceptance and rejection and the various explanations for their existence, it becomes obvious that the method of measurement must be clearly and explicitly described and efforts made to relate method to research results.

Related to the roster and rating versus nomination method comparisons is a distinction in the meaning of each method. Oden and Asher (1977) noted that, whereas the peer nomination method measures friendship choice, the roster and rating method measures general level of acceptance. This distinction proved important in interpreting the results of the study described above (Morrison, 1981a). Although special day class children did not receive nominations indicating friendship, or the lack thereof, some level of acceptance was indicated.

The issue can be raised as to what our expectations for mildly handicapped children are in terms of *levels* of social acceptance. Do we want them to have many friends (probably unrealistic) or just a few? Research on social adjustment indicates that general adjustment is better when a child has at least one friend (Asher and Renshaw, 1981). Do we want the mildly handicapped child to achieve an average level of acceptance so that he or she feels like a part of the classroom group? These questions must be answered with both empirical and philosophical considerations.

IDENTIFICATION AND DEFINITION OF CONTEXTUAL VARIABLES

The third hurdle in studying the social status of handicapped children in educational settings is to identify and define the crucial aspects of the school environment and to document their effects on the social relationships of children. Kaufman et al. (1975) recognized the need to look at within-setting and between-setting variation to account for certain outcomes of mainstreaming. Guralnick (1981) presented a detailed description of the programmatic factors that potentially affect social integration.

Several programmatic factors, including some mentioned by Guralnick, were suspected causes of variation in the contribution of peer and teacher ratings of cognition and behavior to the social status of mildly handicapped children in one of our investigations in Southern California (MacMillan and Morrison, 1980). Our investigation replicated with EMR and educationally handicapped (EH) children a study completed by Gottlieb et al. (1978) focusing on the cognitive and behavioral correlates, as rated by peers and teachers, of the social status of mainstreamed EMR children. Gottlieb et al. (1978) initially found that ratings of cognition of EMR children contributed to social acceptance, whereas ratings of behavior were the main contributors to social rejection. In our study with EMR and EH children who attended self-contained special classrooms, the pattern of contribution to social acceptance and rejection of cognitive and behavior ratings was different. The variations in the pattern were attributed to differences in several factors. One factor was the characteristics of the raters. The pattern of results was affected by whether the raters were handicapped or nonhandicapped and whether teachers were from the regular or special class environment. It is probable that the judgments of these raters were affected not only by their own characteristics and perceptions, but by the characteristics of the target child in relation to the children surrounding that child. The latter factor refers to the relativity of judgments and comparisons. A handicapped child in a mainstreamed classroom is surrounded by more competent children. However, in a special day class, the differences in competencies are less obvious. It is probable that the patterns of perception and acceptance that were evident in our investigation may have been influenced by difference in group composition. Therefore, when exploring the dynamics of social relationships, it is necessary to consider, in addition to child characteristics, the characteristics of the raters and the composition of the group in which the ratings take place.

Another line of investigation associated with the one just described suggests further classroom environment variables that are in need of exploration (Morrison, 1981b; 1982). In these studies, the variables of social acceptance and socioempathy (persons' ability to estimate their own social status) were related in order to understand some of the dynamics of social acceptance. The results indicated that variations in the accuracy of social status estimates of mildly handicapped children were associated with different class placement options (i.e., mainstreamed versus special education classes) (Morrison, 1981b). Mildly handicapped children were more accurate about their social status among their handicapped peers in special classes. They overestimated their status among their nonhandicapped peers in the mainstreamed setting.

Further analysis suggested differences in the social status–socioempathy relationship between types of special education classroom settings. That is, children in special day class settings had a better match between actual acceptance and their estimates than did resource room children. The better match was reflected in higher levels of acceptance for the special day class children.

The results of these investigations indicate that the different administrative placement options for mildly handicapped children are related to differential social consequences for these children. Likely explanations for the influential factors that need further examination are number of children in the class, amount of time spent in various classrooms, amount of social interaction structured within the curriculum, amount and nature of the social feedback received by the handicapped children, and varied characteristics and experiences of the handicapped children themselves.

Stanvik (1979) conceptualized the critical environmental variables differentiating grouping systems as consisting of two major categories: 1) organizational frames, which include number of pupils, number of groups in which a child participates each day, number of teachers that a child is exposed to, education of the teachers, variability in the age of group members, homogeneity of the group in terms of ability, and location of classrooms; and 2) curricular and time frames, which refer to the distribution of time to the different subject areas and other decisions related to teaching processes. These frames influence the conditions of teaching, learning and development, and social interaction to which mildly handicapped children are exposed. Stanvik's conceptualization provides a useful framework from which to structure further research design to study the social status situation for mildly handicapped children.

DISCUSSION

In highlighting some problems in implementing, analyzing, and interpreting research on the social status of mildly handicapped children, the intention has been to emphasize that meaningful results are unlikely to be found by comparing, on a single index of social acceptance, two heterogeneous groups of children attending two very different educational settings. Special education categories and administrative placements are achieved through a dynamic and somewhat unpredictable social process. The resulting groups of children identified as being mildly handicapped do not represent a homogeneous group needed for traditional research design proposed. Given this situation, future investigations need to shift class placement and handicapping categories from controlling variables to variables where variation is documented and related to other factors such as classroom setting characteristics, peer characteristics, and teacher influence.

One such concept that is of potential use is the person-environment fit model (Pervin, 1968). This concept refers to the extent to which characteristics of the person match those of the environment to which he or she is commonly exposed, the assumption being that the better the fit the more favorable the consequences for the person. For instance, mildly handicapped children with a certain combination of behavioral and academic skills might be more successful in a regular classroom environment with certain types of peer and teacher characteristics than would children with a different pattern of skills. The ideal would be to find the best match in as many cases as possible.

Although such systematic matching is futuristic thinking at this time, there is a relevant question that must be answered soon: What educational and social outcomes do we want to ensure for mildly handicapped children and what are the implications for planning educational research and intervention? Do we want to emphasize academic achievement or social and self-development? The realization must be made that development in each area will take intervention in each area. We must not repeat past errors by developing one area and expecting progress in the others (MacMillan and Semmel, 1977). If remedial help is concentrated on academic tasks and delivered in a one-to-one tutoring model (as in the resource room model) we should expect progress in achievement, but not necessarily an improvement in social skills.

It is at the point of prioritizing and apportioning time to tasks that the study of educational outcomes comes face to face with larger societal values. As Stanvik (1979) suggested, social values are reflected in organizational characteristics and structures of schools, which in turn affect the growth and development of children who attend those schools. One job for educators and researchers in the future will be to document the effects that this social system and its values and priorities has on its participants, handicapped and nonhandicapped alike.

REFERENCES

Asher, S. R., and Hymel, S. 1981. Social competence in peer relations: Sociometric and behavioral assessment. In: J. D. Wyne and M. D. Smye (eds.), Social Competence. Guilford Press, New York.

Asher, S. R., and Renshaw, P. D. 1981. Children without friends: Social knowledge and social skill training. In: S. R. Asher and J. M. Gottman (eds.), The Development of Children's Friendships. Cambridge University Press, New York.

Asher, S. R., and Taylor, A. R. 1981. Social outcomes of mainstreaming: Sociometric assessment and beyond. Except. Educ. Q. 1:13–30.

Corman, L., and Gottlieb, J. 1979. Mainstreaming mentally retarded children: A review of research. Int. Rev. Res. Ment. Retard. 9:251–275.

Goodman, H., Gottlieb, J., and Harrison, R. H. 1972. Social acceptance of EMRs integrated into a nongraded elementary school. Am. J. Ment. Defic. 76:412–417.

Gottlieb, J., and Budoff, M. 1973. Social acceptability of retarded children in non-graded schools differing in architecture. Am. J. Ment. Defic. 78:15–19.

Gottlieb, J., and Davis, J. E. 1973. Social acceptance of EMRs during overt behavioral interactions. Am. J. Ment. Defic. 78:141–143.

Gottlieb, J., Semmel, M. I., and Veldman, D. J. 1978. Correlates of social status among mainstreamed mentally retarded children. J. Educ. Psychol. 70:396–405.

Gottlieb, J., and Switsky, H. 1982. Development of school-age children's stereotypic attitudes toward mentally retarded children. Am. J. Ment. Defic. 86:596–600.

Gresham, F. 1981. Validity of social skills for assessing social competence in low-status children: A multivariate investigation. Dev. Psychol. 17:390–398.

Guralnick, M. J. 1981. Programmatic factors affecting child-child social interactions in mainstreamed preschool program. Except. Educ. Q. 1:71–92.

Guskin, S. L., and Spicker, H. H. 1968. Educational research in mental retardation. Int. Rev. Res. Ment. Retard. 3:217–278.

Kaufman, M. J., Gottlieb, J., Agard, J. A., and Kukic, M. B. 1975. Mainstreaming: Toward an explication of the construct. In: E. L. Meyen, G. A. Vergason, and R. J. Whelan (eds.), Alternatives for Teaching Exceptional Children, pp. 35–54. Love, Denver.

Kirk, S. A. 1964. Research in education. In: H. A. Stevens and R. Heber (eds.), Mental Retardation: A Review of Research, pp. 57–99. University of Chicago Press, Chicago.

Lapp, E. R. 1957. A study of the social adjustment of slow-learning children who were assigned part-time to regular classes. Am. J. Ment. Defic. 62:254–262.

MacMillan, D. L., Meyers, C. E., and Morrison, G. M. 1980. System-identification of mildly retarded children: Implications for conducting and interpreting research. Am. J. Ment. Defic. 85:108–115.

MacMillan, D. L., and Morrison, G. M. 1980. Correlates of social status among mildly handicapped learners in self-contained special classes. J. Educ. Psychol. 72:437–444.

MacMillan, D. L., and Morrison, G. M. Sociometric studies. In: R. L. Jones (ed.), Attitudes and Attitude Change in Special Education. University of Minnesota/LTI, Minneapolis. (in press)

MacMillan, D. L., and Semmel, M. I. 1977. Evaluation of mainstreaming programs. Focus on Exceptional Children 9:1–14.

Morrison, G. 1981a. Sociometric measurement: Methodological consideration of its use with mildly learning handicapped and nonhandicapped children. J. Educ. Psychol. 73:193–201.

Morrison, G. M. 1981b. Perspectives of the social status of learning handicapped and nonhandicapped children. Am. J. Ment. Defic. 86:243–251.

Morrison, G. M. 1982. Social perceptual abilities of mildly handicapped children as a function of classroom placement environment. Paper presented at the meeting of the American Association on Mental Deficiency, Boston, June.

Morrison, G. M., MacMillan, D. L., Stohler, S., and Kelleher, S. 1979. The social status of mildly handicapped learners in regular and special class settings: Dynamics from the child's point of view. Unpublished manuscript.

Morrison, G. M., and Peck, C. A. Social status of mildly handicapped children: A developmental perspective. (in preparation).

Oden, S., and Asher, S. R. 1977. Coaching children in social skills for friendship making. Child Dev. 48:495–506.

Pervin, L. A. 1968. Performance and satisfaction as a function of individual-environment fit. Psychol. Bull. 69:56–58.

Rucker, C. N., Howe, C. E., and Snider, B. 1969. The participation of retarded children in junior high academic and nonacademic regular classes. Except. Child. 35:617–623.

Semmel, M. I., Gottlieb, J., and Robinson, N. 1979. Mainstreaming: Perspectives on educating handicapped children in the public schools. In: D. C. Berliner (ed.), Review of Research in Education, pp. 223–279. American Educational Research Association, Washington, D. C.

Stanvik, G. 1979. Self-Concept and School Segregation. Acta Universitatis Gotheburgenis, University of Goteborg, Sweden.

Thurstone, T. G. 1959. An evaluation of educating mentally handicapped children in special classes and in regular grades. U. S. Office of Education Cooperative Research Program Project OE-SAE-6452. University of North Carolina, Chapel Hill.

Wicker, A. W. 1969. Attitudes versus actions: The relationship of verbal and overt behavioral responses to attitude objects. J. Soc. Issues 25:41–78.

PERSPECTIVES AND PROGRESS IN MENTAL RETARDATION
Volume I—Social, Psychological, and Educational Aspects
Edited by J. M. Berg
Copyright © 1984 by I.A.S.S.M.D.

VULNERABILITY OF DEVELOPMENTALLY DELAYED PRESCHOOL CHILDREN TO DEFICITS IN CHILD-CHILD INTERACTIONS

M. J. Guralnick

The Nisonger Center, The Ohio State University, 1580 Cannon Drive, Columbus, Ohio 43210

This paper describes recent research pointing to the fact that mildly and moderately delayed preschool-age children exhibit unusual deficits in their peer-related social behaviors. Possible causes for these deficits are analyzed, as well as intervention efforts designed to improve delayed children's peer interactions by involving nonhandicapped children. Suggestions for both remediation and prevention are provided.

Current interest in the peer relations of handicapped children follows from the growing interest in this area in the field of child development and also appears to reflect a serious and legitimate concern that handicapped children may be especially vulnerable to deficits in peer interactions. Indeed, many developmentally delayed children, in particular, emerge from their infant and toddler experiences shaken by a series of confusing and disruptive events. Parental strain, family dislocations, health complications, fears, and the rapidly changing expectations of those around them are certain to have widespread adverse developmental consequences.

It is not just the traumatic forms of social disruption that are expected to find their way through a child's system of interlocking social relationships to alter the quality of peer relationships. Even with developmentally normal populations the quality of parent-child relationships is predictive of future social relations with peers (Lieberman, 1977; Pastor, 1981). Insecure parent-child relations, it appears, place

53

a child at risk for poor peer relations through two processes. First, exploration of both social and nonsocial objects does not occur as readily, thus discouraging a positive orientation to social encounters. Second, parental encouragement of peer-related experiences is often absent, which prevents the acquisition of child-child social and communicative skills that can only be acquired through active experiences with peers (Hartup, 1978). Clearly, the establishment of productive peer relations is a process that appears to be highly susceptible to disruption.

Despite these and numerous other reasons to suspect that handicapped children are likely to experience unusual difficulties in their relationships with peers, there has not been much interest by researchers in this area (Guralnick, 1981a). In fact, we know virtually nothing about the organization, the content, or the rate of growth of child-child social interactions as they typically occur in group settings such as early intervention programs for preschool-age handicapped children. Nor do we know how the peer interactions of handicapped children correspond to the peer interactions of their nonhandicapped counterparts.

CURRENT RESEARCH AND RESULTS

In an effort to obtain some basic information regarding the peer relations of young developmentally delayed children, Guralnick and Weinhouse (in press) recently conducted a developmental-descriptive study that examined the organization, characteristics, and developmental progression of a range of peer-related behaviors. Briefly, as part of a larger study, 48 developmentally delayed children (mean chronological age approximately $4\frac{1}{2}$ years) enrolled in specialized community programs were observed during free play on two separate occasions; once at the beginning and again at the end of the school year. Two-thirds of the children were mildly delayed, and the remaining third had moderate developmental delays. Approximately 85% of them were $3\frac{1}{2}$ years of age and older, and all were ambulatory.

Sequential interactive measures of individual sequences of social exchanges occurring between children were coded for analysis and ratings were obtained of social participation and constructiveness of play. For the more molecular sequential measures, conventional definitions of socially directed behaviors (Mueller and Brenner, 1977) were followed. Other direct measures of social interactions, as well as derived ones, permitted us to obtain data regarding the frequency, quality (positive or negative), mode (motor or gestural), content (e.g., give/offer/show objects, physical contact), length, complexity (simple or coordinated), reciprocity (correspondence between initiations and responses), and contingencies (related responses to initiations or other socially directed behaviors within a social exchange) of the behaviors that were observed. More global measures of social participation were based on Parten's (1932) classic scale. However, this was used in conjunction with a constructiveness of play measure similar to Rubin (1981).

Analyses of these data suggested that developmentally delayed children exhibited peer interaction patterns similar to those of normally developing children, even though they were acquiring them at a much slower rate. For example, associative play increased and unoccupied play decreased across the year. In addition, the frequency of socially directed behaviors, the number of initiations, the number of simple and coordinated social interactions, and the number of contingent initiations increased significantly over time. Moreover, vocal and verbal interactions came to supplant motor and gestural forms of social communication, interactions became more positive, and a high level of reciprocity was observed, similar to that obtained in normally developing groups (Kohn, 1966; Charlesworth and Hartup, 1967).

Despite similarities to the features, organization, and developmental progression of normally developing children, the most significant outcomes were linked to the unusual deficiencies in peer interactions that were uncovered. In contrast to normally developing children, solitary and parallel play remained the dominant forms of social participation throughout the year. The children in our sample were infrequently able to turn simple two-unit initiation/response sequences into longer, more elaborate social exchanges. Moreover, much of the group play that did occur was the result of interactions by a very small subset (20%) of interactive children. As a consequence, we found that the large majority of moderately and mildly delayed children enrolled in specialized early education settings did not often engage in sustained social exchanges with their peers.

Two additional analyses further confirmed that these deficits were indeed severe and unusual. First, when cognitive level was taken into account, substantial deficits still remained. Comparisons with available normative data revealed that the peer-related social development of these delayed youngsters lagged far behind that which would be expected on the basis of their developmental age. A second and highly deviant pattern was obtained as part of a cross-sectional analysis across chronological age. In particular, this analysis revealed a lack of correspondence between chronological age and level of peer-related social development. That is, the majority of the children seem to reach a plateau early on, showing no substantial growth across the preschool years. It is important to note that, as discussed earlier, delayed children did become more socially interactive with their peers as the school year progressed. However, the data suggest that, for reasons not clear at this time, each new year results in a disruption of any gains that may have occurred, with children making slow improvements across the next few months until the same level established in the previous year is achieved.

These results must, of course, be confirmed through more long-term developmental studies, and certainly not all moderately and mildly delayed children are likely to display deficits of this magnitude. Many, perhaps the highly interactive subset, may not in fact show deficits at all. Yet these data, I think, clearly alert us to the unusual vulnerability of delayed children to peer interaction deficits.

DISCUSSION

Difficulties in interacting with peers by the time children reach pre-school age may in part be traced to generalized deficits in social-communicative interactions that have occurred prior to this time. Even so, entry into the preschool potentially presents opportunities for delayed children to establish new patterns of social relationships that could minimize the impact of these prior problems and form a basis for building toward more satisfying social relationships. Yet, rather than capitalizing on the novelty of the setting and creating an environment that is socially responsive, delayed children often find themselves grouped in highly specialized educational programs serving children with problems similar to their own. As a consequence, encounters with other children are not as likely to be productive, nor are models available to stimulate more advanced forms of communicative and social development. Initial problems in interacting with peers may thereby be compounded, creating an even more substantial deficit throughout the preschool period.

One practice that has been adopted to avoid these problems and to provide a more responsive environment in the preschool has been to involve both handicapped and nonhandicapped children in the same educational or play setting. Although the rationale for mainstreaming, even at the early childhood level, includes humanistic and legal issues, there is little question that there is the expectation that involvement with nonhandicapped children will result in more appropriate and mature forms of social interactions by developmentally delayed children with their peers (Guralnick, 1982).

Developmentally advanced peers have in fact been used successfully to promote a wide range of social behaviors. In these studies, peers typically carry out assigned roles, often highly structured ones, in specially arranged settings (e.g., Strain, 1981). Yet proponents of mainstreaming contend that the more significant and lasting benefits to handicapped children will occur through natural processes of observational learning and social interaction patterns that emerge through day-to-day contact. After all, substantial evidence exists indicating that young children do indeed observe and imitate other more competent playmates (Akamatsu and Thelen, 1974; Abramovitch and Grusec, 1978), and the notion of reciprocity (Cairns, 1979) suggests that a child's companions extensively govern the quality and quantity of a child's social interactions.

Although this approach seems theoretically sound and is supported by related data, the question remains as to whether changes in peer-related social behavior do in fact occur in mainstreamed settings. Perhaps as a result of the difficulty in designing experiments to examine this hypothesis, only two experimental studies have been conducted to date on this issue (Field et al., 1981; Guralnick, 1981b). Moreover, both studies have only been able to examine whether any *immediate* changes in child-child social interactions occurred as a result of repeated changes in the composition of children's playgroups (i.e., the presence or absence of delayed or nondelayed companions). In my own work in this area, the social and play interactions of developmentally delayed and nondelayed preschool children were evaluated when playing in groups homogeneous with respect to developmental level in contrast to a heterogeneous grouping. The heterogeneous grouping included children at similar chronological ages but ranged in developmental level from severely handicapped to nonhandicapped.

When asking the straightforward question of whether children's social behavior with peers changes as a function of the developmental levels of their companions, the answer is substantially no. The data revealed that no effects occurred, positive or negative, on social interaction measures assessed either through social participation or through the frequency of social-communicative behaviors. Improvement in peer-related social behavior did occur over a 1-year period, but the developmental level of a child's possible playmates within a classroom did not alter the usual style or quality of social play. The only exception to this, and an apparently beneficial effect, was that severely delayed children, on a constructiveness of play measure, played less inappropriately when participating with developmentally more advanced playmates (Guralnick, 1981b). A study conducted by Field et al. (1981), which was similar in design (but assessed changes during outdoor recreational periods), did show some increases in the frequency of certain social interactions by handicapped children when nonhandicapped children were present, but the changes were not major ones.

At best, then, the limited data available suggest that involvement with nonhandicapped children can improve social and play interactions to some extent, but even in well-designed programs dramatic improvements are not likely to occur. Process studies have shown that the absence of substantial effects is not due to a lack of opportunities to observe or interact, to failures in developmentally advanced children's ability to properly adjust their communicative interactions to the level of their companion, nor to any undue negative interactions (Guralnick, 1981c). It is, of course, possible that we overestimate the power of advanced peers to bring about change. In one sense, it may be naive to believe that the involvement of nonhandicapped peers could substantially override a history of generalized social, language, and communicative deficits that characterize many delayed children. Alternatively, and more optimistically, perhaps what is lacking is the translation of our existing knowledge into a set of strategies that can be easily used by teachers and clinicians as part of daily classroom activities. Without such programming, subtle as it may be, the potential benefits of mainstreaming may never be realized.

Finally, it should be noted that beyond important future approaches to remediate deficits when they have been identified, additional effort should be directed to gathering information to guide strategies for prevention. Not all children are equally vulnerable, of course, and at this time we know only some of those child-environment characteristics that make some delayed children more susceptible than others to deficits in peer interactions. By identifying conditions and events predictive of future deficits early on, steps can be taken to either minimize or perhaps even entirely prevent their occurrence.

REFERENCES

Abramovitch, R., and Grusec, J. 1978. Peer imitation in a natural setting. Child Dev. 49:60–65.

Akamatsu, T., and Thelen, M. 1974. A review of the literature on observer characteristics and imitation. Dev. Psychol. 10:38–47.

Cairns, R. B. 1979. Social Development: The Origins and Plasticity of Interchanges. W. H. Freeman & Company, San Francisco.

Charlesworth, R., and Hartup, W. W. 1967. Positive social reinforcement in the nursery school peer group. Child Dev. 38:993–1002.

Field, T., Roseman, S., DeStefano, L., and Koewler, J. H., III. 1981. Play behaviors of handicapped preschool children in the presence and absence of nonhandicapped peers. J. Appl. Dev. Psychol. 2:49–58.

Guralnick, M. J. 1981a. The development and role of child-child social interactions. In: N. Anastasiow (ed.), New Directions for Exceptional Children: Socioemotional Development. Jossey-Bass, Inc., San Francisco.

Guralnick, M. J. 1981b. The social behavior of preschool children at different developmental levels: Effects of group composition. J. Exp. Child Psychol. 31:115–130.

Guralnick, M. J. 1981c. The efficacy of integrating handicapped children in early education settings: Research implications. Topics Early Child. Spec. Educ. 1:57–71.

Guralnick, M. J. 1982. Mainstreaming young handicapped children: A public policy and ecological systems analysis. In: B. Spodek (ed.), Handbook of Research on Early Childhood Education. The Free Press/MacMillan, New York.

Guralnick, M. J., and Weinhouse, E. Peer related social interactions of developmentally delayed young children: Their development and characteristics. Dev. Psychol. (in press)

Hartup, W. W. 1978. Peer interaction and the process of socialization. In: M. J. Guralnick (ed.), Early Intervention and the Integration of Handicapped and Nonhandicapped Children. University Park Press, Baltimore.

Kohn, M. 1966. The child as a determinant of his peers' approach to him. J. Genet. Psychol. 109:91–100.

Lieberman, A. F. 1977. Preschoolers' competence with a peer: Relations with attachment and peer experience. Child Dev. 48:1277–1287.

Mueller, E., and Brenner, J. 1977. The growth of social interaction in a toddler playgroup: The role of peer experience. Child Dev. 48:854–861.

Parten, M. B. 1932. Social participation among preschool children. J. Abnorm. Soc. Psychol. 27:243–269.

Pastor, D. L. 1981. The quality of mother-infant attachment and its relationship to toddlers' initial sociability with peers. Dev. Psychol. 17:326–335.

Rubin, K. H. 1981. Manual for Coding Free Play Behaviors of Young Children. University of Waterloo, Waterloo, Ontario.

Strain, P. (ed.). 1981. The Utilization of Classroom Peers as Behavior Change Agents. Plenum Publishing Corp., New York.

PERSPECTIVES AND PROGRESS IN MENTAL RETARDATION
Volume I—Social, Psychological, and Educational Aspects
Edited by J. M. Berg

ANALYSIS OF INTERACTIONS BETWEEN NONHANDICAPPED AND SEVERELY HANDICAPPED PEERS USING MULTIPLE MEASURES

L. M. Voeltz[1] and J. Brennan[2]

[1] *Special Education Programs, Department of Educational Psychology, University of Minnesota, Minneapolis, Minnesota 55455*
[2] *Hawaii Integration Project, Department of Special Education, 1776 University Avenue UA4-5/6 A, University of Hawaii, Honolulu, Hawaii 96822*

A context for investigating peer relations of handicapped children has been provided by several years of educational services for severely handicapped students on public school campuses enrolling primarily nonhandicapped students throughout Hawaii. This paper focuses upon the nature of peer interactions developed through a "Special Friends" program, based upon findings from behavioral observation of peer and teacher-child dyads and a variety of interview and rating measures administered to the children.

Classes for severely handicapped children are increasingly being established on general education campuses (Brown et al., 1979; Wilcox and Sailor, 1980). The proximity of such children to nonhandicapped, same-age peers represents a significant social change compared to pre-

This work was supported in part by Contract No. 300-80-0746 awarded to the University of Hawaii and Contract No. 300-82-0363 awarded to the University of Minnesota (Luanna Voeltz, Principal Investigator) by the Division of Innovation and Development, Special Education Programs, U. S. Department of Education.

vious generations when this interaction might never have occurred during the school years. At present, there is little information regarding the impact of this social contact upon the children involved.

A considerable literature suggests that mildly handicapped children placed in mainstream social and academic situations are not accepted by their nonhandicapped peers, and may even be subjected to exclusion and abuse (MacMillan et al., 1974; Gottlieb and Leyser, 1980). However, there is also evidence that various intervention efforts can positively modify the attitudes and behavior of nonhandicapped children toward their handicapped peers, particularly through changes in the instructional behavior of the teacher and the nature of the task or activity in which the children participate (Johnson et al., 1979; Donaldson, 1980; Gottlieb and Leyser, 1980). Several recent experimental investigations have similarly demonstrated positive attitudes toward and social interaction with severely handicapped peers by nonhandicapped children who were exposed to structured peer interaction programs (McHale and Simeonsson, 1980; Rynders et al., 1980; Voeltz, 1980a, 1980b, 1982).

Although favorable attitudes and behaviors of nonhandicapped children toward handicapped persons may be a laudable outcome of integration efforts, other possible consequences may be of equal or greater importance to the children involved. One such consequence might be increases in both friendship opportunities and enhanced social interaction skills as a result of expanded social expectations for children and adults. Rubin (1980) discussed cross-age friendships among children as a source of various social experiences not otherwise available in more homogeneous, typical "best friend" relationships. In cross-age friendships, younger children who interact with older children may thus be provided a more tolerant and less complex (in comparison to adults) model for socialization. Older children in turn may derive pride and satisfaction—and presumably increased self-esteem—from performance of such a role in interactions with younger children. They might also enjoy the occasional release from particular demands of their parents or a same-age peer. Children in cross-age friendships might sharpen their social skills as a function of the demands of these "heterogeneous" social relationships, likely to differ in unknown but important ways from contingencies associated with homogeneous and nurturant (parent-child) relationships.

Voeltz (1983) has developed a peer interaction program—Special Friends—that promotes mutually enjoyable social and play interactions between nonhandicapped and severely handicapped children who attend separate classes in the same neighborhood public school. The nature of the program and the activities are defined by the concept of heterogeneous friendships: i.e., interactions between same-age severely handicapped and nonhandicapped children that might be called mixed developmental age friendships, paralleling the mixed chronological age friendships discussed by Rubin (1980). A major objective of each peer interaction is to ensure that it represents a mutually beneficial and interesting activity for both the nonhandicapped and the severely handicapped child. The nonhandicapped children are not viewed as tutors or helpers in relation to their handicapped peers, and any connotation that the handicapped child is the "taker" and the nonhandicapped child the "giver" is avoided.

From 1978 to the present, the Special Friends program has been conducted in a dozen schools throughout the state of Hawaii, and previous reports have focused upon changes in attitudes of nonhandicapped students as a function of their participation in program activities (Voeltz, 1980a, 1982). However, Voeltz (1980b) also reported a series of brief interviews with the regular education participants, suggesting that the children perceived certain social interaction benefits occurring because of the program. In order to pursue this issue more fully, evaluation efforts during the 1981–82 school year in several project schools concentrated on obtaining information on the actual behaviors of the children in these social interactions and how they themselves perceived these relationships. This paper highlights some findings from two of the evaluation studies.

METHOD

Setting and Subjects

Two elementary schools on the island of Hawaii and one elementary and two intermediate schools on the island of Oahu were involved in the studies reported here. In addition to serving primarily regular education children, each school also enrolled several classes of severely handicapped children variously diagnosed as severely multiply handicapped, severely to profoundly retarded, deaf-blind, and autistic. Observation data were collected for 43 of these children, and adaptive behavior and other assessment data were collected for these 43 and 20 additional children enrolled in the six schools. Parent permission was obtained to include all severely handicapped children in program and evaluation activities. Parent permission was also sought to collect certain assessments of nonhandicapped children at each school, regardless of whether or not they eventually chose to participate in program activities; from 10% to 35% of the parents of children enrolled at each school consented, and all data for regular education children are based upon this selective sample.

Approximately 1 month after the beginning of school in fall 1981, regular education children could volunteer to participate in the special interaction program after viewing, class by class, a school-specific slide-sound presentation on friendship that included photographs of all severely handicapped pupils enrolled at that school as well as a sample of regular education children. The interaction program consisted of eight weekly group discussions with a program trainer (topics included "How can we play together?" and "What is a prosthesis?") and two or three weekly recess interactions with a severely handicapped peer (for details see Voeltz, 1983). All pretest evaluation data reported below were collected prior to peer recruitment and the program itself, with the exception of data for a minority of the participant regular education children who obtained parent permission after they chose to be involved.

Study 1: The Social Interaction Observations

In order to investigate whether interactions with nonhandicapped peers might offer social interaction opportunities or experiences not currently available to severely handicapped children, behavioral observations of handicapped-nonhandicapped peer dyads were collected over time and in comparison to teacher-child dyads. The Social Interaction Observation System (SIOS) was specifically designed to monitor seven major categories of behavior for both the handicapped and nonhandicapped individuals involved in the interaction, including information on over 44 individual behaviors (Voeltz et al., 1981).

The severely handicapped pupils included in the project exhibited severe to profound developmental delay, and most of them also had severe sensory and/or motor impairments. Prior to the interaction program, their peer socialization experiences were confined to those with other severely handicapped children within the classroom (generally limited because of the structure of the primarily one-to-one, discrete trial instructional strategies as well as the limited mobility of the children themselves) and those that might be available at home with siblings and neighborhood children. Social interaction during the school day was almost entirely restricted, then, to interactions with a caregiver, e.g., the teacher in instructional situations, the aide during feeding. Nonhandicapped children, on the other hand, engage in various non-caregiver social interactions throughout the school day; although explicit data may be lacking, it is generally acknowledged that these peer socialization experiences contribute considerably to the development of children (Rubin, 1980).

Table 1.   Behavior during dyadic interactions between 22 severely
handicapped children and either teachers or nonhandicapped peers[a]

Behavioral category	Behavior toward handicapped				Behavior of handicapped			
	Of peer (%)	Of teacher (%)	F	P	Toward peer (%)	Toward teacher (%)	F	P
Affect								
Neutral	87.1	86.6	0.0	ns	89.7	90.7	0.2	ns
Positive	13.9	17.8	1.0	ns	13.9	12.1	0.6	ns
Negative	0	0.3	1.4	ns	0.4	0.5	0.3	ns
Distress	0	0.1	1.0	ns	1.2	0.8	0.4	ns
Orientation								
To person	55.8	79.1	20.6	<0.01	15.7	17.7	0.3	ns
To object	40.2	33.2	1.0	ns	37.5	53.0	4.6	<0.05
Away	42.2	20.9	13.4	<0.01	57.5	45.7	4.2	<0.05
Play/activity type								
Appropriate	44.5	21.4	7.8	<0.01	41.1	21.5	3.9	ns
Inappropriate	0.1	0.1	0.1	ns	0.2	0.1	0.3	ns
Parallel	15.0	2.7	9.8	<0.01	16.8	7.3	2.4	ns
Cooperative	23.5	11.2	2.4	ns	22.8	10.5	2.4	ns
Interactive	0.7	2.5	2.2	ns	0.5	0.7	0.5	ns

[a] A total of 345 separate observations of 43 severely handicapped children engaged in a dyadic interaction with either a teacher or a nonhandicapped peer were conducted. The comparison here involves means computed across the mean percentage within each behavioral category for dyads involving the 22 severely handicapped children for whom both at least one teacher-child and one child-child observation were available (based upon 278 observations, 191 with a teacher and 87 with a nonhandicapped peer).

We obtained qualitative information on the nature of the behavioral interactions occurring in dyads of nonhandicapped–severely handicapped children. By comparing these observational data to dyads of teacher–severely handicapped child, we could determine if the behavior of the nonhandicapped children differed from that of teachers in some way, and if the behavior of the severely handicapped children was the same or showed differences in the two types of dyads.

Table 1 displays the results of these observations for particular behavioral categories across 22 severely handicapped children for whom we had at least one (each) teacher-child and child-child dyad sample. The table shows that nonhandicapped peers engaged in significantly more Appropriate Activity Type and Parallel Activity Type behavior (i.e., an activity in which the target person parallels the activity of the severely handicapped child) than did teachers; they also engaged in a higher percentage of cooperative activities, although this difference was not significant. On the other hand, nonhandicapped peers spent less time than teachers did looking at the handicapped child, and they spent more time looking away. Behavior patterns for affect and attention to objects in proximity were similar for teachers and peers. The handicapped child's behavior differed significantly across the two dyad types only for two categories; they spent more time looking at the proximal object and less time looking away in the presence of the teacher as compared to the peer.

Because age appropriateness can be an issue in educational placements, we were interested in whether or not regular education children would display different patterns of behavior at the two age levels in interactions with severely handicapped peers who were quite similar. Table 2 summarizes the mean occurrence of certain behavioral categories across 48 observations conducted on two severely handicapped teenage girls in interactions with their teachers and peers. Sandy (chronological age 13) and Marie (chronological age 17) were selected for more frequent observation because they were similar in body type and size (Sandy being slightly taller), adaptive behavior (Marie scoring slightly lower), and severe physical involvement (both had athetoid cerebral palsy). Although both girls are approximately the size of a mature adolescent girl, Sandy is enrolled at an elementary campus with younger and smaller children, whereas Marie attends school at an intermediate school campus where her "peers" are closer to her age and size.

The differences between teacher and nonhandicapped peer behaviors in the Orientation category are even more striking for secondary youngsters than for elementary-age peers; teenagers spent most of the time looking at the joint activity and not at Marie. On the other hand, they did not spend nearly so much time looking away as did elementary children, who differed significantly from the teacher behavior with Sandy. There is a great deal more positive affect occurring at the secondary level (35% as compared to 15% at the elementary level). Teenagers spent more time engaged in cooperative activity with Marie than did the teacher; there is no statistically significant difference in this category for Sandy. The absence of any significant difference between teacher and peer behavior at the secondary level for the Guide/Position category (which involved physically assisting Marie with the activity—almost essential for both girls, given their severe physical involvement) suggests that teenagers were either more sensitive to or simply physically more able to assist a severely handicapped adolescent peer on a task.

Study 2: The Friendship Survey

The intention of the Special Friends Program is to foster mutually beneficial social relationships between nonhandicapped and severely hand-

Table 2. Behavior of elementary/secondary-age nonhandicapped peers in comparison to teacher behavior in dyadic interactions involving two severely handicapped adolescent girls

Behavioral category	Elementary level, with Sandy				Secondary level, with Marie			
	% Peer	% Teacher	t	P	% Peer	% Teacher	t	P
Affect[a]								
Neutral	84.0	83.9	0.01	ns	76.8	98.0	−3.1	<0.01
Positive	15.2	21.7	−0.8	ns	35.0	13.8	2.0	<0.10
Orientation								
To person	55.7	86.5	−2.7	<0.01	10.6	73.5	−9.2	<0.0001
To object	25.8	31.9	−0.4	ns	75.2	26.5	2.8	<0.05
Away	44.6	22.0	2.7	<0.01	26.8	32.9	−0.5	ns
Touch person								
None	63.8	22.6	6.7	<0.0001	47.8	27.5	1.7	ns
Accident/neutral	15.9	17.5	−0.3	ns	3.0	5.0	−0.6	ns
Guide/position	12.4	61.1	−6.8	<0.0001	48.0	63.5	−1.0	ns
Objects								
Demonstrates	30.7	28.3	0.2	ns	14.6	11.1	0.3	ns
Offers	10.0	7.3	0.4	ns	0	28.3	−3.6	<0.01
Adjusts	2.6	16.0	−3.0	<0.01	59.9	46.3	0.7	ns
Play/activity type								
Appropriate	41.9	18.9	1.8	<0.10	69.4	56.7	0.7	ns
Inappropriate	0	0	—	—	1.5	0	0.8	ns
Parallel	24.5	9.0	1.5	ns	14.3	0	1.8	<0.10
Cooperative	17.5	8.6	0.8	ns	47.8	8.3	2.2	<0.05
Interactive	0	0	—	—	4.0	27.6	−2.0	<0.10

[a] With exception of 0.8% teacher negative affect scored for Marie, there were no instances of negative or distress affect observed for either teacher or child dyads.

Table 3.   Relationship function categories listed by children in grades 1–9
(N = 149) for best friend, caregiver (Mom), and Special Friend

Item response to "I like _____because . . ."	Relationship[a]					
	Best friend[b]		Mom[c]		Special Friend[d]	
	n	%	n	%	n	%
Submissive-nurturance: helps me, likes me, is nice to me, cares for me	37	25	79	53	6	4
Dominance-nurturance: help him, do something for him	1	1	2	1	12	8
Appealing: is good person, nice person, personal qualities	43	29	25	17	58	39
Sociable: interactions, fun to be with, enjoy him, good friend	51	34	11	8	44	30
Other: lives by my house, doesn't spank me	12	8	24	16	23	15
Blank—no response	5	3	8	5	6	4

[a] Test of two-way association: χ^2_{10} = 124.89, $P < 0.0001$; approximate proportion association: r^2 = 0.22.
[b] Interrater Kappa = 0.96 (N = 149; 2 raters).
[c] Interrater Kappa = 0.91 (N = 149; 2 raters).
[d] Interrater Kappa = 0.83 (N = 149; 2 raters).

icapped children, yet the nonhandicapped children might nevertheless perceive these interactions as helping situations, and not heterogeneous friendships. In order to investigate their perceptions of the relationship, each program participant was asked to answer three questions (see Tables 3–5) with respect to his/her Special Friend, best friend, and the person at home who fulfilled the caregiver-nurturance role for that child. (The person filling the caregiver-nurturance role was most often the mother, but including other persons such as the father, an older sibling, and other relatives and friends; we determined this information in advance of the survey for each child, and checked on the validity of our information by asking "Who takes care of you at home?" when the survey was completed.) The three questions were completed for each role one at a time, presented in random order.

As can be seen from the tables, there were significant differences in children's responses for the different relationships. As might be expected, children were more likely to say they liked their mother because she performed submissive-nurturance functions for them; they

Table 4.   Activity type listed by children in grades 1–9 (N = 149) for best friend, caregiver (Mom), and Special Friend

Item response to "If I could pick anything I wanted, my *favorite thing to do* with _____would be . . ."	Relationship[a]					
	Best friend[b]		Mom[c]		Special Friend[d]	
	n	%	n	%	n	%
Parallel play: jog, ride bikes, play records	19	13	20	13	18	12
Cooperative play: play with, go places (shopping, etc.) together (joint activities)	102	68	91	61	80	54
Interactive play: hopscotch, talking, cards, video games (turn taking)	17	11	10	7	24	16
Helping: help him, do something for him	4	3	13	9	16	11
Other: do things, hear her tell stories	4	3	11	7	8	5
Blank—no response	3	2	4	3	3	2

[a] Test of two-way association: χ^2_{10} = 19.038, $P < 0.01$; approximate proportion association: $r^2 = 0.04$.

[b] Interrater Kappa = 0.91 (N = 149; 2 raters).

[c] Interrater Kappa = 0.87 (N = 149; 2 raters).

[d] Interrater Kappa = 0.88 (N = 149; 2 raters).

seldom responded with this category for the Special Friend. (Table 3). A small percentage (8%) indicated that they liked their Special Friend because he or she played a dominant-nurturant role for that person. Although the Appealing category response is reminiscent of the positive stereotype of mentally retarded persons, this was also a frequent category selected for the best friend. Approximately one-third of the children indicated that they like both their best and Special friends for sociability reasons, whereas children were far less likely to give this reason for their mothers.

When asked to identify a favorite activity with each person, children were more likely to pick a helping activity for both their mother and their Special Friend in comparison to their best friend; the most frequently identified category across all three relationships was cooperative play or a joint activity of some sort (see Table 4). When asked to provide an adjective describing how they felt in the presence of each person (see Table 5), 17% of the nonhandicapped children expressed some degree of increased self-esteem with respect to their

Table 5. Affect descriptor listed by children in grades 1–9 ($N = 149$) for best friend, caregiver (Mom), and Special Friend

Item response to "When I am with _____, I feel . . ."	Relationship[a]					
	Best friend[b]		Mom[c]		Special Friend[d]	
	n	%	n	%	n	%
Positive-general: Thankful, good, happy, fine, OK	105	71	95	64	96	65
Positive-self: proud, needed, good about myself, important, like older sib	6	4	5	3	25	17
Positive-other: loved, cared for, good friend, like sibling, quality of friendship	12	8	25	17	6	4
Negative: bad, weird, mixed up, some good–some bad	6	4	7	5	8	5
Other: like talking, thoughtful, like I'm learning	15	10	12	8	9	6
Blank—no response	5	3	5	3	5	3

[a] Test of two-way association: $\chi_{10}^2 = 36.73$, $P < 0.0001$; approximate proportion association: $r^2 = 0.08$.

[b] Interrater Kappa = 0.88 ($N = 149$; 2 raters).

[c] Interrater Kappa = 0.86 ($N = 149$; 2 raters).

[d] Interrater Kappa = 0.89 ($N = 149$; 2 raters).

Special Friend; this was seldom mentioned with respect to a best friend or mother (4% and 3%, respectively). Responses in the Positive-General (e.g., "I feel good") category were both the most frequent and quite similar across the three relationships; responses in the Negative (e.g., "I feel weird") category occurred infrequently and again at a similar frequency for the three relationships.

DISCUSSION

Asher and Taylor (1981) emphasized that past research may have obscured the multiple effects of mainstreaming by focusing solely upon changes in a single dependent variable, i.e., children's nominations of their peers for the categories of best friend versus social rejectee. Measures of ongoing social interactions, changes in general acceptance, and the development of alternative friendship patterns may represent integration outcomes of far greater social significance. Furthermore, it is difficult to evaluate data on children's interactions in the absence of information on other (comparison) social relationships experienced by them, such as teacher-child and parent-child interactions. The multiple measures and strategies utilized in our work reveal the rich texture of effects that are possible; a more comprehensive presentation of these and other evaluation findings is forthcoming (Voeltz et al., in preparation).

Clearly, the nonhandicapped children who interacted with their severely handicapped peers perceived value in those interactions, which both resembled and differed from the more typical relationships available to them in crucial ways. Similarly, the interactions with non-handicapped peers provided the severely handicapped children with social (and perhaps learning) opportunities that might not otherwise be available to them and were not present in their interactions with teachers. These data can provide direction for the design of future intervention efforts to facilitate children's adjustment to the major social changes implied by integration. Although none of the information available to us suggests that the effects of integration are negative—indeed, they appear to be overwhelmingly positive—the ultimate importance of such information is in its use to modify existing integration strategies to maximize benefits for each individual child involved.

ACKNOWLEDGMENTS

The authors wish to thank Sue Brown, Royal Fruehling, Norma Jean Hemphill, and Gloria Kishi for assistance with data collection.

REFERENCES

Asher, S. R., and Taylor, A. R. 1981. The social outcomes of mainstreaming: Sociometric assessment and beyond. Except. Educ. Q. 1:13–30.

Brown, L., Branston, M. B., Hamre-Nietupski, S., Johnson, F., Wilcox, B., and Gruenewald, L. 1979. A rationale for comprehensive longitudinal interactions between severely handicapped students and nonhandicapped students and other citizens. AAESPH Rev. 4:3–14.

Donaldson, J. 1980. Changing attitudes toward handicapped persons: A review and analysis of research. Except. Child. 46:504–514.

Gottlieb, J., and Leyser, Y. 1980. Friendship between mentally retarded and nonretarded children. In: S. R. Asher and J. M. Gottman (eds.), The Development of Children's Friendships, pp. 150–181. Cambridge University Press, Cambridge, England.

Johnson, R., Rynders, J., Johnson, D. W., Schmidt, B., and Haider, S. 1979. Producing positive interaction between handicapped and nonhandicapped teenagers through cooperative goal structuring: Implications for mainstreaming. Am. Educ. Res. J. 16:161–168.

MacMillan, D. L., Jones, R. L., and Aloia, G. F. 1974. The mentally retarded label: A theoretical analysis and review of research. Am. J. Ment. Defic. 79:241–261.

McHale, S. M., and Simeonsson, R. J. 1980. Effects of interaction on non-handicapped children's attitudes toward autistic children. Am. J. Ment. Defic. 85:18–24.

Rubin, Z. 1980. Children's Friendships. Harvard University Press, Cambridge, Massachusetts.

Rynders, J. E., Johnson, R. T., Johnson, D. W., and Schmidt, B. 1980. Producing positive interaction among Down Syndrome and nonhandicapped teenagers through cooperative goal structuring. Am. J. Ment. Defic. 85:268–273.

Voeltz, L. M. 1980a. Children's attitudes toward handicapped peers. Am. J. Ment. Defic. 84:455–464.

Voeltz, L. M. 1980b. Special Friends in Hawaii. Educ. Unlimit. 2:10–11.

Voeltz, L. M. 1982. Effects of structured interactions with severely handicapped peers on children's attitudes. Am. J. Ment. Defic. 86:380–390.

Voeltz, L. M. 1983. Program and curriculum innovations to prepare children for integration. In: N. Certo, N. Haring, and R. York (eds.), Public School Integration of Severely Handicapped Students: Rational Issues and Progressive Alternatives. Paul H. Brookes Publishers, Baltimore.

Voeltz, L. M., Brennan, J., and Kishi, G. Multiple effects of integrating severely handicapped learners into public school programs. (in preparation)

Voeltz, L. M., Kishi, G., and Brennan, J. 1981. The Social Interaction Observation System (SIOS). University of Hawaii, Honolulu.

Wilcox, B., and Sailor, W. 1980. Service delivery issues: Integrated educational settings. In: B. Wilcox and R. York (eds.), Quality Educational Services for the Severely Handicapped: The Federal Investment, pp. 277–304. U. S. Department of Education, Washington, D.C.

PERSPECTIVES AND PROGRESS IN MENTAL RETARDATION
Volume I—Social, Psychological, and Educational Aspects
Edited by J. M. Berg
Copyright © 1984 by I.A.S.S.M.D.

PROMOTING COMPETENCIES FOR INTERPERSONAL RELATIONS IN MENTALLY RETARDED CHILDREN

S. Reiter, M. P. Safir, and L. Friedman

School of Social Work, The Center for Rehabilitation and Human Development, University of Haifa, Haifa, Israel

An intensive 5-month program for developing interpersonal relations skills, based on the Structured Learning Approach, was provided to an experimental group ($N = 23$) of moderately and severely mentally retarded children. Following the program, improvements were reported by teachers using a social skills rating scale; children reported a better socioemotional climate in their classrooms and they achieved higher scores on the Adaptive Behavior Scale (ABS), Part 1 (domain of socialization). No changes in overall pattern of behavior were reported by observers and no changes occurred on ABS Part II domains. These results show that children acquired new skills in certain settings and did not show a generalization of learning. A control group ($N = 34$) that did not undergo the program showed no improvements in interpersonal relations skills, thus demonstrating the importance of a systematic teaching of social behaviors. It was concluded that programs in social education should include special generalization training of each skill taught.

With the current emphasis on integration of mentally retarded persons in the community (Nirje, 1969), programs designed to enhance their social adaptation are increasing. Effective social learning programs should 1) promote new skills in relating to and understanding others, and 2) help the student learn to apply these new skills in various situations.

For many mentally retarded persons generalization of skills from the original learning situation is a significant problem (Perry and Cerreto, 1977). There are several theoretical explanations for this phenomenon. It may be that low intellectual functioning inhibits the capacity for transfer of learning. Because social competencies are heavily related to cognitive functioning, this may explain the inability of mentally retarded persons to apply newly acquired social skills in different settings and situations (Edgerton, 1967; Kleck, 1975; Affleck, 1977). Some blame poor social education and unsystematic instruction for social underfunctioning (Gunzburg and Gunzburg, 1973) and others point to a lack of motivation for appropriate social behavior (Zigler, 1969). Few studies, however, have investigated the actual capabilities of mentally retarded persons to learn social interaction skills (Ross, 1970; Perry and Cerreto, 1977).

The present study focused on the effects in moderately and severely retarded children of an intensive instructional program in interpersonal relations skills on improving interpersonal behavior and on having an impact on general social behavior. At the time of the study, there was no formal program for teaching interpersonal relations skills to mentally retarded children in Israel. Indeed, most special education schools for the mentally retarded emphasize academic achievement and do not systematically teach social competencies (Reiter, 1979). We chose Structured Learning Therapy for teaching social skills (Goldstein, 1973; Goldstein et al., 1980) because a previous study by Perry and Cerreto (1977) found this technique suitable for mentally retarded subjects. The program used a group work approach and included the presentation of a specific social skill by the leader, roleplaying by the participants, frequent social reinforcements, and homework assignments. We found this method especially suitable for local teachers because most of them work with pupils in small groups. The aim of the study was to investigate the achievements of an experimental group that received an intensive, systematic program of instruction in interpersonal relations skills and compare them with a control group that did not receive the treatment.

METHOD

Subjects

The experimental group was composed of 23 moderately and severely mentally retarded children (14 boys and 9 girls). They had a mean IQ [Wechsler Intelligence Scale for Children (WISC)] of 44 (range: 30–56), and a mean chronological age (CA) of 14 (range: 10–18). A control group of 34 children (15 boys and 19 girls) was matched to the experimental group on retardation level and age. The control group had a mean IQ (WISC) of 41 (range: 30–56) and a mean CA of 14 (range: 10–18).

Because the program was designed for use by local teachers, whole classes were studied so that the evaluation would represent, to the greatest extent possible, the natural setting in which the program would eventually be implemented. The experimental group included two classes and the control group three.

Background data on all the children ($N = 57$) were gathered from school files. In the experimental group, 10 had low socioeconomic backgrounds, 8 were middle class, and 5 were from high socioeconomic background. All were Jewish, with 17 of Middle Eastern origin, and 6 of European origin. In addition to mental retardation, 8 subjects showed emotional disturbance. Among the control group, 11 had low socioeconomic backgrounds, and 23 were middle class. There were 21 subjects of Middle Eastern origin and 9 of European origin. Three were Arabs. In addition to mental retardation, 5 subjects had emotional disturbances.

Procedure

In order to obtain baseline data on the behavior of all the children, several procedures were used. Structured observations were made on each child in the classrooms by specially trained observers. The technique used followed suggestions of Gregory (1979) for the observation of children with severe handicaps. The following behaviors were recorded: manipulation of objects, talking, wandering around, approaching others or being approached, self-stimulation, and looking around.

Next, all children were individually interviewed on a questionnaire about the socioemotional climate in the classroom. The questionnaire was constructed on the basis of suggestions by Walberg and Anderson (1968). It was designed to tap the childrens' perceptions of their classmates' behavior. Items described the characteristics of this behavior, for example, "in my class children share things willingly." The respondent expressed agreement or disagreement with each of 20 such items, on a 4-point scale.

Teachers were asked to fill in a 16-item rating scale on the behavior of each child. The items represented the major skills included in the instructional program for the interpersonal relations. We were aware that the teachers who took part in the experiment might be subjective in their ratings of pupils' progress; however, it was important to get their own evaluation of the program's effectiveness. To obtain an objective measure of the program's impact on the children's behavior, all the experimental subjects were tested on the Adaptive Behavior Scale (ABS) (Nihira et al., 1974).

Following initial assessments, the experimental group received a systematic and intensive program for the development of interpersonal skills. The program covered the following areas: early social skills, such as listening and responding appropriately to others and introducing oneself to others; more advanced social skills, such as convincing others of one's opinions, asking for help and helping others; and skills for dealing with feelings. Teachers were given a detailed program of instruction and ongoing supervision. The program ran for 5 months, 5 days per week, 15 minutes each time. The main methods of instruction included roleplaying, an intensive use of audiovisual aids, and frequent social reinforcements by teachers.

Following the program, the experimental children were posttested on the ABS, Part I (domain of socialization) and the whole of Part II. All children in the experimental and control groups were observed again in the classrooms and interviewed again on the classroom climate questionnaire, and teachers also completed social skills rating scales.

RESULTS

Factor Analysis for Adaptive Behavior

To ascertain whether or not the primary dimensions of adaptive behavior found by Nihira (1969), and referred to as Personal Independence and Social and Personal Maladaptation, appear in the Israeli sample, a factor analysis was done on all scores obtained on the ABS. In addition, the independent variables of sex, IQ, socioeconomic background, ethnic background, and fathers' and mothers' occupations were computed. Three main factors emerged (on a Varimax rotated factor matrix), together accounting for 64.9% of the variance. Table 1 represents the domains and independent variables included in each factor and their factor loadings.

Table 1 shows that the dimensions proposed by Nihira (1969) appeared in the present study as well. However, the dimension of Personal and Social Maladaptation was subdivided in our study into two distinct areas of behavior: Personal Maladaptation (factor 1) and Social Maladaptation (factor 3). Furthermore, in this study, Personal Maladaptation appeared concurrently with low functioning in Vocational Activity and in Self-direction, two domains that relate to independence skills. Personal maladaptive behavior was also found to be negatively correlated with IQ: the lower the level of intelligence the more maladaptive the behavior. Independence skills (factor 2) were found to correlate with mothers' occupations: the more professional the mothers' occupations the higher the achievements of the children on independent behavior skills.

Table 1.   Factors and factor loadings on adaptive
behavior of moderately and severely mentally
handicapped Israeli children assessed on the Adaptive
Behavior Scale

Factor/domain	Factor loading
Factor 1: Personal maladaptation	
Vocational activity	−0.49
IQ	−0.76
Self-direction	−0.77
Violence	0.67
Rebelliousness	0.61
Stereotyped behavior	0.83
Inappropriate interpersonal manners	0.48
Unacceptable vocal habits	0.74
Eccentric habits	0.72
Hyperactive tendencies	0.88
Psychological disturbances	0.60
Factor 2: Personal independence	
Mother's occupation	0.49
Independent functioning	0.80
Physical development	0.72
Economic activity	0.47
Language development	0.61
Number and time concepts	0.70
Responsibility	0.85
Socialization	0.58
Factor 3: Social maladaptation	
Antisocial behavior	0.80
Untrustworthy behavior	0.76

To learn which areas of behavior were tapped by each of the specially designed measures for this study, a factor analysis was applied
to the baseline data. Table 2 shows the analysis of these data. It yielded

Table 2.   Factors and factor loadings on behavior observed
in the classrooms

Factor/item	Factor loadings
Factor 1: Activity level	
Looking around	0.84
Talking	0.82
Wandering around	0.75
Self-stimulation	0.66
Manipulation of objects	0.61
Factor 2: Social interactions	
Approaching someone	0.67
Being approached by teacher or others	0.41

Table 3.   Factors and factor loadings on classroom behavior as assessed by the children

Factor/item	Factor loadings
Factor 1: Friction	
Fighting	0.80
Insulting	0.77
Being repulsive	0.56
Swearing	0.54
Factor 2: Mutual understanding and help	
Letting others talk	0.62
Accepting corrections	0.59
Helping others	0.55
Factor 3: Freedom of self-expression	
Accepting criticism	0.61
Talking openly and freely with teacher	0.58
Expressing feelings freely	0.51

two independent factors, together accounting for 87.6% of the variability. Only factors with loadings higher than 0.40 were included. The factor analysis indicates that there were two distinct and independent sets of behavior, one related to a general level of activity, and the other to social interaction, such as the number of times a child approached someone, was touched, or was talked to by others.

Factor analysis of scores obtained on the classroom climate questionnaire (See Table 3) yielded three independent factors, which accounted for 61.9% of the variability. Only factors with loadings higher than 0.50 were included. The factors presented in Table 3 indicate that the socioemotional climate in the classrooms had three distinct components: unpleasant behaviors causing friction between children, positive social behaviors like helping and receiving assistance, and freedom of self-expression.

Table 4 shows that the factor analysis of scores on the teachers' rating scales yielded two main factors, together accounting for 100% of the variability. Only factors with loadings higher than 0.60 were included. It appears that the areas of behaviors included in the program were indeed tapped by the scale, which were skills important for 1) interpersonal behavior, and 2) the expression of one's feelings and an understanding of the feelings of others.

Differences between Groups

The control group was matched with the experimental group according to retardation level and age. To find out whether significant differences existed between the groups in social behavior, two-tailed t tests were employed on the factors observed. No differences were found between

Table 4. Factors and factor loadings on social skills assessed by the teachers

Factor/item	Factor loadings
Factor 1: Social integration skills	
Knows how to convince others	0.90
Joins in ongoing activities	0.84
Knows how to present a question	0.81
Helps others	0.81
Knows how to make introductions between people	0.80
Initiates activities	0.77
Knows how to ask permission from others	0.76
Factor 2: Self-expression skills	
Knows how to express fondness for others	0.86
Knows when and how to ask for help	0.68
Knows how to express his/her feelings	0.68
Can listen to others	0.62
Knows how to compliment others	0.62
Knows how to introduce himself/herself	0.60

the experimental group and the controls in the observations in the classrooms. This indicated that the two populations were similar in general level of activity and in amount of time spent in interpersonal contacts. We proceeded to investigate whether changes occurred in the behavior of the experimental group following the program of instruction in interpersonal skills, and compared the experimental group with the control group. A two-tailed t test was done on the scores obtained by the experimental group before and after the intervention programs on the factors found in each measure (Tables 2, 3, and 4).

Highly significant positive differences were noted in the socio-emotional climate of the classrooms, as reported by the children, on Friction ($P < 0.0001$) and on Mutual Understanding and Help ($P < 0.0001$). No differences were found on Freedom of Self-expression. Thus, following the program, the children reported that there was less friction among themselves as well as more understanding between them. Significant improvements in childrens' social-integrational skills were reported by the teachers using the social skills rating scale ($P < 0.008$), and on self-expression skills ($P < 0.0001$). However, no differences were found on the observations done in the classrooms. Children spent the same amount of time in different activities and in social interactions.

Other Comparisons and Assessments

Another measure used to assess the progress of the experimental group was the Adaptive Behavior Scale. Posttests were done only on those parts of the ABS that were relevant to interpersonal behavior. They were Part I (domain of socialization) and the whole of Part II (such items as violent and destructive behavior, untrustworthy behavior, withdrawal, unacceptable vocal habits, eccentric habits, and hyperactive tendencies). Two-tailed t tests were done on the children's scores before and after the intervention program. Significant differences were found in the domain of socialization ($P < 0.01$), where children showed improvement in behavior. No significant changes occurred in children's behavior on any of the Part II domains.

We then investigated whether any variable other than the intervention program could have affected or contributed to the improvements found on socialization. By means of two-tailed t tests and analysis of variance, the independent variables of sex, ethnic origin, social class, and existence of emotional disturbance, in addition to mental retardation, were each tested in relation to socialization. None was found to have influenced the improvements made by the experimental children on socialization. Therefore, we concluded that the program of instruction in interpersonal skills was the major factor influencing the achievements of the study children in this area. Some correlations were found between IQ and socialization ($r = 0.31$, $P < 0.05$), indicating that the higher the IQ the higher were the scores obtained on this domain.

We also investigated the control group's behavior on each of the factors mentioned earlier (Tables 2, 3, and 4) to determine if changes had occurred. Two-tailed t tests were done on the scores obtained by the children in the pre- and posttestings. No significant differences were noted on any of the factors. This finding supports the importance of systematic and intensive programs in social skills for developing social competencies in mentally retarded children.

Comparing the behavior of the experimental children with the controls on scores obtained on each factor in the posttestings, significant differences appeared on the socioemotional climate in the classrooms. Following the intervention program, the experimental children reported significantly less friction than the controls ($P < 0.01$); significantly more mutual understanding and help ($P < 0.001$); and significantly more free expression ($P < 0.01$). The experimental children's social skills were rated higher by their teachers in the posttesting than the control children's behavior in the areas of social integration ($P < 0.0001$) and self-expression ($P < 0.0001$). No differences were found between the experimental group and the controls on the observations done. Indeed, there was no change in either population in their general levels of activities and in the number of times they were involved in social interactions.

In summary, the results of the present study indicate that an intensive program of instruction in social interpersonal skills had a positive effect on children's behavior within that area. However, the program did not affect a more general change in their behavior, as tested on Part II of the ABS and as recorded in the observations done in the classrooms.

DISCUSSION

We found that an experimental group of retarded children who received a 5-month intensive program of instruction, based on the Structured Learning Approach (Goldstein et al., 1980), exhibited marked improvements in social-interpersonal behavior compared to a control group that did not participate in the program. It appeared that, even though all the control children had attended school during the 5-month period between the pre- and posttestings, without the special program for enhancing social behavior children did not develop in this area.

However, it was found that the positive effects of the instruction program were limited to the skills taught. The experimental group showed significant improvements on the ABS domain of socialization, and did not show positive changes on any of the ABS Part II domains. Thus, although they became more cooperative, aware of others, and helpful, and were less selfish, they did not, for example, exhibit less violent and destructive behaviors, or less rebellious behavior. This was further confirmed by the fact that, although the experimental group's social skills were rated better by the teachers following the intervention program, and the children reported a more positive socioemotional climate in their classrooms, no changes occurred in the general levels of activity of the children as recorded by the observers. There was no reduction in wandering around, self-stimulation, looking around, talking, or manipulating objects, nor did the children engage in more social interactions than before the initiation of the program.

A similar finding was reported by King et al. (1980), who reported that, following a systematic program of behavior modification, clients improved on Part I domains of the ABS, and not on Part II domains. A similar finding on the multidimensionality of social behavior (Nihira, 1969; Lambert and Nicoll, 1976) was also reported in a survey on the adjustment of mentally retarded adults to the community (Reiter and Levi, 1980), in which the different aspects of social behavior (social competencies required for independent living, social-interpersonal relations skills, and emotional stability) were each distinct and independent of each other and achievements in one area did not necessarily affect achievements in other areas.

Another finding is that, in our sample of moderately and severely mentally handicapped children, the level of intelligence was negatively correlated with personal maladaptative behavior, and did not correlate with independence skills or antisocial behavior. This finding, which should be further researched on larger samples, supports the contention that cognitive functions relate to social interaction skills (Affleck, 1977).

An additional finding relates to the effects of the general socio-cultural milieu on the social behavior of mentally retarded persons. In spite of the relative independence of each dimension of social behavior, some independent skills appear to be highly correlated with personal maladaptive behavior according to cultural norms. In the present study, vocational activity and self-direction (ABS, Part I) were negatively correlated with personal maladaptation (see Table 1). A possible explanation is that in Israeli society there is an emphasis on "being active and showing initiative." Melach-Pinse and Jimbardo (1977) compared Israeli and American populations on the variable of timidity, and found that Israelis were much less timid. They showed a higher degree of self-confidence and were less inhibited in expressing their feelings and opinions.

The cultural influences on social behavior are also demonstrated in the different meaning given to the term "self-expression" by the children and the teachers. In Israeli society, self-expression means self-assertiveness, being open and direct about one's opinions, ideas, and attitudes. Self-expression does not imply self-disclosure of one's feelings and emotions. Thus, when the teachers in the experimental group reported improvements in "self-expression" following the program, they were referring to the socially encouraged norm of being open and direct. The children, on the other hand, were referring to the self-expression of their feelings. Unlike the teachers, they did not find that their mates improved in this definition of self-expression and they did not report gains following the intervention program.

There are several general implications of the present study for the social education of mentally retarded persons. Programs aimed at social development should cover each dimension of social behavior, independence skills, social interpersonal skills, and personal maladaptation separately, while taking into account local sociocultural patterns of behavior. Such programs should also include special instructions for generalization training. Teachers should aim not only at the technical acquisition of new skills, but also at the internalization of these skills so that they will have a more substantial effect on the subjects' behavior. It is suggested that programs for the development of social skills should be applied concurrently with modifications of maladaptive behaviors. The findings of this study are encouraging in that they indicate that, with careful and systematic introduction, mentally retarded youth can learn adaptive social behaviors. The results also challenge us to design more complete and sophisticated approaches to helping these youth apply the newly acquired skills in the myriad of social situations they encounter in their daily life. Only if they gain the capacity to generalize and transfer these new social competencies will they be able to function effectively in their community.

REFERENCES

Affleck, G. G. 1977. Interpersonal competencies of the mentally retarded. In: P. Mittler (ed.), Research to Practice in Mental Retardation, Vol. II, pp. 85–91, University Park Press, Baltimore.

Edgerton, R. B. 1967. The Cloak of Competence. University of California Press, Los Angeles.

Goldstein, A. P. 1973. Structured Learning Therapy: Toward a Psychotherapy for the Poor. Academic Press, New York.

Goldstein, A. P., Srafkin, R. P., Gershaw, N. J., and Klein, P. 1980. Skill-Streaming the Adolescent. Research Press Company, Champaign, Illinois.

Gregory, O. 1979. Observing children who are profoundly handicapped. Paper presented at 5th Congress of the International Association for the Scientific Study of Mental Deficiency, Jerusalem, Israel, 1979.

Gunzburg, H. C., and Gunzburg, A. L. 1973. Mental Handicap and Physical Environment. Baillière Tindall, London.

King, T., Soucar, E., and Isett, R. 1980. An attempt to assess and predict adaptive behavior of institutionalized mentally retarded clients. Am. J. Ment. Defic. 84:406–410.

Kleck, R. E. 1975. Issues in social effectiveness: The case of the mentally retarded. In: M. Begab and S. Richardson (eds.), The Mentally Retarded and Society: A Social Science Perspective. University Park Press, Baltimore.

Lambert, N. M., and Nicoll, R. C. 1976. Dimensions of adaptive behavior of retarded and nonretarded public school children. Am. J. Ment. Defic. 81:135–146.

Melach-Pinse, A., and Jimbardo, P. G. 1977. On timidity and Israelis. Science 21:273–278. (in Hebrew)

Nihira, K. 1969. Factorial dimensions of adaptive behavior in mentally retarded children and adolescents. Am. J. Ment. Defic. 74:130–141.

Nihira, K., Foster, R., Shelhaas, M., and Leland, H. 1974. AAMD Adaptive Behavior Scale. American Association on Mental Deficiency, Washington, D.C.

Nirje, B. 1969. The normalization principle and its human management implications. In: R. B. Kugel and W. Wolfensberger (eds.), Changing Patterns in Residential Services for the Mentally Retarded. Department of Health, Education, and Welfare, Washington, D.C.

Perry, M. A., and Cerreto, M. C. 1977. Structured learning training of social skills for the retarded. Ment. Retard. 15:31–34.

Reiter, S. 1979. Areas of neglect in the social education of mentally retarded children in special schools. Spec. Educ. (Ministry of Education, Jerusalem) 17:40–44.

Reiter, S., and Levi, A. M. 1980. Factors affecting social integration of non-institutionalized mentally retarded adults. Am. J. Ment. Defic. 85:25–30.

Ross, E. 1970. Effect of intentional training in social behavior on retarded children. Am. J. Ment. Defic. 73:912–918.

Walberg, H. J., and Anderson, G. I. 1968. Classroom climate and individual learning. J. Educ. Psychol. 49:414–419.

Zigler, E. 1969. Developmental versus difference theories of mental retardation and the problem of motivation. Am. J. Ment. Defic. 73:535–556.

PERSPECTIVES AND PROGRESS IN MENTAL RETARDATION
Volume I—Social, Psychological, and Educational Aspects
Edited by J. M. Berg

RESEARCH ON IMPROVING THE SOCIAL ADAPTATION OF CHILDREN WITH DOWN'S SYNDROME

J. E. Rynders

*University of Minnesota Special Education Programs,
Department of Educational Psychology, 249 Burton Hall,
178 Pillsbury Drive S.E., Minneapolis, Minnesota 55455*

Featuring Lewin's (1951) "life space" scheme, this paper examines the validity of three long-standing social stereotypes about Down's syndrome in light of current research findings. Following a historical updating, two areas of research that have implications for social adaptation from a transactions perspective are reviewed in light of their importance for improving educational mainstreaming prospects for children with Down's syndrome.

A current major U.S. law, Public Law 94-142, requires that children with Down's syndrome (DS) and other disabilities be placed in the least restrictive appropriate educational environment, a requirement that often translates to educational mainstreaming with nonhandicapped persons. This law places heavy demands for social adaptation on DS children, who have to learn to be quite adept socially to thrive in a mainstream environment. Thus, educational researchers are challenged to prepare more DS children for successful social adaptation in mainstream environments while designing mainstream environments themselves to be more socially accommodating for them.

In discussing this challenge it should be pointed out that DS children, from the moment of birth, are virtually expected to live up to (or in some cases hoped to outlive) developmental forecasts and social stereotypes that have been set down for them over the last 100 years; infants without handicaps, unless disadvantaged in some way, have no such historical social "baggage" imposed on their lives. To portray the impact of historically determined expectations and stereotypes on

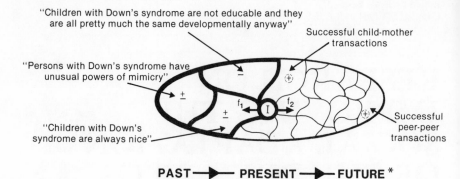

Figure 1.   Conceptualization of the life space of the child with Down's syndrome, with
an emphasis on social adaptation factors. Key:

I   = an infant with Down's syndrome
+   = positively valenced historical stereotype or expectation
−   = negatively valenced historical stereotype or expectation
⊕   = positively valenced opportunity (real or potential)
f_1 = status quo: meeting past expectations
f_2 = movement toward social competence

* This conceptualization is based in part on Myerson (1963).

the DS child's development, I have borrowed from Lewin's (1951) "life
space" scheme of social adaptation (Figure 1). The left side of the figure
depicts the three pieces of historical social baggage that DS children
carry from birth, shown as areas bound by heavy lines to convey the
idea that these long-standing social expectations, or social stereotypes,
probably loom large in the DS infant's life space and are mediating
influences, positively and/or negatively, on the DS person's future development. On the right side of Figure 1 are life space areas that are
smaller and bounded by lighter lines to suggest that a DS person's
future developmental prospects are not well mapped or predictable and
are largely dependent on the success of early social transactions (Schiefelbusch, 1981) such as synchronous mother-child vocal engagement
and, later, mutually satisfying peer-peer social interaction.
    The purposes of this paper are to examine three prevalent histor-
ical social stereotypes or expectations about Down's syndrome (left
side of Figure 1) in light of current evidence about their validity, and
then to look briefly at two research areas that appear to hold particular
promise for improving a DS child's future social transactions (right
side of Figure 1) and, ultimately, his/her prospects for mainstreaming.

HISTORICAL STEREOTYPES

**"Children with Down's syndrome are not educable
and they are all pretty much the same developmentally anyway."**

This prevalent, misinformed expectation has restricted social and educational opportunities of DS children for many years. As recently as 1975, in an article in *Psychology Today*, a prominent physician, chief of the Reproductive Genetics Unit in an eastern university hospital, was quoted as saying, "You show me just one mongoloid that has an educable IQ. . . . I've never seen even one [who is educable] in my experience with over 800 mongols" (Restak, 1975). Disturbed by that statement, we (Rynders et al., 1978) searched the literature to see what evidence of educability exists in studies about DS. Employing a computerized bibliographical search system, we systematically combed the English-language psychological, educational, and medical literature of 1967 to 1976 for studies on DS persons that included data on developmental achievement. The initial search yielded more than 650 references. Of these, 105 studies of DS persons contained psychometric or other educational measures pertinent to the question of educability.

Methodological Problems in Studies   The first thing our search revealed is that studies reporting educability often have serious methodological insufficiencies, appearing to have been conducted as if persons with DS are all very similar. In line with our suspicion of overgeneralization, information on a number of relevant or potentially relevant subject variables is often omitted: 1) confirmation of diagnosis by chromosomal analysis, including the number of subjects with each specific form (i.e., regular trisomy 21, translocation, mosaicism); 2) sex; 3) residence (home or institution) and the period of time in each; and 4) basis on which subjects were selected for study. Such omissions reinforce our suspicion that many researchers may think of Down's syndrome as unitary and invariable, leading to overgeneralization about developmental expectations.

Regarding just the area of sex of subjects, in 63 of the 105 studies (60%), sex of the subjects was not reported. Researchers studying DS persons who ignore sex as a variable seem to reinforce implicitly the stereotype that all such persons are alike, yet few psychologists studying the development and characteristics of nonhandicapped children would fail to take this variable into account. Interestingly, in at least two studies, investigators have found distinct sex differences in psychometrically assessed intelligence in children with DS (Clements et al., 1976; LaVeck, 1977, personal communication), and at least one study has shown sex differences in their social and play behaviors (Schlottmann and Anderson, 1973).

Analysis of Educability Findings   In order to obtain a more conservatively derived picture of the educability of DS persons, we examined data for 103 DS subjects from 15 studies in which karyotypes were specified, chronological age (CA) was greater than 5 years, and

Table 1.   Means, standard deviations (SDs), and ranges of IQ scores for subjects in 15 studies[a] reporting individual IQ scores

Down's syndrome subjects by karyotype	N	IQ		
		Mean	SD	Range
Trisomy 21	39	45	15	18–75
Translocation	14	53	17	28–85
Mosaicism	50	57	22	14–100

[a] The 15 studies are identified with asterisks in the reference section of a previously published article (Rynders et al., 1978).

individual IQs were reported (see Table 1). Several points should be noted about these 103 subjects. First, they represented only 1% of the total subjects in the original 105 studies; obviously, this cannot be described as a representative, random sample of DS persons. Second, we included only studies in which DS persons were past 5 years of age; including subjects younger than that could lead to an erroneous conclusion of higher levels of typical functioning than is actually the case because of the often-reported decline in maturation rate (Carr, 1970; Dicks-Mireaux, 1972). Third, we dealt with IQ scores reported for individuals because means and ranges tell nothing about the actual number of persons who fall into various IQ ranges. Fourth, for 38 of the 39 regular trisomic persons whose data are shown in Table 1 there appeared to be no bias toward selecting subjects with higher IQs. Finally, residence characteristics and sex of subjects were reported for few individuals in these studies; hence, we had two additional reasons to view these individual scores with caution.

Keeping these limitations in mind, it is interesting to note that Table 1 shows an overrepresentation for mosaic DS, compared with the percentage reported in DS populations in general. This discrepancy may be due to interest in whether persons with mosaic DS have higher IQs than do persons with other forms of the syndrome. Therefore, again, one must be extremely cautious in interpreting these data. However, one can conclude from Table 1 that variability in psychometrically assessed intelligence may be more common than is often assumed. Furthermore, a number of individuals in each of the syndrome subgroups fall within the educable range psychometrically. Obviously, much more complete data on individuals are needed to obtain an accurate picture of educability of DS persons.

Project Edge and Other Positive Studies   Some of these individual data are emerging in our own work, Project EDGE, at the University of Minnesota (Rynders and Horrobin, 1980), in which we have studied the development of 35 children with DS from the time they were 6 months old until they reached 5 years of age. These children (17 experimentals, 18 controls) resided in their own homes in the Chicago and Minneapolis–St. Paul areas. All had the regular trisomy 21 form of the syndrome.

At age 5, 10 of 23 males and 10 of 12 females (experimental and control children with DS combined) had IQs at or above 52 on the Stanford-Binet Intelligence Scale. Among these 20, 16 (8 boys, 8 girls) had scores in the mild range (52 to 68) of mental retardation —a range corresponding roughly to the term "educable," as defined in the American Association on Mental Deficiency terminology and classification manual (Grossman, 1973). The remaining 4 of the 20 children whose IQs were 52 or greater had scores higher than 68, which means, according to the AAMD manual, that they should not be labeled mentally retarded.

The 17 children in the EDGE Project's experimental group were not the only ones showing educable-level IQs. In fact, in the group of 18 DS children not receiving our experimental treatment, most of whom received some form of early intervention, fully 45% scored at or above the educable level at 5 years of age.

Also to be noted is that the total group was not representative of all types of families with DS children, because we did not enroll families in either group who were on welfare, had broken homes, or in which the child's mother was mentally retarded. Furthermore, all parents had decided before enrollment to rear their children at home during their child's early years, so one can assume that motivation to maximize their child's development was reasonably high. Despite these limitations on generalization, results of the EDGE Project are encouraging from a developmental expectation perspective.

To add to our encouragement about the DS child's educability, at least 11 contemporary intervention projects for infants and preschool DS children have shown one or more positive developmental outcomes (Jeffree et al., 1973; Pothier et al., 1974; Tawney, 1974; Bidder et al., 1975; Hayden and Dimitriev, 1975; MacDonald et al., 1975; Hanson, 1976; Aronson and Fällström, 1977; Cheseldine and McConkey, 1979; Clunies-Ross, 1979; Rynders and Horrobin, 1980). However, one study (Piper and Pless, 1980) showed no significant developmental differences between an experimental and control group. Most of the intervention studies have methodological problems, and they represent a wide variety of outcomes some of which are limited in applicability and generalizability; however, children with DS in these studies rather commonly show one or more educable behaviors, on a psychometric and/or functional basis, and considerable variability in expression of their educability.

Conclusions   In closing this section on educability, let us return to the statement made by a prominent physician that in all his years he had not seen a DS child with an educable IQ. Based on the data presented here, that physician should at least tell new parents of DS children that: 1) there is a definite possibility that their children will be educable on a psychometric basis; 2) there is a great deal of variability in DS children's early developmental progress as well as in degrees and form of functioning and adjustment beyond early childhood; and 3) the limits of DS children's educability are virtually unknown at this time because past psychometric studies of educability have often been flawed, and results from early education programs for children with DS are just emerging. Such a portrayal is not only appropriately optimistic, it is also appropriately *fair.*

"Persons with Down's syndrome have unusual powers of mimicry."

A long-standing social stereotype is that children with Down's syndrome have unusual imitative (mimicry) powers. If this stereotype were to be verified experimentally, it might be turned to the DS child's advantage because properly modeled important social behaviors might be acquired more readily by the child. Belmont (1971) provided a summary table that highlights the 18 historical clinical-behavioral portrayals of DS persons through 1966, beginning with Dr. Langdon Down's original portrayal in 1866. Interestingly, no less than 13 of these portrayals note mimicry or imitative powers as an important characteristic of persons with DS, although some of the more recent studies Belmont described challenge earlier generalizations. He concluded his extensive review by saying that, although the clinical literature is generally in agreement on the existence of unusual mimicry abilities in DS persons, this trait's existence has not been subjected to a rigorous test experimentally and so remains a hypothesis.

Silverstein et al. (1979) attempted to put Belmont's observation about mimicry to the test with 28 DS persons and 56 persons with retardation of other etiologies, all of whom were institutionalized. Subjects, some of whom were adults, were comparable with regard to sex, CA, and IQ. An abbreviated, modified version of Whalan and Henker's (1971) Social Behavior Test was used to assess imitative behavior. The assessment consisted of 15 nonverbal items (e.g., sticking out tongue), 6 vocal items (e.g., inhale, "ah"), and 14 verbal items (e.g., "baby"). For each item, the examiner said "Do this," gave the response, and then said "You do it." Results showed that persons with DS were not significantly different from other retarded subjects in terms of learning these imitative behaviors.

Silverstein et al. acknowledged that their experiment was beset with methodological problems; for example, diagnosis of DS was made from records without karyotype evidence, and the findings probably lack generalizability because all subjects were institutionalized. Additionally, their study was a less than ideal test of Belmont's observation about the existence of imitative behavior, because their experimental tasks involved considerable verbal cuing and a short number of learning trials, whereas the historical portrayal of mimicry (Belmont's focus) frequently describes imitative behaviors of DS subjects that appear to have been learned with little deliberate verbal cuing and were acquired over a long series of nonlaboratory exposures. Thus, Belmont's challenge to experimentally test the mimicry hypothesis continues to stand.

"Children with Down's syndrome are always 'nice' (e.g., cheerful and passive)."

This expectation is perhaps more of a popular characterization than a genuine historical social stereotype. Little direct evidence exists regarding the characterization, but some evidence bears on it indirectly. Johnson and Abelson (1969) compared 2,606 DS individuals with 20,605 mentally retarded persons representing other etiologies, all of whom were institutionalized. The average age of all subjects was about 22 years; IQs averaged 29 in the population of subjects with DS and 32 in the other subjects. Karyotype data were not provided. The two groups were compared on the frequency with which they exhibited mature social behaviors such as "communicates understandably," "brushes own teeth," "uses toilet independently," and "understands others." Results showed that the DS subjects exhibited higher proportions of socially adaptive, socially competent behavior in most (7 of the 11) categories. However, the DS persons showed markedly inferior performance in items such as "communicates to others understandably." A study by Landesman-Dwyer et al. (1982) involved 53 DS persons (karyotype data not provided). Distributed across several group homes in the state of Washington, these residents with DS engaged in significantly less general social activity than did other residents in the same group homes.

Findings from both of these studies have to be viewed with caution because their subjects, who reside in institutions or group homes, are not representative of all DS persons, especially younger persons living at home who may be functioning with social adeptness (which may be why they are still at home). Furthermore, these two experiments do not fully address the veracity of the assumption that persons with DS are always nice. What they do imply is that the quality of DS persons' social affect has been overgeneralized. Indeed, in the Johnson and Abelson study there was a clear indication that their subjects showed strengths and weaknesses in two different, yet related, types of social activity: peer interaction activity (e.g., verbalizing with others) and self-help activity (e.g., brushing their own teeth). Furthermore, implicit in both of these studies is the notion that DS children are generally nice to have around, i.e., they often have a pleasing demeanor, but that they lack social interaction competencies such as the skilled use of language. Finally, among DS individuals generally, considerable affect variability exists not only across subjects but within individual subjects, who, contrary to another stereotype (that of passivity), can become quite noncompliant (stubborn) when faced with difficult problem-solving tasks (Spiker, 1979).

RESEARCH IN IMPROVING SOCIAL TRANSACTIONS

I turn now to two areas of research that may hold particular promise for improving the future social adaptation of DS children. These areas deal with improvement of social transactions, a fundamental aspect of mainstreaming (see right side of Lewin's life space scheme, Figure 1).

Improving the Early Parent-Child Transaction Process

Spiker (1979) conducted a study that partially addressed a key early intervention question, "How realistic is it for every mother of an infant with Down's syndrome to be asked to assume a structured, formal, teaching role?" Spiker compared the teaching interactions of two groups of 24 mother–DS child pairs, where the children, 26 to 48 months old, varied on IQ level; one group (high-functioning) had IQ scores from 67 to 80 ($\bar{X} = 73.8$), and the other group (low-functioning) had scores between 40 and 62 ($\bar{X} = 54.7$). Groups were matched for CA, sex, and other variables. All the children had regular trisomy 21 and lived in their own homes. Experimental tasks involved the child in learning how to match four different blocks, with pictures on all six sides, to either identical or categorically equivalent pictures displayed on a Plexiglas apparatus. The task for the mother was to teach her child the discriminations involved in a moderately difficult matching task rather than to teach the child the concept of matching per se.

Despite some similarities in the interaction patterns, the two groups of mothers differed in the teaching session, as did the two groups of children, in ways that probably mutually affected each other. For example, mothers of high-functioning children appeared to be more positively encouraging, somewhat less intrusive, more likely to ignore task-inappropriate behavior, and more inclined to take advantage of multiple opportunities to instruct their children about the task and praise their performance. Their children showed more attentive and appropriate involvement by having significantly higher frequencies of on-task responses following both mothers' intervention and mothers' feedback. Overall, the interactions with the high-functioning, as compared with low-functioning, children appeared to have a more synchronous and free-flowing quality, i.e., the involvement of the children was more responsive and appropriate, and the mothers had an easier time engaging their children in the whole task situation.

Spiker concluded her report by suggesting that there may be more than one way to be an effective teacher with DS children, the best method partly depending on the child. In this regard, she found that some children in her study actually resisted maternal intervention, a finding similar to that of Jones (1977, 1980), who noted asynchronous vocal behaviors, e.g., turn-taking interruptions, in some DS infants as they interracted with their mothers [see Spiker (1982) for a comprehensive discussion of issues and possibilities surrounding synchrony as a phenomenon]. Spiker's conclusion is very important from a social adaptation standpoint because successful parent-infant transactions can help to maximize the educational mainstreaming prospects of DS children during their school years.

Improving Peer Acceptance of School-Age DS Children

Simply arranging for handicapped and nonhandicapped students to be in physical proximity with one another does not ensure that positive interaction and interpersonal attraction will result. Indeed, there is considerable evidence that nonhandicapped students often see handicapped peers in negative and prejudiced ways (Jaffe, 1966; Novak, 1975), often feel discomfort and uncertainty in interacting with them (Whiteman and Lukoff, 1964; Siller and Chipman, 1967; Jones, 1970), and, when integrated, sometimes have feelings of rejection toward them (Goodman et al., 1972; Iano et al., 1974).

Rejection or acceptance of students with DS by nonhandicapped peers depends extensively on the way in which learning goals and rewards are structured by the teacher. Within any group learning situation, a teacher can structure positive goal interdependence (cooperation), negative goal interdependence (competition), or no goal interdependence (individualization) (Johnson and Johnson, 1975). There is some evidence that properly structured cooperative experiences result in a greater liking of handicapped students by nonhandicapped peers (Ballard et al., 1977; Johnson et al., 1979; Martino and Johnson, 1979; Cooper et al., 1980).

Recently, we designed a study (Rynders et al., 1980) using bowling alleys and employing three conditions: competitive, individualistic, and cooperative. Subjects were 30 junior high school students, ages 13 to 15, from three different public schools in urban Minneapolis. Twelve of the 30 students were from a school for trainable students and were selected on the basis of a diagnosis of DS*; the other 18 were non-handicapped students (9 from a public and 9 from a parochial school). The 30 students (18 females and 12 males) were assigned randomly to the three conditions, with the restriction that 6 nonhandicapped and 4 DS students were in each condition and that the sex breakdown of nonhandicapped and DS subjects was the same in each condition.

In the cooperative condition, students were instructed to maximize their group bowling score to meet a set criterion (improvement by 50 pins as a group) and to offer each other encouragement (e.g., verbal praise), reinforcement (e.g., a cheer), and assistance (e.g., help in handling a ball). In the competitive condition, students were instructed to maximize their own score so as to outperform the other students in their condition. After each bowling session, students in this condition were rank-ordered, based on their bowling scores, and informed of their rank. They were instructed to seek help only from the instructor and to monitor how well the other bowlers were doing so that they would know whether they were ahead or behind their competitors. In the individualistic condition, students were instructed to maximize their individual score to meet a set criterion (improvement by 10 pins), concentrating only on their own personal bowling performance.

At the outset of the study, all subjects were told that prizes would be awarded for goal structure–appropriate performance improvement. Basic bowling instruction, identical for all three conditions, was given equally to subjects in all conditions throughout the study. Students met for 8 weeks, 1 hour per week, for bowling sessions. The first session was used to demonstrate basic bowling techniques and to familiarize participants with bowling alley procedures. In the second session specific instructions were given to students in the three conditions on how to "do well." During this second session and throughout all the remaining ones a standard format was followed that began when each bowler stepped up to the alley to take his or her turn. At that point, using a frame-by-frame recording sheet, observers categorized all intelligible verbal interactions between the bowler and the other students on a continuous basis until the bowler stepped down from the alley.

The three instructors in the study were given training in maintaining the integrity of their goal structures and were provided with a prompting card for a given condition outlining exactly what they were to do and say. Instructors gave directions specific to each goal structure

---

* Karyotyping of the 12 subjects identified as having DS seemed unnecessary because the experimenters wished only to ensure that they would appear to nonhandicapped students as different from themselves in terms of appearance and behavior. IQs were not reported either because they were not germane to the intent of the experiment; establishing that all 12 subjects were classified as "trainable" was deemed sufficient.

Table 2.   Frequency of daily positive heterogeneous interaction

Interaction/Condition[a]	1	2	3	4	5	6	7
NH toward DS							
Cooperative	46	111	145	42	24	122	154
Competitive	2	9	5	3	0	4	0
Individualistic	7	3	1	12	12	6	13
DS toward NH							
Cooperative	12	19	51	30	11	8	27
Competitive	2	32	1	2	4	2	1
Individualistic	12	12	12	1	5	5	2

[a] NH = nonhandicapped students, DS = Down's syndrome students.

to participants on an every-other-frame basis throughout the study; basic bowling instruction occurred during the alternate frames. Instructors and observers were rotated across conditions.

Results showed that the number of positive heterogeneous (handicapped to nonhandicapped or vice versa) interactions in the cooperative condition differed significantly from the number of positive heterogeneous interactions in either the competitive or individualistic conditions (see Table 2). Interestingly, the relatively high level of positive heterogeneous interaction in the cooperative condition did not obviate relatively high levels of positive homogeneous interaction in the cooperative condition. On the contrary, as Table 2 shows, the entire positive social interaction network increased substantially; i.e., students received more positive interaction both within (homogeneous) and across (heterogeneous) categorical (trainable, nonhandicapped) boundaries in the cooperative condition.

With regard to the effects of the goal structuring on peer attitude, nonhandicapped students in the cooperative condition, looking at photographs of persons with whom they bowled, rated DS students significantly higher than the nonhandicapped students rated DS students in either the competitive or individualistic conditions. Furthermore, DS students in the cooperative condition ranked their nonhandicapped peers significantly higher than did the DS students in either the competitive or individualistic conditions.

Findings of this study say something important for the future of mainstreaming: in the long run, the benefits of mainstreaming will probably be judged, in part, on their ability to benefit *nonhandicapped* as well as handicapped students. This experiment produced the highly desired mutual benefits.

CONCLUSIONS

I trust that the critical review of the literature presented on the validity (and lack of validity) of three long-standing social stereotypes or characterizations will help to clarify and correct some overgeneralized social expectations about DS. This corrected history, coupled with the evidence presented about two promising areas of social transaction research, should lead to better social adaptation in DS children, to improvements in the accommodative capacity of mainstream environments, and, ultimately, to an improved life for children with Down's syndrome and for their parents.

REFERENCES

Aronson, M., and Fällström, K. 1977. Immediate and long-term effects of developmental training in children with Down's syndrome. Dev. Med. Child Neurol. 19:489–494.

Ballard, M., Corman, L., Gottlieb, J., and Kaufman, M. 1977. Improving the social status of mainstreamed retarded children. J. Educ. Psychol. 69:605–611.

Belmont, J. 1971. Medical-behavioral research in retardation. In: N. R. Ellis (ed.), International Handbook in Mental Deficiency, Vol. 5. Academic Press, Inc., New York.

Bidder, R., Bryant, G., and Gray, O. 1975. Benefits to Down's syndrome children through training their mothers. Arch. Dis. Child. 50:383–386.

Carr, J. 1970. Mental and motor development in young mongol children. J. Ment. Defic. Res. 14:205–220.

Cheseldine, S., and McConkey, R. 1979. Parental speech to young Down's syndrome children: An intervention study. Am. J. Ment. Defic. 83:612–620.

Clements, P. R., Bates, M. V., and Hafer, M. 1976. Variability within Down's syndrome. Ment. Retard. 14:30–31.

Clunies-Ross, G. 1979. Accelerating the development of Down's syndrome infants and young children. J. Spec. Educ. 13:169–177.

Cooper, L., Johnson, D. W., Johnson, R., and Wilderson, F. 1980. Effects of cooperative, competitive, and individualistic experiences on interpersonal attraction among heterogeneous peers. J. Soc. Psychol. 111:243–252.

Dicks-Mireaux, M. J. 1972. Mental development of infants with Down's syndrome. Am. J. Ment. Defic. 77:26–32.

Goodman, H., Gottlieb, J., and Harrison, R. 1972. Social acceptance of EMR's integrated into a nongraded elementary school. Am. J. Ment. Defic. 76:412–417.

Grossman, H. J. 1973. Manual on Terminology and Classification in Mental Retardation. American Association on Mental Deficiency, Washington, D.C.

Hanson, M. 1976. Evaluation of training procedures used in parent-implemented intervention for Down's syndrome infants. Am. Assoc. Educ. Sev./Prof. Hand. 7:36–52.

Hayden, A., and Dimitriev, V. 1975. Infant preschool and primary programs for children with Down's syndrome. Paper presented at Children's Psychiatric Research Institute, London, Ontario, Canada.

Iano, R., Ayers, D., Heller, H., McGettigan, J., and Walker, V. 1974. Sociometric status of retarded children in an integrated program. Except. Child. 40:267–271.

Jaffe, J. 1966. Attitudes of adolescents towards mentally retarded. Am. J. Ment. Defic. 70:907–912.

Jeffree, D., Wheldall, K., and Mittler, P. 1973. Facilitating two-word utterances in two Down's syndrome boys. Am. J. Ment. Defic. 78:117–122.

Johnson, D. W., and Johnson, R. 1975. Learning Together and Alone: Cooperation, Competition, and Individualization. Prentice-Hall, Inc., Englewood Cliffs, New Jersey.

Johnson, R., and Abelson, R. 1969. The behavioral competence of mongoloid and non-mongoloid retardates. Am. J. Ment. Defic. 73:856–857.

Johnson, R., Rynders, J., Johnson, D. W., Schmidt, B., and Haider, S. 1979. Producing positive interaction between handicapped and nonhandicapped teenagers through cooperative goal structuring: Implications for mainstreaming. Am. Educ. Res. J. 16:161–168.

Jones, O. M. H. 1977. Mother-child communication with prelinguistic Down's syndrome and normal infants. In: H. R. Schaffer (ed.), Studies in Mother-Infant Interaction. Academic Press, Inc., New York.

Jones, O. M. H. 1980. Mother-child communication with very young Down's syndrome and normal children. In: T. Field, S. Goldberg, D. Stern, and A. Sostek (eds.), Transactions of High-Risk Infants and Children: Disturbances and Interventions. Academic Press, Inc., New York.

Jones, R. 1970. Learning and association in the presence of the blind. New Outlook, December.

Landesman-Dwyer, S., Stein, J., and Sackett, G. 1982. A behavioral and ecological study of group homes. In: G. Sackett (ed.), Observing Behavior, Vol. I. University Park Press, Baltimore.

Lewin, K. 1951. Field Theory in Social Science, Selected Theoretical Papers. Harper & Row Pubs., Inc., New York.

MacDonald, J., Blott, J., Gordon, K., Spiegel, B., and Hartmann, M. 1975. An experimental parent-assisted treatment program for preschool language-delayed children. J. Speech Hear. Disord. 39:395–415.

Martino, L., and Johnson, D. W. 1979. Cooperative and individualistic experiences among disabled and normal children. J. Soc. Psychol. 107:177–183.

Myerson, L. 1963. Somatopsychology of physical disability. In: W. Cruickshank (ed.), Psychology of Exceptional Children and Youth. Prentice-Hall, Inc., Englewood Cliffs, New Jersey.

Novak, D. 1975. Children's responses to imaginary peers labeled as emotionally disturbed. Psychol. Schools 12:103–106.

Piper, M., and Pless, I. 1980. Early intervention for infants with Down syndrome: A controlled trial. Pediatrics 65:463–468.

Pothier, P., Morrison, D., and Gorman, F. 1974. Effects of receptive language training on receptive and expressive language development. J. Abnorm. Child Psychol. 2:153–164.

Restak, R. 1975. Genetic counseling for defective parents: The danger of knowing too much. Psychol. Today 9:21–23; 92–93.

Rynders, J., and Horrobin, J. 1980. Educational provisions for young children with Down syndrome. In: J. Gottlieb (ed.), Educating Mentally Retarded Persons in the Mainstream. University Park Press, Baltimore.

Rynders, J., Johnson, R., Johnson, D., and Schmidt, B. 1980. Effects of cooperative goal structuring in producing positive interaction between Down's syndrome and nonhandicapped teenagers: Implications for mainstreaming. Am. J. Ment. Defic. 85:268–273.

Rynders, J., Spiker, D., and Horrobin, J. 1978. Underestimating the educability of Down's syndrome children: Examination of methodological problems in recent literature. Am. J. Ment. Defic. 82:440–448.

Schiefelbusch, R. 1981. Development of social competence and incompetence. In: M. J. Begab, H. C. Haywood, and H. Garber (eds.), Psychosocial Influences in Retarded Performance, Vol. I. University Park Press, Baltimore.

Schlottmann, R., and Anderson, V. 1973. Social and play behavior of children with Down's syndrome in sexually homogeneous and heterogeneous dyads. Psychol. Rep. 33:595–600.

Siller, J., and Chipman, A. 1967. Attitudes of the Nondisabled Toward the Physically Disabled. New York University Press, New York.

Silverstein, A., Aguilar, B., Jacobs, L., Levy, J., and Rubenstein, D. 1979. Imitative behavior by Down's syndrome persons. Am. J. Ment. Defic. 83:409–411.

Spiker, D. 1979. A descriptive study of mother-child teaching interactions with high- and low-functioning Down's syndrome children. Unpublished Ph.D. dissertation, University of Minnesota, Minneapolis.

Spiker, D. 1982. Early intervention for young children with Down syndrome: New directions in enhancing parent-child synchrony. In: S. Pueschel and J. Rynders (eds.), Down Syndrome: Advances in Biomedicine and the Behavioral Sciences, pp. 331–388. The Ware Press, Cambridge, Massachusetts.

Tawney, J. 1974. Acceleration of vocal behavior in developmentally retarded children. Educ. Train. Ment. Retard. 9:22–27.

Whalan, C., and Henker, B. 1971. Pyramid therapy in a hospital for the retarded: Methods program evaluation, and long-term effects. Am. J. Ment. Defic. 75:414–434.

Whiteman, M., and Lukoff, I. 1964. A factorial study of sighted people's attitudes toward blindness. J. Soc. Psychol. 64:339–353.

PERSPECTIVES AND PROGRESS IN MENTAL RETARDATION
Volume I—Social, Psychological, and Educational Aspects
Edited by J. M. Berg
Copyright © 1984 by I.A.S.S.M.D.

IMPORTANCE OF PEER RELATIONS IN COMMUNITY SETTINGS FOR MENTALLY RETARDED ADULTS

D. Romer[1] and T. Heller[2]

[1] *Department of Psychology, University of Illinois, Chicago Circle, Illinois*
[2] *Illinois Institute for the Study of Developmental Disabilities,
1640 West Roosevelt Road, Chicago, Illinois 60608*

The evidence is reviewed regarding naturally occurring relationships among mentally retarded adults in community settings. This evidence indicates that such adults have an active peer network that is sensitive to various ecological characteristics of community settings. Furthermore, these peer networks appear to have some of the same supportive functions as peer relations among nonhandicapped adults. Thus, a viable goal for promoting adjustment in the community would be the creation of settings in which peer supports can be fostered. Several suggestions for accomplishing this goal are offered.

An important goal of the community mental health movement in the United States is to provide a continuum of care so that disabled persons can ultimately live as independently as nondisabled adults do (Smith and Hobbs, 1966). This independence would be characterized by residence in the community with as little reliance on professional health-care supports as possible. Indeed, most Americans solve their mental health problems without recourse to professional help (Gurin et al., 1960; Gerson and Biller, 1977), and these nonprofessional supports may play a crucial role in enabling people to cope with and to avoid mental health problems (Caplan, 1974; Cassel, 1974; Gottlieb, 1981). However, most of us regard mentally retarded people as exceptions to the rule. Many mentally retarded adults require some assistance in completing daily routines, a problem that can be intensified in the community. As a result, mentally retarded adults would seem to require more professional assistance than nonretarded adults.

Although the policy of normalization encourages reduced dependence on overly restrictive client-professional relations, the development of peer support has not figured heavily in policy formulation and has received less attention than it might deserve. In this paper we consider the possibility that mentally retarded adults may have unrealized resources residing in their peer networks that could enable them to cope more successfully in the community. According to this "ecological" approach to mental health, both naturally occurring peer supports and client-professional helping relationships are critical for independent living in the community (Kelly, 1966).

Much of the impetus underlying this approach derives from research that demonstrates the importance of peer support networks in coping with stress and life problems. This research shows that informal peer supports such as friends and relatives can moderate the effects of life stress (Gottlieb, 1981). Peer support appears to increase one's ability to recover from illness (DiMatteo and Hays, 1981), the loss of a spouse (Hinkle, 1974), and unemployment (Gore, 1978). The number of peer relationships has even been related to increased longevity (Berkman and Syme, 1979). The rapid growth of self-help groups in America attests to the viability of peer relationships as resources for coping with the stress of everyday life (Levy, 1978).

Because peer networks play such an important role for nonretarded adults, the question that arises is how to promote the natural development of peer supports among mentally retarded adults. Answering this question requires knowledge of the environmental and social factors that can increase peer contact and promote social support in the community. It is to these matters that we now turn.

RESEARCH ON PEER RELATIONS

Research conducted by our group and others has recently begun to determine the characteristics of peer relations of the mentally retarded in community settings. This research indicates that: 1) mentally retarded adults maintain friendships and peer relations over time and across situations; 2) intellectual ability is not strongly related to this tendency; and 3) ecological characteristics appear to influence the intensity and range of peer networks.

The earliest studies of adult peer relations were conducted by Edgerton and his colleagues (Edgerton, 1963; McAndrew and Edgerton, 1966). McAndrew and Edgerton (1966) reported an interesting case study of a deep friendship between two severely retarded individuals. The relationship seemed to serve various needs for the couple and appeared to have some of the same characteristics, such as mutuality of regard and similarity of needs, that we associate with friendships between nonretarded adults.

More recently, Landesman-Dwyer et al. (1979) found many enduring friendships identified by both observation and staff reports in group homes. Berkson and Romer (1980) studied client friendships in several sheltered workshop settings and one intermediate care facility. Friendships were identified using observations of affiliation and client and staff reports. All of these measures displayed consistency (from 20% to 26% agreement) over a period of 3 months in one sheltered workshop. Romer and Berkson (1980a) also found that peer relations identified in the workshop were more likely between people who also lived together in their sheltered homes. These studies indicate that peer relations can be relatively enduring and that they are maintained across situations (the home and the workshop). It appears that mentally retarded adults who live in community settings have peer networks that could potentially serve as informal support systems.

An important finding that has been replicated several times is that neither the range nor the intensity of peer relations is related very strongly to the intelligence of clients who live in community settings (Landesman-Dwyer et al., 1979; Romer and Berkson, 1979, 1980a). Individuals over a wide range of intelligence are equally likely to belong to a peer network. Thus, intellectual disabilities of mentally retarded persons need not deter attempts to foster peer support networks in community settings.

Research examining the social ecology of community settings provides further insight into the significance of intelligence. The interesting finding is that individual intelligence only seems related to sociability if individuals are segregated according to ability. Landesman-Dwyer et al. (1979) noted that residents of group homes containing clients who were exclusively of lower intelligence tended to be less sociable than residents of homes with a higher average level of intelligence. Average level of intelligence was also a significant predictor in the community settings studied by Romer and Berkson (1980a). These findings suggest that settings with a wide range of client intellectual abilities might be more conducive to promoting social networks.

Research conducted by Romer and Berkson (1980b) on friendship and affiliation preferences seems to support the heterogeneity principle. Clients in that study appeared to prefer to affiliate with others who were somewhat *different* in intellectual ability. Thus, a severely or moderately retarded person was seen most with a mildly retarded one, and mildly retarded people were seen most with people of greater or lesser intelligence. It appears that "complementary needs" are satisfied in these affiliation preferences. Perhaps mildly retarded people enjoy helping less intelligent persons, and the less intelligent enjoy this relationship. Whatever the needs that are satisfied, it appears that mentally retarded adults have the interests and capacity to affiliate with each other even if they differ in intelligence. This suggests that peer networks might have some of the same support functions for the mentally retarded that have been observed for nonretarded adults.

Other research also indicates that the social ecology has a dramatic impact on individual sociability. Heller et al. (1981) studied the sociability of clients who first entered the sheltered workshop milieu. Some were assigned to a workshop with a sociable group of clients, whereas others were assigned to a less sociable workshop. Although the sociability of the two groups did not differ during a preplacement period in an evaluation center, subsequent sociability approximated the levels of sociability of the workshops to which they had been assigned. It appears that an individual's tendency to develop peer relations depends in part on the sociability of the person's milieu.

Although our research suggests that peer networks are ubiquitous in community settings for the mentally retarded, we do not know how much potential there is for even greater peer network development. Data presented by Berkson and Romer (1981) suggested that residents of group homes spend less time with peers than nonretarded adults spend with peers. If this is so, we must consider the possibility that peer networks among mentally retarded persons are underdeveloped and that greater programmatic encouragement of such networks might be beneficial. Before the development of peer supports is adopted as a viable goal, more will need to be known about the kinds of peer contact that can have supportive functions for mentally retarded people.

IMPLICATIONS FOR COMMUNITY ADAPTATION

There is considerable evidence that peer relationships play a critical role in the successful adjustment of mentally retarded adults in community settings. Failure in community and vocational placements of deinstitutionalized clients has been attributed to lack of interpersonal skills (Goldstein, 1964; Eagle, 1967). There is also evidence that clients with greater degrees of peer contact are more likely to 1) remain in the community (Gollay et al., 1978), 2) transfer to less restrictive settings, 3) demonstrate independence in self-care skills (Heller and Berkson,

1982), 4) earn more money, and 5) transfer out of vocational workshops for positive reasons (Melstrom, 1982).

Gollay et al.'s (1978) interview study of 440 deinstitutionalized clients indicated that three-quarters of them had friends while they were living in the community. Of those who were successfully maintained in the community (nonreturnees), two-thirds still visited or kept in touch with some of their institutionalized friends. The nonreturnees were more likely to have at least one friend than the returnees to the institutions. The most severe problems in adapting to the community identified by both families and clients were interpersonal relations and loneliness.

Heller and Berkson (1982) studied a residential relocation in which administrators were sensitive to the potential disruption of friendship networks following a facility closure. In order to maintain peer relationships, residents were interviewed about their friendship choices and many were moved with their chosen friends or spouses. This relocation offered an opportunity to study the effects of friendship stability on posttransfer adjustment. (The study is particularly important because many clients undergo residential transfers as a result of deinstitutionalization and the closing, opening, and expansion of residential facilities.) Stable friendships were found to be associated with better posttransfer personal adjustment.

Two and a half years after the transfer, 80% of the unmarried people retained their previously chosen friends and all the married couples remained together. Residents moving with chosen friends tended to be rated as more sociable, both 4 months and $2\frac{1}{2}$ years after the transfer, than residents who were separated from friends or who did not express premove friendship choices. Additionally, residents moving with friends were most independent in self-care (in the short and long term) and most likely to move into less restrictive settings. Hence, friendship stability may have resulted in less drastic social disruption and concomitantly in less relocation-related stress. The ongoing friendships provided a support network in which residents helped each other both emotionally and physically.

Peer social behavior has also been shown to be a significant predictor of vocational behavior in community facilities. In an observational study (Melstrom, 1982), clients who demonstrated higher rates of social interaction were more likely to earn more money and to graduate from sheltered workshops to school or competitive employment.

The advantages of peer communication were further demonstrated in a study of small decision-making groups in group homes for mentally retarded adults (Heller, 1978). In that study, resident discussion groups were formed to deal with administrative issues in the home. Participation in these group sessions resulted in subsequent individual decisions that were more socially mature than individual decisions made prior to the group discussion. It appeared that this improvement resulted from information sharing among the residents and from the influence of the most able people.

POLICY IMPLICATIONS

Given that peer contacts have positive consequences, what can be done to promote such contacts? The most popular approach is to involve clients in social skills training programs, which encompass many types of techniques that attempt to increase adaptive social behaviors. Modeling, social reinforcement–feedback, coaching-instructional, roleplaying, and rehearsal techniques have been used separately or in combination to develop and increase various specific behavioral skills of mentally retarded adults (Zisfein and Rosen, 1973; Gibson et al., 1976; Perry and Cerreto, 1977; Stacy et al., 1979; Bates, 1980; Gentile and Jenkins, 1980; Matson and Adkins, 1980). Although these techniques have been generally successful in changing behavior during and shortly after the training period, in most cases these behavior changes have not generalized to settings outside training and have not been measured in longer-term follow-ups. In his review of the social skills training literature, Gresham (1981) noted that generalization and maintenance tend not to be actively programmed. Also, conceptually these programs have been plagued by problems in delineating which skills to teach in which settings. "Skillful" social behaviors vary with the situation, role, sex, class, and age of the individual (Conger and Keane, 1981).

The social skills training approach may not be sufficient for fostering peer relationships. Its main assumptions are that acquisition of social skills plays a prominent role in the development of peer relationships and that inadequate peer contact is a result of skill deficiencies. However viable these assumptions may be, the possibility that the social milieu is as powerful a determinant of social adjustment as individual social skills should not be overlooked. The creation of settings in which peer contact is likely and in which social support can be fostered may be as viable an approach as social skills training.

Our review of the literature on peer relations suggests three means for promoting more effective peer networks among mentally retarded adults in community settings. The first concerns the fate of existing friendship networks when clients are transferred from one residence to another. Heller's (1982) review of the residential relocation literature concluded that disruption of residents' friendship networks is a key factor leading to poor posttransfer adjustment. The fact that broken friendships could have adverse consequences for clients' personal adjustment is often ignored in placement decisions. The relocation of clients described by Heller and Berkson (1982) provides a good example of the benefits accrued from moving clients with their chosen friends. Given the observation that mentally retarded individuals spend more time with peers than with staff (Berkson and Romer, 1980), friendship choice needs to be considered when individuals are transferred.

Another means of boosting the quality of clients' social supports is to develop ongoing client groups with authority to make some binding decisions. If they are structured as support groups, these groups could be beneficial in teaching clients many of the same interpersonal skills (basic communication, self-assertion, problem solving) that are generally taught by professionals in social skills training programs. Advantages of client-led groups are that they provide clients with decision-making and group opportunities typically denied them and that they free up staff time for other activities.

The final focus for encouraging peer supports is the creation of settings in the community where clients with different degrees of disability can have contact. Workshops with heterogeneous clientele and living facilities with a diversity of residents could promote peer networks between clients with differing degrees of disability. These networks might then serve as additional sources of support for successful adjustment in the community. Because nondisabled adults rely on informal peer supports to remain adjusted in the community, there is every reason to believe that peer support can have the same function for mentally retarded adults.

REFERENCES

Bates, P. 1980. The effectiveness of interpersonal skills training on the social skill acquisition of moderately and mildly retarded adults. J. Appl. Behav. Anal. 13:237–248.

Berkman, L. F., and Syme, S. L. 1979. Social networks, host resistance, and mortality: A nine-year followup study of Almeda County residents. Am. J. Epidemiol. 109:186–204.

Berkson, G., and Romer, D. 1980. Social ecology of supervised communal facilities for mentally disabled adults: I. Introduction. Am. J. Ment. Defic. 85:219–228.

Berkson, G., and Romer, D. 1981. A letter to a service provider. In: H. G. Haywood and J. R. Newbrough (eds.), Living Environments for Developmentally Retarded People. University Park Press, Baltimore.

Caplan, G. 1974. Supportive Systems and Community Mental Health: Lectures on Concept Development. Behavioral Publications, New York.

Cassel, J. 1974. Psychological processes and "stress": Theoretical formulations. Int. J. Health Serv. 4:471–482.

Conger, J. C., and Keane, S. P. 1981. Social skills intervention in the treatment of isolated or withdrawn children. Psychol. Bull. 90:478–495.

DiMatteo, M. R., and Hays, R. 1981. Social support and serious illness. In: B. H. Gottlieb (ed.), Social Networks and Social Support. Sage Press, Beverly Hills, California.

Eagle, E. 1967. Prognosis and outcome of community placement of institutionalized retardates. Am. J. Ment. Defic. 72:232–243.

Edgerton, R. B. 1963. A patient elite: Ethnography in a hospital for the mentally retarded. Am. J. Ment. Defic. 69:372–385.

Gentile, C., and Jenkins, J. O. 1980. Assertive training with mildly mentally retarded persons. Ment. Retard. 18:315–317.

Gerson, M., and Biller, H. B. 1977. The Other Helpers. D. C. Heath, Lexington, Massachusetts.

Gibson, F. W., Lawrence, P. S., and Nelson, R. O. 1976. Comparison of three training procedures for teaching social responses to developmentally disabled adults. Am. J. Ment. Defic. 81:379–387.

Goldstein, H. 1964. Social and occupational adjustment. In: H. A. Stevens and R. Heber (eds.), Mental Retardation. University of Chicago Press, Chicago.

Gollay, E., Freedman, R., Wyngaarden, M., and Kurtz, N. R. 1978. Coming Back: The Community Experiences of Institutionalized Mentally Retarded People. Abt Associates, Inc., Cambridge, Massachusetts.

Gore, S. 1978. The effect of social support in moderating the health consequences of unemployment. J. Health Soc. Behav. 19:157–165.

Gottlieb, B. H. 1981. Social Networks and Social Supports. Sage Press, Beverly Hills, California.

Gresham, F. M. 1981. Social skills training with handicapped children: A Review. Rev. Educ. Res. 51:139–176.

Gurin, G., Veroff, J., and Feld, S. 1960. Americans View their Mental Health. Basic Books, Inc., New York.

Heller, T. 1978. Group decision-making among mentally retarded adults. Am. J. Ment. Defic. 82:480–486.

Heller, T. 1982. The effects of involuntary residential relocation: A review. Am. J. Commun. Psychol. 10:471–492.

Heller, T., and Berkson, G. 1982. Friendship and residential relocation. Paper presented at the Gatlinburg Conference on Research in Mental Retardation, Gatlinburg, Tennessee.

Heller, T., Berkson, G., and Romer, D. 1981. Social ecology of communal facilities for mentally disabled adults: VI. Initial social adaptation. Am. J. Ment. Defic. 86:43–49.

Hinkle, L. E. 1974. The effect of exposure to culture change, social change, and changes in interpersonal relationships on health. In: B. S. Dohrenwend and B. P. Dohrenwend (eds.), Stressful Life Events. John Wiley & Sons, Inc., New York.

Kelly, J. G. 1966. Ecological constraints on mental health services. Am. Psychol. 21:535–539.

Landesman-Dwyer, S., Berkson, G., and Romer, D. 1979. Affiliation and friendship of mentally retarded residents in group homes. Am. J. Ment. Defic. 83:571–580.

Levy, L. H. 1978. Self-help groups viewed by mental health professionals: A survey and comments. Am. J. Commun. Psychol. 6:305–313.

Matson, J. L., and Adkins, J. 1980. A self-instructional social skills training program for mentally retarded persons. Ment. Retard. 18:245–248.

McAndrew, C. G., and Edgerton, R. B. 1966. On the possibility of friendship. Am. J. Ment. Defic. 70:612–621.

Melstrom, M. 1982. Social ecology of supervised communal facilities for mentally disabled adults: VII. Productivity and turnover rate in sheltered workshops. Am. J. Ment. Defic. 87:40–47.

Perry, M. A., and Cerreto, M. C. 1977. Structured learning training of social skills for the retarded. Ment. Retard. 15:31–34.

Romer, D., and Berkson, G. 1979. Affiliation and attraction in field settings. In: M. Cook and G. Wilson (eds.), Love and Attraction. Pergamon Press, Inc., New York.

Romer, D., and Berkson, G. 1980a. Social ecology of supervised communal facilities for mentally disabled adults: II. Predictors of affiliation. Am. J. Ment. Defic. 85:229–242.

Romer, D., and Berkson, G. 1980b. Social ecology of supervised communal facilities for mentally disabled adults: III. Predictors of social choice. Am. J. Ment. Defic. 85:243–252.

Smith, M. B., and Hobbs, N. 1966. The community and the community mental health center. Am. Psychol. 21:499–509.

Stacy, D., Doleys, D. M., and Malcom, R. 1979. Effects of social-skills training in a community-based program. Am. J. Ment. Defic. 84:152–158.

Zisfein, L., and Rosen, M. 1973. Personal adjustment training: A group counseling program for institutionalized mentally retarded persons. Ment. Retard. 11:16–20.

SECTION III
Evaluation
and Prognosis

PERSPECTIVES AND PROGRESS IN MENTAL RETARDATION
Volume I—Social, Psychological, and Educational Aspects
Edited by J. M. Berg

A TOOL TO EVALUATE EFFECTIVENESS OF DIAGNOSTIC CLINICS FOR DEVELOPMENTAL DISABILITIES

K. S. Stern[1] and H. Hansen[2]
[1] *250 West 88th Street, New York, New York 10024*
[2] *Division of Epidemiology, University of Connecticut Health Center, Farmington, Connecticut 06302*

A tool has been developed to evaluate effectiveness of multidisciplinary diagnostic clinics for developmental disabilities. The tool operationalizes concepts and defines the outcome of the diagnostic process. It provides the ability to succinctly collect and present data. The results of testing its feasibility by drawing on 100 charts in each of five clinics in New York City indicate its usefulness and demonstrate that tracing patient flow represents a more valid approach than counting case load or service components. The design enables a small clinic or governmental agency to utilize the tool without having access to expensive data equipment. Implications for evaluating outcome of developmental disability programs are discussed.

EVALUATION OF DIAGNOSTIC CLINICS

Diagnostic clinics have become an integral part of community-based services for the developmentally disabled over the 20 years since the benchmark Report to the President of the United States in 1963 (U.S. President's Panel on Mental Retardation, 1963). The purpose of these clinics is to provide both professional and administrative services. Professionally, the clinics offer multidisciplinary team evaluation of children suspected of being retarded; collaborative efforts are required because no single discipline is capable of exploring and planning for the problems involved (Grass and Umansky, 1971; Garrard, 1973; Erenberg et al., 1979; Joint Commission on Accreditation of Hospitals, 1979). Administratively, these clinics are to provide the route to appropriate intervention, including referral, follow-up, planning, placing, and/or providing services (Smith and Van Camp, 1966; Kappleman and Ganter, 1970; Cohen, 1979; New York City Department of Mental Health, Mental Retardation and Alcoholism Services, n.d.).

Cohen (1979) suggested that the diagnostic clinics may not be as effective as could be expected, and Grass and Umansky (1971) noted a discrepancy between appreciation of the team approach and the ability to make it work. However, there have been few systematic efforts to evaluate these clinics. The approach presented here was developed to address this need.

Although Zigler (1978) and others have called for systematic evaluation research, most studies in this area have been of a clinical or applied nature, as noted by Begab (1973). They were usually limited to counting the number of service units or of staff encounters (Rowitz et al., 1974). The report by the U.S. President's Committee on Mental Retardation (1979)—"Service Programs That Work"—gives only descriptive accounts of specific programs, highlighting the lack of evaluation.

The evaluation research literature provides innovative models relating to concepts such as "continuity" (Bass and Windel, 1979) and "through-put" (Baker and Northman, 1979). McAuliffe's (1978) warning that the medical process may be a series of nonadditive "bundles" that have no impact unless all the critical steps, or at least a final step, are completed seems particularly relevant to team diagnosis and the diagnostic clinics. The evaluation tool described below is designed to document the diagnostic process and to evaluate its effectiveness.

THE EVALUATION TOOL

The tool is a combination of an Audit Instrument for describing the diagnostic process, a Flow Chart for tracing an individual clinic's effectiveness, and a Summation Table for comparing effectiveness of different clinics or a single clinic in different time periods.

The 1-page Audit Instrument is designed to summarize information from an individual chart. The auditor marks the progress of the child through the diagnostic process and indicates reasons for incomplete steps, which aid in delineating causes of failure. For instance, the form will show whether the chart contained explanations as to why the process was incomplete, e.g., broken appointments, or whether it was blank. Other variables collected on the form include the dates of events, in order to assess the time spent to complete each step; the professional components comprising the team effort to understand what constitutes

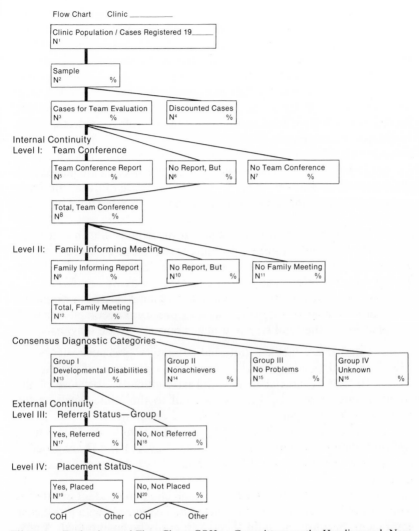

Figure 1. Evaluation tool Flow Chart. COH = Committees on the Handicapped, New York City Board of Education.

"team"; the team's consensus diagnosis; and other types of services that the clinic suggested and rendered for the patient.

The data from each Audit Instrument can be easily tallied and transferred to the Flow Chart (Figure 1) to indicate how effective the clinic was in its diagnostic process. Effectiveness is defined in terms of four levels:

Level I: All children registered by the clinic and considered for a team evaluation (as opposed to being discounted—either rejected or seen for consultation only) are expected to have a subsequent team conference. This constitutes effectiveness for Level I. An exception is the "no-but" category, i.e., cases with *no* record of a team conference *but* with further intervention, such as referral. These cases are credited to the clinic as processed effectively because "services" were rendered, even though professional guidelines may not have been followed.

Level II: All cases who had a team conference should have a family informing meeting. Those cases having the meeting are designated complete and effective for Level II. The cases in the "no-but" category, i.e., those with further intervention, are added as effective.

Level III: All cases with developmental disabilities who had a team conference and a family informing meeting should be referred to special educational classes or programs. Effectiveness for Level III means a referral appropriate to case needs was made.

Level IV: All cases referred to special educational classes or programs should be placed. Effectiveness for Level IV is accomplished with placement, the final step and major purpose of the diagnosis.

Levels I and II are labeled "internal continuity" because success or effectiveness depends primarily on internal operations of the clinics. Levels III and IV are labeled "external continuity" because of the potential interference by factors external to the clinic, such as the Board of Education and its role in placing children.

The Summation Table uses the same definitions as the Flow Chart, and thus allows comparisons. In addition, Levels I and II are grouped for Internal Continuity, and Levels III and IV are grouped for External Continuity.

The design of the tool enables a small clinic to conduct evaluation without need of access to sophisticated and expensive data processing equipment, because the audit sheets can easily be hand tallied. A governmental agency responsible for a number of clinics should find the tool useful for monitoring. A manual explaining the concepts and terms as well as procedures of sampling, data collection, and analysis is in preparation. Tally sheets and other required material will be included in the evaluation kit.

FEASIBILITY STUDY

The Audit Instrument and the Flow Chart were tested by presenting them to a number of clinics and experts to obtain their opinions, and, for its feasibility, by drawing on 100 charts in each of five clinics in New York City. The clinics included two municipal and two voluntary hospital clinics and one voluntary agency clinic, located in three of New York City's five boroughs. The tool was found practical, feasible, and useful by the service providers and experts alike. Although some clinics disagreed on a few points after reviewing the comparative data, they still used the results to examine and improve their services.

The comparative findings indicated a considerable range in performance (Stern, 1981). There were significant differences at all four levels of effectiveness; one clinic attained 96% effectiveness on Level I, whereas another clinic attained only 74%. Most clinics had no or few cases in the "no-but" category, but in one clinic most cases in Level I did not have a team conference—a social worker was assigned the task of interpreting the individual reports and informing the family. One clinic placed 72% of all cases referred, whereas another placed only 33%. The numbers and types of professional components comprising the teams varied considerably for similar populations of cases. One clinic's cases took an average of 45 days from the time of the first professional assessment to the team conference, whereas another clinic required an average of 175 days to do the same.

DISCUSSION

If diagnostic clinics are to play a vital role in the delivery of services, it is critical that their effectiveness be monitored. The evaluation should reflect their concepts and goals; tracing patient flow through the diagnostic process represents a more valid approach than counting case load or service components.

In operationalizing the concepts of diagnostic evaluation and defining outcome of the clinic process, several issues arise. Most will agree that the multidisciplinary team diagnosis is not an end but the means to define programs for children diagnosed as developmentally disabled. Yet professionals and clinics espousing this concept may not embrace all four levels of that process—team conference, family informing meeting, referral, and placement. Furthermore, even those who agree with obtaining placement in special classes or other services as a result of the diagnostic process may not think the clinics have that responsibility. Thus, each clinic may interpret the concepts and their roles and responsibilities differently. A clear definition of goals is needed to make evaluation meaningful. The feasibility study of the tool demonstrated discrepancies between conceptualizing and operationalizing the diagnostic process. Because the concepts generally espoused can be shown to work in some clinics, an understanding of how to make them work can be transferred to other clinics.

In developing the tool, the interdependence of professionals and administrators became apparent, yet their respective roles and responsibilities are not generally discussed or delineated, especially in relation to program effectiveness. For example, without the administrators' facilitating the team conference there is no diagnosis for that child and parent. On the other hand, professionals must understand that their role might go beyond diagnosing, e.g., to ensuring followup, providing family information, planning for referral, and discussing the child's problems with the special program selected. Thus, administrators interact with professionals and professionals assume administrative responsibilities. Most professionals have no administrative training and most administrators have no professional training, which contributes to difficulties in implementing a successful diagnostic process. This problem requires further exploration.

The tool recognizes that the current reporting mechanism of citing new cases and visits, especially for Medicaid reimbursement, is inadequate. Emphasis on the number of new cases, professional encounters, or visits not only has no bearing on service delivery for the child or parent, but may reinforce ineffectiveness because there is no incentive for completion. Service outcomes such as those built into this tool must be part of monitoring.

Presenting evaluation results to professionals and administrators of the clinics can pose problems. Professionals are accustomed to evaluating, but not to being evaluated. Results indicating that what they believe in does not actually occur may be difficult to accept. It should be made clear that evaluation is intended to strengthen the clinics, so that they are better able to provide for the children and parents they serve.

ACKNOWLEDGMENTS

The authors wish to express their appreciation to Lowell E. Bellin, M.D., M.P.H.; Elinor Downs, M.D., M.P.H.; Allen Ginsberg, Ph.D.; and Regina Loewenstein, M.A.

REFERENCES

Baker, R., and Northman, J. E. 1979. Input-throughout-output evaluation of a school mental health clinic. In: H. Schulberg and F. Baker (eds.), Program Evaluation in the Health Fields, Vol. II., pp. 319–334. Behavioral Publications, New York.

Bass, R., and Windel, C. 1979. Continuity of care: An approach to measurement. In: H. Schulberg and F. Baker (eds.), Program Evaluation in the Health Fields, Vol. II., pp. 265–274. Behavioral Publications, New York.

Begab, M. 1973. Guest editorial: Some perspectives on mental deficiency. Am. J. Ment. Defic. 77:483–484.

Cohen, H. J. 1979. Community health planning. In: P. R. Magrab and J. O. Elder (eds.), Planning for Services to Handicapped Persons, pp. 91–120. Paul H. Brookes Publishers, Baltimore.

Erenberg, G., Mattis, S., and French, J. 1979. A multidisciplinary study of 400 children referred to a developmental clinic in an urban ghetto area. Cleveland Clin. Q. 46:57–66.

Garrard, S. D. 1973. Role of the pediatrician in the management of learning disorders. Pediatr. Clin. North Am. 20:737–754.

Grass, C., and Umansky, R. 1971. Problems in promoting growth of multidisciplinary and diagnostic clinics for mentally retarded children in nonmetropolitan areas. Am. J. Public Health 61:698–710.

Joint Commission on Accreditation of Hospitals. 1979. Standards for Services for Developmentally Disabled Individuals, pp. 1–10. Joint Commission on Accreditation of Hospitals, Chicago.

Kappleman, M. M., and Ganter, R. L. 1970. A clinic for children with learning disabilities. Children 17:137–142.

McAuliffe, W. E. 1978. Studies of process-outcome correlations in medical care evaluations: A critique. Med. Care 16:907–930.

New York City Department of Mental Health, Mental Retardation and Alcoholism Services. (n.d.) 1975–76 Annual Plan for Mental Retardation Services, Draft. New York City DMHMRAS, New York.

Rowitz, L., Adams, J., and Barnett, T. 1974. An approach to the evaluation of clinical services. Ment. Retard. 12:6–9.

Smith, R., and Van Camp, D. 1966. The physician, the community and the mental retardation clinic. Rocky Mt. Med. J. 63:39–40.

Stern, K. S. 1981. Evaluating Effectiveness of Multidisciplinary Team Diagnostic Clinics—An Evaluation Tool, Manual and Study. A dissertation presented to Columbia University, School of Public Health, New York.

U.S. President's Committee on Mental Retardation. 1979. MR 78. Mental Retardation: The Leading Edge, Service Programs That Work, pp. 1–70. U.S. Government Printing Office, Washington, D.C.

U.S. President's Panel on Mental Retardation. 1963. Report to the President: A Proposed Program for National Action to Combat Mental Retardation, pp. 73–95. U.S. Government Printing Office, Washington, D.C.

Zigler, E. 1978. National crisis in mental retardation research. Am. J. Ment. Defic. 83:1–8.

PERSPECTIVES AND PROGRESS IN MENTAL RETARDATION
Volume I—Social, Psychological, and Educational Aspects
Edited by J. M. Berg
Copyright © 1984 by I.A.S.S.M.D.

EARLY HANDICAPPING CONDITIONS
Detection and Intervention in Developing Countries

G. M. Kysela and K. Marfo

*Department of Educational Psychology, The University of Alberta,
Edmonton, Alberta T6G 2G5, Canada*

This paper examines the crucial need for early rehabilitative programs in developing countries. Early screening and intervention programs for at-risk and handicapped children are discussed and a model for screening and intervention in a developing country is presented based on the health care system of the West African country of Ghana. Emphasis is placed on procedures that can ensure successful programs at the least possible cost. Existing structures and service delivery systems that can be utilized to attain such low-cost programs have been identified.

It has been estimated that by the year 2000 the proportion of the world's disabled people living in developing countries will increase from the 1975 estimate of 75% to an even more alarming 80% (Noble, Jr., 1981). Despite this gloomy picture, a U.N. expert group meeting in Geneva in December, 1977, to consider the socioeconomic implications of investments in rehabilitation for the disabled reported that planners, particularly in developing countries, tend to overlook the needs of the disabled and give priority to meeting the needs of the majority of the population (United Nations Department of Economic and Social Affairs, 1977). Two invalid assumptions appear to underlie this neglect by governments of developing nations to implement prevention and rehabilitation programs for the disabled (Rehabilitation International, 1981). First, the notion that disability affects only a small and specific segment of the population is prevalent. Second, it is generally held that it takes very expensive and, in many cases, cost-ineffective procedures to institute prevention and rehabilitation programs for disabled individuals.

119

Statistics from several sources, including World Health Organization estimates (Noble, Jr., 1981; Rehabilitation International, 1981) point to a possible 15–20% disability rate in developing countries. These figures are substantial enough to disprove the first assumption. Regarding the second, developing countries need to be assured that the more they recognize the costs of disability and attempt to provide adequate disability prevention and rehabilitation services, the greater is the overall economic return that may be expected (United Nations Department of Economic and Social Affairs, 1977). More importantly, developing countries need assurance that such programs can be instituted at a very low cost by integrating them within the larger normative programs and services established for the general population.

In this paper early screening and intervention are discussed in the context of a developing country and a model is presented for screening and intervention that the authors are developing in cooperation with the University of Cape Coast in Ghana, West Africa. (A former British colony attaining independence in March, 1957, Ghana, with an area of 92,000 square miles, has a population of 12 million people.) The implementation of the model will involve active cooperation among three ministries: Education, Health, and Social Welfare and Community Development. These ministries have in the past 5 years cooperated with the University of Cape Coast and the World Rehabilitation Fund of the United States in sponsoring three biennial international training workshops on the education and rehabilitation of the disabled. At the third workshop, held at the University of Cape Coast in July, 1981 (attended by participants from the West Africa region, the United States and Canada), nine resolutions were passed, the first three of which reflect the increasing recognition of the importance of early intervention:

1. That governments (in the West Africa region) be called upon to undertake, as a matter of urgency, a massive immunization program covering all women of the reproductive age group as well as all children of preschool age, and that every effort be made to attain this target by 1986.
2. That ministries of health, with the help of doctors, nurses, social workers, teachers, and others, should compile national registers of all children at risk for varying forms of developmental disability.
3. That ministries of education (the Ghana Education Service in the case of Ghana) should expedite action on the establishment of regional assessment centers for detection of handicapping conditions in young children.

Inherent in these resolutions is a recognition of two levels of intervention: primary, involving the prevention, in the first place, of the occurrence of physical, mental, or sensory impairments; and secondary, involving the prevention of impairment from causing lasting functional limitation after the condition has occurred.

The model described here falls under secondary intervention and is based upon the knowledge that throughout the West Africa region indigenous governments, with the assistance of international and voluntary organizations, are carrying out various forms of primary preventive intervention. These include improving maternal and early childhood nutrition, improving prenatal and perinatal care, advising on family planning and birth control, and immunizing against bacterial and viral infections. All these services fall within the domain of primary health care. However, very little, if any, secondary intervention is taking place for children who already have some impairment; current programs for handicapped children are offered too late in the lives of the children. Given the alarming statistic that by the year 2000 80% of the world's handicapped population will come from the developing world, early educational and developmental intervention with at-risk and handicapped children appears to be crucial for detection and treatment in developing countries.

RATIONALE FOR EARLY INTERVENTION

The rationale for early intervention with at-risk and handicapped children lies in the crucial need to maximize such children's potential in several developmental domains. It is becoming increasingly evident that medical, nursing, and other forms of pediatric care, although highly desirable, are often not enough to facilitate optimum emotional, mental, and personal development for this population of children. A carefully planned and well-executed program of educational and/or developmental intervention is usually required to overcome the potential debilitating effects of physical, mental, and sensory impairments (Kass et al., 1976).

Theoretical as well as clinical support exists in the developmental literature for carrying out intervention in the child's early years (Colombo, 1982). The high degree of plasticity as well as the rapidity that characterize early growth and development make the early years the best time to correct or arrest developmental problems of both biological and cultural-environmental origin (Bloom, 1964; Barrera et al., 1976; Lipton, 1976; Tjossem, 1976; Gordon et al., 1977; Urban, 1978).

In his report to the U.S. Department of Health, Education, and Welfare following a critical review of early intervention programs in the United States, Stedman (1977) confirmed that environmental effects, either positive or negative, are most powerful in early childhood.

Emphasizing the early years as the most critical period for the development of intelligence, Bloom (1964) advocated increased educational input in the first 4 years of the child's life.

The potential benefits attributed to an early stimulating environment have constituted the conceptual and theoretical basis for the rapid development and implementation of early intervention programs in the Western world. Today, similar programs are being established in several developing countries, the Jamaican projects being good examples (Brown, 1976; Shephard, 1976; Thorburn, 1976, 1981).

GOALS OF INTERVENTION

Broadly speaking, the goal of intervention for children considered at risk for future developmental delay is the prevention of potential threats to the course of normal development. For categories of handicapped children whose developmental trend tends to be characterized by progressive decline in functioning in the absence of intervention, such as many children with Down's syndrome and other types of severe retardation, the goals of intervention include attempts to arrest or reverse such developmental decline and thereby improve the child's quality of life. A number of studies examining the efficacy of early intervention for various categories of handicapped and at-risk children have shown that these goals are attainable. The literature on this subject has been reviewed elsewhere (see Kysela et al., 1980; Marfo et al., 1982).

SCREENING AND DETECTION

Screening is a crucial component in the intervention process; however, it is only the first step in a two-level identification process, the second being diagnosis. Screening involves the application of relatively quick, easily administered procedures to an unselected population for the purpose of determining which individuals are likely to have a specific condition. Thus a screening procedure only selects cases for further investigation directed toward a precise diagnosis (Frankenburg, 1981; Fryers, 1981).

It is pertinent to point out that the goals and intensity of screening may be rather different in a developing country. In many developing countries resources for detailed diagnosis for specific handicapping conditions are not easily available. Facilities for identifying degrees of hearing and visual impairment are more common, but facilities for determining different categories and levels of mental retardation or brain damage, for example, may not be available. This problem has implications for screening and intervention in a developing country. As

Fryers (1981) pointed out, in many communities a two-stage, screening-cum-diagnosis procedure may be impractical, leaving program developers with a one-stage, screening-only procedure. Consequently, the screening procedure in a developing country should be far more rigorous and the subsequent intervention program flexible so as to address the unique needs of each individual client.

Fryers (1981) has identified four practical purposes served by a screening program in a developing country. First, screening serves as a basis for offering effective intervention for children identified either as individuals or as a group located in a community. Second, it is expected to provide evidence of preventable conditions, making it possible to plan appropriate primary prevention measures for the benefit of future generations; thus screening should be seen as an important component in any massive immunization program such as those launched in several developing countries in recent years. Third, it yields information necessary for educating the public on problems that may hitherto have been unknown. Fourth, a screening program provides the demographic and other statistical data necessary to aid the planning and delivery of services. The resolutions emerging from the 1981 Ghana workshop indicate the increasing awareness in the West African region of the place of screening and detection in the prevention of disability. What is required at this stage, perhaps, is the practical implementation of such screening and intervention programs.

Working from a developmental model, we propose that screening in developing countries should focus on gross developmental disabilities or delays rather than on specific diagnostic conditions. Caution must be exercised in identifying problems through screening. For several reasons, Western traditional classifications of handicaps and handicapping conditions may not necessarily be relevant in developing countries. Even in the Western world the limitations that distinct categorizations place upon service delivery are obvious (Jones, 1972; Yoshida and Meyers, 1972). Also, in the absence of appropriate resources for detailed diagnosis it may be dangerous to talk in terms of specific conditions except in certain obvious situations such as hearing, visual, or orthopedic handicaps. Fryers (1981) identified this problem when he noted that "the clinical and pathological models may be less appropriate than developmental models viewed necessarily in the context of the norms, expectations, and cultural characteristics of specific communities."

THE SCREENING PROCESS: REACHING THE TARGET POPULATION

The community resources identified here refer in particular to Ghana, but identical parallels obtain in most other English-speaking West African countries—Nigeria, Gambia, Sierra Leone, and Liberia. As part of the primary health care system in Ghana the following categories of facilities are most closely related to a screening and intervention program:

1. Rural health centers
2. Polyclinics (in the cities)
3. Family health centers
4. Antenatal clinics (attached to most general hospitals)

Rural health centers are located in various parts of the country in an effort to "decentralize" health care. Prior to the establishment of these centers government hospitals and clinics were largely located in regional and a few district capitals. The philosophy behind the increasing number of rural health centers is to bring basic health care to the doorstep of the rural Ghanaian. In addition to basic health care, the rural health centers and the three other facilities listed above provide the following services:

1. Lessons in maternal and child nutrition to expectant mothers
2. Lessons in child-rearing, especially weaning
3. Periodic check-ups to monitor the progress of both mother and fetus
4. Immunization against bacterial and viral infections

In addition to clinic-based consultations, Community Health nurses visit the homes of new mothers as a follow-up to services provided at the clinics. Given the existing role of the Community Health nurse as a liaison between the home and the clinic, we deem it appropriate to train these nurses to carry out screening procedures both at the clinic and in the home during their regular postnatal visits. As part of the screening program antenatal clinics should expand their activities to include educating expectant mothers on the need to send their children to the nearest health center for screening every 6 months.

Figure 1 is an illustration of the screening and assessment process. This would be carried out in three broad areas—biological, developmental, and environmental—involving the following six parameters: medical, sensory, functional, normative, family, and community. The purpose of the biological screening is to determine the degree of disability and the ability of the child to participate in a program if found to require treatment. The developmental screening would seek to confirm developmental delay in functional skills, as well as in normative developmental milestones, and to identify the initial intervention program entry point. The assessment of the family and community environment is aimed at identifying possible supportive structures that

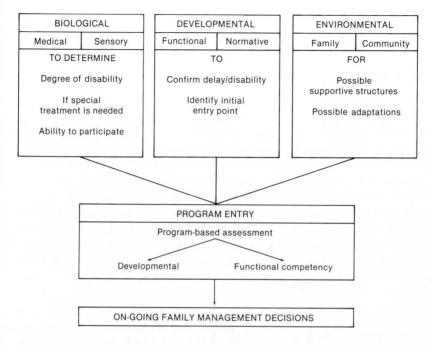

Figure 1.   The screening and assessment process.

can be utilized by program staff in planning individual programs. Also, such assessment would identify necessary adaptations in the child's environment.

Upon admission into the program a more thorough program-based assessment should be carried out to determine in what areas and at what levels programming should begin. Assessment and other relevant information collected on the child will serve as a basis for on-going family management decisions.

Screening Instruments

We have noted that because a two-level diagnostic identification process is, in many cases, not feasible, screening in a developing country may have to be more rigorous than expected. This, coupled with the known differences in early developmental patterns between Western infants and infants in developing countries, suggests that screening devices currently in use in North America and Europe may not necessarily be appropriate in developing countries. An initial exercise to adapt existing devices or develop new ones based on local norms is a necessary prerequisite to the implementation of a screening and intervention program.

THE INTERVENTION PROCESS

The central focus of the intervention process is to prevent general developmental delays that are likely to result from the presence of physical, mental, or sensory impairments. Consequently, emphasis must be placed upon enhancing development in the domains of gross and fine motor skills, self-help skills, personal-social competence, language and communication, and cognitive development.

Several important considerations underlie the approach to intervention being proposed here. These include providing intervention at the least possible cost and ensuring the highest degree of ecological validity. Providing intervention at low cost requires that program tasks should be designed in such a way that the need for highly trained and specialized professional personnel will be reduced to the barest minimum. It also involves the effective use of existing community resources and a de-emphasis upon the creation of new structures and service delivery systems. It calls for a reorientation of workers currently involved in the fields of social welfare, health, nutrition, and education to enable them to take on new roles in the intervention process.

Ensuring the highest degree of ecological validity involves carrying out intervention in the child's immediate community using community resources. It is essential to recognize that the family, by virtue of it being the system that naturally provides the atmosphere and support most likely to foster normal child development, should be seen as the most important instrument in the intervention process. Home-based programs utilizing parents or other relatives as the target child's teacher are highly recommended. The extended family system, which brings together a wide range of family relations under one household, renders home-based programs highly feasible in developing communities. Even when full-time employment and other household duties leave very little time for a parent to assist the target child through the intervention activities, it is usually possible to find some other relative to perform this new role.

Using the infant's natural home environment as the intervention site has several advantages. Among the most controversial issues of our time with regard to the teaching of children with severe developmental disabilities are the twin issues of maintenance and generalization of learned skills and/or behaviors (Stokes and Baer, 1977). One advantage of a home-based intervention program regarding these issues is the absence of the transfer problem, because behaviors will have been learned in the child's natural environment and will have been reinforced by the natural reinforcing agent, the parent.

The psychological gains of having parents teach their own children at an early age have been amplified by Bronfenbrenner (1975). In explaining why programs utilizing parents as teachers tend to be more successful, Bronfenbrenner has postulated:

> The resulting reciprocal interaction between the mother and the child involves both cognitive and emotional components that reinforce each other. When this reciprocal interaction takes place in an interpersonal relationship that endures over time, it leads to the development of a strong emotional attachment that, in turn, increases the motivation of the young child to attend to and learn from the mother. (p. 460)

Evidence is also available to show that the positive effects of parent involvement transcend developmental and behavioral gains by the target child. Several studies have reported benefits to younger siblings of the target child. Klaus and Gray (1968) have referred to this spread of intervention effects as vertical diffusion. Thus home-based early intervention programs can be expected to improve the child-rearing skills of parents for the benefit of younger siblings and subsequent offspring.

Also, in line with the principle of normalization and the concept of least restrictive environment (Wolfensberger, 1972), it is most appropriate that intervention programs for preschool children be offered in what is obviously the least restrictive and most culturally normal environment of an infant—the home. Paraprofessionals such as secondary school leavers should be recruited and given a 3- to 6-month training program as Infant Development Workers (IDWs). The training should cover normal and atypical child development, assessment, behavioral teaching strategies, and family involvement. Each IDW would be assigned to a number of families within a given community, with duties including the planning of a program for each child, the training of parents to set up program goals and teach toward them, the evaluation of the parents' progress during training, and the continuous evaluation of the child's developmental progress during periodic visits. Program directors will need to ensure the development of a package of simple techniques that can be understood and applied by both IDWs and members of the target child's family prior to the training of IDWs.

Referrals to the program may come from several sources. Through the screening procedures carried out at the rural health centers, polyclinics, family health centers, and in individual homes during visits by Community Health nurses, a register of at-risk and handicapped infants and young children should be compiled. Parents of children requiring services have to be advised to register in the program. All other hospitals and clinics across the country should be required to set up a similar register, and pediatricians and other health personnel need encouragement to refer families requiring services to the program. Because it takes an extensive public education campaign to get parents to go after the service themselves, the initial emphasis has to be to take the service to the people. It is therefore necessary to establish a liaison between the program staff and the hospitals, clinics, and polyclinics to enable program staff to reach target families through information from the hospital registers. As the program becomes known to the public the enrollment can be expected to include self-referrals.

CONCLUSIONS

The ever-increasing disability rate in developing countries calls for a multidimensional approach to prevention. In particular, alongside current efforts at primary prevention, there is a crucial need for various forms of secondary prevention. Early intervention for children who are at risk or are confirmed to be developmentally delayed constitutes an important secondary prevention process.

In presenting a model for early screening and intervention in the context of a developing country, we have outlined several important underlying considerations. Emphasis has been placed on ensuring cost-efficient programs through the effective use of existing community resources and service delivery systems. The issue of ecological validity is of special significance; consequently, the provision of intervention programs within the child's immediate environment recognizes the family as the most important instrument of intervention.

Finally, problems relating to screening and intervention in a developing country are outlined. These include the need to adapt existing Western screening devices before use or to develop new instruments based on local norms, the need to make screening more rigorous in view of the difficulty of performing follow-up diagnosis, and the need to develop simple techniques that can be easily understood and applied by both Infant Development Workers and members of the target child's family. Although the model has been presented with Ghana in mind, the similarities in health systems and infrastructure across English-speaking West Africa make it highly applicable in the subregion at large.

REFERENCES

Barrera, M. E. C., Routh, D. K., Parr, C. A., Johnson, N. M., Goolsby, E. L., and Schroeder, S. R. 1976. The Carolina-Abecedarian Project: A longitudinal and multidisciplinary approach to the prevention of developmental retardation. In: T. D. Tjossem (ed.), Intervention Strategies for High Risk Infants and Young Children. University Park Press, Baltimore.

Bloom, B. S. 1964. Stability and Change in Human Characteristics. John Wiley & Sons, Inc., New York.

Bronfenbrenner, U. 1975. Is early intervention effective? In: B. Z. Friedlander, G. M. Sterritt, and G. E. Kirk (eds.), Exceptional Infant, Vol. 3: Assessment and Intervention. Brunner/Mazel, New York.

Brown, J. 1976. Handicapped children in Jamaica benefit from home-based program. Family Involvement 9:9–15.

Colombo, J. 1982. The critical period concept: Research, methodology, and theoretical issues. Psychol. Bull. 91:260–275.

Frankenburg, W. K. 1981. Early screening for developmental delays and potential school problems. In: C. C. Brown (ed.), Pediatric Round Table 5: Infants at Risk: Assessment and Intervention—An Update for Health-care Professionals and Parents. Johnson & Johnson Baby Products Co., Piscataway, New Jersey.

Fryers, T. 1981. Problems in screening for mental retardation in developing countries. Int. J. Ment. Health 10:64–75.

Gordon, I. J., Guinagh, B., and Jester, R. E. 1977. The Florida Parent Education, Infant, and Toddler Programs. In: M. C. Day and R. K. Parker (eds.), The Preschool in Action: Exploring Early Childhood Programs, 2nd ed. Allyn & Bacon, Inc., Boston.

Jones, R. L. 1972. Labels and stigma in special education. Except. Child. 38:553–564.

Kass, E. R., Sigman, M., Bromwich, R. M., and Parmelee, A. H. 1976, Educational intervention with high risk infants. In: T. D. Tjossem (ed.), Intervention Strategies for High Risk Infants and Young Children. University Park Press, Baltimore.

Klaus, R. A., and Gray, S. W. 1968. The early training project for disadvantaged children: A report after five years. Monogr. Soc. Res. Child Dev. 33:(Serial #120).

Kysela, G. M., Marfo, K., and Barros, S. 1980. Early intervention with handicapped children. In: M. Csapo and L. Goguen (eds.), Special Education Across Canada: Issues and Concerns for the 80's. Centre for Human Development and Research, Vancouver.

Lipton, M. A. 1976. Early experience and plasticity in the central nervous system. In: T. D. Tjossem (ed.), Intervention Strategies for High Risk Infants and Young Children. University Park Press, Baltimore.

Marfo, K., Barros, S., and Kysela, G. M. 1982. Rationale and efficacy of early intervention with handicapped and at-risk children: A brief review of the literature. Unpublished manuscript, University of Alberta, Alberta, Canada.

Noble, Jr., J. H. 1981. Social inequity in the prevalence of disability—projections for the year 2000. Assignment Children 53/54:23–32.

Rehabilitation International. 1981. Childhood disability: Its prevention and rehabilitation. Assignment Children 53/54:43–75.

Shephard, G. 1976. A project in Jamaica teaches mothers to help their handicapped children. Family Involvement 8:21–32.

Stedman, D. J. 1977. Important considerations in the review and evaluation of educational intervention programs. In: P. Mittler (ed.), Research to Practice in Mental Retardation, Vol. 1: Care and Intervention. University Park Press, Baltimore.

Stokes, T. F., and Baer, D. M. 1977. An implicit technology of generalization. J. Appl. Behav. Anal. 10:349–367.

Thorburn, M. J. 1976. Working with handicapped children in Jamaica. Family Involvement 8:11–19.

Thorburn, M. J. 1981. In Jamaica, community aides for disabled pre-school children. Assignment Children 53/54:117–134.

Tjossem, T. D. 1976. Early intervention: Issues and approaches. In: T. D. Tjossem (ed.), Intervention Strategies for High Risk Infants and Young Children. University Park Press, Baltimore.

United Nations Department of Economic and Social Affairs. 1977. Rehabilitation for the Disabled: The Social and Economic Implications of Investments for this Purpose. United Nations Department of Economic and Social Affairs, ST/ESA/65. United Nations, New York.

Urban, A. 1978. An early intervention program in a remote area. Aust. J. Ment. Retard. 5:87–93.

Wolfensberger, W. 1972. Normalization. National Institute on Mental Retardation, Toronto.

Yoshida, R. K., and Meyers, C. E. 1972. Effects of labeling as educable mentally retarded on teachers' expectations for change in a student's performance. J. Educ. Psychol. 67:521–527.

PERSPECTIVES AND PROGRESS IN MENTAL RETARDATION
Volume I—Social, Psychological, and Educational Aspects
Edited by J. M. Berg
Copyright © 1984 by I.A.S.S.M.D.

PSYCHOSOCIAL INTERVENTION— POSSIBILITIES AND CONSTRAINTS
What Are the Questions?

A. M. Clarke

Department of Educational Studies, The University, Hull, HU5 2EH, England

Problems of assessing the outcome of intervention are discussed within the context of difficulties in estimating the true prevalence of mild retardation. It is argued that, even with a relatively high level of heritability for IQ, environmental effects can be substantial, but that as yet our understanding of these effects is limited. The combined and continuing influences of home, neighborhood, and school are suggested as powerful factors in determining scholastic and social status in adolescence.

In this paper both general and specific problems are discussed. First, in broad terms I make some general points about our current knowledge as well as indicating areas of uncertainty or ignorance, and, second, I outline what seem to me to be the questions that we can already answer, or are on the threshold of answering, or need to plan in the future to answer. Before so doing, it should be indicated that intervention may be of two types. Primary intervention is designed for children and families deemed to be at risk, but whose children are as yet too young to have exhibited mild retardation. Secondary intervention, on the other hand, is concerned with children or adolescents who have already been shown to be retarded.

GENETICS AND ENVIRONMENT: POSSIBILITIES

Commonly there is some polarization of views about the respective roles of societal factors and familial processes in the etiology of mild retardation. The first is usually taken to imply purely environmental factors; the second, the possibility of genetic as well as environmental agents. In broad terms, I believe we can take the societal view for granted; the development of technological societies and the demands of daily living, especially in urban areas, proves too much for the less gifted of the general population. The least fortunate of these are labeled retarded. However, it may well be in familial processes that the significant etiological agents reside.

In a thoughtful chapter on linking intervention research with policy objectives, Ricciuti (1981) pointed to three temptations to which, for understandable reasons, researchers are exposed: 1) a tendency to emphasize positive findings, even if tenuous and inconsistent, and to overstate their generalizability and practical significance, as well as a reluctance to consider or publish negative findings; 2) a tendency to attribute obtained gains rather uncritically to the intervention itself, without serious consideration of alternative explanations [we (Clarke and Clarke, 1981, 1982) have tried to document this point in connection with the supposed existence of sleeper effects after intervention, indicating alternative explanations as well as the commonly facile and inappropriate use of this concept]; and 3) a tendency to develop an unusual degree of personal and emotional investment in research, and therefore a heightened sensitivity to normal scientific criticism. All these reactions are counterproductive, both scientifically and socially.

One might add that the whole area of intervention has been beset by overoptimistic claims and by reference back to the sometimes powerful effects of total ecological change, as if anything termed intervention might induce equally potent results. Thus the belief that single, restricted, and essentially modest intervention efforts would have lifelong consequences, the history of which has been ably documented by Zigler and Valentine (1979), still lingers on in the minds of many. Within that volume Zigler and Anderson wrote that "great expectations and promises were based on the view that the young child was a plastic material to be molded quickly and permanently by the proper school environment. Over a decade later, Head Start is still recovering from the days of 'environmentalism run amok'," or, in other words, that the *early* environment is critical. However, it is true that the Consortium (Lazar et al., 1977; Lazar and Darlington, 1978) has provided evidence for long-term differences between experimental and control groups on important variables, irrespective of the type of high-quality preschool program, its duration, presence or absence of language goals, training or nontraining of teachers, or age at which intervention occurred within the first 5 years.

In this remarkable situation, it apparently did not matter what was done, nor when, nor for how long. One must surely then invoke intervening variables, indirectly operating from the starting point of the programs. Schweinhart and Weikart (1980) put this extremely well: "as data accumulate, it is clear that we are viewing a complex network of causes and effects. The preschool intervention has been successful over the years because its effects became the cause of other effects as well" and so on down the line. Positive results lead to reinforcements from teachers and others, and it may well be that parents continue the intervention process. Sheldon White (personal communication) has suggested that "schools generally reserve judgments about children in the early grades . . .while beginning serious teaching of children near the middle school years. It is possible that parental involvement in preschools might pay off at this time" (via parental advocacy). He added that in the later years of schooling parental knowledge "enables them to negotiate more effectively with regard to the status and treatment of their offspring."

Is it possible that broad improvements in the social and economic progress of society might alleviate, at least to some extent, the problem of mild retardation? Based on American and British studies we (Clarke and Clarke, 1977) have in the past been pessimistic about this possibility. We have also indicated the undeniable likelihood that even if the whole population shifted upward intellectually, which could well be occurring at the moment, there would still be a tail end of the distribution with members against whom there might be discrimination. Perhaps the dull normal of the present might become the mildly retarded of the future. Recent work from Scandinavia (Hagberg et al., 1981) again raises this question even though it seems very unlikely that in American or British societies the considerable inequalities and disadvantages within their populations will be diminished, as has apparently occurred in Scandinavian countries. It is certainly true that levels of absolute deprivation have greatly diminished in developed societies, but in most there remain widespread relative deprivations (Brown and Madge, 1982).

Prevalence rates for mild retardation are far more often measures of administrative than true prevalence. A very clear positive relationship exists between increased facilities and increased identification of subjects. However, a few researchers have attempted an estimation of true prevalence for mild retardation. Richardson (1981) summarized the findings of detailed research in Aberdeen, a city where there are marked inequalities. All children who were born between 1952 and 1954 and were 7 to 9 years old were routinely given group intelligence tests and studied in detail at ages 8, 9, and 10. Any child scoring below IQ 75 was assessed individually on the Wechsler Intelligence Scale for Children (WISC) and underwent a pediatric neurological examination and a parental social class rating.* The 74% who had IQs of 50 or above were, as usual, heavily overrepresented in the lower socioeconomic groups, and minimally represented in the upper, non-manual classes [and then only where associated central nervous system (CNS) damage was apparent]. Prevalence of mild retardation in social class V was 28 times higher than in classes I–III. Those children without CNS damage were strongly overrepresented in families where there were 5 or more children, those living in the least desirable areas of the city, those in more crowded homes, and those in which the mother's occupation before marriage was a semi-skilled or unskilled manual job. The overall prevalence rate for mild retardation with or without CNS damage was 2.7%. Other surveys [e.g., Jonsson and Kälvesten (1964) in Stockholm] give a similar picture.

A recent Swedish study by Hagberg et al. (1981) using the Terman-Merrill and WISC tests yielded a prevalence of less than 1%; the authors account for this by suggesting a general rise in average child IQ in Gothenburg, with a possible mean of 110–112. In earlier decades large numbers of children scored below IQ 75 on early standardized tests; this is no longer the case for children taking the same early norms. There are, however, a number of difficulties with accepting the suggestion that general social improvement has resulted in lower prevalence of mild retardation. First, there is no clear historical trend, and other *earlier* studies in Edinburgh (Drillien et al., 1966) and in Stockholm (Börjeson and Klackenberg, 1960) also suggest a low prevalence. Furthermore, Jensen (1980) drew attention to possible secular trends in item difficulty within the various revisions of the Stanford-Binet test. These, he said, "would seem almost inevitable for certain culturally loaded test items." In other words it may be hard to discover whether there is a real secular trend with, as Terman and Merrill (1973) put it, a representation of "genuine, important and highly relevant shifts in performance characteristics of children," or it is a matter of children's greater familiarity with test items with which their equivalent age group was less familiar 30 or 40 years earlier. We do not know which is the case; therefore the role of general social progress in diminishing mild retardation—that is, social progress as a psychosocial intervention—is rather unclear. However, if it really is happening then it is worth repeating that the dullard of today may be judged the mildly retarded person of the future.

---

* The United Kingdom Registrar General's 6-point social class classification is as follows: I—higher professional; II—other professional/technical; IIIa—other non-manual; IIIb—skilled manual; IV—semiskilled manual; and V—unskilled manual.

GENETICS AND ENVIRONMENT: CONSTRAINTS

In broad terms one would expect both genetic and environmental factors to have constraining influences. It seems clear that, although many people fail to achieve their potential in a whole range of activities, nonetheless each of us has ultimate limits beyond which it is impossible under long-term optimal conditions to go. Similarly, in the sort of populations for whom intervention is indicated, it is very rare for new circumstances to be optimal. Two limitations are therefore to be found in practice. Moreover, where early intervention is practiced, it is virtually impossible, because of the infant or young child's limited behavioral repertoire, to avoid unwittingly "teaching to the test." Perhaps this is why dramatic responses to modest interventions sometimes occur. It must also be recognized that, for populations at risk for mild retardation, intervention not only attempts to undo or prevent limited development, but also in most cases to counteract the powerful and continuing familial and social pressures that have some etiological role. This is indeed a tall order, which I think can really only be fully met by total ecological change.

The processes underlying positive social changes have been considered by many and eloquently expressed by Kadushin (1970), who reported on a cohort of nonretarded children removed by court order from seriously disadvantaged homes. They were adopted late, at an average age of 7 years. At follow-up Kadushin did not feel the need to offer evidence on the IQs of these children. He felt it was sufficient to look deeply into the social and emotional adjustment of the children to their new parents and the outcome in terms of achievement at school. In seeking to identify the factors responsible for the resilience that so many had shown in recovery from earlier traumas, he offered two: first, of course, the security of the home and the relationships within it, but in addition, and very importantly, he suggested that the wider social context plays a significant part in the recovery process. He pointed out that these children had made *two* important shifts in moving from their own seriously disadvantaged backgrounds via foster homes to the adoptive contexts. They made a change from homes that offered little in the way of meeting their needs in terms of affection, acceptance, support, understanding, and encouragement to homes that offered some measure of these essential psychic supplies. They also changed from deprived, lower-class, multiproblem contexts to respectable, status-conscious, middle-class homes. The child, Kadushin said

. . . now receives messages which proclaim his acceptability, and support, reinforce, and strengthen whatever components, however limited, of self-acceptance he has been able to develop as a result of whatever small amount of affection he received in his former home. The effect of positive parent-child relationships within the home are now buttressed by social relationships outside the home rather than vitiated by the contradiction between the acceptance of the lower-class child in the lower-class home and his rejection by the community.

My own conclusion is that older children adapt toward the academic and behavioral norms of their domestic community, whatever these may be. They may adapt up or down, but the general ecology in which a child is reared almost certainly has an important impact on his achievement and his adjustment: his motivation is bound to be affected as goals change. If this is correct, then the initial reports by Haywood and Arbitman-Smith (1981) on modest cognitive changes following use of Feuerstein's Instrumental Enrichment in retarded adolescents should occasion no surprise. This method had little effect in the areas of school achievement, personality, or motivation after the first year of the intervention program. There were some effects on intelligence test scores, which could be interpreted as narrow transfer from the training material, but in any event these increments were more limited than those reported from Israel (Feuerstein et al., 1980).

ISSUES IN PSYCHOSOCIAL INTERVENTION

I now turn to more specific and interconnected issues, outlined briefly below.

1. There are an unknown number of children in the compulsory schools provided by advanced technological societies who appear to be seriously deficient in either "spontaneous learning ability" or the motivation to acquire those skills that society deems important.

2. There is a high correlation between IQ and attainment—it is not perfect. Thus there will inevitably be apparent overachievers from the bottom and underachievers from the top end of the distribution.

3. Many scientists who are competent both to carry out investigations and to evaluate their findings agree that heritability of IQ is high in humane environments, probably representing a large majority of the homes in which children in developed countries are reared. However, it cannot be reiterated too often that high heritability does not imply unmodifiability.

4. It has been assumed that the causal model involves a path from IQ to achievement. This to some extent remains in the mind of many educators and psychologists, although Crano et al. (1972)

have suggested, somewhat controversially, that among lower working class children attainment precedes (determines) intelligence.

5. Scarr (1981) pointed out that "going straight to the heart of the matter, I think that most evidence points to a 'heritability' of about .4 to .7, in the U.S. white population and .2 to .5 in the black, given that 'heritability' here means the proportion of genetic variance among individuals sampled in twin and family studies, which, as I have repeatedly noted, are not representative of bad environments. If one could include people with really poor environments, the proportion of environmental variance might rise; on the other hand, the genetic variance might also be increased. It is hard to predict whether or not the proportions of variance would change, and in which direction" (p. 458). We do not know a great deal about the limitations imposed by the additive effects of poor genetic backgrounds among disadvantaged families.

6. There is evidence that an unknown but sizeable minority of children in developed countries are brought up in conditions of such gross disadvantage that cumulative deficit occurs (Heber et al., 1968; Jensen, 1977.) We need to know more about the social factors that contribute to this picture, and about the extent to which schools contribute to or fail to prevent these decrements.

7. As yet we know very little about the precise nature of social influences on the development of differences in intelligence and achievement. As Plomin and DeFries (1980) put it, "although we conclude that the new mental test data point to less genetic influence on IQ than do the older data, the new data nonetheless implicate genes as the major systematic force influencing the development of individual differences in IQ. In fact, we know of no specific environmental influences nor combinations of them that account for as much as 10% of the variance in IQ." Furthermore, Scarr (1981) made the important point that "the hypothesis that parent socialization practices have anything to do with children's intellectual development must be tested with genetically unrelated families" (p. 529).

8. Some children who have been exposed to severely depriving environments during their early years have demonstrated dramatic recovery when removed completely from these adverse conditions and given special remedial help (Koluchova, 1976; Clarke, 1982). Once again we know very little about the transactions between these very unusual children and their caretakers, which were the essential agents in the process of change. Furthermore, there are documented cases in which improvement has been sig-

nificant but not sufficient to result in normal development (e.g., Curtiss, 1977). We know very little about the critical factors in these children or their rearing environments.

9. We know that carefully conducted and evaluated preschool education programs for seriously disadvantaged children result in large IQ differences between experimental and control children that normally fade during the school years. We know, too, that benefits of high-level programs may accrue to experimentally treated children in terms of a less common allocation to special classes or retention in grade, but that the difference between treated and untreated children is not nearly so great on standardized achievement tests. It is not clear why there is this difference between teacher ratings and test scores; there could be a number of alternative reasons.

10. From various studies we know that replication may be difficult. Thus one of the Abecedarian groups that had massive intervention starting shortly after birth and continuing until school age did not reach the very high average IQ level of the Milwaukee cohort, although the control children were not very different (Ramey and Campbell, 1980). All these children were selected on the basis of home and parental variables as being at later risk of mental retardation. Unlike the Milwaukee sample, there was no intervention with parents.

The Milwaukee children (Garber and Heber, 1981) at later follow-up showed a narrowing gap in IQ between experimental and control children, but the former group remained above the national average. Their scholastic achievement was superior to the controls across the first 4 years of school in reading and mathematics. However, the major strength of this differential was in the first 2 years of school; by the fourth grade the difference remained in the verbal realm but was much weaker overall. There was a significant decline for both groups on the Metropolitan Achievement Test (MAT) from first through fourth grade, although the decline was greater for the experimental group. For the first year the distribution of the experimental children as a group approximated the national profile on the MAT; the control group was already depressed. The performance of the experimental group since then further declined first to the lower level of the city and then to the still lower one of inner city schools. The experimental groups' IQs were thus not importantly related to later scholastic achievement, and there was little difference between the groups on standardized tests at follow-up.

By contrast, the Perry preschool children (Schweinhart and Weikart, 1980) were selected as toddlers on the basis of having a test IQ

of 85 or below. The experimental children had a much shorter intervention period than the Milwaukee cohort both in terms of weekly
contact hours and years of involvement; there was some intervention
with parents. There was a substantial and highly significant difference
between experimental and control groups in IQ after the preschool
intervention. This disappeared entirely during the years of schooling,
whereas the groups started to diverge in achievement, not only in terms
of allocation to special class or retention in grade, but also in response
to a standardized achievement test. The factors that are responsible
for these discrepant results are unknown.

In an important recent paper Jensen (1981) expressed his position
as follows:

> Environmental interventions that consist only of reallocating the existing
> environmental variation to different individuals will have their effects lim-
> ited by the heritability of trait. But even with heritability in the range .70
> to .80, the magnitude of environmental effects can be considerable. With
> a standard deviation of 7.5 IQ points, for example, and assuming that
> existing environmental effects on IQ are normally distributed (for which
> there is good evidence), the total range of environmental influences would
> be about six SDs or 45 IQ points. Intervention that produces IQ changes
> within that range is not in the least incompatible with present estimates
> of the broad heritability of IQ.
>
> The real problem, however, has been in bringing the environmental
> influences on IQ under experimental control. Even though evidence on
> the genetic analysis of IQ leaves considerable latitude for nongenetic in-
> fluences, psychologists have not yet discovered more than a fraction of
> the nongenetic factors that contribute to IQ variance or how they can be
> experimentally harnessed to raise IQ markedly and permanently. Al-
> though it may come as a surprise to many psychologists, at present we
> know more about the genetics of IQ than we know about environmental
> influences on IQ, except for extreme deprivations and traumas that are
> too rare to contribute importantly to the IQ variance of the general pop-
> ulation. My hunch is that the nongenetic variance in IQ is the result of
> such a myriad of microenvironmental events as to make it extremely dif-
> ficult, if not impossible, to bring more than a small fraction of these in-
> fluences under experimental control. The results of all such attempts to
> date would seem to be consistent with this interpretation. (p. 33)

Jensen's comments may be even more pertinent to the question
of differential achievement within the school context, which is, of
course, along with social adjustment, the main area for concern among
all those who care about disadvantaged children. It might also turn out
to be a considerable problem to change damaging social environments
even if we fully understood the process variables concerned.

CONCLUDING REMARKS: WHAT ARE THE QUESTIONS?

The specific questions raised by this overview seem to me to be as
follows: Does type of program, other things being equal, have a sig-

nificant effect upon outcome? Does duration? Is there an optimal length for intervention, accepting of course that lifelong ecological change is seldom achieved although potentially desirable? Is it the marginally deprived who benefit most? Is, as seems likely, intervention in the home more effective than intervention in the school? Does age, within the range studied, impose any limitations upon intervention effects? Is the best hope for the future to be found in societal change? Is it probable that really effective intervention is impossible within the context that gave rise to its need? Do short intervention programs do anything more than indicate that certain psychological characteristics are or are not easily modifiable on a temporary basis? The fact that all follow-ups into adulthood without any special intervention show on average various degrees of improvement over time (Cobb, 1972) suggests that social influences, prolonged social learning, and delayed maturation play an important role for many. This is perhaps the most hopeful finding in the whole field. Does it reinforce the view that a very long time is needed to shift permanently, if modestly, the characteristics that are to be found in the mildly retarded? These are the sort of questions that will need to be tackled by those seeking to understand the nature of outcomes and processes resulting from intervention.

REFERENCES

Börjeson, M., and Klackenberg, G. 1960. Studies in frequency and prognosis of mentally retarded in Stockholm. Socialmed. Tidskr. 37:243.
Brown, M., and Madge, N. 1982. Despite the Welfare State. Heinemann Educational, London.
Clarke, A. D. B., and Clarke, A. M. 1977. Centennial Guest Editorial: Prospects for prevention and amelioration of mental retardation. Am. J. Ment. Defic. 81:523–533.
Clarke, A. D. B., and Clarke, A. M. 1981. "Sleeper effects" in development: Fact or artifact? Dev. Rev. 1:344–360.
Clarke, A. M. 1982. Developmental discontinuities: An approach to assessing their nature. In: L. A. Bond and J. M. Joffe (eds.), Facilitating Infant and Early Child Development. University Press of New England, Hanover, New Hampshire.
Clarke, A. M., and Clarke, A. D. B. 1982. Intervention and sleeper effects: a reply to Victoria Seitz. Dev. Rev. 2:75–86.
Cobb, H. V. 1972. The Forecast of Fulfillment. Teachers' College Press, Columbia University, New York.
Crano, W. D., Kenny, D. A., and Campbell, D. T. 1972. Does intelligence cause achievement? J. Educ. Psychol. 63:258–275.
Curtiss, S. 1977. Genie: A Psycholinguistic Study of a Modern-day "Wild Child." Academic Press, Inc., New York.
Drillien, C. M., Jameson, S., and Wilkinson, E. M. 1966. Studies in mental handicaps. Part I. Prevalence and distribution by clinical type and severity of defect. Arch. Dis. Child. 41:528–538.

Feuerstein, R., Rand, Y., Hoffman, B., and Miller, R. 1980. Instrumental Enrichment: An Intervention Program for Cognitive Modifiability. University Park Press, Baltimore.

Garber, H. L., and Heber, R. 1981. The efficacy of early intervention with family rehabilitation. In: M. J. Begab, H. C. Haywood, and H. L. Garber (eds.), Psychosocial Influences in Retarded Performance, Vol. II, pp. 71–87. University Park Press, Baltimore.

Hagberg, B., Hagberg, G., Lewerth, A., and Lindberg, U. 1981. Mild mental retardation in Swedish school children, I. Prevalence. Acta Paediatr. Scand. 70:441–444.

Haywood, H. C., and Arbitman-Smith, R. 1981. Modification of cognitive functioning in slow-learning adolescents. In: P. Mittler (ed.), Frontiers of Knowledge in Mental Retardation, Vol. I, pp. 129–140. University Park Press, Baltimore.

Heber, R., Dever, R., and Conry, J. 1968. The influence of environmental and genetic variables on intellectual development. In: H. J. Prehm,, L. A. Hamerlynck, and J. E. Crosson (eds.), Behavioral Research in Mental Retardation, pp. 1–22. University of Oregon School of Education, Eugene.

Jensen, A. R. 1977. Cumulative deficit in IQ of blacks in the rural South. Dev. Psychol. 13:184–191.

Jensen, A. R. 1980. Bias in Mental Testing. Methuen, London.

Jensen A. R. 1981. Raising the IQ: The Ramey and Haskins study. Intelligence 5:29–40.

Jonsson, G., and Kälvesten, A-L. 1964. Two Hundred and Twenty-Two Stockholm Boys. Almqvist and Wiksell, Uppsala.

Kadushin, A. 1970. Adopting Older Children. Columbia University Press, New York.

Koluchova, J. 1976. A report on the further development of twins after severe and prolonged deprivation. In: A. M. Clarke and A. D. B. Clarke (eds.), Early Experience: Myth and Evidence, pp. 45–66. Open Books, London; The Free Press, New York.

Lazar, I., and Darlington, R. 1978. Lasting Effects after Preschool. DHEW Publication No. (OHDS) 79-30178. U.S. Department of Health and Human Services, Washington, D.C.

Lazar, I., Hubbell, V. R., Murray, H., Rosche, M., and Royce, J. 1977. The Persistence of Pre-school Effects: A Long-term Follow-up of Fourteen Experiments. The Consortium on Development Continuity, Education Commission of the States. DHEW Publication No. (OHDS) 78-30130. U.S. Department of Health and Human Services, Washington, D.C.

Plomin, R., and DeFries, J. C. 1980. Genetics and intelligence: Recent data. Intelligence 4:5–24.

Ramey, C. T., and Campbell, F. A. 1980. Educational intervention for children at risk for mild retardation. In: P. Mittler (ed.), Frontiers of Knowledge in Mental Retardation, Vol. I, pp. 47–57. University Park Press, Baltimore.

Ricciuti, H. N. 1981. Early intervention studies: Problems of linking research and policy objectives. In: M. J. Begab, H. C. Haywood, and H. L. Garber (eds.), Psychosocial Influences on Retarded Performance, Vol. II, pp. 293–302. University Park Press, Baltimore.

Richardson, S. A. 1981. Family characteristics associated with mild mental retardation. In: M. J. Begab, H. C. Haywood, and H. L. Garber (eds.), Psychosocial Influences on Retarded Performance, Vol. II, pp. 29–43. University Park Press, Baltimore.

Scarr, S. 1981. Race, Social Class and Differences in IQ. Lawrence Erlbaum Associates, Hillsdale, New Jersey.

Schweinhart, L. J., and Weikart, D. P. 1980. Young Children Grow Up: The Effects of the Perry Preschool Program on Youths Through Age 15. High/Scope Press, Ypsilanti, Michigan.

Terman, L. M., and Merrill, M. A. 1973. Stanford-Binet Intelligence Scale: 1972 Norms Edition. Houghton-Mifflin Company, Boston.

Zigler, E., and Anderson, K. 1979. An idea whose time has come. In: J. Valentine and E. Zigler (eds.), Project Head Start: A Legacy of the War on Poverty, pp. 3–20. The Free Press, New York.

Zigler, E., and Valentine, J. (eds.). 1979. Project Head Start: A Legacy of the War on Poverty. The Free Press, New York.

PERSPECTIVES AND PROGRESS IN MENTAL RETARDATION
Volume I—Social, Psychological, and Educational Aspects
Edited by J. M. Berg

PROSPECTIVE LONGITUDINAL STUDY OF RETARDED CHILDREN

T. E. Jordan

*Graduate School and Office of Research, University of Missouri,
8001 Natural Bridge Road, St. Louis, Missouri 63121*

The St. Louis Baby Study, with particular attention to a birth cohort formed in 1966–67, is described. Related studies around the world are considered. Data from case studies of retarded children are presented to illustrate aggregation of data and multivariate analysis, and also to illustrate that prospective, individualized data files are informative in the study of mental retardation.

In recent years there has been a revival of interest in the technique of prospective longitudinal study in order to examine issues that are developmental. The range of applications has been wide, including quite diverse phenomena and equally diverse spans of time and distance. The phenomena range from microorganisms to people; the time spans have ranged from 24 hours in the case of microorganisms (Speciale et al., 1976) to 50 years in the case of schizophrenics (Bleuler, 1974). The matter of distance is illustrated by an unpublished monograph I finished recently relating the demographics of childhood to subsequent levels of national development within the Third World (Jordan, 1983a).

This reawakened interest in longitudinal study, in the last decade especially, was paralleled by quiet consensus among investigators to set aside stratification by age and retrospective inquiry as two appropriate methods of inquiry. Both techniques have a place, especially when the goal is to assemble a discrete set of data for a narrow but sound purpose. However, a number of people, some years ago, began prospective studies in which inquiry was open-ended but in which they sought specific outcomes at the same time. In some cases, as in my own work in the St. Louis Baby Study (Jordan, 1980b, in preparation) and that of Silva in New Zealand (Silva, 1982), establishment of a birth cohort for open-ended study was a deliberate step. In other instances, of which the first two British cohorts in 1946 and 1958 (but not the third in 1970) are examples, a cohort was really a survey sample to begin with, but follow-ups created the prospective element. Accordingly, it is helpful to separate prospective study and its quiet, probably unpromising beginnings from the mature phase in which criterion ages are reached and explanations of developmental milestones come forth. Prospective studies should cloak themselves in anonymity in their earliest phases in order to avoid premature attention and publicity—with the concomitants of bias and unintended treatments. Only for gerontologists' subjects can the research outcome be predicted with any confidence; even then the timing is rather beyond the locus of one's control.

Two examples of longitudinal data dealing with mentally retarded individuals are the Stevenson et al. (1979) study of treated phenylketonuria and its behavioral consequences and the report by Rodgers (1979) on retarded adults in the March 1946 cohort at age 26 years. An earlier example is Creak's (1969) paper drawn from histories of subnormal children in the Newcastle study of 1,000 families.

ST. LOUIS BABY STUDY

By the end of the 1950s a decade of clinical work on developmental problems of retarded and other children led me to the conclusion that, on the one hand, developmental data offered the promise of explaining disorders of childhood but, on the other, the possibilities of $N = 1$ seemed to be exhausted. In consequence, I decided to embark on an exploration of development using samples of children of robust size; my plan was to create data solely for the research enterprise rather than as a byproduct of clinical work. I set aside the project approach in which limited data are generated from limited samples for limited purposes. The Caterpillar's advice to Alice to ". . . begin at the beginning and go on until you come to the end" seemed salutary. However, the first rather than the second portion of the dictum seems tangible with the passage of time. Data have been analyzed thoroughly to a child age of 10 years (Jordan, in preparation).

Three Cohorts

Our program began in the late fifties and preceded the child-intervention movements of the sixties; indeed, the absence of passionate interventions in this program ran contrary to the prevailing themes of that interesting decade. The first cohort was used for methodological studies between 1960 and 1965. A major outcome was rejection of hospital data gathered by nonspecialists and the decision to take perinatal data through research-oriented people stationed in obstetrical units solely for the purpose. The second (1966) cohort—the subject of this report—was recruited week by week so that subsequent data-taking would be spread out over 4 months. This contrasts with other patterns of cohort formation, such as all cases born on one day (Prokopec, 1960) or within one week (Douglas et al., 1971). No children were excluded, except by noncooperation, and this may be contrasted with exclusion of Francophones (Hopkins, 1947), illegitimate persons (Neligan et al., 1974), children without a male head-of-household (Fogelman and Goldstein, 1976), and boys (Svalastoga, 1976). The third cohort is a small group of infants on whom extensive perinatal data (e.g., Brazelton tests) were taken (Lyon-MacNeil, 1974). They were followed for a brief period until funding was exhausted. [For accounts of major findings please consult Jordan (1980b, 1981, 1983b).]

Relevant Studies

The reader may wish to judge the similarity of the St. Louis Baby Study to other studies. We view it as having the following characteristics, essentially:

1. Prospective case studies of individual children in their homes (*N* = 1008).
2. A cohort drawn from a representative North American metropolitan area.
3. Probands representing the spectrum of the community: rich, poor; black, white; inner city, suburbs; major religions; no children excluded on grounds of illegitimacy, twinning, degree of access or mobility; subjects at biological risk, perinatally; plus controls.
4. Multivariate analyses of data.
5. Computer storage, retrieval, and analysis of approximately 750,000 items of data.
6. Criteria in several domains of child development.
7. Data on social and family variables.

The following programs of research seem most relevant, from the point of view of studying retardation in the context of child development:

1. The Educational Follow-Up Study of Balow in Minneapolis (Balow et al., 1977)
2. The Dunedin (New Zealand) Study of Silva (1982)
3. The Nijmegen (Holland) Study of Prahl-Anderson (1978)
4. Project Metropolitan in Stockholm (Janson, 1978)
5. The Newcastle Study (Miller et al., 1974; Neligan et al., 1974)
6. The Kauai (Hawaii) Studies (Werner and Smith, 1979)

7. The National Child Development Study in Britain (Goldstein, 1980).

Statistical Models

Bottenberg and Ward's technique of multiple linear regression (MacNeil et al., 1975) permits use of regression not merely as a narrow tool but, in Cohen's (1968) phrase, as a *data-analytic system*. The ability to use both discrete and continuous data simultaneously (e.g., test scores plus membership categories) and to introduce quadratic and polynomial terms is most useful. Equally, we need to study interactions and have found Koplyay's (1972) Interaction Regression Analysis quite useful. An innovation called TSAR is our use of multiple regression to schematize the relationships between time-specific predictors and the criterion (Jordan, 1980a).

Some Considerations

Cohorts can be formed relatively easily by seeking subjects who share a common social identity such as attending the same church, or to better effect, are in the same year of schooling. Such groups are captive, in the sense that they are not at large. My families enjoy no common element and do not know each other. This is important in planning because there are no short cuts; each family is contacted at the home address. In the early years each family was visited many times by the same caseworker. In all cases workers and families were matched by race, and occasionally by sex.

Data in child development studies take many forms. From the beginning we have collected data by noninvasive means. There have been no blood samples, and no devices (e.g., skinfold calipers) have been applied. On one occasion small hair samples were taken for lead-poison studies, which proved impractical; the procedures were probably counterproductive in the long run.

As with other studies (Tanner and Israelsohn, 1963) we have had problems with fathers. Our data on fathers are limited to items we obtain from their wives, which has enabled us to avoid some termination of cooperation, but not all, by fathers.

We have employed a noncaptive cohort and worked originally in politically and socially volatile segments of the St. Louis community. We have taken great pains to suppress publicity (Cromwell et al., 1975), and this has not been easy because sponsoring agencies like to see a little recognition for their largesse. Publicity should be delayed until enterprises reach their avowed goals, or it may be premature and unmerited. Field research needs anonymity lest the act of being studied seem glamorous to probands, and so constitute an unintended treatment. A second loss associated with discretion is the absence of recognition that allows funding agencies to associate their philanthropy with visible, fashionable, and apparently successful operations. Obviously, the politics of awarding funds are as delicate as the politics of their pursuit. Benevolent patrons need to justify their support as contributing to major intellectual undertakings. Longitudinal study militates against grantsmanship, unfortunately.

The 1966 Data Set

As a whole, the data set on the 1966 cohort consists of about 750,000 pieces of data stored on tape. More analytically, the data consist of a series of individual case histories acquired through individualized testing and interviewing. In the last several years lack of funds has led to use of correspondence, questionnaires, and school records—techniques that work but are not substitutes for data taking within families by case workers. However, we have observed selected children closely. Major findings are:

1. Through analyses of both continuous and categorical data, we have established that biological risk in the perinatal phase yields significance to environmental factors at about age 2 years.
2. In the matter of other influences, race is barely perceptible and is eliminated by social class data. This does not mean that black-white differences do not exist; they do, but low attainment scores in black preschoolers relate in a statistically significant way to low socioeconomic status scores (SES), but not to race, when both variables are present.
3. Among environmental influences the most consistent for all phases of child development is the aggregate of sex, perinatal SES, ethnic group, and home stimulation (STIM). Among single predictors, within appropriate clusters of independent variables, the most influential in the preschool years by domain appear to be (physical criteria) sex and (cognitive criteria) ethnic group and SES.
4. Some findings are methodological, a topic that is salient in longitudinal study. Criteria of development in the preschool years are not very predictable, according to our regression analyses.
5. Maternal traits that influence the nonsomatic aspects of development are years of schooling and authoritarian-liberal child rearing ideology, especially.
6. We have found two multivariate systems of analysis useful. They are multiple linear regression and interaction regression. Although operating on different assumptions, 200 analyses employing identical data sets show that both techniques identify the same variable as prime sources of criterion variance, generally speaking.

7. In studies of handicapped children we have found developmental histories to be useful tools in the study of biosocial antecedents to physical, mental, and learning disabilities.

Mental Retardation

Children with delayed cognitive development in the St. Louis Baby Study have been studied in two ways. The first and formal method is the classic aggregation of data and its multivariate analysis. We executed this type of study recently (Jordan, 1980b, in preparation). The second is the technique of the case study with its opportunity to study individual children for quite different reasons. I exemplify these two styles of longitudinal research with prospective data to three ages—school entry, age 11 years, and adolescence; the latter, at 16 years, is the most recent episode of data taking.

The first longitudinal approach is illustrated by referring to data reported in 1981 (Jordan, 1981). In that study the verbal and nonverbal performance of children with low cognitive attainment ($> -2\,\sigma$ on the Coloured Progressive Matrices at age 6) was analyzed. Half the subjects were black, most were males, and the perinatal SES level was low. Articulation scores, interestingly, were a little higher than I expected, i.e., not reduced proportional to intellectual test scores. This group was not as low on early assessments at 6 and 12 months as later performance might suggest retrospectively. The number of siblings was above average (mean = 4.4). Half of those children lived in the aging inner city, and a third lived in the suburbs.

In the case of the second longitudinal approach we present prospectively developed files with the original form of all the data. One exemplifies fairly extensive study, the family having sought services from me. In this respect, programmatic longitudinal work establishes special relationships with families. Our data extend further into the developmental span, although with a patchy history of accessibility and cooperation regarding the child in question.

Case Study: A Ten-Year-Old I now present prospective longitudinal information about a white retarded boy (twin *A*). He weighed 7 pounds 1 ounce at birth and had an Apgar score of 9. *A* has a fraternal twin *B* who weighed 6 pounds at birth and also had an Apgar score of 9 at 5 minutes after delivery. Table 1 indicates that *A*'s physical development (height and weight) has been normal. With regard to attainment of functions, the picture that emerged prospectively, as Table 1 shows, is less satisfactory.

Child *A*, the larger of the twins, appeared normal at birth. Fairly soon in the early years he appeared less active than his twin, and language was slow to emerge. A Peabody Picture Vocabulary Test IQ of

68 at age 3 is corroborated by a Wechsler Intelligence Scale for Children IQ of 69 at age 10. In Table 1 two things are apparent via the prospective data. First, there is the nonemergence and late emergence of functions in Twin A. Second, there is the comparative delay as his normal twin met developmental norms. At 7 years 6 months, for example, Twin A failed the Illinois Test of Psycholinguistic Abilities item, "A red light says stop, a green light says _____ ?" Through prospective data the child is seen to be growing in a unique way.

Table 1 is an abstract of a 10-year file. Additional data are derived from our monitoring of the dynamics of the family. A divorce several years ago led to the relative surprise, I surmise, of a new stepmother discovering the limitations of a nice, quiet little boy. In mentioning this I call attention to the idiosyncrasies within families that prospective study catches and refracts.

Case Study: An Adolescent   I now move on to an illustration of a prospective and current study at a third and later age, 15 years, with reference to a black female with Down's syndrome. In this instance, accommodation is seen to a reality that those of us who study the family aspects of retardation as a problem (Jordan, 1976) stress: the development of sexuality in adolescent retarded females. In the 1966–67 cohort the mean age of menses was 12 years 2 months. Shortly after that age comes the potential hazard of pregnancy. In the case of this girl, who is a low-grade Down's syndrome child, the family has adopted a unique strategy: the girl has received injections to suppress the onset of menses for the last several years. Although chronologically a teenager, her intellectual immaturity, which is unavoidable, is paralleled by an induced state of physiological immaturity. At age 16 the girl is maintained at the stage of reproductive immaturity she had attained several years ago. Down's syndrome children have a range of levels and rates of mental growth. In this girl, the rate of mental growth is compounded by behavioral and speech problems. The behavioral problems take the form of much out-of-seat behavior in her classroom, running to other classrooms, and refusing to stay with a group of classmates. Not surprisingly, the parents are concerned about her vulnerability, and suppression of menarche is a consequence of the picture of sustained problems over the period of 16 years.

CONCLUDING REMARKS

In closing, I add a brief comment on the relevance of prospective study to the issues in the field of mental retardation. Very quickly, prospective study of children leads to study of the entire family complex. Siblings and parents become less inhibited and inquiry can enter sensitive

Table 1. Prospective information on twin A from birth to age 10 years

Age	Domain[a]	Information[a]	Physical development information
Birth	Family	Nine children, father is engineer; STIM score on family (Caldwell, 1970) is 30, low average	Apgar = 9, wt = 7 lb. 1 oz. Date of birth: 1/28/67
6 Months	General development	Ad-hoc scale: twin A scores 7, and twin B scores 6	14 lb.; 26 in.
12 Months	Motor development	Mother reports the child is less active than twin B	25 lb. 3 oz.; 31 in.
24 Months	Cognitive development	Twin A scores 12 via maternal interview on Preschool Attainment Record (B scores 27)	33 lb.; 33 in.
30 Months	Cognitive development	Twins both untestable	37.5 lb.; 33.5 in.
42 Months	Cognitive development	A scores 15 on PPVT(A); speech is unintelligible; "immature and infantile"; IQ 68	36 lb.; 39 in.
54 Months	Cognitive development Visual-motor-memory Preschool inventory Boehm concepts	A scores 0, B scores 19 on Copy Forms Test A scores 0, B scores 18 on Preschool Inventory Started performance but started to cry, hid behind mother, and sucked his fingers	

Age	Domain / Test	Result	
66 Months	Cognitive development		50 lb.; 44 in.
78 Months	Cognitive development	A scores 5, B scores 4 on Digit Span	49 lb.; 46.8 in.
90 Months (= 7 yr, 6 mos)	Cognitive development	A scores 7, B scores 11 on Coloured Matrices	
	School	Repeats kindergarten	
	Sensory-motor development	Left-eyed and left-handed	
	General development	A scores 16 problems, B scores 9 on checklist	
	Language development: ITPA-AA	Fails at "Red light says stop, green light says _____?"	
118 Months (= 9 yr, 10 mos)	Cognitive development		
	ITPA	"Overall depressed level of performance"; "single word receptive vocabulary" below 2nd percentile	
	WISC	Full scale IQ = 69	
	PIAT	Grade equivalent = 1.7 grades; Age Equivalent = 6 yr, 11 mos.	
	Beery (Vis-motor)	Age Equivalent = 5 yr, 7 mos.	

[a] Abbreviated test names: PPVT = Peabody Picture Vocabulary Test; ITPA = Illinois Test of Psycholinguistic Abilities; Boehm = Test of Basic Concepts; WISC = Wechsler Intelligence Scale for Children; Beery = Developmental Test of Visual-Motor Integration; PIAT = Peabody Individual Achievement Test.

151

areas. At the same time prospective study obligates the investigator to assist families when they request it. Failure to do so would be unethical, and it would probably lead to a loss of cooperation.

As an aspect of epidemiology, prospective study need not use a single cohort. The opportunity to overlap several cohorts simultaneously should not be ignored, even though my preference is for the leisurely pace and related opportunity for reflection on issues. Should that seem too leisurely, let me add that annual data taking inhibits analysis and write-up of findings. That element illustrates the value of sustained funding so that data taking, however critical to study of spans of developmental interest, does not obliterate timely analysis of data and the obligation to reflect on its meaning. It is essential to structure the management of prospective study so that data taking does not preclude all else. One needs the opportunity to relate individual case studies to the whole cohort. In a phrase, there must be time to sift and reflect, to analyze and write. Failure to do so can lead to mere accumulation of masses of data. What we used to call "file drawer research," that is, determination of the potential answers to nonexistent questions, still exists. Data on computer tapes are no better if we lack the time and opportunity to phrase productive questions and hypotheses.

REFERENCES

Balow, B., Rubin, R., and Rosen, M. J. 1977. Complications of Pregnancy and Birth as Contributions to Personality Development and Aberrant Behavior: Interim Report #26. University of Minnesota, Minneapolis.
Bleuler, M. 1974. The offspring of schizophrenics. Schizophr. Bull. 8:93–107.
Caldwell, 1970. The STIM Scale. University of Arkansas, Little Rock, Arkansas.
Cohen, J. 1968. Multiple linear regression as a general data analytic system. Psychol. Bull. 70:426–433.
Creak, E. M. 1969. Problems of subnormal children studied in the thousand family survey. Lancet 2:282–283.
Cromwell, R. E., Vaughn, C. B., and Mindel, C. B. 1975. Ethnic minority research in an urban setting: A process of exchange. Am. Sociolo. 10:141–150.
Douglas, J. W. B., Ross, J. M., and Simpson, H. R. 1971. All Our Future. Panther House Ltd., New York.
Fogelman, K., and Goldstein, H. 1976. Social factors associated with changes in educational attainment between 7 and 11 years of age. Educ. Stat. 2:95–109.
Goldstein, H. 1980. The Design and Analysis of Longitudinal Studies. Academic Press, Inc., New York.
Hopkins, J. W. 1947. Height and weight of Ottawa elementary school children of two socioeconomic strata. Hum. Biol. 19:68–82.
Janson, C. G. 1978. Research Report #9: The Longitudinal Approach. Project Metropolitan, Stockholm University, Stockholm, Sweden.

Jordan, T. E. 1976. The Mentally Retarded, 4th ed. Charles E. Merrill Publishing Co., Columbus, Ohio.

Jordan, T. E. 1980a. Relationships among predictors in longitudinal data: Temporal-sequential analysis by regression: TSAR. Mult. Linear Regress. View. 10:15–28.

Jordan, T. E. 1980b. Development in the Preschool Years. Academic Press, Inc., New York.

Jordan, T. E. 1981. A persistent problem of mental health in childhood: Delayed mental development—A prospective study. R. Soc. Health J. 101:44–57.

Jordan, T. E. 1983a. Child Development and the Wealth of Nations. Multiple Linear Regression Monographs, No. 12.

Jordan, T. E. 1983b. The St. Louis baby study: Theory, practice, and findings. In: S. Mednick and M. Harway (eds.), Longitudinal Studies in the United States. Plenum Publishing Corp., New York.

Jordan, T. E. Development in the Elementary School Years. (in preparation)

Koplyay, J. 1972. Automatic interaction detector AID-4. Mult. Linear Regress. View. 3:25–33.

Lyon-MacNeil, J. 1974. The refinement and prediction of a measure of infant development. Unpublished doctoral dissertation, Southern Illinois University, Carbondale, Illinois.

MacNeil, K., Kelley, F. J., and MacNeil, J. 1975. Testing Research Hypotheses Using Multiple Linear Regression. Southern Illinois University Press, Carbondale.

Miller, F. J. W., et al. 1974. The School Years in Newcastle Upon Tyne, 1952–1962. Oxford University Press, Oxford, England.

Neligan, G., Prudham, D., and Steiner, H. 1974. The Formative Years: Birth, Family, and Development in Newcastle-Upon-Tyne. Oxford University Press, Oxford, England.

Prahl-Anderson, B. 1978. A Mixed Longitudinal Interdisciplinary Study of Growth and Development. Academic Press, Inc., New York.

Prokopec, M. 1960. Report on the longitudinal follow-up of Prague children (based on the method of the International Children's Center in Paris). In: Proceedings of the Sixth International Congress on Anthropological and Ethnological Science, pp. 519–527. (unpublished proceedings)

Rodgers, B. 1979. Future prospects for ESN(M) school leavers. Spec. Educ: Forward Trends 6:8–9.

Silva, P. A. 1982. The Dunedin multidisciplinary child development study and child health policy in New Zealand. In: T. E. Jordan (ed.), Child Development, Information and the Formation of Public Policy: An International Perspective. Charles C Thomas Publisher, Springfield, Illinois.

Speciale, S. G., Nowoczyk, T., and Jouvet, M. 1976. Longitudinal study of bioelectric activity in the pre- and post-hatch chick. Dev. Biol. 9:539–548.

Stevenson, J. E., Hawcroft, J., Lobascher, M., Smith, I., Wolff, O. H., and Graham, P. J. 1979. Behavioral deviance in children with early treated phenylketonuria. Arch. Dis. Child. 94:14–18.

Svalastoga, K. 1976. Analytic Strategy in Sequential Research: Project Metropolitan Revisited. Report #6, Stockholm University, Stockholm, Sweden.

Tanner, J., and Israelsohn, W. 1963. Parent-child correlations for body measurements of children between the ages of one month and seven years. Ann. Hum. Genet. 26:245–259.

Werner, E. E., and Smith, R. S. 1979. An epidemiological perspective on some antecedents and consequences of childhood mental health problems and learning disabilities. J. Child. Psychiatry 18:292–306.

PERSPECTIVES AND PROGRESS IN MENTAL RETARDATION
Volume I—Social, Psychological, and Educational Aspects
Edited by J. M. Berg
Copyright © 1984 by I.A.S.S.M.D.

CLINICAL PREDICTION OVER A FIFTEEN-YEAR SPAN IN AN EDUCABLE MENTALLY RETARDED POPULATION

G. C. Krantz[1] and G. M. Fox-Reid[2]

[1]*State Department of Public Welfare, Centennial Building, St. Paul, Minnesota 55155*
[2] *Cannon Valley Special Education Cooperative, Northfield, Minnesota 55057*

This paper reports a comparison of the predictive power, over a 15-year span, of certain statistical variables, clinical variables, and clinical predictions in an educable mentally retarded population. All 138 members of a ninth grade educable mentally retarded class in an urban school district were studied. Standard statistical data were recorded, clinical constructs were created, long-term predictions made about each student, and the information was sealed. Fifteen years later, a follow-up located 60% of the former students and ascertained their statuses. The contingencies of seven outcome statuses with the statistical and clinical variables and with the predictions were computed.

Prediction of client outcomes, however much beset by cautions and even by dangers, is an established stock in trade of professionals who deal with the lives of mentally retarded people. At least some grasp of what probable outcomes would be expected, given any particular constellation of client characteristics and circumstances, is a necessary precursor to even an awareness that a concern ought to be taken for the client. Some understanding of what is likely to become of the client if nothing is done—or if something is done—is a kind of prediction that we here intend to take as a legitimate, necessary component of work with handicapped people. The question to be addressed has to do with the defensible acquisition and expression of that understanding.

The study reported here deals with prediction. It reports predictions and predictors that were recorded and sealed when the educable mentally retarded students in our population were in the ninth grade in an urban public school system, and it reports the relationships that those predictions and predictors were found to have with the status of the young adults at follow-up 15 years later. The predictive powers of the clinical predictors and predictions, on the one hand, and of the simultaneously recorded statistical predictors on the other, are the focus of this report.

THE ISSUE

The issue of whether clinical insight has substantive utility is an old one in our field. It was brought to definition in a book that has become a small classic, Paul Meehl's treatise on *Clinical versus Statistical Prediction* (1958). Meehl highlighted predictive power as the touchstone of the validity, and hence of the potential utility, of statistical and clinical analyses of cases.

Pure clinical and pure statistical analyses, Meehl pointed out, are polar approaches with many gradations between them. He described the mechanical or mathematical entry of psychometric and objective data into a predictive table as a clear-cut statistical procedure. Near the other (the clinical) pole, he wrote,

> The most common case of all in clinical practice is that of psychometric plus nonpsychometric data combined nonmechanically, where we have the history, an interview, ward behavior, and the results of standardized and semistandardized psychological examinations combined in a staff conference in the attempt to yield a diagnosis (in the broad sense of that word) which in turn entails some sort of prediction. (p. 18)

In his discussion of the issue, Meehl found the distinction between clinical and statistical analysis or prediction to be more interesting than the distinction between the two kinds of data; it was the clinicity of the combination and the prediction, rather than the clinicity of the data items, on which he focused. That focus will be emulated here.

The issue of the two methods of prediction can be stated simply: which is more effective? Here, we will be even more simple: which method is found, upon examination of its "hit rate," to predict more accurately? Meehl wrote that

> There is only one possible reply to this "silly" question . . . [we] have no recourse except to record our predictions at the time, allow them to accumulate, and ultimately tally them up . . . [then] what have we done? We have carried out a validation study of the traditional kind! . . . Always, we might as well face it, the shadow of the statistician hovers in the background; *always* the actuary will have the final word. (1958, pp. 137–138)

The actuary to whom Meehl referred is the one who applies statistical analysis to the comparison of the relationships between outcome and the clinical and statistical predictions. He did not propose, nor do we, to make the validation study itself a matter of clinical judgment. The intent, then, is to apply statistical analysis to the validation of both clinical activity and statistical predictors, both of them being representative of the common state of the arts.

PROCEDURE

The study reported here is an attempt to do what Meehl proposed: to make predictions based upon the non-mechanical combination of psychometric and nonpsychometric data, to record them at the time, and to later compare their hit rates with the hit rates of the data applied mechanically. The attempt was begun shortly after the publication of Meehl's book. His delineation of the issue in fact inspired the study (although he naturally cannot be charged with the inadequacy with which the study addressed the issue).

In the early 1960s, an attempt was made to describe the characteristics and the school-rehabilitation needs of mentally retarded students in an urban school district (Deno et al., 1965). This was in the course of one of the first federally funded research and demonstration projects at the interface of special education and rehabilitation. Part of the project was the investigation of the 1962–63 ninth grade class of educable mentally retarded students, numbering 138. An organized case study method was worked out, and a substantial body of information was acquired about each of the students. For each of the 138 students, school records were abstracted; referral forms were filled out by the school counselor, shop or home economics teacher, social worker, and special class teacher; and structured interviews were conducted with the counselor and the special class teacher. In addition, new psychological interviews and tests were administered to 88% of the students, and 62% of them were enrolled for 2 weeks in the project's school-rehabilitation center for what was then called prevocational testing following structured interviews with their parents.

While the usual psychometric and objective data were being gathered, certain clinical variables were created by one of the research psychologists who were conducting the study. These clinical variables were statements of student characteristics, formulated by the exercise of clinical judgment in a non-mechanical fashion. These clinical variables, together with statistical variables and clinical predictions to be described shortly, are listed in Table 1 (below). Each clinical variable was defined as to its meaning, although not as to the process of creating the judgment. The definitions covered several pages of text, and are best described here by illustration. For example, the variable called "Family influence upon educability" was defined as follows:

> FAMILY INFLUENCE: the extent to which the family influence (beyond those of the subculture or the neighborhood) contributes to the student's school efficiency.
> Normal: families that are about as supportive of the educational process as the average (actual rather than idealized) middle- or lower-middle class home.
> Unsupportive: passively nonsupportive of school mores or providing a distinctly unstimulating environment.
> Pathological: families that are actively anti-school, have relationships that are destructive to the student's personal integration, or that present circumstances that seriously interfere with the student's school acceptance or attendance.

A statistical variable that corresponded to the clinical variable of family influence, and that thereby highlights its clinicity, was the entry in the student's school record of whether the student's family was intact or broken.

Finally, the psychologist made what amounted to outright predictions. These were clinical statements, each on a 4-point scale, of the student's academic potential, social development potential, potential for benefit from social casework, and employment potential. The last was defined as:

> EMPLOYMENT POTENTIAL: the eventual potential for employment, which may be several years in the future. Present state of employability is to be disregarded.
> Competitive: potential for reasonably regular competitive employment, at any skill level including unskilled, assuming a national unemployment level of 3 to 6%. No special help, such as that of a specialized job placement agency, expected to be necessary.
> Competitive with help: as above, but likely to need transition help from some specialized agency.
> Sheltered: will probably require sheltered workshop employment, for a period of years or terminally.
> Unemployable: not expected to be capable of either sheltered or competitive employment within present rehabilitation technology.

All three classes of variable—statistical, clinical, and prediction—for each of the 138 students were then given the treatment that had been recommended by Meehl. They were recorded "at the time," and the records (identified by number) were sealed in a packet that was then stored beyond the reach of school and agency personnel who subsequently dealt with the students. These personnel of course continued to have access to the statistical variables that were in the school records themselves, but they were not told the ratings on the clinical variables or the predictions. The predicting psychologist himself did not continue to work with these students.

The sealed records were retained for 15 years. They were accessed after 11 years for a partial follow-up by a researcher who had no further connection with the study, and they were then resealed. Then, in 1978–79, a follow-up of the students was undertaken by the junior author. The senior author, who had initially made and recorded the clinical variables and predictions, made available the names, birthdates, and 1963 addresses of the students. The task of locating these people after a lapse of 15 years would be worthy of its own report; of the 138, 83 (or 60%) were located and a structured interview was conducted with them or with their immediate families. Reports were obtained at the interviews of educational history after the ninth grade, present residence, finances, recreational and social activity, community mobility, past and present health, employment 5, 10, and 15 years after ninth grade, and future expectations.

To ensure that the persons located and interviewed were a representative sample of the initial population, t tests were run for the continuous interval data and chi squares for the ordinal and nominal data between the 83 persons located and the population of 138 ninth graders. There were no significant differences on any of the 52 predictor variables; hence, the 83 were considered to be representative of the initial population.

After the follow-up data were recorded, the 1962–63 data packet was unsealed. After the coded data were punched onto cards, the identifiable case records were burned, and subsequent analysis was made under conditions of anonymity. It was then possible to compare the hit rates of the statistical variables, the clinical variables, and the predictions against the students' outcome statuses.

The mathematical tools by which the comparisons could be made were limited by the nature of the data. A few variables, such as IQ, had been recorded in scalar units and covered substantial ranges. Most variables, however, were either categorical or were in three or four ordinal units. The statistical common denominator was necessarily that of nonparametric statistics, and the chi square was chosen for almost all of the comparisons.

FINDINGS

There had been 20 statistical predictor variables recorded in 1962–63, as well as 8 clinical predictor variables and 4 predictions. An additional 10 variables recorded in 1962–63 were not analyzed because of the ambiguity of their clinical versus statistical categorization. Seven follow-up variables were chosen for analysis: the type of 1977–78 living quarters, and employment status and salary bracket 5, 10, and 15 years after ninth grade. This allowed 32 × 7 comparisons of hit rate.

Throughout the series of chi square tests, the sample size remained constant: the 83 former students who were located at follow-up. This constancy allowed the chi squares to be directly compared in those majority of instances in which the degrees of freedom were the same, namely 5. However, because the degrees of freedom were not uniform throughout, the remaining common denominator reported here will be the significance levels of the chi squares, comparable because of the uniform sample size. Those significance levels are shown in Table 1.

At the 0.05 level of significance, 7 of the 20 statistical predictors, 3 of the 8 clinical predictor variables, and 3 of the 4 predictions were contingent with at least one of the outcome variables. At the 0.01 level, 2 of the 20 statistical predictors, 1 of the 8 clinical predictors, and 3 of the 4 predictions were contingent with at least one outcome variable. At the 0.001 level, none of the 20 statistical predictors, 1 of the 8 clinical predictors, and 2 of the 4 predictions were contingent with at least one outcome variable.

A closer look at Table 1 reveals some interesting patterns. Among the statistical predictors, the only two that were robust enough to show contingencies with outcome, and strong enough to yield significance at the 0.01 level with this sample size and degrees of freedom, were sex of the student and age while in ninth grade. Sex was contingent with salary bracket after age 22. The students' ages while in the ninth grade, an index of how retarded they were in academic progress, was contingent beyond the 0.01 level with both employment status and salary bracket, but only 15 years after ninth grade; it was not significantly contingent with status earlier in the occupational career.

Influence of the subculture upon the student's educability was the only clinical predictor robust enough to show contingency, beyond 0.01 significance, with an outcome. It was contingent only with employment status 15 years after ninth grade, and not with salary or with other outcome variables at any reasonable level of significance.

Among the outright predictions, 3 of the 4 showed contingencies with at least one outcome at the 0.01 level, and 2 were contingent at the 0.001 level. Potential for benefit from social casework showed no significant contingencies. Academic potential had one contingency at the 0.01 level, with type of present living quarters. Social development potential was contingent beyond the 0.01 level with three outcomes: employment status and salary bracket 15 years after ninth grade, and current type of housing. The prediction of employment potential was contingent at the 0.01 level with employment status and salary bracket at 10 and at 15 years after ninth grade, and was contingent at the 0.001 level with the 15-year outcomes.

Not very obvious, but evident upon careful inspection, was the somewhat greater tendency for all kinds of predictors to be more contingent with 1977–78 outcome variables than with variables reported for 5 and 10 years earlier.

DISCUSSION

With 224 (32 × 7) contingency calculations, some at least should be expected to show spuriously significant contingencies by chance. At the 0.05 level of confidence, 5% of actually noncontingent relationships should yield erroneous "significance." If the variables were independent of each other—and they almost certainly are not—that would mean an expectancy of 11 (224 × 0.05) false-positive contingencies. Similarly, one would expect about two spurious contingencies at the 0.01 level, and none at the 0.001 level. There were 25 chi squares that exceeded the 0.05 level of probabilities, 15 that exceeded the 0.01 level, and 4 that exceeded 0.001. In view of the probable interrelatedness of the variables, there is no accepted method for translating the available facts into a definite probability of how many of the significance statements are spurious, much less for determining which ones that might be. It is only a factor to be kept in mind in interpreting the findings.

More to the point, the obtained results are plausible. Among statistical predictors, age while in ninth grade (an index of academic retardation) and sex are the most easy to relate logically to employment status and income at approximate age 30, especially when it is known that this study categorized as unemployed full-time homemakers and other family workers.

Among the highest-order 1962–63 variables, it is reasonable to accept that a prediction of employment potential itself would be more contingent with employment outcome than would be predictions of other kinds of potential. Some other results are rather implausible; it would be difficult to explain the lone and highly "significant" contingency of subcultural influence with employment status at approximate age 30.

Three patterns seem to emerge strongly enough to be asserted as findings that would bear further investigation. First, the clinical predictors (these were not predictions) were not more contingent with outcome than were the statistical predictors. In fact, with 0.086 of their possible 140 contingencies significant in contrast to 0.054 of the possible 56 contingencies for the clinical predictors, it is clear that the statistical predictors were in fact more predictive. Second, the predic-

Table 1. Significance levels of the contingencies between 1962–63 variables and 1977–78 follow-up variables, expressed as probabilities that the obtained contingencies are not statistically different from zero (blank spaces represent probabilities greater than 0.05)

Predictor variables and predictions, 1962–63	Follow-up variables obtained, 1977–78						
	Employment status			Salary bracket			Type living quarters, 15 yr
	5 yr	10 yr	15 yr	5 yr	10 yr	15 yr	15 yr
Statistical predictors							
Sex	0.0014				0.0060	0.0066	
Year of birth		0.0367	0.0077			0.0010	
Grade entered special class							
Father's occupation	0.0471						
Reading grade level							
Race	0.0477						
WISC-FS IQ, Project							
WISC-V IQ, Project							
WISC-P IQ, Project							
Binet IQ, Project							0.0101
WISC-FS IQ, pre-Project							
WISC-V IQ, pre-Project							
WISC-P IQ, pre-Project							

	Academic potential	Social development potential	Employment potential	Casework benefit potential
Binet IQ, pre-Project				
Elementary absenteeism				
No. different addresses				
Area of city		0.0422		0.0287
Clinical reports in file				
Family marital status				
No. sibs in special class				
Clinical predictors				
Native intelligence				
Functional intelligence				
Concrete/abstract defect	0.0048	0.0247		
Visuomotor defect				
Emotional status			0.0374	
Family influence				
Subcultural influence	0.0011	0.0006		
Other problems				
Predictions				
Academic potential	0.0173	0.0053	0.0123	0.0018
Social development potential		0.0009	0.0013	0.0000
Employment potential		0.0077	0.0000	
Casework benefit potential				

tions, with 0.357 of their possible 28 contingencies found to be significant, were substantially superior in fact. Third, the 1962–63 variables, especially the predictions, were more contingent with outcome variables for 1977–78 than they were with outcome variables reported for 5 and 10 years earlier. One may speculate that increasing unreliability of self-report with time may have degraded the order of recalled information and thereby degraded contingency, but this does not somehow seem to be a satisfying explanation.

Many related issues and substantially more analysis of these and other data of the study will be found in the junior author's thesis (Reid, 1978). This report is mainly concerned with the issue of clinical versus statistical prediction. One study does not settle such a large issue. On the other hand, this study was so structured as to make a test of the issue quite explicit. The predictors were recorded and sealed at the time, they were retained for 15 years, and the outcome data against which they were checked were gathered by a separate investigator who located a reasonably large portion of the original subjects. Under these conditions, clinical predictions were found to be more strongly contingent with outcome than were the statistical predictors. A fair assertion is that doubt, at least, is cast upon the assumption that only hard and objective data may be defensibly used in providing effective and equitable human service.

Why should effort be made to determine whether clinical judgment may be valid? Has there been denigration of clinical judgment in human services? A glance at the trends of recent years seems to show that there has indeed been such denigration. A very substantial portion of the professional literature is devoted to the low-order data of small-increment behavioral objectives and treatment, often with the frank assertion that more global descripters are indefensible. Single professional judgment has been replaced, by mandate, by team decision in many arenas. Records have even been purged of the entries of professional judgment. These trends are buttressed by assertions that clinical judgment is inherently unreliable and therefore invalid, and probably also unfair and immoral, or at least arbitrary.

If the validation of clinical judgment should therefore be undertaken, the present time is one in which this validation is singularly difficult. It is difficult precisely because it has been under successful attack. The attack has made it burdensome and even sometimes illegal to assemble and keep the records of clinical judgment. Meehl, it must be remembered, was right; we have no recourse but to record our predictions, tally them up, and check their hit rates. The study reported here has been presented as one instance in which it was possible to check a set of hit rates. Our hope is that other such investigations will be carried out.

REFERENCES

Deno, E., Henze, R., Krantz, G., and Barklind, K. 1965. Retarded Youth: Their School-Rehabilitation Needs. Minneapolis Public Schools, Minneapolis, Minnesota.
Meehl, P. 1958. Clinical versus Statistical Prediction. University of Minnesota Press, Minneapolis.
Reid, G. 1978. A Comparative Analysis of Selected Characteristics of Mildly Mentally Retarded Adolescents and their Subsequent Adult Status. Unpublished doctoral dissertation, University of Minnesota, Minneapolis.

PERSPECTIVES AND PROGRESS IN MENTAL RETARDATION
Volume I—Social, Psychological, and Educational Aspects
Edited by J. M. Berg
Copyright © 1984 by I.A.S.S.M.D.

DEVELOPMENT OF DOWN'S SYNDROME CHILDREN FROM BIRTH TO FIVE YEARS

P. Berry, V. P. Gunn, and R. J. Andrews

*Fred and Eleanor Schonell Educational Research Centre,
University of Queensland, Brisbane, Australia 4067*

Mental and motor development in a group of 39 Australian Down's syndrome children, ages ranging from birth to about 5 years, is presented. Results indicate that development in these children is consistently proportional to their chronological age and there is no evidence of plateaus during this period. Such consistent development may be largely due to the early intervention programs that all these children were experiencing.

In his extensive review, Gibson (1978) tentatively extrapolated that "decades of monitoring intelligence in Down's syndrome suggests that intellectual status is improving regardless of home or institutional placement" (p. 40). There are also consistent findings in the syndrome that mental growth decelerates more rapidly as chronological age increases and that there is wide variability between affected individuals.

In this paper developmental data on Down's syndrome children who are taking part in a longitudinal study are presented. This material may be of interest for two reasons. First, the sample comprises a group of Australian-born Down's syndrome children, born between 1976 and 1980, that provides special cross-cultural information relevant to our knowledge and understanding of the development of Down's syndrome infants and young children. Second, the data have been collected on children each of whom has been involved in various ways in a number of newly established intervention programs operated by several public and private agencies; our research team has not been involved at all in the provision of these services. If Gibson's suggestion is correct, it may be possible both to account for general increases in mental development due to such structured programs of early intervention and also to compare these Australian children with those in other countries experiencing similar programs.

There is general agreement concerning the deceleration of mental development over time for Down's syndrome persons. Benda (1949) and Gesell and Amatruda (1964) were among the first to observe increasing developmental delay with age. Zeaman and House (1962) documented the mental ages (MAs) of 97 Down's syndrome children and adults between the ages of 5 and 52 years and formulated an equation based on these data to predict mental development, finding that MA was proportional to 18 × log CA (chronological age). However, as in many earlier studies, these data were based on institutionalized subjects and were collected before there was a significant increase in educational opportunity for the mentally handicapped. A further study by Gibson (1966) of 302 institutionalized Down's syndrome subjects, ages between 18 months and 44 years, produced an interesting MA profile in which three plateaus were apparent—between 4 and 5½ years, when MA stabilized at about 17 months; between 8½ and 11 years, when MA remained at about 31 months; and between 12½ and 17 years, when MA reached an asymptote at about 40 months. Thereafter a decline in MA was evident. Of particular interest here is development at the time of the first plateau, because early intervention (e.g., from birth onward) may well influence mental growth between the ages of 4 and 5½ years.

More recent studies by Carr (1970) and Gath (1978) are also important. Carr undertook an extensive longitudinal study of Down's syndrome infants using the Bayley Scales of Infant Development. The main finding was a substantial decrease in derived IQ (DIQ; derived by the sigma score method) between 1.5 and 10 months. After 10 months, there was a very gradual decline from a DIQ of about 50 at 15 months to less than 40 at about 2 years, when the study terminated. Gath's study did not employ a formal infant assessment test, but some developmental milestones were reported: smiling (median age 10 months), sitting (median age 12 months), walking (median age 24 months), and speaking two meaningful words (median age 18 months). As Gath pointed out, the gap between her Down's syndrome and control infants widened for the later milestones, again corroborating the widely held contention that developmental lag for this group increases with age. Other studies, particularly that of Share and French (1974), also report developmental landmarks in Down's syndrome infants: rolling ($N = 165$, median age 7 months), sitting ($N = 149$, median age 11 months), crawling and pivoting ($N = 123$, median age 13 months) and unsupported walking ($N = 88$, median age 24 months).

These studies have certain limitations because they were undertaken with special groups such as institutionalized children, or because they were cross-sectional rather than longitudinal, or because ratio scores (such as IQ or DIQ) were employed rather than simple mental ages. The present study attempted to overcome some of these problems.

PROCEDURE

Data are presented here on 39 Australian home-reared Down's syndrome infants and 24 control children who are taking part in a longitudinal study of cognitive and social development that began in 1977 (Berry et al., 1981). Developmental data have been collected on the Down's syndrome children (ages 2½ months to 5 years 10 months) and control children (ages 2 months to 5 years) using the Bayley mental and motor scales and the Merrill-Palmer scale. In addition, certain social and motor developmental milestones have been observed.

RESULTS

Figure 1 presents data on the 39 Down's syndrome children tested between 2½ months and 48 months of age; the top of the figure shows the results of 134 assessments on the Bayley Mental Scale of Infant Development. (For practical reasons, not all children could be assessed at the same intervals on the same number of occasions.) These results show consistent overall developmental progression, mental development being generally proportional to chronological age. However, different rates for individual children were clearly evident. There is no evidence of a plateau effect. The bottom of Figure 1 presents the corresponding data for the children on the Bayley Motor Scale of Infant Development from the early months to the toddler years. Again, motor development is consistently proportional to chronological age. The top portion of Figure 2 presents the MA scores of 28 of the older children between the ages of 2 years and 5 years 10 months on the Merrill-Palmer test, the children having been assessed on 57 occasions. Again, it is evident that mental development is consistent and generally proportional to chronological age. The bottom of Figure 2 shows a composite representation of the Bayley mental and motor scales and the Merrill-Palmer data. This includes 136 results for each full Bayley scale and 57 results on the Merrill-Palmer test—thus 193 assessments involving 39 children are presented, undertaken over a period beginning at 2½ months and continuing to a maximum of 5 years 10 months. The three sets of results show the overall pattern of mental and motor development from the early months to about 5 years of age. The best

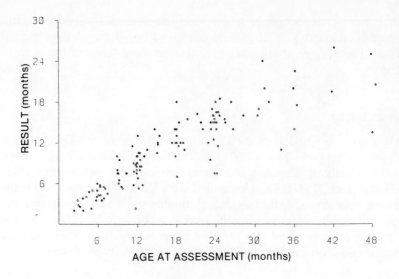

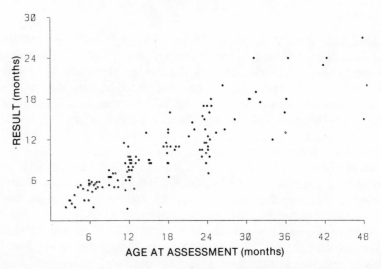

Figure 1.   Scores of Down's syndrome children on the Bayley Mental Scale of Infant Development (**top**) and the Bayley Psychomotor Scale of Infant Development (**bottom**).

representation of this development after 6 months is the simple equation:

$$MA = 3 \text{ months} + \tfrac{1}{2}CA$$

Before 6 months of age most Down's syndrome infants tend to be within or near their MA equivalent.

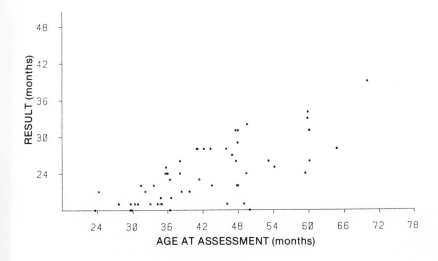

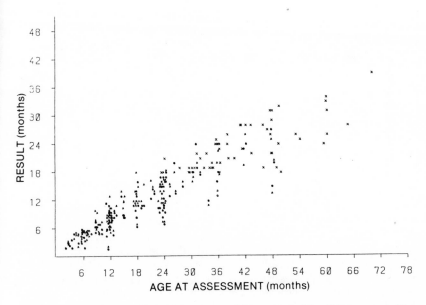

Figure 2. (Top) Scores of Down's syndrome children on the Merrill-Palmer test. (Bottom) Composite scores of Down's syndrome children on the three scales: • = Bayley Psychomotor test; △ = Bayley Mental Test; × = Merrill-Palmer test.

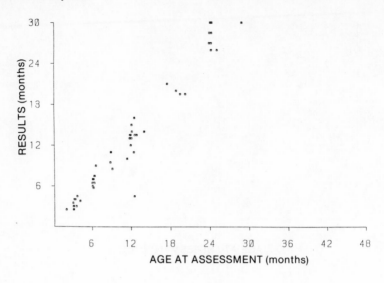

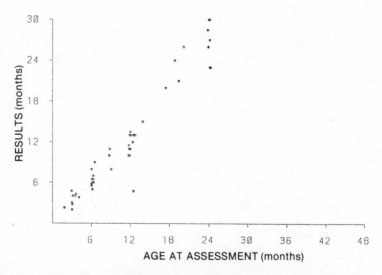

Figure 3.   Scores of control children on the Bayley Mental Scale of Infant Development **(top)** and the Bayley Psychomotor Scale of Infant Development **(bottom)**.

For comparative purposes, a control group was studied during this period and results for this group are presented briefly. Figure 3 shows the results for 24 children ages 2 months to 24 months on the Bayley Mental Scale (top) and the Bayley Motor Scale (bottom). Figure 4 presents results for 22 control children ages 18 months to 5 years on

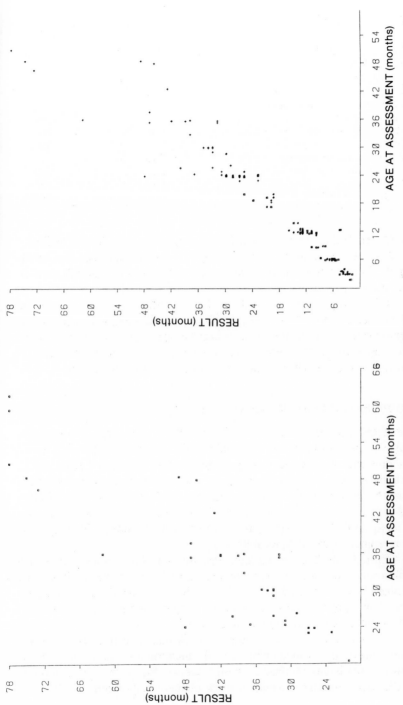

Figure 4. (Left) Scores of control children on the Merrill-Palmer test. (Right) Composite scores of control children on the three scales: ◯ = Bayley Psychomotor test; △ = Bayley Mental test; ✕ = Merrill Palmer test.

Table 1.   Social and motor development in Down's syndrome

Item	Age range (months)		Median (months)
Social milestones			
Social smile	1.5 to	5	2
Says "da-da" or equivalent	5 to	22	10
Says two words (meaningful)	8 to	>45	18
Motor milestones			
Rolls back to front or vice-versa	2 to	12	6
Sits	7 to	12	10
Crawls: nonconventional	7 to	23	11
hands and knees	10 to	25	14
Stands alone	8 to	26	16
Walks independently	15 to	43	24

the Merrill-Palmer test (left) and the compiled results for the children on all three assessments, representing 132 assessment occasions in all (right). Most of the control children fall well within (or slightly above) the "normal" range.

Data are presented in Table 1 for a number of social and motor milestones in Down's syndrome infants. Median ages are shown for each variable, but of interest here are the age ranges when each milestone is attained. It is only when this variability is taken into account that the extent of the heterogeneity in this group can be seen.

COMPARISONS WITH OTHER STUDIES

There are difficulties in relating the results of this study to others because 1) development in "real gain" MA months is presented here, and not data representing proportional scores between CA and MA, such as those of Carr; 2) the study is truly longitudinal and thus differs from the cross-sectional ones of Gibson and of Zeaman and House; and 3) the study is of home-reared Down's syndrome children and not of institutionalized groups, as in most earlier studies. Nevertheless some comparisons are possible.

First, Table 2 shows median ages and ranges for some of the social and motor milestones in three studies. Apart from differences in smiling between our study and Gath's study, there is considerable similarity in median ages for the attainment of "saying two meaningful words" and of sitting and walking in the studies.

Second, there is little evidence in our data that the rate of development decreases as age increases, although the maximum age of these Down's syndrome children is about 5 years. Nevertheless, compared to Gibson's findings no plateaus are observed, and generally the at-

Table 2. Comparison of selected developmental milestones for Down's syndrome children

Landmark	Present study			Gath (1978)			Share and French (1974), cited in Gibson (1978)		
	n	Range (months)	Median (months)	n	Range (months)	Median (months)	n	Range (months)	Median (months)
Smiling	30	1.5–5.0	2	30	2–20	10			
Says two words (meaningful)	27	8–>45	18	21	8–36	18			
Sitting	27	7–23	10	27	7–30	12	149	5–50	11
Walking	17	15–43	24	8	20–30	24	88	14–66	24

tainment in our sample is considerably higher than that reported in his study, thus corroborating his hypothesis that mental development increases.

Third, although again the CA ranges of the children in this study are by no means as wide as those reported by either Zeaman and House or Gibson, there is virtually no evidence that a logarithmic curve best fits developmental progression in our group. Development for the group as a whole is steadily consistent, although rates of development vary considerably between children, as is seen from the age ranges in attaining social and motor milestones in Tables 1 and 2.

CONCLUSIONS

Our data seem to confirm Gibson's finding that the intellectual status of Down's syndrome infants and toddlers, at least, is improving. Perhaps better services, including programs providing opportunities for early intervention in learning, are contributing to this. Certainly for the present group of children a wide variety of programs were available, ranging from occasional home visits by therapists or social workers to intensive programs based on several North American models. It is not possible to say which programs have been most effective because of their variability and the intensity with which they have been followed by the families concerned. However, it is not surprising that most children perform well on the standardized tests because many early intervention programs directly teach the skills required to perform the test items. Perhaps the main effects of better services, which have become more widely available in the 1970s and early 1980s, are to stabilize development in Down's syndrome infants and toddlers and to provide a paradigm for consistent progression for these young children whatever their levels of ability. In addition, the extent to which this contemporary early intervention may influence much later development remains an open question. The long-term effects of early intervention for Down's syndrome youngsters may well be manifested in much later development, not unlike some of the findings in the Head Start program (Bronfenbrenner, 1974). We plan to continue monitoring the development of the present sample and have begun a study of a smaller second cohort of infants in order to replicate this study and provide further data on the earlier development of these children during the present decade.

ACKNOWLEDGMENTS

The authors wish to thank the University of Queensland, Australian Research Grants Committee, and the National Health and Medical Research Council of Australia for their support for this project.

REFERENCES

Benda, C. A. 1949. Mongolism and Cretinism, 2nd ed. Grune & Stratton, New York.

Berry, P., Gunn, P., Andrews, R., and Price, C. 1981. Characteristics of Down syndrome infants and their families. Aust. Pediatr. J. 17:40–43.

Bronfenbrenner, U. 1974. Is early intervention effective? A report on longitudinal evaluations of preschool programs, Vol. 2. Department of Health Education and Welfare, Office of Child Development, Washington, D.C.

Carr, J. 1970. Mental and motor development in young mongol children. J. Ment. Defic. Res. 14:205–220.

Gath, A. 1978. Down's Syndrome and the Family. Academic Press, London.

Gesell, A., and Amatruda, C. A. 1964, Developmental Diagnosis: Normal and Abnormal Child Development, 2nd ed. Harper and Row, New York.

Gibson, D. 1966. Early developmental staging as a prophecy index in Down's syndrome. Am. J. Ment. Defic. 70:825–828.

Gibson, D. 1978. Down's Syndrome: The Psychology of Mongolism. Cambridge University Press, Cambridge, England.

Share, J. B., and French, R. W. 1974. Early motor development in Down's syndrome children. Ment. Retard. 12:23.

Zeaman, D., and House, B. J. 1962. Mongoloid MA is proportional to log CA. Child Dev. 33:481–488.

SECTION IV
Language and Communication

PERSPECTIVES AND PROGRESS IN MENTAL RETARDATION
Volume I—Social, Psychological, and Educational Aspects
Edited by J. M. Berg

A DEVELOPMENTAL STAGE–BASED ASSESSMENT INSTRUMENT FOR EARLY COMMUNICATION DEVELOPMENT

A. E. Hogan[1] and J. M. Seibert[2]
[1] Department of Psychology, University of Miami, P. O. Box 248185, Coral Gables, Florida 33124
[2] Mailman Center for Child Development, University of Miami, Miami, Florida 33101

A developmental stage model is proposed as a framework for organizing a set of scales to assess early social-communication development. The model includes a horizontal organizational aspect that links different behaviors of the same cognitive complexity to the same stage. A vertical organizational aspect leads to a division of the social-communication domain into parallel-developing scale dimensions. Previous research conducted by the authors on the validity of the structural stage construct is briefly reviewed. The paper concludes with recent evidence from a factor-analytic study that supports the subdivision of the social-communication domain into scale dimensions.

THE MODEL

The research we have been engaged in for the past several years has been directed at developing and validating a set of assessment scales for measuring early social-communicative development during the first 2 years of life. The scales differ from typical standardized, norm-

The research reported in this paper was based in part on a master's thesis conducted by the first author. The research was supported in part by the Mailman Foundation and by OSE Grant G007802091.

referenced instruments in that 1) they are explicitly grounded in developmental theory; 2) they are intended to serve as a structured interactive observational system; and 3) their organization is intended to suggest how interventions might be arranged.

In this paper we describe briefly the instrument, called the Early Social-Communication Scales (ESCS) (Seibert and Hogan, 1982a), and discuss research that tests the theoretical model. The ESCS have been developed from a cognitive-developmental framework, meaning that the scales are intended to assess changes in the organization of the infant's interactional competencies. A neo-Piagetian stage model (Uzgiris, 1976; McCall et al., 1977; Fischer, 1980) divides development across the first 2 years of life into five stages. With each successive stage, the child displays greater voluntary control over behavior and increasingly differentiated information-processing capacities. At the fifth stage, symbolic or representational thought emerges, opening new linguistic possibilities for the child's communication system. The stage model is used to organize the ESCS horizontally; it provides a basis for assigning different social and communicative behaviors to the same developmental level if they represent the same organizational structure.

The model's other organizational aspect divides the domain of behaviors to be assessed vertically into several parallel-developing dimensions. The first distinction is between the social-animate and physical-inanimate worlds, i.e., skills directed at people and skills directed at objects (Fischer, 1980). The same global structures are hypothesized to underlie and organize developments in both areas. Skills in both areas emerge through parallel and identical stage sequences. Each area is then further divided into several dimensions. The subdivision into dimensions, which provide the conceptual basis for individual scales, is based on the actual or potential *function* that the interaction is to accomplish.

Within the social-communicative area, three major functions are differentiated: social interaction, joint attention, and behavior regulation. Social interaction includes behaviors that are generally nondirective, gamelike, and playful, with a focus on the pleasure of the dyadic exchange. Joint attention involves a sharing of attention to an object or event of mutual interest, with the pleasure apparently derived from the sharing of a common focus external to the dyad. Behavior regulation is directive and externally goal oriented, with satisfaction generally derived from having a need or want met through the partner's compliant response to a demand or request. Each function has been differentiated into a *responding* and an *initiating* dimension, to reflect the alternative roles the infant may play in any interaction. The capacity to *maintain* for several turns in an interaction is also represented as a distinguishable dimension for social interaction and joint attention. In all, this analysis generates eight parallel dimensions, represented by the eight scales of the ESCS. The evidence for these dimensions should increase with development, reflecting the growth-related processes of differentiation and integration of functions (Werner and Kaplan, 1963). Nevertheless, the origins of these functions should be traceable to the earliest stages of development.

In summary, the ESCS is an interactive observational system that is used to determine at which of five levels of cognitive complexity a child is performing for each of eight functional scale dimensions. The theoretical model predicts that a child's performance across the eight dimensions should fall within a narrow range of stages, and not necessarily all at the same level. Performance-related factors (e.g., experience, motivation, information-processing demands) affect what level of competence is observed in each dimension (Fischer, 1980).

The assessment process requires the presentation of a range of structured eliciting situations in an interesting, child-oriented physical environment. The successful tester is aware of the range of functional categories and can use them rapidly to organize observations of the child's behaviors and respond appropriately to the child's signals at whatever level they are produced.

RESEARCH ON THE STAGES

Most of the research to validate the scales has been directed at testing aspects of the horizontal organization, that is, the cognitive stage model. Because these results are reported in detail elsewhere (Seibert et al., 1982, 1984), they are reviewed only briefly here. Results of more recent analyses aimed at validating aspects of the vertical (scale) organization of the model are discussed in greater detail.

The research has been carried out with a heterogeneous sample of over 100 normal, at-risk, and handicapped infants and toddlers. Handicapped subjects represented a variety of disabilities and degrees of severity. Although sample heterogeneity can create serious problems for some kinds of developmental questions and analyses, it has advantages over homogeneously defined samples for the investigation of universal aspects of development, such as general cognitive organization and stages (Seibert et al., 1984). The advantages should become clearer as the results of our investigations are described.

The data base compiled on these children includes chronological age (CA), Bayley Mental (MA) and Psychomotor ages (PA), individual stage scores for each of the scales of the ESCS and their averages, and similar individual stage scores and their averages for an adapted version of the Uzgiris-Hunt Scales (Uzgiris and Hunt, 1975). The Uzgiris-Hunt Scales assess primarily object-oriented cognitive skills. Our research has adapted them to exclude any socially oriented items (e.g., the imitation scales) in order to avoid confounding item overlap with the ESCS. Each scale has also been organized according to the same five-stage sequence that organizes the ESCS.

The results in support of the model's horizontal organization can be summarized as follows:

1. Correlations between average ESCS level scores and average Adapted Uzgiris-Hunt scores (AUHS) were consistently 0.85 or higher across all subsamples studied, provided that a wide developmental range of scores was represented in the sample (Seibert et al., 1984). Correlations between the cognitive measures persisted despite major reductions in the magnitude of their correlations with CA and PA to near-zero and nonsignificant levels. Deliberate sampling strategies had been employed to construct the samples for which the relationship of CA and PA to the cognitive measures was substantially reduced, in order to investigate the effects of the manipulations on the correlation between the cognitive measures. In one sample, the uniquely shared variance between AUHS and ESCS scores was 70% *after* controlling for the effects of CA and PA.

    A similar pattern of results emerged when the correlations of the individual scale scores of the ESCS with each other, with the AUHS average, and with CA and PA were examined (Seibert et al., 1982). Apparently, level of motor development was not a necessary mediator of the relationship between the social and object cognitive domains, lending support to the model's claim of a specifically cognitive link.

2. Further evaluation of this structural link was examined by comparing each child's average ESCS score with his average AUHS score (Seibert et al., 1984). A frequency histogram of the differences in means revealed an approximately normal distribution, with the mean, median, and mode at zero. Over 40% of the discrepancies fell at zero and more than two-thirds of the scores were less than half a stage from each other. Differences greater than zero were symmetrically distributed on both sides of the zero point, indicating that either domain was as likely to lead in development as the other if a discrepancy existed. These results conformed to the stage model's predictions. Congruence should be common but not universal because performance factors can interfere with the

expression of competence in some dimensions. However, extreme discrepancies of more than a stage were rare, representing less than 4% of the cases.

3. The remaining evidence in support of the horizontal stage organization must be considered in the context of previously reported stagelike patterns in developmental data from normal children (McCall et al., 1977). Because CA could not be used as the measure for organizing our sample along a developmental continuum, we used the Bayley MA, which correlated highly with ESCS and AUHS scores across samples. The percentage of scale scores representative of each of the levels for all subjects at each MA, in monthly intervals, was plotted. The resulting graph displayed the MA at which the different stages emerged, dominated, and receded. The transition from the first to the second stage as the dominant level of organization occurred at an MA of 2 to 3 months, the transition from the second to the third stage at 7 to 8 months MA, the transition from third to fourth stage at 12 to 13 months MA, and the final transition into the fifth stage at about 25 to 26 months MA (Seibert et al., submitted for publication). With the exception of the final transition, all of the mental ages corresponded to the chronological ages that McCall et al. (1977) reported for stage transitions in their Berkeley Growth Study sample. The final transition occurred at about 21, rather than 25, months in their sample.

These results suggested the validity of the model's horizontal organization. More recent findings, not previously reported, supported some of the scale dimension distinctions derived from the model's vertical organization.

RESEARCH ON THE DIMENSIONS

Factor analysis was used to test the a priori theoretical organization of the domains into the various functions and dimensions. If the distinctions made correspond to psychological reality, the scales would be expected to load on factors in ways interpretable within the model. The data for these analyses were 112 completed test batteries on 86 children, ages 8 to 38 months, with MAs between 8 and 25 months. The data pool was divided into two MA ranges: 8–16 months ($n = 51$) and 17–25 months ($n = 61$). A series of factor analyses was then undertaken to investigate the structure of the relationships among the five AUHS scales and seven of the eight ESCS scales (there were insufficient data on Maintains Joint Attention). In all instances, the principal axis method was used with R^2 as the initial communality estimate and a drop in the eigenvalue to less than 1 as the criterion to stop factoring. When more than one factor was extracted, rotation was to the Varimax criterion (Kaiser, 1958).   Results for the analyses are shown in Table 1.

For the developmentally younger sample, three factors emerged that accounted for 49.5%, 10%, and 8.9% of the variance, respectively. The rotated factor loadings in Table 1 suggested the presence of 1) a general social factor; 2) a communication factor; and 3) an object-oriented cognitive factor. The scales that loaded most highly on Factor 1 were the three social interaction scales, with moderate loadings for three of the four other ESCS. The scales that loaded most highly on Factor 2 were the joint attention and behavior regulation scales of the ESCS and the Means-Ends and Schemes scales of the AUHS. The scales that loaded most highly on Factor 3 were the object-oriented scales, i.e., the AUHS scales.

As can be seen in the Table, four factors emerged from the data for the MA 17–25 month sample. These four factors accounted for 27.6%, 14.9%, 11%, and 9.2% of the total variance, respectively. The rotated factor loadings suggested the presence of 1) a communication factor; 2) a social factor; 3) a shared visual attention and reference factor; and 4) an object-oriented cognitive factor. The scales that loaded most highly on Factor 1 were the joint attention and behavior regulation scales of the ESCS and the Causality scale of the AUHS. The scales that loaded most highly on Factor 2 were two of the three social interaction scales of the ESCS. Factor 3 had loadings from both the AUHS and the ESCS, primarily the Space and Schemes scales from the AUHS and the joint attention scales from the ESCS. The scales that loaded most highly on Factor 4 were the three remaining scales of the AUHS: Object Permanence, Means-Ends, and Causality.

Results of these factor analyses cannot be interpreted unequivocally. Total sample size for each is small, so that firm interpretation would be hazardous. Nevertheless, the pattern is intriguing. The shift from three to four factors across the two age groupings can be interpreted as evidence of increasing differentiation of cognitive factors across the developmental span (Werner and Kaplan, 1963). In particular, the communication factor in the MA 8–16 month group (Factor 2) may diverge into two factors (Factors 1 and 3) in the MA 17–25 month group. The factors appear to reflect an instrumental-communication factor and a referential-communication factor. Interestingly, this second referential-communication factor includes two scales from the Uzgiris-Hunt Scales, Space and Schemes, both of which have been mentioned as good predictors of communication abilities at a younger age (Bates et al., 1977). In general, the pattern of loadings intuitively

Table 1. Factor analysis of sensorimotor and social-communication scales

Rotated factor matrix	MA 8–16 months (N = 51)			MA 17–25 months (N = 61)			
	Factor 1	Factor 2	Factor 3	Factor 1	Factor 2	Factor 3	Factor 4
Adapted Uzgiris-Hunt scores							
Object permanence	0.39	0.29	0.49	0.12	0.08	0.04	0.32
Operational causality	0.19	0.16	0.71	0.46	-0.20	-0.04	0.31
Space	0.13	0.38	0.67	0.14	-0.10	0.70	-0.12
Schemes	0.45	0.47	0.44	0.11	0.06	0.56	0.12
Means-Ends	0.23	0.57	0.33	0.00	-0.08	0.05	0.47
Early social-communication scales							
Responds/joint attention	0.02	0.62	0.21	0.59	0.18	0.50	0.21
Initiates/joint attention	0.40	0.48	0.27	0.39	-0.03	0.41	0.08
Responds/behavior regulation	0.38	0.61	0.20	0.63	0.10	0.22	0.29
Initiates/behavior regulation	0.53	0.72	0.12	0.73	0.12	0.31	-0.13
Responds/social interaction	0.62	0.13	0.41	0.14	0.28	0.36	0.19
Initiates/social interaction	0.75	0.24	0.09	0.20	0.86	-0.08	0.01
Maintains/social interaction	0.79	0.22	0.24	-0.11	0.81	0.15	-0.03

supports distinctions made between the object and social domains and among the social-communicative functions within the ESCS.

In conclusion, research provides empirical support for a number of claims made by the theoretical model used to organize the ESCS. Further research to evaluate scale ordinality and stage transition and consolidation over time is currently underway in longitudinal research. A large cross-sectional study is being conducted to replicate and extend the factor analytic findings. The framework, by providing specific observational categories and defining the tester's role explicitly in interactive terms, also provides a foundation for developing interventions (Seibert and Hogan, 1982b).

REFERENCES

Bates, E., Benigni, L., Bretherton, I., Camaioni, L., and Volterra, V., 1977. From gesture to first word: On cognitive and social prerequisites. In: M. Lewis and A. Rosenblum (eds.), Interaction, Conversation and the Development of Language. John Wiley & Sons, Inc., New York.

Fischer, K. W. 1980. A theory of cognitive development: The control and construction of hierarchies of skills. Psychol. Rev. 87:477–531.

Kaiser, H. F. 1958. The Varimax criterion for analytic rotation in factor analysis. Psychometrika 23:187–200.

McCall, R., Eichorn, D., and Hogarty, P. 1977. Transitions in early mental development. Monogr. Soc. Res. Child Dev. 42(3), No. 171.

Seibert, J. M., and Hogan, A. E. 1982a. Procedures manual for the early social-communication scales (ESCS). Unpublished manuscript, University of Miami Mailman Center for Child Development, Miami, Florida.

Seibert, J. M., and Hogan, A. E. 1982b. A model for assessing social and object skills and planning intervention. In: D. McClowry, A. Guilford, and S. Richardson (eds.), Infant Communication: Development, Assessment and Intervention. Grune & Stratton, New York.

Seibert, J. M., Hogan, A. E., and Mundy, P. C. Structure and stages in early cognitive development. (submitted for publication to Intelligence)

Seibert, J. M., Hogan, A. E., and Mundy, P. C. 1982. Assessing interactional competencies: The early social-communication scales. Inf. Ment. Health J. 3:244–258.

Seibert, J. M., Hogan, A. E., and Mundy, P. C. 1984. Developmental assessment of social-communication skills for early intervention: Testing a cognitive stage model. In: R. A. Glow (ed.), Advances in the Behavioral Measurement of Children. JAI Press, Greenwich, Connecticut.

Uzgiris, I. C. 1976. Organization of sensorimotor intelligence. In: M. Lewis (ed.), Origins of Intelligence. Plenum Press, New York.

Uzgiris, I. C., and Hunt, J. McV. 1975. Assessment in Infancy: Ordinal Scales of Psychological Development. University of Illinois Press, Urbana.

Werner, H., and Kaplan, B. 1963. Symbol Formation. John Wiley & Sons, Inc., New York.

PERSPECTIVES AND PROGRESS IN MENTAL RETARDATION
Volume I—Social, Psychological, and Educational Aspects
Edited by J. M. Berg
Copyright © 1984 by I.A.S.S.M.D.

A STUDY OF MOTHER-CHILD VERBAL INTERACTION STRATEGIES WITH MOTHERS OF YOUNG DEVELOPMENTALLY DELAYED CHILDREN

P. Price

School of Education, Macquarie University, North Ryde, New South Wales, Australia

This study has investigated the verbal interaction strategies used by mothers in interaction with their young developmentally delayed children while the children were enrolled in an early language intervention program. Language samples were collected at pre- and posttest with a 6-month interval, and analyzed to provide information regarding mother and child mean length of utterance, ratio of mother:child talk, syntactic complexity of utterances, and the pattern of verbal interaction strategies using an initiation-facilitation-feedback framework. Tentative evidence for changing patterns of strategy usage was found as children move from sound imitation to the 2-word + level of early language acquisition skills.

Recent theoretical explanations of the process of early language acquisition have suggested that the key factor in the acquisition process is the interaction between the child and the primary caregiver (McLean and Snyder-McLean, 1978). This emphasis has given rise to significant research investigating the nature of the behavior of adult caregivers interacting with their normally developing children. Comprehensive reviews of this research have been made by Mahoney and Seely (1976), Moerk (1976), Cross (1981), and Chapman (1981). Convincing evidence for reciprocity in the use of strategies between mother and child has been found in the systematic changes that occur in maternal speech as children grow older. This has been clearly demonstrated by Farrow et al. (1979) and by Bellinger (1980), who concluded that, in the case of children who are progressing normally in language development, it is possible to predict the age (and stage) of the child from the pattern of the mother's speech. The degree to which causality can be ascribed to the relationships that have been identified is an area of continuing controversy.

The identification of specific adult verbal characteristics that may significantly affect language development in the child has important implications for those concerned with facilitating language development in developmentally delayed children. McLean and Snyder-McLean (1978) emphasized that the process of language acquisition for this population tends to follow the normal pattern but at a slower pace. Research information concerning the nature of interactions between this population and its caregivers is relatively limited and has provided controversial evidence on such basic issues as whether mothers of delayed children use strategies different from those used by mothers interacting with normally developing children (Rondal, 1978; Cross, 1981). Rondal, comparing Down's syndrome children with non-retarded children matched for mean length of utterance (MLU), found no significant differences in mother language between the two groups, and concluded that the linguistic environment of these children was "appropriate," if we accept as appropriate the indices from studies of normally developing children and their predominantly middle-class mothers. His implication was that the characteristics of the delayed child did not specifically affect the mother's input.

This finding is at variance with that of Cross (1981), who noted significant differences in linguistic input between fast- and slow-developing children in terms of such factors as following the child's topic, expansions, and partial repetitions (which were associated with accelerated progress) and self-answering, dysfluency, and higher proportions of maternal utterances (associated with slow progress). Cross argued strongly that the child's communicative and linguistic pattern has a determining role in the linguistic and pragmatic adjustments made by parents. Mahoney and Seely (1976) have observed that there may be peripheral evidence to suggest that delayed children do not develop nonverbal behaviors upon which later verbal communication is dependent, and that various responses of caregivers may further impede the language-learning process. Cross's finding that mothers' speech patterns to deaf children were less adequate than those used with normal, younger siblings supports this contention.

Research with developmentally delayed children has clearly demonstrated that this population experiences difficulty in acquiring language and communication skills, and that mere exposure to a normally stimulating environment is inadequate. Several studies have reported success using a more structured approach but within an environmental framework and using parents as language trainers (MacDonald, 1976; Bochner et al., 1980). Increasingly, the caregiver-infant interaction is seen as the central context for the development of communicative skills and ultimately language acquisition, and interventionists have the difficult task of trying to determine from recent research studies which variables may be most significant in facilitating this development, and whether the mother-child interchange is amenable to modification. In a study of six Down's syndrome children, Cheseldine and McConkey (1979) isolated differences between strategies used by "successful" and "unsuccessful" mothers in a language training program, and in a second stage succeeded in modifying the strategies of the "unsuccessful" mothers with a concomitant increase in child progress on the language task. Replication and extension of this approach is needed.

Further experimental investigation of the strategies identified by Cross (1981) as being associated with fast and slow language development may well be significant for intervention procedures focusing on the interaction between mother and developmentally delayed child. Entirely different input strategies may be necessary, and detailed longitudinal study of individual cases of mothers interacting with their developmentally delayed children as they pass through the early stages of language acquisition may provide the information needed to clarify this issue.

The present study was designed as the first stage in a longitudinal investigation of mother-child verbal interaction patterns, with mothers of young developmentally delayed children who were enrolled in a language intervention program that involved training mothers to facilitate the acquisition of early language skills in their children. The specific aims of the study were to determine 1) whether the patterns of verbal interaction strategies used by mothers change as children reach different developmental stages in early language acquisition, and 2) whether there are identifiable differences in the verbal interaction patterns used by mothers of children who make fast or slow progress in the acquisition of language skills, as measured by gains in MLU.

METHOD

The subjects were 10 developmentally and language delayed children, ages between 1 year 9 months and 5 years 10 months, who were enrolled in a language intervention program. The program involvement lasted 6 months, with preprogram assessment conducted in the first 2 weeks, followed by 12 weekly individual appointments for each mother and child, then phased down to fortnightly and then monthly visits followed by postprogram assessment. Data on follow-up testing at 12 and 18 months are not yet available for analysis. Mother-child taped language samples in a free play setting were collected as part of the assessment procedures.

The tapes were transcribed with the assistance of context notes made by an observer who was familiar with the dyad. The transcriptions were analyzed using all the utterances made within a 10-minute period. This procedure was chosen because the amount and rate of mother talk was considered an important variable.

ANALYSIS

Mothers' Speech

The analysis of mothers' speech included:

1. MLU at pre- and posttest using a morpheme count.
2. Ratio of mother to child talk at pre- and posttest.
3. Syntactic complexity, with each utterance classified as phrase without verb, simple sentence, conjoined multiclause sentence and complex multiclause sentence, measured at pre- and posttest.
4. Frequency of mothers' verbal interaction strategies. The strategies selected were based upon Moerk's (1976) reports of nuclear interaction patterns that involved the mother in initiating followed by child responding, mother correcting or facilitating, and further child response receiving feedback. The choice of facilitating strategies selected was influenced by recent studies by Cross (1981). Some categories selected initially occurred with such small frequencies that these were excluded from further consideration. In other cases categories were amalgamated for the purpose of this report, as with different question types and feedback categories. Categories used are listed under strategies in Table 1.

Children's Speech

Measures of children's speech included: 1) MLU at pre- and posttest; 2) rates of mother-to-child talk at pre- and posttest; and 3) syntactic complexity, using the category system applied to mother utterances.

RESULTS

A single case study approach has been adopted for the discussion and interpretation of results, in view of the small sample. In terms of the

Table 1. Mean percentage frequency of verbal interaction strategies used by mothers at three language levels before and after a language intervention program

Strategies	Sound imitation		Single word		2 word +		Mean total usage
	Pre	Post	Pre	Post	Pre	Post	
Verbal demand	0	1	1	4	0	2	1
Control demand	44	45	33	26	19	18	31
Commenting	17	20	10	18	16	9	15
Questions	11	15	18	26	41	43	25
Modeling	7	5	6	6	3	0	5
Expansion	0	1	0	2	2	2	1
Mother-interpretation	1	0	1	2	3	6	2
Mother self-repetition	11	0	9	2	2	0	4
Conversational-interactional	5	4	6	3	4	10	5
Reflection	2	3	3	3	3	2	3
Negation	1	1	3	2	3	2	2
Positive confirmation	0	4	5	4	5	5	4
Praise-nonverbal	1	1	5	2	0	1	2

expressive language levels in the training program, the children were identified at the following stages on entry: 2 children at sound imitation, 5 at the single-word stage, and 3 at the 2+-word stage. Results are discussed in relation to these stages.

Mother and Child MLU

At pretest, 7 of the children were at the sound imitation or 1-word stage, and 3 children at the 2-word stage. These differences were reflected in MLU scores of mothers and children (see Table 2). The average MLU for mothers of 1-word stage children was 3.1 and for children 1.1, a difference of 2.0. For the 2-word group, mother MLU was 4.7 and child MLU 2.0, a difference of 2.7, suggesting that these mothers followed the pattern that has been found with normal dyads of adjusting the length of their utterances to that of their children. At posttest only 4 children were at the 1-word stage with mother MLU 3.2 and child MLU 1.2, a difference of 2.0. For the 6 children at the 2-word level mother MLU averaged 4.0 and child MLU 1.9, a difference of 2.1. The reduced MLU difference between pre- and posttest for the 2-word group may reflect two factors—3 of the 6 children were just entering the 2-word stage, with MLUs lower than those of the 3 children clearly at this stage at pretest, and there was a reduction in MLU for 2 mothers whose MLU was high at pretest.

These findings tend to support those of other studies showing that mothers do modify the lengths of their utterances and adjust them to growth in child MLU, that individual differences are marked, and that some mothers are capable of modifying their MLU in a downward direction during the course of a language intervention program.

Child Opportunity—Ratio of Mother-to-Child Talk

Of the 10 mothers in the program, 8 reduced their proportion of talk from pre- to posttest, with mother:child ratios ranging from 9:1 at pretest to 1:1 at posttest. The mean ratio at pretest was 3.8:1, and 1.9:1 at posttest—a considerable reduction. An increased rate of talking was observed in only one mother whose initial ratio was very low. The 3 mothers with a ratio of 1:1 at posttest were all interacting with children at the 3- and 4-word level, suggesting that as children become more fluent mothers allow them more opportunity.

Syntactic Complexity

Mothers of all 7 children at the 1-word and below stage used only verbless phrases and simple sentences at both pre- and posttest. The results ranged from 20% phrases and 80% simple sentences to 40% and 60%, respectively. Only 2 mothers showed altered patterns at posttest,

Table 2. Mother and child MLUs at pre- and posttest, grouped for language stage on entry

Word stage	Child			Mother		
	Pretest MLU[a]	Posttest MLU[a]	Difference	Pretest MLU	Posttest MLU	Difference
Sound imitation						
Child 1	1.0 (4)	1.1 (22)	+0.1	2.9	3.4	+0.5
Child 2	1.0 (2)	1.0 (20)	0	3.3	3.4	+0.1
Single-word stage						
Child 3	1.1 (30)	1.2 (78)	+0.1	3.9	3.7	−0.2
Child 4	1.0 (16)	1.2 (38)	+0.2	2.6	2.7	+0.1
Child 5	1.0 (23)	1.4 (83)	+0.4	3.3	2.4	−0.9
Child 6	1.2 (71)	1.7 (71)	+0.5	2.8	4.5	+1.7
Child 7	1.5 (35)	2.1 (80)	+0.6	3.1	2.5	−0.6
2 +-word stage						
Child 8	2.1 (22)	2.3 (98)	+0.2	4.0	4.7	+0.7
Child 9	2.0 (64)	2.4 (80)	+0.4	4.0	4.9	+0.9
Child 10	1.8 (33)	2.6 (181)	+0.8	6.2	5.3	−0.9

[a] Numbers in parentheses represent the number of intelligible utterances in the language sample upon which child MLU was calculated.

one having increased the use of simple sentences, in line with her child's gain in MLU of 0.8 and use of 4-word sentences. The other showed a reduction in use of simple sentences, in line with a reduction in her MLU. Six of the children at this level were using 100% phrases at pretest, and one was using 80% phrases. All 6 showed growth in the use of simple sentences up to 30% at posttest. The seventh child made no growth. For the 3 children at the 2-word level the range of phrases was from 20–30% to approximately 70% simple sentences with conjoined multiclause sentences accounting for less than 10% of utterances. Two of the children at this level showed an increase in their use of simple sentences at posttest.

These results strongly support the finding from other studies that mothers simplify the complexity of their utterances when talking to children at the 1- and 2-word stages and that their language increases gradually in complexity in line with child growth.

Verbal Interaction Strategies

The overall pattern of strategy usage was similar for all groups, with 62–80% initiating utterances, 10–14% facilitation, and 4–16% feedback. Frequency of detailed strategy usage is shown in Table 1.

The 2 children at sound imitation level were characterized by a very high level of control demand, above average use of commenting, and low use of questioning. Differences were observed between the 2 children from pre- to posttest, with child 1 (see Table 2) receiving reduced control demand and increased commenting, modeling, expansion, and feedback. Child 2 experienced increased control demand and questioning, and reduced modeling and feedback for nonverbal behavior only. MLU gains were 0.1 and 0, respectively. The high level of control demand at this level is consistent with the expectation that mothers would be more directive and use fewer questions when interacting with a child of very limited vocabulary. The strategy pattern for child 1, with the exception of feedback, is in keeping with the strategies identified by Cheseldine and McConkey (1979) as discriminating significantly between successful and unsuccessful mothers in a language-teaching task.

Five children were at the single-word stage, and the pattern of strategy usage showed considerable variation. Children 4, 5, 6, and 7, with MLU gains of 0.2, 0.4, 0.5, and 0.6, respectively, were characterized by initially high rates of control demand that reduced at posttest, an increased or moderately high use of commenting, and, for children 5 and 7, a low level of questioning in contrast to the marked increase to high levels for children 4 and 6. All 4 children had an increasing or moderately high rate of modeling and expansion, and children 4, 5, and 6 had reduced rates of mother simplification and relatively high feedback rates. Child 7 received low feedback at both pre- and posttest. Child 3, who had an MLU gain of 0.1, had a moderate use of control demand, increased commenting, and reduced questioning, in common with children 5 and 7, but no modeling or expansion, high conversational-interactional, and low feedback, half of which was for nonverbal behavior.

The single most striking factor at the 1-word stage was the variation in strategy pattern. A reduction in control demand was combined with either an increase in commenting or an increase in questioning, increased modeling and expansion, and a high level of feedback. Where a high rate of questioning was not combined with feedback, as was the case for child 4, MLU growth was low, as it was for child 3, where high control demand was combined with a lack of modeling and expansion and a low level of feedback. However, low feedback combined with a high level of commenting, modeling, and expansion proved a satisfactory pattern for child 7, who had an MLU gain of 0.6.

At the 2+-word stage, children 8 and 9 had similar patterns with very high rates of questioning, low rates of control demand and commenting, reduced modeling, expansion, and feedback at posttest and high rates of mother interpretation and conversation-interaction. Children 8 and 9 had MLU gains of 0.2 and 0.4, respectively. Child 10, who had an MLU gain of 0.8, differed from the other two children in that questioning had reduced from pre- to posttest from excessively high to moderate usage, with low commenting and low feedback, and reduced questioning combined with moderate rates of control demand and commenting, low modeling and expansion, and a high rate of feedback. Two clear patterns were evident at this stage—a high rate of questioning combined with low commenting and low feedback, and reduced questioning combined with moderate commenting and high feedback. Low rates of modeling and expansion applied in both cases.

DISCUSSION

The specific purpose of this study was to determine whether mothers change their patterns of verbal interaction as children move through early stages of language acquisition, and to determine whether there are identifiable differences in verbal interaction patterns associated with fast or slow progress as measured by increased MLU. Some tentative evidence for change in strategy pattern has been presented. A high usage of control demand at the sound imitation stage tends to give way to patterns of either increased commenting or increased questioning, with combinations of high and low usage of modeling, expansion, and feedback at the later stages. The high rate of questioning in association with evidence of satisfactory growth in MLU observed at the 1- and 2-word stages is at variance with Cheseldine and Mc-Conkey's (1979) findings, but Farrow et al. (1979) identified yes/no questions as one of the mother strategies significantly related to fast development in normal children. Detailed analysis of question types was not carried out in this study but is obviously necessary. The relationship between questioning and feedback requires further investigation, as does the role played by commenting, modeling, and expansion. Cheseldine and McConkey's (1979) argument for the importance of these strategies is in terms of providing the child with frequent, simple models of the language that he requires to express his needs and describe his activities. Their criticism of a questioning strategy is in terms of its inability to provide this model, but at the 2 + -word level, combined with appropriate feedback, it may be a successful strategy when used by a mother sensitively tuned to the child's level.

Any findings in relation to strategy patterns identifiably associated with fast and slow rates of progress as measured by MLU must be considered extremely tentative for two reasons. First, growth from one stage to the next is a gradual process, and not necessarily an even one. Secondly, the number of children in the present total sample was limited, with only 2 and 3 children, respectively, at the sound imitation and 2-word stage. Within these constraints there is tentative evidence to suggest that an extremely high level of control demand or questioning unaccompanied by commenting, modeling, expansions, or feedback may be associated with slower progress, but the significance of the various strategies is not yet clear; findings from other studies suggest that the key factor may be the extent to which the mother follows the child's topic (Cheseldine and McConkey, 1979; Cross, 1981). Chapman (1981) supported this viewpoint, stating that it is the linguistically responsive environment that should accelerate language acquisition in the early stages, with the mother creating order in the child's world and responding consistently to his/her communicative attempts. Investigation of interaction patterns within this framework may be more fruitful than the many studies involving frequency counts of strategies. Analysis of discourse sequences is needed to tap the nature of the exchange between mother and child. Longitudinal studies are essential for the developmentally delayed, who are slow to move from one stage to the next.

REFERENCES

Bellinger, D. 1980. Consistency in the pattern of change in mothers speech: Some discriminant analyses. J. Child Lang. 7:469–487.

Bochner, S., Price, P., Salamon, L., and Brownell, M. A. 1980. Early language intervention with handicapped children. Aust. J. Hum. Commun. Disord. 8:48–63.

Chapman, R. S. 1981, Mother-child interaction in the second year of life. In: R. L. Schiefelbusch and D. Bricker (eds.), Early Language: Acquisition and Intervention. University Park Press, Baltimore.

Cheseldine, S., and McConkey, R. 1979. Parental speech to young Down's syndrome children: An intervention study. Am. J. Ment. Defic. 83:612–620.

Cross, T. 1981. The linguistic experience of slow learners. in: A. R. Nesdale (ed.), Advances in Child Development. Cambridge University Press, Cambridge, England.

Farrow, D., Nelson, K., and Benedict, H. 1979. Mothers' speech to children and syntactic development: Some simple relationships. J. Child Lang. 6:423–442.

MacDonald, J. D. 1976. Environmental language-intervention. In: F. Withrow and C. Nygren (eds.), Language and the Handicapped Learner. Charles E. Merrill Publishing Co., Columbus, Ohio.

Mahoney, G. J. and Seely, P. B. 1976. The role of the social agent in language acquisition: Implications for language intervention. In: N. R. Ellis (ed.) Research in Mental Retardation. Academic Press, Inc., New York.

McLean, T. E. and Snyder-McLean, L. K. 1978, A Transactional Approach to Early Language Training. Charles E. Merrill Publishing Co., Columbus, Ohio.

Moerk, E. L. 1976. Processes of language teaching and training in the interactions of mother-child dyads. Child. Dev. 47:1064–1078.

Rondal, J. 1978. Maternal speech to normal and Down's syndrome children matched for mean length of utterance. Monograph of the American Association on Mental Deficiency. American Association on Mental Deficiency, Washington, D.C.

PERSPECTIVES AND PROGRESS IN MENTAL RETARDATION
Volume I—Social, Psychological, and Educational Aspects
Edited by J. M. Berg
Copyright © 1984 by I.A.S.S.M.D.

SELECTIVE PREFERENCES TO DIFFERENT SPEECH STIMULI IN INFANTS WITH DOWN'S SYNDROME

S. M. Glenn and C. C. Cunningham

Hester Adrian Research Centre, The University, Manchester, M13 9PL, England

An apparatus has been developed, based on Friedlander's (1968) PLAY-TEST, to study auditory preferences in normal and abnormal infant populations. Using this apparatus, it has been shown that at around 9 months' developmental level nonhandicapped and Down's syndrome infants show similar patterns of responding to speech. However, Down's syndrome infants have longer response durations to preferred stimuli, suggesting auditory processing differences between the two groups. Furthermore at around 18 months' developmental level nonhandicapped infants have significantly increased their response to mother's speech, whereas the Down's syndrome group show a significant decrease. Implications for intervention are discussed.

Many workers have demonstrated a marked delay in language production in the child with Down's syndrome (e.g., Rondal, 1982), yet it is not clear how this delay may relate to perceptual difficulties in the reception of speech. In communicating with infants it is necessary to know what controls their listening behavior. It is known (e.g., Eimas and Tartter, 1979) that by 6 months of age infants can discriminate a wide variety of simple speech stimuli, and that by 12 months comprehension of speech can be demonstrated on standard tests, but to what aspects of the linguistic environment is the 6- to 12-month-old infant paying attention?

This research was supported by a grant from the Department of Health and Social Security Small Grants Committee to the first author.

In this context the study of perceptual preferences is useful. One method is based on the technique developed by Friedlander (1968). Using his PLAYTEST apparatus, infants can choose to listen to one of two auditory stimuli; the infants' patterns of responding thus provide information about selective listening preferences. This device avoids the disadvantages of laboratory-based experimental work by being used in the home as a toy with which the child plays freely.

Modifications were made to the apparatus to enable it to be used by younger and handicapped infants (Glenn et al., 1979). Thirty-seven out of 38 babies so far tested [mental age (MA) range 4.5 to 24.5 months, profoundly mentally handicapped to nonhandicapped] have demonstrated consistent selective responding over time. We then asked three questions:

1. Do infants respond preferentially to speech rather than to other auditory stimuli? Friedlander demonstrated selective response to speech, but failed to match for complexity. We attempted to control for complexity.
2. Do infants attend predominantly to the intonation and rhythm of speech rather than to single word characteristics? Menyuk (1974) suggested that this is so, and that at around 12 months of age, when the infant's production is changing from babble to single words, attention is directed to segmental aspects of speech. We tested this by giving the infants a choice of listening to familiar nursery rhymes or the same rhymes with each word revised such that the suprasegmental aspects were kept intact but the words were nonsense.
3. Do infants respond differently to varying maternal speech patterns? Several studies have reported that mother's speech to babies (BT) is different in many ways from mother's speech to adults (AT), and Sachs (1977) has argued that one of the functions of BT is to gain and hold the child's attention. We tested this by giving the infant the choice of listening to his/her own mother using BT or AT.

As the study progressed it became apparent that total response to mother's speech was significantly less than to the nursery rhyme stimuli. Given that most nursery rhymes have rather complicated words, this preference seems unlikely to encourage single word utterances. We felt that at some stage infants would show a greater preference for mother's speech than for nursery rhymes. This was confirmed by pilot experiments with 18-month-old nonhandicapped infants, and thus a fourth question arose: Do patterns of responding in nonhandicapped and mentally handicapped infants change over time?

METHOD

Subjects

Eleven nonhandicapped infants [mean MA 9.6 months, mean chronological age (CA) 9.3 months] were matched individually to 11 Down's syndrome infants for MA (mean MA 9.2 months, mean CA 12.7 months), sex, number of siblings, and socioeconomic class by father's occupation. Each infant 1) could reach smoothly and consistently, 2) could sit in a stable position for relatively long periods, and 3) had no severe hearing disorder. The Down's syndrome infants had an audiological assessment that showed minimal losses (responding on a distraction test at raised levels of 30–40 dBA). Routine hearing checks revealed no loss in the nonhandicapped infants.

Stimulus Variables

The following pairs of stimuli were available on the two channels:

Variable 1: "Somebody Come and Play" from "Sesame Street" (a television program for preschool children) (CR) versus a piano tone (middle C, frequency 90 per minute).

Variable 2: Nursery rhymes either played by a flute, guitar, or trumpet (INR) or sung by an unaccompanied female voice, matched to the instruments for pitch, rhythm, and sound level (SNR).

Variable 3: Familiar nursery rhymes (FNR) that mothers regularly sang to their infants, recorded by the same unaccompanied female voice for each infant, versus nonsense nursery rhymes (NNR) recorded by the same voice using the same tunes, rhythms, and intonations as the originals and matched syllable for syllable, e.g., "Hickory Dickory Dock, the mouse ran up the clock" and "Oricky Oricky Cod, eth soame nar poo eth clod."

Variable 4: Each mother talking to her own baby (BT) and each mother talking to an adult (AT).

Testing

Full details of the apparatus and procedure are given in Glenn et al. (1979).

Apparatus   This consisted of two red boxes (22.8 × 20.25 × 15.2 cm) each with a yellow touch-sensitive switch situated directly below a loudspeaker. A control box, situated at a distance from the infant, recorded both the frequency and duration (in seconds) of responses.

Procedure   Testing was carried out entirely in the infants' homes and mothers collected the data at the end of each session. Mothers' recording techniques were checked twice weekly. Measures were taken of response duration per session (seconds), response frequency per session, and average duration per response (ADR), i.e., total response duration divided by total response frequency. Testing was carried out in two phases:

Phase 1: Variable 1 was always presented first to ascertain that infants could use the apparatus and respond selectively. Variable 2 was presented next. Variables 3 and 4 were then presented in a counterbalanced order.

Phase 2: Ten of the 11 infants with Down's syndrome were retested 12 months after Phase 1 (mean MA 17.3 months, mean CA 24.5 months). The 10 nonhandicapped infants who had responded in Phase 1 were tested 7 months after Phase 1, to try to achieve a developmental match (mean MA 18.8 months, mean CA 16.6 months).

RESULTS

Mean results are presented in Table 1.

Variable 1 (CR/Tone)

Both groups of infants significantly preferred the children's rhyme to the tone on all measures at both test ages. At both test ages infants with Down's syndrome had significantly longer response durations and ADRs than nonhandicapped infants, although response frequency was not significantly different. There were significant interactions between subjects and stimuli, the major difference between the groups being for the children's rhyme. The same pattern was also found at the second test age but the difference between groups was not as great.

Variable 2 (SNR/INR)

Here the two stimuli were better matched for complexity. Both groups significantly preferred to listen to the human voice for all three measures. This seems to be an important prerequisite for the development of receptive language. It also suggests that a lack of saliency for speech stimuli per se is not a major factor in the language problems of children with Down's syndrome. Again, the Down's syndrome children had significantly longer response durations and ADRs than the nonhandicapped children, although there was no significant difference in response frequency. Nor were there any significant interactions, the difference between the two groups of children being apparent for both stimuli.

Table 1. Mean results for two groups of subjects over time

Subjects	CR		TONE		BT		AT		SNR	INR	FNR	NNR
	Phase 1	Phase 2	Phase 1	Phase 2	Phase 1	Phase 2	Phase 1	Phase 2	Phase 1	Phase 1	Phase 1	Phase 1
Response duration (seconds)												
Infants with Down's syndrome (n = 10)	387.3	230.9	90.5	66.7	216.0	141.2	89.9	67.6	268.9	139.7	290.5	201.0
Nonhandicapped infants (n = 10)	144.9	130.0	75.2	59.4	92.5	150.1	56.2	46.6	120.1	85.5	100.3	86.6
Response frequency												
Infants with Down's syndrome	51.6	38.7	21.8	18.2	27.8	26.8	16.9	16.4	27.3	21.3	28.2	23.9
Nonhandicapped infants	33.6	30.5	24.1	18.7	21.9	22.6	12.1	14.5	25.6	20.1	21.9	17.1
ADR (seconds)												
Infants with Down's syndrome	8.1	6.7	4.2	3.8	8.8	5.4	5.9	4.3	10.0	7.4	10.8	8.6
Nonhandicapped infants	4.7	4.2	3.2	3.4	4.3	7.7	4.5	3.7	5.2	4.2	5.9	5.1

[a] Stimuli and times. Abbreviations: CR = children's rhyme; SNR = sung nursery rhyme; INR = instrumental nursery rhyme; FNR = familiar nursery rhyme; NNR = nonsense nursery rhyme; BT = baby talk; AT = adult talk.

Variable 3 (FNR/NNR)

Significantly longer response durations and significantly higher response frequencies were found for the familiar rhymes compared to the nonsense rhymes. No significant differences were found for ADR. Yet, again, the Down's syndrome children had significantly longer response durations and ADRs than the nonhandicapped children; there were no significant interactions. Individual comparisons indicate that preference for FNR increased with MA (Glenn and Cunningham, 1982). Because only one infant (a nonhandicapped girl) demonstrated comprehension of simple words on standardized tests, it was interesting to find the preference for the familiar words of rhymes; this indicates that infants of this age are beginning to recognize words.

Although it was found that the infants attended to words, this does not imply that suprasegmental aspects of speech stimuli are a less important source of information. Indeed, three sources of evidence strongly suggested the opposite:

1. No significant group difference was found in ADRs to the familiar and nonsense rhymes, in contrast to results from Variables 1, 2, and 4 where preferential responding was reflected in ADR measures.
2. To further explore the lack of group difference in ADRs to rhymes an additional study was carried out with one subject (CA 9.2, MA 7.5 months). He was presented with the choice of nonsense rhymes versus the familiar words of the rhymes, read as a list without intonation. He significantly preferred the nonsense rhymes, suggesting that suprasegmental aspects have more control over listening for infants at this age.
3. We found that, where the nursery rhymes involved actions, the infants would often produce these in response to both sets of stimuli.

Variable 4 (BT/AT)

Both groups of infants significantly preferred to listen to BT on all three measures at both test ages. This supports the hypothesis that one of the functions of BT is to gain and hold the infant's attention. In Phase 1 Down's syndrome infants had significantly longer response durations and ADRs than the nonhandicapped infants and there was a significant interaction between subjects and stimuli. The results indicated that the major differences between the two groups was for BT, with relatively little difference for AT. However, by the time of Phase 2 the two groups of subjects had changed in opposite directions in response to BT, with little change for AT. The nonhandicapped group showed a significant increase in response duration and ADR such that they now responded longer than the Down's syndrome group and longer to BT than to CR. However, the latter group showed a significant decrease in response duration and ADR over time, and still responded less to BT than to CR, as in Phase 1.

DISCUSSION

Comparison of Variables 1, 2, 3, and 4

In the earlier period for both groups nursery rhymes produced more prolonged responding than normal speech stimuli. When we combined response durations for each of the pairs of stimuli, BT + AT had significantly less response duration than any of the other pairs. Total response frequencies were in the same direction. Thus, in Phase 1, nursery rhymes appeared to have more control over babies' listening than did mothers' talk. Although the direct comparison was not made this suggests that babies will listen longer to a stranger singing an unfamiliar rhyme than to their own mothers talking. Familiarity has some effect, because ongoing studies with severely mentally handicapped infants indicate that the most prolonged responding is produced to hearing their own mothers singing familiar nursery rhymes. In one sense this is not a surprising finding: the fact that mothers in many cultures sing nursery rhymes to infants under 12 months suggest that mothers receive positive feedback and infants appear to listen. Results from variable 3 (FRN + NNR) suggests that infants are beginning to recognize familiar words of nursery rhymes at this time. Infants are thus attentive to the characteristic rhythms of nursery rhymes, and this, together with constant repetition, appears to encourage the development of word recognition. The Down's syndrome infants showed this as much as the nonhandicapped infants, which suggests the possibility of using the rhythms of nursery rhymes to teach common words. Nursery rhymes tend to have simple repeated rhythms but complicated words. Using simpler, fewer, and repeated words related to the child's own environment could capitalize on the attention-gaining capacity of rhymes.

In the second phase (17–18 months) we saw a change in the nonhandicapped children to more prolonged listening to their mothers' speech than to nursery rhymes. This seems to imply a switch in relative preference from rhythmical contours to single word characteristics, which parallels the rapidly increasing word comprehension at this age.

Comparison between the Down's
Syndrome and Nonhandicapped Groups

If we look at the significant differences across all variables in phase 1, we find that there is the least difference between the Down's syndrome and nonhandicapped groups for stimuli that are least preferred (i.e., AT and tone). This may imply that the former group had fewer problems at that stage of perceptual processing where input is rejected (Kahneman, 1973). For the other stimuli, whether the least or most preferred of their pair, significant differences were found between the two groups. Thus, differences appear to arise when the input is accepted and passed on for processing.

Other studies show similar results. Berger and Cunningham (1982) found longer average fixation times to mother's eyes for Down's syndrome infants compared to nonhandicapped infants. Miranda and Fantz (1973) also noted longer fixation times in infants with Down's syndrome in their visual preference study. Such findings might suggest that a longer inspection time for perceptual input is needed by these infants before a response is made. Although a longer inspection time would be advantageous in the visual mode, where stimuli are relatively static, it would be disadvantageous for the auditory mode, where increased inspection time for a temporally ongoing stimulus would increase the information load. Infants with Down's syndrome may have a smaller overall processing capacity than nonhandicapped infants, so that increasing the amount of auditory information could have two disadvantageous effects—it could restrict the allocation of attention 1) within the auditory message, and 2) to visual and other contextual aspects of the language learning situation. This may partly explain the language delay in Down's syndrome. The implication for intervention is to use short phrases and long pauses between phrases. Unfortunately, it seems that people do not naturally do this.

Several workers (e.g., Davis and Oliver, 1980) have demonstrated that mentally handicapped children have more language directed at them than do nonhandicapped children of an equivalent developmental level. Experimental manipulation of mothers' responses to their Down's syndrome infants (Berger and Cunningham, 1982) has demonstrated significantly increased responses in 20-week-old children with Down's syndrome when longer response opportunity was given the children by instructing mothers to imitate the infant and not initiate responses. We may have similar experiences to the Down's syndrome child when we are learning a foreign language; the words sound familiar, and we may be just sorting them out, when the speaker continues and we lose the original phrase.

Our results indicate that infants with Down's syndrome show preference patterns similar to those of nonhandicapped infants at a developmental level of under 1 year. At this age duration responding and ADRs were longer in the Down's syndrome infants, suggesting that they need a longer inspection time. However, by the second phase, the nonhandicapped infants had significantly increased response duration to mother's speech, whereas there had been a significant decrease for the infants with Down's syndrome. Sometime in the period from 12 to 24 months of age the stimulus of the mother talking to her Down's syndrome infant had decreased its ability to maintain responding. We tentatively suggest that these two findings might be related and might affect social interaction patterns. This would seem to be a profitable area for future research and intervention.

REFERENCES

Berger, J., and Cunningham, C. C. 1981. The development of eye contact between mothers and normal versus Down's syndrome infants. Dev. Psychol. 17:678–689.

Berger, J., and Cunningham, C. C. 1982. Early development of social interactions in Down's syndrome and non-handicapped infants. In: A. Teirikko, R. Vihavainen, and T. Nenonnen (eds.), Finland Speaks: Report of the EASE 80 Conference, Helsinki. Finnish Association for Special Education with European Association for Special Education, Helsinki.

Davis, H. M., and Oliver, B. 1980. A comparison of aspects of maternal speech environment of retarded and non-retarded children. Child Care Health Dev. 6:135–145.

Eimas, P. D., and Tartter, V. 1979. On the development of speech perception: Mechanisms and analogies. Adv. Child Dev. Behav. 13:155–193.

Friedlander, B. Z. 1968. The effect of speaker identity, voice inflection, vocabulary and message redundancy in infants' selection of vocal reinforcement. J. Exp. Child Psychol. 6:443–459.

Glenn, S. M., Cunningham, C. C., Joyce, P. F., and Creighton, W. T. 1979. An automated system for the study of auditory preferences in infants (Infant Project Paper 10). Hester Adrian Research Centre, Manchester University, Manchester, England.

Glenn, S. M., and Cunningham, C. C. 1982. Recognition of the familiar words of nursery rhymes by handicapped and non-handicapped infants. J. Child Psychol. Psychiatry 23:319–327.

Kahneman, D. 1973. Attention and Effort. Prentice-Hall, Inc., Englewood Cliffs, New Jersey.

Menyuk, P. 1974. Early development of receptive language: from babbling to words. In: R. L. Schiefelbusch and L. L. Lloyd (eds.) Language Perspectives—Acquisition, Retardation and Intervention. University Park Press, Baltimore.

Miranda, S. B., and Fantz, R. L. 1973. Visual preferences of Down's syndrome and normal infants. Child Dev. 44:555–561.

Rondal, J. A. 1982. Language acquisition in Down's syndrome children: Recent studies and problems. In: A. Teirikko, R. Vihavainen, and T. Nenonnen (eds.), Finland Speaks: Report of the EASE 80 Conference, Helsinki. Finnish Association for Special Education with European Association for Special Education, Helsinki.

Sachs, J. 1977. The adaptive significance of linguistic input to prelinguistic infants. In: C. Snow and C. Ferguson (eds.), Talking to Children: Language Input and Acquisition, pp. 51–62. Cambridge University Press, Cambridge, England.

PERSPECTIVES AND PROGRESS IN MENTAL RETARDATION
Volume I—Social, Psychological, and Educational Aspects
Edited by J. M. Berg
Copyright © 1984 by I.A.S.S.M.D.

COGNITIVE TRAINING AND ITS RELATIONSHIP TO THE LANGUAGE OF PROFOUNDLY RETARDED CHILDREN

J. V. Kahn

*College of Education, Box 4348, University of Illinois at Chicago Circle,
Chicago, Illinois 60680*

This study was an attempt to systematically investigate the effects of cognitive training of nonverbal profoundly retarded children on language learning. Twenty-four children between 3 and 10 years of age were matched on age, etiology, and sensorimotor period scores on the Uzgiris-Hunt scales and assigned to one of three groups: 8 children received object permanence training followed by language training, 8 children received means-ends training followed by language training, and 8 children received only language training. Children in both cognitive training programs learned more language than those in the language only group. Finally, a follow-up 10 months after the conclusion of training indicated a good deal of retention among the children in the cognitive training groups.

The study presented here is part of a 3-year project that has just concluded. The first 2 years were the intervention phase, and the third was used to follow up on the durability and generalization of the skills learned in the first 2 years of intervention.

Recent publications (e.g., Piaget, 1970; Bates et al., 1975; Kahn, 1975, 1976; Sinclair, 1975; Bates, 1976; Leonard, 1978; Corrigan, 1979) have indicated an apparent relationship between sensorimotor period functioning and speech. The publications have all suggested that referential speech does not develop until the last stage (stage six) of the

The research was supported by Grant #8043-03 from the Illinois Department of Mental Health and Developmental Disabilities.

sensorimotor period. Many severely and profoundly retarded children are functioning below stage six (e.g., Woodward, 1959; Rogers, 1977; Kahn, in press) and might not be "ready" to learn to speak. Possibly these children might benefit from a cognitive training program prior to speech training. Recent research has indicated that retarded children's rate of sensorimotor period development can be accelerated (Brassell and Dunst, 1976; Henry, 1977; Kahn, 1977a, 1978).

The research reported here was an attempt to systematically study the effects of two different training programs that were designed to accelerate the rate of cognitive development of profoundly retarded children who were functioning at the sensorimotor period. The major question investigated is whether cognitive training in object permanence and/or means-ends, followed by a language training program, will result in the learning of more language (as measured by number of words and syntatic complexity) than the language training program alone. This study also investigated the durability and generalization of the training to other situations and continued learning.

METHOD

Subjects

The subjects were 24 children with profound retardation of varied etiology, whose chronological ages were between 3 and 10 years at the beginning of the study. The American Association on Mental Deficiency definition of profound retardation was used (Grossman et al., 1977). All the subjects were functioning cognitively within the sensorimotor period as measured by the Uzgiris and Hunt (1975) scales, and attended one of three schools in Chicago. None of them exhibited any form of expressive communication (e.g., speech, sign language, Bliss Symbolics) prior to this study or had any sensory impairment that would make it difficult or impossible for them to learn to speak. In addition, although their mobility might have been limited, they were all able to control at least one arm well enough to perform the object permanence and means-ends tasks required of them.

Because of the relatively small sample size, the subjects were matched according to age, etiology, and scores on the language assessment, and assigned to one of three groups (described below).

Procedures and Instrumentation

All the subjects were individually assessed at the beginning of the study with three instruments: assessment in infancy (Uzgiris and Hunt, 1975);

the Bayley scales of infant development (Bayley, 1969); Bricker et al.'s (1976) behavioral probes of linguistic and prelinguistic behaviors. In addition, they were reassessed at the end of the first year of the study and at the end of the cognitive training phase. The third year involved a follow-up study to determine the durability of the training effects.

The Uzgiris and Hunt instrument consists of seven parallel scales that measure moderately correlated components of Piaget's sensori-motor stages. As referred to here, the seven scales are Object Permanence, Means-Ends, Gestural Imitation, Vocal Imitation, Causality, Spatial Relations, and Schemes. Uzgiris and Hunt developed a scoring system that is more finely graded than Piaget's six stages (e.g., Uzgiris and Hunt have 14 steps for Object Permanence, which encompass Piaget's stages two through six).

The language assessment in this study used the behavioral probes devised for use with the Bricker et al. (1976) language training program. This program consists of 26 phases of training from "sitting" and "eye contact" to "production of three word phrases" (see Table 1 for a listing of these phases). Each training phase has a behavior probe that is used to determine which phase of training the child is learning.

The three groups of 8 subjects each consisted of two groups receiving different cognitive training programs followed by language training, and a group receiving just the language training. The two cognitive training programs involved individualized training in object permanence and means-ends. Each of these training programs involved a concentrated, often highly directed, effort to improve the child's performance in the area being trained. Primary (when necessary) and secondary positive reinforcements were used as required to keep the child interested in the tasks. The steps in the training procedures followed the same order as the Uzgiris and Hunt scales of the same name. Training began with the lowest scale step on which the child could not demonstrate criterion. The criterion for each step was considered achieved when the subject demonstrated successful performance on the step, with no errors, for two consecutive sessions. Training then continued to the next step through successive approximations of that step. If repeated efforts on the next step were unsuccessful, overlearning of the preceding step was implemented. The procedures used for object permanence training are those described by Kahn (1977b) and found to be at least moderately successful (Kahn, 1978). The procedures used for means-ends training were developed for the present study.

Each subject in the two cognitive training groups began language training when he/she achieved the criterion for that cognitive training program. The criterion consisted of the highest item on the Uzgiris and Hunt Scale for which the subject received direct training.

Table 1.   Phases of language training[a]

Phase	Learning activity
1	Sit in chair
2	Eye contact
3	Work on task
4	Increase vocalization
5	Early gestural imitation
6	Gestural imitation of familiar actions
7	Gestural imitation of unfamiliar actions
8	Sound imitation—child initiated
9	Sound imitation of familiar sounds
10	Sound imitation of unfamiliar sounds
11	Early word recognition
12	Functional use of objects
13	Appropriate use of objects
14	Verbal imitation of component sounds
15	Imitation of nouns (criterion is 10 nouns)
16	Comprehension of nouns (criterion is 10 nouns)
17	Production of nouns (criterion is 10 nouns)
18	Imitation of verbs (criterion is 10 verbs)
19	Comprehension of verbs (criterion is 10 verbs)
20	Production of verbs (criterion is 10 verbs)
21	Imitation of 2-word phrases (criterion is 10 2-word phrases)
22	Comprehension of 2-word phrases (criterion is 10 2-word phrases)
23	Production of 2-word phrases (criterion is 10 2-word phrases)
24	Imitation of 3-word phrases (criterion is 10 3-word phrases)
25	Comprehension of 3-word phrases (criterion is 10 3-word phrases)
26	Production of 3-word phrases (criterion is 10 3-word phrases)

[a] Adapted from Bricker et al. (1976).

The language training program referred to earlier (Bricker et al., 1976) was constructed to represent the normal language learning process. Operant procedures were used as necessary and behavioral probes were administered every 2 weeks in order to determine the progress being made by the subject. The probes consisted of the trainer requesting the subject to demonstrate the skills that had been taught. For instance, if a subject had been working on the production of nouns, the trainer might ask, "What is this?" while pointing at one of three objects in front of the child. Reliability of these probes was measured in this study and found to range between 91% and 98% agreement between two observers. In addition, data were collected daily in each subject's training session. Each subject began the language training at the most appropriate phase for that subject, based upon the baseline probe given just prior to the initiation of language training. Each of the

24 subjects received individual training for 20 minutes a day, 5 days a week, during the first 2 years of the project.

The object permanence training procedure has 14 steps with individuals beginning training anywhere from step 1 to step 14 depending on their current level of performance. Upon achieving criterion on step 14, the individual begins language training. The language training program has 26 phases with an individual's starting phase depending on his/her performance at the onset of the language program.

During the third year of the project, each subject was observed in various activities (e.g., training activities, lunch, with and without an adult in immediate proximity) in their schools. The observations particularly noted communicative behaviors and the frequency and type of any stereotypes. In addition, the Uzgiris and Hunt scales and language probes, based on the Bricker et al. (1976) program, were administered to each subject twice (4 and 10 months after the completion of training).

RESULTS AND DISCUSSION

Object Permanence Training

The beginning point (9/79), the midpoint (6/80), and the point at which each subject finished training (6/81) are given in Table 2. As can be seen, 4 of the subjects had completed the object permanence training and begun the language training by the end of the first year and the other 4 subjects completed the object permanence training and began the language training thereafter. Thus, the object permanence training was successful in raising the subjects' scores in this area. Of the 8 object permanence–trained subjects, 3 did not achieve the criterion on any of the speech phases (phases 15–26). One subject imitated 10 nouns, comprehended 8 nouns, and produced 2 nouns. Two other subjects completed the imitation and comprehension of nouns phases and were producing 5 and 9 nouns, respectively. Another subject completed the production of 10 nouns in phase 17 and also used one verb for a total of 11 words independently. The highest-achieving subject in this group completed the production of nouns and imitation and comprehension of verbs phases and produced 15 words.

Means-ends Training

The means-ends training procedure has 13 steps with individuals beginning training anywhere from step 1 to step 13, depending on their existing level of functioning. The beginning step, the step at the end

Table 2.   Highest cognitive and/or language phases "passed" at the beginning (9/79), midpoint (6/80), and end (6/81) of training

	Training period		
Subjects	9/79	6/80	6/81
Object permanence group			
1	Obj perm #4	Language #9	Language #11
2	Obj perm #2	Language #6	Language #14
3	Obj perm #9	Language #7	Language #16
4	Obj perm #4	Obj perm #10	Language #16
5	Obj perm #5	Obj perm #10	Language #15
6	Obj perm #4	Obj perm #13	Language #17
7	Obj perm #4	Language #6	Language #19
8	Obj perm #2	Obj perm #10	Language #13
Means-ends group			
1	Means-ends #7	Language #6	Language #18
2	Means-ends #2	Means-ends #8	Means-ends #11
3	Means-ends #5	Means-ends #10	Means-ends #12
4	Means-ends #8	Language #9	Language #20
5	Means-ends #10	Language #8	Language #22
6	Means-ends #10	Language #9	Language #19
7	Means-ends #9	Language #9	Language #16
8	Means-ends #4	Means-ends #11	Language #17
Language group			
1	Language #1	Language #9	Language #11
2	Language #1	Language #11	Language #13
3	Language #1	Language #2	Language #6
4	Language #1	Language #2	Language #7
5	Language #1	Language #2	Language #5
6	Language #1	Language #6	Language #9
7	Language #1	Language #2	Language #6
8	Language #4	Language #5	Language #9

of the first year (6/80), and the step on which each subject finished training (6/81) are given in Table 2. As shown, 5 subjects had completed the means-ends training and begun the language training by the end of the first year, with an additional subject achieving this level by the end of the second year. Thus, the means-ends training has not been as successful as the object permanence training in raising the subjects' scores in this area

However, the language learned by the 6 successful means-ends–trained subjects exceeded that learned by the object permanence–trained subjects. All these subjects achieved the criterion on at least the beginning speech phases. The 6 successfully trained means-ends subjects were producing between 7 and 31 words. In addition, one of these subjects was producing 6 2-word phrases.

Language Training

The subjects in the language training only group did not achieve as much as the subjects who received either object permanence or means-ends training first. As can be seen from Table 2, none of these 8 subjects even began training on any of the speech phases, and only one came close. Thus, it seems clear that both of the cognitive training procedures have prepared the majority of the children to be able to learn speech.

Generalization Follow-up

It was still necessary to demonstrate that the gains made by the subjects in the cognitive training conditions were durable and generalizable to situations other than the one-to-one testing situations. In order to determine the retention and generalization of the training, data were collected using the Uzgiris and Hunt scales and the Bricker et al. language scale probes for all of the subjects 10 months after the completion of training.

The object permanence–trained subjects and the means-ends–trained subjects made significant gains on the scale for which they received training, with a good deal of retention. In addition, these subjects made some small gains on the other scales, particularly the gestural imitation and vocal imitation scales. However, the improvement of imitation can probably be explained by the type of training procedures used in the training programs and by the language program's imitation training phases. The gains made by these subjects on the language training program were generally retained, with a few subjects showing slight gains or losses following the training. The language-trained subjects did not change much on the Uzgiris and Hunt scales in the 31 months between the pretest and the second posttest. Although these subjects did advance in the language training program, not one achieved the linguistic phases of training. Thus, the training of object permanence and of means-ends prior to speech training appears to be a better approach with children who are functioning below stage six of Piaget's sensorimotor period. Further research is needed before similar statements can be made for language systems other than speech (e.g., signs, nonSLIP).

In addition, each subject was observed in his/her school 10 times a month for 6 months during the 9 months of the follow-up. Four of the 8 children in the object permanence group used from 1 to 5 different words independently; 5 of the 8 children in the means-ends group used from 1 to 7 different words independently. None of the subjects in the language-only training group used any speech. Although the number of words used independently by the subjects in the cognitive training groups is not spectacular, and although 7 of these 16 subjects used no speech independently, the use of speech by these subjects compares favorably with the subjects receiving language training alone. Perhaps training of speech in the environment in which we wish it to be used would lead to more generalization.

Finally, each subject was observed in his/her school 10 times a month for 6 of the 9 months of follow-up to see if there was any reduction in stereotypic behaviors. There was a reduction in stereotypies for all 24 subjects. This may simply be a result of one-on-one training in imitation, which all but 2 of the subjects received as part of the language training program. No implications can be drawn regarding the part that cognitive training played in this reduction because the subjects in the language-only training group also experienced a reduction in these behaviors.

REFERENCES

Bates, E. 1976. Pragmatics and sociolinguistics in child language. In: D. M. Morehead and A. E. Morehead (eds.), Normal and Deficient Child Language. University Park Press, Baltimore.

Bates, E., Camaioni, L., and Volterra, V. 1975. The acquisition of performatives prior to speech. Merrill-Palmer Q. 21:205–226.

Bayley, N. 1969. Bayley Scales of Infant Development: Birth to Two Years. Psychological Corp., New York.

Brassell, W. R., and Dunst, C. J. 1976. Comparison of two procedures for fostering the development of the object construct. Am. J. Ment. Defic. 80:523–528.

Bricker, D., Dennison, L., and Bricker, W. 1976. A Language Intervention Program for Developmentally Young Children, Monograph 1. University of Miami Mailman Center for Child Development, Miami, Florida.

Corrigan, R. 1979. Cognitive correlates of language: Differential criteria yield different results. Child Dev. 50:617–631.

Grossman, H. J., Warren, S. A., Begab, M. J., Eyman, R., Nihira, K., and O'Connor, G., 1977. Manual on Terminology and Classification in Mental Retardation. American Association on Mental Deficiency, Washington, D.C.

Henry, J. C. 1977. The effects of parent assessment and parent training of preschool mentally retarded children on Piagetian tasks of object permanence and imitation. Unpublished dissertation, Temple University, Philadelphia, Pennsylvania.

Kahn, J. V. 1975. Relationship of Piaget's sensorimotor period to language acquisition of profoundly retarded children. Am. J. Ment. Defic. 79:640–643.

Kahn, J. V. 1976. Utility of the Uzgiris and Hunt scales of sensorimotor development with severely and profoundly retarded children. Am. J. Ment. Defic. 80:663–665.

Kahn, J. V. 1977a. On Training Generalized Thinking. Paper presented at American Psychological Association, San Francisco. (ERIC Document No. ED 165 348).

Kahn, J. V. 1977b. Procedures for training object permanence with severely and profoundly retarded children. In: M. Thomas (ed.), Developing Skills in Severely and Profoundly Handicapped Children. Very Special Children Series. Council for Exceptional Children, Reston, Virginia.

Kahn, J. V. 1978. Acceleration of object permanence with severely and profoundly retarded children. Am. Assoc. Sev. Prof. Hand. Rev. 3:15–22.

Kahn, J. V. Uses of scales of psychological development with mentally retarded populations. In: I. C. Uzgiris and J. McV. Hunt (eds.), Research with Scales of Psychological Development in Infancy. University of Illinois Press, Champaign, Illinois. (in press)

Leonard, L. B. 1978. Cognitive factors in early linguistic development. In: R. L. Schiefelbusch (ed.), Bases of Language Intervention. University Park Press, Baltimore.

Piaget, J. 1970. Piaget's theory. In: P. H. Mussen (ed.), Carmichael's Manual of Child Psychology, 3rd ed. John Wiley & Sons, Inc., New York.

Rogers, S. J. 1977. Characteristics of the cognitive development of profoundly retarded children. Child Dev. 48:837–843.

Sinclair, H. 1975. Language and cognition in subnormals: A Piagetian view. In: N. O'Connor (ed.), Language, Cognitive Deficits, and Retardation. Butterworths, London.

Uzgiris, I. C., and Hunt, J. McV. 1975. Assessment in Infancy: Ordinal Scales of Psychological Development. University of Illinois Press, Urbana.

Woodward, M. 1959. The behavior of idiots interpreted by Piaget's theory of sensorimotor development. Br. J. Educ. Psychol. 29:60–71.

PERSPECTIVES AND PROGRESS IN MENTAL RETARDATION
Volume I—Social, Psychological, and Educational Aspects
Edited by J. M. Berg
Copyright © 1984 by I.A.S.S.M.D.

NATURALISTIC OBSERVATION OF LANGUAGE USE IN A CLASSROOM FOR SEVERELY RETARDED CHILDREN

K. A. Thrasher and N. W. Bray

*Graduate School of Experimental and Clinical Psychology,
The University of Alabama, P.O. Box 2968, University, Alabama 35486*

The types of communications used during 36 10-minute segments of activity in a classroom for the severely retarded were analyzed. The students did not initiate interactions as frequently as the teachers, and they did not always respond appropriately, but they were able to effectively use language to obtain desired objects and to direct the actions of others. The results suggest that the structural aspects of language (e.g., syntax and vocabulary) are deficient in this population, but that these individuals nevertheless use their limited language structures to accomplish a variety of social and personal goals.

The ability to communicate with others is a powerful and versatile adaptive skill, and at least some minimal communicative skill is clearly essential to social adjustment. The mentally retarded, in general, and the more severely retarded in particular, are frequently characterized as language deficient (e.g., Blount, 1968; Wehman and Garrett, 1978). For the most part, studies supporting this assertion have focused on structural aspects of language. For instance, it has been reported that some mentally retarded persons use less developmentally sophisticated sentences and phrases in comparison to their nonretarded peers (e.g., Cromer, 1974) and that shorter and less syntactically complete utterances are associated with more severe retardation (Martyn et al., 1969; Keane, 1972; Reynolds and Reynolds, 1979).

In an effort to understand possible origins of the deficiencies in the structural aspects of language, other research has focused on the characteristics of speech directed toward retarded individuals. Most often, investigators have studied the speech of mothers to their children. Typical of these studies, Buckhalt et al. (1978) found that mothers of Down's syndrome children spoke at a faster rate than did mothers of nonretarded children of comparable age. Mothers of mentally retarded children also more frequently asked questions to which they already knew the answer or subsequently provided the correct answer (Kogan et al., 1969). Several researchers have also reported a higher frequency of simple requests, demands, and imperative sentences directed toward mentally retarded children by their mothers (Kogan et al., 1969; Marshall et al., 1973; Buium et al., 1974). Gutmann and Rondal (1979) found that mothers of both retarded and nonretarded children simplified their speech in accordance with their children's mean lengths of utterance (MLUs). Mothers of children with shorter MLUs more frequently used simple demands and requests in their speech and also more frequently echoed their children's utterances. Zetlin and Gallimore (1979) suggested that, because the use of simplified speech over an extended period of time provides a limited language model, the functional language of the mentally retarded may be reduced. Also, Marshall et al. (1973) noted that requests and demands typically require a child to *do* something, rather than speak in reply, and that this pattern of interaction could, over time, limit the development of language competency.

In addition to research on deficient structural aspects of language and mothers' speech as a possible origin of these deficiencies, there has been growing interest in the social use of language by the mentally retarded (e.g., Hoy and McKnight, 1977; Layton and Sharifi, 1978; Price-Williams and Sabsay, 1979; Owings and McManus, 1980; Zetlin and Sabsay, 1980). Research in this area has been concerned with the ways mentally retarded individuals use whatever language structures they possess. For instance, Zetlin and Sabsay (1980) found that adolescent students in a classroom for the moderately retarded most often made simple statements or comments to their peers and teachers, but they also asked questions, made commands for action, and even told jokes. Among severely retarded individuals, language use does not seem to be as sophisticated as that for the moderately retarded. Price-Williams and Sabsay (1979), however, observed that severely retarded adults were able to obtain the attention of others for the purpose of initiating communication and they could direct that attention to the topic of discussion.

PRESENT STUDY

Purpose and Methods

The purpose of the present study was to extend the investigation of communicative competency in the mentally retarded by describing naturally occurring interactions in a public school classroom for the severely retarded. In light of previous findings suggesting a fairly high degree of successful communication, the primary focus was on characterizing the function of utterances made in the classroom rather than on detailing the language structures used by the students. Specifically, the selected topics of interest were: 1) who initiated the interactions (students or teachers); 2) toward whom those interactions were directed; 3) the functional nature of the interactions (e.g., statements, requests, and questions); and 4) the topic of utterance (people, objects, or events).

The classroom in which the observations were made had 12 students, 1 teacher, and 4 teacher aides. All the instructors performed similar functions, coordinated by the teacher. Six students were selected at random to participate in the study. The students ranged in age from 8 years 5 months to 19 years 7 months (mean = 15 years 8 months). On adaptive behavior scales and by teacher estimate the students were functioning in the severe retardation range.

Following a 2-week desensitization period during which the experimenters and their equipment were present in the classroom, videotaping was initiated. Each of the 6 students was videotaped for 10 minutes on six consecutive school days. Taping was conducted across various classroom activities, including motor skills training, mealtimes, language training, and free time, in order to provide a variety of opportunities for the students to exercise their communicative abilities. Every student was videotaped in each setting.

The videotapes were viewed by one of the experimenters and an undergraduate assistant. All vocalizations were transcribed verbatim, with the setting, initiator, receiver, and outcome of every interaction described. Boundaries of a communication were defined as natural breaks or pauses between utterances, changes in topic, or elaborations on a topic. For example, "John, pick up the block," would be scored as one communication. "John, pick up the block. Now put it in the box." would be scored as two communications. Any discrepancies in the transcription were resolved through discussion between observers.

Results and Discussion

Analysis of the videotapes yielded 1,722 interactions recorded across the 6 hours of observation. Three types of communications were scored: statements, requests, and questions. Statements were comments on the nature of objects or events in the environment. Requests expressed the speaker's desire that the listener perform some action. Questions were communications in which the speaker desired some information from the listener. Two types of questions were noted: "Real" questions, in which the speaker genuinely sought information (e.g., "Where do you want your stamp?"), and "exam" questions, which were probes to determine whether the listener possessed the information (e.g., "Did you clap your hands?"). The transcripts were read by the experimenters, who independently scored the type of communication used in each interaction. Interrater reliability was 96% and, as with the initial tape transcriptions, disagreements were resolved through discussion.

Thirteen percent of the 1,722 interactions were initiated by students. Both students and teachers initiated nearly half (46% and 44%, respectively) of their interactions via requests. Teachers responded appropriately to student requests by taking some action 77% of the time. In these cases they either attempted to comply or provided some explanation of their failure to comply. In contrast, the students responded appropriately to teachers' requests only 53% of the time.

Students initiated interactions with questions 16% of the time. Virtually all (89%) were "real" questions directed to the teachers. On the other hand, although teachers asked questions more frequently than the students did (26%), less than one-third of these questions (26%) were "real" questions.

Students and teachers began communications with statements 38% and 30% of the time, respectively. These are sizeable percentages, but not as great as the 68% obtained in a comparable study with moderately retarded students (Zetlin and Sabsay, 1980). Also, in the present study statements generally did not facilitate much interaction, [e.g., (student) "It's sticky," or (teacher) "We finished that in a hurry"]. However, the statements may have been useful in gaining the listener's attention so that additional communicative exchanges could be initiated. Price-Williams and Sabsay (1979) found that simple attention-seeking statements made by severely retarded adults were often sufficient to convey the intention to communicate to a listener, who then used context cues for additional information about the topic of discussion. Our results are consistent with their finding.

People provided the principal topic of conversation for both students and teachers (85% and 87% of interactions, respectively). It is notable that, when communicating about people, the students referred to individuals not immediately present in the environment 42% of the time (e.g., "Where's Sheila?" or "Erin is my sister's name"). Teachers spoke about absent persons in 64% of their communications about people. Other topics included objects (e.g., "That's peanuts!"; 6% for students, 7% for teachers) and events (e.g., "Go home now?"; 9% for students, 6% for teachers). When objects were discussed by either students or teachers, 93% of the time they were objects that were present. Teachers also confined most (94%) of their communications to events occurring at the time. However, when students discussed events, 50% of these utterances focused on the future (e.g., "Go to the beach?" or "When we're going home?"). Clearly, these students were not limited to conversations about topics immediately at hand but could conceptualize and communicate about topics removed in time or space.

Another finding of interest concerned the intended listener for a communication. Students interacted among themselves very little, directing 72% of their communication to teachers. In the present sample, teachers directed all of their communications to students. This is not to say that they never spoke to one another, but rather it appeared that they withdrew from the students (and, as a result, the videorecorder) before speaking together. By doing this, teachers were missing opportunities to model appropriate communication for their students.

The present findings also underscore a point made by studies on mothers' speech to retarded children (e.g., Marshall et al., 1973; Zetlin and Gallimore, 1979) and by other studies (e.g., Bloom, 1974; Mittler and Berry, 1977) regarding the importance of situational demands on communicative behavior. The teachers placed relatively little demand for communication upon the students. The largest group of interactions initiated by teachers involved requests, and usually these could be responded to nonverbally (e.g., "Point to the big ball"). Similarly, teachers' questions frequently required only a yes/no response from the student or it was apparent that the teacher already knew the answer (e.g., "John, what's your name?"). This appears to be a common situation in classrooms for the severely retarded (Zetlin and Gallimore, 1979). Mittler and Berry (1977) have noted that "retarded people may be handicapped as much by the underexpectation of those who live and work with them as by their primary disabilities." Indeed, the present study indicates that this group of severely mentally retarded students possesses and exhibits a variety of communicative abilities even when there is slight demand to display them. How much superior their performance would be under conditions of more optimal demand and modeling remains to be explored.

REFERENCES

Bloom, L. 1974. Talking, understanding, and thinking. In: R. L. Schiefelbusch and L. L. Lloyd (eds.), Language Perspectives—Acquisition, Retardation and Intervention. University Park Press, Baltimore.

Blount, W. R. 1968. Language and the more severely retarded: A review. Am. J. Ment. Defic. 73:21–29.

Buckhalt, J. A., Rutherford, R. B., and Goldberg, K. E. 1978. Verbal and nonverbal interaction of mothers with their Down's syndrome and nonretarded infants. Am. J. Ment. Defic. 82:337–343.

Buium, N., Rynders, J., and Turnure, J. 1974. Early material linguistic environment of normal and Down's syndrome language learning children. Am. J. Ment. Defic. 79:52–58.

Cromer, R. F. 1974. Receptive language in the mentally retarded: Processes and diagnostic distinctions. In: R. L. Schiefelbusch and L. L. Lloyd (eds.), Language Perspectives—Acquisition, Retardation and Intervention, pp. 237–267. University Park Press, Baltimore.

Gutmann, A. J., and Rondal, J. A. 1979. Verbal operants in mothers' speech to nonretarded and Down's syndrome children matched for linguistic level. Am. J. Ment. Defic. 83:446–452.

Hoy, E. A., and McKnight, J. R. 1977. Communication style and effectiveness in homogeneous and heterogeneous dyads of retarded children. Am. J. Ment. Defic. 81:587–598.

Keane, V. E. 1972. The incidence of speech and language problems in the mentally retarded. Ment. Retard. 10:3–5.

Kogan, K. L., Wimberger, H. C., and Bobbitt, R. A. 1969. Analysis of mother-child interactions in young mental retardates. Child Dev. 40:799–812.

Layton, T. L., and Sharifi, H. 1978. Meaning and structure of Down's syndrome and nonretarded children's spontaneous speech. Am. J. Ment. Defic. 83:439–445.

Marshall, N. R., Hegrenes, J. R., and Goldstein, S. 1973. Verbal interactions: Mothers and their retarded children vs. mothers and their nonretarded children. Am. J. Ment. Defic. 77:415–419.

Martyn, M. M., Sheehan, J., and Slutz, K., 1969. Incidence of stuttering and other speech disorders among the retarded. Am. J. Ment. Defic. 74:206–211.

Mittler, P., and Berry, P. 1977. Demanding language. In: P. Mittler (ed.), Research to Practice in Mental Retardation. Volume II: Education and Training, pp. 245–251. University Park Press, Baltimore.

Owings, N. O., and McManus, M. D. 1980. An analysis of communication functions in the speech of a deinstitutionalized adult mentally retarded client. Ment. Retard. 18:309–314.

Price-Williams, D., and Sabsay, S. 1979. Communicative competence among severely retarded persons. Semiotica 26:35–63.

Reynolds, W. M., and Reynolds, S. 1979. Prevalence of speech and hearing impairment of noninstitutionalized mentally retarded adults. Am. J. Ment. Defic. 84:62–66.

Wehman, P., and Garrett, S. 1978. Language instruction with severely, profoundly, and multi-handicapped students: Two years of data. Ment. Retard. 16:410–412.

Zetlin, A. G., and Gallimore, R. 1979. An instructural model for the development of comprehension strategies through the regulatory function of teacher questions. Paper presented at the conference on "The Impact of Specific Settings on the Behavior and Development of Retarded Persons." University of California at Los Angeles, Westwood, California.

Zetlin, A. G., and Sabsay, S. 1980. Characteristics of verbal interaction among moderately retarded peers. Paper presented at the Gatlinburg Conference on Research in Mental Retardation, Gatlinburg, Tennessee.

PERSPECTIVES AND PROGRESS IN MENTAL RETARDATION
Volume I—Social, Psychological, and Educational Aspects
Edited by J. M. Berg
Copyright © 1984 by I.A.S.S.M.D.

SHORT-TERM MEMORY STRATEGIES FOR VERBAL AND MANUAL SIGN LABELS USED BY MENTALLY HANDICAPPED CHILDREN

D. Bowler

Thomas Coram Research Unit, University of London Institute of Education, 41 Brunswick Square, London WC1N 1AZ, England

Four experiments are described that were designed to examine retarded children's handling of manual signs and spoken words as names for pictures. Children were presented with signs or words either singly (Experiments I and II) or in groups of 4 (Experiments III and IV) and asked to select the appropriate pictures after a delay of 1, 5, or 10 seconds. Analysis of reaction time and response accuracy data revealed only one overall group difference between signs and words on all four experiments.

The data from Experiments I and II revealed quite large individual differences, not all in the same direction. This pattern of results suggested that more account should be taken of task demands and individual differences when dealing with retarded behavior.

Attempts to explain the poor learning performance of retarded individuals have increasingly emphasized defects in memory, especially in the area of short-term processing. In a series of studies, Ellis (1970) found retarded individuals to lack certain strategies such as rehearsal that are thought to maintain information in short-term store and to aid transfer to a longer term store. Belmont and Butterfield (1969, 1971), Brown (1974), and Hagen et al. (1974) reached similar conclusions and also demonstrated improved memory performance after training in rehearsal strategies. Other research in this area explored short-term memory difficulties in terms of modality-related coding deficiencies.

O'Connor and Hermelin (1978) found that some severely subnormal children experienced difficulty in encoding temporal sequences especially when presented in the auditory mode.

Another salient characteristic of severely retarded individuals is poor vocal language development. Spreen (1965) estimated that 90% of subjects with IQs between 21 and 50 had vocal language disorders. This has led in recent years to an increasing concern with the use of nonvocal language systems such as manual signing systems as aids to communication with these subjects (see Kiernan et al., 1982 for a review).

It is possible to draw parallels between the poor vocal language performance of some retarded people and the finding of an auditory sequential deficit. This provides the rationale behind the present series of studies, which were designed to look at patterns of performance of a group of mentally retarded children when required to remember signs or words as names for objects. A number of different analyses of the data are in preparation, two of which, reaction time and response accuracy, are reported here.

THE EXPERIMENTAL PRETRAINING

The four short-term memory experiments described below all studied children who had learned sign and word names for a set of 12 cartoon pictures of people. Six consonant-vowel-consonant (CVC) nonsense syllables that had low association value and high pronouncability according to Underwood and Schultz (1960) were selected from Archer's (1960) list. The six words selected were MIVE, VUB, YIG, GEX, NOJ, and ZOF. Six one-handed hand configurations were selected from the easy end of the scale of hand configuration difficulty devised by Kiernan and Bowler (in preparation). These are shown in Figure 1 together with their descriptive titles.

EXPERIMENT I

This experiment was designed to examine children's performance when required to remember a single sign or word for a period of 1, 5, or 10 seconds and then to identify its appropriate referent. Reaction time was taken as one measure of ease of processing because items that are easy to process should have a shorter response latency than difficult items. Response accuracy was also measured, because it was expected that more difficult categories of items would be more likely to produce mistakes than easier categories.

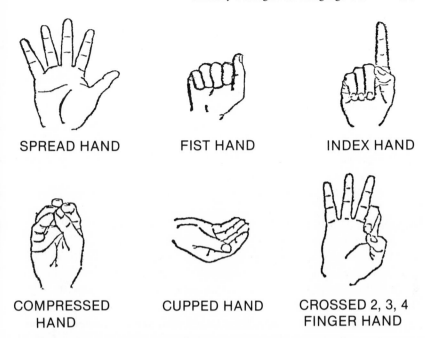

SPREAD HAND   FIST HAND   INDEX HAND

COMPRESSED   CUPPED HAND   CROSSED 2, 3, 4
HAND   FINGER HAND

Figure 1.   Hand configurations used in the four experiments.

Method

Subjects   Nine boys and 9 girls from two Inner London schools for the severely educationally subnormal were used in this experiment. The task required the children to be able to follow simple instructions and attend to the experimenter: the 18 subjects were randomly selected from a pool of such children. They ranged in age from 11 years 6 months to 19 years 2 months (mean 14 years 8 months). Peabody IQs ranged from 28 to 68 (mean 47).

Equipment   A Kodak Carousel slide projector was modified to deliver start pulses to a millisecond timer when slides were projected. Slides were back-projected onto a touch-sensitive screen that stopped the timer when the child pointed to the stimulus. The delay periods were measured by a clockwork timer. Seventy-two slides of random arrangements of the 10 stimulus pictures were loaded onto the projector.

Procedure   This consisted of the following sequence of steps:

1. A sign or word was presented by the experimenter.
2. The prescribed interval of 1, 5, or 10 seconds elapsed.
3. The slide was projected, starting the millisecond timer.

4. Stimulus choice, reaction time, and any activity of the child (e.g., rehearsal) during the delay period was noted.

In all cases, incorrect responses were corrected. Thirty trials were given per day over a 5–school day period, with each pair of conditions having an equal number of trials.

Results

This experiment gave both reaction time and response accuracy data, which were analyzed separately and then compared.

Reaction Time   Analysis of variance on mean reaction times for all signs and words (i.e., both correct and incorrect responses) revealed no significant difference between signs and words ($F_{1,17} = 1.31$, ns), but a significant increase in reaction time with increasing delay ($F_{2,34} = 17.60$, $P < 0.01$). Despite no overall group difference in reaction time between signs and words, inspection of individual subjects' protocols often showed quite marked differences, although not always in the same direction. Separate analyses of each subject's response protocol, using a single-subject analysis of variance developed by Shine and Bower (Shine and Bower, 1971; Shine, 1973), showed that 5 of the 11 subjects with a significant ($P < 0.05$) reaction time difference were quicker at processing signs and 6 were quicker with words. This finding of 11 significant differences out of 18 is higher than would be expected by chance.

Response Accuracy   Analysis of variance of means of subjects' average numbers of incorrect responses under the different conditions yielded no significant effect for the signs/words factor ($F_{1,17} = 0.38$, ns) but a significant effect for the delay ($F_{2,34} = 9.97$, $P < 0.01$). Binomial tests carried out on each subject's accuracy pattern showed that, of the 10 subjects who had a significant sign/word difference in response accuracy ($P < 0.05$), 5 were better at words and 5 at signs. As with the reaction time data, the number of statistically significant tests is higher than would be expected by chance.

Comparison of the Two Measures   Comparison of each subject's response bias for both reaction time and response accuracy measures showed that 7 of the 18 subjects who took part in the experiment showed a bias on both measures in the same direction with both differences significant. Another 4 subjects showed the same bias on both measures with only one difference being significant. No subject was found to have a different bias on the two measures, both of which were significant, and 3 subjects showed a different bias on the two measures with one of them being significant (see Table 1) below.

EXPERIMENT II

Because rehearsal was observed on some trials in Experiment I, the second experiment was designed to look at memory performance when the possibility of rehearsal was reduced. To achieve this, a counter sorting and naming task was performed by the children during the retention intervals.

Method

Subjects   Seventeen of the 18 subjects used in Experiment I were used in this study.

Equipment   The same equipment was used as in the last experiment with the addition of four boxes colored red, green, yellow, and blue, and four sets of 10 counters in the same colors. The boxes and counters were laid out between the subject and the screen.

Procedure   This was the same as that in Experiment I. In addition, during the 5- and 10-second delay periods children were required to sort the counters into the boxes by color using both hands alternately while simultaneously naming the colors. With all subjects the experimenter also called out the colors of the counters. This task was included to interfere with any possible manual rehearsal of signs or vocal rehearsal of words.

Results

Like Experiment I, this experiment yielded both reaction time and response accuracy data. A major difference between the results of the two studies, however, was the very low incidence of misidentification responses in this experiment. Instead, subjects indicated that they had forgotten the item and failed to respond. Analyses exactly similar to those of Experiment I were therefore not always possible.

Reaction Times   As in Experiment I, analysis of variance of means of subjects' average reaction times for both correct and incorrect signs and words gave no main effect for the signs/words factor ($F_{1,16} = 0.49$, ns) but a significant effect for delay ($F_{2,32} = 8.91$, $P < 0.01$). Because of the large numbers of failed trials under the 5- and 10-second delay conditions, two-factor single subject analyses were not possible on all levels of these data. A one-factor single subject analysis of variance (Shine and Bower, 1971) carried out on each subject's 1-second delay data showed that 11 of the 17 subjects were faster with signs than with words, eight of these differences being significant at the 0.01 level. Of the 6 subjects showing a faster reaction time to words, 5 differences were significant at or beyond $P < 0.01$.

Response Accuracy   Because errors consisted of both misidentifications and failures to respond, this section deals with rates of correct responding. Analysis of the means of each subject's average number of correct responses showed significant main effects for both the sign/word factor ($F_{1,16} = 7.67$, $P < 0.05$) and for delay ($F_{2,32} = 84.81$, $P < 0.01$) as well as for the interaction term ($F_{2,32} = 8.93$, $P < 0.01$).

The finding of a significant difference in response accuracy for signs/words contrasts both with the reaction time data from this experiment and with the findings of Experiment I. Inspection of means showed that the accuracy difference was present only under the 5- and 10-second delay conditions, subjects showing better performance on words than on signs. This suggests that the interpolated task was more effective at interfering with sign processing.

Comparison of Results   Comparison of subjects' performance on the two data measures revealed that 9 of the 17 subjects showed a bias in the same direction on both measures. Of these, 2 had significant differences on both measures and 6 had a significant ($P < 0.05$) difference on one of the measures. Of the 8 subjects showing a different bias on each measure, 1 had significant differences on both measures and 6 were significant on one measure only.

EXPERIMENT III

The main aim of this study was to examine how children handled strings of 4 signs or words under different periods of delay. However, this and the fourth study provide data comparable to those in Experiments I and II on biases in recall.

Method

Subjects and Equipment   Restrictions on time permitted the testing of only 8 subjects in this experiment, 7 of whom took part in the previous two experiments. The same equipment as in Experiment I was used.

Procedure   Individual children were presented with strings of 4 signs or 4 words and asked to identify the appropriate pictures 1, 5, or 10 seconds after the last item had been presented. Reaction time for the first response was recorded, and all the child's responses were recorded in order. Twenty-three trials were given per day over a 6-day period, with equal numbers of sign and word trials under each delay condition.

Results

For comparison with the two earlier studies, only the reaction time and response accuracy data are presented here.

Reaction Times   Analysis of means of subjects' average reaction times for all sign and word strings showed no main effect for the sign/ word factor ($F_{1,7}$ = 0.55, ns) but a significant effect for delay ($F_{2,14}$ = 8.44, P < 0.01). Single subject analyses of variance on the reaction time data revealed only one subject showing a sign/word difference that was significant.

Response Accuracy   The measure of accuracy used here was each subject's total number of items correct. This gives each subject a score from 0 to 92 under each pair of conditions. Analysis of the mean numbers of correct stimulus items under the different conditions revealed no main effect for the sign/word factor ($F_{1,7}$ = 3.71, ns), delay ($F_{2,14}$ = 1.36, ns), or interaction ($F_{2,14}$ = 1.87, ns). Analysis of each individual subject's response patterns by binomial test revealed only one subject with a significant sign/word difference.

EXPERIMENT IV

This experiment looked at children's ability to handle strings of 4 signs or words without having to use them as names for pictures.

Method

Subjects and Equipment   Nine subjects, all of whom participated in one or more of the previous experiments, were used in this study. Only a clockwork timer was needed for the experiment.

Procedure   The same design was used as in Experiment III. The procedure involved the experimenter presenting the child with a string of 4 signs or words and, after the prescribed delay of 1, 5, or 10 seconds, asking the child to produce the string by making the signs or speaking the words.

Results

Only response accuracy data are available here because the experiment did not permit the measurement of reaction time. Analysis of variance on the mean numbers of items correct under the different pairs of conditions gave no main effect for signs/words ($F_{1,8}$ = 1, ns) or for delay ($F_{2,16}$ = 4.07, ns). Binomial tests on subjects' individual data showed only one subject to have a significant difference in response accuracy.

COMPARISON OF RESULTS ACROSS STUDIES

Table 1 shows each subject's response bias and its significance for reaction time and response accuracy measures in Experiments I, II, and III and for the response accuracy measures in Experiment IV.

Table 1. Comparison of response biases of individual subjects across measures and experiments

Subject	Experiment I			Experiment II			Experiment III			Experiment IV
	RT[a]	Acc[b]	Agmt[c]	RT[a]	Acc[b]	Agmt[c]	RT[a]	Acc[b]	Agmt[c]	Acc[b]
1	S**	S**	[A]	S**	W	D	—	—		
2	S*	S**	[A]	S**	S	A	S	S	a	S
3	W*	W	A	W**	W**	A	S	W	d	W
4	W	S	d	S	S	D	—	—		
5	S	S	a	S**	S	A	—	—		
6	S**	S**	[A]	S	W	a	—	—		
7	W*	W	A	S**	W*	D	—	—		W
8	S*	S*	[A]	W**	W**	[A]	S	W	d	S**
9	W*	S	D	W**	W	A	—	—		W
10	S	S*	A	S**	W**	[D]	—	—		
11	S	W	d	S*	S*	[A]	—	—		
12	W	W*	A	W	W*	A	—	—		
13	W**	W**	[A]	W**	W	A	—	—		
14	W*	W**	[A]	—	—		—	—		
15	S	S	a	S	W	d	W	W	a	S
16	=	W**	D	S**	W	D	S	W	d	
17	W*	W**	[A]	W**	S	D	S	W**	D	S
18	S**	=	D	S**	W	D	W	=	D	S
19	—			—	—		S*	W	D	S

[a] RT = reaction time; S = sign, W = word; *P < 0.05, **P < 0.01; = indicates equivalent response time for signs and words.
[b] Acc = response accuracy; remaining symbols as for reaction time data.
[c] Agmt = agreement between the two measures; a/d = agree/disagree with neither significant; A/D = agree/disagree with one significant; [A]/[D] = agree/disagree with both significant.

Also shown is the level of agreement for the two measures taken in Experiments I, II, and III.

These data show an almost total absence of significant differences on the two experiments requiring retention of more than one item. This suggests that response accuracy and reaction time are not as sensitive a measure of difference in sign/word processing as in the single-item tasks. Examination of the consistency of each subject's response bias across measures and experiments shows 10 of the 19 subjects who took part in one or more of the series of experiments to have two or more significant sign/word differences in the same direction, and 4 to have two or more significant differences that differ in direction. Of these last 4, only one subject (Subject 10) showed different directional biases that are significant on both measures from the same experiment.

DISCUSSION

The main aim of the present series of studies was to examine the short-term memory performance of retarded children on manual signs or spoken words when presented either singly or in groups of 4. Analysis of reaction time and response accuracy data gave rise to three main findings.

First, differences between signs and words on these two measures were apparent only when single items were presented. Reaction time and response accuracy effects seemed to disappear when strings of 4 items were presented for recall. Other analyses of the data from Experiments III and IV on serial order effects (in preparation) may show up differences not tapped by the measures presented here.

The second finding was the presence on only one measure—response accuracy in Experiment II—of significant sign/word difference for the whole group of subjects. In the other three experiments, no significant group differences were found in spite of often quite large differences for individual subjects, the different direction of which eliminated any overall group difference. The response accuracy group difference in Experiment II may well result from the counter sorting task being more effective at disrupting memory of signs than of words.

A final point, related to the last observation, concerns the consistency of response bias across subjects. Although there was quite a high level of consistency for individual subjects across measures and experiments, the presence of 4 subjects who showed a different bias on different measures prompts a reevaluation of how the demands of a particular task might influence responding in a particular direction.

The main conclusion to be drawn from these studies concerns the need to evaluate individual rather than group patterns of response. This is in line with a suggestion of Ellis (1978) of a need to progress from simple group effect considerations to finer-grained analyses of subgroup or individual subject data.

REFERENCES

Archer, E. J. 1960. A re-evaluation of the meaningfulness of all possible CVC trigrams. Psychol Monogr. 74, No. 10 (whole number).

Belmont, J. M., and Butterfield, E. C. 1969. The relations of short-term memory to development and intelligence. In: L. P. Lipsett and H. W. Reese (eds.), Advances in Child Development and Behavior, Vol. 4. Academic Press, Inc., New York.

Belmont, J. M., and Butterfield, E. C. 1971. Learning strategies as determinants of memory. Cognit. Psychol. 2:411–420.

Brown, A. L. 1974. The role of strategic behaviour in retardate memory. In: N. R. Ellis (ed.), International Review of Research in Mental Retardation, Vol. 7. Academic Press, Inc., New York.

Ellis, N. R. 1970. Memory processes in retardates and normals. In: N. R. Ellis (ed.), International Review of Research in Mental Retardation, Vol. 4. Academic Press, Inc., New York.

Ellis, N. R. 1978. Do the mentally retarded have poor memory? Intelligence 2:41–54.

Hagen, J. W., Streeter, L. A., and Raker, R. 1974. Labeling, rehearsal, and short-term memory in retarded children. J. Exp. Child Psychol. 18:259–268.

Kiernan, C. C., and Bowler, D. M. The imitation and learning of features of sign language. (in preparation)

Kiernan, C. C., Reid, B. D., and Jones, L. M. 1982. Signs and Symbols: A Review of Literature and Survey of Use of Non Vocal Communication Systems. University of London Institute of Education Studies in Education, No. 11., London.

O'Connor, N., and Hermelin, B., 1978. Seeing and Hearing and Space and Time. Academic Press, Inc., New York.

Shine, L. C. 1973. A multi-way analysis of variance for single-subject designs. Educ. Psychol. Meas. 33:633–636.

Shine, L. C., and Bower, S. M. 1971. A one-way analysis of variance for single-subject designs. Educ. Psychol. Meas. 31:105–113.

Spreen, O. 1965. Language functions in mental retardation. A review. I. Language development, types of retardation and intelligence level. Am. J. Ment. Defic. 69:482–494.

Underwood, B. J., and Schulz, R. W. 1960. Meaningfulness and Verbal Learning. J. B. Lippincott Company, Philadelphia, Pennsylvania.

PERSPECTIVES AND PROGRESS IN MENTAL RETARDATION
Volume I—Social, Psychological, and Educational Aspects
Edited by J. M. Berg

ACQUISITION AND RECALL OF SIGNS AND WORDS BY MENTALLY HANDICAPPED CHILDREN

B. Reid

Thomas Coram Research Unit, University of London Institute of Education, 41 Brunswick Square, London WC1N 1AZ, England

Processing of spoken words and manual signs was compared in the context of three paradigms: acquisition of labeling responses, release from proactive inhibition in short-term memory, and recall from short-term memory in response to ambiguous stimuli. There was an advantage in favor of signs in the label acquisition studies, no advantage for either mode in the release from proactive inhibition studies, and a slight advantage in favor of words in the ambiguous stimuli study.

The research program described in this paper began in 1977, by which time there were several reports of successful sign acquisition by mentally handicapped individuals who had been unable to acquire speech (e.g., Sutherland and Beckett, 1969; Levett, 1971). Kiernan (1977) pointed out in his review of these reports that, although they supported the basic claim that mentally handicapped people could learn to sign and use other alternative systems, they provided little explanation for the effectiveness of these systems. Acknowledging that a single explanation for the success of alternative systems was unlikely, Kiernan suggested several lines of investigation that included examination of teaching methods, mechanisms of sign and word production, intellectual and neurological prerequisites, and cognitive processing of vocal and nonvocal input. In response to the last suggestion, the research program described here set out to explore some of the elements involved in the cognitive processing of signs and words by mentally handicapped children.

Spoken words and manual signs are expressed in different modes, the former by sounds produced by the speaker and the latter by hand pictures produced by the signer. Words and signs are also received differently, by the ear and the eye, respectively. Studies involving American Sign Language suggest that this modality difference also extends to the coding of utterances for memory (Bellugi and Klima, 1975). Although both signs and words are coded in terms of formational parameters, these parameters differ according to input mode. Bellugi and Klima found that spoken words were coded in terms of phonological features and manual signs were coded in terms of visuospatial features. Work by Hermelin and O'Connor (1975) and Morris (1975) suggests that severely mentally handicapped subjects may show a preference for visuospatial coding over audiosequential coding. If mentally handicapped people, like Bellugi and Klima's subjects, encode the visuospatial parameters of signs and the audiosequential parameters of spoken words, then we might expect them to be more successful in their preferred processing channel, and to show a greater facility for remembering signs than for remembering words.

Although the experimental work described above suggests differences in short-term memory of signs and words, the signing studies reported in the literature (e.g., Sutherland and Beckett, 1969; Richardson, 1975) involved a different process, the acquisition of signs as a working vocabulary to be stored in long-term memory and used for labeling or requested objects and activities. The present research program investigated both types of processing. The first set of four experiments compared the acquisition of signs and words as labels for objects, and investigated the effect of learning signs on the subsequent learning of words. The second set of experiments investigated short-term memory processes. Two studies used the release from proactive inhibition paradigm (Wickens, 1970) to compare the encoding of signs and words, and one study used ambiguous stimuli that could have been encoded as either signs or words to explore subjects' preferred mode of response.

This report uses data drawn from five of these experiments (two acquisition and three short-term memory) to examine the differences between signs and words in three memory processes: label acquisition, using a paired-associates procedure; short-term recall, using the release from proactive inhibition procedure; and preferred response mode for short-term recall, using an ambiguous stimuli procedure. Although there was no experimental evidence on which to base a prediction about the relative rate of sign and word acquisition for long-term memory, the reports in teaching studies of successful sign learning by subjects who had failed to learn words (e.g., Richardson, 1975; Topper, 1975) suggested that signs might be acquired at a faster rate. Short-term memory experiments with mentally handicapped children (Hermelin and O'Connor, 1975), taken together with the encoding differences for signs and words in deaf and hearing adults (Bellugi and Klima, 1975), suggested that signs would also have an advantage over words in short-term recall.

METHOD

Subjects

Subjects in all five experiments were children attending schools for the severely educationally subnormal in Inner and Greater London. They ranged in chronological age from 4 years 9 months to 15 years 11 months (median 11 years 11 months), and in mental age, measured by the Peabody Picture Vocabulary Test, from 2 years 3 months to 7 years 5 months (median 4 years). All subjects were able to imitate signs and words, as judged by the experimenter. Although many subjects made "articulation" errors in both modes, all met the criterion of a distinguishable consonant-vowel response to a nonsense consonant-vowel-consonant (CVC) stimulus, and a distinguishable handshape or location response to a nonsense manual sign.

The number of subjects varied from study to study. The two acquisition experiments had 12 and 36 subjects, respectively. Analyses for this paper used group data from 6 subjects in the first experiment and 9 subjects in the second. Individual data were used from 12 and 9 subjects, respectively. The bases for choosing this data set are explained below in "Procedures and Results."

The two memory studies that used the proactive inhibition (PI) procedure had the same 6 subjects in each study. The memory study that used the ambiguous stimuli procedure had 7 subjects, none of whom had participated in the PI studies.

Materials

Words were all nonsense CVCs. They were varied within each experiment, so that no one combination of vowel and initial consonant or vowel and final consonant occurred more than once in the list. *Signs* were all nonsense manual signs, which could vary in handshape or location. With a few exceptions in the first acquisition experiment, handshapes used were those that a similar group of mentally handicapped subjects found easiest to imitate correctly (see Kiernan, "Imitation and Learning of Hand Postures," this volume). *Stimulus cards* were cartoon pictures of novel "funny faces." Within each experiment, the color combination for each face was different, and no combination of main color and basic shape occurred more than once in the set.

Location

All work was done with individual children outside the classroom, in a separate room or space in the school.

PROCEDURES AND RESULTS

This paper presents data from five experiments, which have been labeled Acquisition 1 and 2 and Memory 1, 2, and 3 for ease of reference. The procedure and results for each experiment are described separately and in chronological order, because some of the experiments are based on the results of preceding ones. Data sources and results of the present analyses are described at the end of the relevant sections.

Acquisition Experiments

Acquisition 1   The first phase of this experiment consisted of sign-learning by the six subjects in group A and word-learning by the six subjects in group B. In the second phase the modes were reversed, with group A learning words and group B learning signs. This study had been designed as a first experimental investigation of the suggestion from the applied literature that signs were more easily learned by mentally handicapped people than were words. The study confirmed this suggestion, with a significant main effect for signs ($F_{1,8} = 6.27, P < 0.05$).

Acquisition 2   This was a further experiment in the acquisition series, which confirmed the main effect of Acquisition 1.

Combined Analysis—Acquisitions 1 and 2   Data that allowed comparison of sign and word acquisition rates were combined for this analysis. The first phase of Acquisition 1 yielded data on word learning for 6 subjects and sign learning for 6 subjects. The first phase of Acquisition 2 yielded the same sets of data on two additional groups of 9 subjects each. Data are available from seven daily training sessions, and take the form of number of correct, unprompted responses per session.

The acquisition rates for sign and word labels over seven training sessions are presented in Figure 1. Inspection of the graph shows a clear advantage for sign acquisition rates over word acquisition rates, which is more marked in the early stages of training than in the later ones. A 2×7 ANOVA on these data yielded significant main effect for modality, in favor of signs ($F_{1,28} = 20.5, P < 0.01$).

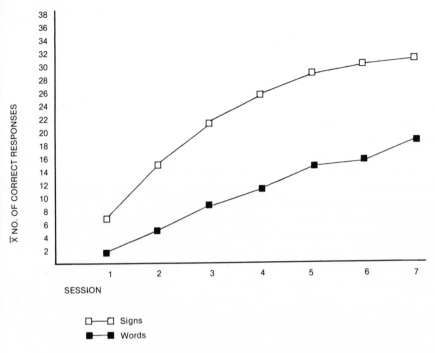

Figure 1.   Mean number of signs and words acquired per daily session.

Memory Experiments

Memory 1   This experiment followed the standard release from proactive inhibition (PI) paradigm (Wickens, 1970). Subjects were presented with three stimuli over a period of approximately 20 seconds. In this experiment they named the stimulus cards (cartoon faces) with the appropriate sign or word label. After a filled interval of 15 seconds subjects were asked to recall the names of the three stimuli that had been presented in that trial. Each subject's score per trial consisted of 1 point for each correct response, with an additional point for recalling all three stimuli in the order of presentation (after Wickens, 1970).

Before the PI tests were conducted each subject learned each stimulus-label pair to a criterion of all labels correct for three consecutive sessions. The PI test phase contained four conditions: two shift conditions (three trials of words followed by one trial of signs, or vice versa), and two nonshift conditions (four trials of words or four trials of signs). The test phase was replicated once after a 3-week interval.

The results showed a significant interaction between trials (1 to 3 versus 4) and conditions (shift versus nonshift) ($F_{1,10}$ = 17.36, $P <$

0.01). This interaction indicated the presence of release from proactive inhibition. An additional release measure, recovery rate in the shift conditions, showed that 91.7% of the information lost through proactive inhibition was "recovered" in the shift conditions (see Reid and Kiernan, 1979 for a full description). These results suggested an encoding difference for short-term memory, but the source of the difference was not clear. Subjects had been presented with two kinds of stimuli—the face cards themselves, and the sign and words that were used to label them. Although the sign-word difference seemed to be the most salient one, it was possible that subjects were encoding labels on the basis of class of stimulus card; this could have been a difference in taxonomic category between the groups of cards. Memory 2 was designed to control for this possibility.

Memory 2   The procedure for this experiment was identical to that for Memory 1, with one exception: no stimulus cards were presented. In place of labeling cards, subjects imitated the relevant signs and words as presented by the experimenter. Results were similar to Memory 1, with a significant difference between shift and nonshift conditions on the last trial ($F_{1,5} = 4.94$, $P < 0.05$), and a recovery rate of 93.8%.

Combined Analysis—Memory 1 and 2   In the two PI experiments, the number of correct responses on the first three trials of each condition yielded a rate of recall of signs and words for each of the 6 subjects; these are shown in Figure 2. The graph shows virtually no difference between sign recall and word recall rates, and this is confirmed by a 2×3 ANOVA, which yielded a nonsignificant main effect for modality ($F_{1,5} = 1.16$, $P > 0.05$).

Memory 3   This experiment was designed to test modality preference in memory more directly by giving subjects a forced choice recall task where they could respond with either a sign-label or a word-label. As in the PI experiments, signs and words were trained to the same criterion and should have been equally available as labels. The 10 training stimuli, cartoon faces, were designed in five related pairs. Each pair shared a similar shape and major features (e.g., hat, hair), but differed in minor features and in color. The cards within each pair were randomly assigned to either list A or list B. Four of the subjects learned words for list A and signs for list B; the remaining 3 subjects had the opposite pattern. Subjects were required to meet criterion of 40 correct responses (four blocks of 10 stimuli) on two consecutive sessions.

Ambiguous test stimuli were five black outlines drawn on white cards. Each ambiguous stimulus included the shared characteristics of its related training stimulus pair (shape, major feature), but did not

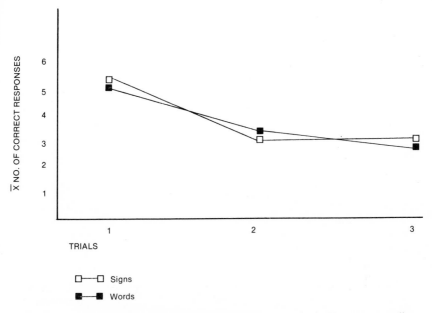

Figure 2.   Mean number of signs and words recalled per trial in PI memory studies.

include any of the differing characteristics of the training stimuli (color, minor features). The test sessions involved eight presentations of the five ambiguous stimuli. Subjects were shown each stimulus in turn and asked "Who is this?" The experimenter recorded whether the subject had given a verbal, signed, or combined response, and whether the response was correct. Only correct, single-mode responses were scored, yielding a sign recall score and a word recall score for each of the 7 subjects; these are presented in Figure 3. Because a response in one mode precluded a response in the other, the two lines on the graph form a mirror image about the mean. The graph shows equivalence of sign and word response rates on the first trial block, followed by increasing disparity over subsequent trial blocks, with words being the preferred response mode. A binomial test on the total scores yields a Z score of 3.30, showing a significant effect in favor of words ($P <$ 0.01).

Individual Differences

Data from these five experiments also permit comparison of the preferred response mode of individual subjects. In the two acquisition studies, measures of total words correct and total signs correct were available for each of 21 subjects. Sign tests on these data indicated that

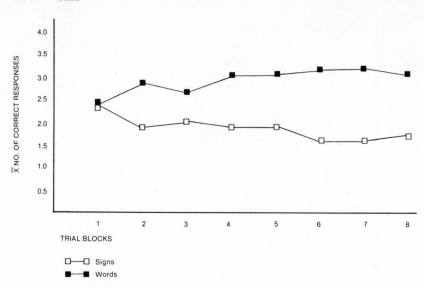

Figure 3.   Mean number of sign and word responses per trial to ambiguous stimuli.

14 subjects (67% of the sample) showed significantly higher rates of sign acquisition, 5 subjects (24%) showed significantly higher rates of word acquisition, and 2 subjects (9%) showed no significant difference in mode. Percentage data are presented in Figure 4.

In the PI memory studies, measures of total words recalled and total signs recalled were available for each of 6 subjects. Sign tests on these data showed no significant modality effects (Figure 4). Finally, individual data on response mode were available for the 7 subjects in the ambiguous stimuli experiment. Only one subject (14%) showed a significant effect for signs and 3 subjects (43%) for words; the other 3 subjects showed no significant modality effects. These data are also presented in Figure 4.

DISCUSSION

The analyses presented in this paper address the question of the effect of stimulus mode (visual or auditory) on label acquisiton and short-term recall in mentally handicapped children. Although the literature suggested a significant advantage for the visuospatial mode (i.e., signs) in short-term memory, in fact this did not emerge. However, signs were the stronger mode in the acquisition of labeling responses. This advantage for signs was found both in group data (overall numbers of correct responses) and in individual data (number of subjects showing significantly higher sign scores).

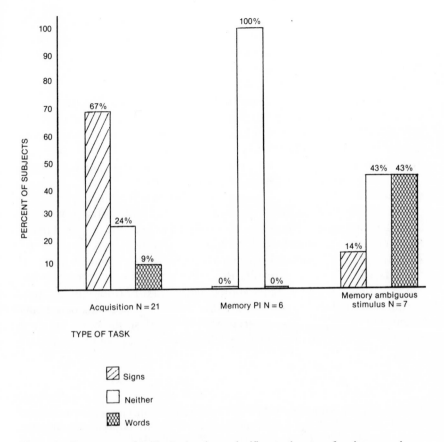

Figure 4. Percentage of subjects showing a significant advantage for signs, words, or neither in each of the three types of study.

This result is consistent with the reported literature on sign acquisition by subjects who had failed to learn speech. Signs have also been used with speaking children as mediators for the acquisition of receptive word labels (Bricker, 1972) and expressive word labels (Kotkin et al., 1978). All of these studies suggest that the processing of manual signs during label acquisition may be less difficult than the processing of spoken words.

However, the memory studies reported in the present paper suggest that this advantage for signs is not a general feature of cognitive processing by mentally handicapped children. Although the two PI experiments did demonstrate a release from proactive inhibition, allowing the conclusion that the two types of stimuli are in fact encoded differently for short-term memory, the implied visuospatial encoding of signs did not give subjects an advantage in short-term recall, nor were signs more readily recalled in the ambiguous stimuli experiment. One subject demonstrated an advantage for signed responses, but the remaining 6 were evenly divided between an advantage for spoken responses and no modality difference.

It is interesting that the substantial advantage for signed responses evident in the acquisition studies virtually disappears in the memory experiments. Both types of memory experiments involved pretraining of spoken and signed labels to a very stringent criterion. This suggests that, although signs have an advantage in the initial acquisition stage, word labels, when overlearned to the same criterion, can be recalled with equal or even greater facility from short-term memory.

It is clear that the effect of stimulus mode on cognitive processing is not a simple one. Although signs may be more readily acquired overall, there are still substantial individual differences among subjects. The two memory paradigms reported here, release from PI and ambiguous stimuli, yielded results that were consistent with each other but at variance with the acquisition experiments. Further studies comparing signs and words in the context of different processing paradigms might help to explain this discrepancy, and to describe more fully the complex interactions between modalities, processes, and individuals.

REFERENCES

Bellugi, U., and Klima, E. S. 1975. Aspects of sign language and its structure. In: J. F. Kavanagh and J. E. Cutting (eds.), The Role of Speech in Language, pp. 171–203. MIT Press, Cambridge, Massachusetts.

Bricker, D. D. 1972. Imitative sign training as a facilitator of word-association with low-functioning children. Am. J. Ment. Defic. 76:509–516.

Hermelin, B., and O'Connor, N. 1975. Seeing, speaking and ordering. In: N. O'Connor (ed.), Language, Cognitive Deficits and Retardation, pp. 129–138. Butterworths, London.

Kiernan, C. C. 1977. Alternatives to speech: A review of research on manual and other forms of communication with the mentally handicapped and other noncommunicating populations. Br. J. Ment. Subnorm. 23:6–28.

Kotkin, R. A., Simpson, S. B., and Desanto, D. 1978. The effect of sign language on picture naming in two retarded girls possessing normal hearing. J. Ment. Defic. Res. 22:19–25.

Levett, L. M. 1971. A method of communication for non-speaking severely subnormal children—Trial results. Br. J. Disord. Communic. 6:125–128.

Morris, G. P. 1975. Language and memory in the severely retarded. In: N. O'Connor (ed.), Language, Cognitive Deficits and Retardation, pp. 143–150. Butterworths, London.

Reid, B. D., and Kiernan, C. C. 1979. Spoken words and manual signs as encoding categories in short-term memory for mentally retarded children. Am. J. Ment. Defic. 84:203–206.

Richardson, T. 1975. Sign language for the SMR and PMR. Ment. Retard. 13:17.

Sutherland, G. F., and Beckett, J. W. 1969. Teaching the mentally retarded sign language. J. Rehab. Deaf 2:56–60.

Topper, S. T. 1975. Gesture language for a non-verbal severely retarded male. Ment. Retard. 13:30–31.

Wickens, D. D. 1970. Encoding categories of words: An empirical approach to meaning. Psychol. Rev. 77:1–15.

PERSPECTIVES AND PROGRESS IN MENTAL RETARDATION
Volume I—Social, Psychological, and Educational Aspects
Edited by J. M. Berg

IMITATION AND LEARNING OF HAND POSTURES

C. Kiernan

Thomas Coram Research Unit, University of London Institute of Education, 41 Brunswick Square, London WC1N 1AZ, England

In planning programs utilizing sign languages and systems, practitioners are faced with questions of selection of vocabulary. Initial signs may be chosen on the basis of functionality for the individual, and receptively, in terms of needs for parents or caregivers to transmit information or requests of choices. This paper describes studies that suggest that, in addition to these considerations, structural features of signs need to be taken into account in vocabulary selection. In particular, the type of hand posture employed in signs and whether the signs require one or two hands to execute is shown to produce significant differences in imitation and expressive learning. It is suggested that easy-to-execute signs may be taught initially.

Until recently language programming for retarded children without speech presented almost insuperable problems. The success rate on even well-developed speech-based programs is modest (Goetz et al., 1979) and the amount of time required is excessive. Kiernan et al. (1979, 1982) found that around a third of children in schools for the severely and profoundly retarded in the United Kingdom were said to be unable to use more than three spoken words to express needs or requests.

The use of alternative or augmentative systems with these children and others offers a possible route for teaching of language and communication skills. Their use not only sidesteps specific speech and hearing problems but offers a "new start" for children who may have found speech training frustrating, and a more readily prompted response mode for the teacher to work with. The relative success of use of such systems also suggests hypotheses relating to modality effects in information processing capacity (Kiernan, 1983).

Evidence from surveys of use of manual sign systems and languages indicates that they are becoming increasingly popular in schools for the severely and profoundly retarded in the U.K. Our most recent

251

data suggest that around 89.5% of such schools are employing a sign language (Reid, Jones, and Kiernan, 1983). Schools report mixed success, with some pupils learning very few signs and others learning over 50 symbols within a few months, and with frequent mention of facilitation of speech within sign programs (Kiernan et al., 1982).

In planning programs utilizing sign languages and systems, practitioners and researchers are faced with questions of selection of vocabulary. Initial expressive signs may be chosen in terms of functionality for the individual and, receptively, in terms of the needs of teachers and caregivers to transmit information or request choices. Within this framework practitioners may utilize one of the several available vocabularies (Fristoe and Lloyd, 1980).

Considerations other than the meaning of signs may be taken into account. Signs, like spoken words, can be analyzed in terms of their form (for example, in terms of hand postures used, whether one or two hands are employed, speed and type of movements made) and accompanying facial expressions. It seems reasonable to suggest that the learner will need to build up an "articulatory framework," possibly involving contrasting features, in much the way that a child learning to speak builds up his knowledge of an ability to use speech sounds (Ingram, 1976). Initial phases of sign programs may need to consider these factors. This paper describes four studies that explore the ease of imitation, expressive and receptive learning of hand postures, and the ease of imitation of signs employing one or two hands in their formation.

IMITATION OF HAND POSTURES

In the first study we examined the ease of imitation of 27 hand postures by mentally retarded and nonretarded children. The hand postures selected were taken from published sources illustrating signs in American Sign Language (ASL) (Wilbur, 1979), British Sign Language (BSL) (Woll et al., 1981), and the Paget Gorman Sign System (PGSS) (Wilbur, 1979).

Sixty severely mentally retarded children and 60 nursery school children were employed. Children with cerebral palsy or other physical disabilities were included if at least one hand was judged as functioning normally. The groups were assessed using the Peabody Picture Vocabulary Test (Dunn, 1965); the retarded group had a mental age of 45.0 months and the nursery group a mental age of 62.4 months. Twenty-seven hand postures were employed (Figure 1). They represented all postures used in a sample of 148 spoken words that were translated into ASL, BSL, and PGSS. The analysis showed that three

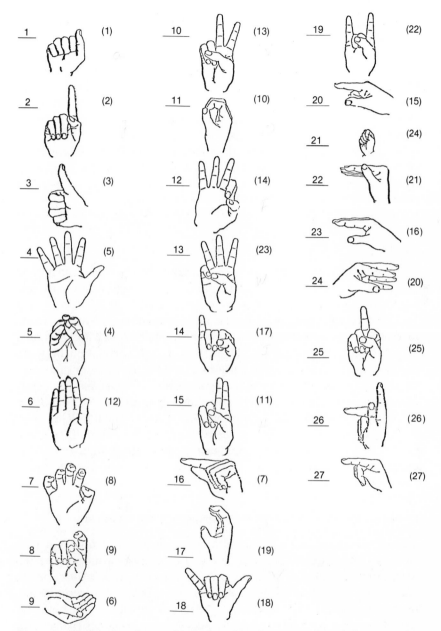

Figure 1. Rank order of ease of imitation of hand postures. Retarded group underscored; normal group in parentheses.

types of posture, flat hands (B and B with thumb parallel to hand), fist hand (A hand), and index finger hands (L and L with thumb parallel to hand) were used by ASL and BSL in 55.1% and 54.1% of signs, respectively, whereas PGSS used them only in 39% of signs (chi square = 16.01, $d.f.$ = 2, $P < 0.01$; see Kiernan, 1983, for further analysis of these and related data).

The procedure involved an initial warm-up phase in which the experimenter introduced the task as a "game with our hands" and demonstrated hand postures for the child to imitate. Physical prompting and correction was used until the child met a criterion of four consecutive correct unprompted trials. The 27 postures were presented in a counterbalanced order. Each child was asked to imitate each posture once.

Results

Rank order of correct responses by mentally retarded (underlined) and nonretarded children (in parentheses) for each posture are shown in Figure 1. Frequency of correct responses ranged from 100%, 80%, and 78.3% correct for fist, index finger, and "spread hand," respectively, to 18.3%, 15%, and 10% for the three postures ranked 25th, 26th, and 27th for the retarded group. There was a high correlation between performance of the two subject groups ($r = 0.96$). Correlations between frequency of occurrence in sign languages and systems and frequency of correct imitations were all positive and significant (ASL, $r = 0.44$, $d.f.$ = 26, $P < 0.05$; BSL, $r = 0.50$, $d.f.$ = 26, $P < 0.01$; PGSS, $r = 0.46$, $d.f.$ = 26, $P < 0.05$). These data suggest that, overall, sign languages and systems tend to employ easy-to-imitate postures more frequently than difficult postures.

EXPRESSIVE AND RECEPTIVE LEARNING OF HANDSHAPES

The relative ease of imitating different hand postures does not necessarily relate to ease of expressive and receptive learning. In particular, postures that are difficult to imitate may be relatively easier to learn once the child has overcome initial problems of discrimination or motor control. Two studies explored this possibility. In both, we taught severely mentally retarded children signs as labels (names) for cartoon pictures. This task was used because it allowed us to select arbitrary signs and to relate these to neutral stimuli without possible contamination from earlier learning of verbal labels or association of gestures with the stimuli.

Expressive Learning

Twelve postures were selected from the previous study, six from the easy end of the scale and six from the difficult end. Fifteen children were employed in the study; all of them were severely retarded. Sign-cartoon pairings were varied across subgroups of children in order to allow for any differential difficulty of sign-word pairing.

Training was conducted over a 5-day period, with three blocks of 12 trials per child per day, in a quiet area in the child's school. The children were told that they were going to learn the "names" of the cartoon figures. On block one, the first picture was held up, the sign demonstrated, and the child encouraged to imitate and physically prompted if necessary. On subsequent blocks, imitation and physical prompts were provided if the child did not label the cartoon on request following presentation. All children learned all cartoon-sign pairings, but, as already noted, pairings were systematically varied.

Results   Data from the study are presented in Figure 2. Analysis of variance gave two significant F values, for ease of imitation, where the easy-to-imitate hand postures were learned more readily ($F_{1,14} = 23.83$, $P < 0.01$), and for days ($F_{4,56} = 46.92$, $P < 0.01$) reflecting acquisition. The interaction between days and difficulty was not significant.

Discussion   These data suggest that the ease of expressive learning of hand postures is related to ease of imitation. The greater the facility in learning the easier postures held for all 15 subjects. On average, children found it possible to learn easy postures around 1.7 times faster than they did the difficult-to-imitate postures.

Receptive Learning

A parallel study assessed receptive learning of hand postures. Here 9 severely mentally retarded children were taught the sign labels for 16 cartoon figures. Four cartoon figures were laid out before the children on each trial. The experimenter then made the sign name of one of the figures and, if necessary, prompted the child to indicate the correct figure or corrected incorrect responses. Signs used as names were identical to those used in the expressive learning study. The frequency of occurrences and position within the set of four stimuli presented for target and distractor items was systematically counterbalanced. In all, 96 trials were given per stimulus per day over a 5-day period.

Results   Data computed in terms of mean number of correct selections per day over the 5-day period are presented in Figure 3. Analysis of variance showed that the main effect of ease of imitation approached, but did not attain, an acceptable level of significance ($F_{1,8} = 4.32$, $0.05 < P < 0.10$), but that the learning effect, days, did attain

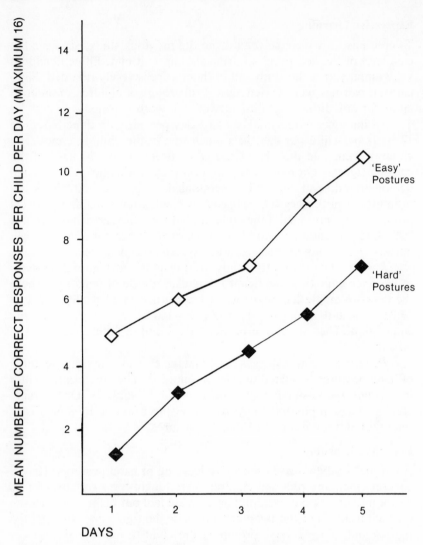

Figure 2.   Expressive learning of "easy"- and "hard"-to-imitate hand postures.

significance ($F_{4,32} = 10.59$, $P < 0.01$). The interaction effect between ease of imitation and days is not significant ($F_{4,32} = 19$, $P > 0.05$).

Discussion   Data from this study suggest that ease of imitation does not relate to ease of receptive learning. This conclusion contrasts with the findings from the expressive learning study. The learning of signs may be approached in terms of a visual perceptual component, reflected in all three studies, and a motor production component, pres-

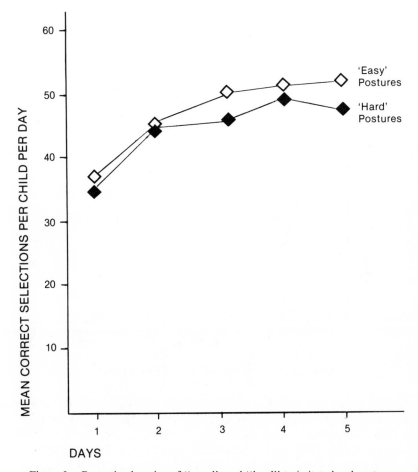

Figure 3. Receptive learning of "easy"- and "hard"-to-imitate hand postures.

ent only in the imitation and expressive learning studies. In terms of this simple analysis, we may suggest that the visual perceptual component has an effect that does not lead to statistical significance in receptive learning but that the motor component, when added to the visual perceptual component, produces such an effect, i.e., in the imitation and expressive learning studies.

HANDS STUDY

Sign languages differ in terms of the requirement for use of one hand (1H), two hands adopting the same posture (2HS), or two hands adopting different postures (2HD). Kiernan (1983) reported analyses of ASL

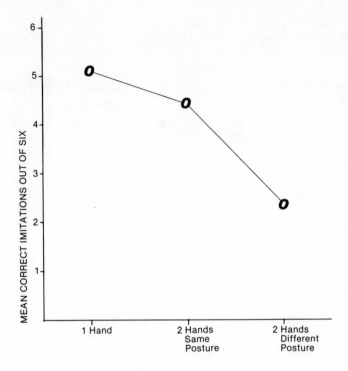

Figure 4.   Imitation of three types of hand postures.

and BSL suggesting that ASL employs more 2HS signs than BSL, with BSL favoring 1H signs (49.1% for ASL, as opposed to 36.7% for BSL, for 2HS signs). These conclusions were based on a sample of 148 signs. Analysis of 322 BSL signs shows that 46.3% were 2HS signs (signs adopted by the British Deaf and Dumb Association, 1960). The 2HD form is used relatively less frequently by ASL and BSL (16.4% and 14.0% respectively) but most frequently by the contrived PGSS system (49.1% of signs).

Two groups of 10 severely mentally retarded children were asked to imitate six hand postures presented singly (1H), with both hands adopting the same posture (2HS), or with the hands adopting different postures (2HD). The groups differed in terms of particular postures used, but all postures were selected from the "easy" end of the scale established in the first study reported here.

Results   Figure 4 presents the mean number of correct imitations for each of the three conditions. Analysis of variance established that the average level of correct imitative responses in the 1H and 2HS was significantly higher than in the 2HD condition, but the 1H versus 2HS difference was not significant ($F_{2,36} = 123.7$, $P < 0.01$).

Discussion   These data suggest that the forms of signs most commonly used in ASL and BSL (1H, 2HS) are significantly easier to imitate than the form of sign more commonly used by the contrived system, PGSS. We might speculate that the easier-to-imitate forms have been selected by users in the evolution of the natural sign languages. Data on expressive learning of this feature reflect these findings (Kiernan and Bowler, in preparation).

DISCUSSION

The results of the studies discussed in this paper suggest that the various postures used in sign languages and systems differ in difficulty of imitation for normal and mentally retarded children alike. Easy-to-imitate postures are easier for retarded children to learn expressively but no easier receptively, suggesting that the motor component of the posture presents problems to the children. Signs employing one hand or two hands adopting the same posture proved easier to imitate than signs employing two hands with different postures in each hand.

The data suggest that postures required and form of signs be considered in addition to functional value in selecting initial sign lexicons, and that there is a need to explore the development of "articulation" training for sign learners (Goodman et al., 1978). Before a systematic structure of features is learned by the child, practitioners may find it necessary to accept "baby forms." The data also suggest that natural sign languages (ASL and BSL) have selected postures and sign forms that are more readily acquired than alternatives but that PGSS has, in some respects, selected more difficult-to-learn options.

REFERENCES

British Deaf and Dumb Association. 1960. The Language of the Silent World. British Deaf and Dumb Association, Oxford, England.

Dunn, L. M. 1965. Peabody Picture Vocabulary Test. American Guidance Service, Minneapolis, Minnesota.

Fristoe, M., and Lloyd, L. L. 1980. Planning an initial expressive sign lexicon for persons with severe communication impairment. J. Speech Hear. Disord. 45:170–180.

Goetz, L., Schuler, A., and Sailor, W. 1979. Teaching functional speech to the severely handicapped: Current issues. J. Autism. Dev. Disord. 9:325–343.

Goodman, L., Wilson, P. S., and Bornstein, H. 1978. Results of a national survey of sign language programmes in special education. Ment. Retard. 16:104–106.

Ingram, D. 1976. Phonological Disability in Children. Edward Arnold, London.

Kiernan, C. C. 1983. The exploration of sign and symbol effects. In: J. Hogg and P. Mittler (eds.), Advances in Mental Handicap Research, Volume 2. Wiley, London.

Kiernan, C. C., Reid, B. D., and Jones, L. M. 1979. Signs and symbols: Who uses what? Spec. Educ: Forward Trends 6:32–34.

Kiernan, C. C., Reid, B. D., and Jones, L. M. 1982. Signs and Symbols. A Review of Literature and Survey of Use of Non Vocal Communication Systems. Studies in Education, No. 11. University of London Institute of Education, London.

Reid, B. D., Jones, L. M., and Kiernan, C. C. 1983. Signs and symbols. The 1982 survey of use. Spec. Ed.: Forward Trends 10:27–28.

Wilbur, R. B. 1979. American Sign Language and Sign Systems. University Park Press, Baltimore.

Woll, B., Kyle, J., and Deuchar, M. 1981. Perspectives on British Sign Language and Deafness. Croom Helm, London.

SECTION V
Education and Training

PERSPECTIVES AND PROGRESS IN MENTAL RETARDATION
Volume I—Social, Psychological, and Educational Aspects
Edited by J. M. Berg

TERMINOLOGY, CLASSIFICATION, AND EDUCATIONAL SERVICES FOR THE MENTALLY RETARDED IN THE U.S.S.R.

I. Z. Holowinsky

*Graduate School of Education, Rutgers University, 10 Seminary Place,
New Brunswick, New Jersey 08903*

This paper provides an overview of terminology, classification, and educational services for the mentally retarded in the Soviet Union. Soviet
defectologists (specialists in mental defects) maintain that mental retardation (oligophrenia) is related to a diffuse maldevelopment or defect of
the cortical hemispheres that leads to the pathological inertia of the central
nervous system. Classification of mental retardation involves medical or
etiological factors, level of intellectual functioning, adaptive behavior,
and an estimate of educational potential. Mentally retarded children are
trained and educated in a variety of facilities such as hospitals, institutions, residential schools, and auxiliary schools.

Currently we are witnessing increased interest in international education and service delivery systems to the handicapped population.
Mass media communication, jet travel, and participation in international conventions and projects brought into focus common problems
faced by handicapped individuals regardless of their nationality or cultural or racial background. Such conditions obviously contributed to
the ever-increasing international exchange of information in the field
of education of the handicapped, as manifested by the First World
Conference on the Future of Special Education, held in Stirling, Scotland, in 1978.

However, there are numerous problems hampering cross-cultural
and international comparisons. Some of the more important problems

can be identified: 1) cultural differences that determine how a deviant behavior is perceived in a given culture; 2) a particular philosophical outlook on life, or "weltanschaung," that influences terminology; 3) the level of sociocultural and economic development of a given society; 4) difficulty in direct translation of terminology; and 5) limited availability of primary source information. The purpose of this paper is to provide a brief overview of terminology, classification, and educational services for the mentally retarded as they exist at the present time in the Soviet Union.

TERMINOLOGY IN THE FIELD OF MENTAL RETARDATION

In most countries terminology in the field of mental retardation could be recognized as being of two types. One is generic, which is easily translatable and similar in many languages, for example "of feeble mind" or "feebleminded" (English), "débilité" (French), "Schwachsinn" (German), "umstvenno otstaly" (Russian), and "umovo nedorozvyneni" (Ukrainian). In addition to generic terminology, there is usually a more specific terminology that reflects cultural and scientific orientation, for example, "mental deficiency," "oligophrenia," and "intellectual subnormality."

The official view of mental retardation in the Soviet Union suggests that it is related to a diffuse maldevelopment or defect of the cortical hemispheres that leads to pathological inertia of the central nervous system. Intellectually impaired individuals are described in the Soviet Union either as "umstvenno otstaly" (Vlasova, 1971), which is a generic term and could be translated as "intellectually backward," or as "oligophrenic" (mentally deficient)—those in whom there is definite evidence of neurological insult (Luria, 1963; Pevzner, 1973). Because Soviet defectology does not acknowledge use of standardized IQ tests for the purpose of quantitative assessment of cognitive abilities, "umstvenno otstaly" as a group would compare to mildly retarded individuals of undifferentiated etiology. Oligophrenia more precisely would describe a condition within the range of profound to moderate retardation. Such individuals might be described in the United States as mentally deficient.

In the Ukraine the acceptable terminology for intellectual subnormality is "umove nedorozvynennia," which translates directly as "intellectual backwardness" or "mental retardation." It should also be pointed out that Soviet publications on defectology and oligophrenia are still using traditional terminology in reference to the levels of mental retardation, for example, "idiocy," "imbecility," and "debility" (fee-blemindedness).

In the late 1960s and early 1970s a new terminology was introduced into defectological literature. Studies began to appear that described children with delayed mental development ("zederzhka psikhitcheskavo razvytya"). Pevzner and Rostiagaylova (1981) reported recently that research with developmentally delayed children began in the Soviet Union in 1965 at the Scientific Research Institute of the Soviet Academy of Pedagogical Sciences. In 1966 a book by Pevzner entitled *Children with Developmental Deviations* was published in Moscow.

Children described as developmentally delayed in the Soviet Union in many respects are similar to those described in the United States as learning disabled. Many etiological factors are also similar to those found among mildly retarded children. Yavkin (1973) indicated that in both clinical groups such etiological factors as mild intrauterine and perinatal trauma, prematurity, chromosomal aberrations, endocrine disorders, and infectious illnesses in early childhood are found. Yassman (1976) agreed with Yavkin that many developmentally delayed children were similar in their performance to oligophrenic children. Comparisons between characteristics of normal, developmentally delayed, and mentally retarded children were made by Tsymbaliuk (1973), Vlasova et al. (1975), Markovskaya (1977), Zharenkova (1981), and Strelkova (1981).

CLASSIFICATION OF MENTAL RETARDATION

Classification of mental retardation usually involves medical or etiological factors, level of intellectual functioning, and adaptive behavior, as well as an estimate of educational potential. In the Soviet Union classification of the mentally retarded has been influenced by writings of Pevzner and Luria. Pevzner (1973) suggested that oligophrenia is related to biological defects of the central nervous system, especially of the most complex and late-developing brain structures. She suggested (Pevzner, 1970) that there were five etiological groups among oligophrenics. The first group is characterized by diffuse maldevelopment of the cortical hemispheres without serious neurological implications. The second involves cortical defects with impaired perceptual abilities. The third involves various sensory, perceptual, and motor defects. The fourth is associated with psychopathological behavior. The fifth group is associated with maldevelopment of the frontal lobes, with behavior similar to that seen in people with serious psychopathologies.

Luria (1963) classified oligophrenics into five groups on the basis of behavioral manifestations of the central nervous system involvement. The basic group, composed primarily of the mildly retarded, has suffered localized damage to the cerebral cortex, with no serious behavioral characteristics. To the second group he assigns those oligophrenics who are uninhibited and poorly controlled. They are "excitable" oligophrenics in whom the balance of the nervous process is disrupted in favor of excitation. The third group consists of listless, weak, passive oligophrenics in whom inhibition predominates over excitation. The fourth group is composed of oligophrenics who suffer from specific impairment in auditory or visual areas in addition to diffuse central nervous system damage. To the fifth group he assigns those oligophrenics who show gross underdevelopment of personality.

Individual intelligence tests are virtually unknown in the Soviet Union and the assessment of cognitive skills is based upon ideographic rather than nomothetic theory (Holowinsky, 1980). Levels of retardation are described primarily according to physiological characteristics (Luria, 1963). Luria suggested that idiots, the most severely deficient of the retarded, have suffered damage to the brain stem and subcortical areas as well as to the cerebral cortex; imbeciles have suffered lesser damage to subcortical and cortical areas. He maintained that feebleminded (mildly retarded) persons have only superficial damage to the cerebral hemispheres.

In the absence of standardized assessment of cognitive skills, achievement, and not a standardized test score, determines whether a child remains in a regular program or is placed in a special class in an auxiliary school. Upon admission to an auxiliary school a youngster is subjected to 2 weeks of cognitive and educational evaluations. The evaluations take place within and outside the school environment. The general purpose of such evaluations is to determine developmental level, knowledge of arithmetic and reading, orientation to the environment, speed of performing practical tasks, level of understanding, and learning potential. Children entering an auxiliary school are divided into two classes based on higher or lower cognitive abilities.

A youngster is placed in the lower special class level if he or she cannot recognize letters, cannot read, has no concept of numbers, has no practical hobbies, and is disoriented within the environment. Children who are placed in the advanced special class can recognize letters of the alphabet, can write letters, have some concept of numbers, have practical hobbies, and are generally well oriented to the environment. Em (1974) described an evaluation and classification process as it has been developed by the staff of the Department of Clinical Study of Abnormal Children, Institute of Defectology, Academy of Pedagogical

Sciences of the U.S.S.R. The evaluation data involved medical history, interviews with parents, interviews with siblings, and psychoeducational evaluation. Psychoeducational evaluation was based upon comprehension of written stories and description of pictorial stories. On the basis of those findings the children were classified into three groups: highly achieving, moderately achieving, and poorly achieving.

In the absence of standardized testing of intelligence, assessment and classification of exceptional children in the Soviet Union has been based upon a variety of informal techniques. Recently, there have been a number of attempts to reassess classification procedures. Yassman (1975) reported on a symposium devoted to the question of psychodiagnosis. In a paper presented at that symposium, Lubovsky argued for the appropriate use of quantitative data and statistical analysis to help determine qualitatively unique characteristics of developmental disabilities. The symposium participants decided to petition the Executive Council of the Soviet Psychological Association and the Academy of Pedagogical Sciences for permission to develop theoretical and practical approaches to psychodiagnosis. In a book written in 1974, Zamsky, although still critical of psychometrics, acknowledged that the long campaign against pedology prevented the development of legitimate attempts to determine the parameters of children's psychological, physical, and social development. In a symposium on psychodiagnosis in 1980 (Bogoyavlenskaya, 1980), over 100 scientists representing 50 scientific institutions resolved to develop a branch of psychodiagnosis within the Association of Soviet Psychologists. The next symposium on psychodiagnosis was scheduled to take place in 1983.

EDUCATION OF RETARDED CHILDREN

In the Soviet Union mentally retarded children are trained and educated in various facilities such as hospitals, institutions, residential schools, and auxiliary schools. However, some areas have not been receiving adequate attention. Yeremenko (1977) identified these as: 1) inadequate emphasis upon research and education of the severely and profoundly retarded; 2) insufficient study of the education of the mentally retarded within the family setting and in preschool facilities; and 3) inadequate attention to intellectually subnormal deaf children. The Council of Ministers of the U.S.S.R. decided, as of January 1975, to improve education, vocational training, and care of individuals with defects of mental and physical development (Provotorov, 1975). The last 5-year plan (1976–1980) emphasized the development of various early childhood facilities as well as improvement in the training of teachers for residential schools of the mentally retarded. Since 1976 a class limit of 12 has been set for children with auditory, visual, and speech defects, and 16 for mentally retarded children. Physical exercise has an important place in the curriculum for mentally retarded children (Babenkova, 1973).

Programs for moderately retarded and trainable children have been described by Selikhova (1973), Kuzmitskaya (1977), and Yudilevich (1981). Selikhova described a curriculum for moderately retarded adolescents 14 to 19 years of age. The curriculum emphasized acquisition of numerical and spatial relationships. The youngsters were trained to comprehend such concepts as larger-smaller, high-low, long-short, similar-different, and one-many. They also were trained to understand basic geometrical concepts such as a square, a triangle, and a circle.

A curriculum discussed by Kuzmitskaya (1977) emphasized the following nine objectives: 1) personal communication (such as how to pay attention, greet someone, know one's own name); 2) orientation to place (house and street number, public transportation); 3) knowledge of occupations of residents of towns and villages; 4) basic ideas of commerce; 5) familiarity with everyday basic food preparation; 6) knowledge of available health services in the neighborhood; 7) use of a post office, telephone, telegraph, and radio; 8) knowledge of available recreation facilities in the neighborhood, such as movies, theater, television, parks, and circus; and 9) familiarity with work habits, work schedule, wages, and salaries. Yudilevich (1981) observed that remedial education of trainable mentally retarded youngsters should take into consideration their individual characteristics. It is important to keep in mind that among trainable youngsters, in addition to the low level of intellectual functioning, defective social adaptation is also a significant problem.

Home instruction, as an appropriate form of education for children with severe personality and character pathology, has been advocated by Formakova (1974). An interesting program for handicapped children attending auxiliary boarding schools was discussed by Gavor (1976). He described how school staff members are required to conduct home visits in order to become familiar with social, cultural, and material aspects of the home environment.

Yeremenko (1976) underscored a need to focus upon individual differences in designing programs for the mentally retarded. He called such a program "a differential instruction approach." This approach is similar to programs that in the United States are referred to as diagnostic-prescriptive teaching. In keeping with Yeremenko's suggestion, Kuzmina (1978) proposed that a differential curriculum is needed for those mentally retarded adolescents who show neurotic and psychotic personality disorders. She emphasized that clinical variations among oligophrenics demand differential teaching and treatment programs.

Parental cooperation plays an important role in the educational service delivery system. Parental responsibilities in the education of mentally retarded children were highlighted by Raku (1981), who recommended that parents should be able to facilitate interaction with children in order to help them in their language development. Raku further suggested that parents should help in the development of curiosity in mentally retarded children and teach them how to ask proper questions; likewise, parents should learn how to respond to questions posed by their mentally retarded children.

An important part in a comprehensive service delivery system for the mentally retarded is training of special educators and defectologists. Although these titles are often used synonymously in U.S. and in Soviet literature, there are historical trends that suggest a difference in their meaning. Initially in the Soviet Union defectologists were trained by means of courses at the State Institute of the Defective Child and the Institute of Advanced Pedagogy, whereas special educators were generally trained at 2-year teacher training institutes (Zhivina, 1974). In 1939, defectological departments introduced dual majors. Students who completed the training in special education also were required to study one subject matter area and were certified to teach in that area at the high school level. Since 1963, the special education curriculum has been organized into a 4-year sequence (Zhivina, 1974) that includes:

First year of study—introduction to defectology, physics, chemistry, biology, anatomy, historical materialism
Second year—psychopathology, psychiatry, neuropathology of children, political economy, geography
Third year—pedagogical psychopathology, developmental psychopathology, practicum
Fourth year—public education in the U.S.S.R., sexual psychopathology, clinical practicum, political education

In the 1970s the importance of defectological training was further emphasized by formation of the Council of Defectology within the Ministry of Education of the Soviet Union (Usanova and Shakhovskaya, 1976). Medicoeducational committees were formed to facilitate cooperation between educators and physicians. Currently, teachers/defectologists are being trained at 14 institutions of higher learning (Lapskin and Zhivina, 1981).

CONCLUSIONS

In conclusion, it should be mentioned that, apart from significant differences determined by ideological and cultural factors, there are also similar trends in classification and educational services in the U.S.A. and the U.S.S.R. One such trend is differentiation of developmentally delayed children from those who have been traditionally described as oligophrenic or mentally retarded. Another trend observed in Soviet defectological literature is increasing attention to the need for more systematic standardized assessment of cognitive and educational skills.

REFERENCES

Babenkova, R. D. 1973. Training of mentally retarded children: How to breathe correctly during physical exercise. Defectologia 3:88–90.
Bogoyavlenskaya, D. B. 1980. Psychodiagnosis and school. Vopr. Psikholog. 4:184–186.
Em, E. B. 1974. Pedagogical study of elementary grade pupils of an auxiliary school. Defectologia 1:33–40.
Formakova, A. I. 1974. Individual upbringing and training of children with complicated form of oligophrenia. Defectologia 2:55–59.
Gavor, I. I. 1976. Work of auxiliary boarding school with parents of students. Defectologia 3:72–78.
Holowinsky, I. Z. 1980. Qualitative assessment of cognitive skills. J. Spec. Educ. 14:155–163.
Kuzmina, V. K. 1978. Specific traits of educational approach to oligophrenic adolescents with neurotic and psychotic manifestations. Defectologia 3:60–68.
Kuzmitskaya, M. I. 1977. Preparation of trainable retardates to practical life (home and social adaptation). Defectologia 5:89–91.
Lapskin, V., and Zhivina, A. 1981. 60 years of higher defectological education in the USSR and the role of Defectological Department of the Lenin Pedagogical College of Moscow in training of diplomate defectologists. Defectologia 6:78–81.
Luria, A. R. (ed.). 1963. The Mentally Retarded Child. Pergamon Press, Inc., New York.
Markovskaya, I. F. 1977. Neuropsychological analysis of clinical types in developmentally delayed children. Defectologia 6:3–11.
Pevzner, M. S. 1966. Children with Developmental Deviations. Education Publishing Co., Moscow.
Pevzner, M. S. 1970. Etiopathogenesis and classification of oligophrenia. (Translated by G. Malasko.) Spec. School 4:289–293.
Pevzner, M. S. 1973. Clinical-Genetic Research on Oligophrenia. Pedagogy Publishing, Moscow.
Pevzner, M. S., and Rostiagaylova, L. I. 1981. Clinical-psychological characteristics of developmental backwardness under compensated hydrocephalus. Defectologia 4:10–17.
Provotorov, V. P. 1975. Another evidence of Party's care for children and adolescents with mental and physical impairments. Defectologia 3:3–7.

Raku, A. I. 1981. Parental responsibilities in the upbringing of mentally retarded students. Defectologia 3:83–86.

Selikhova, O. L. 1973. Experience of treatment of profoundly retarded adolescents in an auxiliary school. Defectologia 3:55–58.

Strelkova, T. A. 1981. Peculiarities of classification operation in developmentally backward preschool children. Defectologia 5:61–70.

Tsymbaliuk, A. N. 1973. Comprehension of topic pictures by developmentally backward children under experimental training. Defectologia 3:25–32.

Usanova, D., and Shakhovskaya, S. 1976. Need to accomplish preparation of teacher defectologists. Defectologia 2:86–90.

Vlasova, T. A. 1971. Toward the new achievements of Soviet defectology. Defectologia 3:3–12.

Vlasova, T. A., Pevzner, M. S., and Lebedinskaya, K. S. 1975. Contemporary problems of clinical study of developmentally backward children. Defectologia 6:8–17.

Yassman, L. 1975. New developments in psychodiagnostic methods. Defectologia 2:89–94.

Yassman, L. V. 1976. Peculiarities of grammatical usage in developmentally delayed children. Defectologia 3:35–44.

Yavkin, V. M. 1973. Developmental backwardness of specific etiology. Defectologia 2:18–23.

Yeremenko, I. H. 1976. On differential instruction in auxiliary schools. Defectologia 4:56–63.

Yeremenko, I. H. 1977. Conditions and perspectives of scientific research in the field of defectology in Ukrainian SSR. Defectologia 5:12–20.

Yudilevich, Y. G. 1981. Remedial education of trainable mentally retarded with regard to their individual characteristics. Defectologia 3:51–57.

Zamsky, W. S. 1974. History of the Education of the Mentally Retarded. Education Publishers, Moscow.

Zharenkova, G. I. 1981. Psycho-educational study of developmentally backward students in special school. Defectologia 2:3–8.

Zhivina, A. I. 1974. Major stages of development of special education teacher training in the USSR. Defectologia 2:68–75.

PERSPECTIVES AND PROGRESS IN MENTAL RETARDATION
Volume I—Social, Psychological, and Educational Aspects
Edited by J. M. Berg
Copyright © 1984 by I.A.S.S.M.D.

INSTRUCTION OF SEVERELY MULTIHANDICAPPED INDIVIDUALS

D. Baine

Department of Educational Psychology, University of Alberta, Edmonton, Alberta T6G 2G5, Canada

With the provision of educational programs for severely multihandicapped persons in Canada and the United States, the issue is now one of ensuring a quality education. This paper describes the population as well as recent and current influences shaping the development of an instructional technology for severely handicapped persons. Some of the issues reviewed are: the relevance of normal developmental sequences in the design of curricula, ecological inventories, partial participation, instructional sequencing, instructional methods, group and individual instruction, massed and distributed practice, and exemplary curricula.

In the 1980s, as a result of passage of The Education for All Handicapped Children Act (1975), most severely handicapped students in the United States are receiving direct educational services (Brown et al., 1981). In Canada, although not all provinces have mandatory legislation, educational programs are being provided for increasing numbers of severely handicapped persons. In Alberta, for example, in the absence of mandatory legislation educational programs have been provided for severely handicapped persons in most areas of the Province. In addition, graduate level specialized training programs have been established at the University of Alberta to train various types of personnel to work with severely multihandicapped persons. The major issue now is generally one of ensuring a quality education to prepare severely handicapped individuals to function as independently and as fully as possible in the largest number and variety of least restrictive environments. This paper describes the nature of the severely multihandicapped population and the recent and current influences shaping the evolution of an instructional technology for these persons.

CONCEPTS IN EDUCATION OF
SEVERELY MULTIHANDICAPPED CHILDREN

An individual classified as severely multihandicapped will have two or more of the following handicaps:

1. *Sensory:* a visual and/or auditory impairment
2. *Intellectual:* severe (IQ 25–39) or profound (IQ < 24) mental retardation or autism
3. *Orthopedic:* impaired motor functioning; for example, associated with cerebral palsy, spina bifida, scoliosis
4. *Health:* chronic conditions; for example, neurological (convulsive), metabolic (e.g., PKU), or cardiovascular disorders
5. *Communication:* impaired receptive and expressive abilities, or an absence of speech
6. *Behavior:* maladaptive behavior pattern; for example, self-injurious, withdrawn, and/or violent

Although the influence of any single disability may range from mild to profound, for an individual to be considered severely handicapped, the combined effects of the disabilities must severely or profoundly impair the individual's general functioning, development, education, and adaptive behavior. Severe or profound mental retardation is a common characteristic. Varying degrees of dependency may occur in all or some of the following areas of performance: self-care, mobility, vocational, academic, social, and adaptive behavior.

Treatment and environmental modification may reduce the number, severity, and extent of influence of the disabilities and the range of dependency. Treatment and education may range between the following extremes:

Substantive intervention
   Intensive and continuous medical management and custodial care
   Training to increase sensory awareness and orientation to the environment
   Prevention, reduction, and/or correction of muscular contractures and abnormal motor reflexes
   Amelioration of self-mutilation, rumination, and self-stimulation
   Basic maintenance: feeding, toileting
Normative education/training
   Improved socialization and mainstreaming
   Refinement of daily living skills
   Prevocational and vocational training
   Preacademic and academic instruction
   Improved motor functioning

Recreational skills
Improved communication (verbal or nonvocal)
Orientation and mobility training

Classroom instruction usually involves 6 to 8 children, one teacher, and from 2 to 3 aides; the actual numbers and ratios depend upon the functional level of the students and the nature of the instruction. Teachers in these classrooms frequently work in conjunction with occupational, physical, and speech therapists as well as with other professional support personnel. McCormick and Goldman (1979) described three models within which these various personnel provide service delivery. In the *multidisciplinary* model each discipline conducts its assessments and remedial interventions in isolation from other personnel. Communication across disciplines is virtually nonexistent. The basic difference between the multidisciplinary and the *interdisciplinary* approach is that, in the latter, a case manager is appointed to facilitate communication between disciplines and to promote group decision-making to develop a unified service plan. With severely handicapped individuals, the typically short and infrequent therapy sessions that occur with adoption of these models may not be sufficient to effect significant behavior change. As a result, McCormick and Goldman have recommended the *transdisciplinary* model of service delivery in which, instead of each discipline implementing its own treatment, all remedial programming becomes the responsibility of one or two team members. For example, teachers, aides, and/or parents may be taught to implement the various therapy programs. Other team members would remain available on a continuing basis for consultation and direct assistance. This approach may lead to an increase in the frequency and consistency of therapeutic interventions and may enhance the rate of acquisition and the extent of maintenance and generalization of therapeutic changes. Further study is required to establish the effectiveness of these and other models, in their current or modified forms, in urban and rural areas where varying numbers and types of support personnel may be available.

As mentioned, many of the programs for severely handicapped persons are housed in school environments. However, Brown et al. (1981) proposed, in view of the obvious difficulties these students have in generalizing acquired skills, that instruction must be conducted in a number of nonschool environments in which the behaviors are ultimately expected to be performed. The authors recommended instruction in homes, stores, streets, restaurants, buses, medical offices, and parks in which nonhandicapped persons function.

Although the majority of programs for severely handicapped students are segregated, there is a trend toward increasing integration with nonhandicapped persons. Brown et al. (1979a) described three types of interaction that are possible in integrated environments. In a *proximal* situation, severely handicapped and nonhandicapped persons are placed together in the same locations, such as riding a school bus, attending school assemblies, and eating lunch in the cafeteria, where they engage in common activities. In *helping* situations, nonhandicapped students assist handicapped persons in feeding, dressing, playing games, and moving to and from activities. In a *reciprocal* relationship, both handicapped and nonhandicapped individuals benefit from being together while engaged in mutually enjoyable activities such as games. Both handicapped and nonhandicapped persons can benefit from integrated activities. The nonhandicapped individual may gain an increased awareness, understanding, and appreciation of the range of human conditions and the role and responsibility of each member of society. The handicapped child may gain from increased stimulation and the provision of a normative model. As a result, the interaction may increase the acquisition and generalization of normative behaviors. Further research is required to establish when, where and how to integrate handicapped persons to optimize the mutual benefits.

DESIGNING CURRICULA

In the absence of a model or models to describe the one or more sequences of development that various types of handicapped children may follow, normative models of development provide a reasonable starting point for the design of curricula for severely handicapped children. However, the developmental logic that focuses on the maturational determination of behavior by assuming that the best way to teach the severely handicapped is to follow the sequence in which normal children learn (Guess et al., 1978; Guess and Noonan, 1982) may not be valid. The sensory, physical, and cognitive deficits of handicapped children influence the nature of their experiences and may alter the rate, sequence (Williams and Gott, 1977), and type of development. For example, Adelson and Fraiberg (1974) found that blind infants, when compared with nonhandicapped infants, exhibited a delay in the acquisition of some behaviors, a resequencing of the order in which some behaviors were learned, and the acquisition of some unique compensatory behaviors. Similarly, Guess et al. (1976) observed that severely handicapped children departed radically from the normal developmental pattern in their acquisition of language and speech skills.

Strict adherence to a normative sequence of instruction leads to teaching skills that are assumed to be important for a particular mental age, but that are functionally irrelevant to an individual's ability to better interact with her/his current or future environments (Guess et al., 1978; Guess and Noonan, 1982). Why must children, unable to feed, dress, and toilet themselves, be taught colors, shapes, numbers, and A-B-Cs or play for long periods with puzzles and pegboards (Burton, 1981)? Because of the variety of deficits possessed by severely multihandicapped children, and their slowness to learn, it is imperative that the responses, skills, and knowledge taught should be those that are essential for increasing the individual's independence. Those skills judged inessential to attainment of this objective should be removed from the curriculum (Haring and Csapo, 1980). Every skill in a curriculum for the severely handicapped should be either prerequisite to the acquisition of skills necessary for an individual's current or future functioning (determined by task analysis) or functional in the individual's current or future environments (determined by an ecological analysis), and should be taught in the same form in which the behavior must eventually be performed in the individual's general life space. For example, teaching a child to raise his/her hand in imitation training is of little value, as the demand for that behavior under those conditions is rare; however, raising one's hand to put on a shirt is a functional form of behavior. Curricula should also be examined to determine if they include all of the prerequisite, functional, and compensatory behaviors required exclusively by individuals with various types of handicaps. Brown et al. (1979b) recommended that the school curriculum, traditionally divided into language, reading, math, motor, and self-help skills, be redivided into vocational, domestic, recreation/leisure, and community functioning domains to focus more on the preparatory nature of the educational experience.

Brown et al. (1980a) have described a 5-step ecological inventory for generating comprehensive, longitudinal and chronological, age-appropriate individual educational plans. The inventory is designed to secure critical information about the skills required to perform as independently and productively as possible in the least restrictive environment in which a severely handicapped person is currently functioning, or in which she/he might function in the future. The first step of an ecological analysis involves a study of the educational, vocational, domestic, recreational, and general community domains to determine in which least restrictive, age-appropriate *environments* a severely handicapped individual is currently functioning or in which environments she/he might be functioning in the future. In the second step of the analysis, the environments listed in step one are divided into *subenvironments*. For example, the home environment may be divided into such places as the kitchen, the bathroom, and the bedroom. Step three involves listing the *tasks* that the individual is required to perform in each subenvironment. Tasks in the bathroom may include, for example, adjusting water temperature and flushing the toilet. In the final step of the analysis, the specific *skills* required to perform each of these tasks is listed. In this stage, one should consider any adaptations that could be made to permit full or *partial* participation in the activity.

INSTRUCTIONAL METHODS

Because of the variety of disabilities a severely handicapped individual may possess, it may be impossible to learn all the skills required to perform independently each of the tasks described in the ecological analysis. However, rather than excluding the individual from participating in the task, Brown et al. (1979c) suggested that it is possible to make a number of adaptations to permit partial participation. The adaptations may be *person*-centered, in which other people provide the necessary assistance to complete the task. Partial participation may also be assisted through adaptation of the *materials* involved, through the use of adaptive devices, or by modification of the *sequence* in which the task is performed.

Guess et al. (1978; Guess and Noonan, 1982) suggested that severely handicapped persons should not be given instruction in which they receive repeated consecutive trials on the same task. Rather, the authors recommended that skills should be taught in clusters of two to six behaviors that are sequenced in the order in which the behaviors commonly occur in the natural environment. In this procedure of "individual curriculum sequencing," rather than teaching skills sequentially within a single domain, skills from various domains are taught concurrently. Guess et al. suggested that skills with similar topographical and/or functional components are best taught together to facilitate response generalization. For example, a child may be concurrently taught to put on his shoes, label his shoes, and sort clothing, including shoes, into categories. The common stimulus "shoe" is designed to facilitate generalization. Within the self-help domain, a child may be taught concurrently to grasp and push a doorknob, grasp and push a wheelchair, and grasp and pull down a shirt to facilitate acquisition of a generalized, functional grasping response.

Traditionally, instructional programs for severely handicapped persons have used massed trial training procedures in which repeated trials of the same task occur in such close succession that no other behavior can be expected to occur between the trials (Mulligan et al., 1980). On the other hand, the instructional procedure suggested by Guess et al. requires distributed sequencing of instruction in which trials from one or more other tasks occur between two repeated trials of the same task. Guess et al.'s research indicates that, for some skills in some stages of instruction, distributed practice is superior to massed practice. Many factors may potentially influence the effectiveness of any instructional schedule. For example, the nature of the tasks being taught, the nature of the alternating tasks, the number of consecutive trials on the same task, the duration and pace of each trial, and the interval between trials may influence the acquisition, generalization, and maintenance of a response. More research is needed in this area.

Severely multihandicapped children characteristically require more teacher assistance during instruction than less handicapped students. Usually instruction is conducted on the basis of one teacher or aide to each student. Also, the instructional methods, based on behavioral techniques, are usually highly structured. The procedures employ shaping, chaining, prompting and fading, differential reinforcement, stimulus control, data-based instructional decisions, and other operant methods. A hierarchy of verbal, gestural, modeling, and physical prompts is systematically introduced and faded to facilitate errorless instruction (Baine, 1982). Research is being conducted on most of these techniques in a continuing effort to develop a more effective instructional technology. For example, Bates et al. (1981) reported research on *group* instruction with severely handicapped individuals. Group instruction as described by Bates et al., Brown et al. (1980b), Alberto et al. (1980), and Johnson et al. (1980) may involve from two to four students in homogeneous or heterogeneous groupings, where children are simultaneously or consecutively instructed in the same/different skills, and where children may or may not interact with each other during instruction. Studies reported by these authors indicate that, for a variety of skills and children, group instruction is an efficient method both in terms of teacher time and the rate of skill acquisition. Group instruction may also increase the opportunity for observational learning, give the teacher the opportunity to use and reinforce various children as models of appropriate behavior, and allow the teacher to focus contingently on other children when a child becomes uncooperative. In some situations, children may also be taught to give rewards and prompt each other or respond in a complementary manner where child A orally requests an item such as juice from child B who then selects and passes the juice to child A, who in turn may pour a drink for child B. Exemplary curricula for severely multihandicapped persons incorporating many of the previously described curricular and instructional features are the Programmed Environments (Tawney et al., 1979) and the Teaching Research Curriculum for Moderately and Severely Handicapped for the self-help, cognitive and motor domains

(Fredericks et al., 1980) and for the language domain (Makohon et al., 1980).

VIEWPOINTS ON TRAINABILITY

A final point concerns trainability of severely and profoundly retarded persons. Burton and Hirshoren (1979a,b) stated that the traditional goals of education are inappropriate and beyond the capabilities of such persons. They suggested that the time and effort necessary to teach "trivial" isolated academic skills, and the limited benefits derived from their acquisition, were not justified; they felt instruction should focus on teaching social and self-help skills such as toileting, feeding, and dressing.

Sontag et al. (1979) suggested that Burton and Hirshoren had an overly restricted perspective of the potentialities of severely and profoundly handicapped individuals. They cited studies in which severely handicapped persons have been successfully taught various academic skills such as reading and writing, and claimed that instructional methods and programs exist that make preacademic and academic goals realistic for many severely and profoundly retarded individuals. Sontag et al. recommended the functional application of these skills in various community, domestic, recreational, and vocational settings.

Answers to the questions "How trainable are severely and profoundly retarded persons?" and "How cost-effective are their training programs?" may determine whether funding for existing and future programs will be maintained. It is crucial that both educators and funding agencies adopt the same realistic expectations that neither underestimate the potential of severely and profoundly handicapped persons nor establish goals that cannot be achieved. The benefits of education must be clearly and convincingly demonstrated.

As Sontag et al. (1979) suggested, techniques and programs are available to permit the achievement of a broad variety of skills that were previously unattainable. Furthermore, methods are continuously being developed and improved. On the other hand, there is a tendency to overgeneralize the results obtained in pilot and demonstration projects to situations where there are significant differences from the original training environment. These differences, including the number, nature, training, and commitment of specialized staff, as well as administrative policies, procedures and philosophies, will determine the success or failure of a program regardless of the potential of the individuals who participate.

REFERENCES

Adelson, E., and Fraiberg, S. 1974. Gross motor development in infants blind from birth. Child Dev. 45:114–126.

Alberto, P., Jobes, N., Sizemore, A., and Doran, D. 1980. A comparison of individual and group instruction across response tasks. J. Assoc. Sev. Hand. 5:285–293.

Baine, D. 1982. Instructional Design for Special Education. Educational Technology Publications, Englewood Cliffs, New Jersey.

Bates, P., Renzaglia, A., and Wehman, P. 1981. Characteristics of an appropriate education for severely and profoundly handicapped students. Educ. Train. Ment. Retard. 16:142–149.

Brown, F., Holvoet, J., Guess, D., and Mulligan, M. 1980b. The individualized curriculum sequencing model (III): Small group instruction. J. Assoc. Sev. Hand. 5:352–367.

Brown, L., Branston, M., Hamre-Nietupski, S., Johnson, F., Wilcox, B., and Gruenwald, L. 1979a. A rationale for comprehensive longitudinal interactions between severely handicapped students and nonhandicapped students and other citizens. AAESPH Rev. 4:3–14.

Brown, L., Branston, M. B., Hamre-Nietupski, S., Pumpian, I., Certo, N., and Gruenwald, L. 1979b. A strategy for developing chronological, age-appropriate and functional curricular content for severely handicapped adolescents and young adults. J. Spec. Educ. 13:81–90.

Brown, L., Branston-McClean, M., Baumgart, D., Vincent, L., Falvey, M., and Schroeder, J. 1979c. Using the characteristics of current and subsequent least restrictive environments in the development of curricular content for severely handicapped students. AAESPH Rev. 4:407–424.

Brown, L., Falvey, M., Vincent, L., Kaye, N., Johnson, F., Ferrara-Parrish, P., and Gruenwald, L. 1980a. Strategies for generating comprehensive, longitudinal and chronological, age-appropriate individual educational plans for adolescent and young adult severely handicapped students. J. Spec. Educ. 14:199–215.

Brown, L., Pumpian, I., Baumgart, D., Vandeventer, P., Ford, A., Nisbet, J., Schroeder, J., and Gruenwald, L. 1981. Longitudinal transition plans in programs for severely handicapped students. Except. Child. 47:624–630.

Burton, J. A. 1981. Deciding what to teach the severely/profoundly retarded student. A teacher responsibility. Educ. Train. Ment. Retard. 16:74–79.

Burton, T., and Hirshoren, A. 1979a. The education of severely and profoundly retarded children: Are we sacrificing the concept to the child? Except. Child. 45:598–602.

Burton, T., and Hirshoren, A. 1979b. Some further thoughts and clarifications on the education of severely and profoundly retarded children. Except. Child. 45:618–625.

Fredericks, H. B. B., et al. 1980. The Teaching Research Curriculum for Moderately and Severely Handicapped—Self Help/Cognitive Volume and Gross Fine Motor Volume. Charles C Thomas Publisher, Springfield, Illinois.

Guess, D., Horner, R. D., Utley, B., Holvoet, J., Maxon, D., Tucker, D., and Warren, S. 1978. A functional curriculum sequencing model for teaching the severely handicapped. AAESPH Rev. 3:202–215.

Guess, D., and Noonan, N. J. 1982. Curricula and instructional procedures for severely handicapped students. Focus Except. Child. 14:1–12.

Guess, D., Sailor, W., and Baer, D. M. 1976. Functional Speech and Language Training for the Severely Handicapped, Parts I & II. H & H Enterprises, Lawrence, Kansas.

Haring, N., and Csapo, M. 1980. Teaching the severely and profoundly handicapped: Some basic issues. B.C. J. Spec. Educ. 4:127–142.

Johnson, J. L., Flanagan, K., Burge, M. E. Kauffman-Debriere, J., and Spellman, C. R. 1980. Interactive individualized instruction with small groups of severely handicapped students. Educ. Train. Ment. Retard. 15:230–237.

Makohon, L., et al. 1980. The Teaching Research Curriculum for Moderately and Severely Handicapped—Language Volume. Teaching Research Publications, Monmouth, Oregon.

McCormick, L., and Goldman, R. 1979. The transdisciplinary model: Implications for service delivery and personnel preparation for the severely and profoundly handicapped. AAESPH Rev. 4:152–161.

Mulligan, M., Guess, D., Holvoet, J., and Brown, F. 1980. The individualized curriculum sequencing model (1): Implications from research on massed, distributed, or spaced trial training. J. Assoc. Sev. Hand. 5:325–336.

Sontag, E., Certo, N., and Button, J. 1979. On a distinction between the education of the severely and profoundly handicapped and a doctrine of limitations. Except. Child. 45:604–616.

Tawney, J. W., Knapp, D. S., O'Reilly, C. D., and Pratt, S. S. 1979. Programmed Environments Curriculum. Charles E. Merrill Publishing Co., Columbus, Ohio.

Williams, W., and Gott, E. 1977. Selected considerations on developing curriculum for severely handicapped students. In: E. Sontag, J. Smith, and N. Certo (eds.), Educational Programming for the Severely and Profoundly Handicapped. Virginia Division of Mental Retardation of the Council for Exceptional Children, Reston.

PERSPECTIVES AND PROGRESS IN MENTAL RETARDATION
Volume I—Social, Psychological, and Educational Aspects
Edited by J. M. Berg

IMPROVING THE ACADEMIC FUNCTIONING OF MILDLY RETARDED INDIVIDUALS
The Impact of Research

L. H. Bilsky

Department of Special Education, Teachers College, Columbia University, New York, New York 10027

Recent developments in both educational practice and research with mildly retarded individuals were examined to assess the extent to which practice has been influenced by research. Educational practice was viewed primarily from the perspective of textbook recommendations on the education of the mentally retarded. Implications of both program evaluation and cognitive research were considered. There was evidence from both the educational and research communities that research is beginning to make a meaningful contribution to practice. It was suggested that focusing research attention directly upon academic tasks might be mutually beneficial to both communities.

Phillips (1980) recently stated that the educational researcher and practitioner have little to offer each other. Similarly negative statements have been recorded regarding special education. Blackman (1972) noted the failure of educational research to exert a major impact upon educational practice. Both Gallagher (1974) and Meyen and Horner (1976) found little evidence that curriculum development had been influenced by research. However, as Blackman (1977) pointed out, the past decade has seen a major commitment to research designed to have a high impact upon educational practice in mental retardation.

In the present paper, an attempt has been made to examine the current state of both educational practice and research in mental retardation in order to determine whether communication between prac-

titioners and researchers has improved. Although such two-way communication is clearly essential to a fruitful educational research
enterprise, this paper is focused upon the influence of research on
practice. The discussion is limited to material relevant to school-age
mildly retarded individuals.

For the present purpose, educational practice is viewed primarily
from the perspective of recommendations found in textbooks on the
education of the mentally retarded. Although textbooks are only one
link in the complex chain of events leading from research to practice,
it is assumed that teachers and administrators do, at least to some
extent, apply what they have been taught in their professional preparation programs. Commonly recommended approaches are highlighted in three areas: setting, curriculum, and method. Within each
of these areas, relevant research findings, mainly concerned with program evaluation or cognitive research, are discussed.

SETTING

In 1906, Thorndike emphatically stated that retarded individuals should
be educated in either institutions or special classes. Until the early
1960s, it was safe to assume that any educational services to mildly
retarded individuals would be delivered in one of those settings. Since
then, the educational setting for mildly retarded individuals has become
the focus of heated controversy, sparked by Johnson (1962) and Dunn
(1968), who raised serious questions about the appropriateness of special class placements. The movement toward regular class or mainstream placement gained momentum through the 1970s, aided in the
United States by court decisions and the advent of Public Law (PL)
94-142. According to PL 94-142 (The Education for All Handicapped
Children Act of 1975), all handicapped children in the United States
are entitled to a "free appropriate public education" in the "least restrictive environment."

At present, there is general agreement among professionals that
mildly retarded individuals do not belong in institutions. However,
debate has centered upon the issue of whether or not the special class
should continue to be considered a placement alternative for this population. Klein et al. (1979) have taken the position that special classes
for mildly retarded individuals fail to meet the least restrictive environment requirement of PL 94-142 and are thus precluded as a placement option. Similarly, Payne and Patton (1981) do not even list the
special class in their continuum of placement alternatives for mildly
retarded persons. A more moderate position is represented by Kolstoe
(1976) and MacMillan (1982), who point out the strengths as well as

weaknesses of special classes and maintain that mildly retarded children should be able to draw upon the full array of placement alternatives. These typically include 1) full-time placement in a regular class without ancillary services, 2) full-time placement in a regular class with ancillary services (e.g., itinerant teachers or resource room), 3) part-time placement in a regular class, and 4) full-time placement in a special class.

Because the "special class efficacy studies" cited by Dunn (1968) had failed to yield evidence of the academic superiority of special-class over regular-class educable mentally retarded (EMR) students, it was predicted that these students would do no worse in a regular than in a special class. Gottlieb (1981) conceded, after reviewing the "mainstreaming efficacy studies," that this prediction has been borne out. However, he noted that the academic performance and social adjustment of EMR individuals have continued to be quite poor in both settings. Gottlieb (1982) emphasized that future research should focus upon *how* to educate the mildly retarded, rather than on *where* to educate them.

CURRICULUM

It seems as if we have come full circle in the search for an optimally appropriate curriculum for mildly retarded learners. A "watered down" regular class curriculum was one of the earliest approaches recommended for use with mildly retarded students in the public schools (Inskeep, 1926). Now, after nearly two decades of intense curriculum development activity, we may be facing a return to the regular class curriculum for mildly retarded learners as an unintended by-product of the mainstreaming movement (Childs, 1979). Meyen and Horner (1976) pointed out that, prior to 1965, there was very little evidence of systematic efforts at developing curricula for mentally retarded individuals. However, since 1965, federal funding has stimulated the development of a variety of curricula specifically for retarded individuals. The majority of those curricula represent one or more of the following approaches:

1. Functional academics (e.g., Teaching Functional Academics, Bender and Valletutti, 1982)
2. Career education (e.g., Life Centered Career Education Curriculum, Brolin, 1978)
3. Social skills training (e.g., Social Learning Curriculum, Goldstein, 1974)
4. Cognitive skills training (e.g., Instrumental Enrichment Program, Feuerstein, 1980)

Despite their differences, the above approaches are all based upon the premise that the optimal curricula for retarded and nonretarded individuals are not the same. There is widespread agreement that the curriculum emphasis for retarded persons should be on the essential skills needed for survival in the community rather than on advanced academic learning (Robinson and Robinson, 1976; Childs, 1979; Kokaska, 1980; Payne and Patton, 1981). However, it should be noted that the advent of mainstreaming as a common programming arrangement for the mildly retarded imposes constraints upon the selection of curricula.

The curriculum approaches discussed above clearly are not mutually exclusive. They share many common objectives. This may explain why there have been few empirical attempts to compare them with each other. Studies aimed at establishing the appropriateness of a particular approach typically have compared that approach to a "traditional" one (Brolin et al., 1975; Rand et al., 1979), and reported some evidence supporting the superiority of the target approach.

There have been suggestions that cognitive research findings may be relevant to the development of curricula for mildly retarded individuals (Kramer et al., 1980). For example, Borkowski and Konarski (1981) discussed how intelligence theory and research may be useful in identifying skills and processes that are both educationally relevant and modifiable in retarded individuals. However, if curriculum is defined simply as the *what* of instruction, it is clear that there is a large value judgment component involved in curriculum selection. As Baumeister (1981) indicated, it seems most likely that research will have its greatest impact on the *how* of instruction, or method. However, in practice it is often difficult to separate curriculum from method. Many curriculum materials are identified with a distinctive teaching method, such as the inductive teaching method that is an integral part of the Social Learning Curriculum (Goldstein, 1974).

METHOD

A seemingly infinite array of instructional techniques has been recommended for use with mildly retarded and other handicapped populations. However, many of these techniques may be subsumed under two general approaches that have dominated the field of special education: 1) diagnostic-prescriptive teaching, which consists of designing specific instructional interventions on the basis of the results of diagnostic tests (Payne et al., 1981); and 2) applied behavior analysis, which involves the direct measurement of observable behavior, the application of an intervention to an applied problem of practical importance, and a clear demonstration that the intervention is responsible for any observed changes in the target behavior (Baer et al., 1968) (this approach is also referred to as operant conditioning or behavior modification). Numerous other specialized methods and techniques have been recommended for teaching the mildly retarded. The one distinguishing characteristic of most of these approaches is that they are geared to individual differences among learners and the individualization of instruction. With the advent of PL 94-142, this focus has been formalized in the Individualized Educational Plan (IEP) required for each handicapped learner.

An examination of a substantial body of research on the effectiveness of diagnostic-prescriptive teaching with learning-disabled children revealed little support for the model (Arter and Jenkins, 1979). The behavior analysis approach is not so vulnerable to this type of wholesale refutation. Its self-evaluative component is a built-in safeguard and ensures that, if a particular technique is not effective with a particular child, other techniques will be tried until the target objective is accomplished. However, the educational usefulness of behavior analysis has been criticized for its limited ability to deal with the complex cognitive processes involved in the application of knowledge in problem-solving situations (Shulman, 1974).

Cognitive research with mildly retarded individuals has been the focus of considerable activity during the past decade. This research has yielded a wealth of information on the components of effective strategy training techniques. Early work revealed that it was fairly easy to train retarded individuals to use a specific strategy and to maintain that strategy over time as long as the task remained the same (Bilsky et al., 1978; Burger et al., 1980); however, generalization to new tasks was not readily attained. More recent studies have reported generalization of strategy use from one task to another and have specified the conditions essential to its occurrence (Butterfield and Belmont, 1977; Borkowski and Cavanaugh, 1979; Burger et al., 1982). These studies have provided precise information on effective instructional approaches that have much to offer the practitioner.

IMPACT OF RESEARCH: PRESENT AND FUTURE

There is evidence from both the educational and the research communities that research is beginning to make a meaningful contribution to educational practice. To the extent that one is willing to accept textbooks on methods and curriculum as a reflection of the state of educational practice, there is ample evidence of research applications. However, one cannot guarantee the appropriateness of all these applications. When curricula and instructional methods are recommended, information on their efficacy or basis in research is rarely given. Furthermore, sometimes it seems as if the textbook writers have tried too hard to draw upon relevant research findings. Often, findings are taken piecemeal and converted into recommendations that are inconsistent with overall research trends. Nevertheless, the textbooks do seem to reflect a sincere effort to incorporate the latest findings.

More promising are indications from the cognitive research community that it has come of age and is ready to extend a helping hand to its colleagues in the field. Articles on the educational implications of cognitive research have become more visible (e.g., Kramer et al., 1980). It even appears that Blackman's (1972) admonition that Mahomet go to the mountain is being heeded. Researchers have begun to find their way into the classroom. A number of researchers, often joining with practitioners, have taken laboratory-developed training packages and applied and field tested them with classroom-relevant skills. For example, Taylor and Turnure (1979) described the development of a package of classroom vocabulary training materials based on a program of research in verbal elaboration and imagery. Similarly, Borkowski et al. (1978) developed a geography program based on elaboration training.

The need continues for both program evaluation and cognitive research in the field of mental retardation. However, our expectations must be adjusted. It is unreasonable to expect program evaluation studies to provide definite answers to global questions such as "Which placement is best for all mildly retarded children?" However, we can and should employ evaluative studies to answer more circumscribed questions in specific situations. Likewise, it is unreasonable to expect that the findings of every cognitive research study will be readily applicable to instructional practice. In fact, it appears that in the special education of the mentally retarded we have to guard against the premature application of isolated findings. However, available research findings can and should be applied to the development of instructional methods (e.g., Taylor and Turnure, 1979) and curricula (e.g., Cawley et al., 1976, 1977).

Although it is encouraging that researchers have begun the step-by-step process of carrying their training techniques to the classroom to test their applicability in academically relevant task environments, I believe that we can eliminate some of the steps from the laboratory to the classroom. We can reduce the distance between research and practice by redirecting our research attention to the more "ecologically valid" (Brooks and Baumeister, 1977) academic tasks themselves. As suggested by Shulman (1974) it is time for a return to the "psychology of school subjects." If our understanding of the performance of school tasks can be increased, future research into effective training techniques can concentrate directly upon those tasks. This shift in research focus would be compatible with a likely trend in educational practice, moving away from diagnostic-prescriptive approaches and toward subject matter approaches. An additional benefit of such a shift is that it would bring the researcher and practitioner into closer communication with each other.

REFERENCES

Arter, J. A., and Jenkins, J. R. 1979. Differential diagnosis–prescriptive teaching: A critical appraisal. Rev. Educ. Res. 49:517–555.

Baer, D. M., Wolf, M. M., and Risley, T. D. 1968. Some current dimensions of applied behavior analysis. J. Appl. Behav. Anal. 1:91–97.

Baumeister, A. A. 1981. Mental retardation policy and research: The unfulfilled promise. Am. J. Ment. Defic. 85:449–456.

Baumeister, A. A., and Brooks, P. H. 1981. Cognitive deficits in mental retardation. In: J. M. Kaufman and D. P. Hallahan (eds.), Handbook of Special Education. Prentice-Hall, Inc., Englewood Cliffs, New Jersey.

Bender, M., and Valletutti, P. J. 1982. Teaching Functional Academics: A Curriculum Guide for Adolescents and Adults with Learning Problems. University Park Press, Baltimore.

Bilsky, L. H., Gilbert, L., and Pawelski, C. E. 1978. Facilitation of class-inclusion performance in mildly retarded adolescents: Feedback and strategy training. Am. J. Ment. Defic. 83:177–184.

Blackman, L. S. 1972. Research and the classroom: Mahomet and the mountain revisited. Except. Child. 39:181–190.

Blackman, L. S. 1977. The contributions of research in cognition to the future of special education practices with the mentally retarded. In: P. Mittler (ed.), Research to Practice in Mental Retardation Vol. 2, Education and Training, University Park Press, Baltimore.

Borkowski, J. G., and Cavanaugh, J. C. 1979. Maintenance and generalization of skills and strategies by the retarded. In: N. R. Ellis (ed.), Handbook of Mental Deficiency, Psychological Theory and Research, 2nd ed., pp. 569–617. Lawrence Erlbaum Associates, Hillsdale, New Jersey.

Borkowski, J. G., Cavanaugh, J. C., and Reichart, G. J. 1978. Maintenance of children's rehearsal strategies: Effects of children's amount of training and strategy form. J. Exp. Child Psychol. 26:288–298.

Borkowski, J. G., and Konarski, E. A. 1981. Educational implications of efforts to train intelligence. J. Spec. Educ. 15:289–305.

Brolin, D. E. 1978. Life Centered Career Education: A Competency Based Approach. The Council for Exceptional Children, Reston, Virginia.

Brolin, D., Durand, R., Kromer, K., and Muller, P. 1975. Post-school adjustment of educable retarded students. Educ. Train. Ment. Retard. 10:144–148.

Brooks, P. H., and Baumeister, A. A. 1977. A plea for consideration of ecological validity in the experimental psychology of mental retardation: A guest editorial. Am. J. Ment. Defic. 81:407–416.

Burger, A. L., Blackman, L. S., and Tan, N. 1980. Maintenance and generalization of a sorting and retrieval strategy by EMR and nonretarded individuals. Am. J. Ment. Defic. 84:373–380.

Burger, A. L., Blackman, L. S., Clark, H. T., and Reis, E. 1982. Effects of hypothesis testing and variable format training on generalization of a verbal abstraction strategy by EMR learners. Am. J. Ment. Defic. 86:405–413.

Butterfield, E. C., and Belmont, J. M. 1977. Assessing and improving the executive cognitive functions of mentally retarded people. In: I. Bialer and M. Sternlicht (eds.), The Psychology of Mental Retardation: Issues and Approaches, pp. 277–318. Psychological Dimensions, New York.

Cawley, J. F., Fitzmaurice, A. M., Goodstein, H. A., Lepore, A., Sedlak, R. A., and Althaus, V. 1976, 1977. Project Math, Levels I–IV. Educational Progress Corporation, Tulsa, Oklahoma.

Childs, R. E. 1979. A drastic change in curriculum for the educable mentally retarded child. Ment. Retard. 17:299–301.

Dunn, L. M. 1968. Special education for the mildly retarded: Is much of it justifiable? Except. Child. 35:5–22.

Feuerstein, R. 1980. Instrumental Enrichment: An Intervention for Cognitive Modifiability. University Park Press, Baltimore.

Gallagher, J. J. 1974. Education. In: J. Wortis (ed.) Mental Retardation and Developmental Disabilities, Vol. 6. Brunner/Mazel, New York.

Goldstein, H. 1974. The Social Learning Curriculum. Charles E. Merrill Publishing Co., Columbus, Ohio.

Gottlieb, J. 1981. Mainstreaming: Fulfilling the promise? Am. J. Ment. Defic. 86:115–126.

Gottlieb, J. 1982. Mainstreaming. Educ. Train. Ment. Retard. 17:79–82.

Inskeep, A. D. 1926. Teaching Dull and Retarded Children. MacMillan, New York.

Johnson, G. O. 1962. Special education for the mentally handicapped: A paradox. Except. Child. 29:62–69.

Klein, N. K., Pasch, M., and Frew, T. W. 1979. Curriculum Analysis and Design for Retarded Learners. Charles E. Merrill Publishing Co., Columbus, Ohio.

Kokaska, C. J. 1980. A curriculum model for career education. In: G. M. Clark and W. J. White, (eds.), Career Education for the Handicapped: Current Perspectives for Teachers. Educational Resource Center, Philadelphia, Pennsylvania.

Kolstoe, O. P. 1976. Teaching Educable Mentally Retarded Children, 2nd ed. Holt, Rinehart & Winston, New York.

Kramer, J. J., Nagle, R. J., and Engle, R. W. 1980. Recent advances in mnemonic strategy training with mentally retarded persons: Implications for educational practice. Am. J. Ment. Defic. 85:306–314.

MacMillan, D. L. 1982. Mental Retardation in School and Society, 2nd ed. Little, Brown & Company, Boston.

Meyen, E. L., and Horner, R. D. 1976. Curriculum development. In: J. Wortis (ed.), Mental Retardation and Development Disabilities, Vol. 8, pp. 258–296, Brunner/Mazel, New York.

Payne, J. S., and Patton, J. R. 1981. Mental Retardation. Charles E. Merrill Publishing Co., Columbus, Ohio.

Payne, J. S., Polloway, E. A., Smith, J. E., Jr., and Payne, R. A. 1981. Strategies for Teaching the Mentally Retarded, 2nd ed. Charles E. Merrill Publishing Co., Columbus, Ohio.

Phillips. D. C. 1980. What do the researcher and the practitioner have to offer each other? Educ. Res. 9:17–24.

Rand, Y., Tannenbaum, A. J., and Feuerstein, R. 1979. Effects of Instrumental Enrichment on the psychoeducational development of low-functioning adolescents. J. Educ. Psychol. 71:751–763.

Robinson, N. M., and Robinson, H. B. 1976. The Mentally Retarded Child. McGraw-Hill Book Company, New York.

Sedlack, R. A., and Fitzmaurice, A. M. 1981. Teaching arithmetic. In: J. M. Kaufman and D. P. Hallahan (eds.), Handbook of Special Education. Prentice-Hall, Inc., Englewood Cliffs,

Shulman, L. S. 1974. The psychology of school subjects: A premature obituary? J. Res. Sci. Teach. 11:319–339.

Taylor, A. M., and Turnure, J. E. 1979. Imagery and verbal elaboration with retarded children: Effects on learning and memory. In: N. R. Ellis (ed.), Handbook of Mental Deficiency, Psychological Theory and Research, 2nd ed. Lawrence Erlbaum Associates, Hillsdale, New Jersey.

Thorndike, E. L. 1906. The Principles of Teaching. Mason-Henry, Syracuse, New York.

PERSPECTIVES AND PROGRESS IN MENTAL RETARDATION
Volume I—Social, Psychological, and Educational Aspects
Edited by J. M. Berg
Copyright © 1984 by I.A.S.S.M.D.

COMPARISON OF THE EFFECTS OF TEACHING DIRECT AND INDIRECT STRATEGIES ON THE ACQUISITION OF READING SKILLS BY MILDLY DEVELOPMENTALLY DISABLED ADOLESCENTS

T. R. Parmenter

Unit for Rehabilitation Studies, School of Education, Macquarie University, North Ryde, 2113, Australia

This study reports the replication, with retarded adolescents, of studies that showed that training on successive and simultaneous information-processing skills improved coding and academic skills of learning-disabled and low-achieving children. Three groups, each with 14 subjects, received training on general coding strategies, reading coding strategies, and a combined general/reading coding program, respectively. After 12 hours of training significant training effects were obtained on classification and recall skills by the general strategy group and on saying sounds and syllables for the reading coding group. No transfer of training to reading skills was noted for any of the groups.

Undoubtedly the dominant themes in special education at present are the thrusts toward modifying the cognitive processes of developmentally disabled persons and the related efforts to generalize the effects of training. Process training has been a consistent theme with special education, with the early emphasis upon modality training now giving way to a more cognitive-process approach (Mann, 1979; Sabatino et al., 1981). Despite the failure of early attempts to find significant aptitude-treatment interaction effects, recent work indicates a greater promise of success.

Central to the current momentum has been the development of fresh approaches to the study of intelligent behavior. Here the work of Campione and Brown (1978), Sternberg (1979), Feuerstein et al. (1979), and Das et al. (1979) is noteworthy. The training of intellectual processes has been explored via an instructional approach (Belmont and Butterfield, 1977; Borkowski and Cavanaugh, 1979); the use of a behavioral technology (Meichenbaum and Asarnow, 1979); instructional enrichment (Feuerstein et al., 1980); the development of meta-memory strategies (Campione and Brown, 1977; Lawson and Fueloep, 1980); and the training of strategies to facilitate academic performance (Burger, 1981).

Although much of this work has been laboratory based, there have been some tentative steps to translate the strategy training implications of these various theories into more natural environments. Utilizing the successive-simultaneous information processing model of Das et al. (1979), Krywanuik (1974) demonstrated that low-achieving third- and fourth-grade Canadian native Cree children improved significantly on serial recall, short-term memory, and sight word recognition tasks after a period of training that emphasized successive strategies. In another study Kaufman (1978), using a variety of training tasks that emphasized both successive and simultaneous strategies, showed that a group of fourth-grade learning-disabled children were able to improve significantly on measures of successive and simultaneous information processing and sight word recognition.

Both of these studies suggested that the training of successive and simultaneous processing strategies had a generalized effect upon basic academic and information-processing skills, but it is difficult to determine the relative contributions each of these training strategies had upon the final outcome. However, Das et al. (1979) pointed out that possibly the most significant achievement was that the training programs had induced children to use cognitive strategies that were effective for these particular tasks. In this respect they are suggesting, in Flavell's (1970) terms, that production and not mediational deficiencies have been ameliorated, or, in terms of the Campione and Brown (1978) model, it is the executive rather than the architectural system that has been modified. Although there is strong support for a relationship between the Das et al. (1979) concept of the successive coding process and basic word attack skills (Cummins and Das, 1977;

Kirby and Das, 1977; Das and Cummins, 1978), it is not clear whether a program to strengthen a reader's successive processing skills or a program directly related to the executive or strategy function would be more beneficial.

Despite suggestions to the contrary (Goodman, 1970), it seems critical that beginning readers develop a fluency in graphophonic skills (Biemiller, 1970, 1973; Gough, 1972; Calfee et al., 1973; Williams, 1977; Levi and Musatti, 1978). This has been shown to be the case particularly for mentally retarded readers who have difficulty in moving beyond an initial stage of memorizing words (Mason, 1978). Because of their poor understanding of phonological patterns and orthographic organization of letters, retarded readers generally persevere with inefficient strategies.

There is also compelling evidence that retarded persons display a verbal-coding processing deficit (Belmont and Birch, 1966; Richman and Lindgren, 1980), which possibly forces them to rely upon concrete rather than abstract referents when attempting to recognize words. It has been shown that programs that emphasize the regularity of graphophonic patterns in written English, and in particular those that stress syllabic rather than phonemic segmentation, are an effective means of initial reading instruction for backward readers (Shankweiler and Liberman, 1972; Liberman et al., 1977; Richardson et al., 1977).

The present study sought to compare the effects on reading skills of teaching successive/simultaneous coding strategies and more direct reading strategies that emphasize syllabic segmentation.

METHOD

Subjects

The subjects were 42 adolescents (mean age = 190 months, SD = 32.9 months) who were undergoing training at a work preparation center for handicapped school leavers in the upper range of the educable mentally retarded category. Earlier studies (Ward et al., 1981) showed that the population accepted into the center generally has a variety of disabilities in addition to intellectual ones.

Design and Procedure

Two sets of tests were administered individually to each subject. The first included those commonly used by Das et al. (1979) as marker tests to indicate successive and simultaneous coding processes. These were Raven's Standard Progressive Matrices (used in lieu of the colored matrices to avoid ceiling effects), figure copying, memory for designs, serial recall, visual short-term memory, color naming, digit span, and word reading. In addition, a sentence repetition test and the SORTS test for sampling children's organization and recall strategies (Reigal, 1976) were administered. A second set of tests, sampling a variety of reading skills, included the Neale Analysis of Reading (Neale, 1966), the GAP test (McLeod, 1978), the Schonell R1 test of word recognition (Schonell and Schonell, 1960), and the Gallistel-Ellis (GE) test of coding skills (Gallistel and Ellis, 1974). The subjects were then randomly assigned to three groups. A one-way analysis of variance indicated that there were no significant differences between the groups on any of the above-mentioned tests.

Group 1 received training on the following tasks, which emphasized successive or serial processing of information and classification skills:

Picture story arrangement: Subjects were prompted to arrange sets of pictures into a meaningful sequence and to tell the story while referring to each picture in sequence. The pictures were then turned over and the subjects were asked to recall the story by referring to each picture in turn.

Matrix serialization: Sets of five digits or letters were presented serially on a matrix. Subjects were asked to read the number as it appeared and to repeat the series from memory. During each session memory strategies were discussed and rehearsed.

Picture classification: After grouping and subgrouping sets of pictures, including objects around the home, the community, and the workforce, subjects were asked to give a rationale for their groups. The numbers of pictures and groups were gradually increased. Finally subjects were asked to recall the items. The use of this strategy for other memory tasks was discussed with each subject.

Visual memory tasks: Sets of slides containing series of digits, upper- and lower-case letters, and geometric shapes were projected. Subjects were prompted to use strategies, such as redundant patterns, as an aid to recall of the stimulus slide. Strategies were orally rehearsed and subjects were prompted to give examples of where these strategies could be used in everyday living.

Subjects in Group 2 received training in the G.F.B. Concept Transfer Sequence (Gallistel et al., 1977), which teaches rules of syllabification. Subjects progressed through this program as they demonstrated mastery (three successive correct trials) at each stage of the sequence. Verbalization and application of the rules to words not directly taught were emphasized. Subjects in Group 3 received training on each of the strategies taught to Groups 1 and 2.

The three groups received 50 training sessions, each lasting 15 minutes, over a period of approximately 4 months. At the end of training the coding and reading tests were readministered. Mean residualized gain scores of the groups were compared using a one-way analysis of variance test.

RESULTS

The only significant differences noted between the groups were on the isolated sounds/syllables of the GE test ($F_{2,39} = 23.74$, $P < 0.001$) and the recall section of the SORTS test ($F_{2,39} = 7.94$, $P < 0.01$). In the case of the sounds/syllables, Group 2 scored significantly higher than either Group 1 or 3 ($P < 0.01$) with Group 3 being significantly higher than Group 1 ($P < 0.05$). On the SORTS recall test Group 2 was significantly higher than either Group 1 or 3 ($P < 0.05$).

In summary, the results suggest that the training effects were noted only on the groups that had received reading skills coding strategy training and on the group that had received the longest training on recall strategies. There appeared to be very little, if any, transfer of training across to skills that had not been directly taught.

DISCUSSION

The aims of this study were to test in a natural setting the effectiveness of training coding strategies on the reading behavior of a group of mildly retarded adolescents and in particular to determine if the acquisition of coding skills generalized to novel material. In the case of those strategies that were based on the Das et al. (1979) model of successive/simultaneous processes no improvement was noted on the marker tests nor on the various tests of reading. However, training on classification strategies resulted in significant gains on a test of recall, supporting a number of earlier findings (Bilsky et al., 1972; Burger et al., 1978). Despite this improvement on organizational skills no carryover to reading performance was noted.

One can only speculate as to the results if training had proceeded beyond the 50 sessions. Observation of the responses of Groups 2 and 3 at posttest on the reading test indicated that most subjects seemed more reflective in their approach. Individual subjects attempted to apply phonic decoding strategies in lieu of their earlier sight word approach. Nevertheless, both groups failed to reach significance on the GE word test, which contained phonically regular words. Here the restricted training time possibly militated against more favorable results, because not all of the coding strategies sampled in the test had been covered in training.

A possible explanation for the failure of Groups 1 and 3 to show an improvement on reading performance is that most of the training emphasized visual cues. Considering the high relationship noted between reading skills and the tests of successive processing (Kirby and Das, 1977), future studies might profitably explore the use of training strategies that stress auditory memory rather than visual memory tasks (Semmel and Bennett, 1970).

The discrepant findings of the present study compared to Krywanuik's (1974) and Kaufman's (1978) results may be explained, in part, by the refractory problems faced in training retarded persons in metastrategic behavior. Here, a number of aspects are worthy of attention. First, people in general tend to utilize simple rather than complex strategies unless the situation demands a higher order strategy. In the case of retarded persons, affective characteristics such as learned helplessness, learned incompetence, or the "I can't" attitude may interact with cognitive processes, resulting in their being loathe to risk the use of newly acquired strategies in novel situations. Perseveration with inefficient or inappropriate strategies in problem-solving situations is a common characteristic of this population.

Second, the groups in the present study may not have learned the strategies to a level of fluency. For instance, Burger (1981) suggested that strategic fluency possibly defines the basis of cognitive normalcy. Here the constraints of a traditional research design that calls for treatments equal in time across individuals and groups are obvious. The necessity for the use of careful and precise instructional methods in strategy training has been amply demonstrated by a number of researchers (Belmont and Butterfield, 1977; Meichenbaum and Asarnow, 1979; Campione et al., 1980). Here, too, questions concerning the quality and sufficiency of training need to be carefully addressed (Borkowski and Cavanaugh, 1979). Future studies also need to monitor sensitively the effects of coding training during the training process to ensure that adequate maintenance of the skills is achieved.

A final issue relates to the heuristic value of the successive-simultaneous processes approach to strategy training for retarded populations. Das' (1980) suggestion that a prerequisite level of coding must be reached before executive functions such as planning may occur is plausible. To an extent, however, this begs the question as to how one achieves this threshhold level and, in the case of retarded persons, whether the coding processes are amenable to change. Further work is required, too, to tease out more adequately those specific reading skills that are related to the successive and/or simultaneous processes.

Although these processes have been delineated via factor analyses, there still remains the task of developing adequate training procedures that might establish their educational utility for retarded learners. Perhaps, because of the wide variability noted on the performance of individual subjects within each group in this study, it is possible that an idiographic research design would clarify the effects of training, providing a valid base for individualized instruction.

REFERENCES

Belmont, L., and Birch, H. G. 1966. The intellectual profile of retarded readers. Percept. Motor Skills 22:787–816.

Belmont, J. M., and Butterfield, E. C. 1977. The instructional approach to developmental cognitive research. In: R. V. Krail, Jr. and J. W. Hagen (eds.), Perspectives on the Development of Memory and Cognition. Lawrence Erlbaum Associates, Hillsdale, New Jersey.

Biemiller, A. 1970. The development of the use of graphic and contextual information as children learn to read. Read. Res. Q. 6:75–96.

Biemiller, A. 1973. Relationships between oral reading rates for letters, words, and simple text, and the development of reading ability. Ontario Research Council, Toronto (ED 092 911).

Bilsky, L., Evans, R. A., and Gilbert, L. 1972. Generalization of associative clustering tendencies in mentally retarded adolescents. Effects of novel stimuli. Am. J. Ment. Defic. 77:77–84.

Borkowski, J. G., and Cavanaugh, J. C. 1979. Maintenance and generalization of skills and strategies by the retarded. In N. R. Ellis (ed.), Handbook of Mental Deficiency, 2nd ed. Lawrence Erlbaum Associates, Hillsdale, New Jersey.

Burger, A. L. 1981. Recent research in the facilitation of academic skill development in educable mental retardates. Paper presented to Annual Convention of American Association on Mental Deficiency.

Burger, A. L., Blackman, L. S., Holmes, M., and Zettlin, A. 1978. Use of active sorting and retrieval strategies as a facilitator of recall, clustering, and sorting by EMR and non-retarded children. Am. J. Ment. Defic. 83:253–261.

Calfee, R. C., Lindamood, P., and Lindamood, C. 1973. Acoustic-phonetic skills and reading—Kindergarten through twelfth grade. J. Educ. Psychol. 64:293–298.

Campione, J. C., and Brown, A. L. 1977. Memory and metamemory development in educable retarded children. In: R. V. Krail, Jr. and J. W. Hagen (eds.), Perspectives on the Development of Memory and Cognition. Lawrence Erlbaum Associates, Hillsdale, New Jersey.

Campione, J. C., and Brown, A. L. 1978. Toward a theory of intelligence: Contributions from research with retarded children. Intelligence 1:279–304.

Campione, J. C., Nitsch, K., Bray, N., and Brown, A. L. 1980. Improving memory skills in mentally retarded children: Empirical research and strategies for intervention. Technical Report No. 196. Center for the Study of Reading, University of Illinois, Urbana.

Cummins, J., and Das, J. P. 1977. Cognitive processing and reading difficulties: A framework for research. Alberta J. Educ. Res. 23:245–256.

Das, J. P. 1980. Planning: Theoretical considerations and empirical evidence. Psychol. Res. 41:141–151.

Das, J. P., and Cummins, J. 1978. Academic performance and cognitive process in EMR children. Am. J. Ment. Defic. 83:197–199.

Das, J. P., Kirby, J. R., and Jarman, R. F. 1979. Simultaneous and Successive Cognitive Processes. Academic Press, Inc., New York.

Feuerstein, R., Rand, Y., and Hoffman, M. B. 1979. The Dynamic Assessment of Retarded Performers. University Park Press, Baltimore.

Feuerstein, R., Rand, Y., Hoffman, M. B., and Miller, R. 1980. Instrumental Enrichment. University Park Press, Baltimore.

Flavell, J. H. 1970. Developmental studies of mediated memory. In: H. W. Ruse and L. P. Lipsitt (eds.), Advances in Child Development, Vol. 5, Academic Press, Inc., New York.

Gallistel, E., and Ellis, K. 1974. Gallistel-Ellis Test of Coding Skills. A Linguistic Reading and Spelling Test for Diagnostic Coding Skills. Montage Press Inc., Hamden, Connecticut.

Gallistel, E., Fischer, P., and Blackburn, M. 1977. G.F.B. Sequence of Objectives for Teaching and Testing Reading in the Concept Transfer Sequence. Montage Press, Inc., Hamden, Connecticut.

Goodman, K. S. 1970. Reading: A psycholinguistic guessing game. In: H. Singer and R. R. Ruddell (eds.), Theoretical Models and Processes of Reading. International Reading Assoc., Newark, Delaware.

Gough, P. B. 1972. One second of reading. In: J. F. Kavanagh and J. G. Mattingly (eds.), The Relationship Between Speech and Reading. M.I.T. Press, Cambridge, Massachusetts.

Kaufman, D. 1978. The relation of academic performance to strategy training and remedial techniques: An information processing approach. Unpublished doctoral dissertation, University of Alberta, Edmonton, Canada.

Kirby, J. R., and Das, J. P. 1977. Reading achievement, I.Q. and simultaneous-successive processing. J. Educ. Psychol. 69:564–570.

Krywanuik, L. W. 1974. Patterns of cognitive abilities of high and low achieving school children. Unpublished doctoral dissertation, University of Alberta, Edmonton, Canada.

Lawson, M. J., and Fueloep, S. 1980. Understanding the purpose of strategy training. Br. J. Educ. Psychol. 50:175–180.

Levi, G., and Musatti, T. 1978. Phonemic synthesis in poor readers. Br. J. Disord. Commun. 13:65–74.

Liberman, I. Y., Shankweiler, D., Camp, L., Heifetz, B., and Werfelman, M. 1977. Steps toward literacy. A report on reading prepared for the Working Group on Learning Failure and Unused Learning Potential. President's Commission on Mental Health, Washington, D.C.

Mann, L. 1979. On the Trail of Process. Grune & Stratton, New York.

Mason, J. M. 1978. Role of strategy on reading by mentally retarded persons. Am. J. Ment. Defic. 82:467–473.

McLeod, J. 1978. GAP Reading Comprehension Test, 3rd ed. Heinemann, Melbourne.

Meichenbaum, D., and Asarnow, J. 1979. Cognitive-behavioral modification and metacognitive development: Implications for the classroom. In: P. C. Kendall and S. D. Hallon (eds.), Cognitive-Behavioral Interventions: Theory, Research and Procedures. Academic Press, Inc., New York.

Neale, M. 1966. Neale Analysis of Reading Ability, 2nd ed. Macmillan, London.

Reigel, R. H. 1976. The SORTS Test for Sampling Children's Organization and Recall Strategies. Montage Press, Inc., Hamden, Connecticut.

Richman, L. C., and Lindgren, S. D. 1980. Patterns of intellectual ability in children with verbal deficits. J. Abnorm. Child Psychol. 8:65–81.

Richardson, E., DiBenedetto, D., and Bradley, C. M. 1977. Relationship of sound blending to reading achievement. Rev. Educ. Res. 47:319–334.

Sabatino, D. A., Miller, P. F., and Schmidt, C. 1981. Can intelligence be altered through cognitive training? J. Spec. Educ. 15:126–144.

Schonell, F. J., and Schonell, F. E. 1960. Diagnostic and Attainment Testing. Oliver and Boyd, London.

Semmel, M. I., and Bennett, S. W. 1970. Effects of linguistic structure and delay on memory span of EMR children. Am. J. Ment. Defic. 74:674–680.

Shankweiler, D., and Liberman, I. Y. 1972. Misreading: A search for causes. In: J. F. Kavanagh and I. C. Mattingly (eds.), Language by Ear and Eye. The Relationship between Speech and Reading. M.I.T. Press, Cambridge, Massachusetts.

Sternberg, R. J. 1979. The nature of mental abilities. Am. Psychol. 34:214–230.

Ward. J., Parmenter, T. R., Riches, V., and Hauritz, M. 1981. Predicting the outcomes of a work preparation program. Aust. J. Dev. Disabil. 7:137–145.

Williams, J. 1977. Building perceptual and cognitive strategies into a reading curriculum. In: A. Reber and D. Scarborough (eds.), Toward a Psychology of Reading. Lawrence Erlbaum Associates, Hillsdale, New Jersey.

PERSPECTIVES AND PROGRESS IN MENTAL RETARDATION
Volume I—Social, Psychological, and Educational Aspects
Edited by J. M. Berg
Copyright © 1984 by I.A.S.S.M.D.

COMMUNITY-BASED RESIDENTIAL TREATMENT MODEL FOR MENTALLY RETARDED ADOLESCENT OFFENDERS

G. C. Denkowski[1] and K. M. Denkowski[2]
[1] *Texas Department of Mental Health and Mental Retardation,
5000 Campus Drive, Fort Worth, Texas 76119*
[2] *Volunteers of America, 4700 South Riverside Drive, Fort Worth,
Texas 76119*

A major challenge for the 1980s will be the development of effective community-based treatment strategies for mentally retarded adolescent offenders. To date, no noninstitutional treatment specific to this aggressive and evasive group has been reported in the literature. This chapter proposes a community-based model that utilizes a point economy and timeout procedures, implemented in an environment engineered specifically to facilitate their consistent application. Preliminary evaluative data are presented that assess the model's efficacy in reducing aggression in this population. Several methodological issues germaine to programming retarded adolescent offenders within the community are discussed.

An important development in the past decade in the United States has been the increasing diversion of mentally retarded (MR) adolescent offenders from the juvenile justice into the mental retardation service system (e.g., Wilson, 1978; Department of Developmental Services, 1981; Timbers et al., 1981). The practical relevance of this movement is that it shifts responsibility for treating a very difficult population to an already beleaguered community services network. This impending

---

The opinions expressed by the authors are not necessarily those of their respective institutions.

task is made even more arduous by judicial rulings that stipulate that anyone receiving such services must be provided the least restrictive treatment (*Lake* v *Cameron*, 1966; *Covington* v *Harris*, 1969). Although consensus has yet to frame the parameters of the least restrictive principle, many have come to consider the right to treatment in small community residences as one of its vital aspects (e.g., Wexler, 1973; Martin, 1975; Nay, 1976). Given the trend to divert MR adolescents from prosecution, in tandem with the emphasis upon local treatment, it seems that mounting pressure will be felt by local MR service providers to establish community-based programs for MR adolescent offenders. In fact, in Texas these forces have already converged, via a federal suit, to elicit a guarantee of community residential treatment for all MR adolescent offenders in that jurisdiction (*Wells* v *Killough*, 1980).

The problem that these events pose for local service providers is that technology specific to the noninstitutional treatment of this MR population has not yet evolved. No professional literature could be located that advises how community residential treatment should proceed with MR adolescent offenders. The approach most frequently mentioned in the context of community programming with delinquent youth, the Achievement Place model, does not seem well suited for this MR subgroup. This approach was designed primarily for youth who had not engaged in violent crimes, and who could adapt to public school (e.g., Phillips, 1968; Liberman et al., 1975; Barkley et al., 1976; Kirigin et al., 1982). Experience indicates that most MR adolescent offenders are highly aggressive, to a point where they cannot function in conventional educational settings (Burchard, 1967). Moreover, preliminary data indicate that this group's aggressive behavior does not decrease under an Achievement Place–type treatment, that vandalism of the group home becomes extensive, and that runaway behavior becomes rampant (Denkowski and Denkowski, in press).

The only treatment formulated specifically for MR adolescent offenders appears to be the program at Murdock Center, North Carolina (Burchard, 1967; Burchard and Barrera, 1972; Burchard and Harig, 1976). In this approach, a token economy and timeout (i.e., removal of reinforcement) techniques were combined to treat antisocial behavior in a closed (locked) setting. Unfortunately, the apparent effectiveness of that treatment was not corroborated empirically. Moreover, the Murdock model has not been duplicated within the community.

In 1981, circumstances permitted an adaptation of the Murdock paradigm to a community-based residence for MR adolescent offenders, and allowed for some systematic evaluation of its efficacy in reducing aggressive behavior. This report outlines the resultant treatment, presents preliminary evaluative data, and identifies several methodological issues that seem central to programming this aggressive and evasive population within the community.

TREATMENT SETTING

Our experience had demonstrated that MR adolescent offenders frequently leave the group home covertly to obtain reinforcers that are being withheld because of inappropriate behavior. Moreover, they tend to slip away to obtain prohibited reinforcers, such as liquor and marijuana. In addition, it became apparent that most will not proceed into timeout voluntarily, at least in the initial stage of treatment. In fact, they tend to make every effort, regardless of its danger to others, to avoid that consequence. Furthermore, running away is this population's usual response when serious efforts are made to gain their compliance with a timeout order. Recurrent demonstrations of these behaviors and their counterproductive consequences led to authorization to convert one section of a 15-bed group home into a closed wing in which treatment could be initiated.

The closed wing was specifically modified to facilitate the observation of client behavior and to prevent evasion of consequences programmed for antisocial behavior. This process involved panelling walls and ceilings with $\frac{1}{4}''$ plywood, installing solid-core wood doors throughout, replacing all window glass with $\frac{1}{4}''$ high-impact clear plastic, and mounting steel (wire mesh-coated) burglar bars over the windows. In addition, all portable furniture and other items that could be used as a weapon were removed from that section. Beds were bolted to the floor, and cafeteria-style dining clusters were placed in the dining room and classroom. Only heavy modular furniture was used in the lounge. Locks were installed on all doors, so that each room and closet, as well as the entire wing, could be fully secured. To assure client safety, a fire alarm pull station and extra fire extinguishers were located in the office of this section, and smoking was stringently controlled.

TREATMENT METHOD

Target Behaviors

Because MR adolescent offenders were placed into residential treatment for committing various crimes, the primary focus of intervention is on those criminal acts or the class of behavior they represent (e.g., the target behavior for car theft would be stealing). In addition, previous experience indicated that this population, to varying degrees and under sundry circumstances, exhibits a rather consistent pattern of antisocial behavior comprised of physical aggression, property destruction, verbal abuse, noncompliance, lying, stealing, and running away. Accordingly, each resident's presenting criminal behaviors were considered alongside the antisocial behaviors to arrive at the treatment targets for that youth. Reduction/elimination of these antisocial acts was the goal of the treatment described below.

Token Economy

A point-based version of the token economy system introduced by Ayllon and Azrin (1968) was installed with a seemingly minor but highly significant modification suggested by Foxx (personal communication, 1981): points were dichotomized into training and social components. In this variation, only training points could be earned through habilitative kinds of behaviors (e.g., bathing, room cleanup, class attendance). These points could purchase only relatively low-value backup reinforcers (e.g., cigarettes, extra snacks, posters, time off from activities). Highly desired backup reinforcers, primarily unusual items and off-site activities, had to be purchased with social points. These could be earned only by refraining from antisocial behavior, and only at a prespecified rate per hour. All fines for antisocial behavior were deducted from the social point balance. The point value of target behaviors was periodically adjusted whenever behavioral objectives were not being attained or were easily exceeded.

The reason for dichotomizing the point economy was to preclude its manipulation. That is, it was devised to prevent residents from purchasing highly desired reinforcers with points earned for relatively low priority habilitative-type behaviors, such as wearing clean clothes, bathing, and performing classwork. Only decrease in antisocial behavior, the focus of treatment, provided access to desired reinforcers under this variation.

Timeout

All physical aggression, including property destruction, was treated with timeout. Additionally, residents who demonstrated that their verbal aggression anteceded physical aggression also received timeout when they indulged in this precursor.

Two forms of timeout were used. In the first type, the timeout room door remained unlocked. This was implemented when residents proceeded into timeout voluntarily (i.e., with no more than two verbal prompts). If there was noncompliance, residents were physically assisted into the timeout room and the door was locked. The least force possible was used to gain compliance; however, no one was permitted to evade timeout, regardless of their resolve to do so. Duration of timeout was 10 minutes, with a 5-minute changeover delay. Residents were monitored unobtrusively during the timeout period.

The timeout room was a former bathroom that had been stripped of fixtures, and paneled entirely (including ceiling and floor) with $\frac{3}{4}''$ plywood. A solid wood door was hinged to open inward, and fitted with a $3'' \times 3''$ high-impact clear plastic viewing window. The room was not padded because experience indicated an absence of self-injurious behavior with this population (and none has occurred to date).

Implementation of Treatment

Upon arrival at the group home, new residents automatically enter the closed wing. That area can be left only when at least 80% of available social points are earned and less than 5 timeouts are incurred in a consecutive 30-day period. Residents who meet these criteria are gradually phased into the open section of the home, initially for less than 1-hour intervals. Any significant relapse into antisocial behavior results in partial or complete return to the closed wing. During their stay at this group home, residents receive all services specified in their individual program plans on-site, with the exception of nonroutine medical care.

PRELIMINARY RESULTS

Preliminary results indicate that this community-based treatment model is effective in reducing the aggression of MR adolescent offenders. Using a basic cohort design (Cook and Campbell, 1979; Denkowski and Denkowski, submitted for publication), it was found that physical aggression was reduced 69% below the level attained with an Achievement Place–type program administered in an open setting with a sample of 16 subjects ($P < 0.012$). Likewise, verbal aggression was observed to decrease by 52% ($P < 0.058$). A corollary behavior, running away, was practically eliminated: 32 adolescents ran away in the comparison group (30 days) versus 3 in the experimental group (90 days).

In a sample of 8 residents, physical aggression was found to stabilize after 40 days of treatment at a frequency of less than one episode every 2 weeks, compared with almost 11 incidents during the 2-week pretreatment period. However, verbal behavior did not stabilize as rapidly, requiring 70 days of treatment; even though an average frequency of less than three incidents per 2-week period was observed for each resident after that time, considerable between-subject and within-subject variability was evident.

DISCUSSION

The treatment model outlined here seems to offer a viable starting point for developing community-based residential programs for MR adolescent offenders. This approach tends to effectively decrease aggression, and essentially eliminates runaway behavior. Moreover, preliminary evidence indicates that these outcomes endure subsequently in a conventional group home setting. Because of the presence of three major treatment components—the point economy, timeout, and a closed area—it is difficult to determine the effect of any one component in reducing aggression. Further research is needed to discern empirically their individual and interactive contributions. Similarly, hypotheses advanced to account for why verbal aggression seems to be less adequately controlled by this approach require testing.

Even though the functional dynamics of this model remain to be explicated, practical utility appears to warrant its consideration. In a conventional, open group home, 8 MR adolescent offenders were observed in 185 physical and 562 verbal aggressions in a 30-day period. A comparable group of 8, programmed with this model, committed only 51 physical and 270 verbal aggressions during the initial 90 days of treatment. On average, the experimental subjects engaged in 2 physical and 11 verbal aggressions per month, whereas their conventionally programmed counterparts exhibited 23 physical and 70 verbal aggressions over the same time interval. A treatment that suggests such prospects of reducing aggression in the MR adolescent offender could be a welcome guidepost in program development for this difficult population.

Of the numerous obstacles encountered during implementation of this model, two were paramount: uncontrolled contingencies and lack of rigorous evaluation strategies. As elaborated earlier by Reppucci and Saunders (1974), natural setting treatment is replete with difficult-to-control factors that frequently elicit and maintain undesired client behavior. Many of these contingencies emanate from the environment per se (e.g., unsuitable physical settings), administrative idiosyncracies (e.g., placating external forces at the expense of programmatic considerations), and institutional constraints (e.g., insufficient resources). Although such impediments were present to varying degrees, the most onerous interference resulted from staff's inconsistent application of treatment. This was noted in terms of fluctuations in the accuracy with which target behaviors were discriminated, in the regularity with which programmed positive and negative consequences were provided, in the propriety of nonprogrammed (i.e., interpersonal) behavior, and in the faithfulness with which schedules were followed.

To increase the quality of staff performance, we initiated didactic instruction (24 hours, in four sessions), instituted a 1-week on-the-job training period, and designed various prompting devices. The most useful prompting device appeared to be the daily staff work schedule, which structures all tasks required of staff during each shift in terms of time, activity, and place. Staff are assigned to specific clients, and required to program them in accordance with the work schedule (which interfaces with the clients' activity schedules). Supervisors randomly check to assess whether staff are programming as intended, and that staff-client interactions are appropriate. Differential consequences are provided for staff performance that exceeds or falls short of the supervisor's standards. In a sense, an effort was made to develop a parallel "treatment" for staff.

Although these endeavors have improved the overall consistency of the staff's program implementation, qualitative variations are still evident within staff across time, and new employees tend to introduce marked inconsistencies. These observations confirm Quilitch's (1975) finding that training itself does not produce increased staff effectiveness, and that residential staff require ongoing supervision.

Relevant to our difficulty in excluding nonprogrammed contingencies was the problem of locating an assessment strategy that controlled artifacts sufficiently to allow a meaningful evaluation of this model's efficacy in reducing aggression. As had been recognized by others (e.g., O'Leary and Borkovec, 1978; Kirigin et al., 1982), some dependent variables, such as violent behavior, prohibit the use of a control group and multibaseline formats because withholding of treatment, which is integral to both, is unethical and impractical. To circumvent these consequences, we adopted Cook and Campbell's (1979) "basic cohort design." Although that procedure concedes some internal validity, it seems adequately suited for assessing the reductive impact of interventions upon aggression in the natural setting.

In using this design, we regarded the sample that receives the initial treatment as the control or "contrast" group. The next generation of clients that enters the group home receives a variation of that treatment, and is considered the experimental group. Between-group differences in frequency of aggression are assessed for significance using the Mann-Whitney U test (Mann and Whitney, 1947). Integral to such a comparison is the assumption that both groups are equivalent along important dimensions (e.g., age, sex, IQ, adaptive behavior, and aggressive behavior). Another consideration is that this design takes some time to implement because the contrast group must be transferred/ discharged from the home to make room for a new sample, the experimental group.

As may be evident from this discussion, community-based residential treatment of MR adolescent offenders is still in its infancy. However, lack of professional expertise is unlikely to deter judicial committments of this population into local MR service systems. Attempting to program these difficult youth with conventional group home procedures seems to invite adversity not only for them but also for the community. To prevent these dire consequences, a concerted effort must be expended to raise the current level of treatment technology to meet the anticipated influx of this population into community programs. Accordingly, a major challenge for the 1980s will be the development of effective community-based treatment strategies for MR offenders from the precursors that exist today.

REFERENCES

Ayllon, T., and Azrin, N. 1968. The Token Economy: A Motivational System for Therapy and Rehabilitation. Appleton-Century-Crofts, New York.

Barkley, R. A., Hastings, J. F., and Tousel, R. E. 1976. Evaluation of a token system for juvenile delinquents in a residential setting. J. Behav. Ther. Exp. Psychiatr. 7:227–230.

Burchard, J. D. 1967. Systematic socialization: A programmed environment for the habilitation of anti-social retardates. Psychol. Rec. 17:461–476.

Burchard, J. D., and Barrera, F. 1972. An analysis of timeout and response cost in a programmed environment. J. Appl. Behav. Anal. 5:271–282.

Burchard, J. D., and Harig, P. T. 1976. Behavior modification and delinquency. In: H. Leitenburg (ed.), Handbook of Behavior Modification and Behavior Therapy, pp. 405–452. Prentice-Hall, Inc., Englewood Cliffs, New Jersey.

Cook, T. D., and Campbell, D. 1979. Quasi-Experimentation: Design and Analysis for the Field Setting. Rand-McNally, New York.

Covington v *Harris*, 491, F. 2d 617 (D.C. Cir. 1969).

Denkowski, G. C., and Denkowski, K. M. Community-based residential treatment of MR adolescent offenders. Phase I: Reduction of aggressive behavior. J. Commun. Psychol. (in press)

Department of Developmental Services. 1981. California State Hospital Directory. Department of Developmental Services, Sacramento, California.

Kirigin, K. A., Braukmann, C. J., Atwater, J. D., and Wolf, M. M. 1982. An evaluation of teaching-family (Achievement Place) group homes for juvenile offenders. J. Appl. Behav. Anal. 15:1–16.

Lake v *Cameron*, 364, F. 2d 657 (D.C. Cir. 1966).

Liberman, R.P., Ferris, C. and Salgado, P. 1975. Replication of the Achievement Place model in California. J. Appl. Behav. Anal. 8:287–300.

Mann, H. B., and Whitney, D. R. 1947. On a test of whether one of two random variables is statistically larger than the other. Ann. Math. Statist. 18:52–54.

Martin, R. 1975, Legal Challenges to Behavior Modification: Trends in Schools, Corrections, and Mental Health. Research Press, Champaign, Illinois.

Nay, W. R. 1976. Behavioral Intervention: Contemporary Strategies. Gardner Press, New York.

O'Leary, K. D., and Borkovec, T. D. 1978. Conceptual, methodological, and ethical problems of placebo groups in psychotherapy research. Am. Psychol. 33:821–830.

Phillips, E. L. 1968. Achievement Place: Token reinforcement procedures in a home-style rehabilitation setting for pre-delinquents. J. Appl. Behav. Anal. 1:213–223.

Quilitch, H. R. 1975. A comparison of three staff-management procedures. J. Appl. Behav. Anal. 8:59–66.

Reppucci, N. D., and Saunders, J. T. 1974. Social psychology of behavior modification: Problems of implementation in natural settings. Am. Psychol. 29:649–660.

Timbers, G. D., Jones, R. J., and Davis, J. L. 1981. Safeguarding the rights of children and youth in group-home treatment settings. In: G. T. Hannah, W. P. Christian, and H. B. Clark (eds.), Preservation of Client Rights. Free Press, New York.

Wells v Killough, No. TY-80-110CA (E.D. Texas, filed April 11, 1980).

Wexler, D. 1973. Token and taboo: Behavior modification, token economies, and the law. California Law Rev. 61:81–109.

Wilson, J. P. 1978. The Rights of Adolescents in the Mental Health System. Lexington Books, Lexington, Massachusetts.

PERSPECTIVES AND PROGRESS IN MENTAL RETARDATION
Volume I—Social, Psychological, and Educational Aspects
Edited by J. M. Berg
Copyright © 1984 by I.A.S.S.M.D.

COMMUNITY-BASED SEXUALITY PROGRAMS FOR DEVELOPMENTALLY HANDICAPPED ADULTS

P. R. Johnson

Vancouver-Richmond Association for Mentally Handicapped People, 2979 West 41st Avenue, Vancouver, British Columbia V6N 3C8, Canada

Although there appears to be increased acceptance of the right of developmentally handicapped adults to enjoy intimate relationships, disturbing increases in the incidence of sexual abuse have been noted. In addition, individualized sexuality assessments indicate considerable need for education and training. However, group counseling appears to be an effective educational technique. There is a need for further research into effective teaching, but this should be allied to the utilization of generic services that offer sexuality programs in many communities.

At a recent parent meeting on sexuality, the mother of a multihandicapped teenager rose to ask a question. "My son has severe cerebral palsy, and has little control over his fine motor movements," she said. "I don't think he can masturbate himself, should I do it for him?" The parent group commended the woman for her frankness, discussed the issue, and suggested other ways of helping the young man meet his sexual and social needs.

Incidents like this appear to reflect a positive change in attitudes toward the sexuality of developmentally handicapped persons. As the principle of normalization (Wolfensberger, 1972) is more widely applied, increasing numbers of these people are now being seen as sexual beings, and the topic of sexuality is being openly discussed by parent and professional alike. Certainly, some outdated and rigid attitudes remain and the old myths of sexual aggression and genetic transmission die hard, but many people now believe the handicapped have a right to intimate relationships (Craft and Craft, 1981).

In fact, society's concern for human rights has highlighted other issues concerning the sexuality of handicapped people. For example, doctors, lawyers, and even parents have been successfully sued by mentally retarded adults who were sterilized as minors (Law Reform Commission of Canada, 1980). The result has been a drastic reduction in this form of abuse, because many doctors are now reluctant to perform the operation. Unfortunately, this is a disadvantage to the small number of handicapped people and their families who have legitimate reasons for requesting this procedure.

Even more disconcerting than the sterilization issue is the dramatic increase in the reported incidence of sexual abuse (Seattle Rape Relief, 1981; British Columbia Ministry of Human Resources, 1981). In the vast majority of these cases, the offender is male and a family member or neighbor. Regretfully, many mentally retarded people are perceived as perfect victims because their passivity, verbal limitations, and memory deficits make the chance of legal retribution unlikely. Cases of incest often have an additional distressing element in that the abuse continues for months and even years before it is reported.

The recognition of the handicapped person's right to be sexual and increasing sensitivity toward abuse have led to an increase in the availability of psychoeducational programs in this area. For example, the Alternative Route curriculum (British Columbia Ministry of Education, 1979) offers courses as varied as "Physical Growth and Development" and the "Implications of Unconventional Sexual Relationships." However, there remains a dearth of information regarding the effectiveness of programs addressing the sexual habilitation of developmentally handicapped adults. This paper addresses the issue in relation to research efforts in British Columbia and Alberta during the past 5 years. It contains three components that focus upon the assessment of training needs, group counseling as a teaching method, and planning for community-based services.

ASSESSMENT

Because comprehensive assessments (Gunzburg, 1969; Marlett, 1971) have formed the basis of many successful training programs (Marlett and Hughson, 1979), the Sexuality Development Index (SDI) was devised (Johnson, 1981). Its purpose is to assess the current status of developmentally handicapped adult trainees in the general areas of gender identity, sociosexual behaviors, and sexual knowledge. The SDI is based upon Piagetian principles, and its design takes into account intellectual capacities as underdeveloped as those of the subperiod of preoperational thought.

The first section is entitled Gender Identity. It contains 10 video-taped segments of groups of people. Each segment lasts for approximately 30 seconds. Trainees are asked to identify the member of each group who is most like them, and to provide reasons for their choices. The section contains items such as a boy and a girl, a family group, three members of the same sex, and a nude male and female.

Socio-Sexual Behaviours is the title of the second section. Here, trainees are asked to watch a series of short videovignettes, and then to respond to a question asked by one of the actors. Segments in this section cover the concepts of privacy, masturbation, contraception, pregnancy, venereal disease, coercion, and homosexuality.

The final section focuses on Sexual Knowledge. In the first five segments, the trainees are asked to name body parts, and describe their functions. In segments six to eleven, they are asked to name various sexual activities, and to describe the next steps in the film sequences.

Because initial investigations relating to the reliability and validity of the SDI were encouraging, 63 sexuality assessments have now been completed. Interviews were conducted with 32 men and 31 women who had received services from community-based agencies for developmentally handicapped people. Their mean chronological age was 24.5 years with a range from 17 to 35, and IQ scores fell between 50 and 89 with a mean of 66.7.

Gender Identity

Three interesting points emerged from the data on Gender Identity. The first was that whereas 23 of the females always identified with models of the same gender, only 13 of the males were equally consistent. From this, it may be inferred that females have a stronger sense of appropriate gender identity. One explanation for this may lie in the young women's preparation for menstruation, which probably leads to an increased awareness of being female. Another might be that male handicapped children have had relatively little exposure to male role models and therefore still tend to identify with their ubiquitous female caretakers. It seems likely that to develop a more realistic gender identity, handicapped boys and men should spend more time with valued adult males.

Second, on at least one occasion, 34 of the trainees identified with children instead of young adults. Although they had a mean chronological age of 24.5 years, many did not see themselves as adults. This self-concept is probably related to the phenomenon of handicapped people often perceiving other adults as being dominant (Rosen et al.,

1975), and consequently complying with both their reasonable and un-reasonable demands.

The trainees had some interesting reactions to sexually explicit materials. Half of the men showed some signs of discomfort; this was also true for 25 of the women. Unfortunately, this kind of anxiety probably inhibits performance in social situations, even when the person is knowledgeable on specific topics. Thus, this inhibition may well be another contributing factor in the sexual exploitation of mentally handicapped people, especially those who are female.

Sociosexual Behaviors

Initially, it appeared that the handicapped women had a better under-standing of the concept of privacy. However, on being asked why they should not exhibit certain behaviors in public places, many women said, "It's not ladylike" or "It's not appropriate." Further questioning revealed these phrases to be largely meaningless to the women. They knew which behaviors to avoid, but lacked a cognitive basis for making the relevant discriminations.

There seemed to be another division between men and women with respect to touching strangers of the opposite sex. Whereas 22 of the men were aware of the social constraints against this activity, only 14 of the women demonstrated a similar awareness. In a society where the myth of the sexually impulsive mentally handicapped male has not yet been put to rest, parents and their substitutes have probably had good reason to make sure their sons do not touch female strangers. Although being physically affectionate may be a more acceptable behavior for females, it appears likely that this activity has led unwitting victims into sexually abusive situations.

Further light was shed on the hypothesis of the promiscuity of mentally handicapped adults. More than three-quarters of the 63 trainees said they would not indulge in "necking" or sexual intercourse with a long-time partner. Approximately 40 of them said they would behave in a similar way even if married. In spite of protestations to the contrary, it appears that many of our trainees have been receiving clear messages that they should not be sexual!

When the effects of persuasion are considered, there is a change in the picture of the sexually unresponsive developmentally handi-capped person. In vignettes where the actors were very persuasive, 28 of the people said they would comply with requests for sexual favors. Because of increased anxiety, one would expect the figure to be higher in real-life situations; this finding suggests that trainees were suscep-tible to persuasive coercion.

There was another interesting discrepancy between the sexes on issues relating to the prevention of pregnancy. Whereas only 9 of the males mentioned pregnancy as a restraint on sexual activity, 17 of the women expressed concerns about becoming pregnant. Again, it appeared that these students were responding to parental admonitions rather than predictions of the consequences. This hypothesis is indirectly supported by the finding that 37 individuals of the total group of 63 appeared to lack even basic knowledge about contraception.

Sexual Knowledge

On this section which covers basic sexual knowledge, overall scores ranged from 18% to 77%, with a mean of 53%. This suggests a considerable lack of functional information among this group of young adults. Although embarrassment at some of the explicit scenes undoubtedly inhibited some trainees' responses, the scores may present an accurate picture of knowledge the handicapped person is likely to apply in sexual situations.

Scores varied tremendously among the various items. For example, 52 of the trainees were able to recognize a pregnant woman, but only 16 identified female masturbation. Generally, trainees were more successful in naming parts of the body than in describing their uses. Names for the penis and breast were known by 49 and 45 of the trainees, respectively. However, only 13 knew the function of the testicles and only 30 described a use of the breast. In addition, items concerning intercourse, contraception, and menstruation proved too difficult for just over half of the group.

There were considerable differences in the sexual knowledge of men and women. For example, as one might expect, 19 of the men but only 9 of the women gave a name for the testicles, whereas these numbers were reversed on items concerning uses of the breast. In addition, the female trainees also knew more about menstruation, sexual intercourse, and birth control pills. Rather surprisingly, more women than men were able to identify a condom, and this possibly reflects greater sexual experience among the females. However, as only 6 of this group identified female masturbation and orgasm, it is also a concern that sexual pleasure may be unknown to a large number of handicapped women.

GROUP COUNSELING

After the individualized sexuality assessment, the trainee attends 20 hour-long sessions of group counseling that take place at least twice weekly. Groups usually consist of 4 men and 4 women with both male and female leaders. From the assessments, the leaders know the strengths and needs of the trainees and try to make sure these are incorporated into the program.

Group sexuality counseling differs from traditional sex education in that it incorporates the affective and psychomotor domains as well as providing information. Initially participation is voluntary, but, after making a commitment to attend, trainees are expected to be active and to demonstrate a concern for other members of the group. In addition, they are expected to participate in decision making relating to the content of each session, and to complete homework assignments, which are largely social in nature.

A sex education slide set (Kempton, 1978) is used extensively for the provision of information on topics as diverse as sexual anatomy and venereal disease. However, it is supplemented by other teaching aids, including sets of contraceptives. Discussion of the slides always begins with the trainees' contributions, which are elicited by open-ended questions such as "What do you see on this slide?" It is crucial that the trust level in the group is sufficient for participants to risk making errors. Indeed, in a well-functioning group, the slides can be an effective stimulus for the discussion of personal concerns.

Roleplaying is another important component of the program. Trainees begin by pretending to invite a partner to a social event. When they have achieved a measure of success in this, they are encouraged to transfer the behavior to a real situation. Next, the roleplaying takes the form of assertively rejecting both polite and persuasive invitations to social events. Finally, both men and women learn assertive behaviors in the face of threatened sexual coercion of various kinds.

The sharing of personal experiences is an elusive, yet potentially powerful, teaching technique. Skilled counselors can sometimes create a milieu that is supportive enough for participants to discuss personal concerns. For example, a female leader's self-disclosure of her feelings about pelvic examinations can legitimize similar expressions of concern from the female trainees. Occasionally, concerns about sexual functioning or abuse are raised, and the associated intense feelings must be accepted, discussed, and understood. In one recent group, two female students confronted each other about the pros and cons of sterilization. The sharing of feelings perhaps forms the basis of the truly integrated learning that involves the cognitive, affective, and psychomotor domains.

Group sexuality counseling has been evaluated a number of times. As measured in pre- and posttests on the SDI, this technique was shown to be more effective than traditional sex education and a control condition in raising scores on all three sections of the assessment instrument (Johnson, 1981). Next, in a single-group design Miller et al. (1981) were able to demonstrate significant, positive changes only on the Sexual Knowledge section of the SDI. However, when the study of Miller et al. was replicated, positive changes were noted in the scores of all 8 students on Gender Identity, Socio-Sexual Behaviour, and Sexual Knowledge (Johnson et al., 1983).

Why, then, this discrepancy in results? Miller et al. found little evidence of group cohesiveness in their study, and a wide variation in pre- and posttest change scores that ranged from −26 to +103. In addition, the leaders, although used to working with mentally handicapped adults, were not experienced group counselors. Furthermore, some trainees appeared to be rather reluctant participants. It could be that these somewhat conflicting results point up the importance of experienced group leaders and enthusiastic trainees together creating a safe, yet stimulating, milieu that is the basis for consistent positive change.

However, the limitations of this discussion must be apparent. Perhaps the scores on an assessment device are not a valid measure of a student's reaction and performance in real-life situations. Because of the private nature of intimate behaviors, the true results of this kind of teaching may never be known. Suffice it to say that so far SDI scores, self-reports, and the remarks of parents and staff have almost always been indicative of positive effects.

COMPREHENSIVE SERVICES IN SEXUALITY

Because human sexuality is a controversial topic, it is necessary for communities to plan carefully for the provision of comprehensive services for developmentally handicapped people. In addition to individual assessments and group counseling, a number of other components are needed, including the establishment of an advisory committee. Experience has shown that the following steps are useful in ensuring effective programming:

1. Establishment of an advisory committee consisting of parents, handicapped persons, senior staff from local agencies, and generic professionals such as doctors, public health nurses, and teachers with the purpose of recommending policy in all aspects of sexuality, from education to reproduction. People who are both generic professionals and the parents of handicapped children seem to be particularly valued by these committees. A broadly based advisory committee tends to legitimize programs in sexuality.

2. Parents who are concerned about issues such as sterilization, sex education, and child abuse often appreciate the opportunity to dis-

cuss these topics with others. Consequently, an advisory committee–sponsored series of parents' evenings with guest speakers, films, and small group discussions can help to meet these needs.

3. The credibility of programs is enhanced if they are directed by competent people. Therefore, it is important to develop a base of expertise within the community. Well-trained professionals, such as psychologists, teachers, and college counselors, can effectively start a sexuality program. As they become comfortable with their performance, other people can be added in "training" positions, thus gradually enlarging the pool of expertise.

4. Comprehensive services are important because learning opportunities are increased when programs overlap and the individual absorbs similar information in a variety of settings. Consequently, it is useful to have a range of learning opportunities in a community. For example, issues relating to sex education, birth control, incest, rape, marriage, sexual dysfunctions, and parenting can be addressed on an individual or group basis in various settings.

Although staff in generic agencies often feel ill-equipped to work with special needs groups, mentally handicapped people have a right to the use of these services. This dilemma can be resolved by having the advisory committee sponsor staff training sessions for the generic agencies. With a little encouragement, many community colleges, birth control clinics, and public health departments have successfully met the needs of handicapped people.

5. Finally, group home and vocational services line staff are usually in need of training in emergency procedures. Often, issues like pregnancy or incest first come to the notice of these people, and they have a critical role to play at this time. Successful training programs have focused on personal attitudes, basic counseling skills, a sound knowledge of community resources, and the provision of clear procedural guidelines.

REFERENCES

British Columbia Ministry of Education. 1979. An Alternative Route toward Adult Education for the Mentally Handicapped. Vancouver Community College, Vancouver, British Columbia.

British Columbia Ministry of Human Resources. 1981. Report of the Fraser Valley Child Abuse Team. British Columbia Government, Victoria, British Columbia.

Craft, A., and Craft, M. 1981. Sexuality and mental handicap: A review. Br. J. Psychiatr. 139:494–505.

Gunzburg, H. C. 1969. Progressive Assessment Charts (PAC) and Manual. National Society for Handicapped Children, London.

Johnson, P. R. 1981. Sex and the developmentally handicapped adult: A comparison of teaching methods. Br. J. Ment. Subnormal. 52:8–17.

Johnson, P. R., Grant, D., and Wilson, J. S. T. 1983. Group sexuality counselling: Further research findings. J. Pract. Appr. Dev. Hand. (in press)

Kempton, W. 1978. Sexuality and the Mentally Handicapped. SFA, Santa Monica, California.

Law Reform Commission of Canada. 1980. Sterilization: Implications for Mentally Retarded and Mentally Ill Persons. Ministry of Supply and Services, Ottawa, Ontario.

Marlett, N. J. 1971. The Adaptive Functioning Index. The Vocational and Rehabilitation Research Institute, Calgary, Alberta.

Marlett, N. J., and Hughson, E. A. 1979. Rehabilitation Programmes Manual. The Vocational and Rehabilitation Research Institute, Calgary, Alberta.

Miller, T., Maunula, S., Parker, A., and Brouillet, B. 1981. An evaluation of group sexuality counselling for developmentally handicapped adults. J. Pract. Appr. Dev. Hand. 5:4–9.

Rosen, M., Floor, L., and Zisfein, L. 1975. Investigating the phenomenon of acquiescence in the mentally handicapped: Situational determinants. Br. J. Ment. Subnormal. 21:1–4.

Seattle Rape Relief. 1981. The King County Developmental Disabilities Project. Seattle Rape Relief, Seattle, Washington.

Wolfensberger, W. 1972. The Principle of Normalization in Human Services. National Institute on Mental Retardation, Toronto, Ontario.

PERSPECTIVES AND PROGRESS IN MENTAL RETARDATION
Volume I—Social, Psychological, and Educational Aspects
Edited by J. M. Berg
Copyright © 1984 by I.A.S.S.M.D.

VOCATIONAL HABILITATION RESEARCH AT THE MANITOBA SCHOOL
Behavioral Assessment, Training, and Production Supervision

G. L. Martin,[1] G. Quinn,[2] and D. Yu[1]

[1] *Department of Psychology, Room 129 St. Paul's College,
University of Manitoba, Winnipeg, Manitoba R3T 2M6, Canada*
[2] *Vocational Training Department, The Manitoba School,
Portage la Prairie, Manitoba, Canada*

During the past 4 years, the Vocational Training Department at the Manitoba School has researched vocational habilitation procedures for severely and moderately mentally handicapped adults in sheltered work settings. We have investigated: 1) an objective behavioral assessment system for evaluating sheltered domestic and prevocational skills and sheltered work performance; 2) behavioral training techniques that can be used to teach varied and complex assembly skills; and 3) production supervisory strategies that can be used, after a task has been learned, to maintain adequate production levels. This paper summarizes our progress to date in these areas.

The Manitoba School is the provincial institution for mentally handicapped persons in the province of Manitoba, Canada. The School has approximately 840 clients and 400 direct-care staff (to cover all shifts). The Vocational Training Department consists of four sheltered workshops, an institutional work placement program, and a community work placement program. With an 8-to-1 client:staff ratio, the workshops serve approximately 130 clients, most of whom show severely

This research was supported in part by a grant (#MA6353) from the Canadian Medical Research Council. Grateful appreciation is expressed to this agency.

or moderately handicapped functioning levels on intelligence tests. Clients participating in the workshops earn money for assembling various items through contracts with private businesses. Most of the research described in this paper was conducted within the workshop program.

During the past 4 years, the general strategy of the Vocational Training Department has been to combine the results of recent research concerning behavior modification (e.g., Martin and Pear, 1978) with modern personnel management techniques (e.g., Albrecht, 1978; Miller, 1978). Developments have occurred concurrently in the following areas:

1. Departmental goals were adopted that emphasized work experience and vocational training for clients that would maximize their preparation for community entry.
2. Operational guidelines and job responsibilities for staff were developed, tested, and adopted.
3. Ethical and legal guidelines for developing an equitable pay system for clients in the work training programs were developed and adopted.
4. An accounting system was developed for revenue generated by the workshops.
5. Needs were established and steps were taken for the development of a new assessment and training technology in three areas: a behavioral assessment system to objectively assess client performance; training strategies to teach vocational skills; and production supervisory strategies to maintain production at high levels once vocational skills are acquired.

BEHAVIORAL ASSESSMENT RESEARCH

A literature search of behavioral checklists available for assessing the competencies of severely and moderately mentally handicapped persons led to three generalizations: 1) although a variety of checklists are available, many of these lack objectivity (Walls et al., 1977); 2) many assessment instruments for measuring adaptive behavior rely on behavior ratings from third-party informants who are familiar with the repertoire of the client being evaluated; 3) there is a scarcity of research that has examined the extent to which ratings of behavioral competencies agree with direct measures of those competencies (Halpern et al., 1979). This state of affairs led us to develop the Objective Behavioral Assessment of the Severely and Moderately Mentally Handicapped (the OBA) (Hardy et al., 1981) for use either as a direct assessment device or as a rating scale. After an introduction to the general features of the OBA, the test manual presents a self-instructional, self-testing program that teaches the reader to accurately and easily use the program. The remainder of the book is devoted to 207 objective behavior test items covering the areas of basic self-care skills, social and advanced self-care skills, sheltered domestic skills, prevocational motor dexterity skills, and sheltered work performance.

The field test (Yu et al., in preparation) indicated that the self-instruction manual teaches individuals to use the OBA accurately after approximately 1.5 hours of study. Administration of the OBA as a rating form for use with third-party informants provides a general profile of a client that is of acceptable reliability for considering transfer and placement of clients. OBA direct testing is recommended when a highly objective and reliable assessment is desired for research and/or baseline measurement prior to training. Designed in a way that permits use by persons with a wide range of experience and education, the OBA provides an objective, field-tested program for assessment of individuals with moderate to severe mental handicaps.

TRAINING RESEARCH

In the early 1970s numerous reports demonstrated that severely and moderately mentally handicapped persons were capable of acquiring vocational skills of surprising complexity, including bicycle brake assembly (Gold, 1972), oscilloscope camswitch assembly (Bellamy et al., 1975), and cable-harness construction (Hunter and Bellamy, 1976). These and similar demonstrations had four common features: 1) a task analysis in which the task was broken into a number of small steps and arranged in a sequence for training purposes; 2) a training format in which the steps were taught by one of the chaining strategies; 3) a method of prompting and fading the prompts for correct performance of clients on each of the steps; and 4) a reinforcement system for reinforcing clients for correct performance. Two of these features (task analysis and methods of prompting) had been the focus of some research and guidelines are available for their application (Bellamy et al., 1979; Rusch and Mithaug, 1980; Wehman and McLaughlin, 1980). However, there was some controversy over which of three chaining formats and which of two main reinforcement systems were most effective (e.g., Blake and Williams, 1969; Gold, 1972, 1973a, 1974, 1976; Nettelbeck and Kirby, 1976; Weber, 1978; Walls et al., 1981).

Concerning the most effective training format, we conducted several experiments to compare forward chaining to total task presentation for teaching assembly tasks to severely and moderately mentally handicapped adults (Yu et al., 1980). We next undertook several experiments comparing backward chaining to total task presentation (Martin et al., in press). Our results indicated that total task presentation is the preferred training format for teaching vocational assembly tasks to severely and moderately mentally handicapped persons. With total task presentation, the client performs all of the steps in a sequential behavioral chain from the beginning to the end of the chain on each trial, and continues with total task trials until all steps are mastered.

Concerning reinforcement systems, Gold (1972, 1973b, 1974, 1976) used only minimal reinforcement in teaching vocational skills to the moderately and severely mentally handicapped, and he questioned the emphasis given by others to the need for various "extra" incentive systems for teaching mentally handicapped persons. Because his emphasis on the value of minimal social reinforcement was made in the absence of comparisons of his training strategies using minimal reinforcement to his (or other) training strategies with supplemental reinforcers, we conducted four experiments to make such comparisons. Our results (Koop et al., 1980) clearly indicated that the extra reinforcement facilitated the learning of a task to criterion in terms of training time, number of trials, total number of errors, and the proportion of errors on learned steps. Moreover, preference tests showed that the majority of clients preferred the extra reinforcement condition.

Our next step was to prepare a training system for teaching vocational skills to clients that combined the results of our research on reinforcement systems and on chaining formats, along with guidelines for performing a task analysis and provision of appropriate prompts during training. This training system was outlined in a manual and we are currently in the process of field testing it.

PRODUCTION RESEARCH

Several literature reviews (Gold, 1973a; Bellamy, 1976; Bellamy et al., 1978) indicated that production rate variability of mentally handicapped persons could be influenced by specific reinforcement contingencies, supervisors' instructions, organization of work area, modeling and social facilitation from partners, and distractions in the work area. On the basis of that literature, Martin and Pallotta-Cornick (1979) suggested the possibility of abstracting a multiple-component production supervisory strategy (PSS) that might be applied by staff to maximize work rates of mentally handicapped clients on certain workshop tasks. A PSS was designed and evaluated in two experiments conducted in one of the workshops at the Manitoba School (Martin et al., 1978, 1980). The PSS included the use of partitions placed on production tables to separate clients into pairs and to reduce distractions, a set of verbal and visual prompts to increase production in order to maximize earnings, ratio reinforcement for production with money as the reinforcer and with the money dispensed throughout the day by staff members, and interval reinforcement for on-task behaviors with the reinforcer consisting of praise from staff moving around the workshop. Production increased significantly during the PSS, and both the clients and the staff preferred working under the experimental conditions, rather than under baseline conditions that approximated those found in typical North American sheltered workshops. The next step was the preparation of a self-instructional manual so that staff in a sheltered work setting could implement a PSS to suit the idiosyncracies of their own work setting. In a field test, the manual was introduced and evaluated in a multiple baseline across three groups of staff and clients (Pallotta-Cornick and Martin, 1983). The PSS that was subsequently developed entirely by workshop staff on the basis of the manual increased the average hourly production for 77 of the 80 clients under the PSS as compared to their mean production during baseline. The average increase for all clients was 68% and ranged as high as 241%. A preference test administered to the clients and a questionnaire administered to the staff indicated that all clients and staff preferred working under PSS to working under traditional workshop conditions.

Considering that some form of sheltered work program is a realistic habilitative goal for severely and moderately mentally handicapped persons (Bellamy et al., 1979), the PSS was designed on the assumption that it could become a regular feature of a sheltered workshop supervisory system and that it could be maintained indefinitely. Nevertheless, there is a high probability that at least a proportion of sheltered workshops in community settings will not adopt a strategy like the PSS. The PSS requires that appropriate partitions be prepared for each production table, that workshop staff frequently interact with clients to a much greater degree than is typical in sheltered workshops, and that feedback charts be maintained for each individual on a daily basis. Some workshop staff will simply not be inclined to participate in such activities to the degree proposed by the research cited above. We therefore conducted several experiments to examine self-management techniques, as an alternative to the PSS, for improving and maintaining sheltered work productivity.

Self-control procedures have been used increasingly as components of training programs for mentally handicapped persons (see reviews by Dennis and Mueller, 1981; Jackson and Boag, 1981). Thus far, we have conducted three experiments in this area. In the first experiment, Goyos et al. (1979) used self-recording training to teach two mentally handicapped adults to reinforce work behaviors of work-

shop clients. The two adults were taught to identify the on-task behaviors of 11 other workshop clients working on three different tasks,
to praise or otherwise interact with the clients as much as possible
whenever they were on task, and to record those interactions using
wrist counters. A multiple baseline design across tasks was used to
evaluate the self-monitoring training program. The self-monitoring
training resulted in large increases in the frequency with which both
workers interacted with clients while those clients performed the workshop tasks.

In our second study, we examined the effects of a self-regulation
package (SRP) incorporating self-monitoring, self-administration of reinforcement, and goal-setting techniques on the productivity of mentally handicapped workers working on a contract assembly task (Hanel
and Martin, 1980). A combination multiple baseline, multielement, rev-
ersal-to-baseline design was used to evaluate the SRP across 8 clients.
As a function of the presence of the SRP, production of the 8 clients
increased by an average of 43%. Preference tests conducted following
the research revealed that clients preferred to work under the SRP
conditions rather than baseline conditions.

The third study in this area (Jackson and Martin, in press) analyzed
the additive effects of the components of the SRP studied by Hanel
and Martin. Specifically, self-monitoring was compared to self-monitoring plus goal setting and to self-monitoring plus goal setting plus
self-reinforcement. The components were introduced sequentially in a
multiple baseline design across three clients working on a contract
assembly task. Self-monitoring by itself had very little effect on two
moderately mentally handicapped clients, and had a negative effect on
a mildly handicapped client. Self-monitoring plus goal setting produced
an average 32% increase in the two moderately retarded clients, and
had a slight negative effect on the mildly retarded client. The package
of all three variables had a positive effect on all three clients, with a
mean increase of 42% in the moderately mentally handicapped clients
and an 11% increase in the mildly handicapped client. Once again, a
social validation preference test revealed that clients preferred to work
under the SRP rather than the baseline conditions.

ACKNOWLEDGMENTS

We wish to thank Mr. Neil Upham, Chief Executive Officer, Dr. Larry Hardy,
Program coordinator, and the staff of the Manitoba School for their excellent
cooperation during the conduct of this research.

REFERENCES

Albrecht, K. 1978. Successful Management by Objectives. Prentice-Hall, Inc.,
    Englewood Cliffs, New Jersey.

Bellamy, G. T. 1976. Habilitation of the severely and profoundly retarded: A review of research on work productivity. In: G. T. Bellamy (ed.), Habilitation of Severely and Profoundly Retarded Adults. University of Oregon Center on Human Development. Eugene, Oregon.

Bellamy, G. T., Horner, N. H., and Inman, D. P. 1979. Vocational Habilitation of Severely Retarded Adults: A Direct Service Technology. University Park Press, Baltimore.

Bellamy, G. T., Inman, D. P., and Schwartz, R. 1978. Vocational learning and production supervision: A review of habilitation techniques for the severely and profoundly retarded. In: N. Herring and D. Bricker (eds.), Teaching the Severely and Profoundly Retarded, Vol. 3. Special Press, Columbus, Ohio.

Bellamy, G. T., Peterson, L., and Close, D. 1975. Habilitation of the severely and profoundly retarded: Illustrations of competence. Educ. Train. Ment. Retard. 10:174–186.

Blake, K. A., and Williams, C. L. 1969. Retarded, normal, and superior subjects' learning of paired associates by whole and parts method. Psychol. Rep. 25:319–324.

Dennis, S. S., and Mueller, H. H. 1981. Self-management training with the mentally handicapped: A review. Ment. Retard. Bull. 9:3–31.

Gold. M. W. 1972. Stimulus factors and skill training of the retarded on a complex task: Acquisition, transfer, and retention. Am. J. Ment. Defic. 76:517–526.

Gold, M. W. 1973a. Research on the vocational habilitation of the retarded: The present, the future. In: N. R. Ellis (ed.), International Review of Research in Mental Retardation, Vol. 6. Academic Press, Inc., New York.

Gold, M. W. 1973b. Factors affecting production by the retarded: Base rate. Ment. Retard. 11:41–45.

Gold, M. W. 1974. Redundant cue-removal in skill training for the mentally and moderately retarded. Educ. Train. Retard. 9:5–8.

Gold, M. W. 1976. Task analysis of a complex assembly task by the retarded blind. Except. Child. 43:78–84.

Goyos, A. C., Michael, J. L., and Martin, G. L. 1979. Self-recording training to teach retarded adults to reinforce work behaviors of retarded clients. Rehab. Psychol. 26:215–227.

Halpern, A. S., Irvin, L. K., and Landman, J. T. 1979. Alternative approaches to the measurement of adaptive behavior. Am. J. Ment. Defic. 84:304–310.

Hanel, F., and Martin, G. 1980. Self-monitoring, self-administration of token reinforcement, and goal-setting to improve work rates with retarded clients. Int. J. Rehab. Res. 3:505–517.

Hardy, L., Martin, G., Yu, D., Leader, C., and Quinn, G. 1981. Objective Behavioral Assessment of the Severely and Moderately Mentally Handicapped: The OBA. Charles C Thomas Publisher, Springfield, Illinois.

Hunter, J. D., and Bellamy, G. T. 1976. Cable-harness construction for severely retarded adults: A demonstration of training technique. AAESPH Rev. 7:2–13.

Jackson, H. J. and Boag, P. G. 1981. The efficacy of self-control procedures as motivational strategies with mentally retarded persons: A review of the literature and guidelines for future research. Aust. J. Dev. Disabil. 7:65–79.

Jackson, D., and Martin, G. The additive effect of components of a self-control package for improving production of mentally handicapped workers. J. Pract. Appr. Dev. Hand. (in press)

Koop, S., Martin, G., Yu, D., and Suthons, E. 1980. Comparison of two reinforcement strategies in vocational skill training of mentally retarded persons. Am. J. Ment. Defic. 84:616–626.

Martin, G., Koop, S., Turner, C., and Hanel, F. Backward chaining versus total task presentation to teach assembly tasks to severely retarded persons. In: Behavior Research of Severe Developmental Disabilities. (in press)

Martin, G., Leonhart, B., Pallotta-Cornick, A., Yu, D., Suthons, E., and Quinn, G. 1978. Investigations of a production technology for improving vocational competency of the trainable mentally retarded. A paper presented to the Third National Congress of the Council for Exceptional Children. Winnipeg, Manitoba, October, 1978.

Martin, G., and Pallotta-Cornick, A. 1979. Behavior modification in sheltered workshops and community group homes: Status and future. In: L. A. Hamerlynck (ed.), Behavioral Systems for the Developmentally Disabled: Institutional, Clinic, and Community Environments, Vol. 2. Brunner/Mazel, New York.

Martin, G., Pallotta-Cornick, A., Johnstone, G., and Goyos, A. C. 1980. A supervisory strategy to improve work performance for lower functioning retarded clients in a sheltered workshop. J. Appl. Behav. Anal. 13:183–190.

Martin, G. L., and Pear, J. J. 1978. Behavior Modification: What It Is and How To Do It. Prentice Hall, Inc., Englewood Cliffs, New Jersey.

Miller, L. M. 1978. Behavior Management: The New Science of Managing People at Work. John Wiley & Sons, Inc., New York.

Nettelbeck, T., and Kirby, M. H. 1976. A comparison of part and whole training methods with mildly mentally retarded workers. J. Occupat. Psychol. 49:115–120.

Pallotta-Cornick, A., and Martin, G. L. 1983. Evaluation of a staff manual for improving work performance for retarded clients in sheltered workshops. Int. J. Rehab. Res. 6:43–54.

Rusch, F. R., and Mithaug, D. E. 1980. Vocational Training for Mentally Retarded Persons: A Behavior Analytic Approach. Research Press, Champaign, Illinois.

Walls, R. T., Werner, T. J., Bacon, A., and Zane, T. 1977. Behavior checklists. In: R. P. Hawkins and J. D. Cone (eds.), Behavioral Assessment: New Directions in Clinical Psychology. Brunner/Mazel, New York.

Walls, R. T., Zane, T., and Ellis, W. D. 1981. Forward and backward chaining and whole task methods: Training assembly tasks in vocational rehabilitation. Behav. Mod. 5:61–74.

Weber, N. J. 1978. Chaining strategies for teaching sequence tasks to mentally retarded adults. Am. J. Occupat. Ther. 32:385–389.

Wehman, P., and McLaughlin, P. J. 1980. Vocational Curriculum for Developmentally Disabled Persons. University Park Press, Baltimore.

Yu, D., Martin, G., Hardy, L., Leader, C., and Quinn, G. Objective behavioral assessment of adaptive behavior of the severely and moderately mentally handicapped. (in preparation)

Yu, D., Martin, G., Suthons, E., Koop, S., and Pallotta-Cornick, A. 1980. Comparisons of forward chaining and total task presentation formats to teach vocational skills to the retarded. Int. J. Rehab. Res. 3:77–79.

PERSPECTIVES AND PROGRESS IN MENTAL RETARDATION
Volume I—Social, Psychological, and Educational Aspects
Edited by J. M. Berg

STAFF TRAINING USING INSTRUCTIONAL AND MANAGEMENT STRATEGIES
A Review of the Literature

M. A. Feldman[1] **and A. J. Dalrymple**[2]

[1] *Behavior Research Program, Surrey Place Centre, 2 Surrey Place, Toronto, Ontario M5S 2C2, Canada*
[2] *Huronia Regional Centre, Orillia, Ontario, Canada*

This paper reviews the research literature involving the training of direct-care staff. The literature is divided into studies primarily examining either instructional or managerial strategies. Performance-based instruction (modeling, feedback, roleplaying) is usually more effective than didactic instruction in improving staff's performance of programming procedures. Management techniques designed to prompt (e.g., memos, duty cards) or promote (e.g., supervisor approval, posted feedback, tangible rewards) staff behavior are often necessary to increase the on-the-job performance of skills learned in instructional settings. Tangible rewards appear to be the most powerful management procedure. Future research should compare the cost-effectiveness of various training strategies and include measures of generalization, maintenance, benefits to clients, job satisfaction, and social validity.

In response to the normalization concept (Wolfensberger, 1972) and the success of behavior modification programs (e.g., Baker and Ward, 1971), mental retardation facilities are now considered to be active training centers. In most facilities the direct-care staff are responsible for carrying out life skills and behavior management programming as well as for providing recreational/leisure activities and custodial care to the clients. However, untrained staff do not typically interact with clients in a manner that promotes learning of adaptive behavior (Blindert, 1975; Mansdorf et al., 1977; Walls et al., 1980).

331

Implementation of an effective habilitation technology requires that line staff learn behavioral programming and interaction skills and use these skills in their work setting (Loeber and Weisman, 1975; Kazdin, 1979). "Instructional" techniques (e.g., lectures, modeling, feedback) are used to teach staff behavioral procedures, whereas staff "management" strategies (e.g., memos, assignments, tangible rewards) are employed to ensure desired job performance.

In this paper, the staff training research literature is divided into experiments where major emphasis was either instructional or managerial. This review is limited to those studies involving the training of direct-care staff in mental retardation and psychiatric settings.

INSTRUCTIONAL STRATEGIES

Didactic Instruction

Lectures, discussions, and textbooks are still the most frequently used tools of training (Kazdin, 1979). Overwhelmingly, however, studies evaluating didactic instruction show increases in knowledge of behavioral principles and techniques but little improvement in actual performance of treatment procedures (e.g., Gardner, 1972; Adams et al., 1980; Watson and Uzzell, 1980). The consistent replication of this effect suggests that changing staff performance requires more than didactic instruction (Gardner, 1972; Kazdin, 1979).

Modeling

Because observational learning is so important in human behavior it is not surprising that many staff training programs employ modeling (Paul et al., 1973; Gladstone and Spencer, 1977; Watson and Uzzell, 1980). However, few studies have made exclusive use of modeling. Modeling typically produces positive results. For example, live modeling increased staff use of praise to clients from approximately 2 to 12 statements per programming session (Gladstone and Spencer, 1977). Likewise, live or filmed modeling improved aides' programming skills by 20% (Panyan and Patterson, 1974). Further research in the use of modeling in staff training should investigate variables (e.g., characteristics of the model, vicarious reinforcement) that are known to enhance modeling effects (Bandura, 1969).

Performance Feedback

Feedback involves providing information to staff on their performance with clients and may be either an instructional or a managerial device. As an instructional technique, feedback takes many forms, including

1) verbal comments and praise from the trainer (e.g., Duker and Seys, 1980; Watson and Uzzell, 1980), 2) presentation of staff or client performance data to staff (Duker and Seys, 1980), and 3) videotapes (e.g., Panyan and Patterson, 1974; Duker and Seys, 1980). Although Panyan and Patterson (1974) reported negative results, most feedback studies show improvement in staff treatment skills. Feldman and Ferenc (unpublished observations) gave 30 minutes of verbal and videotaped feedback to 10 staff while they were teaching self-help skills to profoundly retarded clients. The feedback group showed a 38% increase in eight programming skills, which was significantly greater than in a no-feedback group.

It is unclear whether feedback serves as a discriminative or reinforcing stimulus (Prue et al. 1980). The finding of no difference between immediate and delayed feedback (Bowman, Feldman, and Ball, unpublished observations) suggests a discriminative function. It has also been shown (Dalrymple and Feldman, unpublished observations) that the pattern of rate of staff interactions with clients resembled fixed interval scallop responding (Ferster and Skinner, 1957) when staff received weekly performance feedback. This suggests that feedback has reinforcing properties.

Roleplaying

Roleplaying, as defined here, involves staff practicing skills and receiving feedback in a simulated setting. Roleplaying has the advantage of control of "client" behavior through the use of a mock client. Staff may then be systematically exposed to various increasingly complex tasks. Problem situations can be rehearsed until staff demonstrate competence. A potential disadvantage of roleplaying as compared to live feedback is that the staff must generalize skills trained in simulation to the real-life setting. Positive results have been obtained with mental retardation staff in simulated (Gardner, 1972) and actual (Adams et al., 1980) interactions with clients. Feldman, Bowman and Ducharme, (unpublished observations) observed staff conducting self-help programs with retarded clients and found that 2 to 4 hours of either individual or group roleplaying increased by about 30% the correct programming skills of staff.

Comparison Studies

Few researchers have directly compared instructional procedures or conducted component analyses (Bernstein, 1982). Two studies (Gardner, 1972; Adams et al., 1980) found that didactic instruction increased knowledge, but roleplaying was more effective in increasing staff's performance of behavioral procedures. Other studies have found didactic instruction inferior to modeling and feedback in improving actual use of skills (Martin, 1972; Panyan and Patterson, 1974; Watson and Uzzell, 1980).

Several studies have compared modeling to feedback. Martin (1972) reported that modeling plus feedback increased staff use of behavioral techniques in ward programs more than modeling without feedback. Panyan and Patterson (1974) showed that videotaped modeling (staff viewed competent staff's performance) was better than videotaped feedback (staff viewed their own performance with no verbal feedback from a staff trainer). Feldman and Ferenc (unpublished observations) found that the performance of a group receiving videotaped *plus* verbal feedback, but not of a group receiving modeling, was significantly superior to a written instructions group after 2 days of training. The paucity of comparison studies makes it difficult to draw firm conclusions about the relative effectiveness of techniques, particularly when some methods (e.g., feedback) may take various forms (verbal, videotape, graphic). Training packages that combine procedures may yield the best results (Kazdin and Moyer, 1976), but this assumption has not yet received clear empirical support.

Effects of Staff Instructional Training on Client Behavior

Training-induced staff behavior change should result in improvements in client behavior. Early studies often neglected to include client data (e.g., Bricker et al., 1972; Gardner, 1972; Martin, 1972). Recent efforts have corrected this oversight and have usually demonstrated that client behaviors improve as staff become more adept in behavioral techniques (Panyan and Patterson, 1974; Gladstone and Spencer, 1977; Schinke and Wong, 1977). These results validate both the staff training and the client behavior-change procedures being taught to the mediator. When staff were trained in how to prompt and reinforce, client adaptive behaviors increased (Gladstone and Spencer, 1977; Horner, 1980) and maladaptive behaviors decreased (Horner, 1980). Further evidence of close correspondence between staff's programming skills and client performance is seen in two generalization studies (Bowman, Feldman, and Ball, unpublished observations; Bowman, Feldman, and Bell, unpublished observations) in which client behavior improved in new settings or tasks only if the staff generalized the correct use of programming skills to these new situations. Two other studies failed to find clear relationships between staff and client behaviors: either client performance did not improve as the staff became more proficient (Feldman, Bowman, and Ducharme, unpublished observations) or client adaptive behavior increased despite lack of improvement in staff programming skills (Feldman and Ferenc, unpublished observations).

Generalization

The varied work contexts experienced by direct-care staff require that staff training strive for maximum generalization of training effects across tasks, clients, settings, and time. The evidence regarding generalization of instructional training is equivocal. Some investigators have reported generalization across programs (Gladstone and Spencer, 1977) and settings (Duker and Seys, 1980). No or poor generalization has also been obtained (Duker and Seys, 1980). Generalization enhancement strategies such as "training sufficient exemplars" or "training loosely" (Stokes and Baer, 1977) may need to be incorporated into instructional packages to produce meaningful generalization. Investigations of staff skill maintenance after instructional training are rare. Watson and Uzzell (1980) reported 6 months' maintenance of programming skills when staff continued to receive daily feedback from their supervisor or instructor. The durability of instructional training effects has yet to be established.

Generalization from training sessions to on-the-job performance is a crucial requirement of any in-service program. Few instructional studies have achieved such generalization (Paul et al., 1973; Schinke and Wong, 1977; Duker and Seys, 1980). Most researchers have failed to obtain meaningful changes in staff work performance when training consisted of instructional strategies alone (e.g., Panyan et al., 1971; Quilitch, 1975; Greene et al., 1978). Obtained transfer of skills from instructional to job settings may be due to other factors, such as hidden contingencies (e.g., certification—Paul et al., 1973; Watson and Uzzell, 1980) and the stimulus control exerted by instructors, supervisors, and observers (Duker and Seys, 1980; Watson and Uzzell, 1980). Removal of these external variables or loss of initial enthusiasm following in-service training may result in rapid deterioration of job performance (Panyan et al., 1971). Researchers should avoid confounding instructional and managerial variables by identifying management practices in operation during the training period. Possible interrelationships between existing or newly developed management tactics and instructional training should be investigated. Staff management procedures such as contingencies of reinforcement for particular work behaviors (e.g., Patterson et al., 1976) should be examined as a means to "train to generalize" (Stokes and Baer, 1977) the on-the-job use of skills newly acquired from instructional training.

MANAGEMENT STRATEGIES

Management techniques may consist of either antecedents (e.g., memos, verbal instructions from supervisors, duty cards) designed to prompt behavior or consequences (e.g., supervisor praise, disciplinary actions, posted feedback, tangible rewards) designed to reinforce (or punish) work performance.

Antecedents

Several studies have shown that communication from superiors in the form of memos, directives, verbal instructions, and assignment sheets may affect staff behaviors such as program session attendance and correct client care and treatment (e.g., Andrasik and McNamara, 1977; Andrasik et al., 1978). Frequently the effects of antecedents have not been large, consistent, or durable (Panyan et al., 1971; Quilitch, 1975; Iwata et al., 1976).

Consequences

Feedback   Feedback has been used to increase on-the-job performance. Managerial feedback has included 1) praise and comments from the supervisor (e.g., Montegar et al., 1977; Prue et al., 1980; Ivancic et al., 1981); 2) public postings (e.g., Panyan et al., 1971; Greene et al., 1978; Prue et al., 1980); 3) self-recorded observations (Burg et al., 1979); 4) written notices (Andrasik and McNamara, 1977; Prue et al., 1980); and 5) reports of client performance (Pomerleau et al., 1973; Quilitch, 1975; Greene et al., 1978). One study (Ivancic et al., 1981) assessed generalization and found that staff who received supervisor prompts and feedback to increase verbal interactions with clients during bathing also showed increased interactions during dressing where no feedback was given.

A number of studies have examined maintenance. Increased staff performance has persisted where feedback has remained in effect from 1 to 9 months (e.g., Prue et al., 1980; Watson and Uzzell, 1980; Ivancic et al., 1981). However, feedback removal has resulted in deterioration of staff performance to baseline levels (Pommer and Streedbeck, 1974; Montegar et al., 1977). Feedback to staff on job performance or client progress appears to effectively manage staff behavior. Its feasibility and low cost make feedback an appealing long-term management strategy. The objective measurement and reportage of staff performance may be more powerful if it is part of the organizational appraisal and merit system (Martin, 1972; Bernstein, 1982).

Tangible Rewards   Promoting staff performance with tangible reinforcers appears to be a powerful management technique. Three kinds of rewards are commonly used: 1) money (e.g., Pomerleau et al., 1973; Pommer and Streedbeck, 1974; Patterson et al., 1976); 2) trading stamps (Bricker et al., 1972; Hollander and Plutchik, 1972; Hollander et al., 1973); and 3) work-shift changes (Iwata et al., 1976). Results are often dramatic: Bricker et al. (1972) increased staff-client contacts by 700% when trading stamps were made contingent on staff interactions with clients. High levels of staff performance rapidly decline once the reinforcement contingency is eliminated (e.g., Katz et al., 1972; Hollander et al., 1973; Pommer and Streedbeck, 1974). Long-term maintenance of increased performance may require that the reinforcement system become a permanent sanction. Unlike feedback, extended use of tangible rewards may be too costly (Iwata et al., 1976). Furthermore, because rewards are not typically under the control of behavior analysts (Andrasik and McNamara, 1977), financially limited and nonbehaviorally oriented administrators are unlikely to continue an expensive program designed to get staff to do the work they were hired to do in the first place. Documentation showing that benefits consistently outweigh costs, by using a lottery system (e.g., Iwata et al., 1976) or by thinning the reinforcement schedule to reduce expenses while maintaining performance (Patterson et al., 1976), may make long-term tangible reward systems more feasible.

Effects of Staff Management on Client Behavior

Several of the above studies provide client data (e.g., Quilitch, 1975; Greene et al., 1978; Ivancic et al., 1981). When contingencies were established that increased staff's actual use of behavior modification procedures, client behavior also improved; when consequences were abruptly discontinued both staff and client behavior returned to baseline levels (Katz et al., 1972; Hollander et al., 1973; Pomerleau et al., 1973). Gradual fading of management procedures produced more persistent staff and client gains (Ivancic et al., 1981).

Comparison Studies

Instructional versus Managerial Strategies   Reliance on instructional training alone often does not produce improvements in staff work performance (Katz et al., 1972; Quilitch, 1975; Montegar et al., 1977; Greene et al., 1978). When these investigators introduced staff management strategies (e.g., posted feedback, monetary reward), staff work performance increased substantially. It is not clear in these studies whether the preliminary instructional training was necessary to achieve the staff behavior change that occurred under the new management systems.

Antecedents versus Consequences   Antecedent management strategies (e.g., memos, instructions, assignments) do not usually work as well as provision of consequences (Pommer and Streedbeck, 1974; Iwata et al., 1976; Patterson et al., 1976; Andrasik and McNamara, 1977).

Different Types of Consequences   A few studies have compared various forms of feedback. Welsch et al., (1973) reported no substantial difference between individual and entire-shift feedback in increasing staff assignment completion. Greene et al. (1978) found public postings of staff performance plus individual praise from the supervisor to be superior to individual feedback alone in increasing staff-client interactions and client skills. Brown et al. (1981) found that supervisor feedback was not as effective as supervisor feedback plus approval in increasing staff-resident interactions. Andrasik and McNamara (1977) reported greater reductions in programming errors by aides when feedback was given to the aides and their first-level supervisors than when given only to second-level supervisors. Studies comparing feedback to tangible rewards have consistently found the latter to be more effective (Pomerleau et al., 1973; Pommer and Streedbeck, 1974; Patterson et al., 1976). Given the potentially large cost differential between feedback and tangible reward systems, future comparisons should include relative cost-effectiveness analyses based, for example, on the approximate cost per unit of behavior change in staff and/or client performance. Such an analysis may reveal feedback to be more cost-effective than rewards even when the latter produce larger behavioral gains.

CONCLUSIONS

Although there are still many gaps in our knowledge, a review of experimental studies of staff training has yielded important information to aid in the design of effective training programs for direct-care staff. First, untrained staff require performance-based training (e.g., modeling, feedback, roleplaying) to learn to interact more effectively with clients. Didactic instruction alone does not appear to significantly change staff's actual performance in training situations. Second, instructional training alone is unlikely to produce sustained improvements in on-the-job performance. Inclusion of staff management strategies appears essential in most settings to promote meaningful and long-term staff behavior change. Third, establishing contingencies of reinforcement for desired staff behavior may be more effective than manipulating antecedent conditions. Although tangible rewards are usually more effective than feedback, feedback may be more cost-effective in some circumstances. Termination of a consequence system will probably result in loss of initial benefits. Incentives should remain in place or be gradually faded to increase the likelihood of maintenance.

Further research is needed to investigate the necessary and sufficient conditions to maximize acquisition, generalization, and on-the-job use of procedures by staff that benefit clients. Comparative analyses of effectiveness and cost-effectiveness of various instructional and/or managerial strategies should be conducted. The use of in-house supervisory personnel (e.g., Brown et al., 1981) and pyramid training (Page et al., 1982) should also be studied as means to promote cost-effective training and management. A comprehensive staff training research project should examine: 1) changes in staff behavior on the job (e.g., Quilitch, 1975); 2) generalization (e.g., Ivancic et al., 1981) and maintenance (e.g., Panyan et al., 1971) of these changes; 3) approximate costs of training; 4) correlated changes in client behavior; and 5) job satisfaction (Schinke and Wong, 1977) and social validation (Kazdin, 1977) measures.

REFERENCES

Adams, G. L., Tallon, R. J., and Rimell, P. 1980. A comparison of lecture vs. roleplaying in the training of the use of positive reinforcement. J. Organ. Behav. Manag. 2:205–212.

Andrasik, F., and McNamara, J. R. 1977. Optimizing staff performance in an institutional behavior change system. Behav. Mod. 1:235–248.

Andrasik, F., McNamara, J. R., and Abbott, D. M. 1978. Policy control: A low level interventive procedure for improving staff behavior. J. Organ. Behav. Manag. 1:125–138.

Baker, B. L., and Ward, M. H. 1971. Reinforcement therapy for behavior problems in severely retarded children. Am. J. Orthopsychiatry 41:124–135.

Bandura, A. 1969. Principles of Behavior Modification. Holt, Rinehart & Winston, New York.

Bernstein, G. S. 1982. Training behavior change agents: A conceptual review. Behav. Ther. 13:1–23.

Blindert, H. D. 1975. Interactions between residents and staff: A qualitative investigation of an institutional setting for retarded children. Ment. Retard. 13:38–40.

Bricker, W. A., Morgan, D. G., and Grabowski, J. G. 1972. Development and maintenance of a behavior modification repertoire of cottage attendants through T.V. feedback. Am. J. Ment. Defic. 77:128–136.

Brown, K. M., Willis, B. S., and Reid, D. H. 1981. Differential effects of supervisor verbal feedback and feedback plus approval on institutional staff performance. J. Organ. Behav. Manag. 3:57–68.

Burg, M. M., Reid, D. H., and Lattimore, J. 1979. Use of a self-recording and supervision program to change institutional staff behavior. J. Appl. Behav. Anal. 12:363–375.

Duker, P. C., and Seys, D. M. 1980. The use of verbal prompts by nurses: The effects of feedback on acquisition and generalization. Behav. Anal. Mod. 4:71–76.

Ferster, C. B., and Skinner, B. F. 1957. Schedules of Reinforcement. Appleton-Century-Crofts, New York.

Gardner, J. M. 1972. Teaching behavior modification to nonprofessionals. J. Appl. Behav. Anal. 5:517–521.

Gladstone, B. W., and Spencer, C. J. 1977. The effects of modelling on the contingent praise of mental retardation counsellors. J. Appl. Behav. Anal. 10:75–84.

Greene, B. F., Willis, B. S., Levy, R., and Bailey, J. S., 1978. Measuring client gains from staff implemented programs. J. Appl. Behav. Anal. 11:395–412.

Hollander, M. A., and Plutchik, R. 1972. A reinforcement program for psychiatric attendants. J. Behav. Ther. Exp. Psychiatry 3:297–300.

Hollander, M., Plutchik, R., and Horner, V. 1973. Interaction of patient and attendant reinforcement programs: The "piggyback" effect. J. Consult. Clin. Psychol. 41:43–47.

Horner, R. D. 1980. The effect of an environmental "enrichment" program on the behavior of institutionalized profoundly retarded children. J. Appl. Behav. Anal. 13:473–491.

Ivancic, M., Reid, D. H., Iwata, B. A., Faw, G. D., and Page, J. J. 1981. Evaluating a supervision program for developing and maintaining therapeutic staff-resident interactions during institutional care routines. J. Appl. Behav. Anal. 14:95–107.

Iwata, B. A., Bailey, J. S., Brown, K. M., Foshee, T. J., and Alpern, M. 1976. A performance-based lottery to improve residential care and training by institutional staff. J. Appl. Behav. Anal. 9:417–431.

Katz, R. C., Johnson, C. A., and Gelfand, S. 1972. Modifying the dispensing of reinforcers: Some implications for behavior modification with hospitalized patients. Behav. Ther. 3:578–588.

Kazdin, A. E. 1977. Assessing the clinical or applied importance of behavior change through social validation. Behav. Mod. 1:427–472.

Kazdin, A. E. 1979. Advances in child behavior therapy: Applications and implications. Am. Psychol. 34:981–987.

Kazdin, A. E., and Moyer, W. 1976. Training teachers to use behavior modification. In: S. Yen and R. W. McIntire (eds.), Teaching Behavior Modification, pp. 171–200. Behaviordelia, Kalamazoo, Michigan.

Loeber, R., and Weisman, R. G. 1975. Contingencies of therapist and trainer performance. Psychol. Bull. 82:660–688.

Mansdorf, I. J., Bucich, D. A., and Judd, L. C. 1977. Behavioral treatment strategies in institutional ward staff. Ment. Retard. 15:22–24.

Martin, G. L. 1972. Teaching operant technology to psychiatric nurses, aides, and attendants. In: F. W. Clark, D. R. Evans, and L. A. Hamerlynck (eds.), Implementing Behavioral Programs for Schools and Clinics: Proceedings of the Third Banff Conference on Behavior Modification, pp. 63–87. Research Press, Champaign, Illinois.

Montegar, C. A., Reid, D. H., Madsen, C. H., and Ewell, M. D. 1977. Increasing institutional staff to resident interaction through in-service training and supervisor approval. Behav. Ther. 8:533–540.

Page, T. J., Iwata, B. A., and Reid, D. H. 1982. A pyramidal approach to training behavior modification skills to institutional staff. J. Appl. Behav. Anal. 15:335–362.

Panyan, M., Boozer, H., and Morris, N. 1971. Feedback to attendants as a reinforcer for applying operant techniques. J. Appl. Behav. Anal. 3:1–4.

Panyan, M., and Patterson, E. T. 1974. Teaching attendants the applied aspects of behavior modification. Ment. Retard. 12:30–32.

Patterson, E. T., Griffin, J. C., and Panyan, M. C. 1976. Incentive maintenance of self-help skill training programs for non-professional personnel. J. Behav. Ther. Exp. Psychiatry 7:249–253.

Paul, G. L., McInnis, T. L., and Mariotto, M. J. 1973. Objective performance outcomes associated with two approaches to training mental health techniques in milieu and social learning programs. J. Abnorm. Psychol. 82:523–532.

Pomerleau, O. F., Bobrove, P. H., and Smith, R. H. 1973. Rewarding psychiatric aides for the behavioral improvements of assigned patients. J. Appl. Behav. Anal. 6:383–390.

Pommer, D. A., and Streedbeck, O. 1974. Motivating staff performance in an operant learning program for children. J. Appl. Behav. Anal. 7:217–221.

Prue, D. M., Krapfl, J. E., Noah, J. C., Cannon, S., and Maley, R. F. 1980. Managing the treatment activities of state hospital staff. J. Organ. Behav. Manag. 2:165–181.

Quilitch, H. R. 1975. A comparison of three staff-management procedures. J. Appl. Behav. Anal. 8:59–66.

Schinke, S. P., and Wong, S. E. 1977. Evaluation of staff training in group homes for retarded persons. Am. J. Ment. Defic. 82:130–136.

Stokes, T. F., and Baer, D. M. 1977. An implicit technology of generalization. J. Appl. Behav. Anal. 10:349–367.

Walls, R. T., Zane, T., and Thvedt, J. E. 1980. Trainers' personal methods compared to two structured training strategies. Am. J. Ment. Defic. 84:195–207.

Watson, L. S., and Uzzell, R. 1980. A program for teaching behavior modification skills to institutional staff. Appl. Res. Ment. Retard. 1:41–53.

Welsch, W. V., Ludwig, C., Radiker, J. E., and Krapfl, J. E. 1973. Effects of feedback on daily completion of behavior modification projects. Ment. Retard. 11:24–26.

Wolfensberger, W. 1972. Normalization. National Institute on Mental Retardation, Toronto.

SECTION VI
Deinstitutionalization and Community Living

PERSPECTIVES AND PROGRESS IN MENTAL RETARDATION
Volume I—Social, Psychological, and Educational Aspects
Edited by J. M. Berg
Copyright © 1984 by I.A.S.S.M.D.

DEINSTITUTIONAL-IZATION OF MENTALLY RETARDED PERSONS IN THE UNITED STATES
Status and Trends

S. J. Vitello

Rutgers University, 10 Seminary Place, New Brunswick, New Jersey 08903

A review of some descriptive data indicates that progress toward the deinstitutionalization of mentally retarded persons has occurred in the United States over the last 10 years. Admission rates have decreased, discharges have increased, and institutional conditions have been improved. Further research is needed to determine which environmental settings improve the quality of life of particular groups of mentally retarded people.

In its historical context, the deinstitutionalization of mentally retarded persons in the United States represents a phase of a mid–20th century social reform movement designed to shift the locus of care and treatment of disabled populations (e.g., the mentally ill, the elderly) from total institutions to more normalizing community settings. The ideological shift in the care of mentally retarded persons was first expressed in the passage of the Mental Retardation Facilities Construction Act of 1963. This act encouraged states to develop a "continuum of care" with services delivered to mentally retarded persons "as close as possible to the community." Today, as the facts below indicate, "deinstitutionalization is clearly established within the social services systems as a predominant philosophy" (Lakin et al., 1982a).

FACTS AND TRENDS

Deinstitutionalization has been operationally defined as requiring the attainment of three interrelated goals: 1) the prevention of admissions to public institutions by finding and developing alternative community methods of care and training; 2) the return to the community of all residents who have been prepared through programs of habilitation and training to function adequately in appropriate local settings; and 3) the establishment and maintenance of a responsive residential environment that protects human and civil rights and that contributes to the expeditious return of the individual to normal community living, whenever possible. To what extent have these goals been attained?

New Admissions

The implementation of deinstitutionalization policies has resulted in a dramatic decrease in the number of new admissions to public institutions for the mentally retarded. Whereas in 1970 there were an estimated 16,000 new admissions, in fiscal year 1980–81 the number was down to 5,547 (Scheerenberger, 1982). This represents a 65% decrease in new admissions. This decrease can be attributed not only to the declining birth rate but also to more stringent civil commitment procedures and efforts by mental retardation agencies to place more retarded persons in less restrictive community settings. Although the majority (64%) of new admissions are severely (26%) and profoundly (38%) retarded, a significant percentage (36%) of mildly (17%) and moderately (19%) retarded persons continue to be admitted (Scheerenberger, 1982). Interestingly, the mean chronological age for first admissions increased from 13 years in 1967 to 18 years in 1977 (Lakin et al., 1982b). This finding suggests that the availability of expanded community services may be delaying the need for institutional care.

Discharges

Fiscal year 1967–68 marked the downward trend in the number of retarded persons in public residential facilities. In fiscal years 1970–71, 1975–76 and 1980–81 the average daily population in these facilities was, respectively, 189,546, 153,584, and 125,799 residents (Scheerenberger, 1982). These figures represent a 33.6% decrease in the institutional population over a 10-year period. By the mid-1980s it is projected that the number of retarded persons in public institutions will decrease to below 100,000. Thereafter, it is expected that the discharge rate will slow down because of the greater difficulty in developing community alternatives for more severely retarded persons.

Community Care

Complementing the rapid decrease in the institutional population has been the development of a community care system. Nationwide, in 1977 there were 4,427 community residential facilities serving 62,397 mentally retarded persons (Bruininks et al., 1980). There have been significant increases in the number of group homes and specially licensed foster care homes operated by the private sector (i.e., private proprietary and nonprofit facilities). These community programs are serving an increasing number of severely and profoundly retarded persons. Whereas a large number of mentally retarded persons were inappropriately placed in nursing homes during the 1970s, there is some evidence that this trend has reversed itself in recent years.

In addition to the growth in community-based residential services, there has been an expansion of day programs for mentally retarded persons. Severely and profoundly retarded persons between 5 and 21 years of age (in some states from birth to 21) now have access to free, publicly supported educational programs. In addition, there has been an increase in the number of sheltered workshops and adult activity centers serving lower-functioning adults. The availability of these needed services is necessary not only for the successful community placement of institutionalized mentally retarded persons but also for the retention of retarded persons who have always resided in the community (e.g., children living at home).

Institutional Reform

Institutional reform efforts have been directed toward relieving overcrowded conditions and upgrading the quality of services. Whereas there were 190 public institutions in 1970, in 1980–81 there were 248 such institutions (Scheerenberger, 1982). Most of the recently constructed institutions are smaller and designed to care for fewer residents. In fact, a large number of retarded persons have been transferred from the older, larger, overcrowded institutions to these smaller facilities in order to comply with Title XIX standards for Intermediate Care Facilities/Mental Retardation Facilities. Under Title XIX, federal Medicaid funds are to be used by the states "to insure that the institution provides a range of services adequate to help residents develop maximum independent capabilities and to return to the community at the earliest possible time." Eligibility for funds is contingent upon institutions complying with a set of standards that include active treatment, recognition of resident rights, preparation of an individualized habilitation plan, improvements in staffing, adherence to fire and safety regulations, and specifications for minimum space in programming areas and maximum occupancies in sleeping areas. One hundred seventy-seven institutions have indicated that at least part of their program qualified for Title XIX funding (Scheerenberger, 1982).

QUALITY OF LIFE

A major assumption underlying deinstitutionalization policies is that there will be an improvement in the "quality of life" of mentally retarded persons. Are mentally retarded persons better off today than they were 10 years ago? Although the data cited above offer prima facie evidence that the answer may be yes, it is necessary to go beyond descriptive reports to determine empirically whether or not mentally retarded people are, in fact, "better off."

Quality of life is a multidimensional construct. Its dimensions include normalized and decent living conditions, some degree of autonomy, opportunities for personal growth, and general happiness. All of these dimensions have been operationalized by researchers in their attempts to measure the quality of life of mentally retarded people in institutional and community settings. A careful review and analysis of these studies is beyond the scope of this paper, but several tentative conclusions are offered:

1. The variance on any of these outcome measures is as great within a particular residential option (e.g., group homes) as between options (e.g., institutions versus group homes). That is to say, there are community programs that vary considerably in the quality of care provided. This is also true for institutional programs. Residential size or physical location per se does not determine a retarded person's quality of life. Quality of life outcomes have more to do with the nature of the interactions between mentally retarded persons and their immediate environment.
2. The quality of life (usually determined by gains in measures of adaptive behavior) can be improved in both institutional and community settings.
3. High recidivism rates (approaching 30%) can be attributed to the failure to match the characteristics and needs of an individual retarded person and a particular community setting.

Future research should not be concerned with comparing institutional and community programs to find out which provides a "significantly better quality of life" for retarded persons. Such research is not only difficult to design (random assignment of groups is required) but also of limited social value. What needs to be determined is what factors (e.g., personnel qualifications, availability of services, program philosophy, costs) in a particular setting interact to improve the quality of life of a particular type of retarded person.

REFERENCES

Bruininks, R. H., Hauber, F. A., and Kudla, M. J. 1980. National survey of community residential facilities and residents in 1977. Am. J. Ment. Defic. 84:470–478.

Lakin, K. C., Bruininks, R. H., Doth, D., and Hill, B. K. 1982a. Selected Data on Long-Term Care for Developmentally Disabled People. Department of Psychoeducational Studies, University of Minnesota, Minneapolis.

Lakin, K. C., Hill, B. K., Haiber, F. A., and Bruininks, R. H., 1982b. Changes in Age at First Admission to Residential Care of Mentally Retarded People in a Period of Expanding Community Services. Department of Psychoeducational Studies, University of Minnesota, Minneapolis.

Scheerenberger, R. C. 1982. Public Residential Services for the Mentally Retarded: 1981. National Association of Superintendents of Public Residential Facilities for the Mentally Retarded, Madison, Wisconsin.

PERSPECTIVES AND PROGRESS IN MENTAL RETARDATION
Volume I—Social, Psychological, and Educational Aspects
Edited by J. M. Berg
Copyright © 1984 by I.A.S.S.M.D.

PLACEMENT OF MENTALLY RETARDED RESIDENTS FROM PUBLIC RESIDENTIAL FACILITIES IN THE UNITED STATES

L. W. Heal,[1] K. C. Lakin,[2] R. H. Bruininks,[2] B. K. Hill,[2] and B. Best-Sigford[2]

[1] *Department of Special Education,*
University of Illinois at Urbana-Champaign, 288 Education Building,
1310 South Sixth Street, Champaign, Illinois 61820
[2] *Department of Psychoeducational Studies, University of Minnesota,*
178 Pillsbury Drive, S.E., Minneapolis, Minnesota 55455

A discriminant analysis related 11 geopolitical, institutional, and resident characteristics to six community residential facility (CRF) types for 474 individuals who had been released from a national (United States) sample of 75 public residential facilities (PRFs) in 1978. Large canonical correlations ($\Sigma r^2 = 0.752$) indicated that PRF placement staff had a consistent multivariate standard for selecting residents for one alternative or another. There were major differences in placement facility types in different regions of the country: in the Southeast PRFs relied more often on home placements, whereas the larger, more urban, PRFs in the Midwest released more often to unknown placements.

Deinstitutionalization is now firmly established within many social services systems as a predominant philosophy, a functioning process, and a factually demonstrable social reality (Novak and Heal, 1980). In the

---

Portions of this paper are similar to a paper by Best-Sigford et al. (1982) that reported univariate statistics and cross-tabulations only. This paper reports a multivariate analysis of the various placements predicted by several variables related to the released resident's history and personal characteristics.

United States the total population of state institutions has steadily dropped from 194,650 in fiscal year 1967 to 128,550 in fiscal year 1980 (Krantz et al., 1980; Lakin et al., 1982), and there has been a dramatic growth of nonpublic, community-based residential facilities. For example, in the 4½ years between January, 1973, and June, 1977, the number of nonpublic residential facilities doubled to a total of 4,427 with a resident population of 62,397 (Bruininks et al., 1980). In addition, nearly 80,000 mentally retarded people were counted among the residents of nursing homes in 1977 (National Center for Health Statistics, 1979).

A number of investigators have studied the variables associated with resident release, especially with successful community placement. Heal et al. (1978) and Novak and Heal (1980) have reviewed this research. However, no previous study has investigated the factors in the background of public residential facility (PRF) residents and their facilities that have been associated with their release into particular community alternatives. The present paper has this purpose.

METHOD

Facility Sample

In 1977 a listing of all 263 government-operated PRFs for mentally retarded persons was obtained from the periodically revised directory maintained by the National Association of Superintendents of Public Residential Facilities for the Mentally Retarded. These facilities all fit the operational definition of a PRF: "a state sponsored and administered facility that offers comprehensive programming for mentally retarded persons on a 24-hour, 7 days-a-week basis on June 30, 1977." Basic data on the size, location, administration, and staffing patterns of these facilities, and on their residents, were collected by Scheerenberger (1978).

PRFs from Scheerenberger's (1978) 100% sample were stratified according to total number of residents and region. Seventy-eight facilities were selected through controlled sampling. After selection, 6 declined to participate in the study, but substitutions were possible for 3 of them, leaving 75 in the sample.

Released Resident Sample

Based on the most recent reports on the number of releases from PRFs (Krantz et al., 1978; Scheerenberger, 1978), it was determined that, to obtain an adequate sampling ratio of 1:25, approximately 500 releases should be selected from sample facilities. To ensure comparability of subjects across facilities a standard definition of a released resident was developed:

> . . . a mentally retarded person who has left, been transferred, formally released, or discharged from this particular facility for reasons other than death. The person is no longer on the rolls of the facility; or the facility no longer collects financial reimbursement for the person; and the facility no longer maintains a bed for the person's use.

It was further specified that the former residents to be studied were those released between January 1, 1978, and August 31, 1978, the 8-month period immediately preceding data collection. At each selected facility, a full listing was made of all former residents fitting the definition of released resident. Each of these was then assigned a unique serial number. Experienced interviewers from the Survey Research Center at the University of Michigan then selected sample members by means of random numbers provided by the Sampling Section of the Center.

In total, 497 released residents were selected for inclusion in the sample. Of these, data were obtained from resident files on 474. Projections based on refusals to participate and unusable files placed the true sample size at 513, or 679 annually. Thus the projected population of 1978 released residents from this 1:25 sample (16,975) was reasonably close to that actually reported (16,980) by Krantz et al. (1978).

Data Collection

A Released Resident Record Sheet was developed to collect data on these individuals. It consisted of several multiple choice questions and two open-ended questions, worded so that the form could be completed from resident records by either an interviewer or a facility staff person. Information included data on the individual, the placement facility, the reason for placement, and adjustment in the new setting.

Data Analysis

In order to get a multivariate perspective on resident movement, a discriminant analysis was completed using placement facility to define the groups of the dependent variable. The six placement facility categories were:

0. Unknown (38 persons)
1. Natural (or adoptive) home (97 persons)
2. Independent or semi-independent placement, including apartment and boarding house placement (67 persons)
3. Community residential facility (CRF; not included in the other categories) (136 persons)

4. Nursing homes (41 persons)
5. PRFs (95 persons)

This analysis featured 11 predictor variables, 8 of which were continuous or dichotomous, and 3 of which were categorical. The eight univariate predictor variables were:

1. Sex
2. Resident's age in months
3. The square of the resident's age in months (AGESQ), used to account for simple nonlinear age effects
4. Number of disabilities other than mental retardation (OTHDIS)
5. Follow-up calls made by release facility staff (yes or no)
6. Size category of releasing facility (2 = 50–149 residents, 3 = 150–499 residents, 4 = 500–999 residents, 5 = 1000–1599 residents, 6 = 1600+ residents)
7. Months in residence at the releasing facility
8. Behavior characteristics assessment (BCA) score (scaled adaptive behavior score with a range = 0–65 points)

Resident ability was given only as an American Association on Mental Deficiency classification obtained from PRF records. The average BCA score for a national sample (n = 2271) of CRF and PRF residents in each classification (borderline/mild = 54.21, moderate = 49.20, severe = 41.35, profound = 26.09) was substituted for each subject's classification in the present analyses (see Hill and Bruininks, 1981, for a discussion of BCA scores).

The three categorical variables were converted to orthogonal contrast variables so that they could be included as predictors in the discriminant analysis (e.g., Kerlinger and Pedhazur, 1973). The three categorical variables and their associated orthogonal contrasts were:

1. Census Region
   a. South (138 persons) versus Northeast (104 persons), Midwest (130 persons), and West (102 persons) (SVENW)
   b. Northeast versus Midwest and West (EVNW)
   c. Midwest versus West (NVW)
2. Community Type
   a. City and suburb (278 persons) versus village and rural (196 persons) (CITVCTRY)
   b. Central city (226 persons) versus suburb (52 persons) (both being contained in Standard Metropolitan Statistical Areas—SMSAs) (CCVSUB)
3. Admission Status

a. Current residents (317 persons) versus readmission (118 persons) or new admission (39 persons) (CRVRENU)
b. Readmission versus new admission (REVNU)

With regard to admissions, new admissions were defined as residents who had entered the releasing facility for the first time between July 1, 1977, and August 30, 1978. Readmissions were defined as residents who had been admitted during the same period but who had been previously released by the current releasing facility.

RESULTS

Table 1 shows the means and standard deviations for the six continuous variables in the study, although both BCA score and releasing facility size were coarse estimates based on category averages. It can be seen that facility types differed significantly on all six variables. It appears that younger, more recently admitted residents tended to be placed into their natural homes, whereas older, longer-term residents tended to be placed into nursing homes. Strangely, the whereabouts of older, longer-term residents was frequently unknown. Less able, multiply handicapped residents tended to be placed into nursing homes or other PRFs. Rates of recorded follow-up were scandalously low, ranging from 50% to 60% of the placements except for the definitionally low 18% for unknown placements and the understandable 36% for PRF transfers. Finally, the whereabouts of placed residents tended to be unknown more often when the release had been from a large PRF than from a small one.

The results of the discriminant analysis are summarized in Tables 2, 3, and 4, which are based on the printout produced by the Version 9 SPSS subprogram, DISCRIMINANT. With six groups in the dependent variable, five discriminant functions exist. The purpose of a discriminant analysis is to find coefficients (i.e., weights) for the predictor variables, so that the linear combination of these weighted variables discriminate maximally among groups (i.e., among the six placement facility types). Discriminant functions are calculated in succession, with the linear combinations of each successive step being made orthogonal to (uncorrelated with) those of all previous steps. Table 2 shows that the dependent variables in the present study were extremely effective in predicting group membership. The sum of the squared canonical correlations, which is roughly equivalent to the proportion of variance in group membership that is predicted by five linear combinations of predictor variables, is 0.75. Looking at the chisquares, significant variance in group membership remains predictable after all but

Table 1. Descriptive data for each placement facility type

	Unknown	Natural or adoptive home	Independent/ semi-independent	CRF	Nursing home	PRF	$F_{5,468}^{a}$
Length of stay (months)							
Mean	245	84	147	175	198	141	9.32
SD	190	108	153	145	201	108	
Age (months)							
Mean	421	293	397	411	524	341	12.02
SD	213	154	192	170	230	164	
Estimated adaptive behavior							
Mean	42.6	44.4	48.1	47.3	38.9	38.8	8.90
SD	11.5	9.5	8.3	7.0	11.9	10.6	
Additional handicaps							
Mean	0.500	0.762	0.522	0.625	0.927	0.790	12.01
SD	0.464	0.722	0.785	0.843	1.034	0.977	
Percentage follow-up							
Mean	18.4	56.7	55.2	60.3	53.7	35.8	6.61
SD	39.3	49.8	50.1	49.1	50.5	48.2	
Releasing facility (est. size)							
Mean	1287	934	949	885	957	996	3.58
SD	414	474	664	532	472	529	

[a] $P < 0.01$.

Table 2. Canonical discriminant functions

Function	Eigenvalue	Percent of variance	Cumulative percent	Canonical correlation	(after Function $n - 1$) Wilks' lambda	Chi Square	Degrees of freedom
1	0.333	35.37	35.37	0.500	0.432	386.73[a]	75
2	0.305	32.40	67.77	0.483	0.576	254.35[a]	56
3	0.158	16.83	84.60	0.370	0.751	131.75	39
4	0.106	11.28	95.88	0.310	0.870	64.02	24
5	0.039	4.12	100.00	0.193	0.963	17.54	11

[a] $P < 0.001$.

Table 3.   Rotated standardized discriminant function coefficients[a]

	Function 1	Function 2	Function 3	Function 4	Function 5
SVENW	**−0.665**	0.244	−0.068	0.134	0.023
Score	0.149	**−0.760**	−0.068	−0.104	−0.013
CITVCTRY	0.154	**0.319**	−0.134	0.164	0.116
Disabilities	0.159	**0.227**	−0.222	0.164	0.103
NVW	0.126	0.124	**0.626**	−0.173	0.127
Followup	−0.097	−0.139	**−0.594**	−0.218	0.273
Size of RF[b]	0.069	0.064	**0.473**	−0.225	−0.024
CCVSUB	−0.032	0.099	**0.473**	−0.225	−0.024
Age	0.338	1.056	−0.251	**−1.576**	−1.211
AGESQ	0.044	−0.524	−0.224	**1.433**	1.145
CRVRENU	−0.050	0.063	0.012	**0.690**	−0.037
EVNW	−0.047	−0.096	0.064	0.048	**−0.747**
Months in RF	0.171	−0.130	0.361	0.196	**0.610**
REVNU	0.204	0.028	−0.047	0.349	**−0.456**
Sex	−0.146	−0.219	0.009	0.146	**0.370**

[a] Major variables of each discriminant function are in bold print.

[b] RF = Releasing facility; see variable definitions for other abbreviations.

the last function, although the fifth accounts for only 4.12% of the common variance (i.e., of the 75% mentioned above).

Tables 3 and 4 provide insight into the definition of these functions, which were rotated in order to increase interpredictability. It is noteworthy that after rotation the last of the five functions accounted for 9.09% of the variance that group membership shared with the predictors; thus, after rotation, all discriminant functions were presumably significant at a reasonable statistical criterion. The rotated, standardized (all variables standardized to a one-unit standard deviation) discriminant coefficients are shown in Table 3. Variables are ordered and printed in bold type to assist interpretation. Table 4 shows the position or value of each placement group centroid (i.e., multivariate mean).

The first discriminant function is defined almost exclusively by the regional contrast of South versus all other regions (SVENW). Looking

Table 4.   Canonical discriminant functions evaluated at group means (group centroids)

Group	Function 1	Function 2	Function 3	Function 4	Function 5
Unknown	0.664	0.223	1.245	−0.141	0.041
Natural home	−0.700	−0.181	0.054	−0.544	−0.255
Semi-independent	0.342	−0.492	−0.287	−0.035	−0.480
Other CRF	0.283	−0.409	−0.342	0.173	0.260
Nursing home	0.688	1.095	−0.406	−0.200	0.470
PRF	−0.484	0.563	0.307	0.475	0.014

at the placement facility centroids, we see that relative to the rest of the country the South was more likely to place residents in their natural homes and less likely to place them in nursing homes. Also, there were substantially fewer unknown placements from this region. The second discriminant function is defined primarily by BCA adaptive behavior classification (transformed to a 0–65 scale) (Score). Low scores were especially common for residents who were released to nursing homes or to public residential facilities. Age was also positively correlated with this function.

The third function was defined primarily by the occurrence of follow-up visits by the releasing facility staff. Not surprisingly, the only discernible discrimination made by this factor was between the un-known group and the others. Follow-up was apparently much more common in the far West than in the Midwest. Also, smaller releasing facilities were more likely to have staff follow-up than were larger ones, and follow-up was more likely in suburbs than in central cities.

The fourth function was associated with age. Both age and the square of age were entered as predictors, and both were associated with this factor. The discrimination made among groups on this di-mension was both subtle and counterintuitive. Younger residents tended to be transfered from their releasing facilities to other PRFs, whereas older residents tended to be placed in their natural homes. However, age and age squared were salient variables in Functions 1, 2, and 5 as well as Function 4, so the (trivial) interpretation is that Function 4 reflects a residual relationship that exists after subjects have been statistically equated on such factors as nursing home placement and adaptive behavior (Score).

Like Function 4, Function 5 was a residual dimension remaining after most of the associations among variables had been specified. In-deed, its associations were paradoxical and uninterpretable.

DISCUSSION

The best single statement to summarize the results of this study is that the placement site for residents released from PRFs in the United States is very predictable. The sum of the squared canonical correlations from Table 2 was 0.752, indicating that over 75% of the variance in placement site was associated with the 11 predictor variables (having 15 degress of freedom) used in the present analysis. This predictability is espe-cially remarkable in view of the nature of the data collection and man-agement. The data came from institution records whose quality is ques-tionable when the whereabouts of over 8% of their released residents were unknown only a year after their release. Furthermore, one of the best predictors, the adaptive behavior score, was a simple substitution for four categories of disability (borderline and mild, moderate, severe, and profound) of the Behavioral Characteristics Assessment score obtained on a different random sample of cases. Added to these limitations is the arbitrary assignment of facilities to categories and, indeed, the selection of the categories in the first place.

Although the discriminant analysis was very impressive, the most interpretable profile of the resident placed in each facility type can be obtained from the descriptive data in Table 1. From this table, the lost (unknown) residents are seen as older, longer-term residents of a large facility who have few handicaps in addition to their mental retardation. The home placements are young (although their average age is 24), short-term (although their average stay is 7 years), and fairly capable (although not so capable as those selected for CRF or independent placement) residents. Those selected for CRF and independent (and semi-independent) placement were the most capable of all groups, but average in all other characteristics. Those selected for nursing home placement were the oldest, most handicapped residents, with extremely low adaptive skills. Finally, those selected for PRF transfers were similar to those selected for nursing homes except that they were, on the average, 15.25 years younger.

CONCLUSION

These data must be taken as support for the desirability of various residential alternatives for developmentally disabled citizens. The 75% of the variance that facility type had in common with the 11 predictors is certainly an underestimate of what really exists. Given various alternatives, placement staff apparently make reliable decisions in the selection of placement sites for their released clients. The impressiveness of this decisiveness is reduced by the fact that certain placement decisions are more popular in some sections of the country than others. Nevertheless, it appears that the variety of placement alternatives that have developed during the deinstitutionalization movement have made it possible for placement staff to make consistent placement decisions. The continued pursuit of a variety of alternatives for the handicapped individuals who remain in the nation's institutions is endorsed by the findings of the present study.

REFERENCES

Best-Sigford, B., Bruininks, R. H., Lakin, K. C., Hill, B. K., and Heal, L. W. 1982. Resident release patterns in a national sample of public residential facilities. Am. J. Ment. Defic. 87:130–140.

Bruininks, R. K., Hauber, F. A., and Kudla, M. J. 1980. National survey of community residential facilities: A profile of facilities and residents in 1977. Am. J. Ment. Defic. 84:470–478.

Heal, L. W., Sigelman, C. K., and Switzky, H. N. 1978. Research on community residential alternatives for the mentally retarded. In: N. R. Ellis (ed.), International Review of Research in Mental Retardation, Vol. 9. Academic Press, Inc., New York.

Hill, B. K., and Bruininks, R. H. 1981. Physical and Behavioral Characteristics and Maladaptive Behavior of Mentally Retarded People in Residential Facilities. Department of Psychoeducational Studies, University of Minnesota, Minneapolis.

Kerlinger, F. N., and Pedhazur, E. J. 1973. Multiple Regression in Behavioral Research. Holt, Rinehart & Winston, New York.

Krantz, G. C., Bruininks, R. H., and Clumpner, J. L. 1978. Mentally Retarded People in State-operated Residential Facilities: Year Ending June 30, 1978. 2nd ed. Department of Psychoeducational Studies, University of Minnesota, Minneapolis.

Krantz, G. C., Bruininks, R. H., and Clumpner, J. L. 1980. Mentally Retarded People in State-operated Residential Facilities: Year Ending June 30, 1980. Department of Psychoeducational Studies, University of Minnesota, Minneapolis.

Lakin, K. C., Krantz, G. C., Bruininks, R. H., Clumpner, J. L., and Hill, B. K. 1982. One hundred years of data on population of public residential facilities for mentally retarded people. Am. J. Ment. Defic. 87:1–8.

National Center for Health Statistics. 1979. The national nursing home survey: 1977 summary for the United States. Vital and Health Statistics, Series 13, No. 43, DHEW Pub. No. (PHS) 79–1974, July. U. S. Government Printing Office, Washington, D.C.

Novak, A. R., and Heal, L. W. 1980. Integration of Developmentally Disabled Individuals into the Community. Paul H. Brookes Publishers, Baltimore, Maryland.

Scheerenberger, R. C. 1978. Public Residential Services for the Mentally Retarded, 1977. National Association of Superintendents of Public Residential Facilities for the Mentally Retarded, Madison, Wisconsin.

PERSPECTIVES AND PROGRESS IN MENTAL RETARDATION
Volume I—Social, Psychological, and Educational Aspects
Edited by J. M. Berg
Copyright © 1984 by I.A.S.S.M.D.

COMMUNITY LIVING FOR SEVERELY AND PROFOUNDLY RETARDED PERSONS

E. J. Silver, W. P. Silverman, and R. A. Lubin
*New York State Institute for Basic Research in Developmental Disabilities,
1050 Forest Hill Road, Staten Island, New York 10314*

Profoundly retarded, physically disabled persons living in a developmental disabilities specialty hospital were compared to a similar population living in small community-based settings. Some individuals living
in the community had disabilities and service needs comparable to those
of the most disabled hospital residents, and it appeared that each of the
individual needs of specialty hospital residents could be addressed within
community programs. Additionally, an evaluation of the residential environments of profoundly disabled and less disabled individuals indicated
that both groups seemed to be exposed to comparable normalizing factors
in their residential settings.

In recent years, interest in deinstitutionalization and the prevailing
treatment philosophy of "least restrictive environment" have resulted
in increased placement of severely and profoundly mentally retarded
persons in small group-living situations throughout the United States.
According to recent estimates, admissions to community residential
facilities for these individuals will continue to occur at an accelerated
rate (Bruininks et al., 1981). Although research interest in community
residential programs has increased with the growth of the deinstitutionalization movement, most studies have not been designed specifically to address the factors associated with providing services to profoundly disabled persons. Consequently, the present study examined
resident and program characteristics in community residential environments serving severely and profoundly mentally retarded, physi-

This project was supported by a grant (#C-172494) from the New York State Advisory Council on Mental Retardation and Developmental Disabilities. Copies of research
instruments may be requested from the first author.

cally disabled persons. In this paper, we describe these residents and their living environments in two separate investigations designed to answer the questions: 1) Are there some individuals who are "too disabled" to live without undue risk in the community? and 2) Are community programs for profoundly disabled persons as "normalized" as residential programs designed for less disabled individuals?

INVESTIGATION I

The primary participants in this investigation resided in a large metropolitan developmental disabilities specialty hospital, in family care homes, or in small community-based intermediate care facilities for the developmentally disabled (ICFs/DD). Residents of the specialty hospital were profoundly mentally retarded and physically disabled, and were awaiting placement in smaller, community-based residential programs. These individuals generally were considered to be among the most disabled persons receiving residential services in the state. Persons living in the community programs represented the most seriously developmentally and physically disabled persons already residing in small, noninstitutional settings. Selection of community programs was based upon information provided by the Developmental Disabilities Information System (DDIS), a computerized data base containing information on all persons receiving services from the State Office of Mental Retardation and Developmental Disabilities (Janicki and Jacobson, 1979). Their selection was independently verified by subjective reports of administrators who were familiar with this population.

The sample for the study included 115 residents of the specialty hospital, 102 residents of 14 ICF/DD programs, and 10 persons living in family care homes. Although 15 ICF/DD programs and 14 family care providers were identified, 4 family care providers and 1 ICF/DD program chose not to participate. Data included in the present analyses were collected at the study programs from December 1980 through September 1981.

Functional Deficits

As shown in Table 1, data obtained from the DDIS indicated that hospital residents had greater frequencies of physical and developmental disabilities compared to the average community program resident. The typical specialty hospital resident also was more likely to be nonambulatory, to exhibit no expressive or receptive language skills, and to be completely dependent on others for basic self-care.

Table 1. Comparison of selected characteristics of specialty hospital and community residents

	Hospital	Community[a]	Chi square[b]
Mobility			
Walk	2%	79%(81)	143.6(125.8)[c]
Wheelchair	27%	13%(10)	
No mobility	71%	8%(9)	
Expressive language			
Present	5%	41%(31)	39.8(21.3)[d]
Not present	96%	59%(69)	
Receptive language			
Present	23%	76%(72)	58.1(45.4)[d]
Not present	78%	25%(28)	
Toileting skills—completely dependent	96%	29%(33)	96.2(73.7)[d]
Eating skills—completely dependent	82%	11%(13)	101.4(79.6)[d]
Dressing/grooming skills— completely dependent	94%	25%(26)	99.0(82.1)[d]
Number of physical disabilities			
None	3%	31%(34)	44.1(36.6)[e]
1	19%	30%(24)	
2	33%	18%(19)	
3 or more	45%	21%(24)	
Number of developmental disabilities			
1	30%	57%(63)	17.4(23.0)[c]
2	40%	28%(26)	
3 or more	31%	15%(11)	

[a] Numbers in parentheses indicate values for profoundly mentally retarded (PMR) persons only.

[b] X^2 in parentheses compare hospital residents to community PMR residents.

[c] D.f. = 2; $P \leq 0.01$.

[d] D.f. = 1; $P \leq 0.01$.

[e] D.f. = 3; $P \leq 0.01$.

Several additional comparisons between hospital and community residents were made. Although all the specialty hospital residents were profoundly mentally retarded, some individuals living in community programs were functioning at higher intellectual levels. In order to control for the influence of intellectual level, analyses were repeated comparing only profoundly mentally retarded persons in the two settings. As seen in Table 1, all of the differences described above remained statistically significant.

The data in Table 1 indicate that substantial proportions of both groups were profoundly developmentally and physically disabled. Although the mean characteristics of the groups differed, there were considerable overlaps between the groups in levels of functional deficits.

Adaptive Behavior

Information on adaptive behavior was obtained with two forms of the Minnesota Developmental Programming System (MDPS) Behavioral Scales (Joiner and Krantz, 1979). These Scales are composed of a series of developmentally sequenced descriptions of performance divided among various behavioral domains. Individual items are scored according to the frequency with which the specified behaviors are successfully accomplished. For this study, individuals functioning at relatively advanced levels were evaluated using the MDPS-Abbreviated Form (MDPS-AF), a shortened version of the MDPS-Revised (Joiner and Krantz, 1979). More disabled individuals were assessed using a format specifically designed for low-functioning persons, the MDPS Alternate Form C (Bock, 1979).

Whereas 90% of the community residents could be evaluated using the MDPS-AF, all the hospital residents failed to perform the simplest items on this form of the scales and had to be assessed with Form C. Responses to 11 equivalent items on the two forms also illustrated that hospital residents were more impaired in terms of their adaptive behavior skills than were community residents. Table 2 provides a comparison of the two groups with respect to selected adaptive behavior skills. Whereas most hospital residents could not perform these behaviors, the community group had significantly greater proportions of residents with at least some ability to perform these tasks. However, as with the previous group contrasts, some community residents had behavior impairments similar to those of most hospital residents.

Health Status

Information on resident health status and medical services received was gathered using the Health Status Indicator (HSI), a survey instrument specifically developed for this study. Items were designed to assess frequency of health problems and types of care received during the 6-month period preceding the survey.

As shown in Table 3, significant differences were found between specialty hospital and community program residents with regard to respiratory, musculoskeletal, cardiovascular, and skin conditions. During the 6-month period assessed, specialty hospital residents were more likely than community residents to exhibit one or more indications of respiratory problems (e.g., frequent breathing difficulties, problems with secretions, frequent colds, or regular use of respiratory medication), musculoskeletal problems (e.g., limb contractures), and skin in-

Table 2. Percentages of residents with no ability to perform selected adaptive behavior tasks

	Hospital	Community	Chi square[a]
Moves from lying on stomach to sitting position	81%	13%	91.3
Pulls self to standing position using person or prop for support	96%	22%	117.4
Walks 5 feet (may use braces or crutches)	96%	23%	114.6
Drinks without spilling from a glass or cup with assistance	41%	4%	34.9
Picks up food with fingers and puts food in mouth	84%	7%	118.0
Uses spoon to pick up and eat food	74%	7%	91.1
Picks up glass and drinks from it without spilling	78%	19%	68.5
Uses a fork to pick up and eat food	98%	39%	83.8
Obeys a simple instruction such as "Come here"	68%	21%	42.6
Stops an activity upon request such as "No" or "Stop"	64%	17%	44.9
Says or indicates "Yes" or "No" in response to questions such as "Do you want to go out?"	92%	58%	30.2

[a] D.f. = 1; $P \leq 0.01$.

fections. Community residents, on the other hand, had more cardiovascular problems. As Table 4 indicates, hospital residents also were more likely than community residents to have received services from various professionals other than psychiatrists and psychologists.

Although group differences were significant, there was group overlap. Hospital residents, as a group, exhibited more physical problems than community residents, but some individuals living in the com-

Table 3. Percentages of residents with one or more indicators of medical problems during a 6-month period

	Hospital	Community	Chi square[a]
Respiratory	34%	16%	7.5
Musculoskeletal	94%	36%	70.7
Skin	16%	3%	7.0
Cardiovascular	0%	6%	[b]

[a] D.f. = 1; $P \leq 0.01$.

[b] Fisher's exact probability ≤ 0.01.

Table 4.   Percentages of residents receiving health and therapy services during a 6-month period

	Hospital	Community	Chi-square[a]
Occupational therapist	91%	41%	51.5
Physical therapist	99%	52%	59.6
Licensed practical nurse	100%	64%	42.0
Registered nurse	100%	85%	15.4
Nurse practitioner	49%	25%	11.0
Primary physician	100%	92%	7.2
Psychologist/psychiatrist	26%	89%	65.7
Medical specialists	84%	62%	12.7

[a] D.f. = 1; $P \leq 0.01$.

munity had comparable health problems. In addition, some community residents received each type of health or therapy service provided to hospital residents.

Summary

As a group, persons living in community-based residential programs were less developmentally and medically impaired than were persons living in the specialty hospital. However, some persons living in community settings had disabilities and skill levels similar to those of the most impaired hospital residents. These individuals were provided with daily services and medical treatment as intensive as care received by hospital residents. Although it is likely that no existing program provided all of the services that might be needed by the most fragile hospital residents, we found no service that was received by hospital residents that was not provided in at least one of the community programs we studied.

INVESTIGATION II

In a second investigation, we sought to determine whether community programs for profoundly disabled persons provided residential environments that were as normalized and homelike as those provided by ICF/DD programs and community residences (CRs) serving less disabled individuals. In addition to the 14 ICF/DD programs serving profoundly disabled persons described above, this investigation included a comparison group of 49 facilities randomly selected from 499 ICF/DD and CR programs operating in New York State as of June 1, 1979. Demographic and functional data obtained from the DDIS indicated that, on the average, persons in the 49 randomly selected comparison programs were less developmentally and physically disabled than were persons in the 14 programs serving profoundly developmentally dis-

Table 5. Comparison of CTE, PASS, and GHMS scores for two groups of community residential programs

| | PDD[a] programs | | LDD[b] programs | | | |
	Mean	SD	Mean	SD	t	d.f.
CTE activity scale	7.08	1.1	7.54	0.8	1.7	57
PASS program	−3.69	65.3	−10.35	90.8	0.2	60
PASS setting	−5.69	25.7	−9.10	29.5	0.3	60
PASS administration	−5.54	19.1	−6.35	33.9	1.2	60
GHMS rigidity of routine	9.82	2.5	6.65	2.4	3.9[c]	57
GHMS block treatment	10.00	2.7	7.66	2.5	2.7[c]	56
GHMS depersonalization	13.27	3.0	9.38	2.6	4.3[c]	56
GHMS social distance	6.27	1.9	3.77	1.8	4.0[c]	56

[a] PDD = profoundly developmentally disabled.
[b] LDD = less developmentally disabled.
[c] $P \leq 0.01$.

abled persons (PDD programs). For example, analyses of covariance indicated that, compared to programs serving profoundly disabled persons, the 49 comparison programs served residents with greater mobility and fewer developmental and physical problems, even when intellectual levels of the residents were statistically controlled. For mobility, numbers of developmental disabilities, and numbers of physical disorders, $F_{1,160} = 15.5, 8.8,$ and 10.6, respectively ($P \leq 0.01$).

Environments within community programs were evaluated using: 1) an abbreviated version of the Program Analysis of Service Systems (Flynn, 1980), which measured normalization of setting, program, and administration; 2) the Characteristics of the Treatment Environment/Mental Retardation and Developmental Disabilities Community Home Survey Activity Subscale (Jackson, 1964), which assessed the availability and variety of social and recreational activities; and 3) the Group Home Management Schedule (Raynes et al., 1979), which provided information on whether management activities were resident or facility oriented. Surveys were administered at the 14 PDD programs between June and September, 1981. Data were collected at the 49 randomly selected comparison programs between September 1980 and September 1981. These data were collected as part of a related project (Living Alternatives Research Project, 1981), and were shared with us for this phase of the present investigation.

Environmental Ratings

Table 5 shows the distribution of environmental ratings for the two groups of residences. No group differences were found for two instruments, the Characteristics of the Treatment Environment (CTE) Activity Scale and the Program Analysis of Service Systems (PASS). In both groups, CTE scores ranged from neutral to highly positive. Severely and profoundly disabled and less disabled persons appeared to be provided with similar opportunities to engage in social and recreational activities. In addition, the residential environments of PDD programs were rated as comparable to those serving less disabled individuals in terms of normalization of program, setting, and administration. On the average, programs in both groups approximated a minimally acceptable level of service quality (Flynn, 1980).

Group Home Management Schedule (GHMS) scores, however, were significantly different in the two groups. Management activities in community programs for profoundly disabled persons were found to be more facility oriented than were management activities in programs for less disabled persons. Nevertheless, average scores of the PDD programs were fairly neutral, and there was considerable overlap in the distributions of GHMS scale scores in the two groups.

CONCLUSIONS

In summary, a group of profoundly mentally retarded, physically disabled persons living at a large developmental disabilities specialty hospital were found to have disabilities and service needs within the range of those exhibited by individuals living in small, community-based residential programs. As a group, the most disabled persons living in community programs were functioning at higher levels than were hospital residents. Nevertheless, some community programs appeared to be addressing programming and service needs of persons whose developmental and physical problems were comparable to those of hospital residents. In fact, three of the ICF/DD programs studied served persons almost identical to most of the hospital residents. These individuals were nonambulatory, exhibited little or no language use, were completely dependent on others for self-care, and had seizures and other physical disorders.

As part of this study, we also determined that residential environments of profoundly disabled persons were highly similar to those of less disabled individuals in terms of social and recreational activities, normalization, and management orientation. Profoundly disabled and less disabled persons appeared to be exposed to comparable factors in their residential settings.

Our findings have policy implications for provision of residential services for severely and profoundly disabled persons. There may be some small number of extremely fragile persons who require the intensive level of services available in a hospital-like setting, but normalized environments that provide services to persons with all levels of disabilities can and have been established in the community. Nevertheless, making services available within community settings does not ensure a positive outcome. Thus, an important research question remains as to the extent to which each type of residential setting is most suitable for maximizing the developmental potential of profoundly mentally and physically disabled persons. We intend to address this question on the basis of longitudinal data currently being collected on adaptive behavior and health status of hospital and community residents.

REFERENCES

Bock, W. 1979. Minnesota Developmental Programming System, Alternate Form C. University of Minnesota, St. Paul.

Bruininks, R. H., Kudla, M. J., Hauber, F. A., Hill, B. K., and Wieck, C. A. 1981. Recent growth and status of community residential alternatives. In: R. H. Bruininks, C. E. Meyers, B. B. Sigford, and K. C. Lakin (eds.), Deinstitutionalization and Community Adjustment of Mentally Retarded People, pp. 14–27. American Association on Mental Deficiency, Washington, D.C.

Flynn, R. J. 1980. Normalization, PASS, and service quality assessment: How normalizing are current human services? In: R. J. Flynn and K. E. Nitsch (eds.), Normalization, Social Integration, and Community Services, pp. 323–350. University Park Press, Baltimore.

Jackson, J. 1964. Toward the comparative study of mental hospitals: Characteristics of the treatment environment. In: A. F. Wessen (ed.), The Psychiatric Hospital as a Social System. Charles C Thomas Publisher, Springfield, Illinois.

Janicki, M. P., and Jacobson, J. W. 1979. New York's Needs Assessment and Developmental Disabilities: Preliminary Report. Technical Monograph 79-10, New York State Office of Mental Retardation and Developmental Disabilities, Albany.

Joiner, L. M., and Krantz, G. C. 1979. The Assessment of Behavioral Competence of Developmentally Disabled Individuals: The MDPS. University of Minnesota Press, Minneapolis.

Living Alternatives Research Project. 1981. The Identification and Description of Environmental Conditions Affecting Growth in Personal Competence of Persons with Developmental Disabilities: Phase I (Final Report). New York State Institute for Basic Research in Developmental Disabilities, Staten Island.

Raynes, N., Pratt, M., and Roses, S. 1979. Organisational Structure and the Care of the Mentally Retarded. Croon-Helm, London.

PERSPECTIVES AND PROGRESS IN MENTAL RETARDATION
Volume I—Social, Psychological, and Educational Aspects
Edited by J. M. Berg
Copyright © 1984 by I.A.S.S.M.D.

CHARACTERISTICS AND ADAPTIVE BEHAVIORS OF NEW YORK'S GROUP HOME OCCUPANTS

J. W. Jacobson,[1] E. Sersen,[2] and A. A. Schwartz[3]

[1] *New York State Office of Mental Retardation and Developmental Disabilities, 44 Holland Avenue, Albany, New York 12229*
[2] *New York State Institute for Basic Research in Developmental Disabilities, 1050 Forest Hill Road, Staten Island, New York 10314*
[3] *New York State Office of Mental Retardation and Developmental Disabilities, New York, New York 10047*

As part of an information system updating process in New York State, longitudinal information on the adaptive skills of 1,027 group home occupants with mental retardation became available. This report presents findings regarding the amount of adaptive changes found over the course of a year and predictors of change. Findings suggest that, in general, there are small adaptive changes, even among persons with severe or profound mental retardation.

The state of New York operates an extensive system of group homes (hostels, community residences) that serve developmentally disabled persons (the term developmental disabilities in this context includes mental retardation, autism, cerebral palsy, epilepsy, and neurological impairments such as those associated with spina bifida). A group home is defined in New York State as a residential setting that is integrated into the community and serves from 4 to 14 persons with developmental disabilities. Occupants are provided room, board, and services principally relating to household activities, daily living, health care, recreation, and socialization. Twenty-four hour supervision of occupants is available. Admission to a group home is contingent upon enrollment in a day program (habilitative, vocational, or educational program), and over 96% of all group home occupants participate in off-site day programs (OMRDD, 1980). Residences are either staffed in shifts, by persons who live in, or by a combination of these methods, and are operated either by private, nonprofit agencies or by a state agency. The intent of these programs is to provide a homelike setting, and to serve as either a long-term residence for some individuals or as a transitional residence for others who may move on to less closely supervised situations. Group homes usually are sited in single-family, two-family, and duplex houses, or in apartment clusters, in residential neighborhoods.

As of January 1982, 4,583 persons lived in 494 group homes sites in New York State, for an average of 9.3 persons per site. The occupants of New York's group homes are highly similar to group home occupants described nationally in terms of intellectual level, disability characteristics, and functional attributes (O'Connor and Sitkei, 1975; Baker et al., 1977; Bruininks et al., 1980; Hill and Bruininks, 1981; Jacobson and Schwartz, 1982). Most of the occupants are independent in terms of toileting (82%), eating (80%), and dressing (60%). Some exhibit relatively good ability in independent living; for example, 29% can use a telephone and 23% can shop in stores.

The present study is directed at exploring the relationships of occupant age and intellectual level with adaptive behavior changes over time, i.e., improvements in functional skills that occur during a period of group home residency. Several studies (Aanes and Moen, 1976; Eyman et al., 1977, 1979) have documented longitudinal changes in adaptive behavior in group homes. However, the amount of change has not been generally considered. Given the nature of the disabilities represented, the expectation would be that small adaptive changes would occur over the course of only 1 or 2 years, and would be mediated by age and intellectual level.

METHOD

Subjects

As of April 1982, longitudinal data on the adaptive functioning of New York State group home occupants were available for 1,027 persons evidencing some degree of mental retardation. This group constitutes 22% of the population of supervised community residences. Longitudinal data became available for these individuals during the process of updating an existing information system (see Instrument section), and, as a result, this does not represent a randomly selected group. The characteristics of the sample and of the general group home population are contrasted in Table 1. Persons in the study sample differ from the group home population in that they appear more likely to be younger.

Table 1.   Comparison of percent distributions of characteristics of all group home occupants to study sample

	All group home occupants	Sample group home occupants
Age		
0–21 years	2	10
21+ years	98	90
Gender		
Male	58	56
Female	42	44
Developmental disabilities		
Autism	1	1
Cerebral palsy	8	5
Epilepsy	15	12
Mental retardation	96[a]	100
Neurological impairment	10	8
Intellectual level		
Normal or above	11[a]	0
Mild mental retardation	26	30
Moderate mental retardation	27	33
Severe mental retardation	23	27
Profound mental retardation	14	10
Mobility limitation present	2	1
Hearing impairment present	9	10
Vision impairment present	10	13
Expressive language deficit[b] present	42	39
Receptive language deficit[c] present	54	52
Number of cases	3,986[d]	1,027

[a] Incongruity of intellectual level and diagnosis of mental retardation reflects diagnosis of mental retardation for some persons functioning within the archaic classification of "borderline" mental retardation.

[b] Unable to use phrases of three words or more; or equivalent manual or symbol language.

[c] Unable to follow verbal or manual language instructions of three steps or more.

[d] All group home occupants for whom DDIS data were available as of 2/82; 86.8% of total group home population.

However, the sample can be characterized as equivalent in disability level to the total group home population in New York.

Instrument

Descriptive information for both the group home population and the study sample was collected through the New York Developmental Disabilities Information System (DDIS) (Janicki and Jacobson, 1979, 1982), an information system operated by the developmental disabilities agency of New York State, the Office of Mental Retardation and Developmental Disabilities (OMRDD). The DDIS is a comprehensive needs assessment and screening instrument that consolidates demographic, diagnostic, and functional attributes, program and service needs, and adaptive behavior information on an individual case basis. One component of the DDIS is an abbreviated version of the Minnesota Developmental Programming System Behavior Scales (MDPS-AF) (Bock and Weatherman, 1978). This is an 80-item, eight-domain scale that permits the calculation of scale scores, termed "percent competence scores," in the areas of gross motor development, toileting, dressing/grooming, eating, language, reading/writing, quantitative (numeric) skills, and independent living. Each item in the MDPS-AF is marked to indicate the level of behavioral performance using a 4-point rating. Percent competence scores for each domain range from 0 to 100, with a score of 100% interpreted as equivalent to a minimum competence level within the general, nondisabled population. The MDPS-AF is not normed, although mean percent competence profiles have been presented elsewhere based on age and intellectual level (Janicki and Jacobson, 1982).

For persons in group homes the DDIS is completed by the manager of the home, a case coordinator in the home, or by an OMRDD case worker from outside the home who has responsibility for working with the disabled person. In all instances, the protocol is completed by an individual who is personally familiar with the client. The DDIS was completed the first time for individuals in the study sample during 1979 and 1980 ($\bar{x}$ = 1980.2, = 0.5 years) and a second time during late 1980 and early 1981 ($\bar{x}$ = 1981.2, = 0.2 years). The mean interval between protocols was 1 year, and ranged, based on guidelines promulgated as part of the update process, between 6 months and 18 months.

Procedure

A stepwise multiple regression was performed for each MDPS-AF domain with final domain score as the dependent variable, and age, intellectual level, and time 1/time 2 interval as the independent variables. Age was computed in whole years at the time of the baseline measure, time interval as number and parts of months (in decimal format), and intellectual level as mild, moderate, severe, or profound (an IQ score was not always available). Client data were deleted on a pairwise basis if MDPS-AF domain score values were missing for either time.

RESULTS

Group Characteristics

For the purpose of illustrating the changes observed over time, means and standard deviations of MDPS-AF domains are presented as a function of age, intellectual level, and time tested in Table 2. On all MDPS domains, time 1 scores differed significantly across age/intellectual level groups ($11.36 \leq F \leq 283.11$, $P < 0.001$), as did time 2 scores ($11.77 \leq F \leq 233.44$, $P < 0.001$). By inspection of Table 2 it is apparent that: 1) older persons scored higher than younger persons with similar intellectual skills in both time intervals; 2) older persons scored higher at time 2 than at time 1; 3) adults with severe/profound MR scored higher at time 2 than time 1; 4) persons with mild/moderate MR scored higher than persons with severe/profound MR in both time periods; 5) persons with mild/moderate MR scored higher than persons with severe/profound MR at independent living skills; and 6) all clients together scored higher at time 2 than time 1. Clients under the age of 22 scored higher at time 2 than at time 1 on only two to four of the eight MDPS-AF domains, depending upon intellectual level.

Change Scores and Baseline Scores

Pearson product-moment correlation coefficients were calculated between change scores and baseline scale scores for each MDPS-AF domain. All correlations were significant at the 0.001 level (d.f. = 1026) and ranged from -0.342 for language skills to -0.604 for eating skills. Correlations were universally negative; higher initial domain scores were associated with smaller change scores. Furthermore this relationship appeared more pronounced for groups with higher initial baseline scores: persons age 22 or older and persons with mild or moderate mental retardation. These correlations probably reflect person "topping-off" or scoring at or near 100% competence on the baseline measure. For these individuals change scores would approach zero.

Change Scores and Time

Pearson product-moment correlation coefficients between change scores and time between protocols for each MDPS-AF domain were also computed. Where significant correlations were found, again these were universally negative. In general, relationships were most marked and pervasive for gross motor, toileting, dressing, and reading skills, although even in these instances the proportion of variance accounted for (r^2) was very small (1–2%).

Multiple Regression

Table 3 presents the results of stepwise multiple regressions predicting final scores in each MDPS-AF domain. In all instances, the strongest predictor of final score was the baseline score, accounting for 28% to 70% of variance in final scores. Together, time interval, intellectual level, and age accounted for 1% to 4% of final score variance, although

Table 2. Means and standard deviations of MDPS-AF domain scores as a function of age, intellectual level, and time

	n	Gross motor development		Toileting skills		Dress/grooming skills		Eating skills		Language skills		Read/write skills		Quantitative skills		Independent living skills	
		Mean	SD	Mean	SD	Mean	SD	Mean	SD	Mean	SD	Mean	SD	Mean	SD	Mean	SD
Age 0–21 years																	
Mild/moderate MR																	
Time 1	57	92.5	18.5	94.8	9.6	90.0	14.5	92.0	12.8	84.4	20.2	80.4	24.1	79.6	20.7	78.2	19.7
Time 2	56	92.9	17.1	94.1	12.5	91.2	12.3	91.6	12.2	86.7	18.5	80.2	24.1	80.4	20.7	76.5	21.5
Severe/Profound MR																	
Time 1	47	79.3	22.4	69.7	27.0	62.2	28.8	68.3	25.3	46.6	28.3	41.2	26.9	33.7	28.5	39.9	27.0
Time 2	46	84.0	21.4	68.7	30.2	63.8	30.6	72.3	24.9	41.1	27.4	37.8	25.7	30.7	27.1	37.8	26.2
Age 22 + years																	
Mild/moderate MR																	
Time 1	632	91.2	16.6	95.8	11.1	94.0	11.0	93.8	12.8	88.2	17.0	78.9	22.0	80.9	21.4	82.1	18.4
Time 2	616	92.1	14.6	95.9	8.7	94.7	8.8	94.7	10.1	89.1	15.9	79.7	21.1	82.0	20.7	82.0	17.9
Severe/profound MR																	
Time 1	281	86.2	18.5	83.7	18.1	79.4	21.7	80.8	18.8	58.7	26.1	41.8	21.6	37.3	25.0	51.3	24.2
Time 2	275	86.1	17.2	84.7	15.9	82.4	19.8	84.3	16.2	61.1	27.0	46.1	22.8	42.8	27.1	54.3	24.8
Overall																	
Time 1	1027	89.3	17.8	91.2	16.0	88.2	18.2	88.9	17.1	77.7	25.4	66.8	28.3	66.4	30.7	71.2	25.7
Time 2	993	90.1	16.1	91.4	14.7	89.7	16.4	90.6	14.4	79.0	25.2	68.5	27.4	68.7	29.9	71.9	25.1

Table 3.   Summary of multiple regressions predicting final MDPS-AF scores

MDPS-AF domain[a]	Multiple r	r^2	r	F
Gross motor				
B	0.674	0.454	0.674	351.99[b]
T	0.679	0.460	−0.059	10.18[c]
IL	0.680	0.463	0.135	5.23[d]
A	0.682	0.465	−0.128	4.87[d]
Toileting				
B	0.602	0.363	0.602	452.86[b]
IL	0.624	0.389	0.357	38.31[b]
T	0.632	0.400	−0.117	18.90[b]
A	0.635	0.403	0.073	5.66[d]
Dressing				
B	0.656	0.430	0.656	593.87[b]
IL	0.671	0.451	0.363	33.66[b]
T	0.675	0.456	−0.112	12.62[c]
A	0.679	0.461	0.111	7.40[c]
Eating				
B	0.530	0.281	0.530	298.43[b]
IL	0.547	0.299	0.313	23.19[b]
T	0.553	0.305	0.093	9.98[c]
A	0.556	0.310	−0.089	6.07[d]
Language				
B	0.798	0.637	0.798	1217.36[b]
IL	0.804	0.647	0.478	26.94[b]
A	0.806	0.649	0.090	6.74[c]
T	0.807	0.651	−0.090	5.07[d]
Reading				
B	0.792	0.628	0.792	110.73[b]
IL	0.801	0.641	0.506	33.00[b]
T	0.805	0.648	−0.156	18.58[b]
A	0.806	0.650	0.002	6.92[c]
Quantitative				
B	0.839	0.704	0.839	1481.54[b]
IL	0.844	0.713	0.544	28.75[b]
T	0.845	0.715	−0.132	8.14[c]
A	0.846	0.716	0.024	6.21[d]
Independent living				
B	0.759	0.576	0.759	900.29[b]
IL	0.768	0.589	0.468	31.16[b]
T	0.770	0.592	−0.158	8.28[c]
A	0.770	0.593	0.017	1.89

[a] B = baseline percent competence score on MDPS-AF scale
  IL = intellectual level
  T = time interval between protocols
  A = age
[b] $P < 0.001$.
[c] $P < 0.01$.
[d] $P < 0.05$.

F values for these factors are generally statistically significant. The signs of the beta weights for each variable were consistent with those of the simple r's. Consequently, intellectual level was positively associated with the final score in each domain, whereas age was negatively associated with final scores in gross motor and eating skills, and positively associated with other domain scores. In light of positive associations of intellectual level to final scores, and negative associations of baseline scores and change scores, it appears that persons with lower adaptive scores may have shown the most change, and that change was more pronounced among persons with mild or moderate mental retardation.

DISCUSSION

Our findings are consistent with those of other studies (Aanes and Moen, 1976; Eyman et al., 1977, 1979) in that selected changes in adaptive skills to be found in group homes over time differ based upon intellectual level and age. Lack of marked differences based upon age or intellectual level are noteworthy, because the above-mentioned studies suggested that the benefits of group home placement should differ more on the basis of these variables. However, because MDPS-AF domain scores are generally related to number of life activity deficits (as defined in Public Law 95-602, the Rehabilitation, Comprehensive Services, and Developmental Disabilities Amendments of 1978) and IQ and age are also closely associated with number of deficits (Lubin et al., 1982), it is possible that the use of baseline MDPS-AF scores results in an underestimation of the proportion of variance accounted for separately by age and intellectual level. This interpretation is consistent with the simple r's noted for intellectual level (range = 0.135 to 0.544) in Table 3. Furthermore, given the small proportion of persons ages 0–21 in the sample (10%), and differences apparent in time 1 and time 2 scores for age groups shown in Table 2, it is possible that the simple r's (range -0.128 to 0.111) for age reported in Table 3 are underestimates of age and domain score relationships.

It should be noted that the negative correlations between baseline and change scores suggest maintenance or modest improvement of adaptive skill levels among adult group home occupants, even among persons with severe or profound mental retardation. Maintenance of skill levels in a group home setting, rather than substantive positive change (at least over the short term), should not necessarily be interpreted as a negative finding. Given the diverse nature of the group home population, it appears reasonable to expect that this setting is of use in maintaining the adaptive level of individuals who may be quite disabled.

Several characteristics of the present study design may bear upon the pattern of findings. Although the results provide evidence of very small adaptive changes, it is reasonable to ask whether more substantive changes should be expected within this population over the course of 1 year. Additionally, it is possible that the 80 items in the MDPS-AF do not provide sufficient detail, at least when considered as domain scores, to document the extent of change one would hope to find over this interval. Finally, beneficial effects of group home placement may have been overshadowed by inclusion of persons scoring at the upper end of adaptive functioning (some persons who have mild mental retardation). A number of procedural changes, including a longer test-retest interval, a more extensive behavior assessment instrument, consideration of changes in individual MDPS-AF item scores, or selective analysis of cases excluding individuals with the most developed adaptive skills, might disclose more marked effects.

REFERENCES

Aanes, D., and Moen, M. 1976. Adaptive behavior changes of group home residents. Ment. Retard. 14:36–40.

Baker, B. L., Seltzer, G. B., and Seltzer, M. M. 1977. As Close as Possible: Community Residences for Retarded Adults. Little, Brown & Company, Boston.

Bock, W. H., and Weatherman, R. 1978. Minnesota Developmental Programming System Behavior Scales–Revised. University of Minnesota, Minneapolis.

Bruininks, R. H., Hauber, F. A., and Kudla, M. J. 1980. National survey of community residential facilities: A profile of facilities and residents in 1977. Am. J. Ment. Defic. 84:470–478.

Eyman, R. K., DeMaine, G. C., and Lei, T. 1979. Relationship between community environments and resident changes in adaptive behavior: A path model. Am. J. Ment. Defic. 83:330–338.

Eyman, R. K., Silverstein, A. B., McLain, R., and Miller, C. 1977. Effects of residential settings on development. In: P. Mittler (ed.), Research to Practice in Mental Retardation: Vol. I, Care and Intervention, pp. 305–314. University Park Press, Baltimore.

Hill, B. K., and Bruininks, R. H. 1981. Physical and Behavioral Characteristics and Maladaptive Behavior of Mentally Retarded People in Residential Facilities. Project Report No. 12. Department of Psychoeducational Studies, University of Minnesota, Minneapolis.

Jacobson, J. W., and Schwartz, A. A. 1982. The Evaluation of Community Living Alternatives for Developmentally Disabled Persons (Tech. Mono. 82-4). Living Alternatives Research Project, Staten Island, NY.

Janicki, M. P., and Jacobson, J. W. 1979. New York's Needs Assessment and Developmental Disabilities: Preliminary Report (Tech. Mono. 79-10). Office of Mental Retardation and Developmental Disabilities, Albany.

Janicki, M. P., and Jacobson, J. W., 1982. The character of developmental disabilities in New York State: Preliminary observations. Int. J. Rehab. Res. 5:191–202.

Lubin, R. A., Jacobson, J. W., and Kiely, M. 1982. Projected impact of the functional definition of developmental disabilities: The categorically disabled population and service eligibility. Am. J. Ment. Defic. 86:73–79.

OMRDD. 1980. Comprehensive Plan for Services to Mentally Retarded and Developmentally Disabled Persons in New York State: 1981–1982. Office of Mental Retardation and Developmental Disabilities, Albany.

O'Connor, G., and Sitkei, E. G. 1975. Study of a new frontier in community services. Ment. Retard. 13:35–38.

PERSPECTIVES AND PROGRESS IN MENTAL RETARDATION
Volume I—Social, Psychological, and Educational Aspects
Edited by J. M. Berg
Copyright © 1984 by I.A.S.S.M.D.

A STUDY OF INDEPENDENT LIVING SERVICES IN CALGARY

R. Phillips

Vocational and Rehabilitation Research Institute, 3304 33rd Street N.W., Calgary, Alberta T2L 2A6, Canada; 30 Park Hill Road, Toronto, Ontario, Canada

This study analyzed the residential history of 48 clients in an independent living program. The work of Schalock and Harper (1978) was replicated in an urban Canadian setting. The study did not confirm as significant the variables of age, intelligence, months in training, broadly defined academic skills, and ability in language and motor skills that Schalock and Harper had found to be good success predictors. Several factors were identified as being good predictors of success in independent living: community awareness skills, social maturity skills, functional reading, and the client's perception of his happiness. Some differences were noted in the numbers of critical incidents that occurred in the successful and unsuccessful groups (although not at a significant level). Some client perceptions are presented. Recommendations for further study and for admission criteria for independent living services are suggested.

In the past decade there has been an increase in the number of programs in Canada and the United States that help developmentally handicapped adults to live independently. The Province of Alberta, Canada, for example, has funded such programs, called Independent Living Services (ILS), since 1978. The program model used is a nonlive-in staff working individually with 12–15 clients.

Although there are many training manuals available on teaching mentally handicapped adults how to live in the community, research on the process has not been extensive. Some articles that seem to deal with independent living really discuss adjustment to group homes by those previously institutionalized. However, descriptive studies by Nooe (1975, 1977) found an association between positive self-ratings by mentally handicapped adults on a Q-sort and their readiness for a higher level of independence. Crnic and Pym (1979) found psychological skills, client motivation, behavioral skills, and adequate support to be related to success in independent living. Factors associated with failure were behavioral regressions, overwhelming crises, and social isolation. Reavis (1976, 1977) emphasized the need for clients to have both good behavioral skills and minimal socialization skills.

In an evaluative study of independent living, Schalock and Harper (1978) found success to be significantly related to intelligence, skill in symbolic operations, personal maintenance, clothing care, socially appropriate behavior, functional academics, and length of training.

METHOD

Operational Definitions

According to Katz and Lylerly (1963), successful adjustment to the community should be defined broadly. At one end of a continuum is *total success*; at the other end is a *failure* situation where the client moves back to a more structured environment or drops out of the program. In between these two extremes are two other groups, consisting of those who experience *moderate success* (i.e., do not decrease their need for staff support but do maintain their level of skill competency) and those who have only *partial success* (i.e., where failure is prevented only through massive staff intervention).

According to Crnic and Pym (1979), *crises* are events in an individual's life that put severe stress on him/her (e.g., eviction). Crises may involve real or potential dangers to the client or to the public (Nihira and Nihira, 1974).

Subject Selection

Clients who had entered any phase of an ILS program at two agencies in Calgary from 1979 to 1981 were identified by senior agency staff. Of this group, 48 were selected who met the additional criteria of having lived for at least 2 months in a residence that was not their family's and that had no live-in staff. These clients were then rated as successful or unsuccessful by senior agency staff using the operational definitions. The factors that Schalock and Harper (1978) had found as significant predictors of success were examined, as were others, using a biserial correlation. A random sample of clients was interviewed to obtain their opinions about ILS.

The second part of the study was based on the Cowgill et al. (1973) model of prediction of later difficulties from anecdotal reports. Twenty-two clients who had been judged to be in either the total success or the failure groups were randomly selected. For each subject copies were obtained of the reports in the main files of each agency for a 1-

year period prior to entry to ILS. Each subject's file was then rated by senior agency staff.

RESULTS

Descriptive Information

In this study, 28 of the 48 clients experienced some measure of success, as judged by senior agency staff. The clients were divided fairly evenly in terms of sex. The majority of clients (29/48) were between 20 and 29 years of age. Another 9 were between 30 and 34 years of age. Nineteen clients were in the mild range of mental deficiency and 22 in the borderline range as measured on the Peabody Picture Vocabulary Test. Clients were referred to the agencies from a variety of sources: family, another community agency, or a hospital/institution. Fourteen of the clients had been in an institution at some point in their lives. Half of those who had been in institutions had spent between 7 and 20 years there. None had been in penal institutions or in both hospitals for the mentally ill and for the mentally retarded. Five clients were identified as having entered the ILS program more than once. Four of these were later judged unsuccessful.

There was great variety in the amount of previous noninstitutional, residential training clients had received, with a range of 1 to 20 years. One-half of the clients supported themselves completely or to some degree. Almost one-third relied entirely on a government income program.

Factors Associated with Success (Tables 1, 2)

The factors of social maturity, as measured on the Adaptive Functioning Index (AFI) (Marlett, 1973), and the clients' perception of their happiness in ILS were found to correlate with success (0.66 and 0.50, respectively; $P = 0.01$).

Two factors similar to those that Schalock and Harper (1978) had found to be associated with success were confirmed: total number of skills and amount of community utilization, both measured on the AFI. However, the results differed from Schalock and Harper's on several dimensions. Age, intelligence, and months spent in training did not differentiate between the successful and failure groups. Personal routines and clothing care did not prove significant. In the area of functional academics, only number concepts and reading were significant; motor skills and language were not confirmed. Visual and auditory processing were not assessed. Imprecise agency files prevented work

Table 1. Personal routines, community awareness, and social maturity AFI scores: Correlation with success ratings

Training scores	Original residential AFI scores (n = 25)			Recent residential AFI scores (n = 38)		
	Mean	SD	Correlation	Mean	SD	Correlation
Section I: personal routines						
Personal cleanliness	15.32	3.37	0.00	16.50	3.99	0.47[a]
Appearance/eating	15.44	3.75	0.20	18.50	2.11	0.38[b]
Room management	14.76	8.87	0.20	16.40	4.18	0.46[a]
Time management	15.52	3.41	0.36	17.53	2.94	0.44[a]
Health	9.72	4.53	0.42	16.29	3.32	0.47[a]
Total section I	70.72	13.80	0.33	85.13	12.98	0.56[a]
Section II: community awareness						
Transportation	13.04	6.47	0.30	18.74	2.97	0.33[b]
Shopping	14.00	5.17	0.36	17.95	3.28	0.28
Leisure	11.08	4.36	0.34	13.53	4.92	0.63[a]
Budgeting	8.64	6.05	0.64[a]	13.47	4.00	0.53[a]
Cooking/home management	6.64	6.69	0.37	15.89	4.97	0.60[a]
Total section II	53.12	24.20	0.49[b]	79.58	16.76	0.60[a]
Section III: social maturity						
Communication	12.56	4.99	0.30	17.92	2.76	0.45[a]
Consideration	14.64	3.81	0.25	17.71	2.43	0.50[a]
Getting friends	14.48	3.10	0.21	17.37	3.89	0.52[a]
Keeping friends	12.04	4.75	0.48[b]	15.26	3.31	0.57[a]
Handling problems	10.96	4.14	0.14	15.71	2.73	0.60[a]
Total section III	65.20	16.15	0.38	83.50	13.10	0.66[a]
Grand total	186.50	48.69	0.49[b]	248.20	40.26	0.62[a]

[a] Significant at $P = 0.01$ level.
[b] Significant at $P = 0.05$ level.

Table 2.   Social education AFI scores: correlation with success ratings

	Mean	SD	Correlation
Initial scores (n = 21)			
Reading	12.52	4.96	0.60[a]
Writing	14.24	5.25	0.12
Communication	12.24	4.90	0.16
Concept attention	14.76	3.95	0.37
No. concepts	15.43	3.77	0.23
Time	11.14	5.59	0.09
Money handling	15.90	3.18	−0.02
Community awareness	11.57	5.87	0.13
Motor movements	14.05	7.15	−0.12
Recent scores (n = 25)			
Reading	12.68	5.89	0.23
Writing	14.28	5.82	0.16
Communication	14.24	4.97	0.37
Concept attention	15.16	4.14	0.34
No. concepts	15.64	3.47	0.54[a]
Time	11.84	5.60	0.06
Money handling	16.08	3.14	0.04
Community awareness	12.88	5.29	−0.16
Motor movements	16.32	3.11	0.34

[a] Significant at P = 0.01 levels.

skills scores from being assessed. The variable of scores gained in training could not be accurately assessed given the small sample size.

Additional variables that were not confirmed as good predictors of success were: total time in residential training; whether institutionalized or not; length of time in institutions; referral source if the subject had been in residential training over 5 years; monthly income; source of income (salary or welfare/pension); whether living alone or not; and client self-perception of success in independent living.

Perception of Clients

Some of the problem areas expressed by the clients in the Schalock and Harper study were also concerns of the Calgary clients, albeit at lower levels (money management, loneliness, time management, and parents). Unlike those in the earlier study, the Calgary group did not find housekeeping, meal preparation, or health problematic. Some of the differences were dramatic: 43% of Schalock and Harper's group found meal preparation difficult; none did in Calgary.

Overall there were no major differences between how the successful and the unsuccessful groups of clients liked ILS or rated themselves as to success (Table 3). There were also no major differences between what the two groups liked and disliked about the experience

Table 3. Client versus staff ratings of levels of success and happiness with ILS compared to living in group/family/approved home

	Staff ratings of clients		
	Successful	Failure	Total
Number of clients who saw selves as:			
Successful	8	5	13
Moderately successful	3	4	7
Partially successful	0	1	1
(Subtotal)	(11)	(10)	(21)
Failing	0	1	1
Total	11	11	22
Number of clients who saw selves as:			
Very happy	6	1	7
Happy	4	5	9
Like ILS about the same	1	4	5
Like ILS less than group home	0	1	1
Very unhappy—really dislike ILS	0	0	0
Total	11	11	22

Table 4. Client ($n = 22$) opinions of ILS and staff ratings of clients' success

	Success ratings by staff		
Client opinion	Successful	Failure	Total
"What do you like the best about living on your own?"			
No curfew/free to come and go	9	7	16
No parental interference	1	1	2
No staff interference	2	3	5
Chance to learn new skills and responsibilities	2	3	5
Chance to spend own money	0	1	1
Quiet/privacy	2	4	6
Other	1	2	3
Total			38[a]
"What do you like the least about living on your own?"			
High cost of living—food and/or rent	5	3	8
Loneliness	2	5	7
Boredom in leisure time	0	1	1
Type of apt. (size/location)	4	0	4
Other (e.g., roommate/landlord/neighbor problems)	1	3	4
Subtotal			24[a]
"Nothing wrong—I like it all"	3	2	5
Total			29[a]

[a] May be more than one answer per client.

(Table 4).The most common judgment of all clients was that they are successful and that they are happier in ILS than in their previous residential setting.

Crises Reported in Files

Inter-rater reliability scores of 90% to 97% for the rating of crises were obtained. A relatively small number of incidents occurred to both successful and unsuccessful clients in the year before they entered ILS (mean score: 4.14). The number of incidents did not predict success. There were some differences between the types of incidents that occurred in the two groups: the failed group had more evictions (threatened or actual), more incidents of rent being overdue, theft, or property damage, and more family confrontations that they could not handle alone. These differences were not at a significant level.

The type of incidents that occurred here was far broader than those Nihira and Nihira (1974) had found. The incidents did not fall only in the areas of health and safety; there were 20 incidents reported that involved disorderly conduct in public (drunkenness, property damage), and 25 incidents of overdue rent and subsequent eviction. In addition, clients faced crises when they lost their jobs (22 cases), became involved in a major family confrontation (11), or had severe behavioral/emotional problems (19 incidents).

DISCUSSION

It was possible to examine all the skills that Schalock and Harper had examined—with the exception of visual and auditory processing—using the three parts of the AFI. This instrument, which has high validity and reliability, was shown to be useful in predicting success in ILS. Inspection of the raw scores obtained in the most recent AFI provided specific cutoff scores above which clients tended to succeed in ILS. This was of practical use to the agencies.

Definition of Success

The definition of success in independent living, although important in assessing a program, has not been addressed as an issue by most writers in the field. Schalock and Harper, for example, presented an either/or definition of success with no middle ground. None of the studies reviewed addressed either the issue of possible discrepancy between how the staff views a given client's progress and how the client sees himself, or how to intervene when clients see themselves as successful but staff do not. Although not answering these questions definitively, information presented in the top of Table 3 is of interest. The need for further studies with larger sample sizes is apparent. Future studies should also examine in more detail clients who leave ILS against staff advice, because this group too are functioning as autonomous adults learning to live independently.

Admission Criteria for Independent Living Programs

Admission criteria should pay attention to the factors found to correlate with success. Average scores of every section and of the total obtained on the more recent residential AFI are higher than those obtained when the clients first entered training (Table 1). On the basis of their initial scores, it is hard to predict what new skills clients will gain in training. This study suggests that skillful training can make a difference and that skill level at entry to a residential program may not be the best criterion for selection into ILS. The number of scores gained in training, and the speed at which they are gained, should be examined.

Admission criteria should examine several factors that showed strong relations with success, albeit not at a significant level. For example, whether a client lived alone or with others was not confirmed as a significant predictor variable. Because of the small sample it was necessary to group several subcategories (lives with family; lives in group home; lives with spouse or roommate) into the variable "does not live alone." This may well hide differences between the clients on this variable.

The number and types of crises clients experience in the year before they enter ILS should be noted. Attention should be paid to those individuals who are experiencing problems similar to those reported here. These clients may require "overlearning" (Marlett and Hughson, 1978) in other skill areas to compensate for their specific vulnerability or they may need to show stability before they attempt to live on their own.

The feelings of the individual in an independent living program turn out to be a valid measure to consider. Self-confidence and happiness seem important in determining readiness to try ILS and willingness to risk failure. Staff should be aware of the clients' feelings, not only their objectively measured skills (Rosen et al., 1972). The lack of consistency between correlational studies necessitated turning to measures of emotional functioning (Rosen, 1980, personal communication), such as self-concept and acquiescence, when predicting successful postinstitutional adjustment of mentally handicapped adults.

REFERENCES

Cowgill, M. L., Friedland, S., and Shapiro, R. 1973. Predicting learning disabilities from kindergarten reports. J. Learn. Disabil. 6:577–582.

Crnic, K., and Pym, H. A. 1979. Training mentally retarded adults in independent living. Ment. Retard. 17:13–17.

Katz, M. M., and Lylerly, S. B. 1963. Methods for measuring adjustment and social behaviour in the community. Psychol. Rep. 13:503–535.

Marlett, N. J. 1973. The Adaptive Functioning Index (Section I, II, III). Vocational Rehabilitation and Research Institute, Calgary, Alberta, Canada.

Marlett, N. J., and Hughson, E. A. 1978. Rehabilitation Manual, p. 55. Vocational Rehabilitation and Research Institute, Calgary, Alberta, Canada.

Nihira, L., and Nihira, K. 1974. Jeopardy in community placement. Am. J. Ment. Defic. 7:538–544.

Nooe, R. M. 1975. Toward independent living for the mentally retarded. Social Work 20:286–290.

Nooe, R. M. 1977. Measuring self concepts of mentally retarded adults. Social Work 22:320–322.

Reavis, H. K. 1976. Individual Analysis and Prescription Profiles for Deinstitutionalization. Report, Office of Human Development, Washington, D.C., June.

Reavis, H. K. 1977. Individual Analysis and Prescription Profiles for Deinstitutionalization. Final Report, Office of Human Development, Washington, D.C., June.

Rosen, M., Floor, L., and Baxter, D. 1972. Prediction of community adjustment: A failure at cross-validation. Am. J. Ment. Defic. 77:111–112.

Schalock, R. L., and Harper, R. S. 1978. Placement from community-based retardation programs: How well do clients do? Am. J. Ment. Defic. 83:240–247.

PERSPECTIVES AND PROGRESS IN MENTAL RETARDATION
Volume I—Social, Psychological, and Educational Aspects
Edited by J. M. Berg

COMMUNITY REACTION TO COMMUNITY RESIDENCES
A Study of Factors Related to Community Response

M. M. Seltzer and L. C. Litchfield

School of Social Work, Boston University, 264 Bay State Road, Boston, Massachusetts 02215

This study examined the prevalence and correlates of community opposition to community residences. It was found that approximately half the residences encountered opposition, and that opposition is highest during the period immediately before and immediately after the residence opens (subsequently it diminishes considerably). In addition, opposition was least likely to be encountered when the community was made aware of its existence *after* the residents moved in, suggesting that "low profile" entry strategies may be advantageous.

A key objective of the community residence (CR) movement is to enable mentally retarded persons to interact with the general community to the maximum extent possible. However, a problem commonly encountered is opposition from neighbors, local officials, or others who express various fears about the negative consequences that might result from the location of a residence for mentally retarded persons in a particular neighborhood. In response to community opposition, some governmental agencies that regulate CRs have developed policies to minimize the problem or to handle it when it arises. Certain policies have encouraged or required groups planning to open a CR to conduct

Preparation of this manuscript was supported in part by a grant from the National Science Foundation through a subcontract from the Boston Neighborhood Network.

public education activities. Although public education is assumed to have a positive effect, there is little evidence available about its actual effectiveness in reducing community opposition.

A few empirical studies about the broader issue of community opposition have been published. These studies have reported the percentage of CRs experiencing community opposition to be between 25% and 35% (Johnson, 1976; O'Connor, 1976; Baker et al., 1977; Lubin et al., 1982). These rates undoubtedly underestimate the magnitude of the problem, because they do not include CRs that failed to open or that closed prematurely because of community opposition. O'Connor (1976) and Lubin et al. (1982) reported that opposition decreases dramatically after a CR begins operation. However, the reasons for this decrease in opposition over time, and the reasons for opposition prior to the opening of the CR, remain largely unknown.

PURPOSE AND METHODOLOGY

The purpose of this study was to provide descriptive data about community acceptance of and opposition to CRs, and about the various types of community education efforts that have been utilized. The sample of CRs included in the present analysis consisted of 43 facilities that had the following features: 1) provision of room and board to clients; 2) provision of some degree of staff supervision to clients; 3) paid staff members; 4) private nonprofit or for-profit sponsorship; 5) no provision of medical care to clients; and 6) no provision of a formal treatment program during daytime hours. The 43 participating CRs constituted 86% of all facilities serving mentally retarded clients in the city of Boston and in six neighboring cities and towns.

In order to gather information about these CRs, telephone interviews were conducted by trained research assistants. In more than three-quarters of the sample, these interviews were conducted with the executive director or program director of the residence. In some instances, a second person (usually a board member) was contacted to provide supplemental information not available to the primary interviewee. The interviews were structured, and consisted of five sections including questions about: 1) the residents of the facility; 2) the staff; 3) the facility itself; 4) the neighborhood in which the residence was located; and 5) the history of community responses to the CR (both support and opposition).

FINDINGS

Description of the Residents and Staff

The average number of residents per CR was 5.9, of whom 4.8 had previously lived in institutions. Of the 43 CRs, most (32) had at least one moderately retarded client, and almost half (18) had one or more mildly retarded clients. Only 5 had one or more severely retarded clients. Over half (25) served both men and women, and all but one CR served adult clients. The mean age of the clients was 33.8 years. The average length of stay in the residences was 41.8 months, with a client turnover rate of 12.5% during the year prior to the study.

An average of four full-time staff worked at each residence; one staff person on the average came from the neighborhood in which the residence was located. In 35 of the CRs, staff coverage was either 24 hours a day or all of the time when the residents were present. During the year before the research was conducted, the average staff turnover rate was 34%.

Description of the Facility and Neighborhood

The majority of the CRs (26) in the sample occupied either all or part of multiple-unit dwellings (apartment buildings, duplexes, two- and three-family houses), reflecting the urban character of the geographic area of the study. The condition of the exterior of the building was reported to be good or excellent in 41 cases. The average CR had 11 rooms (range 5–32), of which an average of five were used as client bedrooms. Most (26) of the buildings in which the residences were located were rented by the sponsoring organization; the remainder were owned by the sponsoring corporation. At the time of the research, the residences had been open for an average of 2.6 years.

The CRs were located an average of two blocks from public transportation, seven blocks from a fire station, and eight blocks from shops. Neighborhoods were evenly divided between lower class/lower-middle class and middle class/upper-middle class. Most respondents (32) characterized the neighborhood in which the CR was located as being either stable or somewhat stable.

History of Community Opposition, Support, and Education

Opposition from the community was encountered by slightly less than half (21) of the residences. The opposition generally was relatively mild; the two most frequent types of opposition were general lack of acceptance and complaints to government officials (each experienced by one-third of the sample). In contrast, the following more severe types of opposition were encountered by fewer than 10% of the residences: protest letters, negative newspaper articles, lobbying, negative testimony at public hearings, petitions, legal actions, zoning disputes, vandalism, verbal threats, and picketing of the facility. Reasons given for community opposition were fears about resident behavior (15 CRs), safety (10 CRs), lowered property values (6 CRs), and an increased

Table 1. Mean rating of opposition, support, and public education at four points in time

	Time 1 (>6 months prior)	Time 2 (0–6 months prior)	Time 3 (0–6 months after)	Time 4 present
Opposition	1.60	1.89	1.92	1.38
Support	2.17	2.57	2.68	3.15
Education	2.32	2.46	2.42	2.04

crime rate (3 CRs). Interestingly, over half (24) of the CRs had previously attempted to open in a location other than the one in which they were located at the time of the research. In 12 of these cases, the change in location was reported to be provoked by community opposition.

Public education was conducted by 25 of the residences. The more commonly reported types of public education were informal contact with neighbors (17 CRs), open houses (13 CRs), contact with civic groups (11 CRs), and contact with local government officials (10 CRs).

Most community residences (35) reported receiving at least one type of support from the community. All of these CRs reported that the neighbors were friendly. In addition, a number of specific supports were reported by some CRs, including help from neighbors with the upkeep of the facility (25 CRs), invitations to community activities (13 CRs), and positive telephone calls made to government officials (9 CRs).

Table 1 presents estimates obtained from respondents regarding the extent of opposition encountered, support received, and public education activities conducted at four points in time: 1) more than 6 months before the CR opened, 2) between 6 months before the CR opened and the time of opening, 3) between the time the CR opened and 6 months after it opened, and 4) at the time of the research. These estimates were made on a 4-point scale ranging from 1 (none) to 4 (a great deal).

As shown in Table 1, opposition from the community was reported to increase slightly from Time 1 to Time 2 and from Time 2 to Time 3, with a decline in opposition between Time 3 and Time 4. The extent of community education followed a similar pattern. In contrast, support from the community was estimated to have increased at each successive time period, with the increase from Time 3 to Time 4 being most pronounced. These data suggest that relationships between CRs and communities are most problematic prior to the opening of the residences and during the first 6 months of operation; subsequently, support appears to grow and opposition to diminish.

Table 2.   Neighbors' initial and current attitude toward the CR

	Initial attitude (%)	Current attitude (%)
Very negative	11.1	2.4
Somewhat negative	25.0	0.0
Neutral	36.1	31.8
Somewhat positive	22.2	51.2
Very positive	5.6	14.6
	100.0	100.0

The respondents were also asked to characterize the neighborhood's first reaction to the CR and the neighborhood's attitude at the time of the research. These ratings appear in Table 2 and further support the existence of a shift in community attitude over time from negative to positive. Respondents reported that an average of 1 year elapsed before community attitudes began to change to their current level.

Time of First Community Awareness and
Subsequent Community Relationship with Community Residence

Respondents were asked to indicate when the community first became aware of the intended or actual existence of the CR. In 12 of the CRs, community awareness occurred more than 6 months before the CR opened. In 16 of the cases, the community became aware during the 6-month period that preceded the opening of the CR. In 15 of the CRs, the community did not become aware of the CR until after it opened. As shown in Table 3, the least opposition was reported for communities that became aware of the CR *after* it began operation. Significant differences were also reported among the three groups in the number of types of opposition encountered, with the fewest types of opposition encountered by CRs for which community awareness came *after* their opening. Surprisingly, the relationship between time of first community awareness of the CR and the probability that a

Table 3.   Time of first community awareness and opposition

	Resistance encountered	# Types of resistance
Group 1 (>6 mos. prior)	0.546	1.909
Group 2 (0–6 mos. prior)	0.733	2.333
Group 3 (0–6 mos. after)	0.214	0.429
F	4.574	3.271
P	0.0168	0.0492

community would be *supportive* of the residence was found not to be statistically significant; over 70% of the CRs in all three groups reported some community support.

Those who are opening the residence must ultimately be responsible for selecting the best strategy regarding how and when to inform the community. This decision will vary according to specific circumstances and individual preferences. However, it should be noted that the risks of community opposition are probably more serious than those of failing to gain community support, because the former risks are likely to be more detrimental to the existence of the CR and hence to the clients themselves. Such risks are undoubtedly even greater than is evident in findings presented in this paper, because the study did not gather data about residences that attempted to open but failed to do so because of community opposition.

CONCLUSIONS

In conclusion, the findings of this study suggest that if the community becomes aware of the proposed CR shortly before it opens, opposition is most likely to be encountered. In light of these findings, it appears that the best way to minimize opposition is either by informing the community very early (more than 6 months before opening) or at some time after the residents have moved into the facility.

Finally, as was discussed earlier, once a CR is established, the relationship between the community residence and the community in which it is located becomes increasingly positive. Over time, opposition was reported to decrease and support was reported to increase irrespective of any initial opposition that may have been encountered. These findings suggest that policymakers would be wise to carefully select the point in time at which the community is first made aware of the CR. Additional research focusing on the reasons for shifts in community attitudes over time would be useful for policymakers, as well as for those who operate community residences.

REFERENCES

Baker, B. L., Seltzer, G. B., and Seltzer, M. M. 1977. As Close as Possible: Community Residences for Retarded Adults. Little, Brown & Company, Boston.
Johnson, G. R. 1976. Sources of neighborhood opposition to community residence programs. Unpublished doctoral dissertation, Harvard University.

Lubin, R. A., Schwartz, A. A., Zigman, W. B., and Janicki, M. P. 1982. Community acceptance of residential programs for developmentally disabled. Appl. Res. Ment. Retard. 3:191–200.

O'Connor, G. 1976. Home is a Good Place: A National Perspective on Community Residential Facilities for Developmentally Disabled Persons. Monograph No. 2, American Association on Mental Deficiency, Washington, D.C.

PERSPECTIVES AND PROGRESS IN MENTAL RETARDATION
Volume I—Social, Psychological, and Educational Aspects
Edited by J. M. Berg

GROUP HOME EMPLOYEE JOB ATTITUDES AND SATISFACTIONS

W. B. Zigman,[1] **A. A. Schwartz,**[2] **and M. P. Janicki**[3]
[1] *New York State Institute for Basic Research in Developmental Disabilities, 1050 Forest Hill Road, Staten Island, New York 10314*
[2] *New York State Office of Mental Retardation and Developmental Disabilities, New York, New York 10047*
[3] *New York State Office of Mental Retardation and Developmental Disabilities, 44 Holland Avenue, Albany, New York 12229*

This study identified group home employee characteristics, and related these characteristics to the homes' social environment and resident characteristics. A significant relationship was noted between the mean number of resident developmental disabilities, mean staff work hours, and the provision of a more normalized group home program. The absence of relationships among staff characteristics and other characteristics of the social environment was noted. Comments were offered about the need for further research. The relationship between resident disability characteristics and low job satisfaction was described, along with the need to address the problem of low job satisfaction levels among employees in residences for severely disabled persons.

The major goal of the deinstitutionalization of persons with mental retardation has been to replace the isolated and sheltered environment of the institution with a more normalized system of community care and services. In the United States, for example, the national institutional population has been steadily declining, while the number of persons living in community residential options has been increasing (Braddock, 1981). The community residence or group home is one of the community living options that has seen a dramatic increase in development and utilization (Janicki et al., 1983).

There has been much speculation as to which aspects of group homes contribute most to resident well-being and skill attainment (Hull and Thompson, 1980; Lakin et al., 1981). Clearly, certain aspects of the social environment, such as normativeness (Hull and Thompson, 1981) and management style (Pratt et al., 1980), are major factors differentiating residential setting effectiveness. However, it may be that the factor mediating social environmental effects is the staff employed within the settings. Indeed, it has been proposed (McCord, 1981) that staff are a major determinant of the style and quality of life in residential settings. Hence, the characteristics, attitudes, and job satisfaction of persons employed in community residences should be considered when assessing the effects of group home living on mentally retarded or developmentally disabled persons.

Descriptions of characteristics of group home employees can be found in a number of reports (e.g., O'Connor, 1976; Baker et al., 1977; Dellinger and Shope, 1978; Felsenthal and Scheerenberger, 1978; Pratt et al., 1980; George and Baumeister, 1981). These studies have mainly presented data regarding demographic and/or attitudinal characteristics of group home staff. For example, both Dellinger and Shope (1978) and George and Baumeister (1981) described staff demographics (e.g., gender, age, and marital status). George and Baumeister further analyzed staff turnover, absenteeism, and job satisfaction but did not present the relationships among demographics, attitudes, and the group home environment or its residents. Felsenthal and Scheerenberger (1978) reported descriptive information relating both to demographic and attitudinal characteristics of residence staff, but they too did not discuss the relationships between these factors and additional characteristics of the residence environment. A limited relationship between staff attitudes and care practices was noted by Pratt et al. (1980); they found that staff professing equality with residents were employed in more resident-centered homes. Several national surveys (e.g., O'Connor, 1976; Baker et al., 1977) have provided descriptive data on staff demographics and attitudes, but did not address the social environment of the residential settings.

The generalizability of this body of research is limited by a number of factors. For example, with the exception of the larger national surveys, many reported outcomes were based upon: 1) relatively few residential programs; 2) a small number of staff; 3) staff who performed various job functions; 4) programs of different types and sizes; or 5) data that did not measure additional aspects of the environment or its residents. The national surveys, despite having a more representative data base, were also limited in depth. Given these limitations, the present investigation was designed to provide a more comprehensive analysis of demographic and attitudinal characteristics of group home staff. Specifically, this investigation describes the demographic and attitudinal characteristics of group home staff, and identifies associations between staff characteristics and aspects of both the residences' social environment and resident demographics.

For the purpose of this research, group homes were defined as residences that provide supervised housing and therapeutic care for up to 14 mentally retarded/developmentally disabled persons in a community setting. The term "group home staff" refers to any person providing services within the residence environment.

METHOD

As part of a larger study (Zigman et al., 1982) of the approximately 500 group homes existing in New York State as of August, 1980, selected data were collected from a random sample of 50 of these settings. The group homes were located throughout the state of New York and had been in operation prior to June, 1979. They were operated by both the state's developmental disabilities agency (10%) and by nonprofit voluntary agencies (90%). The homes were certified as either supervised living facilities (SLFs) or as intermediate care facilities for the developmentally disabled (ICFs/DD). SLFs are cooperative group living homes providing board, supervision, and a range of training experience. ICFs/DD differ from conventional group homes in that they are designed for residents with more severe disabilities and are more service intensive.

Measures of staff demographic characteristics were provided by the Demographic Questionnaire (DQ). This instrument is a 20-page survey booklet comprised of 86 items within nine sections (Living Alternatives Research Project, 1981). DQ information used in the present investigation was collected as part of an earlier statewide survey of all group homes. The questionnaires were completed by the administrator of each home during the period August, 1980, to February, 1981.

Two measures provided data on staff attitudinal characteristics: the Job Descriptive Index (JDI: Smith et al., 1969); and the Residence Personnel Opinion Scale (RPOS; Living Alternatives Research Project, 1981). The JDI is comprised of five subscales that measure staff satisfaction with work, supervision, pay, promotions, and coworkers. High scores on any subscale indicate satisfaction with that particular aspect of the job situation. The RPOS is a modification of the Attendant Opinion Scale (Bensberg and Barnett, 1966) used to assess staff attitudes toward mentally retarded persons and their care in institutional settings. The Attendant Opinion Scale was modified to more accurately reflect the employment situation in a group home setting. Twelve categories, containing five statements each, constituted the RPOS. JDI and RPOS data were completed by individual staff members and were collected during on-site visits to each group home during the period August 1980 to October 1981.

Measures of resident adaptive functioning and disability status were provided by the Developmental Disabilities Information System (Janicki and Jacobson, 1979; 1982), a needs assessment and client information instrument that collects a broad spectrum of data on developmentally disabled persons within New York State.

RESULTS

In order to retain the residence as the unit of analysis, the data regarding staff demographics and attitudes as well as resident characteristics were aggregated from means of each variable for each home in the sample.

Descriptive Analyses

Group Home Residents   The mean number of residents per home was 10; the range was between 6 and 14. The mean resident age ranged from 18 to 66, with a grand mean (i.e., an average across all of the group homes) of 36.0. The mean level of functioning of residents ranged from mild to profound intellectual impairment, with a grand mean in the range of moderate impairment. Individuals in the residences had disabilities including mental retardation, autism, cerebral palsy, epilepsy, and other types of neurological impairments. The mean number of such categorical developmental disabilities per resident ranged from 0.9 to 2, with a grand mean of 1.2.

Staff Demographic Characteristics   The group homes employed an estimated 400 individuals in staff positions; 70.7% were female and 29.3% male. Mean staff age ranged from 22.4 to 48.7, with a grand mean of 30.8. Employees reported a grand mean of 14.6 years of education; over 68% of the homes had staff with a mean of 2 or more years of college education. Mean years of work experience in developmental disabilities among staff ranged from 0.5 to 8.6, with a grand mean of 2.9.

The mean staff work week reported was 34.2 hours with a range between 8.4 and 60 hours. Regarding salaries for direct care staff and group home program administrators, 100% and 84% earned less than US$13,000 and US$16,000, respectively, per annum.

Staff Attitudes and Job Satisfaction   Table 1 presents the means and ranges for each staff attitude and job satisfaction subscale. Although attitudes varied across homes, in general group home staff reported positive attitudes toward the care of mentally retarded/developmentally disabled persons. For example, staff disagreed with scale items ad-

Table 1.   Staff attitudinal measures

	Mean	Range
Residence Personnel Opinion Scale[a]		
Negative physical care	11.8	7.3–15.5
Job rejection	9.6	5.5–14.0
Push to accelerate development	14.0	10.0–20.0
Negative ward management	13.3	9.0–18.0
Comradeship with residents	17.8	15.7–19.7
Job insecurity	10.3	6.0–17.0
Institutional identification	14.4	11.8–19.0
Encourage verbalization	18.3	14.0–20.0
Irritability with residents	11.1	8.3–16.0
Equality	15.3	12.8–17.8
Strictness	11.2	7.3–17.5
Fostering dependency	8.9	5.5–12.7
Job Descriptive Index[b]		
Work	37.7	22.5–48.0
Supervision	46.4	28.4–54.0
Promotions	12.0	3.3–23.8
Pay	9.0	2.5–22.0
Coworkers	45.2	37.6–54.0

[a] Scores range from 5 to 20, indicating strong and total disagreement to strong and total agreement.
[b] Scores on the Work, Supervision, and Coworkers subscales range from 0 to 54; scores on the Promotions and Pay subscales range from 0 to 27. Higher scores indicate greater satisfaction.

dressing negative aspects of residence employment (e.g., job rejection), and beliefs that staff should abridge residents' autonomy (e.g., fostering dependency). Staff reported mild to strong agreement with items depicting positive aspects of residence care, such as comradeship with residents, equality, and a subscale measuring residents' freedom of expression.

Mean staff job satisfaction data also revealed variability. Staff reported general satisfaction with three aspects of their employment situation: the work itself, supervision, and coworkers. However, the mean and minimum scores for the two subscales measuring promotions and pay were much reduced, indicating a lesser degree of satisfaction.

Social Environment and Resident Correlates
of Staff Demographics and Attitudes

A two-stage series of analyses were performed to determine which characteristics of group home employees were associated with certain features of the group homes' social environment and residents. Initially, a factor analysis of the mean residence scale scores for the RPOS and the JDI was conducted in order to reduce the number of staff

Table 2.   Factor structure of attitudinal staff variables

Attitudinal staff variables	Factors				
	I	II	III	IV	V
Negative physical care			0.65		
Job rejection	−0.57				
Push to accelerate development		0.63			
Negative ward management			0.44		
Comradeship with residents				0.52	
Job insecurity		0.83			
Institutional identification	0.52				
Encourage verbalization				0.83	
Irritability with residents			0.64		
Equality				0.71	
Strictness		0.73			
Fostering dependency					0.94
Work	0.52				
Supervision	0.65				
Promotions			−0.39		
Pay	0.56				
Coworkers	0.68				

attitudinal variables. Principal factoring with Quartimax rotation was utilized. Five resultant factors had eigenvalues greater than 1, and accounted for 68% of the total variance of the staff attitudinal variables. Subscales loaded on the five factors as outlined in Table 2.

Six subscales loaded highly on the first factor and seemed to define a construct measuring "positive job attitudes." For example, four JDI subscales measuring attitudes toward work, supervision, pay, and coworkers were all highly and positively related to this factor. The second factor appeared to relate to issues of "staff control" as measured by three RPOS subscales (Push to Accelerate Development, Job Insecurity, and Strictness). Together, these subscales indicate a desire by employees to control the work environment and the group home residents for whom they care. The construct underlying Factor III appeared to be related to "negative job demands." Specifically, subscales measuring negative attitudes toward the home and its residents (e.g., Negative Physical Care and Irritability with Residents) tended to load highly on this factor. Factor IV appeared to be related to "staff-resident affiliation," because the three subscales that loaded on this factor were all measures of affiliation. Finally, Factor V ("restriction of autonomy") was highly loaded on by one subscale, Fostering Dependency, which measured the extent to which staff believe in the need to restrict residents' autonomy.

The second stage of the analyses, designed to determine the social environment and resident correlates of staff demographic and attitudinal characteristics, included two separate statistical procedures. Three social environment variables and two resident variables were the dependent measures used for these procedures. The variables defining the social environment were derived from previous research that investigated the social-environment of group home settings (Zigman and Silverman, 1982). These variables were derived through a factor analysis of three research instruments: the Group Home Management Schedule (Pratt et al., 1977), the Characteristics of the Treatment Environment (Jackson, 1964), and a short form of the Program Analysis of Service Systems (Flynn and Heal, 1981). The three variables were: 1) "institutional identification," which assesses the degree to which group homes restrict residents' individuality, independence, and self-sufficiency; 2) "normalization," which measures the normativeness of residence settings; and 3) "recreational activities," which assesses the variety and frequency of social and recreational activities available to home residents. The two resident variables included a measure of the mean group home level of resident intellectual functioning and the mean number of categorical developmental disabilities per resident. These two variables were selected on the basis of prior research that related the attitudes of staff to resident disability level (Zaharia and Baumeister, 1978).

The first data-analytic procedure included a series of four stepwise multiple regression analyses. The dependent variables in these analyses consisted of the three social environment factors and the mean number of resident disabilities. The independent predictor variables (i.e., staff demographics and attitudinal factor scores) included in these analyses were those variables that were found to be significantly related (i.e., $P < 0.05$) to the dependent variables. To control for the significant correlations of administrative (i.e., certification type—either supervised living facility or intermediate care facility) and resident (i.e., mean functional level) variables with certain characteristics of the homes' social environment, these variables were included as independent predictor variables in the regression equation involving "institutional identification." Additionally, because of significant correlations between these variables, the mean number of resident categorical developmental disabilities was included as a predictor variable in the regression equation dealing with "normalization."

Table 3 presents the results of the four regression analyses. The analyses regarding social environment factors ("institutional identification," "normalization," and "recreational activities") yielded two significant prediction equations. Mean resident level of intellectual functioning was a significant predictor of "institutional identification." Specifically, group homes in which the mean level of resident intel-

Table 3.   Multiple regression analyses

Variable	Beta	Multiple r	r^2	F
Institutional identification				
Mean resident functional level	0.51	0.62	0.38	15.5[a]
Restriction of autonomy	0.21	0.66	0.43	2.3
Mean staff education	−0.14	0.67	0.45	1.4
Certification type	0.02	0.67	0.45	0.1
Normalization				
Mean number of resident developmental disabilities	−0.33	0.32	0.10	5.6[b]
Mean staff hours	0.30	0.44	0.19	4.6[c]
Recreational activities				
Mean staff hours	0.25	0.28	0.08	2.6[d]
Staff resident affiliation	−0.14	0.31	0.10	0.9
Mean number of resident developmental disabilities				
Restriction of autonomy	0.39	0.39	0.16	8.6[e]

[a] D.f. = 1, 40; $P < 0.01$.
[b] D.f. = 1, 41; $P < 0.05$.
[c] $P < 0.05$.
[d] D.f. = 1, 40.
[e] D.f. = 1, 47; $P < 0.01$.

lectual functioning was low scored higher on this factor. It was found that these homes tended to provide services in a regimented manner that restricted residents' individuality and independence. The prediction equation involving the "normalization" factor revealed that homes in which staff worked a greater mean number of hours and in which the residents had a lesser mean number of developmental disabilities tended to be more normalized. The regression equation involving the social environment factor "recreational activities" revealed no significant predictor variables. The regression equation relating staff characteristics to the mean number of resident disabilities yielded one significant predictor variable. Group homes scoring high on the factor measuring "restriction of autonomy" tended to have residents that had a greater mean number of developmental disabilities.

The second data-analytic procedure was conducted to explore the relationship between mean resident level of functioning and the significantly correlated independent staff variables "positive job attitudes" and "restriction of autonomy." In order to control for the significant correlation of certification type with each of these variables, two separate analyses of variance were conducted. The staff attitude variables served as the dependent measures and certification type and mean level of resident intellectual functioning served as the indepen-

Table 4. Analyses of variance

Source of variation	Sum of squares	d.f.	Mean square	F
Dependent variable: positive job attitude				
Functional level	4.102	1	4.102	5.876[a]
Certification type	1.502	1	1.502	2.151
Functional level by certification type	0.098	1	0.098	0.140
Dependent variable: restriction of autonomy				
Functional level	1.951	1	1.951	2.464
Certification type	5.928	1	5.928	7.484[b]
Functional level by certification type	1.000	1	1.000	1.262

[a] $P < 0.05$.
[b] $P < 0.01$.

dent variables. A median split of the group homes' score on mean level of resident intellectual functioning served to dichotomize the total sample of 50 homes into two groups: homes with higher-functioning residents, and homes with lower-functioning residents. Table 4 presents the results of these two analyses. There was a significant relationship between mean level of resident functioning and "positive job attitudes." Homes in which the mean resident level of functioning was higher tended to have staff who expressed more positive attitudes about their work. The factor "restriction of autonomy" did not vary as a function of mean resident level of functioning; however, it did vary significantly as a function of certification type. Staff in ICFs/DD professed greater agreement with statements regarding the need to restrict residents' autonomy.

DISCUSSION

The present study identified group home staff characteristics, and related these characteristics to aspects of the homes' social environment and their resident population. In general, staff employed within the sampled homes were young, well educated, and experienced. These data both agree and conflict with other studies describing demographic characteristics of group home staff (e.g., Dellinger and Shope, 1978; Felsenthal and Scheerenberger, 1978; George and Baumeister, 1981). However, it is believed that the differences in reported staff characteristics reflect variations in both sampling strategies across studies and hiring and staff patterns among the various jurisdictions in which the studies were conducted. Staff attitudes toward mentally retarded/developmentally disabled persons and their care in community residential settings were generally found to be positive, although sufficient variability was observed in the data to indicate that these attitudes were not necessarily pervasive. Satisfaction was reported with those aspects of the employment situation related to the work itself, supervisors, and coworkers; lower levels of satisfaction were associated with pay and promotions. Dissatisfaction with these latter aspects may reflect discordance between the educational level and occupational expectations of residence staff and the existing pay scale and lack of promotional possibilities in the homes.

Noteworthy among our findings was the evidence of a significant relationship between the mean number of resident developmental disabilities, mean staff work hours, and the social environment factor "normalization." This finding indicates that the provision of normative community residential services is a function of both resident and staff attributes. Specifically, our results showed that persons who are multiply disabled tend to live in less normative settings. We found also that homes in which staff work a greater mean number of hours appear to be more normative. This may be indicative of a pattern in which staff who were more concerned about creating and sustaining a normalized environment were also the kind of individuals who were willing to work more hours. Presently, however, this hypothesis must be considered as conjecture. Further research needs to be conducted to examine this association.

The absence of findings relating other staff characteristics to social environment characteristics (i.e., "institutional identification" and "recreational activities") may have occurred for several reasons. The process of aggregating staff data may have affected the analytic procedures that we used by reducing variability. However, the option of assigning group home environment data to each staff member would have artificially increased the degrees of freedom, thereby creating spurious relationships. It may also be that the independent variables employed were not sensitive to these aspects of the social environment. Further research might focus on other variables that may affect these aspects of the social environment.

Our findings also indicated that staff employed in group homes in which residents had a greater mean number of disabilities tended to hold beliefs that residents should be dependent on staff. These data are not surprising given that residents who are multidisabled are likely to be more dependent on staff. In fact, this expressed attitude of staff may be a realistic outgrowth of actual resident needs. Consistent with other reports (e.g.,Dellinger and Shope, 1978; Zaharia and Baumeister, 1978), our findings indicated that job satisfaction is related to resident functional level. Specifically, staff employed in homes with lower-functioning residents tended to exhibit less positive attitudes toward their jobs. Zaharia and Baumeister (1978) and Sarata (1974) have hypothesized that a resident's disability level is an important determinant of growth and development; therefore working with persons who are significantly impaired may be less satisfactory. Because a greater number of more severely disabled persons are being placed in community settings, and will continue to be so placed, it is vital that appropriate staff attitudes and expectations be fostered through training so as to minimize job dissatisfaction resulting from slow resident progress.

REFERENCES

Baker, B. L., Seltzer, G. B., and Seltzer, M. M. 1977. As Close As Possible: Community Residences for Retarded Adults. Little, Brown & Company, Boston.

Bensberg, G. J., and Barnett, C. D. 1966. Attendant Training in Southern Residential Facilities for the Mentally Retarded. Southern Regional Educational Board, Atlanta.

Braddock, D. 1981. Deinstitutionalization of the retarded: Trends in public policy. Hosp. Commun. Psychiatry 32:607–615.

Dellinger, J. K., and Shope, L. J. 1978. Selected characteristics and working conditions of direct service staff in Pennsylvania CLAs. Ment. Retard. 16:19–21.

Felsenthal, D., and Scheerenberger, R. C. 1978. Stability and attitudes of primary caregivers in the community. Ment. Retard. 16:16–18.

Flynn, R. J., and Heal, L. W. 1981. A short form of PASS 3: A study of its structures, interrater reliability, and validity for assessing normalization. Eval. Rev. 5:357–376.

George, M. J., and Baumeister, A. A. 1981. Employee withdrawal and job satisfaction in community residential facilities for mentally retarded persons. Am. J. Ment. Defic. 85:639–647.

Hull, J. T., and Thompson, J. C. 1980. Predicting adaptive functioning of mentally retarded persons in community settings. Am. J. Ment. Defic. 85:253–261.

Hull, J. T., and Thompson, J. C. 1981. Factors contributing to normalization in residential facilities for mentally retarded persons. Ment. Retard. 19:69–73.

Jackson, J. 1964. Toward the comparative study of mental hospitals: Characteristics of the treatment environment. In: A. F. Wesson (ed.), The Psychiatric Hospital as a Social System. Charles C Thomas Publisher, Springfield, Illinois.

Janicki, M. P., and Jacobson, J. W. 1979. New York's Needs Assessment and Developmental Disabilities: Preliminary Report. (Technical Monograph #79-10). New York State Office of Mental Retardation and Developmental Disabilities, Albany.

Janicki, M. P., and Jacobson, J. W. 1982. The character of developmental disabilities in New York State: Preliminary observations. Int. J. Rehab. Res. 5:191–202.

Janicki, M. P., Mayeda, T., and Eppel, W. 1983. Availability of group homes for persons with mental retardation in the United States. Ment. Retard. 21:45–51.

Lakin, K. C., Bruininks, R. H., and Sigford, B. B. 1981. Deinstitutionalization and community-based residential adjustment: A summary of research and issues. In: R. Bruininks, C. Meyers, B. Sigford, and K. Lakin (eds.), Deinstitutionalization and Community Adjustment of Mentally Retarded People. American Association on Mental Deficiency, Washington, D.C.

Living Alternatives Research Project. 1981. The Identification and Description of Environmental Conditions Affecting Growth in Personal Competence of Persons with Developmental Disabilities: Phase One (Final Report). New York State Institute for Basic Research in Developmental Disabilities, Staten Island.

McCord, W. T. 1981. Community residences: The staffing. In: J. Wortis (ed.), Mental Retardation and Developmental Disabilities, Vol. 12. Brunner/Mazel Publishers, New York.

O'Connor, G. 1976. Home is a Good Place: A National Perspective of Community Residential Facilities for Developmentally Disabled Persons. Monograph No. 2. American Association on Mental Deficiency, Washington, D.C.

Pratt, M. W., Luszcz, M. A., and Brown, M. E. 1980. Measuring dimensions of the quality of care in small community residences. Am. J. Ment. Defic. 85:188–194.

Pratt, M. W., Luszcz, M. A., and Roses, S. 1977. Organizational characteristics and their relationship to quality of care. In: P. Mittler (ed.), Research to Practice in Mental Retardation: Vol. 1. Care and Intervention. University Park Press, Baltimore.

Sarata, B. 1974. Employee satisfaction in agencies serving retarded persons. Am. J. Ment. Defic. 79:434–442.

Smith, P. C., Kendall, L. M., and Hulin, C. 1969. The Measurement of Satisfaction in Work and Retirement. Rand McNally and Co., Chicago.

Zaharia, E. S., and Baumeister, A. A. 1978. Technician turnover and absenteeism in public residential facilities. Am. J. Ment. Defic. 82:580–593.

Zigman, W. B., Lubin, R. A., and Janicki, M. P. 1982. Characteristics of community residences for developmentally disabled persons. Technical Monograph 82-2. New York State Institute for Basic Research in Developmental Disabilities, Staten Island.

Zigman, W. B., and Silverman, W. P. 1982. Socio-environmental characteristics of community residential environments. Paper presented as part of a symposium at the 106th Annual Meeting of the American Association on Mental Deficiency, Boston, Massachusetts.

SECTION VII
Parental Perceptions and Needs

PERSPECTIVES AND PROGRESS IN MENTAL RETARDATION
Volume I—Social, Psychological, and Educational Aspects
Edited by J. M. Berg

PARENTS' PERCEPTIONS OF THE BEHAVIORAL CHARACTERISTICS OF THEIR SCHOOL-AGE CHILDREN WITH DOWN'S SYNDROME

D. Spiker, C. P. Peterson, and G. F. Smith
Illinois Masonic Medical Center, 836 W. Wellington Avenue, Chicago, Illinois 60657

To look for stereotypes of distinct personalities within the population of children with Down's syndrome, data were examined using cluster analysis techniques. Subgroups of Down's syndrome children were based on the total sorting patterns done by their mothers. These data suggest that there may be significant variations in the ways that parents describe the personality characteristics of their Down's syndrome children. The amiable, cheerful stereotype of the Down's syndrome child may not represent a unique style, at least when compared with mental age–matched normal children who are also described as amiable and cheerful. The existence of a higher than expected tendency for stubbornness needs to be explored further. Finally, these data suggest that self-esteem, social comparison, and self-knowledge of school-age Down's syndrome children are important areas for further research.

Stereotypes about special or unique personality patterns of persons with Down's syndrome (DS) have persisted since Langdon Down's (1866) original description, which included the observations that:

> They have considerable powers of imitation, even bordering on being mimics. They are humorous . . . a lively sense of the ridiculous often colours their mimicry; . . .They have a strong sense of the ridiculous; . . . Another feature is their great obstinacy—they can only be guided by consummate tact. . . . They are always amiable both to their companions and to animals. They are not passionate nor strongly affectionate.

Gibson (1978) summarized persistent personality descriptions of persons with DS and discussed empirical evidence for their validity. He noted that persons with the syndrome have been described as "affable, mischievous, docile, aggressive, affectionate, stubborn, pleasing and self-willed"; some of these traits are contradictory. He reviewed the evidence for the possibility of two distinct types: a lively, amiable, docile, and cheerful type, and a reticent, aggressive, negativistic type.

The evidence for a unique DS personality (or a dichotomous typology) is far from conclusive. Several important points regarding previous research in this area must be considered. The variable educability in DS populations has been noted, but much of the current knowledge is based on individuals reared in institutions (Rynders et al., 1978). The same problem exists in studies about personality (Smith and Berg, 1976; Gibson, 1978). This problem is important because there are at least two major differences in the life experiences of persons reared in institutions that have much relevance for the development of personality: 1) the general lack of consistent, significant interpersonal attachments, which provide for the emotional, social, and motivational foundations of personality development (Ainsworth et al., 1978); and 2) the often unstimulating, unchallenging, routinized daily living experiences of institutional living, which may lead to a limited range of expression of social or emotional behavioral styles.

Because many studies about the personality characteristics of DS individuals have focused on institutionalized persons, it is important to examine personality and behavioral characteristics in contemporary populations that are reared in a home environment. Of interest are both the similarities and the variability in personality descriptions in school-age children with Down's syndrome.

METHOD

Fifty-three mothers with home-reared DS children (37 males and 16 females) between the ages of $5\frac{1}{2}$ and $15\frac{1}{2}$ years (mean age of almost 10 years) were asked to complete a Q-sort. The Q-sort method was originally devised by Stephenson (1936) and has been expanded for other uses by the Blocks (Block, 1961; Block and Block, 1980b). It involves arranging descriptive items about a person according to their degree of salience for the person. Items are arranged into categories; those most and least characteristic of the person are given high and low scores, respectively. In this study, mothers sorted the California Child Q-Sort (Block and Block, 1980a). This instrument consists of 100 widely ranging statements of personality/psychological characteristics that are descriptive of normal preschool-age children, and correspond with the mental ages of the children in this sample. [All children were given the Peabody Picture Vocabulary Test—Revised (Form L); their mean age equivalent was 4.3 years (SD = 1.5 years).]

Mothers were instructed to sort the cards into categories from one to nine, according to how characteristic or uncharacteristic each one was of their own child. They were asked to rate their child relative to all other children of the child's age. The arrangement of the cards followed a normal distribution: 1) extremely uncharacteristic (5 cards); 2) quite uncharacteristic (8 cards); 3) fairly uncharacteristic (12 cards); 4) somewhat uncharacteristic (16 cards); 5) relatively neutral/unimportant (18 cards); 6) somewhat characteristic (16 cards); 7) fairly characteristic (12 cards); 8) quite characteristic (8 cards); and 9) extremely characteristic (5 cards).

The socioeconomic status of the participants was determined using Hollingshead's Four-Factor System (1975). Based on the combined educational and occupational status of mothers and fathers, the majority of the families (33 families; 62.3%) were in the middle range (levels II and III). Twelve families were classified at the lowest end of the scale (level I, 22.6%), and 8 families (15.1%) were classified at the highest end of the scale (levels IV and V). Educationally, most (21) mothers were either high school graduates (39.6%) or had partial college educations (12 mothers; 22.6%). Ten mothers (18.9%) were college graduates, 3 (5.7%) had a graduate degree, and 7 (13.2%) had less than a high school education. Overall, the sample can be classified as a middle to lower-middle socioeconomic group on the average, with typical variability.

RESULTS AND DISCUSSION

Three types of analyses with the Q-sorts are presented here. Highest and lowest mean ratings for each of the 100 items and the mean ratings for our sample of 53 mothers were calculated. Table 1 shows those items that were rated as the highest on the average and those items that were assigned the lowest ratings. Many of the highly rated items related to some of the common descriptions of children with DS, such as cheerful, amiable, and responsive, but there was a great deal of variability. This variability was greater for the items with the highest mean ratings, e.g., "Is warm and responsive" (rating range = 2 to 9).

There was also variability on the uncharacteristic end of the ratings, but the range was not as great. The items that were ranked as fairly uncharacteristic of the children involved the expression of negative feelings and of making social comparisions with others. For example, the items "Tends to be suspicious of others" and "Is jealous

Table 1.   Q-Sort items, highest and lowest ratings[a]

Item description	Mean	Range[b]
Is warm and responsive	7.7	2–9
Tends to be proud of accomplishments	7.7	5–9
Is cheerful	7.4	1–9
Responds to humor	7.0	4–9
Is eager to please	7.0	3–9
Tends to arouse liking in adults	6.8	1–9
Appears to feel unworthy	2.4	1–5
Tends to be suspicious of others	2.5	1–5
Tends to be sulky or whiny	2.9	1–6
Is jealous or envious of others	2.9	1–6
Is inhibited or constricted	3.0	1–9
Has a readiness to feel guilty; tends to blame self	3.1	1–6

[a] By 53 mothers of school-age children with Down's syndrome.

[b] Ratings are from 1–9: 1 = extremely uncharacteristic, 9 = extremely characteristic.

or envious of others" involved a comparison with others requiring certain cognitive and social skills as well as somewhat negative feelings. Three other items ("Appears to feel unworthy," "Tends to be sulky or whiny," and "Has a readiness to feel guilty; tends to blame self") may be seen as items that describe self-evaluations or the expression of negative emotions.

Comparison of Sample Sort with Criterion Sorts

Development of Criterion Sorts   This requires an explanation of a method of comparing the individual sorts made by the mothers with the criterion sorts. The sorting pattern of each mother represents a general description of the characteristics of her child—an individual personality description whereby individual items are judged as being characteristic or uncharacteristic relative to all other items. The pattern of rankings describes an individual profile. The individual profiles are compared with a normative or criterion sort of the items based on particular personality. We compared our data with data used by Waters et al. (submitted for publication). These researchers asked a group of developmental psychologists with extensive experience with normally developing preschoolers to sort the California Q-sort items for hypothetical preschool-age children.

The sort reflects a description of a hypothetical highly socially competent normal preschool child. By taking the average of each item for this group, a criterion sort for the highly socially competent child was obtained (Social Competence Criterion Sort). Other psychologists did the sort in a way that described a hypothetical preschool child with

Table 2. Comparison of criterion and DS sample: social competence construct

Item description	Mean rating[a]	
	C	DS
Is admired and sought out by other children	8.9	4.9
Gets along well with other children	8.4	6.4
Is self-reliant	8.1	5.4
Is competent, skillful	8.0	4.6
Is resourceful in initiating activities	7.9	4.9
Is visibly deviant from peers	1.4	4.4
Emotional reactions are inappropriate	1.9	3.8
Has transient interpersonal relationships	2.0	4.1
Cries easily	2.1	3.6
Tries to be the center of attention	5.1	5.3
Expresses negative feelings directly and openly	5.1	5.6
Is reflective, thinks and deliberates before acting	5.1	4.3

[a] From extremely characteristic (9) to extremely uncharacteristic (1); C = criterion, DS = Down's syndrome.

high self-esteem (Self-Esteem Criterion Sort). A third group sorted the cards according to how a person would rate certain characteristics if the child were to be presented in a highly favorable or socially desirable manner (Social Desirability Criterion Sort). The intercorrelations and empirical validity of these sorts have been reported by Waters et al. (submitted for publication).

Social Competence   Table 2 shows the comparison for the construct of social competence. Mean ratings for the highest, lowest, and middle items from the criterion sort are shown, along with the mean ratings obtained for the sample of mothers of children with DS. The criterion sort shows that the highly socially competent preschool child was judged to be admired and sought out by other children, to get along well with other children, to be self-reliant and competent, and to be resourceful in initiating activities. Likewise, characteristics that were judged to be quite uncharacteristic of this child are also shown. The items listed at the bottom of the table were considered to be relatively unimportant or neutral relative to the construct of social competence.

Comparatively, the high-ranking items from the criterion sort were ranked significantly lower by the mothers in this sample. Those items were on the slightly uncharacteristic side of distribution. Similarly, the low-ranking items in the criterion sort were ranked more highly by the mothers, although they were still on the uncharacteristic side of the rankings. The middle items were rated fairly similarly by the two groups. These data indicate that the mothers in this sample described their children as having lower social competence than the hypothetical age-matched normal child.

Table 3.   Comparison of criterion and DS sample: self esteem construct

Item description	Mean rating[a]	
	C	DS
Is self-reliant	9.0	5.5
Can recover after stressful experiences	8.3	5.9
Tends to be proud of accomplishments	8.1	7.7
Seeks to be independent, autonomous	8.0	5.7
Has high standards of performance for self	7.9	4.5
Is open, straightforward	7.9	5.9
Tends to feel unworthy	1.1	2.4
Is easily victimized by other children; often scapegoated	1.7	4.3
Seeks reassurance from others about worth	2.1	5.5
Is easily offended; sensitive to criticism	2.1	4.9
Is fearful, anxious	2.3	3.6
Is stubborn	5.0	6.1
Is obedient and compliant	5.0	5.5
Is neat and orderly in dress and behavior	5.0	5.7

[a] From extremely characteristic (9) to extremely uncharacteristic (1); C = criterion, DS = Down's syndrome.

Self-esteem   Table 3 presents similar data for the comparison of the criterion and the mothers' sorts for the self-esteem construct. On the criterion sort, the highly self-esteemed preschool child was described as being self-reliant, with the ability to recover after stressful experiences, tending to be proud of accomplishments, seeking to be independent, setting high standards of performance, and being open and straightforward. The opposite low-ranking categories are also shown, as are characteristics judged to be unimportant for defining this construct.

Down's syndrome children were rated as having lower self-esteem. Many of the high-ranking items from the criterion sorts were rated in the middle of the distributions for DS children and the low-ranking criterion items were ranked higher. The middle items were ranked similarly.

Social Desirability   Table 4 shows similar data for the comparison of the sorts for the social desirability construct. In contrast to the previous two tables, the ratings for the criterion and the DS sorts were more similar. The high-ranking items from the criterion sort were rated slightly lower for the DS children, but they more closely resembled the ratings for normal children.

Partial Correlations between Sample and Criterion Sorts   Table 5 shows an alternative way to compare the criterion sorts with those done by the mothers. Each mother's sort was correlated with the social competence criterion sort and with the self-esteem criterion sort, with

Table 4. Comparison of criterion and DS sample: social desirability construct

Item description	Mean rating[a]	
	C	DS
Gets along well with other children	8.0	6.4
Tends to give, lend, and share	8.0	6.1
Shows a recognition of other's feelings, empathetic	8.0	6.0
Is helpful and cooperative	7.9	6.2
Is warm and responsive	7.7	7.7
Appears to feel unworthy	1.7	2.4
Tends to be suspicious of others	1.7	2.5
Emotional reactions are inappropriate	1.7	3.8
Is jealous and envious of others	2.1	2.9
Tends to brood or worry	2.4	3.1
Is talkative	5.1	6.1
Seeks physical contact with others	5.3	5.9
Is neat and orderly in dress and behavior	5.3	5.7
Has a rapid personal tempo	5.4	4.5

[a] From extremely characteristic (9) to extremely uncharacteristic (1); C = criterion, DS = Down's syndrome.

social desirability controlled for, to determine the degree of similarity between the two patterns of ratings. The mean correlations with Z transformations are shown. For example, the mean correlation between the mothers' sorts and the social competence criterion sort was 0.02 and the range of correlations was from -0.33 to 0.30, with the majority of correlations being low or negative. Similarly, the average correlation between the mothers' sorts and the self-esteem criterion sort was 0.03. There was also notable variability in the correlations, with more instances of positive correlations for this construct than for the social competence construct. Nevertheless, these results show that these mothers were rating their children, on the average, as having lower social competence and lower self-esteem when compared to developmental age–matched normal children. It is also noteworthy that variability exists in the patterns of descriptions given by this group of mothers.

Table 5. Partial correlations between criterion Q-sorts and DS sample Q-sorts[a]

Criterion sort	Correlations with DS sample		
	$\bar{x}$	SD	Range
Social competence	0.02	0.15	-0.33–0.30
Self-esteem	0.03	0.14	-0.35–0.46

[a] Controlling for social desirability.

Table 6. DS stereotypes: comparison with social competence sort

Item description	Mean rating[a]	
	C	DS
Is warm and responsive	7.1	7.7
Is cheerful	6.9	7.4
Responds to humor	6.7	7.0
Is obedient and compliant	5.4	5.5
Is eager to please	6.0	7.0
Is emotionally expressive	6.3	6.0
Is stubborn	4.4	6.1
Is aggressive (physically or verbally)	3.4	4.5
Characteristically tries to stretch limits, see what she/he can get away with	4.4	5.7
Tends to be sulky or whiny	2.4	2.9
Cries easily	2.1	3.6

[a] From extremely characteristic (9) to extremely uncharacteristic (1); C = criterion, DS = Down's syndrome.

Down's Syndrome Stereotypes

To look for possible unique personality styles, an examination of certain items relevant to DS stereotypes was done. The mean ratings for the mothers were compared with the mean ratings from the social competence criterion sort (Table 6). These data show that for certain of the amiable and friendly types of items, e.g., "Is warm and responsive," "Is cheerful," "Is eager to please," the mothers rated their children highly. The ratings are not very different from those assigned to a socially competent mental age–matched normal child. Negative emotions were rated low for two categories, "Tends to be sulky or whiny" and "Cries easily." On two of the items dealing with stubbornness ("Is stubborn" and "Characteristically tries to stretch limits"), the children with Down's syndrome were rated somewhat higher than the hypothetical normal child. These data did not compare DS children with non-DS mentally retarded children, and it must be recalled that there was notable variability on how individual mothers rated their children.

REFERENCES

Ainsworth, M., Blehar, M., Waters, E., and Wall, S. 1978. Patterns of Attachment. Lawrence Erlbaum Associates, Hillsdale, New Jersey.

Block, J. 1961. The Q-sort Method in Personality Assessment and Psychiatric Research. Consulting Psychologists Press, Inc., Palo Alto, California. (Reprinted in 1978)

Block, J. H., and Block, J. 1980a. The California Child Q-sort. Consulting Psychologists Press, Inc., Palo Alto, California.

Block, J. H., and Block, J. 1980b. The role of ego-control and ego-resiliency in the organization of behavior. In: W. A. Collins (ed.), Minnesota Symposia on Child Psychology, Vol. 13. Lawrence Erlbaum Associates, Hillsdale, New Jersey.

Down, J. L. H. 1866. Observations on an ethnic classification of idiots. Clin. Lect. Rep. Lond. Hosp. 3:259.

Gibson, D. 1978. Down's Syndrome: The Psychology of Mongolism. Cambridge University Press, Cambridge, England.

Hollingshead, A. B. 1975. Four-factor index of social status. Unpublished manuscript, Department of Psychology, Yale University.

Rynders, J. E., Spiker, D., and Horrobin, J. M. 1978. Underestimating the educability of Down's syndrome children: Examination of methodological problems in recent literature. Am. J. Ment. Defic. 82:440–448.

Smith, G. F., and Berg, J. M. 1976. Down's Anomaly, 2nd ed. Churchill Livingston, London.

Stephenson, W. 1936. Introduction to inverted factor analysis, with some applications to studies of orexis. J. Educ. Psychol. 27:353–367.

Waters, E., Noyes, D. M., and Ricks, M. Social competence, self-esteem and social desirability: A Q-sort analysis of conceptual and empirical similarities among related constructs. (submitted for publication)

PERSPECTIVES AND PROGRESS IN MENTAL RETARDATION
Volume I—Social, Psychological, and Educational Aspects
Edited by J. M. Berg
Copyright © 1984 by I.A.S.S.M.D.

ELEMENTS OF PROFESSIONAL HELPFULNESS
Profiles of the Most Helpful and Least Helpful Professionals Encountered by Mothers of Young Retarded Children

L. N. Huang[1] and L. J. Heifetz[2]

[1] *School of Social Welfare, University of California at Berkeley, Berkeley, California 94720*
[2] *School of Education, Syracuse University, 805 S. Crouse Avenue, Syracuse, New York 13210*

Mothers of young, organically retarded children were asked to recall the most helpful and least helpful professionals encountered in their travels through the service network. Interviews and rating scales generated data on the important components of helpfulness. These included the personal, affective quality of the relationship and openness to a collaborative partnership that drew upon mothers' current strengths. Also considered important by the mothers were the professionals' specialized (versus generic) competence and experience in retardation. On the average, educational professionals were disproportionately represented among the most helpful group, whereas medical professionals were disproportionately represented among the least helpful.

Retarded children often require a complex array of developmental services spanning a range of disciplines and located in far-flung corners of the service network (Anderson, 1971; Koch and Dobson, 1971; Greenfeld, 1972; Heifetz, 1980). It can be an overwhelming task for parents to track down and assemble the components of a comprehensive package of services. Guidance in this task is seriously limited by the isolation of different professions and organizations from each other. Consequently, parents can be very much on their own in trying to solve this labyrinth of services (Matheny and Vernick, 1968).

PARENTAL VIEWS OF PROFESSIONALS

What do parents look for in casting professionals in the various roles of service providers to their children? Although there is an enormous literature on parents of retarded children, answers to this question are rather piecemeal, approaching the question either indirectly or incompletely. One area of research has dealt with parents' evaluations of various services (e.g., Caldwell et al., 1961; Justice et al., 1971). As might be expected, reactions have ranged from highly satisfied to extremely disappointed (Ehlers, 1966; Jacobs, 1969). Some of these evaluations have been sponsored by the service agencies themselves, a fact that may have jeopardized parental objectivity. Also, to the extent that the investigators have selected the particular portion of parental experience to be evaluated, they have missed a potentially informative base of comparison in other experiences that may have been either more satisfactory or more disappointing.

Another source of information has been case studies and personal narratives of individual families (Kysar, 1968; Gorham, 1975; Greer, 1975; Stigen, 1976). Because critical voices tend to be louder than satisfied ones, it is not surprising that the recurrent themes in these accounts have been frustration, impatience, helplessness, and anger, often directed not only by parents toward specific professionals and the service system as a whole, but also by parents toward themselves. The obvious problem with data of this type is their idiosyncratic and nonrepresentative nature, despite the rich and often compelling quality of the material.

A third area of the literature draws upon the clinical experience of professionals who work with families of retarded children (Wolfensberger, 1967; Matheny and Vernick, 1968; Menolascino, 1968). These reports frequently offer guidelines for professional practice— some of them insightful and useful, but others verging on the platitudinous. The major drawback of these views is that they do not come *from* parents, and, in attempting to speak *for* parents, they may overlook alternative but equally valid interpretations of the same reality.

Many important questions regarding the nature of the parent-professional relationship remain unanswered. For example, the very basic issue of the parents' conceptions of helpfulness and their perceived and experienced roles in a helping relationship have not been systematically examined. The present study attempted to gain a better understanding of parents' conceptualization of "helpfulness." Mothers provided both qualitative and quantitative data about their experiences with their most helpful and least helpful professionals. Data from interviews and rating scales were integrated in order to begin to document parental criteria for helpful professional relationships.

METHOD

Subjects

The participants in this study were 28 mothers of organically retarded children, living in U.S. metropolitan areas of medium to large size. The mothers ranged in age from 21 to 46 years (mean age = 31.7 years). In all cases the mother was the biological parent and lived at home with the child. Socioeconomically, the families were skewed toward the middle and upper classes as defined by Hollingshead's (1957) two-factor index (Class I, 20%; Class II, 27%; Class III, 43%; Class IV, 7%; Class V, 3%). The racial composition was 2 blacks and 26 Caucasians.

The mean age of the retarded children of these 28 mothers was 5.1 years. Thirteen of the children had received a diagnosis of some form of organic retardation within the first month of life; all of the children had been diagnosed by 36 months. The most frequently reported diagnoses were "brain damage," Down's syndrome, and retardation of unknown etiology. Twelve of the children had multiple diagnoses.

The mothers were recruited by the senior author through four public agencies: two preschools for retarded children and two developmental disabilities nurseries. The investigator was identified as an independent researcher, connected with a university but not affiliated with any service agency or program. The overall participation rate was 73.7%, with 28 of 38 mothers agreeing to participate. Among the 10 who declined there was no particular pattern in their refusal.

Interview Procedure

Interviews were conducted in the home and averaged 2 hours. The interview consisted of open-ended questions focusing on mothers' experiences with specific professionals. A professional was defined as any individual whose training was directly relevant to the enhancement of child development and/or family functioning, either generically (e.g., pediatrician) or specifically in regard to mental retardation (e.g., developmental disabilities counselor). Each mother was asked to recall (but not identify by name) two professionals who stood out in her experience as the "most helpful professional" and the "least helpful professional." In conjunction with the interview, each mother completed two structured scales pertaining to the substance and style of her interactions with the most helpful and the least helpful professional.

Rating Scales

A Professional Characteristics Scale was used to assess the mothers' perceptions of the interpersonal and substantive aspects of their relationships with the two professionals. The scale consisted of 30 adjectives and descriptive phrases that the mother was asked to rate according to the degree to which they characterized the professional being discussed (0 = not at all like him/her; 1 = slightly like him/her; 2 = moderately like him/her; 3 = very much like him/her).

The second instrument was a checklist containing 36 service functions. Each item on the Functions Checklist corresponded to a need frequently mentioned by parents of retarded children (Group for the Advancement of Psychiatry, 1963; Condell, 1966; Carver and Carver, 1972; Holroyd, 1974). A wide range of functions, crossing the domains of various professionals and disciplines, was represented. Each mother first checked the items that she had expected the professional to provide, then checked those items that had actually been provided. The Functions Checklist was used to obtain mothers' expectations of each professional and to determine how completely these expectations had been fulfilled.

RESULTS

Helpfulness and Profession

In recalling the high points and low points of helpfulness, mothers had a strong tendency to single out either medical professionals (mainly physicians) or educational professionals (mainly teachers). Medical professionals made up 35.7% of the "most helpful" category and 71.4% of the "least helpful" category. On the other hand, educational professionals made up 53.6% of the "most helpful" group and 10.7% of the "least helpful" group. The higher level of helpfulness attributed to educational professionals over medical ones was statistically very significant (Yates $\chi_1^2 = 9.36 \; P < 0.01$).

Characteristics of Most Helpful and Least Helpful Professionals

Rating Scale Data   Table 1 shows the mean scores assigned to the most helpful professionals (MHPs) and the least helpful professionals (LHPs) on each item of the Professional Characteristics Scale. The

Table 1.   Characteristics attributed to the "most helpful" professional (MHP) and the "least helpful" professional (LHP) by mothers of mentally retarded children

Characteristic[a]	Mean score of MHPs[b]	Mean score of LHPs[b]	Mean difference[c]
More typical of the most helpful			
Supportive, reassuring	2.93	0.50	2.43[d]
Warm	2.96	0.57	2.39[d]
Enthusiastic, positive outlook	2.89	0.52	2.37[d]
Involves you in decision making	2.85	0.48	2.37[d]
Treats you as an equal	2.93	0.63	2.30[d]
Personally involved and interested	2.75	0.46	2.29[d]
Encourages your suggestions	2.68	0.46	2.22[d]
Likeable	2.96	0.93	2.03[d]
Experienced in dealing with your needs	2.68	0.65	2.03[d]
Open-minded	2.74	0.73	2.01[d]
Dependable, trustworthy	2.93	1.36	1.57[d]
Honest	2.96	1.48	1.48[d]
Generally well informed	2.89	1.41	1.48[d]
Specifically well informed about your child's problems	2.79	1.37	1.42[d]
Intelligent	2.93	2.16	0.77[e]
Persuasive	1.82	1.55	0.27
More typical of the least helpful			
Too busy to spend much time with you	0.04	2.50	−2.46[d]
Insensitive to your worries	0.25	2.30	−2.05[d]
Challenging, makes you feel defensive	0.07	2.00	−1.93[d]
Makes you feel nervous	0.04	1.96	−1.92[d]
Insists on doing things his way	0.46	2.15	−1.69[d]
Doesn't listen to what you have to say	0.11	1.74	−1.63[d]
Dominating, always "the boss"	0.29	1.71	−1.42[e]
Inexperienced	0.14	1.50	−1.36[d]
Inefficient	0.11	1.36	−1.25[d]
Lacks confidence	0.14	1.25	−1.11[d]
Disorganized	0.29	1.39	−1.10[d]
Tense, nervous	0.07	1.00	−0.93[d]
Uses technical, professional words	0.93	1.77	−0.84[e]
Demanding	0.86	1.64	−0.78

[a] Characteristics are listed in two groups: those that were more typical of the "most helpful" professional and those that were more typical of the "least helpful" professional. Within each group, characteristics are listed in descending order of the difference between the two types of professionals.

[b] Characteristics were given the following ratings: 0 = not at all like him/her; 1 = slightly like him/her; 2 = moderately like him/her; 3 = very much like him/her.

[c] Mean differences were tested for significance by means of two-tailed t tests for correlated samples.

[d] $P < 0.001$.

[e] $P < 0.01$.

first group of items are those that were considered more typical of the MHPs and the second group of items were seen as more typical of the LHPs. The differences between MHPs and LHPs were uniformly in favor of the MHPs. Only two items were not statistically significant in differentiating MHPs and LHPs. These items—"demanding" and "persuasive"—did not have a clearly positive or negative connotation.

It is reasonable to suspect that these profiles may have been somewhat influenced by a "halo effect"—a tendency for those variables that truly distinguished the MHPs and LHPs to also positively distort other features of the MHPs and negatively distort other features of the LHPs. Closer examination of Table 1 reveals that, on the average, mothers gave the MHPs a near-maximum rating on almost all of the positive features and a near-minimum rating on almost all of the negative features. The LHPs received a less extreme pattern of ratings. Many of their features, both positive and negative, averaged in the midrange between "slightly" and "moderately" like him/her. In other words, the mothers protrayed the MHPs in near-perfect, almost saintly terms, and they viewed the LHPs not as evil or totally deficient, but rather in terms of low mediocrity.

Despite the possibility of a halo effect, Table 1 still provides insight into the relative importance of different kinds of characteristics, i.e., the extent to which they differentiate MHPs from LHPs. The most critical dimension appears to be one of affect. Of the 10 characteristics that showed the greatest difference between MHPs and LHPs, most involved a general quality of *warmth, concern, and support*. The next most important dimension dealt with parent-professional collaboration. Three items in the top 10 distinguishing features, and five in the middle 10, reflected the extent to which the professionals valued and applied the mothers' ideas in a genuine *spirit of partnership*. The least most important (but still statistically significant) items in distinguishing MHPs from LHPs mainly involved *intra*personal (as opposed to interpersonal) qualities of the professionals, including their *experience, confidence, and efficiency*.

Interview Data. During the interviews, after the mothers had chosen a MHP and a LHP, they were asked: "What was it about this professional that you found most helpful (least helpful)?" Four distinct categories of response to this open-ended question emerged. The most frequent type of response—including 84.6% of the MHPs and 76.9% of the LHPs—dealt with *personal relatedness*. The MHPs were typically recalled as being "interested," "concerned," "understanding," and "sensitive," whereas the LHPs were "discouraging," "insensitive," and "cold and businesslike."

The second most common response—covering 53.8% of the MHPs and 46.2% of the LHPs—dealt with the *perceived competence* of the professionals. MHPs were seen as highly competent in mental retardation and related areas. The LHPs were often seen as generically competent, but deficient in issues specifically related to retardation. One mother spoke for many others when she said: "Maybe he was good with well babies, but not with babies with problems."

The next most frequent response category—including 23.1% of MHPs and 42.3% of LHPs—addressed the *balance of power* between parent and professional. The MHPs "accepted me as an equal" or "elicited a lot of our own priorities," whereas the LHPs were criticized as "condescending," "demeaning," or "unwilling to let you participate in decisions." The smallest category—which covered 30.7% of the MHPs and 15.4% of the LHPs—reflected aspects of the professionals' *efficiency*. A typical MHP "discussed goals and practical management issues," in contrast with a LHP, who "talked in circles, not specific, just never came to the point."

Services Provided by Most Helpful and Least Helpful Professionals

Mothers had expected overall about the same number and kinds of services from their MHPs and their LHPs at the beginning of their relationships. As might have been predicted, the MHPs were reported to have delivered a much higher proportion of these expected services (75.9% for MHPs versus 20.8% for LHPs; correlated $t_{25} = 6.37, P < 0.004$). Next, the MHPs and LHPs were compared on the frequency with which they had provided each of the 36 items on the Functions Checklist. Three functions most clearly differentiated between MHPs and LHPs: 1) "handled my worries about my child" (done by 85.7% of the MHPs, but only 3.6% of the LHPs); 2) "dealt with my feelings about having a child with special needs" (85.7% of MHPs, 7.1% of LHPs); and 3) "helped me accept my child and his/her disability" (71.4% of MHPs, 7.1% of LHPs). In other words, there was a massive discrepancy between the performances of the MHPs and LHPs in dealing with the emotional, expressive needs of parents.

DISCUSSION

The qualitative and quantitative data from the mothers in this study converged almost perfectly, yielding a consistent and detailed profile of the professionals who had been truly helpful. The interviews, the Professional Characteristics Scale, and the Functions Checklist all highlighted the primary importance of the *personal, affective relationship* between parents and professionals. Dealing with parents' emotional reactions to the hard realities of retardation—and doing so in an atmosphere of warmth, concern, and respect—were the paramount requirements of a helpful professional.

Following closely in importance were issues concerning the working relationship between parents and professionals. Mothers were consistently clear about wanting a collaborative partnership. The roles of grateful supplicant, clinical patient, or naive apprentice were disdained in favor of a functional partnership that drew upon parents' resources instead of focusing upon their deficiencies.

Also considered important were the experience and efficiency of the professional. Mothers often made a point of distinguishing the generically competent professional from one whose skills and perspectives were directly relevant to the needs of retarded children and their families. They tied this distinction to the much greater ability of the "most helpful" professionals to meet parents' expectations for service.

On each of the three core elements of helpfulness, mothers generally ranked educators higher than medical professionals. In many cases this was related to the behavior of the physician at the time that the mother was informed of her child's retardation. Mothers vividly recalled this event, and many described with bitterness the devastating impact of a physician whose technical expertise and precision were exceeded only by his lack of personal sensitivity.

The greater helpfulness of educators may also be related to the fact that for most retarded children day-to-day needs are much more developmental and educational than medical—more concerned with charting and striving for the next small steps in a continuum of skills than with restoring a disrupted physiological system to a state of homeostasis. In this regard, it is important to consider the recently accumulating evidence of parents' ability to carry out a wide range of educational and therapeutic functions for their own children (Heifetz, 1977, 1980). This represents a potentially dramatic increase in the quality and quantity of developmental resources available to retarded children. Tapping this vast potential would seem to require professionals who are generally supportive of parents, who acknowledge parents' current knowledge and capacity, who have specialized training and experience to complement the parents' expertise in their own children, and who are prepared to help interested parents further develop their own potential as service providers. These qualities are precisely the ones that mothers in this study emphasized in distinguishing the "most helpful" professionals from the "least helpful."

REFERENCES

Anderson, K. 1971. The "shopping" behavior of parents of mentally retarded children: The professional person's role. Ment. Retard. 9:3–5.

Caldwell, B., Manley, E., and Seely, B. 1961. Factors associated with parental reaction to a clinic for retarded children. Am. J. Ment. Defic. 65:590–594.

Carver, H., and Carver, N. 1972. The Family of the Retarded Child. Syracuse University Press, Syracuse.

Condell, J. 1966. Parental attitudes toward mental retardation. Am. J. Ment. Defic. 71:85–92.

Ehlers, W. 1966. Mothers of Retarded Children: How they Feel; Where They Find Help. Charles C Thomas Publisher, Springfield, Illinois.

Gorham, K. 1975. A lost generation of parents. Except. Child. 41:521–525.

Greenfeld, J. 1972. A Child Called Noah. Holt, Rinehart & Winston, Inc., New York.

Greer, B. 1975. On being the parent of a handicapped child. Except. Child. 41:519–526.

Group for the Advancement of Psychiatry. 1963. Mental Retardation: A Family Crisis: The Therapeutic Role of the Physician. Group for the Advancement of Psychiatry, New York.

Heifetz, L. J. 1977. Behavioral training for parents of retarded children: Alternative formats based on instructional manuals. Am. J. Ment. Defic. 82:194–203.

Heifetz, L. J. 1980. From consumer to middleman: Emerging roles for parents in the network of services for retarded children. In: R. R. Abidin (ed.), Parent Education and Intervention Handbook. Charles C Thomas Publisher, Springfield, Illinois.

Hollingshead, A. B. 1957. Two-Factor Index of Social Position. Unpublished manuscript, Department of Sociology, Yale University, New Haven.

Holroyd, J. 1974. The questionnaire on resources and stress: An instrument to measure family response to a handicapped family member. J. Commun. Psychol. 2:92–94.

Jacobs, J. 1969. The Search for Help: A Study of the Retarded Child in the Community. Brunner/Mazel, New York.

Justice, K., O'Connor, G., and Warren, N. 1971. Problems reported by parents of mentally retarded children—who helps? Am. J. Ment. Defic. 75:685–691.

Koch, R., and Dobson, J. 1971. The Mentally Retarded Child and His Family. Brunner/Mazel, New York.

Kysar, J. 1968. The two camps in child psychiatry: A report from a psychiatrist-father of an autistic and retarded child. Am. J. Psychiatry 125:103–109.

Matheny, A., and Vernick, J. 1968. Parents of the mentally retarded child: Emotionally overwhelmed or informationally deprived? J. Pediatr. 74:953–959.

Menolascino, F. 1968. Parents of the mentally retarded: An operational approach to diagnosis and management. J. Am. Acad. Child Psychiatry 7:589–602.

Stigen, G. 1976. Heartaches and Handicaps: An Irreverent Survival Manual for Parents. Science and Behavior Books, Inc., Palo Alto, California.

Wolfensberger, W. 1967. Counseling the parents of the retarded. In: A. A. Baumeister (ed.), Mental Retardation: Appraisal, Education and Rehabilitation. Aldine Publishing Company, Chicago.

PERSPECTIVES AND PROGRESS IN MENTAL RETARDATION
Volume I—Social, Psychological, and Educational Aspects
Edited by J. M. Berg

PARENTAL INVOLVEMENT COURSES
Contrasts between Mothers Who Enroll and Those Who Do Not

R. McConkey and J. McEvoy
St. Michael's House, Upper Kilmacud Road, Stillorgan, Dublin, Republic of Ireland

Families with a mentally handicapped child between the ages of 2 and 12 years were invited by letter to participate in an evening course on helping children learn through play. Thirty-eight families volunteered, and from the pool of nonvolunteers a group of 29 mothers was selected. They and the course-attenders were visited at home prior to the course and data were collected from them on their child's play patterns, playmates, and daily routines. Information was obtained also on family background, mothers' attitudes to play, and mothers' interactions with their children. A discriminant analysis highlighted marked and significant differences between the two groups of mothers, especially in their attitudes to play and the way they played with their children. Recommendations are made on tailoring courses to best suit parents' needs.

The ambition of most intervention programs with developmentally delayed children is to involve and educate the parents. Various methods are used to do this, ranging from home visits by a professional worker to group meetings in a central location. Several studies have noted that, irrespective of the approach used, the most interested, enthusiastic, and effective parents tend to be those from higher socioeconomic groups (Baker et al., 1981). Thus far, attempts to elucidate the reasons for this have been overshadowed by the more pragmatic shift to working with parents on an individual basis within their own homes,

This research was wholly supported by St. Michael's House Research Fund.

the attitude being, "if they don't come to us, we'll go to them." Nevertheless, even these home-based schemes cannot be wholly effective unless an attempt is made to understand better the parents' perceptions of their child's development, their attitudes to involvement in teaching interactions, and the conflicting demands that may be made on their time.

A COURSE ON PLAY: STUDY OF INVOLVEMENT ATTITUDES

The opportunity to undertake a systematic study of mothers' attitudes to involvement arose during the evaluation of a new course for parents on nurturing the play of handicapped children (McConkey et al., 1982). Not only was the topic novel, but the course was based around a series of specially made videoprograms, each dealing with a different type of play (e.g., energetic, social, pretend) and the making of simple toys for use at home (McConkey and Jeffree, 1983). The course consisted of a series of 6 weekly meetings held in the evenings to enable fathers to attend.

Methods and Sample Characteristics

A letter of invitation, along with a pamphlet describing the course, was sent by post to *all* the families (*N* = 101) with children attending or wait-listed for two developmental day centers in Dublin city, each one serving a defined geographical area. These centers serve preschool-age moderately and severely handicapped children and school-age severely handicapped children. The content of the course was developed with this ability range in mind.

Out of 101 families, 38 enrolled for the course. Briefly, their characteristic were as follows: 64% had children 5 years and under and 36% had children over 5; there were equal numbers of boys and girls represented; 40% of the children had Down's syndrome; and 32% had at least one additional sensory or physical handicap. The median age of the mothers and fathers was 39 years (range 25–54) and 42 years (range 25–60), respectively. In terms of fathers' occupations, 20% were in the professional/managerial category, 15% were self-employed, 40% worked in semiskilled/clerical jobs, and 20% were in manual/routine occupations. In 5% of families, the fathers were deceased. Overall this group was reasonably representative of the families served by the centers.

Prior to the course starting, all the mothers were visited at home and background information about the family was obtained along with details of the child's play activities at home and the mothers' perceptions of play. This was done through structured interviews and questionnaires. Unfortunately, our resources did not permit us to contact and interview all the course "refusers" ($N = 63$); instead a random sample of 29 (almost half) was taken. These mothers also were visited at home and the same information was obtained from them as from the course enrollers.

RESULTS OF GROUP COMPARISONS

The two groups of mothers interviewed—enrollers ($N = 38$) and refusers ($N = 29$)—were compared on a wide range of variables relating to child characteristics, family background, play patterns, mothers' attitudes to play, and mothers' interactions with their children. Such a spread of variables is necessary when the reasons affecting enrollment can be varied and idiosyncratic. Nonetheless, particular attention was focused on variables relating to play, because the topic of the course offered to parents must be a major influence on the decision of discriminating parents.

Enrollment Decision Factors

Reasons for Not Enrolling   Interviewers probed for this in a sympathetic way, at the end of the interview, with mothers who had not enrolled for the course. The interview had been described to the mothers as a study of children's play at home, which indeed it was. The most frequently given responses were that: the child would not benefit (22%); family circumstances prevented it, e.g., moving house (22%); there were problems in finding a babysitter (14%); it was too far to travel (14%); the mother worked in the evenings (6%); the family would be on holidays (3%). In addition, 5 families (14%) claimed that they had not heard of the course and a further 2 (6%) stated that they had tried to enroll after the course had started. (By contrast, parents who did enroll for the course were asked afterward if they had made any special arrangements in order to attend. In all, 52% reported no special arrangements, 37% hired a babysitter, 6% shifted mealtimes, and 4% had to rearrange times at work.)

Reasons for Enrolling   Although mothers gave a diversity of responses to this enquiry, the replies could be grouped into the following categories: it would benefit my child (61%); I wanted to learn more about my child (13%) or to generally learn more (13%); because I was asked (9%); and for encouragement (4%).

Contrasts between Enrollers and Refusers   Obviously, all the reasons mothers gave for attending or not attending may be quite valid, but in themselves they do not account for why some parents perceive a course as benefiting their child and make special arrangements to attend, whereas other parents from apparently similar circumstances will feel the course is of little benefit and will not try to surmount any practical difficulties in order to attend. In order to determine if there were any characteristics in common to mothers who enroll and those who do not, the groups were compared on a series of different variables using chi square or t tests as appropriate. First, there were *no* differences between the two groups in terms of the children's characteristics (age, etiology, degree of handicap, additional handicaps), or in terms of family background (socioeconomic status, parents' ages, family size). The only difference to emerge was a higher incidence of lastborn handicapped children among the course enrollers (chi square = 9.95, $P < 0.05$).

However, there were more striking differences between the two groups when the play pattern of the children at home was examined. Mothers enrolling for the course reported a greater number of different play activities (chi square = 9.24, $P < 0.05$) and a higher frequency of play activities within a typical day (chi square = 12.4, $P < 0.05$), whereas mothers who refused cited a higher incidence of the child engaging in nonplay activities such as hand-waving and opening and closing doors (i.e., stereotyped actions) (chi square = 10.43, $P < 0.05$). Furthermore, when mothers were asked about their and the fathers' play activities with the child, the course enrollers had a higher incidence of active games, such as gross-motor play (40% of mothers), looking at books (29%), and pretending (26%), whereas mothers who did not join the course reported more passive pursuits such as talking or watching television with the child (48% of refusers compared to 16% of enrollers). Interestingly, mothers reported a similar pattern of play interactions between fathers and the handicapped children.

Mothers' Attitudes to Play

A specially designed questionnaire consisting of 21 items about play in general, the role of toys in play, interactions between children, and characteristics of the individual child's play was presented to the parents during the interview and they were invited to indicate their agreement by giving each comment a mark ranging from 0 to 10. They were shown a card indicating that 0 meant "very much disagree," 5 was "unsure," and 10 was "very much agree."

On 9 out of the 21 items there were significant differences between the scores of the two groups of mothers. The most marked differences occurred on the following items: course refusers felt their child was quite happy left doing nothing (median for refusers = 4.7; for enrollers 2.3); that the new toys of today are so much better for children (medians 7.5 and 4.9, respectively); that the other children are not interested in playing with the handicapped child (medians 5.9 and 4.1); and that the child gets more fun out of playing with other children than with toys (medians 7.3 and 4.9) (chi square tests $P < 0.01$). By contrast, the course enrollers seemed to view play as an important interactive experience whether it occurs with children or simple toys.

Mothers' Reactions to Interactions with Child

A specially designed inventory was used to tap mothers' feelings about the various sorts of interactions they have with their children. This consisted of a listing of 15 bipolar items such as "I have lots of fun with child/I don't have fun with child" or "I get harassed/A relaxing situation for me" (Judson and Burden, 1980). Mothers were asked to mark, on a 5-point scale, the comments that best described their feeling. This was done for three different contexts: when *playing*, when *dressing*, and when *shopping* with the child. A Varimax factor analysis yielded one main factor—termed "enthusiasm"—on which five items loaded highest: "lots of fun," "relaxed," "do this often together," "feel I'm doing a good job as parent," "try to create new experiences." The foregoing is a description of mothers who score highest on the enthusiasm factor; opposites to these statements would score low.

As Figure 1 shows, mothers who refused the invitation scored significantly higher on the enthusiasm factor in all three contexts, although it was most marked in the shopping context (two-way analysis of variance $P < 0.01$). Thus the course refusers appeared to be more confident and enthusiastic about their role as parents compared to the course enrollers.

DISCRIMINANT ANALYSIS

A number of variables have been identified above that distinguish between the two groups of mothers; it could well be that these variables are related to each other. Also, an estimate is needed of the proportion of the variance that these variables account for in mothers' decisions to enroll in courses. The statistical procedure of discriminant analysis was used to execute both tasks. All the variables found to distinguish significantly between the two groups were entered into the analysis based on the stepwise method of Wilk's lambda (Nie et al., 1975). This showed that, together, all the variables accounted for 58% of the variance between the two groups (canonical correlation = 0.769). This is a sizeable but incomplete accounting of the differences between the groups, which suggests that for some mothers reasons may be idiosyncratic.

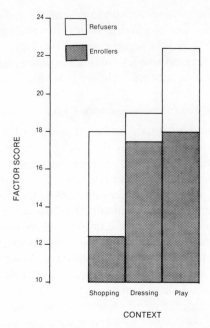

Figure 1.   Mean scores for the two groups of mothers on the enthusiasm factor.

The discriminant analysis also orders the variables according to those that best discriminate between the groups. The rank order for the eight main variables were as follows: course refusers have high enthusiasm scores in the shopping context; feel their child is happy to be left doing nothing; regard the best toys as expensive ones; cite few instances of fathers joining in children's play activities; have a high enthusiasm score in play situations; believe that other children are not interested in playing with the handicapped child; report more instances of the child using stereotyped behaviors as amusement; and cite few instances of their joining in the child's play activities. Other variables, such as child's age and socioeconomic background, did not significantly contribute to the analysis for our sample of 67 mothers.

To summarize, the main distinguishing features of the mothers who enrolled for the play course were, first, a feeling that they could be better parents (particularly in situations such as shopping when they cannot give the child their full attention) and, second, a feeling that it was important for their children to play and for them to join in the activities. By contrast, the course refusers felt comfortable about their role as parents but gave the impression that their children did not play and that they, the fathers, or the other children were less likely to play actively with the handicapped child. This presents a paradox; the mothers who enrolled for the course felt they needed help yet they already appeared to be doing much to nurture their child's play, whereas those mothers who did not join the course were not active players with their children and yet felt that they were doing a good job as parents.

BEYOND SOCIOECONOMIC FACTORS

Past studies of parental participation have generally found a relationship with socioeconomic factors, i.e., middle-class parents are more likely to enroll and to complete courses than are lower-class parents. Of course, this finding is not explanatory; it is merely descriptive. Some investigations have suggested that low-income families with only basic education find it difficult to follow and understand the information presented in courses, especially if it is presented verbally (Baker et al., 1981). However, the present study, although it did not find a strong relationship with socioeconomic factors, suggests another plausible explanation that may be linked with social ethos.

A central issue—at least for Irish mothers participating in a play course—seemed to be their differing perceptions of nurturing their children's development. Our course, like many other intervention programs, was based on two presumptions that apparently some parents did not share—that the behavior of a mentally handicapped child is modifiable and that parents' interactions can affect their child's development. It has been suggested that middle-class parents are more likely to emphathize with these views than are families from lower socioeconomic backgrounds (Bernstein, 1970), yet to date little has been done to break down the myths and routines about children that are handed down from one generation to the next. Parental involvement cannot be wholly effective unless it is based on mutual understandings.

This study goes some way to pointing out the need for professionals to observe and listen to parents. For too long we have expected them to learn only from us. In this respect, home-based involvement schemes offer an opportunity for mutual learning that is difficult to achieve with organized courses in service settings. Nonetheless, we professionals need a greater sensitivity to parents' feelings about the effects of their interactions with their children before we can effectively harness their skills to further their children's development.

ACKNOWLEDGMENT

We are grateful to our colleagues Finola Gallagher and Mary Naughton for their assistance throughout.

REFERENCES

Baker, B. L., Clark, D. B., and Yasuda, P. M. 1981. Predictors of success in parent training. In: P. Mittler (ed.), Frontiers of Knowledge in Mental Retardation, Vol. 1, pp. 281–291. University Park Press, Baltimore.

Bernstein, B. 1970. Education cannot compensate for society. New Society 387:344–347.

Judson, S. L., and Burden, R. L. 1980. Towards a tailored measure of parental attitudes: An approach to the evaluation of one aspect of intervention projects with parents of handicapped children. Child Care Health Dev. 6:47–55.

McConkey, R., and Jeffree, D. M. 1983. Making Toys for Handicapped Children: A Guide for Parents and Teachers. Prentice-Hall, Inc., Englewood Cliffs, New Jersey.

McConkey, R., McEvoy, J., and Gallagher, F. 1982. Learning through play: The evaluation of a videocourse for parents of mentally handicapped children. Child Care Health Dev. 8:345–359.

Nie, N. H., Hull, C. H., Jenkins, J. G., Steinbrenner, K., and Bent, D. H. 1975. Statistical Package for the Social Sciences. McGraw-Hill Book Company, New York.

PERSPECTIVES AND PROGRESS IN MENTAL RETARDATION
Volume I—Social, Psychological, and Educational Aspects
Edited by J. M. Berg
Copyright © 1984 by I.A.S.S.M.D.

SERVICE NEEDS OF DEVELOPMENTALLY DISABLED PARENTS

P. L. Johnson and S. R. Clark

*Maxwell Health Studies Program, Syracuse University,
712 Ostrom Avenue, Syracuse, New York 13210*

The relationship between parenting problems and the cognitive and emotional deficits of developmentally disabled parents is examined, and the impact of social environmental conditions on parenting is discussed. Data for the study consist of observations of developmentally disabled parents participating in a parent group program of a family service agency and interviews with parent aides about their experiences of working with developmentally disabled parents. Advocacy, special educational, and group supportive services are suggested to help developmentally disabled persons to fulfill parenting responsibilities.

Relatively few studies have asked questions about the special needs of developmentally disabled parents for parenting education, child development information, and other supportive services. Heber and Garber (1975) demonstrated the importance of early detection of, and intervention services for, mothers and their children with "cultural-familial mental retardation." They demonstrated positive effects, for both the mother's and child's development, of a maternal rehabilitation program (job training, employment, homemaking, and child-rearing skills) and an infant intervention program (day care with a curriculum including perceptual, motor, cognitive, language, and social-emotional development goals). More importantly, their study identified some of the maternal behavior of mildly retarded women; for example, the tendency to use imperatives and restricted communication in mother-child interaction. Robinson's (1978) study of parental attitudes of retarded mothers also identified particular characteristics. He found that mildly retarded mothers were more likely to hold protective, control-

This study is supported by the Administration for Children, Youth and Families, U.S. Department of Health and Human Services, Grant No. 90 CW 661/01.

ling, and punitive attitudes toward their children compared with mothers of average intelligence.

Although studies of developmentally disabled parents for the most part identify common problems of homemaking, child care, and family functioning, their basic descriptive approach does not lead to a clearer understanding of the relationship between developmental disabilities and parenting. Portraits drawn of the difficulties faced by developmentally disabled parents can leave the impression that each parenting problem somehow relates back to the label of being mentally retarded, intellectually limited, or developmentally delayed. For some parenting problems associated with developmentally disabled mothers, false generalizations are common. For example, parent impulsivity and overdependence on the children for emotional support are easily interpreted as being uniquely related to cognitive deficits of the parent. However, the literature on child abuse and neglect shows these problems to be common for abusive or neglectful parents (Polansky et al., 1981), regardless of level of intellectual functioning. Although some studies using comparison groups of mothers with average intelligence have substantiated that some characteristics are more likely to be found in developmentally disabled parents, questions about the linkage of particular parenting problems to particular cognitive and emotional deficits remain unanswered.

Researchers must go beyond blanket descriptions of developmentally disabled parents and begin in-depth analyses of the relationship between cognitive and emotional deficits and parenting problems. Each significant parenting problem requires close scrutiny so that the skill deficits and social contextual factors directly associated with it can be identified. The earlier research of Mickelson (1947, 1949) is interesting because it used a multivariate analytical perspective to identify factors that were statistically associated with successful and unsuccessful parenting. Significant factors found were: parents' mental health, marital harmony, number of pregnancies, number of children, and adequacy of income. More importantly, Mickelson's research demonstrated that it is the combination or interaction of these factors that better explains the success or failure of parenting.

The first purpose of this paper is to move beyond pure description of developmentally disabled parents and explore the relationship between particular parenting problems and particular deficits of cognitive and emotional functioning. The relationship is also examined for how conditions of family and social environment modify the association. The second purpose is to identify particular service needs of developmentally disabled parents. Suggestions are presented of the services that can address each parenting problem by taking into account the associated cognitive and emotional deficits and social environmental conditions.

METHOD

The research tools of group process observation and informal structured interviewing were chosen as the best methods for collection of data on parenting, cognitive and emotional skills, and social environmental conditions of developmentally disabled parents. The study population consisted of the clients of two family service agencies. The parents are referred to the agencies by the county child protective agency.

In one agency parents receive the services of individual counseling, home visits, and a parent group program. Observations of weekly meetings of three groups of parents, ranging in size between 3 and 8 members, were conducted for 3 months. Observation notes of each parent group meeting were recorded and shared with the group leaders. The compilation of 3 months of observation notes provided the data in this study for reaching conclusions and supporting illustrations about service needs of developmentally disabled parents.

In a second agency, parents receive the services of a parent aide. The parent aide makes an average of three weekly visits to each family and is available for emergency assistance and counseling at any hour. To document the parenting problems and skill deficits of the developmentally disabled parent, a series of informal structured group interviews were conducted with those parent aides who have substantial experience and success in working with developmentally disabled parents. The group interviews enabled the parent aides to richly describe the different kinds of difficult situations that these parents face in raising their children. Transcriptions of the interview tapes represented the second source of data for the findings.

Generalizability of Results

This study of developmentally disabled parents has limited generalizability. The most precise description of the study population is that it consists of parents with observed cognitive, emotional, and social skill deficits who have parenting problems of suffcient seriousness that intervention was deemed necessary by child protective service workers. Previous surveys of mentally retarded parents (Mickelson, 1949; Shaw and Wright, 1960) have reported that between 33% and 39% of those surveyed had received child protective services or had faced proceedings in family courts. Although this reported incidence rate is high compared to the incidence rates of child maltreatment for other population groups in the United States (Burgdorf, 1980), it does indicate that most developmentally disabled parents should not be assumed to be experiencing serious parenting problems that would necessitate child protective intervention. Thus, the findings and conclusions presented below should be generalized only to those developmentally disabled parents who are clients of child protective services.

FINDINGS

The developmentally disabled parents in this study were observed to have significant deficits in the areas of cognitive development, emotional functioning, and social environmental conditions. These three primary deficits were found to directly contribute to particular problems in parenting. Also, a need for individual services that would address both the specific skill deficits and the parenting problems of these parents was clearly evidenced.

Cognitive Development Problems

For cognitive development, limited communication and learning skills serve to intensify parenting problems for the developmentally disabled adult. Furthermore, as the children of these parents mature, their intellectual capabilities generally surpass those of the parents. Thus, the parents' ability to become actively involved in their child's education becomes progressively diminished. For example, expressive and receptive language deficits frustrate the parents' ability to effectively intervene in the school system on behalf of their children. Also, learning deficits confound the parents' efforts to assist with their children's educational needs. The parent who cannot read has difficulty choosing appropriate reading materials for the child. At one agency, a number of donated children's books were offered to the members of a parent group. As the mothers sorted through the box of books, they talked about choosing the ones they wanted on the basis of cover design and color rather than by title or subject matter.

It is readily apparent that a need exists for advocacy services that will help parents negotiate effectively with educational institutions in order to obtain appropriate services for their children. The advocacy service can be provided by the parent aide, who can work with school social workers to assess the child's needs and assist the parents in articulating their needs and desires for their child.

The cognitive disparity between parent and child results in problems in the areas of parental control and discipline. One woman's lack of skills in financial management left her vulnerable to her children's efforts to extort her money. Gradually, the children usurped major control of household finances. They used their powerful position to exert control over their mother, and were unresponsive to her attempts at discipline. After repeatedly failing to regain control, this woman became apathetic to her children's behavior.

These events illustrate the need of developmentally disabled parents and their children for supportive therapeutic services. Support groups for the children would enable them to better understand their parents' disabilities. The school system could assume responsibility for organizing and leading this type of group for children. Additionally, family therapy services that would be able to address the parent-child cognitive disparity through clarification of family roles should be made available.

Learning deficits were found to generally inhibit the developmentally disabled adults' ability to benefit from most current parent education resources. The parents have difficulty internalizing information conveyed through traditional teaching methods such as reading material and classroom presentations. As a result, transfer of learning, if it occurs, is manifested inappropriately. For example, one parent aide suggested to one woman that she take her infant outside for some fresh air when possible. The parent interpreted the aide's suggestion to mean taking her baby outside daily, regardless of the weather (e.g., in pouring rain, in snowstorms). If the aide had actively demonstrated how and when to take an infant outside, the parent might have responded in a more appropriate manner.

Emotional Functioning Problems

For deficits in emotional functioning, two domains of parent behavior observed to be related to parenting problems are impulsivity and maternal overprotection. In the case of impulsivity, the inclination of some developmentally disabled parents to react rashly in response to critical situations of child management puts strain on the parent-child relationship. For example, one woman had difficulty distinguishing her child's emotional needs from her own. When confronted by her 7-year-old son during a dispute, she would respond to him by mirroring his aggressive behavior. When he teased and taunted, she would do likewise. In a short period, what began as a minor disagreement had escalated into a full-blown emotional battle between mother and child. The inability of a parent to control the impulse to respond to a parent-child confrontation in a childish manner places a heavy burden on the child to compensate for the parent's emotional immaturity.

This illustration demonstrates a need of developmentally disabled parents for improved problem-solving skills. Enhancement of these skills would help parents to increase their coping capacity through developing more appropriate ways of responding to stressful parenting situations. For mentally retarded persons, the learning of problem-solving skills has been proved to be effective within a peer support group setting (Richards and Lee, 1972; Davis and Shapiro, 1979; Szymanski and Rosefsky, 1980). Also, group work can enable developmentally disabled parents to form mutual support systems with other parents and thereby reduce social isolation in the community (Triplett, 1965; Grunewald and Linner, 1979; and Rosenberg and McTate, 1982).

Maternal overprotection is manifested through excessive controlling and restrictive parental behavior. Examples observed in this study include: 1) a parent who never allowed her children to play outdoors, 2) a parent who overdressed her child for the weather, to the point of restricting the child's physical movements, and 3) a parent who slept with her children because she feared that they might suffocate or gag during the night by themselves. These inappropriate behaviors reflect the developmentally disabled parents' lack of child development information and their tendency to overinvest emotionally in their children. This emotional overinvestment is commonly associated with reverse dependency, often found in abusive parents (Morris and Gould, 1963). When this condition exists, the parent relies upon the child to provide needed emotional support, in the form of the child's high performance of the parents' behavioral expectations and the child's returned love and respect to the parent.

One method of reducing parental overprotectiveness and breaking the cycle of reverse dependency is to introduce a parent aide into the home environment (Gifford et al., 1979). First, the parent aide serves as a role model for appropriate parenting behavior. Second, the aide provides emotional support, enabling the parent to depend temporarily upon another adult, and thereby minimizing the parent's need to depend on the child. Similar to the impact of the support group, the parent aide also reduces the effects of loneliness and social isolation.

Social Environmental Conditions

The social environmental condition of some developmentally disabled parents frequently serves to aggravate their problems in parenting. For example, the inability and sometimes unwillingness of service providers to adjust communications to a level of understanding for these parents, coupled with the parents' tendency to remain silent (the "cloak of competence"; Edgerton, 1967), results in situations in which the parents are unable to make effective use of available services. At the same time, service professionals feel that their help is unwanted or unneeded. One parent aide told of a woman who had brought her ill son to a pediatric health clinic. The woman had not understood the doctor's instructions about how and when to administer her child's medications and monitor his temperature with a thermometer, nor had she asked for instruction while at the clinic. The aide had to explain the medication procedure and how to use a thermometer.

Communication breakdowns like these can be avoided in two ways. First, when parents have an advocate for their need of services, such as parent aides, the advocate can assist them in communicating with service providers. Second, when service providers learn to recognize the learning disabilities of their clients, they can adjust their mode of service delivery accordingly. Providers would do well to follow the example of one pediatric developmental clinic in the Bronx, New York, that developed screening procedures to identify clients with learning disabilities and instructed its staff in communicating with them (Kaminer et al., 1981).

Another important condition of the social environment of developmentally disabled parents observed in this study is their dependency on public income maintenance programs (U.S. Supplemental Security Income, Home Relief, and Aid to Dependent Children). The generally low subsistence levels of these programs, combined with the likelihood of cognitive deficits in family budgeting and money management, places the developmentally disabled parent in a more vulnerable position by drawing attention of child welfare workers to their poor housekeeping and improper feeding and clothing of children. Consequently, these children are more likely to be defined as "at risk of going into foster care" (Haavik and Menninger, 1981). The poor socioeconomic conditions of some developmentally disabled parents and their inability to effectively utilize community health, social, and educational resources must be recognized as factors explaining why their children are placed in foster care, and why some parents face family court proceedings to terminate rights to their children.

CONCLUSION

The relationship between parenting and developmental disability discussed here is complex because the connection is often conditional on the presence or absence of social or environmental factors. Although this paper has suggested several service interventions for particular parenting problems, a single prescriptive formula for meeting the service needs of developmentally disabled parents would oversimplify the issue. Further development of services will require a continual exchange of services knowledge and experience by those providers who are presently meeting the individual and ongoing needs of parents with developmental disabilities.

ACKNOWLEDGMENTS

The authors are grateful to the parent aides of Alliance and the group leaders of the Family Service Department of The Salvation Army in Syracuse, New York for their contributions to our findings.

REFERENCES

Burgdorf, K. 1980. Recognition and Reporting of Child Maltreatment. National Center on Child Abuse and Neglect, Washington, D.C.

Davis, K. R., and Shapiro, I. J. 1979. Exploring group process as a means of reaching the mentally retarded. Soc. Casework 60:330–337.

Edgerton, R. B. 1967. The Cloak of Competence: Stigma in the Lives of the Mentally Retarded. University of California Press, Berkeley, California.

Gifford, C. D., Kaplan, F. B., and Salus, M. K. 1979. Parent Aides in Child Abuse and Neglect Programs. National Center on Child Abuse and Neglect, Washington, D.C.

Grunewald, K., and Linner, B. 1979. Mentally retarded: Sexuality and normalization. Current Sweden, No. 237.

Haavik, S. F., and Menninger, K. A. 1981. Sexuality, Law, and the Developmentally Disabled Person. Paul H. Brookes Publishers, Baltimore.

Heber, R., and Garber, H. 1975. The Milwaukee Project: A Study of the use of family intervention to prevent cultural-familial mental retardation. In: B. Friedlander, G. Sterritt, and G. Kirk (eds.), Exceptional Infant: Assessment and Intervention, Vol. 3, pp. 399–433. Brunner/Mazel, New York.

Kaminer, R., Jedrysek, E., and Soles, B. 1981. Intellectually limited parents. J. Dev. Behav. Pediatr. 2:39–43.

Mickelson, P. 1947. The feeble minded parent: A study of 90 family cases. Am. J. Ment. Defic. 51:644–653.

Mickelson, P. 1949. Can mentally deficient parents be helped to give their children better care? Am. J. Ment. Defic. 53:516–534.

Morris, M. G., and Gould, R. W. 1963. Role-reversal, a necessary concept in dealing with the "battered child" syndrome. In: The Neglected Battered Child Syndrome. Child Welfare League of America, New York.

Polansky, N. A., Chalmers, M. A., Buttenwieser, E., and Williams, D. P. 1981. Damaged Parents. University of Chicago Press, Chicago.

Richards, L. D., and Lee, K. A. 1972. Group process in the social habilitation of the retarded. Soc. Casework 53:30–37.

Robinson, L. H. 1978. Parental attitudes of retarded young mothers. Child Psychiatry Hum. Dev. 8:131–144.

Rosenberg, S. A., and McTate, G. A. 1982. Intellectually handicapped mothers: Problems and prospects. Child. Today 11:24–26, 37.

Shaw, C., and Wright, C. 1960. The married mental defective: A followup study. Lancet 1:273–274.

Szymanski, L. S., and Rosefsky, Q. B. 1980. Group psychotherapy with retarded persons. In: L. S. Szymanski and P. E. Tanquay (eds.), Emotional Disorders of Mentally Retarded Persons, pp. 174–194. University Park Press, Baltimore.

Triplett, J. L. 1965. A women's club for deprived mothers. Nurs. Outlook 13:33–35.

PERSPECTIVES AND PROGRESS IN MENTAL RETARDATION
Volume I—Social, Psychological, and Educational Aspects
Edited by J. M. Berg

TRAINING PARENTS AS ADVOCATES FOR THEIR DEVELOPMENTALLY DISABLED CHILDREN

R. P. Brightman

Department of Psychology, University of California, 405 Hilgard Avenue, Los Angeles, 90024

In the United States, the Education for All Handicapped Children Act of 1975 promises all disabled children a free and appropriate public education to be provided in accordance with an Individualized Educational Program (IEP). Although the status of parents on the IEP planning team is equal to that of professionals, few possess the skills to assertively exercise their mandated responsibility. To assist parents, a Parents as Advocates course was developed and evaluated. Results of the evaluation reveal that trained parents learn the information and behavioral skills required to advocate effectively.

In the United States, the Education for All Handicapped Children Act of 1975 (Public Law 94-142) promises all children with disabilities a free and appropriate education in the least restrictive environment. Services are to be provided in accordance with an Individualized Educational Program (IEP), developed for each child by persons familiar with his or her unique educational needs. A major provision of the Act is the stipulation that parents serve on the IEP committee with status equal to that of the committee's professional members. Such status formalizes the role of parents as advocates, yet, clearly, few parents possess either the requisite knowledge of complex special education law or the appropriate assertiveness skills required to fully engage in the IEP process, especially when parent opinion regarding the merits

This research was sponsored by Grant 5 R01 HD10962 from the National Institute of Child Health and Human Development to Dr. Bruce L. Baker. In addition, the author received support from Grant 5 T24 MH15901-03 from the National Institute of Mental Health.

of a given educational program differs substantially from professional opinion. It is therefore not surprising that, although parent attendance at IEP meetings is quite high, parent participation is often minimal (Goldstein et al., 1980; Salett and Henderson, 1980). Although some parents may adopt a passive role at IEP meetings, others may choose to act fully on their Public Law 94-142 rights and responsibilities. Without adequate preparation, however, these parents may find themselves intimidated and ineffectual (Brightman and Sullivan, 1980).

Although professionals have studied aspects of the parent-as-advocate role (Hartwell-Meyers and Haynes, 1978), there has not been empirical evaluation of their attempts to facilitate this role. The present study evaluates the effectiveness of a Parents as Advocates program, a training program designed to enhance parents' abilities to advocate effectively for their developmentally disabled children.

METHOD

Overview of Procedures

Parents of developmentally disabled children were assigned to experimental or delayed training control conditions. Families were formed into groups within constraints imposed by parent schedules and geographic distance and groups were randomly assigned either to one of two Parents as Advocates groups or to a delayed training control group. Measures of parent knowledge of special education law, of performance in simulated advocacy situations, and of trait level assertiveness were obtained from all parents 2 weeks before and 1 week after the training period.

Subjects

Parents from 19 families with developmentally disabled children attended an orientation-assessment meeting wherein the goals and format of the Parents as Advocates program and the requirements for participation were explained. All agreed to participate. Each of the Experimental groups consisted of 5 mothers and one couple, a total of 14 subjects representing 12 children. The Control group consisted of 3 mothers and 4 couples, a total of 11 subjects representing 7 children. Two of the mothers in the Experimental condition did not complete postmeasures and are considered dropouts from training. The results are based on complete data from 12 Experimental subjects and 11 Control subjects.

Table 1 presents demographic and advocacy experience data by condition. Independent t tests revealed no significant differences be-

Table 1. Family demographic and advocacy experience data

	Experimental			Control		
	Mean	SD	Group	Mean	SD	Group
Age (years)						
Mother	39.4	6.8		39.3	7.0	
Father	45.0	9.4		43.1	7.4	
Child	11.0	5.3		7.1	4.1	
Education (years)						
Mother	14.4	2.9		14.4	3.3	
Father	14.8	3.3		13.4	3.4	
Advocacy experience (years attending IEP meetings)	2.5	1.7		2.1	1.7	
Marital Status (%)						
Single			16.7			0.0
Intact			83.3			100.0
Employment (%)						
Mother						
Full time			40.0			0.0
Part time			10.0			14.3
Unemployed			50.0			85.7
Father						
Full time			62.5			100.0
Part time			25.0			0.0
Unemployed			12.5			0.0

tween Experimental and Control subjects on these variables. On the average, mothers and fathers in the sample were 39.4 and 44.1 years of age, respectively. Both mothers and fathers had completed a mean of 14.3 years of school. Annual family income averaged approximately $25,000.

The 11 boys and 6 girls represented in the sample ranged in age from 3.0 to 16.3 years, with a mean age of 9.1. The children had generally received the diagnosis of their disability by 2 years of age; retardation (47.1%), multiple handicap (17.6%), and specific learning disability (11.8%) were the most frequently cited disability categories. When the study began, all children were receiving special education services, with placement occurring most frequently in private day schools (41.2%) or in a special class located within a special school (35.3%).

Parents as Advocates Program

The primary objectives of the Parents as Advocates program were to improve parents' understanding of PL 94-142 rights and procedures and to improve their ability to apply and utilize that knowledge, particularly when planning for and participating in their child's IEP meeting. In order to meet these broad goals the program utilized a small group format and numerous instructional approaches, including didactic inputs, small group problem-solving exercises, videotape analysis, behavioral rehearsal with peer feedback, filmstrip presentations, and action-oriented homework assignments. In addition, parents were given many handouts that further specified their rights regarding the conduct and content of educational assessments, IEP meetings, and fair hearings. The Parents as Advocates course consisted of 6 weekly evening meetings, each lasting 2 hours. Early sessions focused on learning relevant special education statutes and regulations; later sessions focused on learning to behave in an appropriately assertive fashion during parent-teacher conferences and IEP meetings.

MEASURES

Outcome Measures

The outcome measures seek to assess the degree to which parents learn the material presented in the Parents as Advocates course and the degree to which they are able to use that knowledge in simulated situations in which their PL 94-142 rights are challenged or violated. Toward these ends, the following outcome measures were used (all but the Behavior Review Scale were developed for the present study):

1. *Information Questionnaire:* this 20-item multiple choice questionnaire assessed knowledge of PL 94-142. Cronbach's alpha, calculated on pretraining scores, was 0.54. Despite this relatively low level of internal consistency, the face validity of the items suggested that the measure is useful in assessing the degree to which subjects learn the material presented in training. This measure was administered at the pretraining and posttraining assessment sessions.

2. *Problem Identification:* this measure presented parents with five vignettes, each characterized by the abridgement of at least one right guaranteed by PL 94-142. Parents were asked to specify which rights have been overlooked in each vignette. Inter-rater reliabilities for a subsample of 10 Problem Identification measures scored independently by two coders were 0.98 for Vignette 1, 0.95 for Vignette 2, 0.98 for Vignette 3, 0.93 for Vignette IV, 0.93 for Vignette V, and 0.99 for the Problem Identification Total Score. This measure was administered at the posttraining assessment session only.

3. *Parent Talk Measure:* this analog measure sought to assess the effectiveness of parents' responses to a series of simulated ad-

vocacy situations. Each parent viewed a videotape in which he/she met three special education professionals: a school administrator, a school psychologist, and a special education teacher. Each "professional" presented parents with five advocacy-related stimulus statements (e.g., school administrator: "We can provide your child with 30 minutes of speech therapy per week. Now I understand you'd like to have 90 minutes of speech therapy, but we have only one speech therapist and there are many children to serve.") Parents had 30 seconds to respond to the stimulus statement and were instructed to respond as if the statement actually applied to their child. Audiotapes of parents' responses were then coded along eight scales: I, Response Latency; II, Subjective Impression; III, Empathy; IV, Law; V, Desired Outcome; VI, Acquiescence; VII, Assertiveness; and VIII, Voice Tone. Inter-rater reliabilities based on scores from two coders who independently scored a subsample of 30 Parent Talk tapes were 0.78, 0.85, 0.50, 0.79, 0.78, 0.70, 0.46, and 0.84 for Parent Talk Scales I–VIII respectively. This measure was administered at the pretraining and posttraining assessment sessions.

4. *Behavior Review Scale:* Developed by Rathus (1973), this is a widely used self-report measure that assesses general assertiveness. The split-half reliability based on pretraining scores was 0.80. This measure was administered at pretraining and posttraining assessment sessions.

Descriptive Measures

Two descriptive measures were used to gain information:

1. *Demographic Questionnaire:* this sought information regarding parent education, parent income, child diagnosis, and school placement.
2. *Advocacy Questionnaire:* this sought information regarding parents' previous experiences with PL 94-142 procedures. The focus of the questionnaire is on parents' perceptions of their child's most recent IEP meeting.

RESULTS

Knowledge of PL 94-142

Information Questionnaire The pre-and posttraining mean scores for each condition are presented in Table 2. The groups did not differ at pretraining. A two-way ANOVA conducted on experimental and control scores revealed a significant condition × time interaction ($F_{1,21}$

Table 2.   Information questionnaire mean scores

Time of administration	Experimental		Control	
	Mean	SD	Mean	SD
Pretraining	10.3	2.9	8.8	2.7
Posttraining	14.9	2.4	10.0	3.0

= 8.91, P = 0.007), indicating that experimental parents demonstrated significantly greater gains than control parents.

Problem Identification   Results from this post-training-only measure are presented in Table 3. Experimental parents scored significantly higher than control parents on each of the five vignettes and on a total score.

Parent Performance

Parent Talk   The mean pretraining and posttraining scale scores are presented in Table 4. Two-way ANOVAs using repeated measures were conducted on mean scale scores. Analysis of Scale I (Response Latency) revealed a significant main effect for time of administration ($F_{1,21}$ = 6.73, P = 0.017), indicating that parents in both conditions were able to respond significantly more quickly at the posttraining assessment session. The condition × time interaction was not significant.

Analysis of Scale II (Subjective Impression) revealed a significant condition × time interaction ($F_{1,21}$ = 14.19, P = 0.001). At pretraining, both groups were judged to have responded in a mildly influential manner. Whereas control parents continued to be perceived as largely ineffectual at posttraining, trained parents were judged as responding in a manner that was "quite likely to influence and impress." Analysis of Scale IV (Law) also revealed the condition × time interaction to be significant ($F_{1,21}$ = 8.54, P = 0.001). At pretraining, parents in both conditions generally failed to allude to their PL 94-142 rights in their responses. Whereas control parents continued to fail to cite the law at posttraining, experimental parents offered responses that, on the average, conveyed an awareness of their legal rights.

Table 3.   Problem identification means and independent t tests

Vignette	Experimental	Control	t	d.f.	P (1-tailed)
I	2.5	1.1	3.47	21	0.001
II	2.6	1.5	3.13	21	0.003
III	2.7	1.4	2.08	21	0.025
IV	3.0	1.7	2.63	21	0.008
V	3.0	0.5	5.92	21	<0.001
Total	13.8	6.2	4.97	21	<0.001

Table 4.   Mean scale and item scores for Parent Talk Scales I–VIII

Parent Talk Scale	Time	Experimental		Control	
		Scale	Item	Scale	Item
I Response latency	Pre	55.7	3.7	53.4	3.6
	Post	42.1	2.8	45.9	3.1
II Subjective impression	Pre	21.3	1.4	18.8	1.3
	Post	32.5	2.2	18.5	1.2
III Empathy	Pre	4.9	0.3	4.6	0.3
	Post	5.8	0.4	4.8	0.3
IV Law	Pre	9.9	0.7	9.0	0.6
	Post	16.3	1.1	8.3	0.6
V Desired outcome	Pre	23.5	1.6	23.3	1.6
	Post	33.6	2.2	22.5	1.5
VI Acquiescence	Pre	15.2	1.0	15.6	1.0
	Post	16.4	1.1	16.8	1.1
VII Assertiveness	Pre	25.9	1.7	24.9	1.7
	Post	27.6	1.8	24.1	1.6
VIII Voice tone	Pre	26.4	1.8	27.1	1.8
	Post	27.4	1.8	27.4	1.8

Analysis of Scale V (Desired Outcome) also revealed the condition × time interaction to be significant. Prior to training, parents in both conditions generally failed to specify their proposed solution to the stimulus situation in a specific manner. Whereas control parents were perceived as continuing to respond in a vague manner at posttraining, experimental parents were judged, on the average, as responding in a behaviorally specific manner. Analyses conducted on the remaining Parent Talk Scales revealed no significant condition × time interactions or main effects.

Behavior Review Scale   At pretraining, experimental and control parents received mean scores of 14.25 and 10.55, respectively. At posttraining, the mean score of experimental parents rose to 21.58 and the mean score of control parents dropped slightly to 9.55. Despite the apparent trend in the expected direction, a two-way ANOVA revealed that the condition × time interaction failed to reach significance ($F_{1,21} = 2.15$, $P = 0.16$).

DISCUSSION

The results of the Parents as Advocates evaluation are easily summarized. On measures of knowledge (Information Questionnaire, Problem Identification) and verbal performance (Parent Talk), experimental parents demonstrated gains significantly greater than those evidenced by control parents. Overall, the short-term objectives of the Parents as Advocates program were met. Parents were able to learn the specifics of special education laws and to utilize that knowledge effectively when the educational rights of their children were violated.

The degree to which the results of the present study can be extended to parents of disabled children in general is not clear. Parents in this sample were generally well educated, of middle socioeconomic status, and had intact relationships. Inasmuch as these demographic characteristics have been positively associated with outcome in behavioral programs training parents as teachers (Clark et al., 1982), they are probably predictive of performance in advocacy training as well. Indeed, the sophisticated intellectual, conceptual, and verbal skills required for effective advocacy may render advocacy training especially sensitive to these demographic characteristics. Nonetheless, the results of the present evaluation are encouraging. It is hoped that, as has been the case in behavioral parent training, future replication and innovation will result in additional advocacy training models well suited to the special needs of parents of developmentally disabled children.

REFERENCES

Brightman, A. J., and Sullivan, M. B. 1980. A Report of Findings. The Cambridge Workshop, Belmont, Massachusetts.

Clark, D. B., Baker, B. L., and Heifetz, L. J. 1982. Behavioral training for parents of mentally retarded children: Prediction of outcome. Am. J. Ment. Defic. 87:14–19.

Goldstein, S., Strickland, B., Turnbull, A. P., and Curry, L. 1980. An observational analysis of the IEP conference. Except. Child. 46:278–286.

Hartwell-Meyers, L. K., and Haynes, J. D. 1978. A data based approach to training parents of handicapped children as effective advocates. Arizona State University, Tempe, Arizona. (Eric Document Reproduction Service No. ED157316).

Rathus, S. A. 1973. A 30-item schedule for assessing assertive behavior. Behav. Ther. 4:398–406.

Salett, S., and Henderson, A. 1980. A Report on the Education for All Handicapped Children Act: Are Parents Involved? National Committee for Citizens in Education, Columbia, Maryland.

PERSPECTIVES AND PROGRESS IN MENTAL RETARDATION
Volume I—Social, Psychological, and Educational Aspects
Edited by J. M. Berg
Copyright © 1984 by I.A.S.S.M.D.

LOWER SOCIOECONOMIC STATUS FAMILIES AND PROGRAMS FOR TRAINING PARENTS OF RETARDED CHILDREN

B. L. Baker, M. Prieto-Bayard, and M. McCurry
*Department of Psychology, University of California, Los Angeles,
California 90024*

Four model programs are examined in training lower socioeconomic status (SES) parents of retarded children. An underrepresentation in training programs for lower-SES families is found, and parent's education is a strong predictor of performance on verbal measures, but changes in the training model can increase gains. Suggested modifications are discussed in competency-based progress, minimizing didactic presentation, involving parents and observers and teachers, and providing incentives for participation. Posttraining follow-through problems are highlighted both with English- and Spanish-speaking families.

Training programs for parents of mentally retarded children have by now justified their place in our system of service delivery. Parents have long asked professionals for answers to questions that arise daily with a retarded child—obvious questions, like how to toilet train, or what to do about a tantrum. Programs built upon a behavior modification foundation, albeit varying considerably in their specifics, have demonstrated changes in parental skills and child behavior, at least in the short run (Baker, 1976). This paper addresses the question: How do lower socioeconomic status families fare in parent training programs? A disproportionate number of lower socioeconomic status families have a retarded child; yet, to anticipate our discussion, they may receive less training, and benefit less from it, than middle-class families.

In addressing this question, we immediately encounter difficulties. First, how should socioeconomic status (SES) be defined? This construct has several components, variously used in different studies. Our measure of SES follows Hollingshead's (1957) in combining father's education and occupation. Mother's education, however, is important because parent training programs typically involve only mothers. Although family income is no longer widely used as an index, it too appears as a correlate in several studies. Beyond the issue of measuring SES, there is also the problem of defining cutoff points. For some authors low SES means families below a cutoff point on one dimension (e.g., receiving welfare payments, or unemployed, or not high school educated), whereas for others it means only that the families are low relative to others in the sample.

A further difficulty is that few studies have directly examined the relationship between SES and parent training, partly because parent training has been largely a middle-class venture. Programs to increase skills in parenting normal children (e.g., Parent Effectiveness Training; Gordon, 1970) have attracted mainly middle class parents. Hargis and Blechman (1979) reviewed reports of behavioral parent training and found lower-SES families underrepresented here as well. We cannot say whether lower-SES families are less interested in such programs or are systematically excluded by recruitment methods and program attributes.

In marked contrast to the limited representation of low-SES families in published reports is the interest expressed by service providers in every audience we address. Professionals who work with these families often feel frustrated and devalued. Many tell us that the lower-SES families they see for counseling or training do more poorly at every stage—that they are less apt to keep initial appointments, to complete assignments, to complete the program, to master the content, and to effectively teach their children. Although there is some empirical evidence to support these impressions, it is not without contradictions. It is important to check these assumptions further, so that we can adapt programs as necessary to involve lower-SES parents better. To address this question, we first review here three common models of parent training. We then consider the evidence for how low-SES families fare in them, and describe some promising adaptations of these models.

COMMON PARENT TRAINING MODELS

Model 1: Individual Training

Individual training appears to be the most prevalent model. The trainer, usually a mental health professional, has a series of meetings with parent(s) and child at the clinic or home. The trainer typically demonstrates teaching methods and supervises the parent's teaching. Individual training sometimes follows a well-defined curriculum that aims to teach specific knowledge and skills. However, it is difficult in this model to keep training focused on general principles and to keep from lapsing into more diffuse therapy. It is also awkward to present didactic lectures to an audience of one. In practice, the individual model often proceeds more loosely, with the trainer helping the parent to problem solve about her own child's behavior and to implement programs. Individual training is costly; it often lasts until the trainer and parent agree that their goals have been accomplished, sometimes for one or more years of weekly or biweekly visits.

Model 2: Group Training

Reports of successful individual training led to experiments with groups of 5 to 10 families. The advantages include reduced per-family cost, greater parent-to-parent exchange and support, more stimulation for trainers (who usually work together in this model), and a wider range of possible training techniques. Groups require more preparation; they are likely to follow an established curriculum and be limited in time (usually about 10 weeks). They usually do not include the child, thereby placing a greater burden on parents to generalize what they have learned to their interactions with the child at home. This generalization is usually facilitated by use of visual modeling—live and with media—and by a series of homework assignments. Most groups also go beyond consideration of current problems to teach some social learning principles, and this has been demonstrated to enhance generalization (McMahon et al., 1981).

Model 3: Media Training

Training parents through media is the least researched of these models but has the greatest potential impact. Professional guidance can be delivered in more cost-effective ways than on a one-to-one or small group basis. One need only think of the impact of a book like Benjamin Spock's (1976) *Baby and Child Care* on the child-rearing practices of millions of people, or the impact of a television series like "Sesame Street" on preschool children's development, to realize that psychological knowledge, imaginatively packaged, can be a powerful intervention.

Few data bear directly on media-based training for parents of retarded children. Although most programs utilize videotapes or films, the only comparison of training by visual media only versus training by other modalities has been in brief (30 minute or less) analog programs; here visual media were very successful (O'Dell et al., 1982). The primary focus of study has been written media. Bernal and North (1978) reported on 26 behavioral manuals or series; of these five are specifically for parents of handicapped children. Unfortunately, these five are written at a much higher reading level than the manuals for general parent use (13.1 versus 8.7 years of education). Nonetheless, there is evidence that manuals can be a cost-effective alternative for parents with requisite skills. We have produced nine manuals for parents of retarded children; these cover self-help skills, independent living skills, speech and language, play skills, and behavior problems (Baker et al., 1976, 1977, 1978, 1980). We evaluated these manuals as training models when used alone and when used in conjunction with professional consultation by telephone, in groups, and in groups with home visits. Surprisingly, parents who had only manuals gained as much in their knowledge of teaching principles, and their children improved as much in self-help skills, as those in the more costly professional conditions (Baker and Heifetz, 1976; Heifetz, 1977).

LOWER-SES FAMILIES AND THESE MODELS

Our examination of these three models suggests several reasons why lower-SES families are less likely to be in parent training. Most individual and group training takes place at agencies, which are often some distance from the family's home. Daytime sessions conflict with work and child-care demands. Groups are conducted with a curriculum, homework, and the expectation of regular attendance—too much like school to appeal to parents with limited education. Training manuals, our own included, may have been written at too high a reading level to be used comfortably without additional professional help.

Low-SES parents who do join training programs generally have been reported to fare less well than middle-class families. In families with child conduct disorders, Rinn et al. (1975) found that lower income parents attended fewer group sessions and attained fewer goals; Sadler et al. (1976) and Patterson (1974) found that families with low education and SES, respectively, produced less reduction in deviant child behavior following individual training. In families with a retarded child, Rose (1974) found that mothers on welfare who were trained in groups took longer than middle-class mothers to carry out programs and hence completed fewer. Our studies have found that both income and education relate to measures after training of how well parents understand behavioral principles and teach their retarded child (Clark and Baker, 1983).

How could training be altered to attract low-SES parents, to keep them in the program, and to increase their gains? When agency staff feel a mother may not benefit from a group, one inclination is to see her individually. We have compared the same 10-session training curriculum implemented individually and in groups, and found that these models produced equivalent outcomes at considerably different costs (Brightman et al., 1982). To see if lower-education mothers might do better in individual training, we analyzed these data further, dividing the groups by mother's education. We measured parents' knowledge of behavioral principles and actual teaching skills with their child after training. For knowledge of behavioral principles there was no differential relationship with education in the two training models. Yet our measure of teaching skills showed a borderline significant interaction (time × model × education: $F_{1,40} = 3.81, P = 0.058$). However, we found that lower-education mothers did *more poorly* in the individual model than they did in groups. This argues against simply presenting the same curriculum individually for low-SES families. However, we note that Rogers et al. (1981) found no relationship between SES and child or parent outcome in an individual training program that had one important difference from ours: it had a graded series of tasks and required parents to master each one before moving on. Unfortunately, Rogers et al. do not report whether or not training proceeded more slowly for lower-SES parents. Their study does suggest that competency-based progress through training may be one way to enhance effectiveness.

Another possible change is to make presentation of program content less didactic and more action-oriented, with modeling and/or direct involvement in teaching. O'Dell et al. (1982) found SES and education correlated with parent skills attained when training used a written manual, audiotaped manual, or live modeling with rehearsal. No such correlation was found when training was done by videotape alone. We must be cautious in generalizing from this one-session training program, but these results suggest the need for further study of training through media. A further change is to introduce specific incentives. A number of investigators have demonstrated increased attendance and compliance with training demands when an incentive was provided. Incentives have included a parenting salary, a "contract deposit" (money paid to be refunded upon completion), toys, additional services, and even written summaries of soap operas for mothers in a daytime program. In our own programs we have successfully used a lottery, whereby parents earn tickets for attending and completing assignments; at each meeting there is a drawing wherein one parent wins a prize (e.g., a plant, a toy for the child, a canned ham). Incentives have been found to be effective with middle- as well as lower-SES families; however, they may be a particularly valuable addition for the latter (Fleischman, 1979).

ADAPTATIONS OF TRAINING MODELS

Alternative Training: Spanish-speaking Families

As an illustration of the group model's potential flexibility to accommodate lower-SES families, consider a program we recently conducted with low-SES parents who speak only Spanish. For these families, the myriad of ongoing adjustments and difficulties inherent in raising a retarded child are exacerbated by lack of bilingual services, low incomes, limited education, institutional discrimination, and immigration concerns. Frequently they are simply unaware of existing services.

We collaborated with the South Central Los Angeles Regional Center for the Mentally Retarded, which told parents about our program and provided meeting space. Twenty low-SES families began training. All were monolingual Spanish speaking and 80% had annual incomes below $11,000. Most (75%) were intact, with fathers working at unskilled jobs. The mean education for mothers was fifth grade, usually completed in Mexico. Most (70%) immigrated from Mexico within the last 10 years. Target children were mildly to severely retarded, with a mean age of 6.7 years (range 3–16), and a mean of 2.65 siblings.

To conduct training, typical barriers to utilization by low-SES and/ or Spanish-speaking families had to be reduced. Tangible barriers include language, location, transportation, cost, and child care. Intangible barriers include misinformation about the child's retardation, ambivalence about going to agencies, religious beliefs that emphasize accepting the child as he or she is, and uncertainly about oneself as a learner, let alone a teacher.

We were able to reduce the tangible barriers and at least address the intangible ones. Bilingual University of California (Los Angeles) and Regional Center staff jointly conducted groups, and manuals and handouts were translated into Spanish. Groups were located centrally at the Regional Center, and met in the evenings so that mothers did not have to come alone. Groups were offered without cost, and as an incentive, parents were reimbursed $2 for each meeting attended to defray transportation costs. As it turned out, diplomas given at the end of the program were a much more sought-after incentive. To further enable attendance we provided child care. The child group was staffed by undergraduate volunteers, who quickly learned basic behavioral techniques under the authors' supervision. As our first group progressed we made increasingly greater use of the child group as a place to model good teaching for parents; in the second group, parents observed teaching and were supervised by staff while teaching in every session.

Fifteen families (75%) completed the 10-week training program, and they increased significantly ($P < 0.05$) on each of five measures of outcome (no measure required the parent to read or write):

1. Knowledge of behavioral principles, measured by a series of vignettes posing teaching or behavior management problems to which the parent verbally gave solutions, which were coded
2. Teaching skill, measured by the Teaching Proficiency Test (TPT) (Clark and Baker, submitted for publication), a coded teaching session conducted by the parent and videotaped
3. Teaching at home, measured by an interview
4. Child behavior problems measured by a parent-completed checklist administered verbally
5. Child self-help skills, measured by a parent-completed checklist administered verbally.

Overall, these results were encouraging with a group predicted to do poorly. The posttraining level of actual teaching skill on the TPT was almost equal to the level attained by middle-class parents. We have no comparable data from middle-class families on the verbally administered vignettes test. The one discouraging note is that these Spanish-speaking families showed little increase in their actual teaching at home—the gains on our measure reflected better teaching but not more teaching. We still face the problem of how to help parents put their increased teaching knowledge and skills to work.

Model 4: School-based Training

As a further adaptation of individual or group training, we considered a school-based model. It seems obvious that training parents in conjunction with a school program for their child would enhance both learning and follow-through, and it is surprising that this model is so rarely reported. Fredericks et al. (1974) developed a system whereby every few weeks the parent briefly watches the teacher and then carries out teaching of one skill at home. There is no formal training, and record-keeping just involves a data sheet that goes back and forth in the child's lunch box. For the approximately 50% of families that participated, the child's rate of learning for targeted skills was doubled. A simple system like this that does not require parents to learn behavioral principles may be particularly adaptable to low-SES families.

We experimented with a 3-week mini-camp for children of parents who had completed 10 sessions of group training but had shown only minimal gains on our measures. The results indicated that an intensive school-based program that emphasizes active teaching can increase low-gain parents' teaching proficiency (Brightman et al., 1980). We developed a second mini-camp in the summer of 1981, described briefly below. The program enrolled 21 low-SES black and Hispanic families selected according to predictors of low gain if they were in group training. Predictors were determined through discriminant analysis of over 100 families' outcome in our previous research (Clark and Baker, 1983). These were low mother's education, low family income, no previous behavior modification experience, and high expectation of problems in teaching.

Families participated in a 6-week program, with one half-day to a day's involvement each week; their children attended mini-camp 4 days a week for 3 or 6 weeks. Parent training emphasized action inputs: observation of teaching, practice teaching under supervision with other children as well as their own, and review with trainers of videotaped teaching sessions. Principles and future planning generally were worked into teaching supervision, although, because these parents entered without previous training, small group sessions were conducted for didactic inputs, viewing of videotapes, and group discussion. Because 12 families were monolingual Spanish speaking, training for them was conducted in Spanish.

The program produced generally satisfying results, with one reservation. The completion rate was good; all families attended some of the training, and posttraining data were obtained from 17 families. Four families (19%) had spotty attendance and were considered dropouts (two dropouts had serious emotional problems that interfered with training to the extent that we considered it best that they discontinue). Participating families showed significant gains on a measure of behavioral knowledge, although in this program we used the Behavioral Vignettes Test (Baker and Heifetz, 1976), which gives four possible alternatives for each item. This format is more difficult than the open-ended one used in our previous Spanish-speaking groups, and scores were correlated highly with education ($r = 0.56$). In retrospect, the open-ended verbal format is a better way to assess knowledge in families with limited education.

Participating parents increased significantly on measures of teaching skill (the Teaching Proficiency Test) and child self-help skills. Parents also increased significantly on the interview about home teaching. However, as with our Spanish-speaking groups, this increase reflected better teaching but not more teaching. We still cannot point to evidence that, following this mini-camp, parents were more involved in teaching their retarded child than they had been before. Such problems of follow-through are not limited to lower-SES families; in fact, they plague all behavioral intervention work.

CONCLUSIONS

The literature and our own experiences in training lower-SES parents lead us to one observation and three conclusions. The observation is that within the population of low-SES families there is considerable heterogeneity. This is, of course, obvious, but it warrants mention because we have talked mainly of how low-SES families in general behave and have only begun to address some of the important dimensions within the low-SES population that relate to training and outcome. We have noted, for example, that education is still a strong predictor of performance on verbal measures, even within a sample with no high school graduates. Furthermore, there may well be differences between English- and Spanish-speaking low-SES families that would relate to program outcome. Clearly an important direction for future research is toward understanding how other characteristics influence receptivity to, and performance in, training. With this caveat, we offer three general conclusions about lower-SES families and parent training:

1. Lower-SES families are underrepresented in parent training programs. However, they will join and complete such programs if barriers to utilization are reduced.
2. Lower-SES parents, it has been reported, complete fewer programs than middle-class parents and attain lower levels of proficiency and child change. Here, too, changes in the training model can increase gains. Suggested changes include competency-based progress, minimizing didactic presentations, involving parents as active observers and teachers, and giving incentives for participation.
3. The problem of follow-through after training, so that parents implement the skills they have acquired in daily routine at home, is far from solved.

REFERENCES

Baker, B. L. 1976. Parent involvement in programming for the developmentally disabled child. In: L. L. Lloyd (ed.), Communication Assessment and Intervention. University Park Press, Baltimore.
Baker, B. L., Brightman, A. J., Heifetz, L. J., and Murphy, D. M. 1976, 1977, 1978, 1980. Steps to Independence Series. Research Press Co., Champaign, Illinois.

468 Baker et al.

Baker, B. L. and Heifetz, L. H. 1976. The READ Project: Teaching manuals for parents of retarded children. In: T. D. Tjossem (ed.), Intervention Strategies for High Risk Infants and Young Children. University Park Press, Baltimore.

Bernal, M. E., and North, J. A. 1978. A survey of parent training manuals. J. Appl. Behav. Anal. 11:533–544.

Brightman, R. P., Ambrose, S. A., and Baker, B. L. 1980. Parent training: A school-based model for enhancing teaching performance. Child Behav. Ther. 2:35–47.

Brightman, R. P., Baker, B. L., Clark, D. B., and Ambrose, S. A. 1982. Effectiveness of alternative parent training formats. J. Behav. Ther. Exp. Psychiatry 13:113–117.

Clark, D. B., and Baker, B. L. 1983. Predicting outcome in parent training. J. Consult. Clin. Psychol. 51:309–311.

Clark, D. B., and Baker, B. L. The Teaching Proficiency Test: A measure of skill in applying behavior modification techniques for parents of retarded children. (submitted for publication)

Fleischman, M. J. 1979. Using parenting salaries to control attrition and cooperation in therapy. Behav. Ther. 10:111–116.

Fredericks, H. D., Baldwin, V. L., and Grove, D. 1974. A home-center based parent training model. In: J. Grim (ed.), Training Parents to Teach: Four Models. First Chance for Children 3:11–24.

Gordon, T. 1970. Parent Effectiveness Training. Wyden Press, New York.

Hargis, K., and Blechman, E. A. 1979. Social class and training of parents as behavior change agents. Child Behav. Ther. 1:69–74.

Heifetz, L. J. 1977. Behavioral training for parents of retarded children: Alternative formats based on instructional media. Am. J. Ment. Defic. 82:194–203.

Hollingshead, A. B. 1957. Two-factor Index of Social Position. Unpublished manuscript, Department of Sociology, Yale University, New Haven.

McMahon, R. J., Forehand, R., and Griest, D. L. 1981. Effects of knowledge of social learning principles on enhancing treatment outcome and generalization in parent training program. J. Consult. Clin. Psychol. 49:526–532.

O'Dell, S. L., O'Quin, J. A., Alford, B. A., O'Brient, A. L., Bradlyn, A. S., and Giebenhain, J. E. 1982. Predicting the aquisition of parenting skills via four training methods. Behav. Ther. 13:194–208.

Patterson, G. R. 1974. Interventions for boys with conduct problems: Multiple settings, treatments, and criteria. J. Consult. Clin. Psychol. 42:471–481.

Rinn, R. C., Vernon, J. C., and Wise, M. J. 1975. Training parents of behaviorally-disordered children in groups: A three years' program evaluation. Behav. Ther. 6:378–387.

Rogers, T. R., Forehand, R., Griest, D. L., Wells, K. C., and McMahon, R. J. 1981. Socioeconomic status: Effects on parent and child behaviors and treatment outcome of parent training. J. Clin. Child Psychol. 10:98–101.

Rose, S. 1974. Group training of parents as behavior modifiers. Soc. Work 19:156–162.

Sadler, O. W., Seyden, T., Howe, B., and Kaminsky, T. 1976. An evaluation of "Groups for Parents": A standardized format encompassing both behavior modification and humanistic methods. J. Commun. Psychol. 4:157–163.

Spock, B. M. 1976. Common Sense Book of Baby and Child Care, Rev. ed., E. P. Dutton & Company, Inc., New York.

ADDITIONAL SUBMITTED PAPERS GIVEN AT THE 6th I.A.S.S.M.D. CONGRESS

The list below provides the professional addresses of the speakers whose submitted papers could not be published in the two volumes of this set. The Editor thanks all the Congress participants who forwarded copies of their papers for consideration. The Editor considered every article forwarded to him, and for those manuscripts in an area outside his competence he sought assistance from the Editorial Board and independent reviewers. It is regretted that space could not be found for many excellent papers.

Abu Ghazeleh Gaza, H. *Handicapped Children in the Gaza Strip.* Society for the Care of Handicapped Children, Sun Day Care Centre, P.O. Box 146, Gaza

Adima, E. E. *The Mentally Retarded in Nigeria: The Problems.* Department of Special Education, University of Ibadan, Nigeria, West Africa

Albanese, A. *From Social Integration to Participation: Handicapped People at School.* Istituto di Psicologia, Istituto Universitario di Bergamo, Via Salvecchio 19, Bergamo 24100, Italy

Allen, A. A. *The Mildly Retarded: What Price Neglect? What Profit Programming?* Ohio University, 7 Watt Street, Athens, Ohio 45701

Aloia, G. F. *Ethics, Medicine and the Mentally Retarded Infant.* Department of Special Education and Speech Pathology, Arkansas State University, P.O. Box 2762, Arkansas 72467

Alonso Seco, J. M. *Mentally Handicapped Persons in Spain and the Social Integration of Disabled Persons Act.* Social Service for Disabled Persons, Department of Labour and Social Security, Maria de Guzman 52, Madrid 3, Spain

Ambrosie, F., Debona, D., and Hochreiter, G. *The Onondaga-Madison Board of Cooperative Educational Services Multi-occupational Educational Program for Students with Handicapping Conditions.* Onondaga-Madison BOCES, 310 Lakeside Road, Syracuse, New York 13209

Andrews, R. J. *Focus on the Aging and Aged Mentally Retarded Person: Implications for Administrators and Supervisors.* Commonwealth Schools Commission, P.O. Box 34, Woden, Canberra ACT 2606, Australia

Andrews, R. J., Berry, P. B., and Elkins, J. *The Development of an Accreditation Program for Services to Handicapped Persons in Australia.* Commonwealth Schools Commission, P.O. Box 34, Woden, Canberra ACT 2606, Australia

Andron, L., and Scheer, R. *Mentally Retarded Parents: Roles, Relationships and Realities.* Social Work Department, University of California at Los Angeles, 760 Westwood Plaza, Los Angeles, California 90024

Antonelli, C. J. *Community Placement of the Mentally Retarded: Population Characteristics and Behavioral Trends.* Macomb-Oakland Regional Center, 16200 Nineteen Mile Road, St. Clemens, Michigan 48044

Apolloni, T., and Roeher, G. A. *Establishing a Private Sector Power Base to Improve the Continuity of Services for Dependent Persons.* California Institute on Human Services, Sonoma State University, 1801 East Cotati Avenue, Rohnert Park, California 94982

Armfield, A. *Applying Psycholinguistics when Planning Alternative Communication for Persons with Severe Communication Impairment.* Psychology Teaching Group, South China Teachers' College, Guangzhou (Canton), People's Republic of China. (On assignment from University of Nebraska at Omaha)

Arya, R. P. *Step Back into the Real World.* "Arya Niwas", 3 Skipton Avenue, Crossens, Southport, Merseyside PR9 8JP, England

Bader, D., and Woodruff, M. D. *The Effects of Corrective Lenses on Various Behaviors of Mentally Retarded Persons.* School of Optometry, University of Waterloo, 1681 Bayview Avenue, Suite B, Toronto, Ontario M4G 3C1, Canada

Bairrao, J., Castanheira, J. L., Felgueiras, I., Abreu, J. G., and Lucas, J. *A Multivariate Analysis of Biomedical, Psychological, and Sociological Data Obtained in the First Epidemiological Study of Mental Deficiency in Portugal.* Ministerio Dos Assuntos Sociais, Centro de Observação e Orientação Médico-Pedagógico (COOMP), Rua de Santana à Lapa 52, Lisbon 1200, Portugal

Bakke, J. *Monozygous Male Triplets with Mental Retardation, Fragile X Chromosome, Large Testicles and Hyperactivity: A Preliminary Report.* Tordsvei 7, 1370 Asker, Norway

Barrera, F. J., Bucher, B., and Boundy, G. *Dependence on Shock-producing Stimuli.* P.O. Box 1000, Blenheim, Ontario N0P 1A0, Canada

Beasley, D. M. G. *Mobilisation of Resources: New Zealand Experience in the South Pacific.* 1 Bedlington Street, Whangarei, New Zealand

Beatty, H. *Human Rights Legislation in Ontario: Its Application to Persons with Mental Retardation.* Ontario Association for the Mentally Retarded, 1376 Bayview Avenue, Toronto, Ontario M4G 3A3, Canada

Beauchesne, M. A., and Gruppo, P. A. *The Role of the Nurse Practitioner in Institutions for the Mentally Retarded.* 6T-2 Lake Shore Terrace, Brighton, Massachusetts 02135

Belmont, L., Nemeth, S., and Stein, Z. *The International Pilot Study of Severe Childhood Disability.* New York State Psychiatric Institute and Gertrude H. Sergievsky Center, Columbia University, 630 West 168th Street, New York, New York 10032

Bennett, G. *Managing the D. D. Planning Council for Effective Coordination of Services.* West Virginia D.D. Planning Council, State Health Department, State Capital, Charleston, West Virginia 25305

Bennett, H. S., Dunlop, T., and Ziring, P. *Reduction of Polypharmacy of Epilepsy in an Institution for the Retarded.* Pediatric Neurology Department, The Brookdale Hospital Medical Center, Linden Boulevard at Brookdale Plaza, Brooklyn, New York 11212

Benson, F. A. M., Fox, R., King, E., Fish, T., and Gerenser, J. *A Problem Oriented Training Process for Interdisciplinary Clinical Teams.* The Nisonger Center, The Ohio State University, 1580 Cannon Drive, Columbus, Ohio 43210

Bergman, J. S. *An Eight Year Report on a Productive Interdisciplinary Project.* Center for Developmental and Learning Disorders, University of Alabama in Birmingham, Box 313, University Station, Birmingham, Alabama 35294

Berkell, D. E. *Generalization of Training Effects in Developmentally Disabled Children.* Department of Special Education, C. W. Post Center of Long Island University, Greenvale, New York 11548

Berko, F. G. *What is Advocacy—Who Are the Advocates?* New York State Office of Advocates for the Disabled, Agency building One—10th Floor, Empire State Plaza, Albany, New York 12223

Berman, L. J. *Rehabilitation Engineering and Language Development.* Department of Clinical Communicology, Flower Hospital, 1249 Fifth Avenue, New York, New York 10029

Bhatt, P. S., Swehli, M., and Senoussi, S. *Febrile Convulsions in Children: A Follow Up Study of 207 Children.* Faculty of Medicine, Alfatah University, P.O. Box 13483, Tripoli, Libya.

Bickford, A. T., and Wickham, E. R. *Attitudes toward the Mentally Retarded: Preliminary Results from Four Countries.* Department of Social Work, Wilfrid Laurier University, Waterloo, Ontario N2L 3C5, Canada

Binford, J. H., and Stone, J. A. *Developing a State-wide Training Program to Provide Community Services to People with Mental Retardation.* Bureau for Health Services, Department for Human Resources, Commonwealth of Kentucky, Frankfort, Kentucky 40621

Black, J. L., and Roelofs, A. R. *Independent Living Systems: Realistic Risk-taking.* Adult Learning Systems, Inc., 812 Williamsbury Ct 177, Pontiac, Michigan 48054

Blomquist, H. K., Gustavson, K.-H., and Holmgren, G. *Mild Mental Retardation in Children in a Northern Swedish County.* Department of Pediatrics, University Hospital, Umea, Sweden

Bochner, S., Ward, J., Price, P., and Linfoot, K. *Protolinguistic Behaviour in Institutionalised Infants.* Special Education Centre, Macquarie University, North Ryde, New South Wales 2113, Australia

Bornstein, H., and Jordan, I. K. *The Relationship Between Sign Characteristics and Understandability of Simpler Sign Forms.* Department of Psychology, Gallaudet College, 800 Florida Avenue N.E., Washington, D.C. 20002

Bouchard, J.-M. *Modèle Universitaire de Formation Professionnelle et de Recherche Integrant les Réalités Familiales des Parents de Jeunes Infants Déficients Mentaux.* University of Quebec, Montreal, Canada

Braddock, D. *Using Accreditation Survey Results for Statewide Program Evaluation.* Institute for the Study of Developmental Disabilities, University of Illinois at Chicago, 1640 West Roosevelt Road, Chicago, Illinois 60608

Bradley, T. B. *Remediation of Cognitive Deficits: A Critical Appraisal of the Feuerstein Model.* Department of Special Education, Shippensburg State College, Shippensburg, Pennsylvania.

Briese, B. D. *Friendship in the Balance . . . Friend or No Friend.* Department of Special Education, Brisbane College of Advanced Education, 54 Cranes Road, North Ipswich, Queensland 4305, Australia

Brown, B., and Rosenbaum, L. *Stress and Intelligence.* Evaluation Division, Administration for Children, Youth and Families, Box 1182, Washington, D.C. 20013

Brown, R. I., and Bayer, M. B. *A Follow-up Study of Developmentally Handicapped Adults—An Examination of Later Life Experience in Canada.* Department of Educational Psychology, The University of Calgary, 2500 University Drive N.W., Calgary, Alberta T2N 1N4, Canada

Castell, J., and Hemming, H. *The West Glamorgan Relocation Study.* The Psychology Department, Swansea University, Swansea, South Wales

Champagne, M. P., and Walker-Hirsch, L. W. *A Tool for Organizing Appropriate Social/Sexual Behaviors.* Rhode Island Division of Retardation, 600 New London Avenue, Cranston, Rhode Island 02920

Charron, R. *New Directions in Community Systems.* Programs for the Mentally Retarded, 838 Louisa Street, Lansing, Michigan 48910

Cheney, D., and Foss, G. *Social Competence and Employment for Mentally Retarded Workers.* Rehabilitation Research and Training, Center in Mental Retardation, University of Oregon, Eugene, Oregon 97403

Cherkes-Julkowski, M., Guskin, S., Schwarzer, C., and Okolo, C. *Attitude Formation: A Case of Loose Logic.* Box U-64, University of Connecticut, Storrs, Connecticut 06268

Christie, J. R. *Guardianship: The Alberta Model.* Office of the Public Guardian, Province of Alberta, P.O. Box 5002, Red Deer, Alberta T4N 5Y5, Canada

Clark, E. T., St. John, J. H., and Pecchenino, E. H. *Physical Response Education Systems—Acupressure for Persons with Handicaps.* Santa Cruz County Office of Education, 809 Bay Avenue, Suite H, Capitola, California 95010

Cohen, H. J., and Diamond, D. L. *Training and Preparing Physicians to Care for Mentally Retarded and Handicapped Children.* University Affiliated Facility, Albert Einstein College of Medicine of Yeshiva University, 1410 Pelham Parkway South, Bronx, New York 10461

Cohen, J. *The Resettlement of Institutionalized Retarded Individuals.* Institute of Applied Human Dynamics, 3526 Bainbridge Avenue, Bronx, New York 10467

Coven, L. *The Special Olympics as a Teaching Tool.* New Trier High School, 385 Winnetlea Avenue, Winnetlea, Illinois 60093

Coyner, A. B. *Nursing Services to Developmentally Disabled Children in the United States of America, 1982.* Family Health Services Division, Utah Department of Health, 44 Medical Drive, Salt Lake City, Utah 84112

Creedon, M. P. *Program Follow-up Report: Using Simultaneous Communication Model.* Dysfunctioning Child Center, Michael Reese Hospital and Medical Center, 29th Street and Ellis Avenue, Chicago, Illinois 60616

Cremers, M. J. G. *The Management of Cerebral Palsy/Mental Retardation.* Hooge Burch, Spoorlaan 19, 2471 PB Zwammerdam, The Netherlands

Crook, P. *Hospital Based Community Nursing Service for the Mentally Handicapped.* Truro Unit, Stoke Park Hospital, Stapleton, Bristol BS16 1QU, England

Crosby, K. G. *Development of an Accreditation Program to Evaluate and Improve Services for Developmentally Disabled Persons.* Accreditation Council for Services for Mentally Retarded and Other Developmentally Disabled Persons, 5101 Wisconsin Avenue N.W., Suite 405, Washington, D.C. 20016

Cupaiuolo, A. A. *Planning Community Residences: Legal and Community Relations Issues.* Public Administration Department, Pace University, White Plains, New York 10603

Dahlman, A. Y. and Tymchuk, A. J. *Parental Attitudes in Prader-Willi Syndrome;* and *Epidemiology of Prader-Willi Syndrome.* Dubnoff Center, 10526 Victory Place, North Hollywood, California 91606

Darbyshire, J. O. and Brooks, F. D. *The Design of an Original (Pre) Communication Inventory Related to an Integrated Model of Program Delivery for Mentally Retarded and 'Normal' Children Under Two Years.* Human Communications Research Unit, Queen's University, Kingston, Ontario K7L 3N6, Canada

Day, K. *A Psychiatric Unit for the Adult Mentally Handicapped.* Northgate Hospital, Morpeth, Northumberland, England

De Grandmont-Fortier, N. *Pédagogie du Jeu Atelier de Manipulation Élève Déficient Mental Moyen.* 1025 Est Boulevard, St. Joseph, Montreal, Quebec H2J 1L2, Canada

Dever, R. B. *Sequencing Instruction in English Grammar: A Theory for Guiding First Language Instruction.* Department of Special Education, Indiana University, 2805 East Tenth Street, Suite 170, Bloomington, Indiana 47405

Deweaver, K. L. *The Social Work Role in Maintaining Community Support Systems for Mentally Retarded Individuals: A New Focus for Social Work Education.* College of Education and Social Services, Social Work Program, 449A Waterman Building, Burlington, Vermont 05405

Dirks, J. A. *Using Group Activities to Decrease Maladaptive Behavior Among Institutionalized Retarded Adolescents and Adults.* Southgate Regional Center for Developmental Disabilities, 16700 Pennsylvania Road, Southgate, Michigan 48195

Doernberg, N. L. *Child-bearing Attitudes of Parents of Developmentally Disabled Preschool Children.* Albert Einstein College of Medicine, Rose F. Kennedy Center, 1410 Pelham Parkway South, Bronx, New York 10461

Drapo, P. J. *Using a State School for the Mentally Retarded as a Clinical Site for Senior Nursing Students.* Texas Woman's University, College of Nursing, TWU Box 23026, TWU Station, Denton, Texas 76204

Dupont, A. *Epidemiology in Mental Retardation.* Institute of Psychiatric Demography, Aarhus Psychiatric Hospital, 8240 Risskov, Denmark

Dutta, S. K. *From Institution to Freedom. A Research Project of Rehabilitation of the Mentally Handicapped from Hospital to Independent Community Living.* Dovenby Hall Hospital, Cockermouth, Cumbria, England

Dybwad, G., Jones, W. E., Hogan, M. F., Phillips, A., and Kendrick, M. *The Planning and Development of Comprehensive Community Based Services for People with Mental Retardation.* Florence Heller Graduate School, Brandeis University, Waltham, Massachusetts 02154

Dzenowagis, J. *Recruitment of Foster Parents for Mentally Retarded Adults and Children.* State of Michigan Department of Mental Health, Macomb-Oakland Regional Center, 16200 Nineteen Mile Road, Mount Clemens, Michigan 48044

Edwards, J. P. *Social/Sexual Training for Persons with Retardation.* Department of Special Education, Portland State University, Box 751, Portland, Oregon 97207

Elder, J. K. *The Private/Public Partnership: A New Recipe for a New Mix.* Department of Health and Human Services, Administration on Developmental Disabilities, Washington, D.C. 20201

El Ghatit, Z. *Community Development. Non-institutionalization/Deinstitutionalization of the Mentally Retarded. An Ontario Experience.* Children's Services Area Office, Ministry of Community & Social Services, 2197 Riverside Drive, Ottawa, Ontario K1H 7X3, Canada

Ellis, D. W. *Psychotherapy of the Head Injured–Emotionally Disturbed Adolescent.* The Devereux Foundation, Devon, Pennsylvania 19333

Evans, B. *Evaluation in a Service-oriented Infant Stimulation Programme.* CPRI, Box 2460, London, Ontario N6A 4G6, Canada

Felix, T. *Parents' Movement and Their Role in a Developing Country (India).* Central Institute and Information Centre on Mental Retardation, All Kerala Association for the Mentally Retarded, Cotton Hill, Trivandrum 695 010, South India

Ferngren, H., and Sjogren, O. *Application of the New WHO Classification to Selected Groups of Mentally Retarded Admitted to the Service of Stockholm County in 1973, 1976 and 1981—Its Usefulness to Describe Impairments and Disabilities.* Board for Provision of Service to the Mentally Retarded, Stockholm County Council, Box 20033, S-104 60 Stockholm, Sweden

Fields, D. L., and Gibson, D. *The Institutional Record: A Half-century of Habilitation Outcomes.* Psychology Department, University of New Brunswick, Fredericton, New Brunswick, E3B 6E4, Canada

Fletcher, R. J. *Program Model to Meet the Needs of a Multiply Disabled Population: Mental Retardation and Mental Illness.* Beacon House, 110 Prince Street, Kingston, New York 12401

Foshee, J. G. *Use of the Accreditation Process in a State System of Services for Developmentally Disabled Persons.* Tennessee Department of Mental Health and Mental Retardation, 501 Union Building, Nashville, Tennessee 37219

Fox, R., Burkhart, J. E., and Rotatori, A. F. *Obesity in the Mentally Retarded: Prevalence, Characteristics and Intervention.* The Nisonger Center, Ohio State University, 1580 Cannon Drive, Columbus, Ohio 43210

Frank, J., and Pilon, B. *Study of a Practical Team Approach to Cerebral Palsy.* Clinic for Children with Cerebral Palsy, Orthopaedic Hospital, 2400 South Flower Street, Los Angeles, California 90007

Fraser, W. I., Leudar, I., Gray, J., and Jeeves, M. A. *Studies of Behaviour Disturbance in Mentally Handicapped Persons.* Gogarburn Hospital, Glasgow Road, Edinburgh EH12 9BJ, Scotland

Frausto, S. *The Normalization Principle.* 4212 Greenfield Road, Berkley, Michigan 48072

Friedman, E., Wolf, E. G., and Cohen, I. L. *Early Infantile Autism: The Diagnostic Puzzle.* New York State Institute for Basic Research in Developmental Disabilities, 1050 Forest Hill Road, Staten Island, New York 10314

Friese, A. J. *Perspectives of Mental Retardation in a Third World Country. Implications for Teacher Education.* Department of Special Education, Jamia Millia Islamia, New Delhi, India

Fryns, F. P. *X-linked Mental Retardation and the Fragile X-chromosome. A Personal Experience.* Academisch Ziekenhuis Sint-Rafaël, Kapucijnenvoer 33, 3000 Leuven, Belgium

Garber, M., and Green, G. *Teaching Parents of Developmentally Handicapped Children with a Paraprofessional Home Visiting Program.* Ontario Institute for Studies in Education, 252 Bloor Street West, Toronto, Ontario, Canada

Gath, A., *Psychiatric Disorder and Mental Retardation, with Special Reference to Down's Syndrome.* West Suffolk Hospital, Bury St. Edmunds, Suffolk, England

Gladkowski, G. J. *Allocating Human Resources: A Task Analysis.* Specialized Treatment Services, Southwestern Regional Centre, P.O. Box 1000, Blenheim, Ontario NOP 1AO, Canada

Goldberg, B. *Principle of the Least Restrictive Alternative; Management of Aggression in the Emotionally Disturbed Retarded;* and *Anti-psychiatry and Anti-professionalism.* Children's Psychiatric Research Institute, P.O. Box 2460, London, Ontario, Canada

Goodnough, P. *Helping Hand—A Developmental Story;* and *Language, Physical Therapy, and Care Intervention for Children with Multiple Handicaps.* Trend Community Mental Health Services, 318 Fourth Avenue East, Hendersonville, North Carolina 28739

Göstason, R. *Mental Retardation and Its Psychiatric Complications. Preliminary Report of an Epidemiological Study on an Adult Population in Sweden.* Kopparberg County Council, Box 712, 79129 Falun, Sweden

Gray, A. S. *S.P.E.E.C.H. The Saint Peter's Eclectic Expressive Communication Habilitation Program.* St. Peter's Child Development Center, 4127 Brownsville Road, Pittsburgh, Pennsylvania 15227

Gray, J. M., Roberts, J., and Jeeves, M. A. J. *Cognitive Factors in the Experience of Emotion in Mental Handicap.* Department of Psychology, The University, St. Andrews, Fife KY16 9JU, Scotland

Griffith, P.L. *Perceptions of Tactile and Visual Iconicity by Blind and Sighted Groups.* Department of Special Education, Kent State University, 401 White Hall, Kent, Ohio 44242

Groeneweg, G., Nunziato, D., Laffin, M., and Winkelaar, D. *A Strategy for the Development of an Informal Communication Screening Procedure for the Developmentally Handicapped Adult.* The Vocational and Rehabilitation Research Institute, 3304 33rd Street N.W., Calgary, Alberta T2L 2A6 Canada

Gross, A. M. *Deinstitutionalization—A Good Idea (?) at the Wrong Time (?)* Baerwald School of Social Work, Hebrew University, Mount Scopus, Jerusalem

Grotberg, E. H. *Limitations of Current Theories of Mental Retardation.* Administration for Children, Youth and Families, Department of Health & Human Services, P.O. Box 1182, Washington, D.C. 20013

Grover, S. C. and Wight Felske, A. *Metalearning in the Mentally Retarded Adult: Implications for Teaching.* Department of Educational Psychology, University of Calgary, 2500 University Drive N.W., Calgary, Alberta T2N 1N4, Canada

Grubar, J.-C. *Sleep and Mental Deficiency.* IUT "B", Laboratoire de Psychologie des Acquisitions Cognitives et Linguistiques, Université de Lille, Lille 3, France

Gruppo, P. A. and Foley, J. P. *Families of Institutionalized Developmentally Disabled. Unresolved Grief.* Eunice Kennedy Shriver Center for Mental Retardation, Inc., 200 Trapelo Road, Waltham, Massachusetts 02154

Gudalefsky, A. B. *Nepal Meets Mental Retardation: A 'Hands' Experience.* HANDS-Nepal, G.P.O. Box 1668, Kathmandu, Nepal

Gugino, H., Dasgupta, M. E., and Shore, F. *Survey of Records for Significant Etiological Variables Associated with Mental Retardation.* Medical College of Georgia—SONAT, Heritage Building, Milledge Avenue, Athens, Georgia 30601

Gugino, J. C. *Day Treatment. A Legal and Direct Care Program.* The Rehabilitation Center, RD1, Box 61, N. Nine Mile Road, Allegany, New York 14706

Harrison, A. *Nursing Education and Mental Retardation in the United States.* Department of Nursing, Wilkes College, Wilkes Barre, Pennsylvania 18766

Hasan, R. *Problems Potential and Prospects of a Comprehensive Approach in Meeting Service Needs of Mentally Deficient in Pakistan.* Department of Psychology, University of the Punjab, Lahore, Pakistan

Hauritz, M. *A Critical Review of Vocational Training Packages.* Unit for Rehabilitation Studies, Special Education Centre, School of Education, Macquarie University, North Ryde 2113, New South Wales, Australia

Hayden, F. J. *Issues and Answers in International Sport for the Mentally Handicapped.* School of Physical Education, McMaster University, Hamilton, Ontario L8S 4X1, Canada

Hayes, S., and Hayes, R. *An Overview of Legal and Policy Issues in Mental Retardation.* The Australian Law Reform Commission, 99 Elizabeth Street, Box 3708—GPO Sydney 2001, Sydney, New South Wales 2000, Australia

Haywood, H. C., Arbitman-Smith, R., Bransford, J. D., Delclos, V. R., Towery, J. R., Hannel, I. L., and Hannel, M. V. *Cognitive Education with Adolescents: Evaluation of Instrumental Enrichment.* The John F. Kennedy Center for Research on Education and Human Development, Box 40, Peabody College, Vanderbilt University, Nashville, Tennessee 37203

Henderson, M. L., and Triplett, J. *Incorporating Mental Retardation Nursing into an Undergraduate and Graduate Curriculum: A Collaborative Effort of a University Affiliated Facility and Collegiate Nursing Program.* Children's Hospital of Los Angeles, 4650 Sunset Boulevard, Los Angeles, California 90027

Hewitt, S. E. K. *Retarded Persons and the Law—The Interface.* British Institute of Mental Handicap, 1 Oxney Place, Peasedown St. John, Near Bath, Avon, England

Hill, J. W. *Utilizing Incompatible Alternatives in the Language Arts Assessment of a Hyperactive Child.* Meyer Children's Rehabilitation Institute, University of Nebraska Medical Center, 444 South 44th Street, Omaha, Nebraska 68131

Hjärpe, J. *Normalization in Sweden: Quality and Limitations.* Mental Retardation Project, Psychiatric Research Center, University of Uppsala, S-750 17 Uppsala, Sweden

Hodges, P. M. and Schwethelm, B. *A Comparison of the Effectiveness of Graphic Symbol and Manual Sign Training with Nonverbal Profoundly Retarded Children.* Department of Psychology, California State University, 5151 State University Drive, Los Angeles, California 90032

Hovav, M. *Services for the Mentally Retarded: Four-year Plan.* Department of Services for the Mentally Retarded, Ministry of Labour and Social Affairs, 10 Yad Harutzim Street Talpiot, P.O.B. 1260, Jerusalem, Israel

Howard, M. *An Anthropological Study of Patterns of Interaction Between Staff and Residents in a Group Home for Mentally Retarded Persons.* Department of Anthropology, Michigan State University, East Lansing, Michigan 48824

Howlett, R., and Hill, L. A. *The Application of Primary Prevention in the Community: A Case Study.* Infant Development Programme, Suite 104, 477 Queen Street E, Sault St. Marie, Ontario, Canada

Huene, S. A. *Trends in Career Education for the Educable Mentally Retarded High School Student.* 5624 Freshaire Lane, Columbia, Maryland 21044

Hughes, J. *Integration of Developmentally Delayed Children into a Regular Pre-school Setting.* Faculty of Education, The University of Manitoba, Winnipeg, Manitoba R3T 2N2, Canada

Hughes, J. M. *Educational Services for the Mentally Retarded in Developing Countries.* School of Special Education, Gwent College of Higher Education, College Crescent, Caerleon, Newport, Gwent, Wales

Hughson, E. A. *Rehabilitation Programming.* Behavioral Support Unit, Faculty of Education, University of Calgary, Calgary, Alberta T2N 1N4, Canada

Hutchinson, P., and Lord, J. *A Critical Analysis of the Portrayal of Mental Retardation in Canadian Newspapers.* University of Waterloo, Waterloo, Ontario, Canada

Ibrahim, B., Dhadphale, M., and Gajjar, M. *Epidemiological Survey of Embakasi Village in Kenya.* Aga Khan Hospital, Nairobi, Kenya

Inoue, F. *Impact of Clinical Pharmacy Service to Reduce Psychotropic Drug Use.* Ministry of Community & Social Services, Prince Edward Heights, P.O. Box 440, Picton, Ontario KOK 2TO, Canada

Jacobs, J. *The Role of the Physician in Mental (Developmental) Retardation.* Department of Pediatrics, McMaster University, 1200 Main Street West, Hamilton, Ontario L8N 3Z5, Canada

Jacobson, J. W. and Janicki, M. P. *Demographic, Functional and Adaptive Characteristics of Persons with Severe and Profound Mental Retardation in New York State.* New York State Office of Mental Retardation and Developmental Disabilities, 44 Holland Avenue, Albany, New York 12229

Jageman, L. W. *Community Residential Personnel Training.* Department of Special Education, Ohio University, College of Education, Athens, Ohio 45701

Jancar, J. *Familial Mental Handicap.* Stoke Park Hospital, Stapleton, Bristol BS16 1QU, England

Jegard, S. *Educational Methods for the Multiply Handicapped.* Alvin Buckwold Centre, Department of Pediatrics, University Hospital, Saskatoon, Saskatchewan S7N 0X0, Canada

Jegard, S., and Zaleski, W. A. *Regional Resource Centre for Multi-handicapped Retarded Children.* Alvin Buckwold Centre, Department of Pediatrics, University Hospital, Saskatoon, Saskatchewan 57N 0X0, Canada

Johnson, V. P. *Ethical Issues in Medical Genetics.* Center for the Developmentally Disabled, Departments of Obstetrics, Gynecology, Pediatrics and Laboratory Medicine, School of Medicine, University of South Dakota, Vermillion, South Dakota 57069

Jones, N. *A Legacy of Mental Retardation.* 320 Queen Street, Strathroy, Ontario N7G 2J2, Ontario, Canada

Juul, K. D. *Programs, Progress and Problems in Services for Mentally Retarded Persons in Scandinavia.* Department of Special Education, Southern Illinois University at Carbondale, 134 Pulliam Hall, Carbondale, Illinois 62901

Kaufman, M. E. and Alberto, P. A. *Transfer of Training in Severely Autistic and Severely Retarded Children.* Department of Special Education, Georgia State University, University Plaza, Atlanta, Georgia 30303

Kealy, S., and Lawless, A. *Intervention with Children with Known Syndromes of Mental Handicap and Developmental Delays.* Moore Abbey, Monasterevan, County Kildare, Ireland

Kebbon, L. *Normalization in Sweden: Quality and Limitations. Model of Analysis;* and *Future of Community Services: Ideology versus Economy.* Psychiatric Research Center, University of Uppsala, S-750 17 Uppsala, Sweden

Kennett, K. F., and Kennett, B. E. *Autism: Profiles for Individual Development at Home and School.* Nepean College of Advanced Education, Box 10, Kingswood, New South Wales 2750, Australia

Ketcheson, L., and Daminato, P. *The Evolution of Community-based Leisure Opportunities in Canada.* Canadian Parks/Recreation Association, 33 River Road, Ottawa, Ontario K1L 89B, Canada

Khalil, E. F. *Analysis of Functional Abilities of 364 Severely and Profoundly Retarded children in Central California.* Central Valley Regional Center for the Developmentally Disabled, 4747 North First Street, Ste 195, Fresno, California 93726

Killip, M. C. *Sexuality Training for the Developmentally Handicapped Adult: Present Curriculum Guidelines and Future Considerations.* Social Education Unit, The Vocational and Rehabilitation Research Institute, 3304 33rd Street N.W., Calgary, Alberta T2L 2A6, Canada

Killip, M. C., and Speer, C. D. *Towards a Multi-disciplinary Approach to Personal Adjustment Training.* Social Education Unit, The Vocational and Rehabilitation Research Institute, 3304 33rd Street N.W., Calgary, Alberto T2L 2A6, Canada

King, E., Arms, D., Heiskell, N., Sherman, R., and Peppe, K. *National Workshop on Nursing Criteria Sets: A Report.* Department of Nursing, Ohio State University, The Nisonger Center, 1580 Cannon Drive, Columbus, Ohio 43210

Kipper, P. A. *Diagnosis, Evaluation and Treatment in Mental Deficiency: A Description of Styles in Canada, Mexico and the United States. Canadian Procedures as Implemented in Southwestern Ontario.* Southwestern Regional Centre, P.O. Box 100, Blenheim, Ontario N0P 1A0, Canada

Kirman, B. H., and Hamilton-Hislop,* H. *X-linked Mental Retardation with Fragile X (q27-28) site. Three Families Affected by the Condition.* *Botleys Park Hospital, Chertsey, Surrey, England

Kowalski, G. *Application of Learning System Design to Teaching the Mentally Retarded Student.* Cardinal Stritch College, 6801 N. Yates Road, Milwaukee, Wisconsin 53217

Kranz, G. *Sample from Let's Play to Grow Materials.* 1701K Streek N.W., Suite 205, Washington, D.C. 20006

Krupski, A., Burstein, N. D., and Rubinstein, C. *The Experiences of Handicapped Children Who Have Been Integrated into Regular Preschool Settings: A Report of an Observational Study of Two Preschools.* Graduate School of Education, University of California, Los Angeles, California 90024

Kulik, T. J., and Campo, S. *A Critical Issue Concerning the Integration of Severely and Profoundly Retarded Individuals into the Community.* Special Children's Village, Route 2, Box 146, Zachary, Louisiana 70791

Kumta, N. B. *An Etiological Analysis of 696 Cases of Mental Retardation in India.* Department of Paediatrics, Seth G. S. Medical College and K. E. M. Hospital, Parel, Bombay 400 012, India

Kvist, A., Larson, S., Miller, H., and Nelson, D. *Familial Retardation: Its 'Causes' and Three Treatment Models.* Parenting Program, Reuben Lindh Learning Center, 3616 12th Avenue S., Minneapolis, Minnesota 55407

Kylén, G., Göransson, K., Granlund, M., and Hedman-Hallin, L. *Profoundly Mentally Handicapped Adults at the Sensorimotor Stage (A-stage).* Stiftelsen ALA, Box 5410, 114 84 Stockholm, Sweden

Lalemand, K. *Non-abusive Physical Intervention.* NAPI, 339 Central Avenue, Lewiston, Maine 04240

Lazuardi, S., Lestari, H., Hendarto, S. K., Purboyo, R. H., and Ismael, S. *Madopar Treatment of Retarded Children.* Subdivision of Pediatric Neurology, Department of Child Health, Medical School, University of Indonesia, Jakarta

Lee, R. *Curriculum Development for Students with Special Needs in Colleges of Further Education in England and Wales.* Further Education Curriculum Review and Development Unit, Elizabeth House, London S.E.1., England

Lefebvre, L., and Gallinger, J. *A Study of Skill Acquisition in Leisure Planning with Multihandicapped Adults.* The Vocational and Rehabilitation Research Institute, 3304 33rd Street N.W., Calgary, Alberta T2L 2A6, Canada

Lerner, H. *Use of Clinical Facilities in Educating Nursing Students in Mental Retardation.* Department of Nursing, Lehman College, Bedford Park Boulevard West, Bronx, New York 10468

Leudar, I. *Speech Acts and Communication of the Mentally Handicapped Person.* Psychology Laboratory, The University, St. Andrews, Fife KY16 9JU, Scotland

Levy, B. *The Incidence of Oculo-visual Anomalies in an Adult Population of Mentally Retarded Persons.* 700 University Avenue, Toronto, Ontario M5G 1Z5, Canada

Liberoff, L. M. *El Sistema Simbolico de Bliss y Otros Sistemas Aumentativos. Estado Actual de su Difusion y Utilizacion en la Republica Argentina.* Instituto de Lenguate y Educacion Especial, Conesa 2051, 1428 Buenos Aires, Argentina

Lipman, L. *The Relevance of Piaget for Teachers of Retarded Children.* 29 Congo Road, Emmarential 2195, Johannesburg, South Africa

Little, M. T. *To Each His Own.* Social Work Department, Cramond House, 2 Prescott Terrace, Toorak Gardens, South Australia 5065

Lloyd, L. L., and Karlan, G. R. *Nonspeech Communication Symbols and Systems: Where Have We Been and Where Are We Going?* Department of Special Education, Purdue University, South Campus Courts—E, West Lafayette, Indiana 47907

Loadman, W. E., Benson, F. A., McElwain, D., and Schnell, S. *Development and Testing of an Interdisciplinary Screening Tool.* The Nisonger Center, The Ohio State University, 1580 Cannon Drive, Columbus, Ohio 43210

Long, E., and Irmer, L. D. *Peer-teaching: A Positive Approach to Physical Education for Handicapped Students in Adapted or Regular Classes Through Physical Education Opportunity Program for Exceptional Handicapped Learners (PEOPEL).* PEOPEL Project, 2910 North 19th Avenue, Phoenix, Arizona 85015

Love, A. J. *Basic Characteristics of Emotionally Disturbed Mentally Retarded (EDMR) Adolescents: Presenting Problems and Service Needs.* Community Concern Associates Ltd., Suite 503, 112 St. Clair Avenue West, Toronto, Ontario, Canada

Lowden, J. A., and Hutton, E. *Ethical Aspects of Genetic Screening and Prenatal Diagnosis.* Neurosciences Department, 9th Floor, Elm Wing, The Hospital for Sick Children, 555 University Avenue, Toronto, Ontario M5G 1X8, Canada

Lupacchino, R. W. *Infant Euthanasia: A Gravid Dilemma.* 1420 N. Meridian Road, Apt. 201, Tallahassee, Florida 32303

Lusthaus, C. S., and Lusthaus, E. W. *Parents and Their Involvement in the Educational Process.* Department of Educational Administration and Policy

Studies, McGill University, 3700 McTavish Street, Montreal, Quebec H3A 1Y2, Canada

Lynch, A. *The Amniocentesis–Abortion–Advocacy Discontinuum.* University of Toronto, St. Michael's College, 81 St. Mary Street, Toronto, Ontario M5S 1J4, Canada

Lyon, P. E., Medved, R. M., Messier, H., and Wessels, M. *Professionals and Parents: Partners in Programming and Service.* Department of Special Education, College of Saint Rose, 432 Western Avenue, Albany, New York 12203

Lysander, N. *Parental Involvement—Decisive Factor in the Success of Programs for the Developmentally Handicapped.* Rideau Regional Centre, P.O. Box 2000, Smiths Falls, Ontario K7A 4T7, Canada

McCabe, A. E. *Language Acquisition and Mental Retardation: A Question of Style.* Department of Psychology, University of Windsor, Windsor, Ontario N9B 3P4, Canada

McConkey, R., and O'Connor, M. *Videocourses: An Effective and Economic Approach to the In-service Training of Staff in Mental Handicap Services.* St. Michael's House, Upper Kilmacud Road, Stillorgan, Dublin, Ireland

McCormack, B., and McConkey, R. *Changing Young People's Perceptions of Mentally Handicapped Adults.* St. Michael's House, Upper Kilmacud Road, Stillorgan, Dublin, Ireland

McCormack, F. A., and Mandel, D. *How to Manage an Institution During Litigation.* Long Island DDSO, Box 788, Melville, New York 11747

McCreary, B. D. *The Development and Activities of an Academic Division of Mental Retardation at Queen's University.* Division of Mental Retardation, Department of Psychiatry, Queen's University, Kingston, Ontario, Canada

McGee, J. J., and Menolascino, F. J. *Gentle Teaching Techniques for Severely Retarded Persons with Severe Behavior Problems;* and *Community Services for Persons with Severe Disabilities. From Ideology to Practice.* Nebraska Psychiatric Institute, University of Nebraska, 602 South 45th Street, Omaha, Nebraska 68106

McGlamery, R. D. and Guldager, L. *Alternatives to Institutionalization for Severely and Profoundly Handicapped Adults.* Oak Hill School, 120 Holcomb Street, Hartford, Connecticut 06112

McKibbin, E. *Enhancing Development and Learning for Children with Developmental Disabilities through Occupational Therapy Sensory Motor Programs.* Center for Developmental and Learning Disorders, University of Alabama in Birmingham, 1711A Valley Avenue, Birmingham, Alabama 35209

McLean, J., and Snyder-McLean, L. *Application of Normal First-language Learning Data and Speech Acts Theory to the Mentally Retarded.* Bureau of Child Research, Parsons Research Center, Parsons, Kansas 67357

McQueen, C. *Priorities for Prevention of Mental Handicap: Use of Epidemiological and Economic Data.* Atlantic Research Centre for Mental Retardation, Dalhousie University, Halifax, Nova Scotia B3H 4H7, Canada

Maharaj, S. C. *A Non-verbal System of Communication;* and *Plastic (Cosmetic) Surgery for Mentally Retarded Persons (Down's Syndrome): Attitudes and Opinions of Professions.* Valley View Centre, Box 1300, Moose Jaw, Saskatchewan S6H 4R2, Canada

Malik, G. *Community Support System and Deinstitutionalization.* Developmental Services, Pine Ridge, Box 130, Aurora, Ontario L4G 3H3, Canada

Malin, N. A. *Group Homes for Mentally Handicapped Adults.* Department of Health Studies, Sheffield City Polytechnic, 36 Collegiate Crescent, Sheffield S10 2BP, England

Mandel, D. *Information Systems Coordinator Role and Function in a Human Service Agency.* Long Island DDSO, Box 788, Melville, New York 11747

Marge, M. *Principles and Practices in the Prevention of Mental Retardation.* Division of Special Education and Rehabilitation, School of Education, Syracuse University, 805 South Crouse Avenue, Syracuse, New York 13210

Margolis, J. *Theoretical Difficulties Regarding the Moral Status of the Severely and Profoundly Retarded.* College of Liberal Arts, Temple University, Philadelphia, Pennsylvania 19122

Marko, K. B. *Implications for Teacher Training Institutes as a Result of Mainstreaming: Perspectives for Third World Countries.* 101 East 75th Street, New York, New York 10021

Marlett, N. J. *Competency in Making Decisions—A Psychological Perspective.* Rehabilitation Studies, The University of Calgary, 2500 University Drive N.W., Calgary, Alberta T2N 1N4, Canada

Marlow, J. *Mental Retardation and Physical Disabilities: A Survey and Critique—Program Development.* Wassaic Developmental Center, New York State, New York.

Mason, L. *A Community Development Project for the Mentally Handicapped in the London Borough of Southwark: The Scheme and Its Evaluation.* Hilda Lewis House, The Bethlem Royal Hospital, 579 Wickham Road, Shirley, Croydon CR0 8DR, England

Matin, M. A., Anderson, M. I., Dickerson, J. W. T., and Carter, J. K. *Vitamin and Mineral Study in Down's Syndrome.* Leybourne Grange Hospital, West Malling, Kent ME19 5HS, England

Matser, J., and Geus, R. *Project for the Development of Objectives: Background of the Project and Development of a Method to Determine Objectives which are Realizable for Inmates of an Institution for the Mentally Handicapped.* Sterrenberg, Amersfoortseweg 56, 3712 BE Huis ter Heide, The Netherlands

Matsui, I. *Cohort Study of Birth Defects and Mental Retardation in Infancy and Early Childhood.* Department of Genetics, Institute for Developmental Research, Aichi Prefectural Colony, Japan

Mavrin-Cavor, L., Levandovski, D., and Teodorovic, B. *The Attitudes of Mothers of Non-handicapped Children to Their Child, Compared to the Attitudes of Mothers of Mentally Retarded Children to Their Child in Relation to Certain Characteristics of School Behaviour of the Child.* Department of Defectology, University of Zagreb, Kuslanova 59a, 41000 Zagreb, Yugoslavia

Mearig, J. S. *Ethical and Psychological Aspects of Surgical Intervention for Down's Syndrome Children.* St. Lawrence University, 17 Bay Street, Potsdam, New York 13676

Mendelson, I. S., Zaleski, W. A., Wellner, V. P., and Meister, A. *5-Oxoprolinuria (Glutathione Synthetase Deficiency) Therapy.* Alvin Buckwold Centre, Department of Pediatrics, University Hospital, Saskatoon, Saskatchewan S7N 0X0, Canada

Meyers, S., and Geller, D. *Mentally Retarded People and Their Right to Risk.* VARCA, Coon Hollow Road, Derby, Connecticut 06418

Miller, M. B., and Yager, H. L. *Effective Educationally Focused Transdisciplinary Programming for Students with Profound Retardation.* Project

TIDE, Yeshiva University, School of Professional Psychology, 1165 Morris Park Avenue, Bronx, New York 10461

Moodie, M., Apolloni, T., and Hayes, A. *Institutes and Resource Centres in the Field of Developmental Disabilities. A Call for International Collaboration.* Challinor Centre, Ipswich, Queensland, Australia

Moore, J. L. *Curriculum Development for the Moderately Mentally Handicapped in Alberta.* Calgary Regional Office of Education, 1200 Rocky Mountain Plaza, 615 Macleod Trail S.E., Calgary, Alberta T2G 4T8, Canada

Morgan, R. H. *Professional Assessment of the Family with a Retarded Member.* Department of Pediatrics, University of Miami Mailman Center for Child Development, P.O. Box 016820, Miami, Florida 33101

Morgan, R. R. *Use of the Accreditation Process to Improve the Quality and Integration of Services Provided by Agencies in a Community Service System.* Summit County Board of Mental Retardation and Developmental Disabilities, 140 East Market Street, Akron, Ohio 44308

Mühl, H. *Integrating Mentally Handicapped Students into the Regular School System in the Federal Republic of Germany.* Geistigbehinderten–Pädagogik, University of Oldenburg, Birkenweg 3, 2900 Oldenburg, West Germany

Mulcahy, M. *Observations on a Community Based Record System for Mental Handicap.* The Medico-Social Research Board, 73 Lower Baggot Street, Dublin 2, Ireland

Nagel, J. *Developing Communication Skills Through Music with Non-verbal Students.* 1135 Kim Street, Ann Arbor, Michigan 48103

Napolitan, J. T., and Lee, M. C. *The Coordination of Medical and Behavioral Services in the Treatment of Severe Self-injurious Behaviors in a Group Home Setting.* Ray Graham Association for the Handicapped, 266 W. Fullerton, Elmhurst, Illinois 60101

Nehring, W. M. *A Comparison of Toy Selection Between Preschool Children with Down's Syndrome and Preschool Children with No Mental Retardation.* School of Nursing, University of Wisconsin–Madison, 4859 Sheboygan Avenue No. 317, Madison, Wisconsin 53705

Neuhauser, G. *Medical Aspects of Early Intervention in Mentally Retarded Children.* Department of Pediatric Neurology, Justus-Liebig-Universität Giessen, Feulgenstrasse 12, D-6300 Giessen, West Germany

Newman, E., Reiter, S., and Pinkovitch, A. *Evaluation of Vocational Training in Construction and Agriculture in an Israeli Kibbutz Village for Retarded Adults.* Temple University, 1801 N. Broad Street, Philadelphia, Pennsylvania 19122

Nilsson-Embro, A.-C. *Critical Factors in Leisure Time for Mentally Retarded.* Psychiatric Research Center, University of Uppsala, S-750 17 Uppsala, Sweden

Nirje, B. *The Basis and Logic of the Normalization Principle.* Psychiatric Research Centre, Psychological Unit, Ulleraker Hospital, S-750 17 Uppsala, Sweden

Norsman, A. *'Opportunities and Challenges'. A Report on a Study Project: Facilitating Viability in the ARC through Organizational Restructuring.* Wisconsin Association for Developmental Disabilities, 5522 University Avenue, Madison, Wisconsin 53705

Nuffield, E. J. *Treatment of Social Isolation in Disturbed Retarded Children.* Western Psychiatric Institute and Clinic, 3811 O'Hara Street, Pittsburgh, Pennsylvania 15261

O'Connell-Mason, C. Y. and Stilwell, B. *Adaptive versus Appropriate Behavior: Informal and Formal Assessment and Implications for Instruction.* Institute for Habilitation Services, Eastern Montana College, Billings, Montana 59101

Olsen, M. R. *The Case for the Radical Reform of the Training of Nurses in Mental Handicap in Britain.* Department of Social Work, University of Birmingham, P.O. Box 363, Birmingham B15 2TT, England

Omari, I. M., and Kisanji, J. A. N. *Screening and Intervention with Young Mentally Retarded Children in East Africa.* Department of Education and Psychology, University of Dar Es Salaam, Tanzania

Oshima, M., and Takahashi, A. *A Survey Study of Present Condition of Early Diagnosis for Handicapped Children.* Aichi Prefectural Colony, Kamiya-cho, Kusugai, Aichi 480-03, Japan

Paour, J.-L. *Piagetian Learning as a Tool for Research and Intervention in Mental Retardation.* Laboratoire de Psychologie de l'Enfant et de Psychologie Génétique, Université de Provence à Aix-en-Provence, 29 Avenue R. Schuman, 13621 Aix-en-Provence, France

Parker, A. W., Bronks, R., and Snyder, W. *Gait in Down Syndrome.* Department of Anatomy, University of Queensland, Brisbane 4067 Australia

Parker, T., and Cooper, R. M. *A Systems Approach to Treating the Family with a Mentally Retarded Child: Clinical Practice Related to Facilitating Effective Family and Family-professional Relationships.* Meyer Children's Rehabilitation Institute, University of Nebraska Medical Center, 42nd and Dewey, Omaha, Nebraska 68105

Parnes, B. F., and Murto, N. S. *Reaching Untapped Potential Through SOI— Success Oriented Instruction.* 214 Wedgewood Drive, Williamsville, New York 14221

Paul, F. M. *Chromosomal Abnormalities in a Survey of Mentally Subnormal Children in Singapore.* Department of Paediatrics, Faculty of Medicine, University of Singapore, Singapore 0316, Singapore

Paul, L. *Appropriate Education for Students Who Are Severely and Profoundly Retarded: The Personnel Problem.* Department of Educational Psychology, University of Alberta, 6-102 Education North, Edmonton, Alberta T6G 2G5, Canada

Paulhus, E. *Right or Wrong Use of Image in the Field of Training Mentally Defective Children in Spiritual and Religious Values.* College Mont Ste. Anne, RR 1 Sherbrooke, Sherbrooke, Quebec J1H 5G9, Canada

Peniston, E. G. *A Comparison Study: Characteristics of Previously Institutionalized Clients Presently Placed in Community-based Settings.* Veterans Administration Medical Center, Fort Lyon, Colorado 81038

Penovici, A. *The 'Death' of an Institution and the 'Birth' of a New Settlement.* Directory, Kafr Tikva, Tivon, Israel

Perrin, B., and Nirje, B. *Setting the Record Straight: A Critique of Some Frequent Misconceptions of the Normalization Principle.* Mental Retardation Service Provision, Uppsala County, Börjeg 31C, S-752 29 Uppsala, Sweden

Peterson, C. P., Spiker, D., and Smith, G. F. *Patterns of Intellectual, Motor and Social Abilities in School-aged Children with Down Syndrome.* Illinois Masonic Medical Center, 836 W. Wellington Avenue, Chicago, Illinois 60657

Petronko, M. R., Nezu, A., and Pos, A. *Natural Setting Therapeutic Managements (NSTM) as an Alternative to Institutionalization for the Severely Mentally Retarded.* Fairleigh Dickinson University, 139 Temple Avenue, Hackensack, New Jersey 07601

Pilkington, T. L. *An Historical Perspective on Movie Films and the Development of the Mental Retardation Services in the United Kingdom.* Whixley Hospital, Whixley, York Y05 8DR, England

Pivato, E., and Hermanson, C. *GRIT: A New Approach to Serving Young Severely Handicapped Children.* Gateway Association for the Mentally Handicapped, 201 Financial Building, 10621-100 Avenue, Edmonton, Alberta T5J OB3, Canada

Pluymers, R. J. *Medical Sport Advising for the Mentally Retarded.* National Institute for Sports Health Care, Van Weedestraat 11, Soest, The Netherlands

Posner, B. *An International Overview.* The President's Committee on Employment of the Handicapped, 1111 20 St. N.W., Washington, D.C. 20036

Powell, M. L. *Maternal Teaching Strategies of Mothers of Preschool Children with Mental Retardation.* College of Nursing, University of Utah, Salt Lake City, Utah 84112

Powis, J. N. *The Forgotten Gynecology Client.* Pennsylvania Hospital, 301 South Eighth Street, Philadelphia, Pennsylvania 19107

Pressman, H. *Expanding Competitive Employment Opportunities for People who Are Labelled Retarded: The WORC (Work Opportunities for Retarded Citizens) Model.* Transitional Employment Enterprises, Inc., 184 High Street, Boston, Massachussets 02110

Priest, M. R. *Model Training Program for Related Service Personnel in Occupational and Physical Therapy in Public Education.* University Affiliated Center for Developmentally Disabled Children, 3801 Herschel Street, Dallas, Texas 75219

Ramey, C. T., Yeates, K. O., and MacPhee, D. *Risk Variation in Disadvantaged Families: A Systems Approach to Conceptualizing and Preventing Developmental Retardation.* Frank Porter Graham Child Development Center, University of North Carolina at Chapel Hill, Highway 54 Bypass West 071 A, Chapel Hill, North Carolina 27514

Rand, Y. *Mediated Learning Experience: Emotional Aspects of Down's Syndrome Subjects in Pre- and Post-reconstructive Facial Surgery.* Department of Psychology, University of Montreal, C.P. 6128 Succursale "A", Montreal, Quebec H3C 3J7, Canada

Rand, Y., Feuerstein, R., Ben Shachar, N., and Tzuriel, D. *LPAD Tests: New Versions. Some Empirical Data.* Department of Psychology, University of Montreal, C.P. 6128 Succursale "A", Montreal, Quebec H3C 3J7, Canada

Reeves, P. *The Role of Vocational Aspirations in the Occupational Choice of Adults Who Are Developmentally Handicapped.* Metropolitan Toronto Association for the Mentally Retarded, Harry E. Foster Employment Training Centre, 30 Birch Avenue, Toronto, Ontario M4V 1C8, Canada

Reutter, J. W. *Modifying Verbal Behavior Using Visual Light Feedback.* Speech Pathology and Audiology Department, Muscatatuck State Hospital and Training Center, Butlerville, Indiana 47223

Rezmierski, L. R., Jones, L., and Shiffler, N. *A Curriculum Project for the Developmentally Disabled—Design, Implementation and Evaluation: One School District's Approach.* Special Education Services, Northville Public Schools, 501 West Main Street, Northville, Michigan 48167

Rezmierski, L. R., Schwarze, T. H., and Wangrud, D. C. *Northville Public Schools. Administrative Procedures Dealing with Child Abuse and Neglect.* Special Education Services, Northville Public Schools, 501 West Main Street, Northville, Michigan 48167

Richardson, M., and West, M. *Assessing Human Resources Within Mental Retardation Service Systems.* Department of Health Services, Clinical Training Unit, Child Development and Mental Retardation Center, University of Washington, Seattle, Washington 98105

Rimmerman, A. *Parental Social Status and Realism About Their Developmentally Disabled Infants or Toddlers as Predictors of Continuance in the Early Evaluation and Intervention Program.* School of Social Work, Bar-Ilan University, Ramat-Gan, Israel

Rivier, M. *Etiological and Neuropsychological Correlates of Minor Physical Anomalies in Mentally Retarded, Cerebral Palsied and Normal Adults.* Department of Psychology, Rideau Regional Centre, P.O. Box 2000, Smiths Falls, Ontario K7A 4T7, Canada

Rix, B. *The Changing Role of Voluntary Organisations.* Royal Society for Mentally Handicapped Children and Adults, MENCAP National Centre, 123 Golden Lane, London EC1Y ORT, England

Roberts, J. R. *Can Legislation End Discrimination in Employment for the Handicapped?* Kiva Professional Plaza, 7110 East McDonald Drive, Suite A-1, Scottsdale, Arizona 85253

Robson, C. *The Development of Language Intervention Programs.* Behavioral Sciences Department, Huddersfield Polytechnic, Queensgate, Huddersfield HD1 3DH, England

Rodrigues, M. M. *The Nature of Self-Injurious Behavior Among Visually Impaired Residents of Mental Retardation Facilities.* Operational Support Branch, Ministry of Community and Social Services, Room 205, 700 Bay Street, Toronto, Ontario M5G 1Z6, Canada

Roessler, R. T. *Comprehensive Vocational Preparation Strategies for Individuals with Severe Mental and Physical Disabilities.* Arkansas Rehabilitation Research and Training Center, University of Arkansas, Fayetteville, Arkansas 72701

Rosen, H. S., Eidelman, S. M., and Walker, J. C. *Training Community Residential Facility Staff: Effects on Staff and Mentally Retarded Residents.* Blick Clinic for Developmental Disabilities, Inc., Akron, Ohio 44303

Rosenbaum, L., and Brown, B., *Stress and the Growth of Competence.* Biofeedback Programs, Georgetown University Family Center, 4380 MacArthur Boulevard N.W., Washington, D.C. 20007

Rucksdashel, S. V., and Harlan, N. T. *Language Development: An Interactive Process.* Scottish Rite Parent-Child Language Program, University of Nebraska Medical Center, 444 South 44 Street, Omaha, Nebraska 68131

St. Louis, E. E. B. *State Agencies Can Work Together to Serve Children.* Kansas University Affiliated Facility, Bureau of Child Research, University of Kansas, Parsons, Kansas 67357

Salbreux, R. *Multiple Handicaps: Structure, Number and Nature of the Association.* Comité d'Étude, de Soins et d'Action Permanente en Faveur des Déficients Profonds (CESAP), 81 rue Saint Lazare, 75009 Paris, France

Salter-Bimm, M. *Marriage and Parenthood for the Developmentally Handicapped.* Vocational and Rehabilitation Research Institute, 3304 33rd Street N.W., Calgary, Alberta T2L 2A6, Canada

Salzberg, C. L., and McCuller, W. R. *Generative Acquisition of Receptive Language in Severely Mentally Retarded People.* Exceptional Child Center, Utah State University, UMC 68, Logan, Utah 84322

Schlotterer, G. R. *A Decentralized, Community-based Mental Retardation Service Delivery Network: A Model for the Future.* Developmental Services, 119 Sydney Street, Cornwall, Ontario K6H 3H1, Canada

Schmidt, D. *Postural Seating for the Severely Involved Multihandicapped Child.* Developmental Services, Brantwood Residential Development Center, 25 Bell Lane, Brantford, Ontario N3T 1E1, Canada

Schneider, S. V. *Hypnosis and the Mentally Retarded.* Southern Wisconsin Center for the Developmentally Disabled, Union Grove, Wisconsin 53182

Schreiber, S. *Vocational Preparation of Blind Mentally Retarded Persons.* Visually Impaired Persons' Services, 125 Neptune Drive, Suite 1010, Toronto, Ontario M6A 1X3, Canada

Schwethelm, B., Taylor, R., Villarruel, F., and DeCooke, P. *The Development of Sex-role Knowledge and Gender Constancy in Mentally Retarded Boys and Adolescents.* Department of Developmental Psychology, 3433 Mason Hall, University of Michigan, Ann Arbor, Michigan 48109

Settles, R. B. *Are the Retarded Really Relegated in Employment? If So—Who Did It?* Georgia Retardation Center, 850 College Station Road, Athens, Georgia 30610

Shafer, E. L. *Staff Development: A Systemic Approach to Training/Retraining in Western Massachusetts.* Belchertown State School, Region I, Department of Mental Health, Belchertown, Massachusetts 01007

Shapiro, J., *The Potential of Agriculture in Vocational Rehabilitation and Employment for the Mentally Retarded.* Selwyn Segal Hostel, Johannesburg, South Africa

Shennan, V. *Some Implications of Current Research Findings for Families with a Mentally Handicapped Member.* Royal Society for Mentally Handicapped Children and Adults, MENCAP National Centre, 123 Golden Lane, London EC1Y ORT, England

Shipe, D. M. *An Infant Stimulation Program: The Earliest Intervention.* The Ontario Institute for Studies in Education, The University of Toronto, 252 Bloor Street West, Toronto, Ontario M5S 1V6, Canada

Silverman, W., and Wisniewski, H. M. *Research Applications for Primary Prevention.* New York State Institute for Basic Research in Developmental Disabilities, 1050 Forest Hill Road, Staten Island, New York 10314

Slonim, M. B. *Casefinding/Basics for Interdisciplinary Efforts.* Health/Education Collaborative Project, Health Services for Handicapped Children Section, Connecticut Department of Health Services, 79 Elm Street, Hartford, Connecticut 06115

Smedshammar, H. *Integrated Group Housing for the Mentally Retarded.* Royal Institute of Technology, Vetenskap Och Konst Section for Architecture, S-100 44 Stockholm, Sweden

Sonnander, K. *Normalization in Sweden: Quality and Limitations. Mentally Retarded and Quality of Life.* Psychiatric Research Center, University of Uppsala, S-750 17 Uppsala, Sweden

Sorensen, D. A., Frese, F. J., and Waechter, L. *Establishment and Certification of Units Serving the Developmentally Disabled in a State Psychiatric Center.* Western Reserve Psychiatric Habilitation Center, P.O. Box 305, Northfield, Ohio 44067

Soudek, D. *Fragile X Disease: Is Chromosomal Mosaicism Involved?* Cytogenetics Laboratory, Kingston Psychiatric Hospital, P.O. Box 603, Kingston, Ontario K7L LX3, Canada

Sproger, S. R. *Is There a Future for the Deinstitutionalization Movement? An Analysis of Trends in North America and Elsewhere.* 437 Jamacha Road No. 12, El Cajon, California 92021

Stavrakaki, C., and Pond, D. *An Investigation of the Pattern of Epilepsy in the Different Diagnostic Categories of Mentally Deficient Children.* Regional Children's Centre, Royal Ottawa Hospital, 1145 Carling Avenue, Ottawa, Ontario K1Z 7K4, Canada

Stephens, B. *Parents of Severely/Profoundly Mentally Retarded Persons Serve as Parent Trainers.* Department of Defense Dependents Schools, 2461 Eisenhower Boulevard, Alexandria, Virginia 22331

Sternlicht, M. *Normalization: Altered Living Arrangements for Retarded Clients with Special Needs.* Department of Psychology, Yeshiva College, 500 West 185th Street, New York, New York 10033

Stone, R., Berson, N., and Moore, S. *Staff Perceptions of Their Aging Mentally Retarded Clients.* Institute for Human Services, Kean College of New Jersey, Morris Avenue, Union, New Jersey 07083

Strassmeier, W. *The System of Early Intervention in the Federal Republic of Germany.* Wettersteinstrasse 11, 8910 Landsberg, Federal Republic of Germany

Striefel, S. *A Rural Service Delivery Model.* Division of Services, Utah State University, Exceptional Child Center, Logan, Utah 84322

Tamlyn, D. L. *Shaping the Future: The Role of the Community Health Nurse in Home Care of the Mentally Retarded.* Dalhousie University School of Nursing, 5963 College Street, Halifax, Nova Scotia B3H 4H7, Canada

Taskar, K. T. *Personality Development Mechanism of Mentally Retarded Children.* Directorate of Social Welfare, Maharashtra State, Avanti, 50 Shailesh Housing Society, Ganeshinagar, Pune 411029, India

Thomas, E. D. *A Respite Aide Home Program as Part of a Prescriptive Team Program for Deaf-blind and Multihandicapped Children and Families.* Section of Developmental Pediatrics, Child Study Center, 1100 N. E. 13th Street, Oklahoma City, Oklahoma 73117

Thomas, M., and Conte, M. *Self Awareness and Interpersonal Relations Group.* New Haven Regional Center, 455 Wintergreen Avenue, New Haven, Connecticut 06415

Thorburn, M. J. *Training of Child Care Staff in Early Detection and Intervention.* Caribbean Institute on Mental Retardation and Developmental Disabilities, 94C Old Hope Road, Kingston 6, Jamaica

Tilley, A. D. *Sport and the Mentally Handicapped Participant.* School of Physical Education and Recreation, University of British Columbia, 6081 University Boulevard, Vancouver, British Columbia V6T 1W5, Canada

Titrud, K. *Communications with the Family About the Findings of Your Evaluation.* Child Development Section, St. Paul–Ramsey Medical Center, St. Paul, Minnesota 55101

Tjosvold, D., and Tjosvold,* M. M. *Residential Facilities: Co-operative Techniques, Conflict Resolution, Collaborative Management.* *Camilia Rose Group Home, 11800 Xeon Boulevard, Minneapolis, Minnesota 55433

Tomiyasu, Y., Oshio*, C., and Nakane, K. *Organization Care Pattern and Direct Staff Behavior in Residential Institutions.* *Institute for Developmental Research, Aichi Prefectural Colony, Kamiya-Cho, Kasugai, Aichi 480-03, Japan

Tomkiewicz, S. *A French Study About Adopted Children: The Influence of Family Environment on Scholastic Status and IQ.* Institut Nationale de la Santé et de la Recherche Médicale (INSERM), 1 rue du 11 Novembre, 92120 Montrouge, France

Tu, J.-B., and Smith, J. T. *Eastern Ontario Survey: The Evolution of a Study of Mental Disorder in Mental Handicap.* Ongwanada, Penrose Division, 752 King Street W, Kingston, Ontario K7M 2G2, Canada

Vanbiervliet, A., and Morton, M. W. *An Empirical Determination of Direct Observation Procedures for Residential Program Evaluation: A Preliminary Report.* University of Otago, Dunedin, New Zealand

Van Coppenolle, H., Van den Broek, A., and Billen, W. *The Effects of Movement Education Programs on Social and Self-help Skills in Moderately and Severely Mentally Retarded Adults.* Department of Physical Education, Katholieke Universiteit, Tervuursevest 101, B-3030 Heverlee, Leuven, Belgium

Van Hal, A. J. C. *Barriers and Consequences of Competitive Sport.* Netherlands Sports League for the MH/Foundation Sport for the Handicapped SGK, Koninginnegracht 101, The Hague, The Netherlands

Velche, D. *The Use of an Assessment Method for the Needs of Mentally Handicapped Workers in Sheltered Work Centres in France.* SNAPEI, 15 rue Coysevox, 75018 Paris, France

Verburg, G. *Towards Computer-assisted Blissymbol Assessment.* Ontario Crippled Children's Centre, 350 Rumsey Road, Toronto, Ontario M4G 1R8, Canada

Vermeer, A., De Winter, C. E., De Winter, E., De Bruin, W. J., and Kemper, A. B. A. *Opinions on the Desirability of Competitive Sport for the Mentally Retarded.* Interfaculty of Human Movement Science and Education, Postbus 7161, 1007 MC Amsterdam, The Netherlands

Verniers, W. *A Theoretical Approach Towards Communication in the Care of the Mentally Handicapped.* Clinic for Child Psychiatry, Herlaarhof, Boxtelsweg 32, 5161 NE Vught, The Netherlands

Verpoorten, R. A. W. *A Therapeutic Application of Total Communication Principles in the Care of the Profoundly and Severely Mentally Handicapped.* Piusoord, J. van Himbergenlaan 16, 2380 Ravels, Belgium

Vesprani, G. J., Veatch, W. C., and Goulet, M. W. *Using Telecommunications Media to Provide Regionalized Professional Training in Mental Deficiency.* Cincinnati Center for Developmental Disorders, University of Cincinnati, Elland and Bethesda Avenues, Cincinnati, Ohio 45229

Wade, P. A. *Weight Awareness Program for Mentally Retarded Adults.* Butler County Board of Mental Retardation and Developmental Disability, 282 No. Fair Avenue, Hamilton, Ohio 45011

Walbran, B., Campbell, D., and Hartman, B. *A Comparison of the Piagetian and Bayley Scales in the Assessment of the Severely Handicapped, Mentally Retarded Person.* Hawthorn Children's Psychiatric Hospital, 5247 Fyler Avenue, St. Louis, Missouri 63139

Walker, S. *A Look at the Needs of Preschool Handicapped Children in Ghana and Nigeria.* School of Education, Howard University, Washington, D.C. 20059

Wallingford, H., Topo, C., and Romanko, S. *The Effects of a Sensorimotor Program on Repetitive Behavior of Six Retarded Preschoolers.* Centre for Sensory Motor Maximization, Site 12, Box 33, S. S. No. 1, Sudbury, Ontario P3E 4S8, Canada

Walsh, G. F. *Report on Sports for the Mentally Handicapped Survey for the International League of Societies for the Mentally Handicapped.* Mount Olivet Rolling Acres, 7200 Rolling Acres Road, Excelsior, Minnesota 55331

Walujo, S. *Group-dynamic Activities at Some Residential and Group Homes for Mentally Retarded Adults in Sweden. An Experiment to Apply the So-called SIVUS Method.* Socialstyrelsen, The National Board of Health and Welfare, Division of Services for the Handicapped, S-106 30 Stockholm, Sweden

Ward, J. *Studies in Program Effectiveness.* School of Education, Macquarie University, North Ryde, New South Wales 2113, Australia

Way, M. C., *The Symptoms of Affective Disorder in Severely Retarded Children.* Earls House Hospital, Durham, England

Weaver, V. S., Zimmerman, W. W., Kinnison, L. R., and Johnson, D. *A Comparison of Full Day Urban with Half-day Rural Educational Programs for Preschool Multihandicapped Students.* University of Tulsa, 4351 S. Madison Plaza, Tulsa, Oklahoma 74105

Weber, S. J. *Improving Information Resources in Mental Retardation and Related Disabilities.* 93 Fonthill Park, Rochester, New York 14618

Weikart, D. P. *Early Education Today.* High/Scope Educational Research Foundation, 600 North River Street, Ypsilanti, Michigan 48197

Weisberg, P. *The Mentally Retarded in Life and as Depicted in Literature.* Department of Special Education, Trenton State College, CN550 Pennington Road, Trenton, New Jersey 08625

Weiss, A. I. *Televised Core Curriculum on Developmental Disabilities.* Special Education Department, University of South Carolina, Columbia, South Carolina 29208

Wilkinson, P. F. *Providing Integrated Play Environments for Disabled Children.* Faculty of Environmental Studies, York University, 4700 Keele Street, Downsview, Toronto, Ontario M3J 2R2, Canada

Willer, B., and Intagliata, J. *Unintended Effects of Deinstitutionalization and Suggestions for Future Planning.* Department of Psychiatry, State University of New York at Buffalo, 2211 Main Street, Building E, Buffalo, New York 14214

Wisniewski, K., French, J. H., and Wisniewski, H. M. *Age Associated Changes in Down's Syndrome Nervous System.* New York State Institute for Basic Research in Developmental Disabilities, 1050 Forest Hill Road, Staten Island, New York 10314

Wolgard-Hageman, P. *Two Psychomotor Approaches for the Mentally Retarded.* 500 Riverside Drive, P.O. 35, New York, New York 10027

Wolinsky, G. F. *Prevention of Mental Retardation and Developmental Disabilities: No Easy Answers.* Department of Educational Foundations, Hunter College, 695 Park Avenue, New York, New York 10021

Wright, J. M. C., Nasser, C. G., Packer, J. M., Bemi, C., and De Glas, G. *Community Living for Severely Intellectually Handicapped Persons in Queensland, Australia.* Department of Health, Intellectual Handicap Services Branch, Legacy House, 56 Mary Street, Brisbane 4000, Australia

Wright, J. S. *A Model of Parental Involvement.* Early Childhood Intervention Program, Institute for the Study of Developmental Disabilities, University of Illinois at Chicago Circle, 1640 West Roosevelt Road, Chicago, Illinois 60608

Zacarias, J. *Model Services for Mentally Retarded Adults Placed in Their Community.* Department of Special Education, Universidad Iberamericana, Heriberto Frias 1046-2, Mexico 12, D.F. 03700

Zaman, S. S., and Akhtar, S. *Effects of Early and Late Intervention Among Retarded Children: Bangladesh Experience.* Department of Psychology, University of Dacca, 50 Purana Paltan Line, Dacca 2, Bangladesh

Zanfordino, J. P., and Jerrels, E. G. *Environmental Sign Language and Phonological Acquisition with Mentally Retarded Adults.* Orient Developmental Center, Orient, Ohio 43146

Zarfas, D. E. *Issues in Mental Retardation (Sterilization of Retarded People).* Department of Psychiatry, Faculty of Medicine, The University of Western Ontario, London, Ontario N6G 2K3, Canada

Zoller, M. K. *Tympanometry Screening in Developmentally Delayed Individuals.* Huronia Regional Centre, P.O. Box 1000, Orillia, Ontario L3V 6L2, Canada

AUTHOR INDEX

SUBJECT INDEX